THE ROUTLEDGE HANDBOOK OF PRIVACY AND SOCIAL MEDIA

This volume provides the basis for contemporary privacy and social media research and informs global as well as local initiatives to address issues related to social media privacy through research, policymaking, and education.

Renowned scholars in the fields of communication, psychology, philosophy, informatics, and law look back on the last decade of privacy research and project how the topic will develop in the next decade. The text begins with an overview of key scholarship in online privacy, expands to focus on influential factors shaping privacy perceptions and behaviors – such as culture, gender, and trust – and continues with specific examinations of concerns around vulnerable populations such as children and older adults. It then looks at how privacy is managed and the implications of interacting with artificial intelligence, concluding by discussing feasible solutions to some of the more pressing questions surrounding online privacy.

This handbook will be a valuable resource for advanced students, scholars, and policymakers in the fields of communication studies, digital media studies, psychology, and computer science.

Sabine Trepte is a full professor of Media Psychology in the Department of Communication at the University of Hohenheim in Stuttgart, Germany.

Philipp K. Masur is an assistant professor in the Department of Communication Science at the Vrije Universiteit Amsterdam, The Netherlands.

ROUTLEDGE HANDBOOKS IN COMMUNICATION STUDIES

The Routledge Handbook of Positive Communication
Edited by José Antonio Muñiz Velázquez and Cristina M. Pulido

The Routledge Handbook of Mass Media Ethics
Edited By Lee Wilkins and Clifford G. Christians

The Routledge Handbook of Comparative World Rhetorics: Studies in the History, Application, and Teaching of Rhetoric Beyond Traditional Greco-Roman Contexts
Edited By Keith Lloyd

The Routledge Handbook of Media Use and Well-Being: International Perspectives on Theory and Research on Positive Media Effects
Edited By Leonard Reinecke and Mary Beth Oliver

The Routledge Handbook of Queer Rhetoric
Edited by Jonathan Alexander and Jacqueline Rhodes

The Routledge Handbook of Nonprofit Communication
Edited by Gisela Gonçalves and Evandro Oliveira

The Routledge Handbook of Intercultural Mediation
Edited by Dominic Busch

The Routledge Handbook of Corporate Social Responsibility Communication
Edited by Amy O'Connor

The Routledge International Handbook of Research on Writing, Second Edition
Edited by Rosalind Horowitz

The Routledge Handbook of Privacy and Social Media
Edited by Sabine Trepte and Philipp K. Masur

For a full list of titles in this series, please visit www.routledge.com/series/RHCS

THE ROUTLEDGE HANDBOOK OF PRIVACY AND SOCIAL MEDIA

Edited by Sabine Trepte and Philipp K. Masur

Designed cover image: oxygen / © Getty Images

First published 2023
by Routledge
605 Third Avenue, New York, NY 10158

and by Routledge
4 Park Square, Milton Park, Abingdon, Oxon, OX14 4RN

Routledge is an imprint of the Taylor & Francis Group, an informa business

Library of Congress Cataloging-in-Publication Data
Names: Trepte, Sabine, editor. | Masur, Philipp K., editor.
Title: The Routledge handbook of privacy and social media / edited by Sabine Trepte, Philipp K. Masur.
Description: New York, NY : Routledge, 2023. | Includes bibliographical references and index. |
Identifiers: LCCN 2022060785 (print) | LCCN 2022060786 (ebook) | ISBN 9781032111612 (hardback) | ISBN 9781032155555 (paperback) | ISBN 9781003244677 (ebook)
Subjects: LCSH: Social media and society. | Privacy. | Data protection.
Classification: LCC HM742 .R684 2023 (print) | LCC HM742 (ebook) |
DDC 302.23/1--dc23/eng/20230109
LC record available at https://lccn.loc.gov/2022060785
LC ebook record available at https://lccn.loc.gov/2022060786

ISBN: 978-1-032-11161-2 (hbk)
ISBN: 978-1-032-15555-5 (pbk)
ISBN: 978-1-003-24467-7 (ebk)

DOI: 10.4324/9781003244677

The Open Access version of chapter 22 was funded by Bavarian Research Institute for Digital Transformation (bidt).

CONTENTS

PREFACE

In this handbook, we discuss and reflect on two intricately interwoven concepts: privacy and social media. Using social media is fun, allows us to stay connected, to socialize, to be entertained, to seek out news, and to stumble across content we didn't know we were interested in. Social media are platforms for exploration, games, and the unlikely beauty of the mundane, the ridiculous, and the funny. Further, they are vehicles for political discussions, entire social movements and trends, networking, and learning. For most people, they represent a convenient way of virtually traveling across one's social networks. For others, they are a lifesaving connection to other people sharing the same disease. For some, they offer the chance to perform in front of large audiences. All of this is possible because user-generated content is the heart of social media. But sharing authentic, personal, and at times intimate information on social media goes hand in hand with the need to regulate and negotiate access; it is therefore crucially influenced by users' ruminations about what to share, with whom, in what way, and when. In other words, all sharing of information is accompanied by privacy-relevant cognitions and emotions, resulting in complex interpersonal boundary management processes. Users thoughtfully reflect about the content they share, who is allowed to have access, and how it should be used. Sharing authentic and intimate information thus requires privacy protection strategies as well as proactive communication and deliberation around political and normative privacy issues. Further, social media providers themselves impose questionable norms and practices, intrude on their users' privacy, and commodify personal information. Maintaining an appropriate level of privacy on social media is no easy task, and it is all too understandable that some users feel overwhelmed or even frustrated at times. Protecting one's privacy requires specific knowledge and skills as well as the ability to communicate and negotiate with others. We have observed a continuously growing and vibrant research community over the last ten years whose aim was and still is to tackle these manifold aspects, issues, dimensions, contexts, and paradoxes pertaining to privacy on social media. Thousands of studies have been published, diverse theoretical accounts have emerged, and heterogeneous – at times contradictory – findings paint a granular, but complex picture of the privacy research landscape. We believe that the current status quo requires us to pause and take stock. We therefore are proud to present this comprehensive handbook, which aims to substantiate existing privacy work by systematizing and summarizing the most important findings, offering novel theoretical approaches, and outlining desiderata for future research.

To this purpose, the book is divided into five parts. In Part 1 – *Perspectives on Social Media Privacy,* prominent research streams and theoretical approaches to privacy on social media are introduced. Existing theories are presented and analyzed, their strengths and weaknesses are highlighted, and potential for redirection, transformation, and adaptation is suggested. Whereas the first eight chapters provide a theoretical foundation, the chapters in Part 2 zoom in on relevant *Factors Shaping Social Media Privacy*. Experts on affordances, trust, literacy, privacy breaches, cynicism, gender, and culture offer fruitful insights into the entanglement of these factors with privacy on social media. It is here that current research is discussed and findings are put into perspective. In Part 3, the focus is on particular *Populations and Their Social Media Privacy*. Ranging from young children's privacy in light of "sharenting" to the challenges of managing privacy in later life, and from privacy of minority groups to general inequalities that shape privacy experiences on social media, the chapters offer more situated, population-specific perspectives on privacy on social media and highlight specific user groups, social margins, and contexts. Part 4 – *Algorithms and Privacy* then directs our focus to technological advances affecting privacy in one way or the other: Experts on AI, robots and intelligent machines, social crediting, microtargeting, and the use of algorithms in health systems disentangle related privacy issues and offer important directions for future research. Finally, Part 5 offers potential *Solutions to Preserve Social Media Privacy*. Here, the authors try to answer pressing questions such as how to successfully change social media users' behavior to meet their most prevalent needs and how privacy and secure online behaviors might be nudged, regulated, and protected. It closes with some reflections on how to conduct ethical privacy research. After all, we – as privacy scholars – often intrude on participants' privacy when we conduct our research.

In this handbook, we summoned the wisdom and expertise of many great privacy scholars, renowned voices in their fields, all with long-standing experience in studying privacy and social media use. We wish to express our deepest gratitude to all authors and to express our appreciation for their unique perspectives and analyses that make up this handbook. Their work goes far beyond existing work and offers exciting new angles for research and intriguing solutions to some of the most pressing issues and problems surrounding privacy on social media. It is our hope that this volume provides the basis for contemporary and future privacy research and, in turn, informs global as well as local initiatives to address privacy in social media technology and design, policymaking, regulation, and education. We dedicate this book to our children, who are our greatest inspiration in how they experience social media and who, at this point in time as well as at any time in the future, are always welcome to intrude on our privacy.

Sabine Trepte & Philipp K. Masur
Stuttgart and Amsterdam
March 2023

WHAT IS PRIVACY

Zizi Papacharissi, University of Illinois at Chicago, USA

I begin with a provocation, which I hope will sound rational by the conclusion of this introduction. There is no such thing as private. There is no such thing as public. Both concepts are abstractions of convenience that serve to organize our social lives. We use them to configure the temporal and spatial boundaries of our relationships. We then develop shared understandings that have always been contextual in some form. Consider how many norms, habits, and laws would be invalidated were it not for the shared imaginaries of publicity and privacy that societies cultivate and thrive on. There is much to be gained from defining privacy. More to the point, a lot more becomes accessible if we conceive of publicity as its binary counterpart. Private and public, as opposites, present an imagined binary around which we formulate ways of living together, sharing information, forming relationships, delineating boundaries, organizing trade and commerce, and presenting arguments for regulation, among many other things.

And yet, this binary exploits as much as it conveniences. It invites us to develop shared ways of labeling behaviors that are deeply subjective. What some people consider to be private information, others feel comfortable talking about openly. Many of these decisions are culturally bound. Where I grew up in Greece, for instance, private life and personal relationships are not considered a permissible subject for casual conversation. Similar canons prevail in neighboring countries or regions in Europe. It is rude to ask us who we are dating, if we are in a relationship, and what our private life is like. And yet in the United States, this information is a convenient icebreaker in informal conversations, and one that often creates discomfort and confusion when I respond by saying that it is private. Co-conversants feel like they have offended and must apologize. Many of us navigating multiple cultural contexts find ourselves sharing information that is private just so we do not offend. Consider a bench in a public park, a busy street in a city, or a bar or restaurant. Though placed in public, these spaces support private conversation. When I moved to the United States, I was startled to encounter interruptions from strangers in the park, on the street, or at a bar. This was a different cultural canon that I had to get used to, while traversing through spaces publicly private and privately public.

Why do I start with these personal, colloquial recollections while writing for a volume that is scholarly? Well, because it has become customary for us social scientists to use the privately public and publicly private context collapse primarily when we talk about public and private behaviors in online spaces. Yet all social spaces afford privacy and publicity. A home with massive windows opens up the domestic to the public sphere, making it both accessible and vulnerable. A public park with tabled seating encourages private conversation, but does not offer confidentiality or protection. So, the first point I want to make in setting the tone for this volume is this: We have never been private and we have never been public. We have always existed in ambient, always on social spaces that are sometimes private, sometimes public, and most often a little bit of both.

Yet we develop ways of dealing with the paradoxes in which our cultures and our spaces intersect. We are socialized into dealing with the manner in which the movie theater demands respect for private habits while co-existing in a public space. When we enter the public spaces of transportation we find ways to respect the privacy of others and look down upon those who do not. Consider how we conduct ourselves in the crowded confines of an elevator. In fact, it is socially acceptable for us to reprimand those who are disrespectful to the privacy of others in public spaces. We shush loud attendees at the symphony. We chastise manspreaders on public transportation and have developed massive meme cultures to help make that point. In restaurants, when seated close to others, we try our best to not overhear conversation, even when it is impossible not to. In loud and crowded bars, we find ways to respect the ways of others. In the event that we do not engage in disrespectful behavior, then we might get thrown out. So the second point I wish to make is that we have gone through a long, layered, and continuous process of socialization that helps us navigate our behaviors skillfully as we traverse spaces private and public.

In the same vein, we design our spaces to align with our cultural customs and to lockstep with our socialization practices. For example, we enhance security when we want to ensure privacy in high rises located on busy streets. We utilize curtains and shading when we want to moderate how much sun to let in and how much onlooking to permit through windows. We construct imbricated visual and gestural vernaculars of privacy that we learn to interpret and respect: an open office; a half-open office door; a nearly shut office door; a closed office door; a locked door. All guarantee different levels of privacy that we are socialized to read. Our world is filled with design that prompts, reminds, permits, discourages, and allows for nuance. Architecture around the world varies to accommodate cultural difference, so that when we are traveling, even if not familiar with local custom, we are often guided by the shape highways take on, by the size of streets, by the form of houses, by the presence, absence or design of corridors and hallways, by seating arrangements, and by a number of subtle nudges. Why is it that we design offline spaces with nudges in mind and abandon the utility of soft design intervention when we design online spaces? Some spaces have built-in reminders that soften the sharp edges of our behaviors. Online spaces do not. One cannot lock a door online with the ease one does so offline. One cannot grab a bouncer and ask them to throw the bigot who has been throwing insults around the online discussion space out. We cannot call the police when someone abuses us online with the ease at which we reach to our phone to report an offline incident. We often say that all traces of our behavior attain digital permanence online. That is not true. All of our behaviors have the potential to attain digital permanence, but in reality, some behaviors are more valuable than others to the infrastructure of an attention economy. And as a result, some behaviors are more permanent and tradeable than others.

Online spaces are designed to collect some traces of digital behavior and easily forget others, ones not so easily monetizable. We bring our traits, our habits, and our predispositions with us, and they accompany us into all the spaces we enter. There is no sign that reads, "leave your problems at the door, right next your racist, sexist and classist attitude; you are entering cyberspace." We carry those problems with, in a space that lures us in because it is shapeless. It is an empty stage that affords maximal theatricality and drama, and we find that incredibly seductive. Much of the mystique of cyberspace derives from capabilities perceived as both exotic and mundane at the same time. It is a vast and alluring performative stage that has been platformized and commodified with our own mundane everyday social exchanges unitized and monetized in way that sustains traffic, activity, networks, and companies that drive a stock market. Each platform, be it Twitter, Mastodon, or Instagram then affords its own potentiality for reimagining the mundane rituals of connection in everyday life. The terms may change, as we no longer talk about cyberspace but platforms. The places may evolve, and so platforms like Friendster mean little to millennials. Yet the central idea of entering an elsewhere looking for an other, in order to make ourselves familiar with it will always be there. We are explorers and that is part of human nature.

I find it meaningful to think of technology as architecture. By architecture, I refer to the subtle shape of the textures that surround us, with an emphasis on how they tease out and put a certain glean on our behaviors. Think about the zoom rooms that we all found ourselves in during the Covid-19 pandemic, and how they confine and enable us at the same time. Consider how our mood and the tone of conversations change if we were in a room with open windows and high ceilings and nice ventilation. Or how we might feel talking about these things in a room with low ceilings and dark lighting. Ponder the movie theater that I mentioned earlier – what about its design commands silence? Think about a loud bar – and the insanity of having a private conversation there, or a private dinner and how we are subtly discouraged to adopt loud bar behaviors there. Move beyond affordances and consider how technology sets the tone. Tone is so important to us when we design the spaces we live in. Décor, and decorum, are key. Cultures have nuanced vocabularies that describe these tendencies. Take for example the idea of hygge, the Danish word for the quality of coziness and comfort that ensures well-being. So here is my final point: we used code to create spaces that do not set a tone. Online spaces do not possess any type of geomancy, or to put it in terms all recognize, feng shui. We left all hygge behind as we entered online spaces and this is a problem. Online spaces do not possess an architecture, and this makes it difficult to regulate, to educate, to create literacies, and to enhance well-being. Online spaces have codes. Technologies that network us possess something that resembles design, but comes nowhere near the intuitiveness other objects in our everyday life possess, especially when it comes to allowing us to draw our own privacy boundaries. To define publicity on our own terms. And to find the in-between space, that allows us to foster community in publicly private and privately public settings. I am not suggesting that all design of offline space is perfect or enhances well-being. That is not the case. I place emphasis on the recognition that good design involves more than structures, or in the case of online spaces, codes that do not crash.

So, to circle back to my opening statement: There is no fixed collective understanding of privacy. There never has been. Privacy is meaningful because it is just that; privately established. It's not privacy if someone else is setting the boundary. It is a construct that is subjective. Offline and online spaces; spaces, period, are meaningful to us because they afford us the autonomy to decide what is private to us. This autonomy is maintained by law, habits, and atmosphere that set the tone. It is safeguarded by an architecture bound by regulation, standards, and understanding of human nature. So the solution to our privacy problem cannot just be regulatory. It must be regulatory, behavioral, and grounded in design. Laws must safeguard. Socialization must remind us to develop, adjust, and maintain standards of behavior everywhere, including online. The internet was not created to serve as the wild west to all of our exploits. Finally, the design of digitally networked spaces must reinforce, reproduce, and enhance the standards of civil society. The overarching architecture of our society should nudge civility; should support well-being; should feel democratic. The atmosphere of all spaces, including all ones, must set this tone.

A while back, I was drawn to describe a number of contemporary tendencies and tensions in behavior as formative of *a networked self*. I wrote about the networked self in the context of online platforms, but never thought of it as specific to online environments. On the contrary, in my early work, I was drawn to reality TV, as I found much similarity between how people behaved when placing the self on display on TV and tendencies that were developing in how people were beginning to diary the fascinating mundaneness of everyday life online. I defined the networked self as drawing from a more porous connective environment, facilitated by digital technologies. This environment is promising, because it is new and unexplored. Identity expression has always been a performative and connective exercise, and any new place presents a potential stage for us, even more so one of interconnected, overlapping, and globally capable platforms. Autonomy of expression and connection is key. Heightened potential for performativity is a draw. Sociability is and always will be networked, although increasingly in a saturated, porous, and often overwhelming manner. We will create, sustain and break ties and relationships in this environment, and in so doing we will offer some private information, exchange secrets, and say things of a private nature in a public environment. But just because we utter something in public does not immediately render it the public property of others, in the same manner that my private act of entering a public space can be viewed but is not the property of others. Let me put it plainly: you may view but you may not exploit. On the interpersonal level, something someone posted online is not always an appropriate conversation starter for an offline interaction. We must apply and adapt nuance. We are invited to become much more self-reflexive through these technologies, and so must develop the same kind of acumen that we are socialized to apply in offline interaction. This is important, because our autonomy is an essential part of human nature.

Doing privacy work is not easy. We often dismay that our privacy is neglected online, but we forget how much progress has been made in the short past 25 years. Safeguarding autonomy is not easy in life, and evermore so when entering new, unfamiliar spaces. It is a life project that involves polymedia storytelling of the self in a world that is both post-colonial and techno-colonial. The work of social scientists was key in bringing privacy concerns to fore and getting policymakers and industry stakeholders to place them at the center of the conversation. We increasingly come into being in structures that impart an atmosphere of strong capitalism and soft democracy. The foundational architecture is grounded by profit-making with civil society as an afterthought. Sociality is commodified via capitalist structures that were invented centuries ago to serve societies with social habits very different from ours. Not only does economic interest shape the atmosphere of online environments, but it does so in a way that is extremely dated and colonial. Our very use of the terms public and private translates poorly in so many languages and cultures, presenting further challenges for privacy research. This provocation is by no means a pardon card, meant to release technology companies of their responsibility. On the contrary, it is meant to invite these companies to rethink how they design spaces meant to be social; to design spaces with sociality and democracy as more than an afterthought.

My writing is further meant to engage educators in conversations that reconsider the meaning of privacy in ways that are aligned with social impulses of young adults today. Finally, lawmakers must adopt a vocabulary that is current and informed, so that regulatory efforts work. The solution will be regulatory, but it cannot just be regulatory. It needs to also be behaviorally motivated, architecturally supported, and educationally encouraged. The luminaries who contribute to this volume have many ideas to this end, and I leave you to be further inspired by their insights. As the editors of this volume tellingly explain, the volume and richness of research questions developing around privacy are suggesting of a lively and important field. They signal that scholars understand the complexity of the problem and that they possess the knowledge to present viable solutions. Never has the field of privacy been more populated by vibrant analyses. They follow, and they have inspired this prologue to the volume. They affirm that privacy is emerging as a formidable area of research, and one that utilizes but also challenges typical intra and interdisciplinary and boundaries. The game is afoot.

PART 1

Perspectives on Social Media Privacy

1
DEFINITIONS OF PRIVACY

Sabine Trepte[1] *and Philipp K. Masur*[2]

[1]UNIVERSITY OF HOHENHEIM, GERMANY
[2]VRIJE UNIVERSITEIT AMSTERDAM, THE NETHERLANDS

Introduction

Very often, scholarly work starts with the claim that the field has not yet settled on a uniform definition. We believe that struggling to define a core concept is not necessarily a problem, but rather a symptom of a lively and active field. Uniform definitions, in contrast, reflect that the concept is not important, draws little attention, or worse, is owned by a handful of scholars reigning over this field and normalizing its research. Fortunately, none of this is the case in research on privacy, online privacy, or social media privacy. Over the last 60 years, privacy has become a vibrant area of research, with a significant peak in research activities regarding privacy on social media after 2010. Since this time, many flagship articles, books, and chapters have been published (Eichenhofer, 2019; Masur, 2018; Nissenbaum, 2010; Papacharissi, 2010; Sevignani, 2016; Trepte & Reinecke, 2011). Consequently, we can conclude that privacy research is growing and very much alive, as evidenced by the existence of many different definitions of privacy.

With this chapter, we provide an overview of the most popular definitions of privacy and discuss these with regard to i) their theoretical background, ii) model of humanity, iii) their suitability for capturing social media privacy, and iv) how well they facilitate communication regarding aspects and issues related to social media privacy in applied contexts (i.e., to the press, the public). In line with our arguments above and the inherent nature of the term privacy, this chapter does not seek to establish a single, final definition, but rather discusses definitions that meet different criteria and as such add to the body of knowledge in the field of privacy and social media.

Seminal Definitions of Privacy

For several decades and even centuries, scholars have grappled with the task of defining privacy. To the non-academic reader, this may come as a surprise. After all, the meaning of something described as "private" is readily understood by everyone: We call something private that belongs to us and that is kept separate from others, such as our homes, our thoughts and feelings, or our intimate family life. Here, we use the descriptive meaning of the word. However, we also seek to emphasize that the private thing *should* not be accessed or known by others, certainly not by the general public. If we consider something private, it belongs to us and we get to decide what happens with it. Here, the word privacy is used in its normative meaning.

Nevertheless, pinpointing an exact scholarly definition of privacy is almost impossible, at best difficult. From an academic point of view, the variety of definitions reflects the different disciplinary

DOI: 10.4324/9781003244677-2

backgrounds and purposes for which concepts of privacy have been created. It is thus understandable that privacy is often conceived as a *right* when legal issues are at stake, as a *form of control* if behavioral processes are under investigation, and as *a state of seclusion* when psychological perceptions of privacy are studied.

That being said, there are nonetheless commonalities between the different approaches that are worthwhile to highlight before we review some of the seminal definitions of privacy. For example, almost all modern, Western concepts of privacy are rooted in the work of liberal theorists such as Hobbes (1651/2011), Locke (1689/2005), and Mill (1859/2015). In describing the boundaries of a state's or sovereign's power, they coined the idea of negative freedom: The sole purpose of intervening with people's liberty of action is protection (e.g., Mill, 1859/2015). Negative freedom is thus freedom from external (i.e., the state's) intervention. This idea often translates to concepts of privacy that emphasize protection from external influences (Masur, 2020; Rössler, 2001).

Legal scholars Warren and Brandeis (1890) paved the way to defining the actual term privacy when they demanded "the right to be let alone" (p. 195), meaning that privacy translates to freedom from intrusion by the press. Their essay inspired an international conversation on how to define privacy in law and beyond. Interestingly, their motivation was a changing media environment. Warren and Brandeis claimed that personal attitudes, sentiments, and interactions would be protected by the law, but that recording and publishing would not. Nevertheless, their definition is somewhat imprecise with regard to what privacy actually is. Is "being let alone" the right itself? Or is it "being let alone" that the right aims to protect? We will see that protection of being let alone and managing access to oneself constitute the basis for most of the seminal work on privacy. One of the most commonly cited definitions of privacy building on Warren and Brandeis stems from Westin who proposed the following definition from a legal point of view:

> Privacy is the claim of individuals, groups, or institutions to determine for themselves when, how, and to what extent information about them is communicated to others [...]. Viewed in terms of the relation of the individual to social participation, privacy is the voluntary and temporary withdrawal of a person from the general society through physical or psychological means, either in a state of solitude or small-group intimacy or, when among larger groups, in a condition of anonymity or reserve.
>
> *(Westin, 1967, p. 5)*

We thus again observe ambiguity as Westin defines privacy as a broad legal claim, but also as a rather descriptive, reduced state of withdrawal. Furthermore, four states of privacy are introduced: Solitude, intimacy, anonymity, and reserve (Westin, 2003). Withdrawal as a function of privacy has become the basis for many psychologically inspired theories of privacy (Altman, 1975; Dienlin, 2014; Masur, 2018; Petronio, 2002).

The ambiguity in Westin's definition is also reflected in the growing amount of privacy literature in the 1960s–1990s. Over the years, a fruitful debate between what could be termed an anti-reductionist perspective (e.g., DeCew, 1997; Prosser, 1960; Solove, 2008) vs. a reductionist perspective (Allen, 1988; Gavison, 1980; Miller, 1971) emerged. The former argued that privacy touches upon too many aspects and areas and can therefore not be boiled down to a single definition. In other words, anti-reductionists highlight the necessity of taking the circumstances of a specific situation and contextual factors into account when trying to identify privacy values and interests. Solove (2008), for example, proposed a pluralistic understanding of privacy, stating that we should no longer search for one unifying common trait in all privacy violations, as one "can identify many specific elements of privacy without sacrificing inclusiveness" (Solove, 2008, p. 44).

Reductionists, in contrast, often held extreme positions such as abandoning the term privacy altogether for its lack of precision and overall vagueness. Their reduced definitions describe privacy as a state or condition. Gavison (1980), for example, defined privacy as "the limitation of others' access to an individual" (p. 428). Reductionists often argued that such a reduced, primarily descriptive concept of privacy can help to establish objective criteria for different levels of privacy.

Within the social sciences, work by Altman (1975) has been most influential in shaping definitions of privacy:

> For my purpose, privacy will be defined as the selective control of access to the self or to one's group.
>
> *(Altman, 1975, p. 18)*

Again, we observe a vagueness as to what privacy actually is. Is privacy really an individual's active control of access, or is it again a condition of limited access to this person, or both? Altman (1975) of course disentangles these questions in his work. And Irvin Altman inspired the analysis of privacy as a constant process of interpersonal boundary control aimed at optimizing levels of access to the self in alignment with one's personal needs for seclusion and interaction. The metaphor that "Privacy regulation by persons and groups is somewhat like the shifting permeability of a cell membrane" (Altman, 1975, p. 10) continues to be a useful metaphor for the shifting needs and circumstances that people deal with today (e.g., as laid out in Communication Privacy Management Theory, by Petronio, 2002; see further as follows).

With the rise of computers and later the internet, privacy scholars began to emphasize what Warren and Brandeis had earlier discovered as a conceptual gap in lawmaking, that is, the flow of information and "informational privacy." For example, Miller (1971) noted

> [...] that the basic attribute of an effective right of privacy is the individual's ability to control the circulation of information relating to him—a power that often is essential to maintaining social relationships and personal freedom.
>
> *(Miller, 1971, p. 25)*

Privacy definitions from this time reflect growing concerns over governments' and institutions' ability to collect and store personal information.

Consolidating different perspectives on privacy and relying on the work of the scholars denoted above, Burgoon (1982) proposed a multi-dimensional concept of privacy that differentiates between individuals' control over information, physical distance, social interaction, and the psychological experience of privacy. Here, *informational privacy* is defined as an individuals' ability to control the initial release of information about themselves and its subsequent distribution and use. Burgoon highlights that the amount of information in others' hands, its content, and the nature and relationships with those possessing the information are relevant. This also relates to the dimension of *social privacy*, an individual's ability to control the pattern of social contacts on an individual, dyadic, or group level. Social privacy varies with the "degree of personalness of conversational topics and language" (p. 222). *Psychological privacy* is defined as an individual's "ability to control affective and cognitive input and outputs" (p. 224). Finally, *physical privacy* refers to an individual's ability to control and choose the limits of one's physical boundaries to others, the "freedom from intrusion to one's self-defined body-buffer zone" (p. 211).

According to Margulis (2011), one of the most valuable theories for studying privacy in online environments is Communication Privacy Management Theory (Petronio, 2002):

> In this theory, privacy is defined as the feeling that one has the right to own private information, either personally or collectively; consequently, boundaries mark ownership lines for individuals.
>
> *(Petronio, 2002, p. 6)*

This idea of ownership is central to the theory. Privacy management thereby entails sustaining and controlling private boundaries with other people. The limits of such boundaries are defined by specific rules that coordinate the level of accessibility of the information that flows between group members defining the boundary.

As the above literature review has shown, general definitions of privacy are manifold. Over time, they have been refined, adapted, and adjusted. In light of this, the best course of action may well be to adopt an anti-reductionist approach and consider all of these definitions as worthwhile starting points and fruitful in their own right. As Margulis noted: "If you intend to use a behavioral theory of privacy, you should determine whether its definition of privacy meets your requirements" (Margulis, 2011, p. 15). We believe that the plurality of definitions is not necessarily a weakness, but rather a strength of our field. The richness of the ideas in the work referred to above and the many more we could not cite due to the word limitations of this chapter have undoubtedly shaped the work of the authors in this volume. As has been done in the past, we believe that we should continue to place our definitions of privacy under scrutiny and examine their potential to explain and describe current practices, phenomena, and processes. In what follows, we highlight how scholars have used these seminal definitions of privacy and adapted them to reflect the specificities of online environments and specifically the reality of managing privacy on social media.

Defining Online Privacy

We have demonstrated how seminal privacy research has laid the groundwork for our current understanding of privacy and can be understood as the first pillar of current privacy research. We would consider early research in computer-mediated communication the second pillar of our current understanding of privacy (Joinson, 2001; Joinson et al., 2006; Tidwell & Walther, 2002). Ironically, this early work seldom explicitly mentioned the term privacy. It was strongly centered around the individual agent, processes of how an individual reacts to certain circumstances with disclosure or withdrawal, and of course, the context was not yet social media, but rather online forums (Barak & Gluck-Ofri, 2007). Here, computer-mediated interpersonal communication could be observed and investigated in a nutshell.

Privacy was pivotal to communication science in the first decade of the millennium because it was at risk. The commercial internet had started to develop and jurisprudence was always one step behind what developers had invented (Sevignani, 2016). Data was considered the new oil (The Economist, 2017). Hence, the most important scholarly work on online privacy in these early years was published with respect to individual regulation on the one hand and e-commerce on the other (Acquisti, 2005; Acquisti & Grossklags, 2004; Ben-Ze'ev, 2003; Dinev & Hart, 2004, 2006; Dommeyer & Gross, 2003; Jensen et al., 2005; Metzger, 2004; Palen & Dourish, 2003; Patil & Kobsa, 2005; Preibusch, 2006; Tavani & Moor, 2001; Viegas, 2005). Here, scholars strove to understand the ways in which privacy was perceived, enacted, controlled, or violated in "cyber-space," the "networked world," or simply "the internet." Thus, the internet was conceptualized in a rather abstract way.

What do these developments tell us with regard to definitions of privacy? In retrospect, it seems that the full force of research was directed towards understanding privacy in online realms in the very broadest sense, with no further adaptations of privacy definitions for this new context. Definitions were mostly drawn from the seminal theories we referred to in the previous section and applied to how individuals regulate privacy with regard to service providers.

Only later, when social media became as dominant as the mass media, did scholars realize that privacy experienced in online media cannot always be fully captured by the definitions already in use. Only then did they suggest privacy definitions specifically tailored to the online applications, services and experiences(Acquisti & Gross, 2006; Barnes, 2006; Gross & Acquisti, 2005; Nissenbaum, 2010;

Papacharissi, 2010, 2011; Reinecke et al., 2008; Sevignani, 2016). Interestingly, these online privacy definitions were tremendously influencedby social media practices and scholarship. Hence, the term online privacy did not have a definition in its own right that we would consider a well-established or important step of privacy theorizing.

Defining Privacy for the Social Media Context

Central to this handbook is the question of how privacy can be defined for the context of social media. In what follows, we therefore first seek to establish the context and discuss the existing definition of social media in general and social networking sites in particular. We then discuss how the specific characteristics, affordances, and boundary conditions of social media need to be considered when defining privacy for social media. We thereby particularly emphasize that social media and privacy are inherently social, dynamic, and at their core rooted in communication between individuals as well as with companies and institutions. We will discuss the nature and flow of social media use based on the central tenets of the Social Media Privacy Model (Trepte, 2021) and illustrate each step with associated research. This will allow us to review definitions of privacy for the social media context that we believe incorporate the particularities of privacy in social media and provide sufficient complexity for future research.

Social Media

To start with, it is important to better understand the context in which privacy became relevant after 2005, when the social media emerged as a global, popular, and ubiquitous phenomenon. What defines the technology and as such the context in which users now find themselves spending many hours of the day? A very commonly cited definition underlines users' activities and social media affordances:

> Social media are Internet-based channels that allow users to opportunistically interact and selectively self-present, either in real-time or asynchronously, with both broad and narrow audiences who derive value from user-generated content and the perception of interaction with others.
>
> *(Carr & Hayes, 2015, p. 50)*

In their definition, Caleb T. Carr and Rebecca A. Hayes underline that social media have four discrete requirements. They 1) consist of online platforms that 2) support synchronous and asynchronous communication, 3) are social in nature, and 4) are primarily based on user-generated content. We endorse the definition because it views technology as a context affording interaction. This definition encompasses what we think is key to understanding social media privacy as well: Technology is co-developed through interactions among users themselves, but also by developers reacting to these users' interactions. In social media, there is no clear "regime" of technology (see chapter 6 by Masur on situational privacy and chapter 9 by Treem, van Zoonen, and Sivunen on social media affordances and privacy). Rather, technology is both socially shaped and socially shaping (Williams, 1974), and its uses are negotiated among individuals, society, and the technology itself (Papacharissi, 2012). Similarly, how privacy is perceived and negotiated is shaped by technology *and* through social media users' practices.

Whereas social media can be seen as an umbrella term including various platforms and services, the perhaps most prominent examples are social networking sites such as Instagram, Twitter, Mastodon, BeReal, Snapchat, and Facebook.

> A social networking site is defined as a "[...] networked communication platform in which participants 1) have uniquely identifiable profiles that consist of user-supplied content, content provided by other users, and/or system-level data; 2) can publicly articulate connections that can be viewed and traversed by others; and 3) can consume, produce, and/or interact with streams of user-generated content provided by their connections on the site".
>
> *(Ellison & boyd, 2013, p. 158)*

In this definition of social networking sites, the interactional and social aspects of use practices are emphasized, highlighting users' profiles, connections, and behaviors. Here, social media are understood as an inherently social matter. Interestingly, although Carr and Hayes' social media definition as well as Ellison and boyds' definition of social networking sites seek to conceptualize a technology, most words actually refer to people and their practices in using it. From our point of view, this is no coincidence and is an important feature of definitions aiming to capture the fluctuating and dynamic nature of both social media and (as described in the following section) privacy, respectively.

Defining Privacy in Social Media

In the next step, we can investigate which interactions among individuals, dyads, groups, and collectives are relevant for the experience and practice of privacy on social media. From 2010 on, individuals negotiating and managing their personal privacy needs in light of the internal and external demands of social media use have been at the core of privacy research. In the "Privacy Online: Perspectives on Privacy and Self-Disclosure in the Social Web" (Trepte & Reinecke, 2011) – the book preceding this handbook – each of the 18 chapters refers to the negotiation of social media privacy. Authors describe social media users' struggles to attain or regain privacy on the one hand and to engage in self-presentation, emancipation, and inclusion on the other. In the introduction to the book, Margulis (2011) critically notes that the three most popular seminal definitions of privacy by Westin, Altman, and Petronio are of limited generalizability, because they cannot sufficiently be applied to the social media context.

A pivotal perspective on how privacy could be understood and defined in a networked, modern democracy was proposed by Zizi Papacharissi (2010) in "A private sphere: Democracy in a digital age," in which the convergence of economic, cultural, social, and political contexts is discussed along the lines of three themes: First, that "the privacy realm as a personal domain [is] presently contested by profit-driven objectives, thus leading to a potential commodification of *privacy*" (p. 42ff); second, that we are witnessing a "privatization of the public space" (p. 37ff) and "a progression towards a more intimate society" (p. 42); third, that "the rejection of both public and private spaces for the pursuit of a malleable space in between, characterized by activity that is *social* at heart, but that could embed political/civic merit and consequences" (p. 37). Social media use can well be seen as a key driver of the phenomena described in these themes. Although not specifically providing a definition of social media privacy, this analysis clearly paved the way for more specific and contextualized conceptualizations.

Nissenbaum (2010), who discussed privacy in the context of modern information and communication technologies, likewise provides a new perspective on privacy that takes the fluctuating and social nature of social media into account. In an attempt to emphasize the contextuality of privacy, Nissenbaum (2010) advanced the theory of contextual integrity, in which privacy is an individual's claim to an appropriate flow of information in a given context, arguing that there is great variability in a person's privacy needs that are systematically linked to the prevailing social context. A privacy violation is thus not necessarily a form of unwanted access, as often suggested by earlier theories (see above), but rather inappropriate access given a respective context:

> We have a right to privacy, but it is neither a right to control personal information nor a right to have access to this information restricted. Instead, it is a right to live in a world in which our expectations about the flow of personal information are, for the most part, met [...].
>
> *(Nissenbaum, 2010, p. 231)*

In 2010, Nissenbaum reflected on privacy against the backdrop of new technologies, including social media. This definition claims privacy as a right, as claimed 120 years earlier by Warren and Brandeis. It also coincides with Altman's and Westin's idea that individuals should strive to meet their ideal level of personal information flows. Yet, it further specifies contextual factors, including role perceptions, norms, and values that determine the principles of information flow in a given context.

The importance of acknowledging the specific context and affordances of social media use was underlined by danah boyd, who argued that

> [...] achieving privacy requires the ability to control the social situation by navigating complex contextual cues, technical affordances, and social dynamics. Achieving privacy is an ongoing process because social situations are never static.
>
> *(boyd, 2014, p. 60)*

Of course, situations are never static. Situational experiences also differ in non-mediated environments. However, early research on social media and privacy often assumed that these platforms are somewhat static, with everything remaining just as it was designed by the platform developers, unless the same or another developer steps in to make a change. This perspective often failed to acknowledge that within social media, people experience vastly different situations although using the exact same technology. Some communicative acts have small, others large or even unknown audiences. Some conversations are not accessible to others (e.g., in signal via end-to-end encryption), while others are protected by the cloak of anonymity (e.g., posting something under a pseudonym). Thus, no social media use episode (even within a single platform) is the same, which requires users to constantly evaluate their level of privacy and the options they have available to control it. This idea of fluctuating context is highlighted in Masur's (2018) situational definition of privacy:

> Privacy is a subjective perception resulting from the characteristics of the environment in which an individual happens to be at a given time. More precisely, the entirety of interpersonal and external circumstances (and their interactions) determines what level of privacy an individual perceives.
>
> *(Masur 2018, p. 312)*

Privacy practices thus are deeply embedded in the technical and social architecture of social media platforms. These specific contexts and the situations they typically produce have to be considered when aiming to understand how social media users perceive, enact, and regulate their privacy. But what exactly does this intricate interplay between social media use and privacy look like?

We outline the major tenets of the Social Media Privacy Model (Trepte, 2021) and adjacent research to highlight more explicitly how privacy is perceived and enacted on social media (Dombrowski & Trepte, 2023; Schäwel et al., 2021; Trepte & Dombrowki, 2023).

The privacy-relevant process of social media use starts with an initial assessment: Individual users assess their *ideal level of access* to the self, as laid out by the theorists referred to above (Altman, 1975; Gavison, 1980; Petronio, 2002). The ideal level of access refers to people's preference for how much should be known about themselves at a given moment in time. It is quantifiable in the sense of more or less (or alternatively, high or low). It results from individuals' dispositions (e.g., their individual need for privacy, personality, and experiences) and more external requirements and situational demands.

Then, social media users have different privacy-relevant *communication goals*, such as information retrieval, exchange of content, or simply socializing with other users. These goals come along with different challenges for privacy regulation and vary with regard to the gratifications to be expected from others (Trepte et al., 2020). Furthermore, time pressure is often an issue in privacy regulation and can crucially alter communication goals (see chapter 8 on heuristics in privacy decision-making by Liao, Sundar, and Rosson). In sum, one's initial assessment of the ideal level of access and one's communication goals set the expectations and motives, they are the glasses that social media users wear when evaluating social media interactions.

Social media boundary conditions exist in terms of content, the flow of content, and uses. First, what content social media users find online is the most important and first issue they deal with. Then comes the *flow of content* and how it is, will, or might be monitored and used, both by other social media users and also by third parties such as companies, service providers, or even state authorities. The exchange of information with other users on social networking sites is stored on servers owned by the platform providers and saved on other users' profiles; it can be forwarded, published to a wider audience, deleted, or move outside the internet.

Affordances set the boundaries of what is possible with regard to privacy regulation and what social media users can do to safeguard and regulate their privacy in alignment with their individual level of access and communication goals (Trepte, 2015). Affordances can be defined as the result of the interaction between the possibilities and features of the social media context on the one hand, and how social media users breathe life into these features on the other (Fox & McEwan, 2017; Treem & Leonardi, 2012). The affordance of anonymity, for example, means that social media users participate, get in touch with one another, interact, and retrieve information with varying degrees of identifiability, but this comes at the price of not being identifiable and thus not oneself. Editability means that in the course of using social media, individual actions are changeable and can be edited and altered. Association, as the core social media affordance, means that the content of social media and its flow allows for and demand interaction with others. Only those deliberately sharing their identity and more will be rewarded with what has been shown to make social media users happy and healthy: Social contacts (Dienlin et al., 2017). Persistence means that content is more or less available over time. All of these affordances are deeply social. They are rooted in social processes and are expressed as such. Consequently, not only how the structures of social media are designed for social encounters, but also how they are used in practice, are driven by social processes. Social encounters determine how social media features work.

Affordances such as anonymity, editability, association, and persistence define *privacy mechanisms*, or in other words, the options individuals have at their hands to regulate their privacy and to rely on: Control, trust, norms, and interpersonal communication. With the emergence of social media, it became clear to both scholars and users that control is only one of the privacy mechanisms (Hargittai & Marwick, 2016; Tavani & Moor, 2001). Accordingly, control, but also trust and norms, can be considered the most important privacy mechanisms that social media users tend to rely on. Then, the option to communicate about one's privacy has been discussed as an important mechanism in more current privacy theorizing and empirical studies (de Wolf, 2020; Trepte, 2021).

Users want to share personal information with others in order to celebrate life or share sadness and sorrow. To do so, they have to rely on social and legislative norms asserting that these pieces of information will not find their way into information flows that betray them and these purposes. When assessing the boundary conditions, they think about whether they can trust other users, how much they can rely on established norms, or whether it would be better to get in touch with other users in order to personally explain that this specific picture or piece of information should not be shared with (certain) others. Privacy mechanisms are nothing more than options in this step. Each individual's assessment of their communication goals and of the social media boundaries results in an assessment of what can be done, what is necessary, and what is available with regard to privacy regulation. Then, in the next step, the situational and experienced level of access is re-assessed, leading to the individual perception of privacy in this certain situation, as outlined in Masur's (2018) definition of privacy. Only if an individual is aware of their individual goals and the social media boundaries can they determine how they feel about their individual privacy and whether and how they should regulate their privacy in the following.

Privacy regulation behaviors have often been used synonymously with privacy in respective definitions. According to the Social Media Privacy Model, such behaviors include "interdependent" and more "ego-centered" forms of regulation (Trepte, 2021). First, interdependent privacy regulation behaviors include deliberation, institutionalized, and often public communication. Here individual privacy regulation can become a part of the democratic process. Deliberation is widely known and theorized in the field of political communication, and scholars always found that privacy is political (Ochs, 2018; Papacharissi, 2010). Privacy refers to the freedom of social media users and of larger networks and as such has important political dimensions. Second, the most important form of privacy regulation on social media is *interpersonal communication*. Examples of this include a brief check-in among colleagues about how to handle sharing private pictures after a work event or a longer talk about pictures of a young couple on one of their Instagram's (de Wolf, 2020).

Ego-centered forms of privacy regulation, including control and self-disclosure, are much more commonly discussed in theorizing and definitions. *Control* means that social media users take advantage of their option to consent, correct information, or adjust access and protection (Tavani, 2007). On social media, there is only a very narrow space for controlling who shares what with whom. Although not much control is available, social media users still feel that controlling information is one of the most efficient and certainly the easiest way of obtaining the experience of privacy they expect (Sarikakis & Winter, 2017).

Self-disclosure has been key to understanding privacy online and on social media ever since (Dienlin & Metzger, 2016; Joinson, 2001). Self-disclosure is thus the most researched form of privacy regulation because, without self-disclosure, social media participation is not visible and not executable. Each and every step of social media use involves self-disclosure, from registration to logoff. Hence, self-disclosure is often not a conscious or pro-active form of privacy regulation, but first and foremost active participation on social media implying granular forms of disclosure and withdrawal.

Although we believe these are the most important regulation behaviors, there are of course more. Withdrawal has been introduced as the counterpart to self-disclosure (Dienlin & Metzger, 2016; Meier et al., 2020). Also, legal measures are sometimes a necessary step of privacy regulation when other regulation behaviors fail. Furthermore, cognitive or emotional regulation accompanies other forms of regulation behavior and is sometimes only available approach (Dombrowski & Trepte, 2023). Cynicism and resignation do not encompass privacy behaviors, but can also be considered a type of privacy regulation because they involve a form of coping (see chapter 13 by Ranzini, Lutz, and Hoffmann). These privacy regulation behaviors – and this is a challenge for its empirical investigation – are not used in an on- or off-fashion, but rather intertwined.

Based on these considerations, Trepte (2021) developed a definition of social media privacy that specifically acknowledges the social, dynamic, and fluctuating nature of privacy during social media use:

> I define privacy by an individual's assessments of (a) the level of access to this person in an interaction or relationship with others (people, companies, institutions) and (b) the availability of the mechanisms of control, interpersonal communication, trust, and norms for shaping this level of access through (c) self-disclosure as (almost intuitive) behavioral privacy regulation and (d) control, interpersonal communication, and deliberation as means for ensuring (a somewhat more elaborated) regulation of privacy. In social media, then, the availability of the mechanisms that can be applied to ensure privacy are crucially influenced by the content that is being shared and the social media affordances that determine how this content is further used.
>
> *(Trepte, 2021, p. 561)*

In accordance with seminal and also most current theories, we consider the initial individual assessment of needs, access, and communication goals as the first step in defining the ideal level of privacy. We then argue that social media realms impose three relevant aspects for consideration – the other people involved, the content being shared, and the affordances encountered – and that social media users regulate their privacy in light of these aspects.

Conclusion

This chapter has pursued three goals. One was the rather service-oriented idea of reviewing definitions for other scholars, perhaps particularly those new to our field and seeking to gain first insights. Our second goal was to critically reflect on how these definitions serve different purposes. Lastly, we discuss the specific nature of privacy in the context of social media and finally suggest a definition that reflects social media privacy specifically. A definition is nothing more than a first attempt to find common ground and a starting point. Some are specific to certain aspects of privacy on social media, others are broad and all-encompassing. However, all definitions make it possible to conduct comparative research, which in turn advances the opportunity to conduct replication studies and compare findings. Most importantly, we believe it is important to embrace complexity in future privacy theorizing.

References

Acquisti, A. (2005). Privacy in electronic commerce and the economics of immediate gratification. In J. Breese, J. Feigenbaum, & M. Seltzer (Eds.), *EC ' 05: Proceedings of the 6th ACM conference on electronic commerce, June 5–8, 2005* (p. 21). Vancouver, Canada, ACM. https://doi.org/10.1145/988772.988777

Acquisti, A., & Gross, R. (2006). Awareness, information sharing, and privacy on the Facebook. In *56th Annual Meeting of the International Communication Association*, June 21–24, 2006, Dresden, Germany.

Acquisti, A., & Grossklags, J. (2004). Privacy attitudes and privacy behavior: Losses, gains, and hyberbolic discounting. In L. J. Camp & S. Lewis (Eds.), *Advances in information security: Vol. 12. Economics of information security* (pp. 165–178). Kluwer. https://doi.org/10.1007/1-4020-8090-5_13

Allen, A. L. (1988). *Uneasy access: Privacy for women in a free society. New feminist perspectives series*. Rowman & Littlefield.

Altman, I. (1975). *The environment and social behavior: Privacy, personal space, territory, crowding*. Brooks/Cole Publishing Company.

Barak, A., & Gluck-Ofri, O. (2007). Degree and reciprocity of self-disclosure in online forums. *CyberPsychology & Behavior, 10*(3), 407–417.

Barnes, S. B. (2006). A privacy paradox: Social networking in the United States. *First Monday, 11*(9). https://doi.org/10.5210/fm.v11i9.1394

Ben-Ze'ev, A. (2003). Privacy, emotional closeness, and openness in cyberspace. *Computers in Human Behavior, 19*(4), 451–567. https://doi.org/10.1016/S0747-5632(02)00078-X

boyd, d. (2014). *It's complicated. The social lives of networked teens*. Yale University Press.

Burgoon, J. K. (1982). Privacy and communication. *Communication Yearbook*, *6*(4), 206–249. https://doi.org/10.1080/23808985

Carr, C. T., & Hayes, R. A. (2015). Social media: Defining, developing, and divining. *Atlantic Journal of Communication*, *23*(1), 46–65. https://doi.org/10.1080/15456870.2015.972282.

de Wolf, R. P. (2020). Contextualizing how teens manage personal and interpersonal privacy on social media. *New Media & Society*, *22*(6), 1058–1075. https://doi.org/10.1177/1461444819876570

DeCew, J. W. (1997). *In pursuit of privacy: Law, ethics, and the rise of technology*. Cornell University Press.

Dienlin, T. (2014). The privacy process model. In S. Garnett, S. Halft, M. Herz, & J. M. Mönig (Eds.), *Medien und Privatheit* (pp. 105–122). Karl Stutz.

Dienlin, T., Masur, P. K., & Trepte, S. (2017). Reinforcement or displacement? The reciprocity of FtF, IM, and SNS communication and their effects on loneliness and life satisfaction. *Journal of Computer-Mediated Communication*, Advance online publication. https://doi.org/10.1111/jcc4.12183

Dienlin, T., & Metzger, M. J. (2016). An extended privacy calculus model for SNSs—Analyzing self-disclosure and self-withdrawal in a U.S. representative sample. *Journal of Computer-Mediated Communication*, *21*(5), 368–383. https://doi.org/10.1111/jcc4.12163

Dinev, T., & Hart, P. (2004). Internet privacy concerns and their antecedents - measurement validity and a regression model. *Behaviour & Information Technology*, *23*(6), 413–422. https://doi.org/10.1080/01449290410001715723

Dinev, T., & Hart, P. (2006). An extended privacy calculus model for e-commerce transactions. *Information Systems Research*, *17*(1), 61–80. https://doi.org/10.1287/isre.1060.0080

Dombrowski, J., & Trepte, S. (2023). Predicting privacy regulation behavior on social media. *Under Review*.

Dommeyer, C. J., & Gross, B. L. (2003). What consumers know and what they do: An investigation of consumer knowledge, awareness, and use of privacy protection strategies. *Journal of Interactive Marketing*, *17*(2), 34–51. https://doi.org/10.1002/dir.10053

The Economist (2017). *The world's most valuable resource is no longer oil, but data*. https://www.economist.com/leaders/2017/05/06/the-worlds-most-valuable-resource-is-no-longer-oil-but-data

Eichenhofer, J. (2019). *e-Privacy - Theorie und Dogmatik eines europäischen Privatheitsschutzes im Internet-Zeitalter [Theoretical and doctrinal foundations of a European privacy protection regulation in the internet age]*. University of Bielefeld.

Ellison, N. B., & boyd, d. (2013). Sociality through social network sites. In W. H. Dutton (Ed.), *The Oxford handbook of studies* (pp. 151–172). Oxford University Press.

Fox, J., & McEwan, B. (2017). Distinguishing technologies for social interaction: The perceived social affordances of communication channels scale. *Communication Monographs*, *84*(3), 298–318. https://doi.org/10.1080/03637751.2017.1332418

Gavison, R. (1980). Privacy and the limits of law. *The Yale Law Journal*, *89*(3), 421–471.

Gross, R., & Acquisti, A. (2005). Information revelation and privacy in online social networks. In V. Atluri, S. Di Capitani Vimercati, & R. Dingledine (Chairs), *The 2005 ACM Workshop*, Alexandria, VA, USA.

Hargittai, E., & Marwick, A. E. (2016). "What can I really do?" Explaining the privacy paradox with online apathy. *International Journal of Communication*, *10*, 3737–3757.

Hobbes, T. (1651/2011). *Leviathan*. Pacific Publishing Studio.

Jensen, C., Potts, C., & Jensen, C. (2005). Privacy practices of users: Self-reports versus observed behavior. *International Journal of Human-Computer Studies*, *63*(1–2), 203–227. https://doi.org/10.1016/j.ijhcs.2005.04.019

Joinson, A. N. (2001). Self-disclosure in computer-mediated communication: The role of self-awareness and visual anonymity. *European Journal of Social Psychology*, *31*(2), 177–192. https://doi.org/10.1002/ejsp.36

Joinson, A. N., Paine, C., Buchanan, T., & Reips, U.-D. (2006). Watching me, watching you: Privacy attitudes and reactions to identity card implementation scenarios in the United Kingdom. *Journal of Information Science*, *32*, 334–343.

Locke, J. (1689/2005). *A letter concerning toleration*. Digireads.com Publishing.

Margulis, S. T. (2011). Three theories of privacy: An overview. In S. Trepte & L. Reinecke (Eds.), *Privacy online. Perspectives on privacy and self-disclosure in the social web* (pp. 9–17). Springer.

Masur, P. K. (2018). *Situational privacy and self-disclosure: Communication processes in online environments*. Springer International Publishing.

Masur, P. K. (2020). How online privacy literacy supports self-data protection and self-determination in the age of information. *Media and Communication*, *8*(2), 258–269. https://doi.org/10.17645/mac.v8i2.2855

Meier, Y., Schäwel, J., Kyewski, E., & Krämer, N. C. (2020). Applying protection motivation theory to predict Facebook users' withdrawal and disclosure intentions. *SMSociety'20: International Conference on Social Media and Society*, 21–29. https://doi.org/10.1145/3400806.3400810

Metzger, M. J. (2004). Privacy, trust, and disclosure: Exploring barriers to electronic commerce. *Journal of Computer-Mediated Communication, 9*(4). https://doi.org/10.1111/j.1083-6101.2004.tb00292.x
Mill, J. S. (1859/2015). *On liberty*. CreateSpace.
Miller, A. R. (1971). *The assault on privacy: Computers, data banks, and dossiers*. University of Michigan Press.
Nissenbaum, H. (2010). *Privacy in context: Technology, policy, and the integrity of social life*. Stanford University Press.
Ochs, C. (2018). Self-protection beyond the self: Collective privacy practices in (big) datascapes. In *Routledge research in information technology and society: Vol. 21. The politics and policies of big data: Big data, big brother?* (1st ed., pp. 265–291). Routledge.
Palen, L., & Dourish, P. (2003). Unpacking 'privacy' for a networked world. In V. Bellotti (Ed.), *CHI letters: Vol. 1, CHI 2003: Proceedings of the SIGCHI conference on human factors in computing systems* (5th ed., pp. 129–136). ACM Press. https://doi.org/10.1145/642611.642635
Papacharissi, Z. (2010). *A private sphere: Democracy in a digital age*. Polity Press.
Papacharissi, Z. (2011). *A networked self: Identity, community, and culture on social network sites*. Routledge.
Papacharissi, Z. (2012). A networked self: Identity performance and sociability on social network sites. In F. L. F. Lee , L. Leung J. L. Qiu ,& D. S. C. Chu (Eds.), *Frontiers in new media research* (pp. 207–221). Routledge Taylor & Francis.
Patil, S., & Kobsa, A. (2005). Uncovering privacy attitudes and practices in instant messaging. In M. Pendergast, K. Schmidt, G. Mark, & M. Ackerman (Eds.), *Proceedings of the 2005 international ACM SIGGROUP conference on supporting group work - GROUP '05* (p. 109). ACM Press. https://doi.org/10.1145/1099203.1099220
Petronio, S. (2002). *Boundaries of privacy*. State University of New York Press.
Preibusch, S. (2006). Implementing privacy negotiations in E-commerce. In X. Zhou (Ed.), *Lecture notes in computer science: Vol. 3841. Frontiers of WWW research and development: Proceedings* (Vol. 3841, pp. 604–615). Springer. https://doi.org/10.1007/11610113_53
Prosser, W. L. (1960). Privacy. *California Law Review, 48*(3), 383–423. https://doi.org/10.2307/3478805.
Reinecke, L., Trepte, S., & Behr, K.-M. (2008). Web 2.0 users' values and concerns of privacy. In *58th Annual Conference of the International Communication Association (ICA), May 22–26, 2008*, Montreal, Canada.
Rössler, B. (2001). *Der Wert des Privaten* (1530th ed.). Suhrkamp.
Sarikakis, K., & Winter, L. (2017). Social media users' legal consciousness about privacy. *Social Media + Society, 3*(1), 1–14. https://doi.org/10.1177/2056305117695325
Schäwel, J., Frener, R., & Trepte, S. (2021). Political microtargeting and online privacy: A theoretical approach to understanding users' privacy behaviors. *Media and Communication, 9*(4), 158–169. https://doi.org/10.17645/mac.v9i4.4085
Sevignani, S. (2016). *Privacy and capitalism in the age of social media. Routledge research in information technology and society: Vol. 18*. Routledge.
Solove, D. J. (2008). *Understanding privacy*. Harvard University Press.
Tavani, H. T. (2007). Philosophical theories of privacy: Implications for an adequate online privacy policy. *Metaphilosophy, 38*(1), 1–22. https://doi.org/10.1111/j.1467-9973.2006.00474.x
Tavani, H. T., & Moor, J. H. (2001). Privacy protection, control of information, and privacy-enhancing technologies. *ACM SIGCAS Computers and Society, 31*(1), 6–11. https://doi.org/10.1145/572277.572278
Tidwell, L. S., & Walther, J. B. (2002). Computer-mediated communication effects on disclosure, impressions, and interpersonal evaluations. Getting to know one another a bit at a time. *Human Communication Research, 28*(3), 317–348. https://doi.org/10.1111/j.1468-2958.2002.tb00811.x
Treem, J. W., & Leonardi, P. M. (2012). Social media use in organizations. Exploring the affordances of visibility, editability, persistence, and association. *Communication Yearbook, 36*, 143–189. https://doi.org/10.1080/23808985.2013.11679130
Trepte, S. (2015). Social media, privacy, and self-disclosure: The turbulence caused by social media's affordances. *Social Media and Society, 1*(1), 1–2. https://doi.org/10.1177/2056305115578681
Trepte, S. (2021). The social media privacy model: Privacy and communication in the light of social media affordances. *Communication Theory, 31*(4), 549–570. https://doi.org/10.1093/ct/qtz035
Trepte, S., & Dombrowki, J. (2023). Testing the social media privacy model. A meta-analysis. *In Preparation*.
Trepte, S., & Reinecke, L. (Eds.). (2011). *Privacy online. Perspectives on privacy and self-disclosure in the social web*. Springer.
Trepte, S., Scharkow, M., & Dienlin, T. (2020). The privacy calculus contextualized: The influence of affordances. *Computers in Human Behavior, 104*, 106115. https://doi.org/10.1016/j.chb.2019.08.022

Viegas, F. B. (2005). Bloggers' expectations of privacy and accountability. An initial survey. *Journal of Computer-Mediated Communication*, *10*(3), article 12. https://doi.org/10.1111/j.1083-6101.2005.tb00260.x
Warren, S. D., & Brandeis, L. D. (1890). The right to privacy. *Harvard Law Review*, *4*(5), 193–220.
Westin, A. F. (1967). *Privacy and freedom*. Atheneum.
Westin, A. F. (2003). Social and political dimensions of privacy. *Journal of Social Issues*, *59*(2), 431–453. https://doi.org/10.1111/1540-4560.00072
Williams, R. (1974). *Television: Technology and cultural form*. Fontana.

2

INDIVIDUALISTIC PRIVACY THEORIES

Natalie N. Bazarova and Pengfei Zhao

CORNELL UNIVERSITY, USA

The origin of individualistic approaches to privacy traces back to the legal conception of privacy as a human right integral to society's moral value systems (Warren & Brandeis, 1980). Its deeper roots go even further into the public/private distinctions in ancient Greece where privacy and the private sphere were conceptualized as a backdrop for participation in the public sphere (public in the sense of political, as in the life of the Polis), fulfilling an important social function (Komamura, 2019; Solove, 2008). The rise of the modern age and the expansion of the social sphere, as distinct from both political and private (household) lives, have brought into light a new dimension of privacy as a "shelter for intimacy," whereby privacy holds an intrinsic value for individuals (Komamura, 2019, p. 1346). The social realm has blurred the lines between the public realm and the private sphere, forcing individuals into "the ambivalent spaces between disclosure and concealment" in which people constantly choose what to share and what to conceal in every aspect of their daily lives (Komamura, 2019, p. 1350). How people navigate these ambivalent spaces by making decisions about disclosure and concealment, the role of socio-psychological factors in determining their choices, and perceptions of privacy risks and rewards have become the bread-and-butter questions for research conducted within the individualistic paradigm, guided by underlying assumptions of individual control, agency, and rationality in privacy management.

In what follows, we first consider the core assumptions of individualistic theories and how these assumptions hold in today's digital environments. Then we review foundational privacy theories, followed by a discussion of rationality vs. bounded rationality in privacy decision-making. Throughout the chapter, we raise questions and challenges that have emerged for individualistic privacy in a networked environment. Finally, the chapter concludes with emergent directions and extensions in an individualistic understanding of privacy.

Control and Agency as Core Assumptions of Individualistic Theories

The focus of individualistic approaches on privacy as the right of autonomous individuals with a voluntary choice and self-determination foregrounds individual control and agency in privacy decisions. Control has been tightly coupled with privacy as either a core mechanism through which individuals attain privacy (Westin, 1967a) or as a precondition for privacy such that people feel safe to share personal information when they perceive enough control over information content, flow, and use (see for review, Trepte, 2021). In a recent analysis of privacy control, control is equated with "informational self-determination," which refers to "power over information and agency in

DOI: 10.4324/9781003244677-3

decisions regarding this information" (Trepte, 2021, p. 555). With informational control closely tied to individuality, agency, and power, it is not a surprise that individualistic approaches resting on the premise of control have embraced privacy ego-centrality (Trepte, 2021), or having an individual at the center of privacy regulation, reflecting "ego-centered needs and ... practices structured around the self" (Papacharissi, 2010, p. 144).

In today's digital society, however, the roles and functions of control in privacy decisions have been profoundly altered. Social media have amped up the obscurity and ambiguity of online social spaces creating *hyper-ambivalent spaces* for privacy navigation by blurring the lines between mass and personal communication, different audiences, and contexts (French & Bazarova, 2017; Marwick & boyd, 2014; O'Sullivan & Carr, 2018). The ambiguous and often unobstructed information pathways across audiences, contexts, and time complicate individuals' ability to contextually regulate their privacy by adjusting what, when, and with whom to share personal information. With the rise of the new type of social media publicness – the "personal publics" (Schmidt, 2014) – individuals find themselves, paradoxically, with both more control and less control over their personal information. On the one hand, personal publics opens up a communicative space where people are in control of selecting and sharing information of personal relevance (Schmidt, 2014). On the other hand, they largely lack awareness and control over information flow and use. Once shared, personal data control and ownership become quickly fragmented across multiple actors and entities, including other users and companies who can, in turn, share it with other unintended users and third parties, such as apps and advertisers, and use it in contextually unintended ways (Bazarova & Masur, 2020; Nissenbaum, 2010). For instance, someone's picture can become easily detached from its primary owner and the original context in which it was shared and turn into a viral meme in a matter of hours or even minutes. As asserted by privacy legal scholars (Richards & Hartzog, 2016, p. 444), when users enter an asymmetrical power relationship with social media platforms by consenting to share personal data there, what they are left with is only "the illusion of control" rather than a real control over their personal information.

The limits and losses of individual control undermine the privacy-as-control and privacy-as-rights-based models (Komamura, 2019; Nissenbaum, 2004). However, rather than equating a loss of control with the "death of privacy" (Preston, 2014), recent theorizations have emphasized interpersonal and relational aspects of privacy regulation (Trepte, 2021), offered conceptualization of privacy based on information flow rather than control (Nissenbaum, 2010), called for the integration of different levels and layers of privacy controls and information flow (Bazarova & Masur, 2020), and espoused trust-based instead of control-based models of privacy (Komamura, 2019; Richards & Hartzog, 2016). We will come back to these theorizations in the last section on future directions and potential extensions of individualistic approaches.

Individualistic Privacy Theories and Frameworks: Foundations

With an individual at the center of privacy agency and control, individualistic privacy research has made significant strides in understanding individual privacy decision-making, individuals' perceptions of risks and factors that shape them, privacy management and self-disclosure behaviors, and, finally, how individuals navigate and mitigate risks through preventive and corrective behaviors. Most individualistic theories have built on the theoretical foundations of the works by Westin (1967a) and Altman (1975), both of which, especially Altman's theory, paved the way for Petronio's (2002) communication privacy management (CPM) theory (see for a detailed review of these theories, Margulis, 2011).

Westin ascertained the individual right and autonomy to determine what personal information can be communicated to, and used by, others. Drawing on the distinctions between the public and private spheres and increasingly concerned with a growing data surveillance (Westin, 1967b), he conceptualized privacy as a voluntary withdrawal state and "freedom from the observation of others" (Westin, 2003, p. 432). While later research, by and large, contested Westin's conceptualization of privacy as a voluntary withdrawal state, his concern for informational control and understanding of privacy as a dynamic process serving individuals' momentary needs and social roles made a significant imprint on future privacy research.

The dynamic approach to privacy has been further refined by social psychologist Irvin Altman. He conceptualized privacy as a selective control to self through an interpersonal boundary regulation in response to one's changing internal states and external circumstances (Altman, 1975). This process is inherently dialectical, reflecting individuals' desires for openness and closedness to others. His conceptualization of privacy integrated interpersonal aspects of relationships, behavioral mechanisms of privacy regulation, and temporal and situational dimensions, at the center of which all is an individual as a social actor embedded in an environment. Thus, Altman's analysis advanced both psychological and social aspects of privacy by recasting privacy in a dialectical, rather than oppositional, relationship to social interaction. Furthermore, his approach to privacy as a psychological process inseparable from social and physical environments and temporal dynamics propelled future research's focus on situational and individual factors that shape privacy perceptions and privacy regulation behaviors (see for review, Knijnenburg et al., 2022; Trepte & Reinecke, 2011).

In one of the early applications of Altman's framework to digital environments, Palen and Dourish (2003) described online spaces within which people manage privacy as "conditions of circumstance" (p. 131). These conditions of circumstance are created by a combination of technology in use, physical environments, audiences, tasks, intentions, motivations, social status, and other factors. By outright rejecting a static or rule-based approach to privacy management, Palen and Dourish conceptualized online privacy boundary regulation as a dynamic response to the conditions of circumstance. Recognizing the disruptive role of technology in shifting the lines between public and private and individuals' diminishing control over disclosed information, Palen and Dourish emphasized the importance of privacy management in relation to the *possibilities* offered by technologies in addition to their actual use. The idea of managing privacy in the context of possibilities afforded by technology, which may never be possible for ordinary users to fully comprehend, further underscores the challenge of individual privacy management in hyper-ambivalent online spaces.

A comprehensive account of people's dialectical management of privacy boundaries was offered in Petronio's (2002) CPM theory, which integrated the dynamic perspective with a rule-based approach to privacy. According to this theory, people continuously manage individual privacy boundaries by controlling the flow of private information. The individual privacy boundary management is based on a malleable and dynamic rule-based system determined by both stable and variable decision criteria, including cultural and family privacy orientations, individual characteristics, situational needs and motivations, and risk-benefit ratio criteria. By presenting a comprehensive analysis of individual privacy decision-making, CPM also made evident the limitations of a purely individualistic privacy approach: A collective privacy ownership begins where a personal boundary ends because an act of self-disclosure transforms a personal boundary into a collective boundary (Petronio, 2002). Therefore, the analysis of individual privacy decision-making must account for how people manage both personal and collective privacy boundaries, and CPM stipulates rules for regulating collective privacy boundaries. While the disclosed information is co-owned with authorized recipients, CPM makes it clear that collective rules should adhere to the primary owner's expectations about third parties' access to the disclosed information and control over the information flow (Petronio & Child, 2020). This presupposition, however, comes under question in social media environments where access to and control over the disclosed information become fragmented across multiple parties, with increasing separation of information from the primary owner, who often has limited awareness, and even less influence, over how the data are being used (Bazarova & Masur, 2020).

To sum up, there is a strong theoretical tradition of individual agency and control in privacy research, putting individuals at the center of privacy management. At the same time, privacy is recognized as an inherently social process (Margulis, 2011), where the centrality of self goes hand-in-hand with "the centrality of others" who are both recipients and co-owners of entrusted information (Petronio & Child, 2020, p. 80). We also discussed how privacy management had been made increasingly complicated by online socio-technical environments, which we identified as hyper-ambivalent social spaces because of the fluidity and obscurity of actions, audiences, and information flows and controls. From the individualistic privacy foundations, we now move to other models and frameworks that build on these foundations to understand individual privacy decision-making and behavior online.

Individual Decision-Making and Behaviors: Rationality or Bounded Rationality?

The efforts to account for privacy decision-making and behaviors can be characterized as chasing the question of rationality and departures from it, in how people evaluate privacy risks, perceive disclosure rewards, and act upon their risk-reward valuations. Individualistic privacy research has approached this question from two directions: A rational approach according to which individuals engage in a rational and systematic cost-benefit analysis and disclose personal information when perceived benefits outweigh perceived risks (Dinev & Hart, 2006; Krasnova et al., 2010) or the bounded rationality perspective (Simon, 1956) where people fall short from perfect rationality and instead resort to cognitive shortcuts and heuristics (e.g., Acquisti & Grossklags, 2005; Sundar et al., 2020). The former approach is best exemplified by the privacy calculus theory grounded in an "anticipatory, rational weighing of risks and benefits" (Kehr et al., 2013, p. 2), while the latter is represented by privacy paradox – a mismatch between privacy perceptions and disclosure behaviors, which is often (although not always) assumed to be a product of biased and irrational decision-making (Barnes, 2006; Baruh et al., 2017; Kokolakis, 2017).

While privacy calculus and privacy paradox theories are often cast as opposites, their recent re-interpretations and empirical findings point to what we see as a common vector of situational privacy within the constraints of bounded rationality or *situationally bounded privacy*. First, because of the constraints of information, cognition, and time, perfect rationality is virtually unattainable in real-life situations (Simon, 1956, 1990). Second, bounded rationality does not imply that people act irrationally, unreasonably, or inferiorly, but that their rationality is bounded by information availability, cognitive capacities, situational environment, time, and other factors that cause their decision-making calculus to shift from perfectly rational to "good enough" or "satisfying" to the specific circumstances (Simon, 1956). Third, recent work has extended privacy calculus into a "situational privacy calculus" (Kehr et al., 2013, p. 610) and "contextualized" privacy calculus (e.g., Bol et al., 2018; Dienlin & Metzger, 2016). Both emphasize the role of contextual factors (e.g., affordances, perception of other users, situational cues via primes and nudges, and social media contexts) in the perceived privacy risk-benefit tradeoff, which can override general/global privacy attitudes and tendencies. At the same time, "mitigating situational factors" have also been proposed to account for the privacy paradox because they induce disclosure by highlighting gratifications (Wilson, 2015, p. 23), and proximate perceived benefits are weighed more heavily than uncertain and distal risks (Krasnova et al., 2010). Furthermore, Dienlin and Trepte (2015) provided convincing evidence that a gap between privacy concerns and privacy behaviors exists only when generic privacy concerns are mapped onto specific privacy behaviors but disappears when privacy attitudes and intentions are aligned with privacy behaviors in terms of action, target, context, and time, following the principle of compatibility from the theory of planned behavior (Fishbein & Ajzen, 2010). In other words, "broad and abstract attitudes such as privacy concerns are less likely to predict narrow behaviors such as the use of public vs. private profile on social network sites" (Dienlin & Trepte, 2015, p. 287).

The fact that privacy concerns have to be situationally grounded – as argued by both privacy calculus and privacy paradox research – is highly significant from the point of view of bounded rationality. Simon (1990, p. 7) used the metaphor of scissors to describe bounded rationality, with one blade referring to humans' cognitive capabilities and their limitations and the other to the structure of the environment. Just as it takes both blades for the scissors to work, people use cognitive optimization strategies adapted to the structures of the environment to arrive at satisfying solutions (see also, Gigerenzer & Selten, 2002). In contrast, looking at generic or global privacy concerns is similar to using only one blade of the scissors, which does not help us understand how people behave in a particular environment. The environment is the "life space" of an organism determined by one's perceptions, needs, and goals, and people behave "approximately rationally, or adaptively, in a particular environment" by responding to its structural characteristics, suggested by salient clues and choice points (Simon, 1956, p. 130). This kind of bounded rationality as an adaptation to the structures of social and physical environments has also been referred to as "ecological rationality" to emphasize functional and environmental perspectives (Gigerenzer, 2002, p. 37).

Now consider the significance of situational cues for privacy decision-making adaptation in hyper-ambivalent spaces of online environments. In addition to the enormous knowledge gaps with regard to the information flow and access in social media platforms, people in these spaces lack customary sensorial cues, which serve as "the baseline privacy safeguards" in physical environments (Acquisti et al., 2022, p. 271). Amid information gaps and lack of sensorial cues, combined with the malleability and uncertainty of people's own privacy preferences (Acquisti et al., 2015), situational cues serve as usable signposts in otherwise largely uncharted terrains of social media. These cues can be furnished in the form of privacy nudges and primes, social norms, social media affordances, audience cues, or other social or technological features, which can raise awareness of privacy risks or, alternatively, amplify anticipated rewards, thereby moving the privacy needle toward more risk-averse or more sharing behaviors, respectively (e.g., Masur et al., 2021; Sundar et al., 2020). The pathways from situational cues to disclosure rewards to disclosure behaviors have been further developed within the functional disclosure paradigm, according to which situational cues in the form of audience representations and social media affordances spotlight certain disclosure rewards and subjective risks, which, in turn, account for general disclosure intimacy (Bazarova & Choi, 2014; Choi & Bazarova, 2015) and distress disclosure on social media platforms (Zhao et al., 2021).

The challenge in situational bounded privacy is the intertwined and multilayered nature of different internal and external factors and how to disentangle their impacts and interplays in privacy decision-making and behavior (Acquisti & Grossklags, 2006). One of the recent efforts to tackle this challenge is Masur's (2018) theory of situational privacy and self-disclosure (see also chapter by Masur on situational privacy in this volume). According to this theory, self-disclosure is predicted by one's psychological perception and experience of a given situation shaped by a combination of different factors, including situationally salient needs or feelings (situationally variable internal factors), interpersonal assessments of other people present in this situation, and environmental factors. Other empirical work has also started to address situational factors more holistically by incorporating a broad array of situational factors into one's online disclosure ecology, as well as more general situational (e.g., external stressors) and non-situational factors (Zhang et al., 2021).

In addition to interdependencies between cognitive processes and a variety of situational factors, it is important to account for the fluidity of situations as they unfold, confronting people with new situational cues that can shift their perceptions of socio-technical environments. Furthermore, as argued in the networked privacy model (Marwick & boyd, 2014), social media users are actively co-constructing situations, and "context slips and changes according to fluctuating social norms and technological affordances" (p. 1064). Capturing this dynamic unfolding and co-construction is critical for understanding the joint influence of situational and non-situational factors in order to disentangle why different people perceive and behave differently in the same situation (between-person level) and why a given person may behave consistently to some extent across different situations (within-person level) (e.g., Meier et al., 2022). Although we emphasize the situational perspectives in this chapter, the impact of relatively stable individual factors, such as demographics, personality, and literacy, should not be overlooked for understanding privacy perceptions and behaviors.

Finally, while people are most apt to respond to the structures of the situation at hand based on salient social and situational cues, online privacy, as argued above, must be managed in the context of possibilities offered by technologies (Palen & Dourish, 2003), as data use and access are not restricted to a specific point in time, interaction context, and immediate conversational participants in social media exchanges. Thus, another challenge laid bare by the bounded rationality perspective is how to reconcile the myriad of possibilities enabled by technologies, including an ever-growing use of algorithms and AI tools, with situationally bounded privacy. We now turn attention to the emergent directions in individualistic privacy research that extend our understanding of individual privacy management by tackling the challenges of limited individual control and situationally bounded privacy.

Emergent Directions and Extensions in Individualistic Privacy Research

Several recent frameworks have addressed the decline of individual privacy control by re-conceptualizing and de-emphasizing its role in privacy management. Nissenbaum's (2010) contextual integrity theory has individual control as one of many possible transmission principles or constraints, which, along with reciprocity, confidentiality, etc., regulate the flow of information, as prescribed by informational norms. Trepte's (2021) new social media privacy model incorporates individual control as one of the lesser core privacy mechanisms, in addition to trust, norms, and interpersonal communication. Challenging the "access-control" model, Marwick and boyd (2014) argue that control is no longer in the purview of an individual user because anyone connected to the user can violate privacy, and the only viable privacy regulation mechanisms are social norms and social ties. Bazarova and Masur (2020) further layered control into three levels: A primary control held by original disclosers who decide what to share and with whom, a proximal control held by intended information receivers who become information co-owners, and a distal control by collateral third parties, such as companies and platforms, who are not intended recipients of information but receive authorized access through terms of use and data sharing agreements. Recognizing that privacy is not just one's own business and instead taking a relational view on privacy, Richards and Hartzog (2016, p. 432) introduced the idea of "information relationships" based on trust and expectations around information transactions, arguing for the need to move from control-based to trust-based models of privacy where tech companies would have fiduciary-like responsibilities toward users' data.

In acknowledging the interdependent nature of privacy, an emergent trend that we see in interdisciplinary scholarship is putting a premium on social and relational aspects of privacy in a networked ecology or "the social turn in privacy theory" (Trepte, 2021, p. 561). It is worth noting, however, that even though the above approaches de-center individual control in privacy management, many of them are built around individual privacy, which becomes extended and reconfigured through adding relational privacy mechanisms and interdependent privacy regulation behaviors (Trepte, 2021), integrating it with networked and institutional mechanisms (Bazarova & Masur, 2020), establishing its inherently social value for enabling long-term, sustainable information relationships based on trust (Richards & Hartzog, 2016), and representing individual functions of privacy through relational and networked activities and configurations (Bannerman, 2019). This presents a promising pathway for a conceptual bridging of different facets of privacy toward an integrative and fuller picture where individual privacy is reconstructed through understanding the limits of individual control, the nature of situationally bounded privacy, and its interdependency with relational and institutional mechanisms in a networked ecology.

Finally, in considering situationally bounded privacy, we see three potential ways forward. One is via a critical digital literacy that should emphasize the limits of individual control over personal data instead of promoting complete privacy self-determination and autonomous control. People should be made aware of privacy interdependence and shared responsibility and taught to think of privacy choices and consequences in the context of information relationships they enter when they share their data on social media platforms. Furthermore, digital literacy should empower people to exercise their personal agency by requiring companies whom they entrust their data to uphold standards and values appropriate for trust-based, "fiduciary-like contexts" (Richards & Hartzog, 2016, p. 468). Second, tech companies should make people aware of relevant possibilities when people decide to share their data to enable a more accurate understanding of the socio-technical structures to which they should adapt their privacy. However, tech privacy safeguards cannot be implemented without policy interventions, and the third route should be privacy policies that incentivize and foster building privacy tools and safeguards into the fabric of digital systems (Acquisti et al., 2022). Only by recognizing the limitations of individual privacy can we find acceptable solutions for helping people manage privacy in the digital age.

References

Acquisti, A., Brandimarte, L., & Hancock, J. (2022). How privacy's past may shape its future. *Science, 375*(6578), 270–272.

Acquisti, A., Brandimarte, L., & Loewenstein, G. (2015). Privacy and human behavior in the age of information. *Science, 347*(6221), 509–514. https://doi.org/10.1126/science.aaa1465

Acquisti, A., & Grossklags, J. (2005). Privacy and rationality in individual decision making. *IEEE Security and Privacy Magazine, 3*(1), 26–33. https://doi.org/10.1109/MSP.2005.22

Acquisti, A., & Grossklags, J. (2006). Privacy and rationality: A survey. In K. Strandburg & D. S. Raicu (Eds.), *Privacy and technologies of identity: A cross-disciplinary conversation* (pp. 15–30). Springer.

Altman, I. (1975). *The environment and social behavior: Privacy, personal space, territory, crowding*. Monterey: Brooks/Cole.

Bannerman, S. (2019). Relational privacy and the networked governance of the self. *Information, Communication & Society, 22*(14), 2187–2202. https://doi.org/10.1080/1369118X.2018.1478982

Barnes, S. B. (2006). A privacy paradox: Social networking in the United States. *First Monday, 11*(9). 10.5210/fm.v11i9.1394

Baruh, L., Secinti, E., & Cemalcilar, Z. (2017). Online privacy concerns and privacy management: A meta-analytical review. *Journal of Communication, 67*(1), 26–53. psyh. https://doi.org/10.1111/jcom.12276

Bazarova, N. N., & Choi, Y. H. (2014). Self-disclosure in social media: Extending the functional approach to disclosure motivations and characteristics on social network sites. *Journal of Communication, 64*, 635–657.

Bazarova, N. N., & Masur, P. K. (2020). Towards an integration of individualistic, networked, and institutional approaches to online disclosure and privacy in a networked ecology. *Current Opinion in Psychology, 36*, 118–123. https://doi.org/10.1016/j.copsyc.2020.05.004

Bol, N., Dienlin, T., Kruikemeier, S., Sax, M., Boerman, S. C., Strycharz, J., Helberger, N., & de Vreese, C. H. (2018). Understanding the effects of personalization as a privacy calculus: Analyzing self-disclosure across health, news, and commerce contexts. *Journal of Computer-Mediated Communication, 23*(6), 370–388. https://doi.org/10.1093/jcmc/zmy020

Choi, Y. H., & Bazarova, N. N. (2015). Self-disclosure characteristics and motivations in social media: Extending the functional model to multiple social network sites. *Human Communication Research, 41*(4), 480–500. https://doi.org/10.1111/hcre.12053

Dienlin, T., & Metzger, M. J. (2016). An extended privacy calculus model for SNSs: Analyzing self-disclosure and self-withdrawal in a representative U.S. sample. *Journal of Computer-Mediated Communication, 21*(5), 368–383. 10.1111/jcc4.12163

Dienlin, T., & Trepte, S. (2015). Is the privacy paradox a relic of the past? An in-depth analysis of privacy attitudes and privacy behaviors: The relation between privacy attitudes and privacy behaviors. *European Journal of Social Psychology, 45*(3), 285–297. https://doi.org/10.1002/ejsp.2049

Dinev, T., & Hart, P. (2006). An extended privacy calculus model for e-commerce transactions. *Information Systems Research, 17*(1), 61–80. https://doi.org/10.1287/isre.1060.0080

Fishbein, M., & Ajzen, I. (2010). *Predicting and changing behavior: The reasoned action approach*. New York, NY: Psychology Press.

French, M., & Bazarova, N. N. (2017). Is anybody out there?: Understanding masspersonal communication through expectations for response across social media platforms. *Journal of Computer-Mediated Communication, 22*(6), 303–319. https://doi.org/10.1111/jcc4.12197

Gigerenzer, G. (2002). The adaptive toolbox. In G. Gigerenzer & R. Selten (Eds.), *Bounded rationality: The adaptive toolbox* (pp. 37–50). The MIT Press.

Gigerenzer, G., & Selten, R. (2002). Rethinking rationality. In G. Gigerenzer & R. Selten (Eds.), *Bounded rationality: The adaptive toolbox* (pp. 1–12). The MIT Press.

Kehr, F., Wentzel, D., & Mayer, P. (2013). Rethinking the privacy calculus: On the role of dispositional factors and affect. *Proceedings of International Conference on Information Systems*, 15–18.

Knijnenburg, B. P., Page, X., Wisniewski, P., Lipford, H. R., Proferes, N., & Romano, J. (2022). *Modern socio-technical perspectives on privacy*. Springer Nature.

Kokolakis, S. (2017). Privacy attitudes and privacy behaviour: A review of current research on the privacy paradox phenomenon. *Computers & Security, 64*, 122–134. https://doi.org/10.1016/j.cose.2015.07.002

Komamura, K. (2019). Privacy's past: The ancient concept and its implications for the current law of privacy. *Washington University Law Review, 96*(6), 1337–1366.

Krasnova, H., Spiekermann, S., Koroleva, K., & Hildebrand, T. (2010). Online social networks: Why we disclose. *Journal of Information Technology, 25*(2), 109–125. https://doi.org/10.1057/jit.2010.6

Margulis, S. T. (2011). Three theories of privacy: An overview. In S. Trepte & L. Reinecke (Eds.), *Privacy online: Perspectives on privacy and self-disclosure in the social web* (pp. 9–18). Springer.

Marwick, A. E., & boyd, D. (2014). Networked privacy: How teenagers negotiate context in social media. *New Media & Society*. https://doi.org/10.1177/1461444814543995

Masur, P. K. (2018). *Situational privacy and self-disclosure: Communication processes in online environments*. Springer.

Masur, P. K., DiFranzo, D. J., & Bazarova, N. N. (2021). Behavioral contagion on social media: Effects of social norms, design interventions, and critical media literacy on self-disclosure. *PLOS One, 16*(7).

Meier, Y., Meinert, J., & Kramer, N. (2022). One-time decision or continual adjustment? A longitudinal study of the within-person privacy calculus among users and non-users of a COVID-19 contact tracing app. *Media Psychology*, 1–18.

Nissenbaum, H. (2004). Privacy as contextual integrity. *Washington University Law Review, 79*(1), 119–158.

Nissenbaum, H. (2010). *Privacy in context: Technology, policy, and the integrity of social life*. Stanford: Stanford Law Books.

O'Sullivan, P. B., & Carr, C. T. (2018). Masspersonal communication: A model bridging the mass-interpersonal divide. *New Media & Society, 20*(3), 1161–1180. https://doi.org/10.1177/1461444816686104

Palen, L., & Dourish, P. (2003). Unpacking "privacy" for a networked world. *Proceedings of the SIGCHI Conference on Human Factors in Computing Systems*, 129–136.

Papacharissi, Z. (2010). *A private sphere: Democracy in a digital age*. Polity Press.

Petronio, S. (2002). *Boundaries of privacy: Dialectics of disclosure*. Albany: State University of New York Press.

Petronio, S., & Child, J. T. (2020). Conceptualization and operationalization: Utility of communication privacy management theory. *Current Opinion in Psychology, 31*, 76–82. https://doi.org/10.1016/j.copsyc.2019.08.009

Preston, A. (2014). *The death of privacy*. https://www.theguardian.com/world/2014/aug/03/internet-death-privacy-google-facebook-alex-preston

Richards, N., & Hartzog, W. (2016). Taking trust seriously in privacy law. *Stanford Technology Law Review, 19*(3), 431–472.

Schmidt, J. H. (2014). Twitter and the rise of personal publics. In K. Weller, A. Bruns, J. Burgess, M. Mahrt, & C. Puschmann (Eds.), *Twitter and society* (pp. 3–14). Peter Lang.

Simon, H. A. (1956). Rational choice and the structure of the environment. *Psychological Review, 63*(2), 129–138. https://doi.org/10.1037/h0042769

Simon, H. A. (1990). Invariants of human behavior. *Annual Review of Psychology, 41*(1), 1–20.

Solove, D. J. (2008). *Understanding privacy*. Harvard University Press.

Sundar, S. S., Kim, J., Rosson, M. B., & Molina, M. D. (2020). Online privacy heuristics that predict information disclosure. *Proceedings of the 2020 CHI Conference on Human Factors in Computing Systems*, 1–12. https://doi.org/10.1145/3313831.3376854

Trepte, S. (2021). The social media privacy model: Privacy and communication in the light of social media affordances. *Communication Theory, 31*(4), 549–570. https://doi.org/10.1093/ct/qtz035

Trepte, S., & Reinecke, L. (Eds.). (2011). *Privacy online*. Springer Berlin Heidelberg. https://doi.org/10.1007/978-3-642-21521-6

Warren, S., & Brandeis, L. (1980). The right to privacy. *Harvard Law Review, 4*(5), 193–220.

Westin, A. F. (1967a). *Privacy and freedom*. Atheneum.

Westin, A. F. (1967b). Legal safeguards to insure privacy in a computer society. *Communications of the ACM, 10*(9), 533–537.

Westin, A. F. (2003). Social and political dimensions of privacy. *Journal of Social Issues*, *59*(2), 431–453. https://doi.org/10.1111/1540-4560.00072

Wilson, D. W. (2015). *Overcoming information privacy concerns: Learning from three disclosure contexts*. The University of Arizona. https://www.proquest.com/dissertations-theses/overcoming-information-privacy-concerns-learning/docview/1672951886/se-2

Zhang, R., Bazarova, N., & Reddy, M. (2021). Distress disclosure across social media platforms during the COVID-19 pandemic: Untangling the effects of platforms, affordances, and audiences. *Proceedings of the 2021 CHI Conference on Human Factors in Computing Systems*, 1–15. https://doi.org/10.1145/3411764.3445134

Zhao, P., Lapierre, M. A., Rains, S. A., & Segrin, C. (2021). When and why we disclose distress on SNSs: Perceived affordances, disclosure goals, and anticipated negative evaluations. *Computers in Human Behavior*, *125*, 106964. https://doi.org/10.1016/j.chb.2021.106964

3

PRIVACY THEORY – SOCIAL, NETWORKED, RELATIONAL, COLLECTIVE

Sabine Trepte

UNIVERSITY OF HOHENHEIM, GERMANY

Introduction

Is social media used socially and networked? Yes, of course. Is privacy social? Yes, absolutely. Polemically put: Privacy is not a private affair. Privacy in each and every context, on and off social media, is networked and inherently social. Individuals perceive and regulate their privacy with regard to other agents in roles such as relationship partners, wardens of boundaries, co-owners of information, and third parties with interests. The list is endless. What is clear is that privacy is a relational concept. Privacy is social and almost always relational, very often networked. But how social, relational, and networked are our theories, measures, IT solutions, policies, and legislation? How do they refer to socially mediated contexts *and* socially determined privacy regulation? And to what extent do we as privacy scholars care about understanding the social and networked nature of privacy not only from the perspective of the individual, but also as an endeavor of the dyad, the group, and the collective? In what follows, I will review and discuss social perspectives on privacy and how they may guide future perspectives on social media use, privacy by design, policymaking, and legislation.

Social Privacy – Ego Agents

The focus of individual privacy theories is how individuals control others, what disclosures they make to others, and how they withdraw from others (see chapter 2 by Bazarova & Zhao on individual-level privacy theories). This perspective focuses on the individual "regulator" of privacy. Similar to a DJ, this individual stands at the turntables while observing the crowd and reacting to others' movements and inquiries. Despite reacting to and being in touch with others, this person is still controlling, protecting, disclosing, and withdrawing information as an ego-centered agent, who tends to take the spotlight in our academic research. In the first generation of privacy research, much emphasis was placed on individual persons' perception, processing, and reactions. In this research tradition, an individual's control and protection were the key mechanisms for ensuring privacy, and control and controllability were often used as synonyms for privacy. That being said, these theories include a stark emphasis on the social aspects of privacy. We could read and interpret seminal work on privacy as inherently social, and some scholars suggest re-reading and re-interpreting certain privacy theories along these lines (Palen & Dourish, 2003; Sacharoff, 2012). The most influential

DOI: 10.4324/9781003244677-4

privacy scholars, including Altman (1974, 1975), Burgoon (1982), Margulis (1974), Petronio (2016), and Westin (1967), defined privacy with regard to others. But, privacy is understood as social from the perspective of individuals, focusing on how they react as individual persons.

Privacy research concerning social media tremendously benefits from this first generation of privacy research, but it does not sufficiently grasp the networked nature of social media. It is "too anthropocentric (only natural persons count) and atomistic (only the single individual counts)" (Floridi, 2013). The individual or ego-centered privacy perspective in this line of research systematically neglects (i) how others shape an individual's privacy; (ii) how others shape social media technology and, in turn, the individual's privacy; (iii) how groups or collectives actively work out their privacy together; and (iv) how the individual deliberates or communicates with others "about" their privacy.

Hence, in a second generation of privacy research, scholars tried to understand and find solutions for the networked nature of privacy in social media. At this point, a social turn in privacy scholarship emerged, slowly but steadily. This turn acknowledges how social media users are social actors by taking into account their needs for autonomy, expression, and connection through the "convergence" of social media technology and its audiences (Papacharissi, 2010). A convergence of technology takes place, for example, on the level of service providers, which are often part of the same company (e.g., Meta, Alphabet) and as such have greater insight than an individual seemingly grants when sharing their data on a single social networking site. The convergence of audiences is experienced, for example, by individuals trying to manage the collapsing of different contexts, such as work life and personal life, on a single social networking site. Users routinely accept that their need for privacy is challenged by this convergence and have found different ways to react to it. Based on this desire to better understand the social in social media privacy, I reviewed over 140 articles that have been published using the terms social, group, relational, networked, collective, or interdependent privacy. I will critically discuss, define, and reflect on what they contribute with regard to social media privacy (see Table 3.1 for an overview) and what I think is still missing.

Social Privacy

Social privacy has been defined as privacy processes referring to situations where other individuals are involved (Burgoon, 1982; Jozani et al., 2020; Lutz & Ranzini, 2017; Raynes-Goldie, 2010) and "to the revealing or sequestering of personal information from social display" (Abdul-Ghani, 2020). Social privacy was a tremendously necessary term because it helped capture "the social" in social media privacy research. It was necessary to emphasize that people are challenged by what others expect from them and what they themselves should expect (Burgoon, 1982). It was necessary to understand that most struggles around privacy result from the need for social support, social capital, or inclusion (for an overview, cf. Trepte & Reinecke, 2011). Finally, the term was necessary because we needed to understand how important it is for individuals to establish boundaries and thereby define their private spaces in social media (boyd & Marwick, 2011).

Definitions of social privacy are abstract and often include everything falling under "the social," but then fail to further define what social actually means. Social privacy is more of a mantra or a "model of humanity" than a clear-cut term. It is broadly defined as referring to social encounters of any kind. Then, taking up this broad definition, scholars re-define, use, and apply social privacy in ways that optimally align with particular study designs and disciplines. As such, the term social privacy is sufficiently flexible for all uses. It does not come as a surprise that it is likely the oldest term associated with the social turn in privacy research. What is surprising is that social privacy is not currently the most prevalent term. We will see in the following that the terms group or collective privacy are not only more clearly specified, but have also accumulated more scholarship across disciplines.

Table 3.1 Group, Relational, Networked, and Collective Privacy on Social Media – Definitions and Relevance for Social Media Contexts

	Definition	*Social Media Relevance*
Group Privacy	Privacy of more than one individual. A group is defined as such as soon as it is identified by its members (self-ascription) or by others (other-ascription). Groups may but need not per se have a common basis, identity, or leitmotif (as in → collective privacy). All of the following terms refer to group privacy by emphasizing different aspects of the group.	Most necessary, basic, and prevalent term, and also most neutral one as compared to → collective or → networked privacy. Important term for the critical perspective on social media use, as it stresses the need to consider group privacy for lawmaking and social media design.
Relational Privacy	Privacy referring to and with relevance for the interaction of entities (individuals, groups, and institutions) that are tied together by a known and obvious bond (e.g., parent-child, life partners, coach-coachee, doctor-patient, service user, and provider). Often refers to dyads, families, and close friends. The term "relational" expresses interactions between known interaction partners, whereas → networked privacy expresses that not all participants are known and observable to one another.	Important term indicating that and how privacy is negotiated within relations. Relational privacy is still under-researched and under-used in computer-mediated communication.
Networked Privacy	Referring to and with relevance for the interaction of a number of entities (individuals, groups, and institutions), some of whom are tied together by a known and obvious bond, others tied together by loose bonds, and still others by bonds unknown to the network members. When referring to obvious and known bonds use → relational privacy.	Terms and theory very well express the most important aspects of social media privacy: Privacy is determined by whether and how individuals collaboratively use social media technology, by how they interact in their network, and by the often unknown nature of this network and its participants.
Collective Privacy	Privacy of a group with a leitmotif (i.e., risk, plan, or action) which is ascribed to members of the collective. For example, the collective can refer to shared unknown risks (e.g., discrimination because of algorithmic classification), to obvious and explicitly stated goals, or deliberative action and activism (e.g., LGBT privacy). A group is categorized by criteria, a collective is characterized by a motif.	The term collective privacy underscores that all groups with an explicitly stated or ascribed leitmotif also share collective privacy on social media, whether they decide to collectively regulate it or not.

Theorizing around social privacy can be traced back to the first privacy studies relevant for communication science, such as Judee Burgoon's work on self-disclosure (Burgoon, 1982), in which social privacy was defined as control over social encounters. Then, social exchange theory and utility theory highlighted privacy costs vs. social rewards on social media (Wang & Midha, 2012). These theories suggested differentiating between costs and rewards of disclosure and how they affect the desire to get in touch with others (Altman & Taylor, 1973). This idea of rational choice profoundly influenced theorizing on social media privacy (see chapter 7 by Dienlin on the privacy calculus).

In previous empirical research, social privacy has often been applied as a foil to institutional privacy (Abdul-Ghani, 2020; Jozani et al., 2020; Lutz & Ranzini, 2017; Raynes-Goldie, 2010; Young & Quan-Haase, 2013). In that sense, social privacy refers to humans such as other users, peers, family, or employers, whereas institutional privacy refers to faceless entities such as service providers, platforms, companies, governments, and even algorithms (Sujon, 2018). Social and institutional privacy are used synonymously with horizontal and vertical privacy, respectively (Masur, 2019). Adjacent research demonstrated that early social media users cared more about privacy regulation with regard to their peers than with regard to institutions (Sujon, 2018; Young & Quan-Haase, 2013). The opposite has been found in more recent research (Masur et al., 2021). Furthermore, the term social privacy is most often used in conjunction with a variety of emotions or behaviors, such as social privacy concerns (Jozani et al., 2020) or social privacy literacy (Bartsch & Dienlin, 2016). To date, there is an ambiguous picture regarding whether social or institutional privacy concerns are experienced as more threatening, but results demonstrate that the two are strongly interrelated (Jozani et al., 2020; Schwartz-Chassidim et al., 2020).

Hence, social privacy refers to (i) situations in which the individual encounters other individuals and (ii) individual choices around social encounters (Abdul-Ghani, 2020; Lutz & Ranzini, 2017). Consequently, social privacy measures are user centric; they ask individual users for their perspective on social encounters via quantitative surveys, qualitative interviews, or diary studies (Li, 2020; Sujon, 2018; Sujon & Johnston, 2017; Young & Quan-Haase, 2013). For example, in quantitative surveys, social privacy has been measured by asking whether users restrict access to their profiles and the visibility of their social media content (Dienlin & Trepte, 2015). Social privacy behavior has been measured by asking users whether only themselves, friends, or friends of friends could see their status updates, date of birth, religion, or location on social media (Bartsch & Dienlin, 2016).

How does the term social privacy help us better understand social media use, regulate privacy, and design privacy measures? I acknowledge that we need the term social privacy to highlight that privacy has experienced a social turn since the early 2000s, most certainly inspired by online media use. However, privacy has always been and will always be social. Hence, I have come to the conclusion that we can refrain from distinguishing social privacy from other forms of privacy. Privacy is social, and that is sufficient to acknowledge. If the term social privacy is used to draw a contrast to institutional or physical privacy (as I also did in my own previous research), I would today instead use a more specific term. For example, when investigating how social media users experience privacy issues with regard to their peers (previously termed social privacy) vs. privacy with regard to social media providers (previously termed institutional privacy), terms such as privacy with regard to peers vs. privacy with regard to the service seem useful. The following section will review and discuss more specific terms that better specify "the social" and as such are better suited to advance privacy theory.

Group Privacy

Group privacy refers to the privacy of more than one individual, i.e., a group that is labeled as such by the group members themselves or by others. Group membership thus results from individuals' self-ascriptions as group members (i.e., self-ascribed groups) or the ascriptions of others not belonging to the group (i.e., other-ascriptive groups). For example, some Twitter users might perceive other users tweeting the #metoo hashtag as a group, but the latter would not necessarily share this perspective themselves (see chapter 5 by Petro & Metzger on group privacy).

Group privacy has evolved as a synonym for social privacy and is also the most current label for the social turn in privacy research. I would consider group privacy the most necessary, basic, and neutral term: It is necessary, because it highlights that social media users are in this together no matter what. It is basic, because it expresses the defining condition of the individual person "plus one" more, which may then be further specified, for instance, with regard to how active a group is or which processes are the object of focus. It is normatively neutral, as it does not allude to co-dependence or interactions among group members and/or with third parties.

Group privacy has been investigated by asking social media users whether they are concerned about their own and the group's privacy while using a fitness app (Suh et al., 2018) and by surveying members of a youth organization (de Wolf et al., 2014). The results of this previous research have demonstrated that individual and group privacy are highly empirically interrelated. Are group privacy and individual privacy really two separable constructs, then? And do we need both of them for policies, lawmaking, and privacy by design? I think it will become necessary to specify what constitutes the group for each and every application and context before we start finding solutions for group privacy. We should always define group privacy with regard to what is most characteristic of the particular group at hand. This approach will presumably lead to more complex solutions, but offers the chance to better grasp and differentiate what inherently defines and characterizes a group.

Along these lines, ethnographic research on privacy negotiations has endeavored to explore group identities as a precondition for group privacy, for example, in private Facebook groups (Mansour & Francke, 2021), minority groups (see chapter 19 by de Wolf & de Leyn on minorities' privacy), or self-help groups (Helm, 2018). This line of research demonstrates what group membership means to its members. Furthermore, it demonstrates that conflicts around privacy do not stem from within the group, but predominantly from interactions with outgroups, the public, or with unknown others. Also, it underscores that the group's position and ongoing privacy negotiation processes allow for and require a "critical and playful subjectivity" (de Wolf et al., 2022), with blurred boundaries between the privacy needs of the agents and the groups to which they belong.

In sum, for group privacy, our most important task is to understand and respect the identities, processes, and hierarchies within a group under consideration. How is the group constituted, and what are its aims and motives, norms and rights, concerns, and risks? What is the flow of interactions? And, most importantly, which of these aspects do we want to focus on? Group privacy is the first, most basic term that may then be specified with respect to the processes in question.

Relational Privacy

Relational privacy refers to how people actively negotiate and communicate with each other about their privacy. It has been investigated for dyads such as parent-child relationships (Ebersole & Hernandez, 2016; Hernandez & Ebersole, 2022), romantic relationships (Craddock, 1997; Petronio et al., 1989), relationships between older people and their adult children serving as caregivers (Berridge & Wetle, 2019), and relationships between nursing home residents and care staff (Petronio & Kovach, 1997). For example, an interview study with young adolescents and their parents focused on health-related privacy (Ebersole & Hernandez, 2016; Hernandez & Ebersole, 2022). Most studies that use the term relational privacy are not situated in social media or online settings. An exception is the study by de Wolf (2020) investigating communication among groups of friends. It assesses privacy management by asking whether "my friends and I talk about what can and cannot be shared" or "discuss the appropriate privacy settings" (de Wolf, 2020, p. 1074).

What does the term relational privacy have that other privacy-related terms do not? Do we need the term relational privacy for future reflections and debate around social media privacy? Let me start with an example study that seeks to answer these questions (Berridge & Wetle, 2019): Adult children often function as caregivers for their aging parents and use surveillance measures such as location tracking, in-home activity sensors, and Webcams running 24×7. The adult children weigh their parents' safety, privacy, and freedom. In this process, caregivers seek to find a balance between valuing privacy on the one hand side and their parents' safety on the other. Privacy is clearly at risk with location tracking and 24-hour surveillance. But how would parents' privacy be infringed in a 24×7 nursing home setting, which may be the only alternative to the joint efforts by the children and cameras? When reading this study, it struck me that family caregivers have been suddenly placed in the situation of service providers. They are the ones infringing on privacy for the sake of efficiency, maybe even for financial reasons if a nursing home would be too expensive. In this sense, the term relational privacy brings an important perspective to the spectrum of privacy terms, as it highlights the privacy balance in peer-to-peer relationships and their influence on power relations . Considering relational privacy means emphatically listening to both sides of the relationship.

My judgment on relational privacy is that the concept is important for future reflections on social media privacy for two reasons. First, it highlights the processes that are inherent to social media use and relationships: Communication, interaction, trust, social support, and power relations. The term relational privacy specifies which of these processes we are looking at when designing our research, policies, or laws. Secondly, and even more importantly, the term relational privacy takes into account the perspective of "the other." Peers or parents suddenly become a voice in research on relational privacy. Very often in previous research, such "others" are understood merely as social media benefits or privacy risks. Only seldom did we specifically ask about their communication goals and privacy needs. Relations with others are the foundation of privacy reflections; they are the place to solve privacy issues via communication. Hence, listening to both sides of such relationships will shed further light on the nature of social media privacy.

Networked Privacy

The term networked privacy refers to the interrelated nature of social media privacy (boyd & Marwick, 2011). A network is characterized by bonds and interactions among a number of entities. These entities can be individuals, groups, or institutions, some of which are tied together by known and obvious bonds (e.g., parent-child), some by looser bonds (e.g., acquaintances from work), and some of which do not know each other (e.g., friends of friends). Interactions in a network usually take place through the more or less conscious sharing of mutually owned information. The network and its interactions are not fully known to its users, though, and this opaque nature is exactly what helps us distinguish the term networked privacy from relational privacy (Marwick & boyd, 2014). Relational privacy refers to visible, measurable interactional processes of concrete agents. In contrast, networked privacy refers to how the privacy of the network as a whole is co-developed by actors who differ with regard to their visibility, activity, and strength of connection. For example, teens collaboratively use a range of measures to limit access to meaning via social steganography – "only those who are in the know have the necessary information to look for and interpret the information" (boyd 2012). Here, networked privacy means that teens disclose information within the network while withdrawing it from parents (boyd, 2012, 2014). Networked privacy also means that parents and adults often do not know that and how they participate in this kind of privacy regulation. That, for example, by asking certain questions about the social media content of their children or evaluating it, they force their children into more access regulation. Research on networked privacy tries to equally address known and unknown bonds. The teens in this example collaboratively regulate privacy, sometimes without knowing each other. Interactions in a network spread out to the more distant nodes of the network, where they encounter other, denser nodes that connect this network to the next. Not only are the network, its communication channels, and content unknown to most network participants, but so too are each network participant's privacy needs.

Networked privacy theory holds that social media is characterized by frequently changing technologies, social norms, and collapsing audiences (Marwick & boyd, 2014). The negotiation of privacy thus goes hand in hand with the negotiation of contexts (Vitak, 2012). The meaning of the context for privacy is different in networked privacy theory and contextual integrity theory. Networked privacy theory suggests that privacy regulation cannot be tailored to a certain context, because social media contexts are opaque and, as such, moving targets. For example, the network of people sharing genetic code is affected by each and every person sending in their personal data and genetic code to the respective agencies and by investigative genetic genealogy (Samuel, 2021). The network depends on each member's privacy regulation, but cannot actively communicate about it as in relational privacy (King, 2019). In contrast, contextual integrity theory holds that each context requires particular forms of privacy regulation (Nissenbaum, 2010). Privacy is understood as an appraisal process in which individuals assess the context and (should) try to act accordingly.

For future research, social network analysis would be an interesting way to measure networked privacy on social media. Lewis (2011) analyzed the mechanisms and behavioral dynamics of privacy on Facebook and demonstrated how students' social networks significantly influence their privacy regulation behaviors during their first year of college. The first-year college students assimilated their privacy behaviors in social media networks early in the term and in ways that depended on the size of their network (Lewis, 2011). Students with larger networks were more likely to manage their privacy by using private profiles than students with smaller networks.

In summary, I would consider networked privacy one of the most important terms furthering our understanding of privacy on social media. Social media technology is not only designed, but constantly shaped by humans. Moreover, social media users are in touch with others, but a large share of these relationships are unknown and changing. These two presuppositions challenge privacy theory. They highlight that when we as researchers or practitioners define groups, certain social media contexts, or relevant persons, it is only one very tiny part of the picture. Privacy research, policies, and lawmaking should focus on relational privacy, because relations are observable parts of the network. But they should also acknowledge networked privacy, because privacy regulation is affected by the larger network and its unknown parts. Our utmost aim should always be to programmatically work to better understand both direct relations and the networks in which they are embedded.

Collective Privacy

The term collective describes a group with a leitmotif. The collective consists of more than two people who are either self- or other-defined as a group and share a leitmotif, which could be a plan, goal, fate, or even risk (Jia & Xu, 2016a; Mittelstadt, 2017). This leitmotif binding the group members together and defining them as a collective might be situational or ongoing. As such, a collective is more than a group because collective privacy involves understanding privacy in light of this leitmotif. The bond, goal, or calling of the group can be aware to all group members, to some group members, or even just to spokespersons or to an external individual.

Previous research on collective privacy has addressed social media communication in LGBTQ+ communities (Blackwell et al., 2016) or groups of friends (Cho et al., 2018; Li et al., 2022) (Cho & Filippova, 2016). As soon as individuals collaboratively manage their privacy with an eye to their shared motif, they move from group to collective status.

Theoretically, research on collective privacy mostly relies on Communication Privacy Management Theory, while transferring the theory's presuppositions from the individual person to collectives (Choi & Jiang, 2013; Jia & Xu, 2016a, 2016b). Communication Privacy Management Theory is based on Altman's (1975) conception of boundaries and how the individual person coordinates such boundaries with others, the co-owners of information. When transferred to collective privacy, boundaries are coordinated either by all members of the collective, by self-nominated parts of it, or even by external forces seeking to protect the collective (Cho et al., 2018).

As introduced above, I see the leitmotif as the critical momentum creating the collective. This leitmotif, in turn, is closely tied to the urge of boundary coordination which can be experienced, for example, by members of groups experiencing discrimination. Blackwell et al.'s (2016) study shows in an almost shocking way how intertwined collective and personal boundaries and as such privacy are. Here, communication on social media is considered a "second job" for parents of LGBT youngsters, because ongoing negotiation within the group and to out-groups is perceived as stressful, time consuming, and extremely risky for all family members. Of course, privacy regulation by the individual person and the collective is intertwined. But in the collective, more is at risk as for the individual person (Bruhn, 2014).

On social media, collective privacy is an important term to focus on, because it has the potential to politicize privacy (Ochs, 2018; Samuel, 2021): The last ten years of research on individual privacy have tremendously enriched our field. We know quite well what individuals want and need and how they regulate privacy through disclosure, control, and communication (see chapter 2 by Bazarova & Zhao on individualistic privacy theories). Now, scholarship on group privacy is demonstrating that groups surrounding and encompassing the individual person have relevance for the individual as well (see chapter 5 by Petro & Metzger on group privacy). Then, taking this as a point of departure, it must be decided whether a group qualifies as a collective – consistently or in a certain situation. The collective adds to group members' identity and becomes of particular relevance for privacy regulation. This final step has been clearly demonstrated in the social media privacy research referred to above on LGBT communities as privacy collectives (Blackwell et al., 2016). Here, each member can become an incidental advocate for the collective, for a minute or a lifetime. The simplest sharing of a photo can become advocacy work for the collective, and privacy management is a collective responsibility. If we are aware of this, we are ready to answer the most important political and normative questions regarding privacy.

Future Perspectives

Now that privacy has experienced a social turn, now that we embrace the social and relational aspects of privacy, it is worth asking whether we are already measuring, regulating, and designing social, relational, interpersonal, group, networked, and collective privacy using the same measures. The answer is no. Despite its social turn, privacy is not yet regulated, researched, and designed in the community-based way it is experienced and practiced on social media. For the future, we need measures and methods of social media privacy that are as social as social media and its uses. I will try to contribute to this endeavor by only using the "best of" and developing them a little further. I will start with empirical measures, then address technology, and finally norms – in a cross-disciplinary journey, traveling on the shoulders of the many scholars I have referred to in this chapter.

For *research in communication science*, we will need a more granular understanding of the social group we are interested in. Research on relational privacy needs dyadic analysis, research on collective privacy needs conjoint approaches, and networked privacy needs social network analysis. Currently, in our surveys, we assumesimilar experiences for all study participants, such as the experiences of registering with a new social network, posting pictures on this network, or encountering privacy breaches. Our field is dominated by survey research asking individual persons to evaluate ostensible individual experiences without giving them the chance to individually elaborate on this particular experience. We know a lot about individual concerns as reported by the individuals themselves. Ironically, we do not know much with regard to what individuals encounter online (technology as the context) and whom (relationship, group, or network as the context). The question is whether we can understand privacy if we do not fully understand the scenarios in which and for which privacy is co-developed, negotiated, or a point of concern. Social privacy research in communication science requires a methodology displaying the *same* use scenario to a variety of people instead of asking a variety of people for their individual scenarios and *then* assuming that these are comparable. That being said, first attempts have of course been made to better understand groups and collectives. They are presented throughout this chapter, in many other chapters of this volume and in Taylor, Floridi and van der Sloot (2017). But they remain underrepresented. What if we move from surveys to studying scenarios, vignettes, or beta versions? We will of course encounter the problemthat they are not representative of the wide array of social media scenarios. Hence, when referring to concrete uses and groups, we are only studying a tiny portion of social media reality. That said, I would stillargue to let in more social media experiences of the individual user instead of neglecting their experiences.

Furthermore, if we conceptualize privacy behavior regarding social media as communication, we should ask how users talk about it. Only a very small number of privacy theories explicitly address communication as a mechanism for privacy regulation. For example, the social media privacy model and the first studies investigating it refer to communication about privacy (Trepte, 2021). Privacy regulation on social media does not work without communication. When social media users need social support from friends or acquaintances, they need to communicate their needs (Trepte et al., 2020). When social media users seek to regulate their privacy, the same applies. Hence, communication is key to social media privacy (Trepte, 2021). Now the next steps are to strengthen our theoretical understanding of actual communication about privacy as an important privacy regulation behavior and, of course, measuring communication and deliberation as two distinct forms of privacy regulation (see chapter 1 by Trepte & Masur on the social media privacy model). Our research and theorizing are in a very good place with regard to understanding the social in social media privacy. Now we can take the time to pick out specific communication processes and further explore their meaning. Better understanding of the complex nature of privacy communication can help us design social media that cater to our need for both privacy and sociality.

The desire for boundary coordination in groups and collectives has been initially addressed in efforts concerning *privacy by design* on social media (Caliskan-Islam et al., 2014; Mosca et al., 2020). Collective privacy by design solutions often work on the back end, unknown to users (Xu & Sun, 2014). For example, they might obfuscate individual users' locations on location-based social media such as Snapchat or Twitter without degrading the service these location-based services have to offer. The underlying algorithm recursively minimizes the number of users providing location-based data to the necessary minimum. An anonymous crowd of users is represented by ambassadors and developers in order to protect the collective against unwanted intrusion and data use by the marketplace. The collective has a shared ideal of privacy, even though they do not know each other. For example, with the "Privacy Flag" project, users assess objects of concern based on a predefined method and criteria, share and accumulate their knowledge in a database maintained by independent web developers from the European Union (EU) funded project, and then reach out to service providers (Ziegler & Chochliouros, 2015). Service providers can, in turn, commit to responding to data security problems of this kind, which is a particularly interesting option if the service providers are not subject to EU legislation.

I would consider relational privacy the most important construct to discuss with regard to *regulation and legislation*. Relational privacy naturally relies on social norms. And of course, privacy norms are subject to excessive socialization within relationships beginning at a very young age (Masur et al., 2021). However, even though social norms are co-developed in relationships, there is no sufficient notion of relational privacy in current lawmaking (Eichenhofer, 2019). Relational privacy underscores that it is important who "the other" is. Confidentiality in conversations with doctors and therapists is protected by law. What we disclose to a romantic partner or friend is not public either, but is in most cases not protected as such. It is worthwhile to look at such relationships in order to better understand social media privacy. Information that is shared on social media and thus enduring might need safeguards that ensure the privacy of the other party to this relationship (Reviglio & Alunge, 2020). A dyad very often is a group of two that is committed to each other, an active group, an identifiable group, and as such, its members should have a right to be protected.

Social media privacy should be considered relational, interpersonal, networked, and collective. Hopefully, this chapter motivates us to increase the complexity of our debates and designs and supports us in deciding which aspects to explore further.

References

Abdul-Ghani, E. (2020). Consumers' online institutional privacy literacy. In F. J. Martínez-López & S. D'Alessandro (Eds.), *Springer proceedings in business and economics. Advances in digital marketing and e-commerce* (pp. 40–46). Springer Nature. https://doi.org/10.1007/978-3-030-47595-6_6

Altman, I. (1974). Privacy: A conceptual analysis. In S. T. Margulis (Ed.), *Man-environment interactions: Evaluations and applications* (pp. 3–28). Dowden, Hutchinson & Ross.

Altman, I. (1975). *The environment and social behavior: Privacy, personal space, territory, crowding*. Brooks/Cole Publishing Company.

Altman, I., & Taylor, D. A. (1973). *Social penetration: The development of interpersonal relationships*. Holt, Rinehart & Winston.

Bartsch, M., & Dienlin, T. (2016). Control your Facebook: An analysis of online privacy literacy. *Computers in Human Behavior, 56*, 147–154. https://doi.org/10.1016/j.chb.2015.11.022

Berridge, C., & Wetle, T. F. (2019). Why older adults and their children disagree about in-home surveillance technology, sensors, and tracking. *The Gerontologist, 60*(5), 926–934. https://doi.org/10.1093/geront/gnz068

Blackwell, L., Hardy, J., Ammari, T., Veinot, T., Lampe, C [C.], & Schoenebeck, S. (2016). LGBT parents and social media: Advocacy, privacy, and disclosure during shifting social movements. In J. Kaye, A. Druin, C. Lampe, D. Morris, & J. P. Hourcade (Eds.), *Proceedings of the 2016 CHI conference on human factors in computing systems* (pp. 610–622). ACM. https://doi.org/10.1145/2858036.2858342

Börsting, J., Frener, R., & Trepte, S. (2023). Privacy and political targeting on social media in the light of the federal election 2021 in Germany. *Under Review*.

boyd, d. (2012). Networked privacy. *Surveillance & Society, 10*(3/4), 348–350.

boyd, d. (2014). *It's complicated. The social lives of networked teens*. Yale University Press.

boyd, d., & Marwick, A. E. (2011). Social privacy in networked publics: Teens' attitudes, practices, and strategies. *A Decade in Internet Time: Symposium on the Dynamics of the Internet and Society*. https://ssrn.com/abstract=1925128

Bruhn, J. (2014). Identifying useful approaches to the governance of indigenous data. *The International Indigenous Policy Journal, 5*(2), Article 5. https://doi.org/10.18584/iipj.2014.5.2.5

Burgoon, J. K. (1982). Privacy and communication. *Communication Yearbook, 6*(4), 206–249. https://doi.org/10.1080/23808985

Caliskan-Islam, A., Walsh, J., & Greenstadt, R. (2014). Privacy detective: Detecting private information and collective privacy behavior in a large social network. In G.-J. Ahn & A. Datta (Eds.), *Proceedings of the 13th workshop on privacy in the electronic society* (pp. 35–46). ACM. https://doi.org/10.1145/2665943.2665958

Cho, H., & Filippova, A. (2016). Networked privacy management in Facebook. In D. Gergle, M. R. Morris, P. Bjørn, & J. Konstan (Chairs) (Eds.), *CSCW '16: Computer Supported Cooperative Work and Social Computing*, San Francisco, California, USA.

Cho, H., Knijnenburg, B., Kobsa, A., & Li, Y. (2018). Collective privacy management in social media: A cross cultural validation. *ACM Transactions on Computer-Human Interaction, 25*(3), 1–33. https://doi.org/10.1145/3193120

Choi, C. F. B., & Jiang, Z. J. (2013). Trading friendship for value: An investigation of collective privacy concerns in social application usage. In *The 34th International Conference on Information Systems' Proceedings*.

Craddock, A. E. (1997). The measurement of privacy preferences within marital relationships: The relationship privacy preference scale. *The American Journal of Family Therapy, 25*(1), 48–54. https://doi.org/10.1080/01926189708251054

de Wolf, R. (2020). Contextualizing how teens manage personal and interpersonal privacy on social media. *New Media & Society, 22*(6), 1058–1075. https://doi.org/10.1177/1461444819876570

de Wolf, R., van Hove, S., & Robaeyst, B. (2022). Exploring Flemish Muslim children's experiences and negotiation of offline and online group privacy. *European Journal of Cultural Studies, 25*(4), 1030–1046. https://doi.org/10.1177/13675494211005440

de Wolf, R., Willaert, K., & Pierson, J. (2014). Managing privacy boundaries together: Exploring individual and group privacy management strategies in Facebook. *Computers in Human Behavior, 35*, 444–454. https://doi.org/10.1016/j.chb.2014.03.010

Dienlin, T., & Trepte, S. (2015). Is the privacy paradox a relic of the past? An in-depth analysis of privacy attitudes and privacy behaviors. *European Journal of Social Psychology, 45*(3), 285–297. 10.1002/ejsp.2049

Ebersole, D. S., & Hernandez, R. A. (2016). "Taking good care of our health": Parent-adolescent perceptions of boundary management about health information. *Communication Quarterly, 64*(5), 573–595. https://doi.org/10.1080/01463373.2016.1176939

Eichenhofer, J. (2019). *e-Privacy – Theorie und Dogmatik eines europäischen Privatheitsschutzes im Internet-Zeitalter [Theoretical and doctrinal foundations of a European privacy protection regulation in the internet age]*. University of Bielefeld.

Floridi, L. (2013). *The ethics of information*. Oxford University Press. https://doi.org/10.1093/acprof:oso/9780199641321.001.0001

Helm, P. (2018). Treating sensitive topics online: A privacy dilemma. *Ethics and Information Technology, 20*(4), 303–313. 10.1007/s10676-018-9482-4

Hernandez, R., & Ebersole, D. (2022). Parents' and children's privacy management about sensitive topics: A dyadic study. *Journal of Family Issues, 43*(1), 73–95. https://doi.org/10.1177/0192513X21993192

Jia, H., & Xu, H. (2016a). Autonomous and interdependent: Collaborative privacy management on social network sites. In J. Kaye, A. Druin, C. Lampe, D. Morris, & J. P. Hourcade (Eds.), *Proceedings of the 2016 CHI conference on human factors in computing systems* (pp. 4286–4297). ACM. https://doi.org/10.1145/2858036.2858415

Jia, H., & Xu, H. (2016b). Measuring individuals' concerns over collective privacy on social networking sites. *Cyberpsychology: Journal of Psychosocial Research on Cyberspace, 10*(1). 10.5817/CP2016-1-4

Jozani, M., Ayaburi, E., Ko, M., & Choo, K.-K. R. (2020). Privacy concerns and benefits of engagement with social media-enabled apps: A privacy calculus perspective. *Computers in Human Behavior, 107*, 106260. https://doi.org/10.1016/j.chb.2020.106260

King, J. (2019). "Becoming part of something bigger": Direct to consumer genetic testing, privacy, and personal disclosure. *Proceedings of the ACM on Human-Computer Interaction, 3(CSCW), Article 158.* https://doi.org/10.1145/3359260

Lewis, K. (2011). The co-evolution of social network ties and online privacy behavior. In S. Trepte & L. Reinecke (Eds.), *Privacy online. Perspectives on privacy and self-disclosure in the social web* (pp. 91–110). Springer.

Li, H. (2020). Negotiating privacy and mobile socializing: Chinese university students' concerns and strategies for using geosocial networking applications. *Social Media + Society, 6*(1). https://doi.org/10.1177/2056305120913887

Li, Y., Cho, H., Anaraky, R. G., Knijnenburg, B., & Kobsa, A. (2022). Antecedents of collective privacy management in social network sites: A cross-country analysis. *CCF Transactions on Pervasive Computing and Interaction, 4*(2), 106–123. https://doi.org/10.1007/s42486-022-00092-8

Lutz, C., & Ranzini, G. (2017). Where dating meets data: Investigating social and institutional privacy concerns on Tinder. *Social Media + Society, 3*(1). https://doi.org/10.1177/2056305117697735

Mansour, A., & Francke, H. (2021). Collective privacy management practices: A study of privacy strategies and risks in a private Facebook group. *Proceedings of the ACM on Human-Computer Interaction, 5(CSCW2), Article 360.* https://doi.org/10.1145/3479504

Margulis, S. T. (Ed.). (1974). *Man-environment interactions: Evaluations and applications*. Dowden, Hutchinson & Ross.

Masur, P. K. (2019). *Situational privacy and self-disclosure: Communication processes in online environments*. Springer International Publishing.

Masur, P. K., DiFranzo, D., & Bazarova, N. N. (2021). Behavioral contagion on social media: Effects of social norms, design interventions, and critical media literacy on self-disclosure. *PLOS One, 16*(7). https://doi.org/10.1371/journal.pone.0254670

Mittelstadt, B. (2017). From individual to group privacy in big data analytics. *Philosophy & Technology, 30*(4), 475–494.

Mosca, F., Such, J. M., & McBurney, P. (2020). Towards a value-driven explainable agent for collective privacy. In *19th international conference on autonomous agents and multiagent systems*. AAMAS.

Nissenbaum, H. (2010). *Privacy in context: Technology, policy, and the integrity of social life*. Stanford University Press.

Ochs, C. (2018). Self-protection beyond the self: Collective privacy practices in (big) datascapes. In *Routledge research in information technology and society: Vol. 21. The politics and policies of big data: Big data, big brother?* (1st ed., pp. 265–291). Routledge.

Palen, L., & Dourish, P. (2003). Unpacking 'privacy' for a networked world. In V. Bellotti (Ed.), *CHI letters: Vol. 1, CHI 2003: Proceedings of the SIGCHI conference on human factors in computing systems* (5th ed., pp. 129–136). ACM Press. https://doi.org/10.1145/642611.642635

Papacharissi, Z. (2010). *A private sphere: Democracy in a digital age*. Polity Press.

Petronio, S. (2016). Communication privacy management theory. In C. R. Berger & M. E. Roloff (Eds.), *ICA international encyclopedias of communication. The international encyclopedia of interpersonal communication*. Wiley Blackwell.

Petronio, S., & Kovach, S. (1997). Managing privacy boundaries: Health providers' perceptions of resident care in Scottish nursing homes. *Journal of Applied Communication Research, 25*(2), 115–131. https://doi.org/10.1080/00909889709365470

Petronio, S., Olson, C., & Dollar, N. (1989). Privacy issues in relational embarrassment: Impact on relational quality and communication satisfaction. *Communication Research Reports, 6*(1), 21–27. https://doi.org/10.1080/08824098909359828

Raynes-Goldie, K. (2010). Aliases, creeping, and wall cleaning: Understanding privacy in the age of Facebook. *First Monday, 15*(1). 10.5210/fm.v15i1.2775

Reviglio, U., & Alunge, R. (2020). "I am datafied because we are datafied": An Ubuntu perspective on (relational) privacy. *Philosophy & Technology, 33*(4), 595–612. https://doi.org/10.1007/s13347-020-00407-6

Sacharoff, L. (2012). The relational nature of privacy. *Lewis & Clark Law Review, 16*(4), 1249–1303. https://papers.ssrn.com/sol3/papers.cfm?abstract_id=2201903 (University of Arkansas research paper No. 13-08).

Samuel, G. (2021). Investigative genetic genealogy: Can collective privacy and solidarity help? *Journal of Medical Ethics, 47*(12), 796–797. https://doi.org/10.1136/medethics-2021-107960

Schwartz-Chassidim, H., Ayalon, O., Mendel, T., Hirschprung, R., & Toch, E. (2020). Selectivity in posting on social networks: The role of privacy concerns, social capital, and technical literacy. *Heliyon*, 6(2), e03298. https://doi.org/10.1016/j.heliyon.2020.e03298

Suh, J. J., Metzger, M. J., Reid, S. A., & El Abbadi, A. (2018). Distinguishing group privacy from personal privacy: The effect of group inference technologies on privacy perceptions and behaviors. *Proceedings of the ACM on Human-Computer Interaction, 168*, 1–22.

Sujon, Z. (2018). The triumph of social privacy: Understanding the privacy logics of sharing behaviors across social media. *International Journal of Communication, 12*, 3751–3771. https://ijoc.org/index.php/ijoc/article/view/9357/2453

Sujon, Z., & Johnston, L. (2017). Public friends and private sharing. In *Proceedings of the 8th international conference on social media & society* (pp. 1–13). ACM. https://doi.org/10.1145/3097286.3097305

Taylor, L., Floridi, L. & van der Sloot, B. (Eds.) (2017). Group privacy. New challenges of data technologies. Springer.

Trepte, S. (2021). The social media privacy model: Privacy and communication in the light of social media affordances. *Communication Theory, 31*(4), 549–570. https://doi.org/10.1093/ct/qtz035

Trepte, S., Scharkow, M., & Dienlin, T. (2020). The privacy calculus contextualized: The influence of affordances. *Computers in Human Behavior, 104*, 106115. https://doi.org/10.1016/j.chb.2019.08.022

Trepte, S. & Reinecke, L. (Eds.) (2011). *Privacy Online. Perspectives on Privacy and Self-disclosure in the Social Web*. Springer.

Vitak, J. (2012). The impact of context collapse and privacy on social network site disclosures. *Journal of Broadcasting & Electronic Media, 56*(4), 451–470. https://doi.org/10.1080/08838151.2012.732140

Wang, Y., & Midha, V. (2012). User self-disclosure on health social networks: A social exchange perspective. In *International conference on information systems 2012: (ICIS 2012)*, 16–19 December 2012 (Vol. 5, pp. 4259–4269). Orlando, Florida, USA, Curran.

Westin, A. F. (1967). *Privacy and freedom*. Atheneum.

Xu, H. & Sun, Y. (2014). Toward collective privacy using coordinative path planning. In: D. Hutchison, T. Kanade, J. Kittler, J. M. Kleinberg, A. Kobsa, F. Mattern et al.*Pervasive computing and the networked world*. Cham: Springer Nature (Lecture notes in computer science). pp. 698-710.

Young, A. L., & Quan-Haase, A. (2013). Privacy protection strategies on Facebook. *Information, Communication & Society, 16*(4), 479–500. https://doi.org/10.1080/1369118X.2013.777757

Ziegler, S., & Chochliouros, I. (2015, December 14 – 2015, December 16). Privacy flag – collective privacy protection scheme based on structured distributed risk assessment. In *2015 IEEE: 2nd world forum on internet of things (WF-IoT)* (pp. 430–434). IEEE. https://doi.org/10.1109/WF-IoT.2015.7389093

4
INSTITUTIONAL PERSPECTIVES ON PRIVACY

Elizabeth Stoycheff

WAYNE STATE UNIVERSITY, USA

Another frontier in privacy research mounts an affront to large, multinational technology corporations, like Facebook and Google, that transact with the public using data as currency. These "free" digital platforms have risen to global dominance with a business model that eradicates direct monetary costs to consumers, instead levying users' time, information, and privacy. Such costs are often far less tangible for individuals, which elicits important questions about the fairness and transparency of these economic exchanges. Moreover, user data has an afterlife that can be obtained by government agencies, further complicating privacy concerns in democracies and nondemocracies alike. In the current landscape, it is easier to discuss the institutional *threats* to one's online privacy than institutional protections of it. Thus, this chapter dives into the research on these less visible, but incredibly profound, institutional encroachments of individual privacy and their consequences for internet users and society.

Definitions

The migration of social activity to digital spaces brought about a new paradigm known as *datafication*, wherein all facets of social life – relationships, interests, emotions, and information seeking – can be reduced to numerical form. This quantifiable data can then be used to predict future behavior. The rise of datafication has made *institutional privacy* more salient. Institutional, or vertical, privacy is control of one's personal information and data from public and private entities, like corporations, schools, healthcare providers, and government agencies. Such institutions have implemented systems for collecting user data and information that can operate invisibly to the user. Individuals are typically notified about the collection of their online data through website terms of service and privacy policies. But these long, technically laden agreements are incompatible with diligent consent, such that internet users typically ignore their provisions and mindlessly comply with any requests provided therein (Obar & Oeldorf-Hirsch, 2020; Stoycheff, 2022). After all, failure to comply with specified terms often denies one access to the service entirely.

Information continually gleaned from individuals without their full understanding is called *dataveillance* (van Dijck, 2014). Like traditional forms of surveillance, dataveillance confers data, and therefore power, to institutions and people in authority while further disassociating individuals from information needed to make well-informed decisions. (See Figure 4.1 for complete definitions.) The corporate entities that possess these large databases have pivoted to the business of extracting and analyzing data in order to generate profit, condition users for repeated behavior, and retain market control, practices Zuboff (2019) refers to as *surveillance capitalism*. As online surveillance becomes

DOI: 10.4324/9781003244677-5

Chilling Effects: The deterrence of speech and other forms of legal behavior as a result of fear and uncertainty that they will incur legal penalty.

Datafication: Converting facets of social life (relationships, interests, emotions, information seeking) into numerical form, which can then be quantified and used to observe trends and predict future behavior.

Dataveillance: Collection and retention of data streams without individuals' full understanding of the information being collected and stored.

Figure 4.1 Institutional privacy definitions

more expansive, legal and professional communities are increasingly concerned about how violations of institutional privacy create *chilling effects*, which is the deterrence of lawful behavior out of fear and uncertainty that such actions may be viewed as suspicious. Together, the mass quantification of data and its harvesting for commercial intent have created an environment that is systematically antithetical to user privacy. How did we get here?

Institutional Illiteracy

Social network sites, and now apps, were originally intended to facilitate communication between peers. As a result, privacy considerations on these channels prioritized technical design features that gave individuals control over how other users would view their information. This led to an enduring bias that other users were the primary audiences of people's posts, rather than the institutional entities that mediate them (Quinn et al., 2019). Early public opinion revealed that ordinary internet users were confused about institutional privacy; simultaneously believing that corporations would protect their data yet may also sell it to third parties without their consent (Turow & Hennessy, 2007).

Up until recently, much of the scholarly literature on privacy in communication science was similarly situated in the context of social threats, concerns, and protective behaviors. One of the topic's most established theoretical frameworks, communication privacy management theory (CPM), can certainly apply to institutional privacy, but has overwhelmingly been used to examine boundaries, rules, and information ownership among peers, rather than with institutions and governments (e.g., Petronio & Child, 2020). Normative websites promote privacy-protective behaviors that control the flow of information between users, but not from online platforms themselves. And even a recent meta-analysis of research using CPM scarcely mentioned its institutional applications (Baruh et al., 2017).

Scholars were quick to suggest that individual-level variables of online privacy literacy were important to reconciling the disconnect between privacy concerns and protective behaviors, known as the privacy paradox. But the average user possesses a poor understanding of institutional data collection practices, technical jargon, and privacy-specific policies (Park, 2013). To better assess individuals' privacy literacy, Trepte and colleagues (2015) developed an online privacy literacy scale that not only acknowledged, but prioritized, institutional privacy knowledge. This marked an important milestone to quantify how much individuals know about institutional data practices and the policies that can protect them. It has since inspired new research on how privacy literacy is a function of one's sociodemographic profile and is producing new inequalities in our digital environments (Epstein & Quinn, 2020; Hagendorff, 2018).

Edward Snowden and the US National Security Agency

Institutional privacy concerns exploded on the global stage in 2013. An American intelligence contractor for the US National Security Agency leaked millions of classified files that unearthed top-secret government surveillance programs that spied on citizens and public officials in the United States, across Western Europe, Asia, and South America. Both world leaders and regular internet users had been previously unaware of these programs' existence, let alone the sheer scope and volume of how their internet and telephone data could be harvested for state use. These disclosures prompted users to seriously contend with vertical privacy threats and reform their online behavior. News of the Snowden leaks triggered an uptick in the adoption of DuckDuckGo, a privacy-oriented search engine (Rosso et al., 2020), and reduced internet search through less secure channels (Penney, 2016). After whistleblowing on the United States government, Snowden feared for his safety and fled, prompting a thrilling worldwide manhunt for either a champion of internet privacy or traitor, depending on where one stood.

Cambridge Analytica Scandal and Privacy Social Contracts

Institutional concerns about internet privacy erupted again in 2018 when a whistleblower from Cambridge Analytica came forward accusing the political consultancy of illegally gleaning Facebook data from 87 million Americans. The breach occurred when Cambridge Analytica amassed quiz results from a Facebook app called "This is your digital life." The app assessed "Big Five" personality characteristics from about 270,000 consenting users, but it also accrued information from the private profiles of quiz takers' virtual friends. Cambridge Analytica then used this data to design political microtargeting strategies for US Republican candidates Ted Cruz and Donald Trump during the 2016 US Presidential election. Barack Obama's team used a burgeoning version of psychographic profiling in 2012 to target prospective voters.

Outside the United States, Cambridge Analytica partnered with governments and political campaigns to use online data to tailor political messaging in countries from Kenya to Brazil. A second Cambridge Analytica whistleblower said these revelations "showed global manipulation [of user data] is out of control" (Cadwalladr, 2020). Widespread fears prompted concern that the company also interfered in the 2016 United Kingdom referendum on European Union (EU) membership, known colloquially as Brexit, but an independent commission later determined that Cambridge Analytica did not operate illegally, but merely exploited "systemic vulnerabilities in our democratic systems."

News of the company's scandals were reported around the world, sending Facebook into a reputational crisis and reaffirming its commitment to the protection of user privacy. There were social media calls to #QuitFacebook, but it has had little impact on overall user behavior. In the wake of the Cambridge Analytica scandal, users continued to maintain their Facebook accounts and those on its subsidiary platforms, Instagram and WhatsApp. Studies of Facebook users from around the world revealed heightened privacy concerns (Brown, 2020), but at the same time they experienced privacy fatigue, as news reports on commercial breaches to user privacy are not uncommon, and an overall lack of efficacy on how to continue to participate on social media platforms while protecting their privacy from institutional actors (Hinds et al., 2020). Lutz et al. (2020) also observed social media users' cynicism toward online privacy, classifying it as a multidimensional contrast that includes components of distrust, uncertainty, powerlessness, and resignation. This pessimism is perhaps (rightly) derived from understanding that even if psychodemographic targeting is mired in ethical considerations, it is integral to the business models of these platforms and widely deployed for other commercial purposes.

Other research found that the Cambridge Analytica incident marked an important turning point in public opinion. Internet users shifted from thinking about privacy as a fundamental human right to the belief that it's a necessity of participating in the digital world, and as such, it is the responsibility of individuals to protect their own privacy and interests (Afriat et al., 2020). This sentiment was replicated in comparative research that showed social media posts from English-speaking users tended to hold large institutions, like Facebook and Google, responsible for protecting user privacy; whereas Spanish-speaking voices were more likely to place blame on individual users for being negligent with their personal information (González et al., 2019).

The belief that one's privacy protection is their own responsibility stems from social contract theory, which contends that harmonious society is predicated on reciprocal moral obligations and agreements (Martin, 2016). Applied in this context, the contract operates through an exchange of individual information for commercial services provided (e.g., searching for information on Google, using Instagram to connect with friends, and tailoring advertising content to fit one's specific needs). The moral clause of this theory contends that, as part of this exchange, individuals need to trust that their data will be protected and not used outside the context for which it was acquired; what Nissenbaum (2004) termed contextual integrity.

New research has looked at the extent to which individuals do indeed trust institutions or perceive privacy risks in such online exchanges. Kruikemeier and colleagues (2020) derived five archetypes of internet users based on how people perceived social contracts with online technology companies – the highly concerned, wary, ambivalent, neutral, and carefree. Most of their participants either found such agreements unreliable or expressed distrust entirely. More compellingly, less than 5% of respondents had confidence that institutions would uphold the contextual integrity of their data. And predictably, their findings showed that the highly concerned, wary, and ambivalent groups were more likely to implement privacy-protective behaviors as a result. Kruikemeier et al. (2020) employed longitudinal data, important for acknowledging that social contracts with online technology companies are continuous relationships. It supports previous findings that institutional assurances of data security can assuage privacy concerns (Xu et al., 2011), but the more often one's privacy is violated by a platform – through data breaches or unsanctioned data mining – the more skeptical individuals become about assurances and the social contract more broadly (Wang et al., 2019).

One critique of this framework is that it assumes all parties entering into an agreement do so rationally and in good faith. In the absence of these conditions, social contracts are essentially nullified. Abdul-Ghani (2020) argues this is the case for most online data exchanges, wherein individuals are unaware of the scope of data being collected about them, the purposes as to why this information was collected, and the parties with whom it will be shared. Moreover, rarely do such social contracts encourage individuals to reconsider or later withdraw their consent. Quite the opposite – they are designed to elicit indefinite compliance (Stoycheff, 2022) – so as not to disrupt access to a steady stream of information.

Renegotiating these terms and allowing users to shut off the data pipeline was central in the construction of Article 17 of the General Data Protection Regulation (GDPR) that governs data collections within the EU. This provision grants individuals the "right to be forgotten," such that they can request that institutions erase their personal data. It predominantly applies when data is no longer being used in accordance with its original intent, not in the public interest, or for data that was obtained illegally. This measure is credited with allowing individuals to recoup some of their privacy rights and limit institutions' expansive reach; however, it does not apply to information gleaned outside of the EU. While its implementation raises important questions about the need to balance privacy protections with freedom of expression, it set a global precedent that continues to influence legislation outside Europe (Youm & Park, 2016).

Governmental Privacy and Chilling Effects

Individuals require privacy from other people and corporate entities, but they also need to be able to control their disclosures to governments. Like technology firms that employ user data to optimize experiences, governments have ramped up their own data collection efforts to improve public services, assess security risks, and trace communicable diseases. Confronted with COVID-19, many governments designed their own apps to track and notify residents of potential exposures. Most were bound by federal privacy laws and required individual consent (Seto et al., 2021), but still prompted public concerns about mass governmental surveillance, which lowered adoption rates (Chan & Saquib, 2021; Zhang et al., 2020).

In the US, media harbor deep suspicion toward state agencies that employ the same data collection techniques as corporate institutions. Their reporting tends to hold government to a higher moral standard, accusing such actions of violating the public trust and obscuring transparency (Connor & Doan, 2021). The Cambridge Analytica scandal is an excellent example. In less democratic environments, state-sponsored dataveillance can pose a dire threat to civil and political liberties, as well as basic human rights. Kabanov and Karyagin (2018) termed such efforts "data-driven authoritarianism" which refers to extensive data harvesting that is used solely to reinforce the autocratic regime, rather than improve the country's digital infrastructure or otherwise benefit the citizenry. Such efforts seek to bolster the regime's legitimacy by publicly embracing technology, using cooptation to associate the regime with powerful tech players, and then using dataveillance to systematically find and repress opposition voices.

Governments can intercept private user data in two ways: Indirectly, by filing a request for user data with technology companies, which typically targets specific information and leaves a traceable record; or directly, by circumventing service providers using legal and technical loopholes. Direct access allows governments to engage in mass surveillance, collecting indiscriminate data from a large number of users. It also tends to operate extralegally, and as a result, the content and sheer scale of data collected are often not publicly disclosed (Global Network Initiative, 2021). In 2021, more countries around the world implemented laws to weaken or eradicate privacy-protection tools like encryption and virtual private networks, as well as regulations that require technology companies to store user data on local servers, granting state agencies easier jurisdiction to it (Freedom House, 2022). This follows an 11-year decline in global internet freedom and political deterioration in some of the most stable democratic systems, including India, Hong Kong, and the United States. Western Europe grappled with how to balance online privacy with COVID-19 contact tracing and immigration policies, as they fought to contain the virus.

The ability to maintain privacy boundaries and control how one's data is disclosed to government underpins democratic principles of free speech, freedom of movement and assembly, and peaceful opposition. Perceptions of dataveillance are known to produce political chilling effects, whereby individuals refrain from various forms of civic engagement due to fear and uncertainty of how their information could be used. Chilling effects originated in the legal community and are now routinely cited in privacy law. Judgments that employ the chilling effect contend that an action must "anticipate the implications of future behavior outside the case under consideration" (Townend, 2017, p. 5). In other words, chilling effects occur when the threat to one's privacy is so profound that it alters many subsequent actions.

Chilling Effects Research

Empirical chilling effects research has revealed a systematic suppression in the following types of democratic activities: Expressing minority political opinions on social media (Stoycheff, 2016; 2022), online searches for politically sensitive keywords (Penney, 2016), disclosing one's religious identity (Stoycheff et al., 2019), and restricting others' political and civil liberties (Stoycheff et al., 2017). These online chilling effects are not deterred by promises to delete one's personal information or protections like the right to be forgotten (Hermstrüwer & Dickert, 2017). Moreover, individuals who reside in countries with heavy dataveillance engage in less *offline* political participation, like attending protests and forming unions (Stoycheff, Burgess, & Martucci, 2019).

Chilling effects research investigates a counterfactual – when individuals choose *not* to participate in civic life. Very often, the decision to refrain from online social and political activity is far less conscious than one's choice to participate. This can be explained through a concept known as mindless compliance, which is conforming one's behavior to social norms without first weighing the costs and benefits of doing so (Anaraky et al., 2020).

On social media, mindless compliance often manifests when users quickly consent to a platform's terms of service without reading how organizations intend to use their data. Most social media users grant unconditional consent to tracking within seconds of appearing on the platform (Obar & Oeldorf, 2020). This can have big and permanent consequences. For example, last year TikTok updated its privacy policy to allow the collection of biometric identifiers, including face and voiceprints. It didn't specify how this data could be used, but it can be harvested by encouraging users to experiment with filters and effects.

To determine how these cryptic privacy policies can contribute to chilling effects, I recently conducted a large, nationally representative experiment in the US. (Stoycheff, 2022). Study participants were presented with a boilerplate pop-up message asking for permission to track user cookies, as is required by the EU's GDPR and the California Consumer Privacy Act. Exposure to these cookie notifications triggered emotional responses of anger and fear, which translated into an unwillingness to engage in various types of civic engagement, like posting about one's ideas and seeking out more information. Thus, on a day-to-day basis, website cookie notifications are acting much the same way the Snowden and Cambridge Analytical scandals did to increase both desirable (privacy protective) and undesirable (chilling) behaviors.

Fearing the consequences of insufficient institutional privacy is not unfounded; in 2021 alone, individuals from 56 countries were arrested for information they disclosed on internet platforms (Freedom House, 2022). It has become increasingly clear that governments around the world are seeking greater access to private user data to maintain power asymmetries and better control their holds on power. And their citizens have no better recourse than to stay silent.

A Culture of Chilling

The institutional threats delineated in this chapter and throughout this volume underscore the complexity of managing multiple spheres of privacy. Individuals must navigate emerging privacy threats from governments and big tech; they present individual concerns as well as collective ones. And while we have evidence of expansive dataveillance producing individual chilling effects, more problematic is its undocumented culture of chilling. In mass, this manifests as less tolerance for those who do not conform to social expectations, as well as less inclusive social and political structures that reinforce hierarchies rather than permit new ideas (Büchi et al., 2022).

New research on institutional privacy literacy, efficacy, and privacy-protective behaviors is promising, but these threats are simply too big for individuals to tackle themselves. In fact, institutional privacy is no longer just an individual right; it is a collective one. As governments and corporations analyze swaths of user data to determine patterns of ideas and behaviors, the public has a right to understand how it is grouped and classified, to ensure the protection of collective rights. Mantelero (2017) recommends shifting the narrative away from confidentiality and control of one's personal data to questioning institutions about how they use aggregate data to systematically discriminate or govern entire groups.

Technology companies and social media platforms, like Facebook, YouTube, and TikTok, would like users to believe that they provide free, transparent channels for producing and consuming content alongside network friends and connections. But in actuality, they are powerful, multinational corporations that mediate information consumption, interpersonal relationships, and online behavior like never before.

References

Abdul-Ghani, E. (2020). Consumers' online institutional privacy literacy. In *Advances in digital marketing and e-commerce* (pp. 40–46). Cham, Springer.

Afriat, H., Dvir-Gvirsman, S., Tsuriel, K., & Ivan, L. (2020). "This is capitalism. It is not illegal": Users' attitudes toward institutional privacy following the Cambridge Analytica scandal. *The Information Society*, *37*(2), 115–127.

Anaraky, R. G., Knijnenburg, B. P., & Risius, M. (2020). Exacerbating mindless compliance: The danger of justifications during privacy decision making in the context of Facebook applications. *AIS Transactions on Human-Computer Interaction*, *12*(2), 70–95.

Baruh, L., Secinti, E., & Cemalcilar, Z. (2017). Online privacy concerns and privacy management: A meta-analytical review. *Journal of Communication*, *67*(1), 26–53.

Brown, A. J. (2020). "Should I stay or should I leave?": Exploring (dis) continued Facebook use after the Cambridge Analytica scandal. *Social Media+ Society*, *6*(1).

Büchi, M., Festic, N., & Latzer, M. (2022). The chilling effects of digital dataveillance: A theoretical model and an empirical research agenda. *Big Data & Society*, *9*(1).

Cadwalladr, C. (4 January 2020). Fresh Cambridge Analytica leak 'shows global manipulation is out of control'. *The Guardian*. Retrieved from: https://www.theguardian.com/uk-news/2020/jan/04/cambridge-analytica-data-leak-global-election-manipulation?utm_term=Autofeed&CMP=twt_gu&utm_medium=&utm_source=Twitter#Echobox=1578158795

Chan, E. Y., & Saqib, N. U. (2021). Privacy concerns can explain unwillingness to download and use contact tracing apps when COVID-19 concerns are high. *Computers in Human Behavior*, *119*, 106718.

Connor, B. T., & Doan, L. (2021). Government and corporate surveillance: Moral discourse on privacy in the civil sphere. *Information, Communication & Society*, *24*(1), 52–68.

Epstein, D., & Quinn, K. (2020). Markers of online privacy marginalization: Empirical examination of socioeconomic disparities in social media privacy attitudes, literacy, and behavior. *Social Media+ Society*, *6*(2), 2056305120916853

Freedom House (2022). Freedom on the Net 2021: The global drive to control big tech. Retrieved from: https://freedomhouse.org/report/freedom-net/2021/global-drive-control-big-tech

Global Network Initiative (3 June 2021). Defining direct access: GNI calls for greater transparency and dialogue around mandatory, unmediated government access to data. Retrieved from: https://globalnetworkinitiative.org/defining-direct-access-2/

González, F., Yu, Y., Figueroa, A., López, C., & Aragon, C. (May 2019). Global reactions to the Cambridge Analytica scandal: A cross-language social media study. In *Companion Proceedings of the 2019 World Wide Web Conference* (pp. 799–806).

Hagendorff, T. (2018). Privacy literacy and its problems. *Journal of Information Ethics*, *27*(2), 127.

Hermstrüwer, Y., & Dickert, S. (2017). Sharing is daring: An experiment on consent, chilling effects and a salient privacy nudge. *International Review of Law and Economics*, *51*, 38–49.

Hinds, J., Williams, E. J., & Joinson, A. N. (2020). "It wouldn't happen to me": Privacy concerns and perspectives following the Cambridge Analytica scandal. *International Journal of Human-Computer Studies*, *143*, 102498.

Kabanov, Y., & Karyagin, M. (2018). Data-driven authoritarianism: Non-democracies and big data. In *International conference on digital transformation and global society* (pp. 144–155). Cham, Springer.

Kruikemeier, S., Boerman, S. C., & Bol, N. (2020). Breaching the contract? Using social contract theory to explain individuals' online behavior to safeguard privacy. *Media Psychology*, *23*(2), 269–292.

Lutz, C., Hoffmann, C. P., & Ranzini, G. (2020). Data capitalism and the user: An exploration of privacy cynicism in Germany. *New media & society*, *22*(7), 1168–1187.

Mantelero, A. (2017). From group privacy to collective privacy: Towards a new dimension of privacy and data protection in the big data era. In *Group privacy* (pp. 139–158). Cham, Springer.

Martin, K. (2016). Understanding privacy online: Development of a social contract approach to privacy. *Journal of Business Ethics*, *137*(3), 551–569.

Nissenbaum, H. (2004). Privacy as contextual integrity. *Wash. L. Rev.*, *79*, 119.

Obar, J. A., & Oeldorf-Hirsch, A. (2020). The biggest lie on the internet: Ignoring the privacy policies and terms of service policies of social networking services. *Information, Communication & Society*, *23*(1), 128–147.

Park, Y. J. (2013). Digital literacy and privacy behavior online. *Communication Research*, *40*(2), 215–236.

Penney, J. W. (2016). Chilling effects: Online surveillance and Wikipedia use. *Berkeley Tech. Law Journal*, *31*, 117.

Petronio, S., & Child, J. T. (2020). Conceptualization and operationalization: Utility of communication privacy management theory. *Current Opinion in Psychology*, *31*, 76–82.

Quinn, K., Epstein, D., & Moon, B. (2019). We care about different things: Non-elite conceptualizations of social media privacy. *Social Media+ Society*, *5*(3).

Rosso, M., Nasir, A. B. M., & Farhadloo, M. (2020). Chilling effects and the stock market response to the Snowden revelations. *New Media & Society*, *22*(11), 1976–1995.

Seto, E., Challa, P., & Ware, P. (2021). Adoption of COVID-19 contact tracing apps: A balance between privacy and effectiveness. *Journal of Medical Internet Research*, *23*(3).

Stoycheff, E. (2016). Under surveillance: Examining Facebook's spiral of silence effects in the wake of NSA internet monitoring. *Journalism & Mass Communication Quarterly*, *93*(2), 296–311.

Stoycheff, E. (2022). Cookies and content moderation: Affective chilling effects of internet surveillance and censorship.

Stoycheff, E., Liu, J., Xu, K., & Wibowo, K. (2019). Privacy and the panopticon: Online mass surveillance's deterrence and chilling effects. *New Media & Society*, *21*(3), 602–619.

Stoycheff, Elizabeth, Burgess, G. Scott, & Martucci, Maria Clara (2018). Online censorship and digital surveillance: the relationship between suppression technologies and democratization across countries. Information, Communication & Society, 23, 474–490. https://doi.org/10.1080/1369118x.2018.1518472

Stoycheff, E., Wibowo, K. A., Liu, J., & Xu, K. (2017). Online surveillance's effect on support for other extraordinary measures to prevent terrorism. *Mass Communication and Society*, *20*(6), 784–799.

Townend, J. (2017). Freedom of expression and the chilling effect. *The Routledge companion to media and human rights*. Chicago, Routledge.

Trepte, Sabine, Teutsch, Doris, Masur, Philipp K., Eicher, Carolin, Fischer, Mona, Hennhöfer, Alisa, & Lind, Fabienne (2015). Do People Know About Privacy and Data Protection Strategies? Towards the "Online Privacy Literacy Scale" (OPLIS), Law, Governance and Technology Series,Reforming European Data Protection Law (pp. 333–365). https://doi.org/10.1007/978-94-017-9385-8_14

Turow, J., & Hennessy, M. (2007). Internet privacy and institutional trust: Insights from a national survey. *New Media & Society*, *9*(2), 300–318.

van Dijck, J. (2014). Datafication, dataism and dataveillance: Big data between scientific paradigm and ideology. *Surveillance Society*, *12*(2), 197–208.

Wang, L., Sun, Z., Dai, X., Zhang, Y., & Hu, H. H. (2019). Retaining users after privacy invasions: The roles of institutional privacy assurances and threat-coping appraisal in mitigating privacy concerns. *Information Technology & People*.

Xu, H., Dinev, T., Smith, J., & Hart, P. (2011). Information privacy concerns: Linking individual perceptions with institutional privacy assurances. *Journal of the Association for Information Systems*, *12*(12), 798–824.

Youm, K. H., & Park, A. (2016). The "right to be forgotten" in European Union law: Data protection balanced with free speech? *Journalism & Mass Communication Quarterly*, *93*(2), 273–295.

Zhang, B., Kreps, S., McMurry, N., & McCain, R. M. (2020). Americans' perceptions of privacy and surveillance in the COVID-19 pandemic. *PLOS One*, *15*(12), e0242652.

Zuboff, S. (2019). *The age of surveillance capitalism: The fight for a human future at the new frontier of power*. Profile Books.

5

GROUP PRIVACY

Gwen Petro and Miriam Metzger

UNIVERSITY OF CALIFORNIA SANTA BARBARA, USA

Developments in privacy legislation over the past decade, including the European Union's General Data Protection Regulation and California's Consumer Privacy Act, grant individuals greater control over their personal data. These protections aim to prevent actors with malicious intentions from identifying a needle in a haystack by preserving people's anonymity and protecting their identities online. However, Taylor et al. (2017) argue that there is not always safety in numbers: Sometimes, it is necessary to keep bad actors from identifying the haystack itself. Advancements in data-driven technologies have made it easier to identify groups of similar individuals – those most likely to purchase a certain type of car, vote for a particular political candidate, or join a union, for example – rather than individuals themselves. Such groups are often extremely valuable to advertisers, political strategists, corporate executives, and law enforcement agents, among others, who might exploit the privacy of groups to advance their own interests. Nevertheless, the actions that legislators, media platforms, and users have undertaken to protect the privacy of individuals often do not protect the privacy of groups.

Throughout this chapter, we differentiate group privacy from personal privacy, describe situations that may threaten group privacy, and argue that privacy scholarship must pay greater attention to understanding how to manage group privacy. To this end, we explain how current privacy theory may or may not apply to group privacy and summarize existing research in this area upon which future scholars might build. In doing so, we hope to help motivate further discussions of privacy and social media beyond the individual level.

Conceptualizing Group Privacy

In this section, we begin to define group privacy by describing various ways to conceptualize groups and how new information technology has altered the notion of what constitutes a group. We then explain why groups themselves, in addition to their individual members, have a right to privacy and may experience threats to their privacy. In doing so, we conceptualize group privacy and group privacy concern with a focus on informational privacy.

What Makes a Group?

Before defining group privacy, we ought to define what we mean by a "group." There is debate surrounding the extent to which a collection of individuals may be considered a group. Floridi (2017) discusses two viewpoints on the issue: That groups are defined by objective, "natural" traits or by more subjective, arbitrary characteristics. Ultimately, Floridi argues that social groups are not

DOI: 10.4324/9781003244677-6

naturally occurring, nor are they socially constructed; rather, "they result from the choices we make of the observables we wish to focus on, for specific purposes, and from the constraining affordances (data) provided by the systems we are analysing" (p. 86). Thus, although individuals exist on their own, they do not constitute a group until they are labeled as such by themselves or others, and commonalities between group members may only be observable to the party gathering the data.

Furthermore, Mittelstadt (2017) identifies three types of groups based on the nature of the connections between group members: Collectives, ascriptive groups, and ad hoc groups. *Collectives* are groups that people with shared interests, goals, or other characteristics join intentionally, such as trade unions or book clubs. *Ascriptive groups* are groups that people belong to automatically because they possess a common trait, including ethnic groups or those with a particular health condition. *Ad hoc groups* are fleeting, unstable groups, and similarities between group members may be as trivial as waiting for the same bus to arrive. Often, however, ad hoc groups are defined by third parties for specific, time-bound purposes (e.g., marketing segments). According to Mittelstadt, collectives and ascriptive groups often have a collective identity held by group members or the group itself. Moreover, both types of groups may possess agency, for which self-awareness is required; members of collectives are self-aware by definition, and although members of ascriptive groups are not necessarily aware of their ethnic identity or other underlying characteristics, self-awareness may nevertheless exist at the group level. Ad hoc groups, on the other hand, need not share a collective identity or possess self-awareness.

Social media scholars have used additional terms to describe various types of groups in prior work. For instance, Suh and Metzger (2022) distinguish between self-constituted groups and algorithmically-determined groups, also referred to as active and passive groups, respectively. They describe *self-constituted groups* as those "recognized as groups by their members or by outsiders" (p. 93), whereas *algorithmically-determined groups* are ad hoc groups assembled for purposes ranging from the tailoring of song recommendations to the dissemination of targeted marketing campaigns to the surveillance of rule-breaking citizens or employees. To create these groups, machine-learning algorithms are applied to social media user data to assign individual users to various groups by inferring their probability of having some trait or set of traits. This process results in groups who are not self-aware and yet, as we will argue, are susceptible to significant group-level privacy threats.

The Right to Group Privacy

In 1977, Bloustein discussed the "right to huddle," which he defined as the privacy of individuals' associations with one another. The focus in his conceptualization is on individual group members' privacy rather than the privacy of the group itself. However, a group can have its own identity and interests that are distinct from those of their individual members (Bélanger & Crossler, 2011). Thus, Taylor et al. (2017) argue that in addition to considering *their* privacy, or the privacy of "a collection of individuals with individual interests in privacy" (p. 2), it is necessary to consider *its* privacy – the privacy of the group itself as a whole. They assert that the latter is especially important in light of new data analytic techniques which have shifted the focus from individual users to crowds of users (i.e., algorithmically-determined groups). Mittelstadt (2017) posits that groups, like individuals, may possess *moral patienthood* so far as one might consider them an object of moral concern with the potential to suffer harm. Moreover, Floridi (2017) asserts that individuals have a right to *inviolate identity*– to control information that constitutes their identity – which should also apply to group identity. Therefore, we define group privacy as a group's ability to control data or information about itself, with the possible goal of protecting the identity of the group from discovery by outsiders, rather than only protecting the privacy of individual group members.

Those who believe that groups have a right to privacy consider the ways in which this right might be threatened. Bélanger and Crossler (2011) define *group information privacy concern* as "the collective concern that group members have regarding the privacy of the information the group possesses and has access to" (p. 1032). According to Metzger et al. (2020), "Anything that negatively impacts the group or that shifts control of the group away from group members can be considered a threat to group privacy ('its privacy') that resides either separately or alongside individual privacy threats" (p. 7). This includes third-party access to and use of information that results in the discovery, surveillance, harassment, domination, or termination of a particular group. Loi and Christen (2020) distinguish between the risk of confidential information being spread outside of a select group of people (a threat to "what happens in Vegas" privacy) and the risk of sensitive information being inferred about individuals or groups based on publicly available data about them (a threat to "inferential" privacy). For example, a health insurance provider might infer that someone is a member of a group that is at a higher risk of lung cancer because he has purchased cigarettes, and there is a higher incidence of lung cancer among smokers (Loi & Christen, 2020).

The question of whether a group has a right to privacy, and in what circumstances, continues to generate debate. Loi and Christen (2020) argue that "what happens in Vegas" group privacy may be a matter of *their* (group members') or *its* (the group's) privacy, whereas inferential privacy concerning algorithmically-determined groups is strictly a matter of *their* privacy unless members of these groups become self-aware of their being grouped. In contrast to Loi and Christen, we believe that inferential privacy poses threats to individuals as well as groups, whether or not they are self-aware. If an algorithmically-determined group remains hidden (i.e., it was not found because the algorithm was never applied to find it), then both *its* privacy and *their* privacy are protected. For instance, the Children's Online Privacy Protection Act in the US prohibits companies from collecting, using, and disclosing personal information from children under the age of 13 in an attempt to protect the privacy of a vulnerable group in its entirety, as well as the privacy of individual children. Furthermore, class-action lawsuits, which occur on behalf of groups without the awareness of many group members, demonstrate that groups have legal rights and that threats to group privacy (*its* and *their*) can occur despite a lack of group self-awareness.

Group Privacy Theory

Allusions to the concept of group privacy appear throughout the work of foundational privacy theorists. For example, Westin defines privacy as "the claim of individuals, *groups*, or institutions to determine for themselves when, how, and to what extent information about them is communicated to others" (1967, p. 5, emphasis added), and Altman defines it as, "selective control of access to the self or to one's group" (1975, p. 18). Subsequent privacy scholarship has primarily focused on the individual level, although there have been some exceptions. One such exception is communication privacy management (CPM) theory (Petronio, 2002). CPM argues that groups such as families can have *unified privacy boundaries* whereby they collectively own their private information, and group members can jointly manage this information in the process of *unified boundary coordination* (Petronio, 2002). While CPM is useful for understanding how groups co-manage private information in general, is it less applicable to the novel and complex group privacy challenges posed by social media and data mining technologies.

Other theoretical perspectives on privacy more expressly consider the online environment. Nissenbaum (2009), for example, developed the framework of contextual integrity as a normative approach to understanding information flow off- or online. According to Nissenbaum, different contexts have *context-relative informational norms* dictating which types of information should be shared with which actors according to which values or principles. *Contextual integrity* "is preserved when informational norms are respected and violated when informational norms are breached" (p. 140). Thus, people may feel that their privacy is violated when an embarrassing photo of them is posted on social media or when viewing a personalized advertisement based on a prior web search because these situations violate the principle of contextual integrity. In other work, Marwick and boyd (2014) propose the concept of *networked privacy* to explain how "privacy in social media cannot be entirely maintained and established by individuals, as it is not wholly dependent on individual choices or control over data" (p. 1062). According to these authors, people must actively and adeptly navigate a multitude of audiences, social norms, and technical features to maintain their privacy despite the blurring of contexts online. Although neither Nissenbaum (2009) nor Marwick and boyd (2014) explicitly reference group privacy, their work recognizing that informational norms are co-constructed is an important step towards understanding privacy beyond the individual level. In fact, the framework of contextual integrity and the concept of networked privacy are just a couple of examples of how privacy scholarship is moving in this direction.

Recent Theoretical Developments

Recently, scholars have begun to modify and combine existing theoretical perspectives on privacy to apply them to the study of group privacy. Bélanger and James (2020) propose the theory of multilevel information privacy (TMIP), which explains how people make multilevel information privacy decisions. They define *multilevel information privacy* as "the ability of an individual (I-privacy) or group (we-privacy) to construct, regulate, and apply the rules (i.e., norms) for managing their information and interaction with others" (p. 3). TMIP extends CPM by explaining how groups can come to co-own information through intentional boundary linkage (i.e., sharing with group members), boundary turbulence (i.e., non-consensual disclosure to a group), or content co-creation (i.e., group members creating and sharing content together).

Further, TMIP combines principles of CPM with the social identity approach, which encompasses social identity theory (Tajfel & Turner, 1979) and self-categorization theory (Turner et al., 1987). These approaches posit that social interactions range from the interpersonal, where personal identities are more salient, to the intergroup, where group-based social identities are more salient. When a particular context activates a certain identity, then one is likely to abide by the norms associated with that identity. In TMIP, Bélanger and James argue that the characteristics of one's present online or offline environment affect the salience of different social identities, their related informational privacy norms or rules, and the perceived risks and benefits of disclosure, which all ultimately influence one's privacy behavior. Although the privacy norms associated with one's personal and group identities may contradict one another, the extent to which one identifies with different social identities and the extent to which they are situationally salient will determine which norms will have the strongest influence on the privacy decision at hand. While TMIP clearly provides utility for studying group privacy decision-making in self-constituted online groups, its applicability (as well as all other existing privacy theories) to algorithmically-determined groups is less obvious.

Current and Emerging Empirical Findings

To date, most research pertaining to group privacy on social media has involved self-constituted groups. Scholars have paid less attention to ad hoc or algorithmically-determined groups thus far, although this is a growing area of research. In this section, we begin by discussing studies on privacy management in self-constituted groups. Next, we move on to discussing privacy in algorithmically-determined groups.

Interpersonal Relationships and Self-Constituted Groups

Much of the research related to group privacy has focused on interpersonal privacy and privacy management in self-constituted groups. One area of this research focuses on understanding when and how people experience privacy challenges involving multiple people. Another area of research concerns the strategies that people use to co-manage their privacy and cope with interpersonal privacy issues on social media. As we will explain here, much of this research has yet to thoroughly explore privacy threats involving an entire group rather than individual group members.

Understanding Relational and Group Privacy Threats

Research has identified types of situations that can lead to privacy challenges involving multiple individuals and the factors associated with people's reactions to these situations. Litt et al. (2014) argued that self-presentation on social networking sites can become a collective process when users post content implicating others and, at times, produce face threats for those who are not depicted in a desirable manner. Birnholtz et al. (2017) and Litt et al. (2014) both found that people's responses to face-threatening social media posts depend on individual (e.g., internet skills), relational (e.g., closeness), and situational factors (e.g., audience size), confirming that the networked nature of social media provides unique challenges to privacy and self-disclosure which involve multiple individuals (see also chapter 3 by Trepte on social, relational, and networked privacy).

Despite the involvement of more than one person, most of the examples identified in prior research better illustrate threats to individual privacy rather than threats to group privacy because they do not threaten any particular group as a whole. Nevertheless, a 2018 study by Guberek et al. on privacy management among undocumented immigrants found that participants seldom considered the potential privacy risks associated with participating in social media groups for sharing information related to immigration; though, one participant considered how, in the case of a group privacy breach, belonging to such groups might lead to members getting arrested. Moreover, the Chinese government reportedly deleted numerous individual accounts and groups associated with feminist and LGBTQ activism, including some private group chats (Ni & Davidson, 2021). And workers in the US attempting to unionize have encountered threats to group privacy, such as anti-union managers secretly infiltrating employee WhatsApp groups and managers crashing zoom calls discussing organizing (Constanz, 2021). Research is needed to understand the situations that threaten the privacy of vulnerable groups (and their members) on social media with diverse sets of concerns, and how people evaluate these threats.

Collectively Managing Privacy and Coping with Challenges

In contrast to the research on group privacy threats, the research on collaborative privacy management is more applicable to both individual privacy *and* group privacy. This work has examined how people manage privacy collaboratively and cope with privacy challenges involving more than one person. Lampinen and colleagues found that people use behavioral strategies (e.g., self-censoring, restricting who can see certain content) and mental strategies (e.g., trusting others, considering boundaries with respect to different groups) to manage the co-presence of multiple groups and social identities on SNSs (Lampinen et al., 2011). In addition, researchers have distinguished between preventative strategies intended to avoid unwanted outcomes, such as obfuscation or creating secret groups, and corrective strategies enacted to mitigate the negative impact of a collective threat, such as untagging or deleting a post. Finally, there are strategies for individuals to manage shared privacy boundaries on SNSs (e.g., using different sites to interact with different audiences) as well as collaborative strategies (e.g., asking for approval before posting, negotiating privacy rules with others), and the two are often intertwined (Cho & Filippova, 2016; DeWolf, 2016; Jia & Xu, 2016; Lampinen et al., 2011).

The literature also contains examples of group privacy management strategies designed to protect *its* (the group's) privacy rather than *their* (group members') privacy. Research on users of

Couchsurfing, a platform that allows hosts to connect with potential houseguests, found that members of multi-person households offering to host had to determine "how to present multiple people in a single profile and, especially, how to repurpose originally individual profiles for shared use" (Lampinen, 2015, p. 27). This example reflects the challenges of group identity presentation, which involves choosing aspects of a shared identity to disclose or conceal. Elsewhere, research on group privacy management among members of youth organizations similarly demonstrated how group members aimed to maintain a positive group identity by creating slideshows of their best photos to post on the organization's website, for example, or deleting information from Facebook that was potentially harmful to their group (DeWolf, 2016). In the future, researchers should devote more effort towards designing solutions that protect the privacy of groups themselves; for example, new technology might help group members assert their group privacy preferences and manage their personal and collective identities more efficiently.

Research in this area has not only identified various types of collaborative online privacy management strategies, but it has also examined the antecedents and effects of different strategies. For instance, Jia and Xu (2016) found that awareness of collective privacy values and collective efficacy predicted the adoption of collaborative privacy practices. A study by Pan et al. (2017) found that greater group impression management behavior among online community members predicted lower group privacy concern, which then predicted greater group cohesion and vitality. Together, these studies show that some sense of collective identity and efficacy is necessary for groups to manage their privacy collaboratively, and that collaborative privacy management strategies can in turn strengthen intra-group relations and foster positive attitudes towards one's group.

Privacy Threats Posed by Algorithmically-Determined Groups

Despite the modest body of research examining how people conceive of and manage their privacy within their self-constituted (or active) groups, there is currently little research with respect to privacy for passive groups formed or identified by algorithms. Group-inference technologies present privacy risks at both the group and individual levels. Here, we describe two such cases where these technologies threaten group privacy: Microtargeted advertising and trending topics analysis. See Part 4 of this book for further discussion of algorithms and privacy.

Microtargeted Advertising

Microtargeted advertising has been the subject of frequent controversy due to the threats it poses to individual privacy (see chapter 23 by Dobber on behavioral targeting and privacy) and, we now argue, to group privacy. The ability to target advertising to groups of users with inferred sensitive characteristics threatens group members' individual privacy by posing potential risks to their well-being. For example, in 2018, the Guardian reported that Facebook's advertising tools algorithmically classified thousands of Russian users as "interested in treason" based on their activity on the platform. Although a list of users in this group is not directly available to advertisers, according to Hern (2018), one could ostensibly run an ad campaign targeted at this particular group of users and identify the IP addresses of individuals who clicked on the ads. This is clearly an issue of individual privacy because it puts the safety and welfare of specific users at risk, but it is also an issue of group privacy because it allows for the discovery of a group of users who would prefer to remain hidden.

Microtargeting advertising also potentially harms group privacy because it may perpetuate stereotypes and limit a group's ability to control how it is viewed by others. In this sense, privacy is *identity constitutive*, meaning that it involves the right of a person or group to construct its own identity (Mittelstadt, 2017), and microtargeted advertising threatens group privacy by taking some of this power away from groups and their members. As Bol and colleagues (2020) explain, "unlike in the traditional media, only the targeted groups will see these particular messages (e.g., women see beauty advertisements), while being excluded from others (e.g., women see no advertisements about cars or technology), which could further reinforce stereotyping of a particular group to the extent that also social media play a role in shaping people's perception about themselves" (p. 2011).

Because of these issues, some digital media platforms have taken steps to protect groups from negative privacy-related consequences of microtargeted advertising. Facebook's recent decision to remove many of its sensitive ad categories (e.g., those pertaining to one's sexual orientation, race, and ethnicity, health, or religion) prevents the identification of certain groups of users in the first place, thereby eliminating at least some privacy risks for those groups. The company also discontinued recommendations for health groups as a means to prevent outsiders from infiltrating these groups, and thereby threaten the privacy of both group members and the group itself. Still, increased transparency is needed from social media platforms concerning how users are classified into various groups and what purposes these groupings serve. Moreover, stricter corporate codes of ethics and governmental regulation surrounding the identification of groups using data inference techniques might prevent issues of group privacy from occurring in the first place.

Trending Topics Analysis

Trending topics analysis is another case where group-inference technologies may pose a threat to group privacy. Trending topics analysis is a technology implemented by social media platforms that identifies clusters of individuals with shared characteristics such as demographics or geographic location who happen to be discussing the same topic at the same point in time. Many groups today, such as worker union advocates or political activists, use social media to organize. Employers and law enforcement agencies, however, may use trending topics analysis for identifying and surveilling groups of workers or political activists attempting to organize via social media. One example appeared when HelloFresh employees attempted to unionize, and the company responded by using a social media monitoring tool to identify users sharing union-related posts (Gurley, 2021). This tactic threatens the privacy of this group of workers by violating the contextual integrity of their social media activity. Specifically, it threatens group members' individual privacy because they could be fired as a result of their employer discovering their union affiliation, and it threatens the privacy of the group itself because HelloFresh management intended to disband the developing union.

Very few studies have examined how people respond to the privacy threats posed by trending topics analysis. An experiment conducted by Metzger et al. (2020) considered the extent to which trending topics analysis raises personal and group privacy concerns. Interestingly, people were moderately concerned about threats to both personal and group privacy, especially in the case of sensitive topics. Another study by Suh et al. (2018) found that people did not distinguish personal from group privacy threats, and only the salience of personal privacy threat affected people's evaluation of an app that used trending topics analysis. Together, these studies suggest that although people are concerned about the privacy risks that trending topics analysis poses for algorithmically- determined groups, they have difficulty perceiving group-level threats associated with this technology. The authors argue that this makes people more vulnerable to privacy violations at the group level and underscores the need for expanded legal protection of groups' right to privacy in the big data age.

Coping with Inferential Privacy Threats

Despite the potential for algorithmically-determined groups to experience privacy threats and their limited agency to mitigate such threats, there is limited research illuminating how people discover and respond to group privacy threats. Loi and Christen (2020) suggest that when online platforms enable any sort of interaction between members of algorithmically-determined groups, and this results in some sense of group self-awareness, then these groups evolve into self-constituted groups. Such groups might then feel empowered to take collective action to counter group privacy threats, such as garnering media coverage of the issue or filing a class-action lawsuit against the company responsible for the algorithmic grouping. Other potential solutions include a legal regulatory framework curtailing companies from group profiling and privacy literacy that educates the public about group-level threats to privacy posed by advanced information technology (see also Suh & Metzger, 2022).

Conclusion

Throughout this chapter, we have emphasized that current privacy protections for individuals on social media platforms typically fall short of safeguarding group privacy. However, there are actions that social media platforms, policy makers, and individual users can take to help maintain the privacy of groups; these solutions include increasing transparency surrounding how platforms use people's data, designing features that promote group privacy, developing stricter regulations surrounding data collection and identification of vulnerable groups, and, most importantly, educating the public about threats to both group privacy and personal privacy. We believe that future scholarship on group privacy in social media will advance each of these efforts and help move the discussion – and protection – of privacy beyond the individual.

References

Altman, I. (1975). *The environment and social behavior: Privacy, personal space, territory, crowding*. Brooks/Cole.

Bélanger, F., & Crossler, R. E. (2011). Privacy in the digital age: A review of information privacy research in information systems. *MIS Quarterly, 35*(4), 1017–1041.

Bélanger, F., & James, T. L. (2020). A theory of multilevel information privacy management for the digital era. *Information Systems Research, 31*(2), 510–536. https://doi.org/10.1287/isre.2019.0900

Birnholtz, J., Burke, M., & Steele, A. (2017). Untagging on social media: Who untags, what do they untag, and why? *Computers in Human Behavior, 69*, 166–173. https://doi.org/10.1016/j.chb.2016.12.008

Bloustein, E. J. (1977). Group privacy: The right to huddle. *Rutgers Camden Law Journal, 8*(2), 219–283.

Bol, N., Strycharz, J., Helberger, N., van de Velde, B., & de Vreese, C. H. (2020). Vulnerability in a tracked society: Combining tracking and survey data to understand who gets targeted with what content. *New Media & Society, 22*(11), 1996–2017. https://doi.org/10.1177/1461444820924631

Cho, H., & Filippova, A. (2016). Networked privacy management in Facebook: A mixed-methods and multinational study. In *Proceedings of the 19th ACM Conference on Computer-Supported Cooperative Work and Social Computing (CSCW '16)* (pp. 503–514). San Francisco, CA, ACM.

Constanz, J. (2021, December 13). 'They were spying on us': Amazon, Walmart, use surveillance technology to bust unions. *Newsweek*. https://www.newsweek.com/they-were-spying-us-amazon-walmart-use-surveillance-technology-bust-unions-1658603

De Wolf, R. (2016). Group privacy management strategies and challenges in Facebook: A focus group study among Flemish youth organizations. *Cyberpsychology: Journal of Psychosocial Research on Cyberspace, 10*(1). https://doi.org/10.5817/CP2016-1-5

Floridi, L. (2017). Group privacy: A defence and interpretation. In L. Taylor, L. Floridi, & B. van der Sloot (Eds.), *Group privacy: New challenges of data technologies* (pp. 83–100). Springer. https://doi.org/10.1007/978-3-319-46608-8_5.

Guberek, T., McDonald, A., Simioni, S., Mhaidli, A. H., Toyama, K., & Schaub, F. (2018). Keeping a low profile? Technology, risk and privacy among undocumented immigrants. In *Proceedings of the 2018 CHI Conference on Human Factors in Computing Systems* (pp. 1–15). https://doi.org/10:1145/3173574:3173688

Gurley, L. K. (2021, November 19). Internal slacks show HelloFresh is controlling talk of unionization. *Motherboard*. https://www.vice.com/en/article/n7nb9w/internal-slacks-show-hellofresh-is-controlling-talk-of-unionization

Hern, A. (2018, July 11). Facebook labels Russian users as 'interested in treason'. *The Guardian*. https://www.theguardian.com/technology/2018/jul/11/facebook-labels-russian-users-as-interested-in-treason

Jia, H., & Xu, H. (2016). Autonomous and interdependent: Collaborative privacy management on social networking sites. In *Proceedings of the 2016 CHI Conference on Human Factors in Computing Systems* (pp. 4286–4297). https://doi.org/10.1145/2858036.2858415

Lampinen, A. (2015). Networked privacy beyond the individual: Four perspectives to 'sharing'. In *Proceedings of the Fifth Decennial Aarhus Conference on Critical Alternatives* (pp. 25–28).

Lampinen, A., Lehtinen, V., Lehmuskallio, A., & Tamminen, S. (2011, May). We're in it together: Interpersonal management of disclosure in social network services. In *Proceedings of the SIGCHI Conference on Human Factors in Computing Systems* (pp. 3217–3226).

Litt, E., Spottswood, E., Birnholtz, J., Hancock, J. T., Smith, M. E., & Reynolds, L. (2014). Awkward encounters of an "other" kind: Collective self-presentation and face threat on Facebook. In *Proceedings of the 17th ACM Conference on Computer Supported Cooperative Work & Social Computing* (pp. 449–460). https://doi.org/10.1145/2531602.2531646

Loi, M., & Christen, M. (2020). Two concepts of group privacy. *Philosophy & Technology*, *33*(2), 207–224.

Marwick, A. E., & boyd, d. (2014). Networked privacy: How teenagers negotiate context in social media. *New Media & Society*, *16*(7), 1051–1067

Metzger, M. J., Suh, J. Y., Reid, S., & El Abbadi, A. (2020). *New threats to privacy in social network environments* [Unpublished manuscript]. Department of Communication, University of California at Santa Barbara.

Mittelstadt, B. (2017). From individual to group privacy in big data analytics. *Philosophy & Technology*, *30*(4), 475–494. https://doi.org/10.1007/s13347-017-0253-7

Ni, V., & Davidson, H. (2021, July 8). Outrage over shutdown of LGBTQ WeChat accounts in China. *The Guardian*. https://www.theguardian.com/world/2021/jul/08/outrage-over-crackdown-on-lgbtq-wechat-accounts-in-china

Nissenbaum, H. (2009). *Privacy in context: Technology, policy, and the integrity of social life*. Stanford University Press.

Pan, Y., Wan, Y., Fan, J., Liu, B., & Archer, N. (2017). Raising the cohesion and vitality of online communities by reducing privacy concerns. *International Journal of Electronic Commerce*, *21*(2), 151–183.

Petronio, S. (2002). *Boundaries of privacy: Dialectics of disclosure*. Suny Press.

Suh, J. J., & Metzger, M. J. (2022). Privacy beyond the individual level. In B. Knijnenburg, X. Page, P. Wisniewski, H. Lipford, N. Proferes, & J. Romano (Eds.), *Modern socio-technical perspectives on privacy*. Springer.

Suh, J. J., Metzger, M. J., Reid, S. A., & El Abbadi, A. (2018). Distinguishing group privacy from personal privacy: The effect of group inference technologies on privacy perceptions and behaviors. *Proceedings of the ACM on Human-Computer Interaction*, *2*, 1–22. https://doi.org/10.1145/3274437

Tajfel, H., & Turner, J. C. (1979). An integrative theory of intergroup conflict. In W. G. Austin & S. Worchel (Eds.), *The social psychology of intergroup relations* (pp. 33–47). Brooks/Cole.

Taylor, L., Floridi, L., & van der Sloot, B. (2017). Introduction: A new perspective on privacy. In L. Taylor, L. Floridi, & B. van der Sloot (Eds.), *Group privacy: New challenges of data technologies* (pp. 83–100). Springer. https://doi.org/10.1007/978-3-319-46608-8_5

Turner, J. C., Hogg, M. A., Oakes, P. J., Reicher, S. D., & Wetherell, M. S. (1987). *Rediscovering the social group: A self-categorization theory*. Blackwell.

Westin, A. (1967). *Privacy and freedom*. Atheneum.

6

A SITUATIONAL PERSPECTIVE ON PRIVACY IN SOCIAL MEDIA

Philipp K. Masur

VRIJE UNIVERSITEIT AMSTERDAM, THE NETHERLANDS

In the psychological literature, there is a well-documented bias known as the *fundamental attribution error* (Nisbett & Ross, 1980; Ross & Nisbett, 2011). It describes the general human tendency to attribute another person's action to their character or personality instead of attributing it to situational factors outside of their control. As researchers, we often tend to overestimate the effect of dispositional factors and, vice versa, underestimate the power of situations in shaping behavioral outcomes. This bias can also be found in the field of privacy research. Whereas many theories acknowledge (albeit often underspecify) the contingency of privacy-related behaviors on contextual or situational factors (e.g., Altman, 1975; Laufer & Wolfe, 1977; Nissenbaum, 2010; Omarzu, 2000), the vast majority of empirical work investigates relationships on an aggregate, non-situational level. For example, Westin (1967) already argued that "individuals are constantly engaged in an attempt to find sufficient privacy to serve [...] their individual needs of the moment" (p. 44). More recently, Nissenbaum (2010) perhaps made the most convincing case for the contextual and situational dependency by noting that privacy expectations "are systematically related to characteristics of the background social situation" (p. 129). Yet, much empirical research, such as, e.g., investigations of the privacy paradox (Kokolakis, 2017) or the privacy calculus (Krasnova & Veltri, 2010; see also chapter 7 by Dienlin in this volume), neglects contextual or situational contingencies. Here, variables such as privacy concerns are assumed to be stable across time, but to vary between people. These between-person differences are then assumed to be systematically linked to general behavioral tendencies, that is between-person differences in privacy-related behaviors. Whether concerns or privacy-related behaviors vary across contexts or situations is rarely, if ever, investigated.

In 2018, I, therefore, published the book *Situational Privacy and Self-Disclosure* (Masur, 2018) in which I argued that such an "aggregating" approach neglects the considerable variance in behaviors across situations, contexts, and media environments. Neglecting situational dependency ultimately fails to predict under what circumstances people engage in self-disclosure and privacy protection behavior. I attempted to provide a comprehensive theoretical framework for studying privacy and self-disclosure from a situational perspective, or more precisely, tried to make the manifold situations people encounter in their daily lives amenable to empirical investigation. Building on person-situation research in psychology (cf. Rauthmann et al., 2015), the theory of situational privacy and self-disclosure emphasized situations as pivotal units of analysis, identified relevant situationally

 DOI: 10.4324/9781003244677-7

varying factors related to both the person *and* the environment and asked how these interacted with more stable person characteristics in predicting and explaining situationally observable disclosure decisions. Based on the theory, I investigated self-disclosure in smartphone-based communication situations and found that only a third (28%) of the variance in disclosure was explainable by stable, person-related characteristics (Masur, 2018, p. 274). In contrast, a much larger part of the variance was attributable to situational variance – a finding that was consistent with similar investigations of other behaviors (Ross & Nisbett, 2011, p. 3). I further found that *who* one is disclosing to in a particular situation and *how much* one wants to disclose something at a given time are much better predictors of self-disclosure than stable privacy concerns or privacy literacy.

Yet, I also realized the limitations of the theory: The somewhat crude differentiation of situational and non-situational factors related to both person and environment was empirically appealing (as it easily translates into data-gathering methods such as experience sampling and statistical approaches such as multilevel modeling), but grossly oversimplifying. It completely ignored other sources of variation in self-disclosure including, for example, contextual influences such as norms, role perceptions, or transmission principles (Nissenbaum, 2010). Further, although assuming that only what people perceive in a situation becomes relevant for their behavior, the distinction between the objective situation (objectively measurable external cues of the environment) and the psychological situation (the subjective construal of a situation in a person) was underspecified – a quite common problem in situational research (Rauthmann et al., 2015). The theory further rested upon a rather strong assumption that the individual processes the environment without disruption and that the decision to disclose results from a purely rational decision-making process. An assumption that is quite vividly falsified by work on heuristics and biases in privacy decision-making processes (see chapter 8 by Liao et al. and chapter 25 by Acquisti et al. in this volume).

With this chapter, I aim to reinvigorate the situational analysis of privacy and self-disclosure processes, with a particular focus on its applicability to social media. To this end, I first summarize the major tenets of the theory of situational privacy and self-disclosure (Masur, 2018) and discuss its usability for studying privacy perceptions and self-disclosure on social media specifically. I then proceed to outline potential extensions of the theory that address the limitations outlined above. Finally, I discuss theoretical and empirical implications for future research.

The Theory of Situational Privacy and Self-Disclosure

In simple terms, the theory argues that focusing on the changing characteristics of situations allows for better predictions of when people perceive different levels of privacy and, in turn, feel able to disclose themselves. Although this may sound simple and intuitive, it has major implications for how we think about, conceptualize, and study privacy processes. It requires us to define the situation as a unit of analysis and identify relevant situational factors that can be investigated as predictors of privacy-related behavior across all potential situations. The major challenge is the following: How can we investigate the manifold universe of possible situations without resorting to clustering similar situations into conceptual buckets, which are by definition simplifications and abstractions? In the following, I will lay out the major tenets of the theory while already pinpointing at potential limitations and weaknesses.

Situations as Units of Analysis

Rather unnoticed in communication science, there is an entire field that investigates how situations can be conceptualized and operationalized for empirical research (for overviews, see, e.g., Magnusson, 1981b; Rauthmann et al., 2015; Rauthmann & Sherman, 2020; Saucier et al., 2007). Although social scientific theories tend to acknowledge that the person and the situation at any given moment are inextricably interwoven, there is less consensus about how to describe, explain, and predict person-situation interactions (Rauthmann et al., 2015). The exact mechanisms remain underspecified or vary considerably depending on the theoretical lens that is applied. For example, vibrant debates relate to the question of whether situations exert direct influence or whether it is only the environment "as it is perceived" (Magnusson, 1981a) that determines people's behavior. At the same time, it remains rather unclear how exactly situations are interacting with more stable person variables, where situations begin and end, and whether there are any meaningful taxonomies for comparing different "classes" of situations (Rauthmann & Sherman, 2020).

For the purpose of the theory and aligning with quite traditional approaches in situations research (e.g., Lewin, 1951; Rauthmann et al., 2015; Reis, 2008), I defined situations as "the entirety of circumstances that affect the behavior of a person at a given time" (Masur, 2018, p. 136). The situation itself is thereby construed by the perception of the individual, yet determined by external cues (physically present, scalable, and relatively objectively quantifiable stimuli; Block & Block, 1981). This definition may have been surprising given the central emphasis on *behavior*. However, it turned out that starting from an observable behavioral act of a person at a given time is a good baseline for identifying relevant circumstances and factors that matter in that situation. We thus need to ask how we can break down the "entirety of circumstances" at a given time. The solution is what I call a "grid approach"[1]: In the first step, we differentiate personal and environmental factors on one axis and situational and non-situational on a second axis. This two-dimensional matrix thus consists of non-situational person factors (e.g., personality, skills, knowledge, etc.) and situationally varying person factors (e.g., internal factors such one's own motives, needs, mood, etc.) on the one hand and stable environmental factors (e.g., cultural context) and situationally varying environmental factors (e.g., interpersonal assessment of other people present such as trust or closeness and perceptions of external factors such as perceptions of the situational cues) on the other hand. Attempting to explain variation in, for example, self-disclosure across social situations then requires us to identify variables in each of these cells that are present and measurable in any potentially occurring situation (cf. Omarzu, 2000). Which specific variables are relevant depends on the studied behavior. For self-disclosure, personality facets such as extraversion or risk aversion may be more meaningful factors than the need for cognition. Similarly, the need for closeness and intimacy may be stronger situational drivers of self-disclosure than the need for relaxation and escapism. The combination of factors then reflects *situational profiles* that should have a particular influence on the behavior of interest. As shown in Figure 6.1, situations are thus characterized by a potentially infinitely precise combination of, and at the same time rather limited number of, parameter values.

This approach circumvents the problem of clustering certain situations into labeled classes to simply compare behavior across them (what we typically do when we use a scenario-based approach; e.g., Facebook vs. WhatsApp, online shopping vs. social media). This focus on relevant factors that characterize situations makes *any* situation amenable to empirical investigation, while directly offering explanations for why different situations lead to different behavioral outcomes.

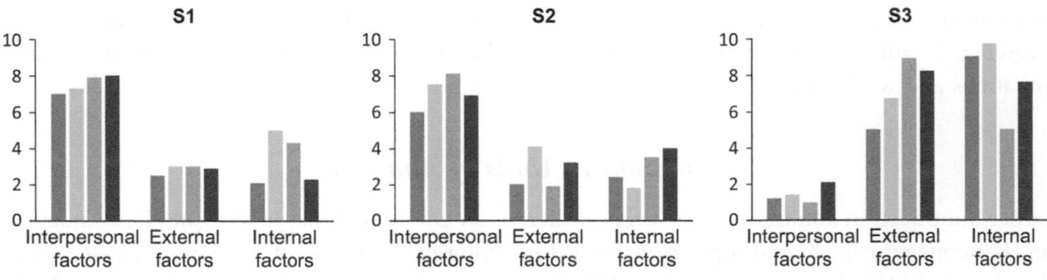

Figure 6.1 Situational Profiles Based on Environmental and Personal Factors

Such an approach is particularly useful for studying behavioral differences on social media platforms because, instead of comparing, e.g., TikTok with Instagram or Facebook with Twitter, it creates profiles for all situations *within* these platforms. An important implication is that it is perfectly possible that similar situations (S1 and S2 compared to S3 in Figure 6.1) occur on different platforms, but elicit the same behavioral response due to their similar situational profile. The grid approach is also useful to account for potential interactions between the identified factors. For example, it allows us to consider the moderating effect of a stable person characteristic such as privacy cynicism (see chapter 13 by Ranzini et al. in this volume) on the influence of some external cues such as presence of a large and unknown audience. As often argued (Hoffmann et al., 2016), a general cynicism may make potentially privacy-threatening situational factors (such as a large audience or no encryption) less important for the decision to self-disclose. In other words, it allows investigating how between-person differences determine the power of situational influences.

Pre-Situational, Situational, and Post-Situational Processes

Based on the situation definition outlined above, the theory outlines how individuals a) at times actively choose or manipulate the environment to create situations that align with their desired level of privacy or simply stumble into new situations, b) evaluate the environmental circumstances (external and interpersonal factors) in combination with their own personal needs and motives to determine whether it is safe and appropriate to disclose themselves, and c) post-situationally evaluate the effectiveness of their pre-situational privacy regulation, their environmental assessment, and their self-disclosure outcomes (see Figure 6.2 for a simple overview).

The theory thereby rests on several assumptions that align with prior research (e.g., Altman, 1975; Dienlin, 2014; Omarzu, 2000; Westin, 1967; for a more thorough discussion of prior research, see Masur, 2018, chap. 7.2): First, it assumes that the level of privacy is determined by the

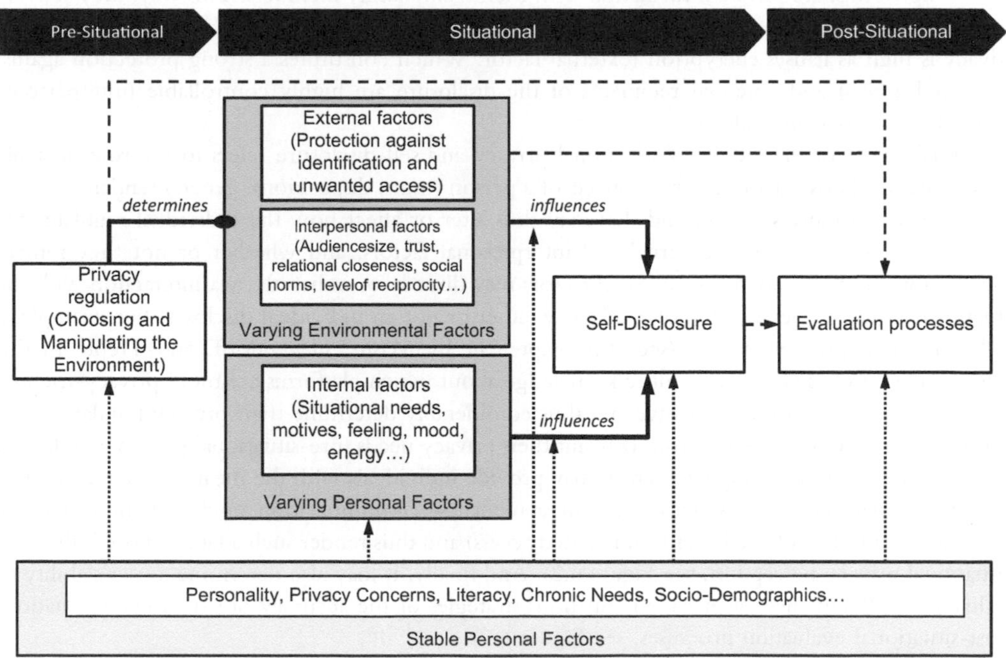

Figure 6.2 Simplified Overview of the Theory of Situational Privacy and Self-Disclosure

perception of environmental factors in a given situation. More specifically, the level of privacy is determined by those external cues that constitute a form of limited access or limited identification (e.g., Altman, 1975; Dienlin, 2014; Laufer & Wolfe, 1977; Westin, 1967). For example, if potential recipients of my disclosures are all deemed trustworthy (an interpersonal environmental factor), this should heighten the perceived level of privacy. Using the real name instead of a pseudonym (an external factor) in a public environment (such as, e.g., Twitter), in contrast, should lower the perceived level of privacy. A second assumption of the theory is that people require a certain level of privacy in order to be able to satisfy more fundamental needs, such as being able to self-disclose (Dienlin, 2014; Omarzu, 2000). Thus, only if the combination of environmental factors suggests an appropriate level of privacy (rather than always a high level; cf. Nissenbaum, 2010), do people feel able and will engage in self-disclosure. Otherwise, they will refrain from doing so (a form of privacy regulation by withdrawing into what Westin called "reserve"). However, the theory does not suggest that people always disclose if they find themselves in a situation with an appropriate level of privacy. The third assumption argues that people's self-disclosure is determined by both the perceived level of privacy and relevant personal factors such as their motivation, mood, and needs in the respective situation. It is here, where the interaction between the person and the environment becomes particularly salient on a situational level: It is both an appropriate level of privacy, as determined by the combination of environmental factors and the person and his/her needs and motives that drive behavior. The interaction of both types of factors, however, may be more complex than that. For example, the level of energy at a given situation may explain whether or not people actually correctly perceive environmental cues. Similarly, some environments may elicit particular motives and needs and vice versa, people may seek certain environments based on their momentary needs (see also chapter 3 by Trepte in this regard). In the theory, this is accounted for by the pre-situational privacy regulation mechanism. Based on their privacy needs, people choose or actively construct situations that fit their needs (the fourth assumption of the theory). With regard to social media, for example, people may actively choose to use a dyadic, encrypted messenger service such as Signal to share private information with friends and family members. This way, they actively manipulate the situation to align with their privacy needs. Within Signal, the perceived level of privacy is high as it uses encryption (external factor: Which constitutes a strong protection against unwanted access) and potential recipients of the disclosure are highly controllable (interpersonal factor: Only trusted individuals).

A final aspect of the theory of situational privacy and self-disclosure refers to the role of stable person factors. Those factors refer to aspects of a person (traits, dispositions, general tendencies) that people bring into any situation and that may thus alter or affect how the individual regulates situations, how s/he perceives external and interpersonal factors, and whether or not they remain relevant for the disclosure decision. Such factors may directly or indirectly, via interaction with the situational processes described above, affect whether or not an individual discloses. For example, a higher level of privacy literacy (see also chapter 11 by Masur, Hagendorff, and Trepte in this volume) may provide users with more knowledge about which platforms are more privacy-friendly and which are more privacy-invasive and thus considerably determine their privacy regulation and thus their ability to choose situations that suit their privacy needs (pre-situational privacy regulation, see Figure 6.2). Similarly, higher literacy may provide individuals with the means to better evaluate certain external cues (e.g., whether or not a mediated communication environment is actually encrypted and thus protected against unwanted access) and thus render such a factor more influential (situational privacy perception, see Figure 6.2). And finally, it may also determine a user's ability to evaluate the effectiveness of privacy regulations strategies or the accuracy of situational evaluations (post-situational evaluation processes, see Figure 6.2).

The theory outlined above serves well to provide first insights into how personal and environmental factors interact in influencing disclosure decisions. In fact, it proved valuable in designing a multi-method study that combined survey methods, smartphone tracking, and event-based experience samplings to gain a rich resource for modeling situational profiles (Masur, 2018, chaps. 9 and 10). In this study, I found that disclosure decisions depend much more on situational factors than stable person factors. Interpersonal assessments of the situation, including how trustworthy, similar, and relationally close potential recipients were in a given situation (compare, e.g., dyadic conversation with a close friend via the Facebook Messenger with a public tweet on Twitter), how many other people could gain access to the disclosures (compare the potential audience of a Facebook status update with a message posted in a WhatsApp group chat), and whether or not the disclosure was a response to an earlier disclosure by the recipient (users are generally more open to share if someone else opened up to them), explained a considerable amount of the variance and more than stable person characteristics. Further, internal factors such as how much a person wanted to disclose in that situation were a comparatively strong positive predictor – it could even be seen as a basic requirement for self-disclosure.

Extensions and Challenges

After several years, I realized that the theory has certain limitations or gaps, which at the same time provide ample opportunities for extensions. A first weakness relates to the somewhat artificial dichotomy between situational and non-situational factors, which does not capture or represent the manifold factors with varying stability. The theory remained ambiguous with regard to how concepts such as, for example, "episodes" or "contexts," which are often used and discussed in the media use literature, could be integrated. Second, the difference between what constitutes the objective situation (the environment "as it is") and the psychological situation (the environment "as it is perceived") was acknowledged but underspecified. More granularity is needed to describe the within-person processes that explain the true mediating effect from external cues via information processing to rational vs. heuristic decision-making and actual behavioral outcome. Third, the focus remained too much on the specific factors themselves and failed to acknowledge that particular situations may have their own interesting (meta-)characteristics such as, e.g., complexity, similarity, or strength. Adding this extra conceptual level may be useful, for example, to identify situations that are particularly prone to lead to privacy violations/turbulences, particular behavioral outcomes, or types of information processing (e.g., rational vs. heuristic decision-making). In the following, I will discuss and reflect on each of these three potential extensions.

Stability and Duration

In defining the situation as "the entirety of circumstances that affect the behavior of a person at a given time" (Masur, 2018, p. 136), I consciously reduced the complexity of what a situation can represent down to an empirically fruitful baseline. However, the reality of situation research in psychology is much more complex, albeit as a natural consequence, more confusing and conflating as it is desirable. In fact, defining what exactly constitutes a situation has been a difficult issue in the literature because scholars tend to use and conflate different concepts (Reis, 2008). Table 6.1 provides an overview of typically used terminology in relation to situationally inspired research. What this overview shows quite vividly is that we can often organize different situation-related concepts with regard to their stability (or duration) in time. This is an important organizing principle that is tremendously helpful for theorizing situational influences.

In the theory of situational privacy and self-disclosure, I already alluded to this principle by differentiating *stable* person and environmental factors from *more fleeting* factors. Yet, if we really start to identify the sources for this variation in the stability of factors, we realize that stability is rather a continuum on which various sources of situationally relevant factors can be placed. In the same way,

Table 6.1 Overview of Different Concepts in Relation to Situational Research

Concept	*Stability/Duration*	*Example*
Occurrence	− −	Receiving a message by another user
Situation	−	Chatting with another user, multiple messages back and forth
Episode	+	Using social media to chat with others, browse the news feed, post something
Contexts	+ +	Facebook, a particular group of friends
Environment	+ + + +	The Netherlands, 21st century

Note: This table is inspired by Table 1 in Rauthmann and Sherman (2020). Minus signs represent less stability, and plus signs indicate longer duration and higher stability. Characteristics related to each term thus differ in their duration and stability across time.

as we look at comparatively stable person factors such as personality or skills (which are in fact not that stable and are subject to change across a person's lifespan), we can look at, e.g., contextual factors that likewise exhibit a certain stability beyond each situation (I here refer to the sociological concept of context as described by, e.g., Nissenbaum, 2010). For example, whenever I meet my family, the type of interactions, the specific people present, and the topics we talk about are fairly similar. So there are indeed a number of potential contextual influences that are more stable (or re-occurring) than truly situational factors. Yet, switching between contexts is something that happens daily (e.g., if I leave my family and go to work) and relevant factors are thus nonetheless less stable in how they influence my behavior compared to my personality, which I always carry with me from situation to situation.

The appeal of using stability as an organizing principle becomes even more clear if we go back to the situational profiles (see again Figure 6.1) and how they are composed of factors with varying stability. They can be made up of person characteristics (black color in Figure 6.1, stability: +++), contextual factors (medium gray, stability: ++), almost non-changing environmental factors such as cultures (dark gray, stability: ++++), and truly situationally varying person and environmental factors (light gray, stability: −). By incorporating even more granularity by further distinguishing occurrences and situations, we could even start to take within-situation processes into account (stability: − −).

Another interesting aspect of distinguishing such concepts and their associated stability is the possibility of "nesting" or "grouping" situational measures within them. Based on the theory of situational privacy and self-disclosure, I argued that we need to sample situations within people (similar to repeated measurements) as it allows us to group these situations within individuals (conceptually similar to a multilevel approach). But the dichotomy between situations (the lower level) and the person (the higher level) is artificial. We could basically go so far as to postulate more of such concepts (e.g., situations, contexts, persons, environments …) and investigate their true explanatory power in predicting the behavior or outcome of interest. Such concepts do not even have to be nested in one another (e.g., nesting = situations in person, which in turn, are nested within cultures), but could exhibit similar levels of stability (and thus represent independent sources of variation). For example, media environments (somewhat akin to contexts) can likewise be seen as a somewhat stable organizing concept (stability: ++). By grouping situations in media environments, we do not lose a situational lens, but rather provide yet another level from which factors can be extracted that can, in turn, be included in situational profiles. For example, if we group situations into various social media platforms, we can then ask which factors define these platforms (e.g., anonymity, persistence of content, …) and include them in the situational profiles. This has interesting implications for empirical investigations and the way we generally specify models for predicting behavior (which I will discuss in the future perspectives section further as follows). By grouping potential antecedents of behavior and the behavior itself in various concepts of varying stability (situations, context, persons, environments, media environments), we might become more sensitive for potentially influential sources of variation in behavior and also might ask more specifically which of those sources matter the most. Given the possibility of grouping in different variables, we are further sensitized to explore potential interactions between such grouping factors.

Going back to the example of self-disclosure on social media, for example, it could make sense to consider (1) truly situational characteristics (personal factors such as motives, needs, and mood; environmental factors such as specific audience for an individual post), (2) contextual factors (personal factors such as role perceptions in a group chat with friends vs. work colleagues or family; environmental factors such as exhibited norms and transmission principles, but also external cues such as time of the day, location), (3) platform/media-related characteristics (e.g., environmental factors such as norms on a platform), (4) person characteristics (e.g., personality, general concerns, literacy ...), and (5) environment characteristics (e.g., culture in which the interaction takes place). Not only do we start to truly consider relevant factors that may drive people's behavior in a situation, we also ask which source of variation is most important and how different sources of variation interact in shaping behavioral outcomes. Remaining with the example suggested above, we could, for example, investigate how certain comparatively stable person factors (e.g., personality) are particularly activated in certain contexts (a person-context interaction) or how norms are made salient in particular situations (a context-situation interaction). That said, if we truly want to capture such interactions, it becomes important to reconcile objective and subjective perspectives on situations, which I will discuss as another potential extension of the theory in the following.

Subjective vs. Objective Situations

In the theory of situational privacy and self-disclosure, I assumed that all factors are individuals' psychological perceptions of external and environmental cues and their internal, cognitive, and affective responses. Such a perspective aligns with the so-called "processing principle" (Rauthmann et al., 2015), which argues that environmental factors (physically or digitally present, scalable, and relatively objectively quantifiable stimuli) only matter and become influential for people's behavior if they are perceived. Yet, the question of how individuals interpret and process situations is more complex and deserves more scrutiny. By focusing only on the psychological representation of external cues and explaining how this psychological situation drives people's behavior, we ignore that the psychological representation is the consequence of *information processing* of environmental and external cues and thus also fail to acknowledge both objectivist and subjectivist perspectives in situation research (cf. Rauthmann et al., 2015). This is problematic as information processing may not always work perfectly and instead may be restricted depending on other situational factors (including both traits and states and the external cues themselves).

By integrating external cues and information processing as potential within-person processes, a more complete picture emerges. Figure 6.3 represents an extension of Figure 6.2's middle part and provides an overview of how information processing can be integrated as a mediator between the objective and the subjective/psychological situation.

In the first step, environmental cues (outside of a person, thus alluding to an environmental-ecological perspective on situations that aims to identify objective stimuli) are processed by individuals. This refers to the selection, filtering, evaluation, interpretation, and meaning assignment as described in common dual-process models (e.g., Kahneman, 2013; Strack & Deutsch, 2004). This processing can be rather implicit (impulsive–affective) or explicit (reflective–cognitive) (Rauthmann et al., 2015). At the same time, both stable and situationally varying person factors (the difference between traits and states; i.e., factors with different stability) guide, influence, and change how such cues are, selected and

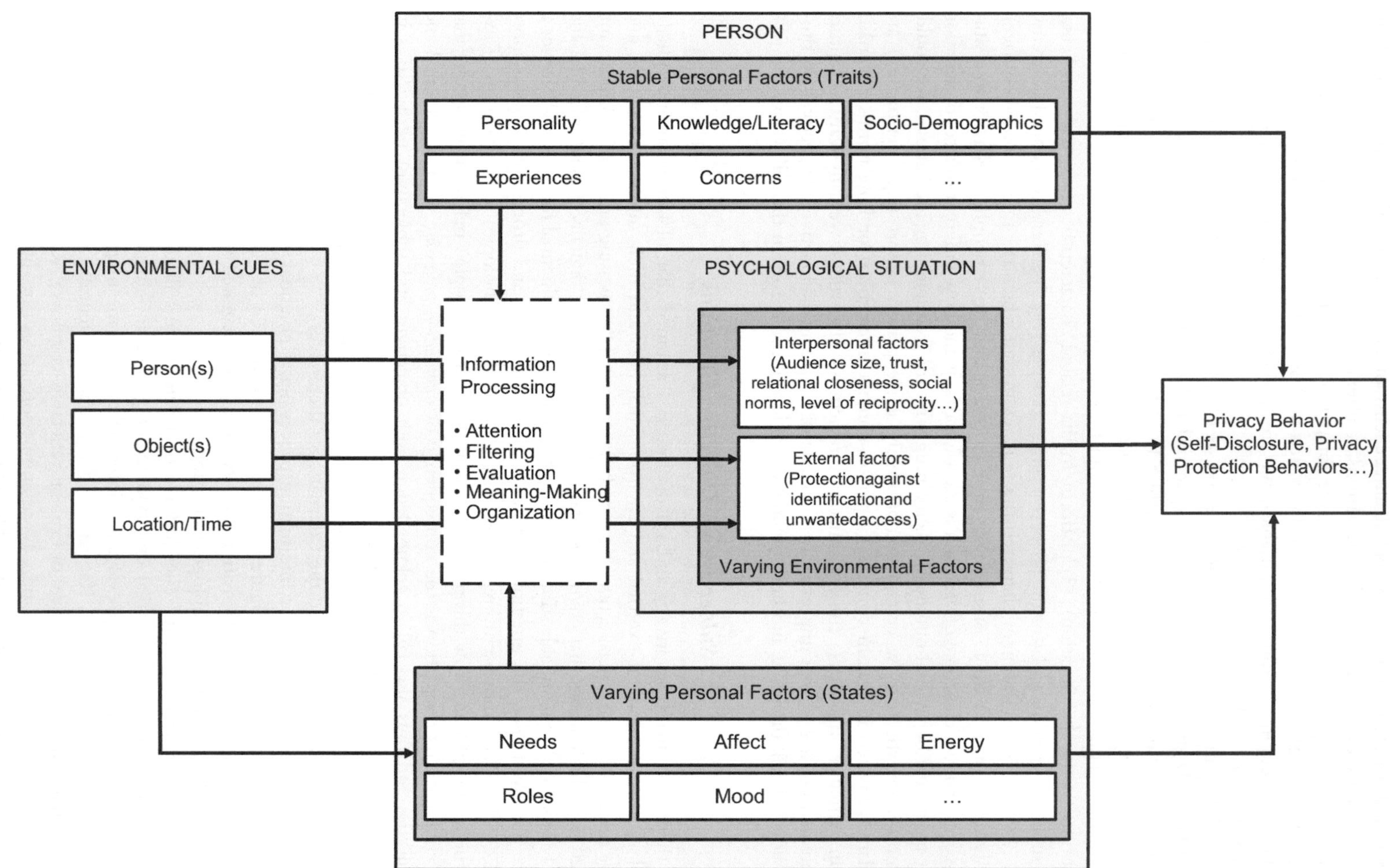

Figure 6.3 A Simple Process Model of Situation Perceptions and Their Relationship to Behavioral Outcomes

interpreted (Magnusson, 1981b) and thus likewise determine a person's psychological representation of the situation (Block & Block, 1981; Rauthmann et al., 2015; Reis, 2008).

By adding this extra layer or mediating process, new insights can be gained: First, we can investigate differences in how people perceive situationally varying environmental cues as the information processing (including amount of attention payed to particular cues, filtering principles, evaluative process, meaning-making, and cognitive organization) is influenced by both stable and more varying person factors. The interaction between person and environment is thereby more explicitly included, resulting in some beneficial implications: The model becomes less based on a rational-choice paradigm as non-rational information processing such as the use of heuristics (see chapter 8 by Liao et al. in this volume) or the influence of cognitive biases can be integrated. For example, in situations in which a user of a social media platform is rather tired (situationally varying person factor) and has previously made only positive experiences (a comparatively stable person factor that this person brings into every situation), the attention towards environmental cues may be low and some cues may even be unconsciously filtered out. The evaluation may thus be limited to a single factor (e.g., who is the recipient of my disclosure) and trigger a simple heuristic (e.g., bandwagon heuristic: "Everybody does it, so it must be safe" or positivity bias: "I never had negative privacy experiences, hence it will be safe now as well") that, in turn, produces a behavioral response (a high level of disclosure).

Second, the inclusion of objective external stimuli opens up the possibility to investigate the differences between persons in construing the psychological representation of a situation and thus very explicitly focuses on person-environment interactions in explaining behavior (see also chapter 3 by Trepte). As already mentioned earlier, this provides a lot of possibilities to include prior research that primarily investigated person characteristics (e.g., privacy concerns, privacy literacy, privacy cynicism ...) into a more holistic model that accounts for how such stable person characteristics influence and determine behavior in a specific situation. Most importantly, however, it does so without flattening situational variance in the outcome variable into aggregates and general behavioral tendencies and remains granular and on the situational level.

Situation (Meta-)Characteristics

Another implication of the situational perspective and particularly the use of the "grid approach" to identify situational profiles is the possibility of investigating meta-characteristics of situations. Although situational profiles represent a combination of relevant factors, certain combinations may stand out as they represent particular types of situations that foster, limit, hinder, or even inhibit certain behavioral responses or, at an earlier stage, the information processing. For the study of privacy and self-disclosure on social media, meta-characteristics such as the complexity or strength of a situation as well as their promotional vs. inhibitory character represent another level of abstraction that can help to explain irrational or paradoxical behavioral outcomes (Rauthmann & Sherman, 2019).

If we go back to potential situational profiles, it should be obvious that there could be situations that are more *complex* than others. Let's imagine a person A engages in a conversation with another person B via WhatsApp and would like to share some private pictures of a vacation. Judging the level of privacy based on environmental cues is comparatively simple: Only one, potentially trustworthy recipient is present (interpersonal assessment comparatively easy), the conversation is comparatively well protected against outside access (end-to-end encryption), and there is hardly much more to take into account. Compare this to a situation in which a person wants to share the same pictures on Instagram. Here, the evaluation of the level of privacy is inherently more complex: A potentially unlimited and unknown audience (if the person has a public profile) makes interpersonal judgments difficult or at least uncertain, external cues that would suggest protection against identification and access by other users are blurry and (without literacy) difficult to understand, and there may be considerable uncertainty what the provider does with the information. This complexity of mediated situations, in fact, may explain some of the irrational, privacy-risky behavior of social media users. Given the manifold factors that need to be considered, many may resort to heuristic processing or limit their attention to very specific, but often insufficient factors (e.g., what is the benefit?) and thereby inappropriately judge the true level of privacy. The often-described context collapse on social media (Marwick & boyd, 2011; Vitak, 2012) is a good example describing the complexity of judging situations on social media where multiple, traditionally distinct social contexts converge into one large, heterogeneous audience. Accordingly, perhaps the situational meta-characteristic "complexity" may account for a large amount of the variance we observe in media users' privacy behavior or moderate the information processing in the situation.

A second meta-characteristic that is related to complexity can be termed *similarity* (alternatively, it can also be thought of as familiarity vs. novelty). A situational lens also helps us understand the level of similarity between some situations (see again Figure 6.1; S1 is rather similar to S2, but quite different to S3) and, vice versa, the *uniqueness* of some particular situations. For example, sharing a tweet on Twitter, a status update on Facebook, or a public post on Instagram are comparatively similar situations in that the combination of factors that make up the situational profiles are fairly similar (e.g., large heterogeneous audience, low protection against unwanted access). The similarity of these situations thus explains similar disclosure observations or engagement in privacy protection strategies. Sharing a video on TikTok or SnapChat similarly shares a common combination of relevant factors (e.g., ephemerality of the posts, protection through "being lost in the crowd"). In contrast, we can also imagine situations that are rather unique (and thus rare) and therefore represent unusual combinations of situational factors. What is unique or common, of course, depends on the person. For example, a person that uses Instagram and Facebook several times a day may constantly encounter somewhat similar situations on these platforms, but the moment this person uses SnapChat (something this person rarely does), the subsequent situations on this platform are, in comparison, rather unique. At the same time, the uniqueness of a particular situation may also stem from an unusual strength of a parameter: For example, being approached by a stranger via a social media platform (supposedly a rather rare occurrence) emphasizes interpersonal assessments (e.g., trustworthiness) to a degree that it represents a unique situation. In sum, it seems reasonable to assume that familiar situations should activate habitual, heuristic responses, while novel situations may require more active cognitive processing.

A third meta-characteristic is related to what has been known as the "strong situation hypothesis" (Cooper & Withey, 2009; Mischel, 1977). According to Mischel (1977), strong situations are those that "lead everyone to construe the particular events the same way, induce uniform expectancies regarding the most appropriate response pattern, provide adequate incentives for the performance of that response pattern, and require skills that everyone has to the same extent" (Mischel, 1977, p. 347). In contrast, rather weak situations are less uniform and thus less homogeneously perceived, they do not generate similar expectancies concerning behavior and generally do not offer sufficient incentives for its performance and may require specific skills or abilities. A common assumption in the literature was that strong situations negate trait influences on behavior and weak situations increase their power in shaping behaviors. Although there is little evidence for this rather common claim (Cooper & Withey, 2009), the strength of a situation in shaping a particular behavior (independent of whether it activates personality traits or negates their influence) can nonetheless be a useful unit of analysis. In the context of privacy and self-disclosure on social media, one could argue that there are situational profiles that are particularly strong in driving people's behavior. Although a mere hypothesis at this point, it could be worthwhile to identify those situations that uniformly lead to high levels of self-disclosure for one person or even different people – or in contrast to low levels of disclosure and high levels of privacy protection behaviors. Are there particular combinations of situational, contextual, and media-related characteristics that elicit the same behavioral outcomes in (almost) all users? An example might be the general high willingness to disclose very private (medical) information to a doctor, even if this person is not particularly close.

Future Perspectives

With the potential extensions and considerations outlined above, my aim was to reinvigorate the situational analysis of privacy and self-disclosure processes in social media. For the time being, I hope they serve as inspiration and potentially interesting stepping stones for further theoretical development and potentially innovative empirical investigations that go beyond traditional survey or experimental methods to truly capture situational variance. In this last section, I develop some future perspectives for theory building and further some considerations for empirical investigations and methodology.

Theoretical Desiderata

Despite many calls for acknowledging the cultural and political (e.g., Masur et al., 2021; Wang et al., 2011), contextual (Nissenbaum, 2010), and situational dependency (Acquisti et al., 2015; Masur, 2018) of privacy processes, the ways in which privacy is investigated remains mostly on the aggregate, between-person level. As mentioned before, this may be due to the fact that a lot of related theories acknowledge situational dependency, but remain vague with regard to how situations, contexts, and environments should be operationalized. To overcome these challenges, I propose several theoretical perspectives for future research.

First, although I outlined several angles from which situations can be defined and operationalized to make them amenable to empirical investigation, there are still gaps and missing pieces. For example, temporal concepts such as occurrence and episodes are difficult to account for theoretically (and empirically). The temporal and spatial boundaries of situations remain vague as they are only defined by the presence of a combination of factors. More research is needed to clarify these concepts and organize them in a coherent theoretical model.

Second, the consolidation of objective and subjective perspectives on situations is of utmost importance. My theory already acknowledged that only subjective perceptions matter for behavioral outcomes, but neglected how people construct psychological situations. This is unfortunate because, as outlined above, it ignores the information processing between external cues and the cognitive representation of these cues within persons. A stronger focus on subjective information processing will help to understand how people differ and how situational constraints (whether originating from the environment itself or from within the person) affect, limit, or increase attention and filtering of external cues.

Third, I proposed meta-characteristics of situations as potentially interesting factors that so far have not yet been considered when trying to explain privacy outcomes. Although they seem intuitively fruitful in explaining certain phenomena, their derivation (both theoretically and empirically) is unclear. Is it really just the combination of factors that account for differences in complexity and strength? More research is needed to better understand the role of such meta-characteristics within broader situational frameworks.

Fourth, I argued that media environments themselves can be interesting, somewhat stable organizing units for explaining variance in privacy-related behaviors. Defining relevant factors related to media environments is an important endeavor and scholars can draw from the rich literature on defining and characterizing media environments.

Empirical and Methodological Considerations

At this point, you may wonder how the ideas expressed throughout this chapter translate into practical research. To make the theoretical ideas expressed in this chapter empirically investigatable, we need to find novel methodological solutions, often requiring the combination of different methods such as survey, experience sampling, behavioral observation, and log data. The experience sampling method (Barrett & Barrett, 2001; Csikszentmihalyi & Larson, 1987), which allows sampling from people's real-life experiences, provides situational measures that can then be nested in different concepts of varying stability. Granular log data of browsing behavior or app use can similarly be seen as an intensive longitudinal sampling that allows the nesting into different concepts of varying stability. The interesting implication is that we can then use a multilevel framework (Geiser et al., 2015; Hox, 2010) to account for variance in our variables of interest (e.g., situationally assessed self-disclosure, privacy behavior, use of certain websites, ...) on various levels (see Figure 6.4). By cross-classifying them into concepts such as persons ($P_1, \ldots, P_n$), contexts ($C_1, \ldots, C_n$), media environments ($M_1, \ldots, M_n$), or even higher level grouping factors such as environments, nations, cultures, and political systems ($E_1, \ldots, E_n$), we gain the ability to quantify their relative influence on the privacy outcome of interest in a multilevel framework. We can, for example, specify an intercept-only model where self-disclosure is nested in persons, contexts, and media environments (I purposefully leave out the higher order level of environments to simplify) as follows (Hox, 2010, p. 173):

$$Y_{i\,(pcm)} = \beta_{0\,(pcm)} + e_{i\,(pcm)},$$

where the level of self-disclosure $Y_{i\,(pcm)}$ of an individual i with the cross-classification of persons p, contexts c, and media environments m is modeled by the intercept (or overall mean) $\beta_{0\,(pcm)}$ and a residual error term $e_{i\,(pcm)}$. The subscripts (pcm) are written in parentheses to indicate that they are on the same (cross-classified) level. They indicate that we assume that the intercept varies independently across persons (each person has generally a different average level of self-disclosure), contexts (general disclosure levels differ between contexts such as work or family), and media environments (disclosure levels generally differ between public, such as Facebook, and

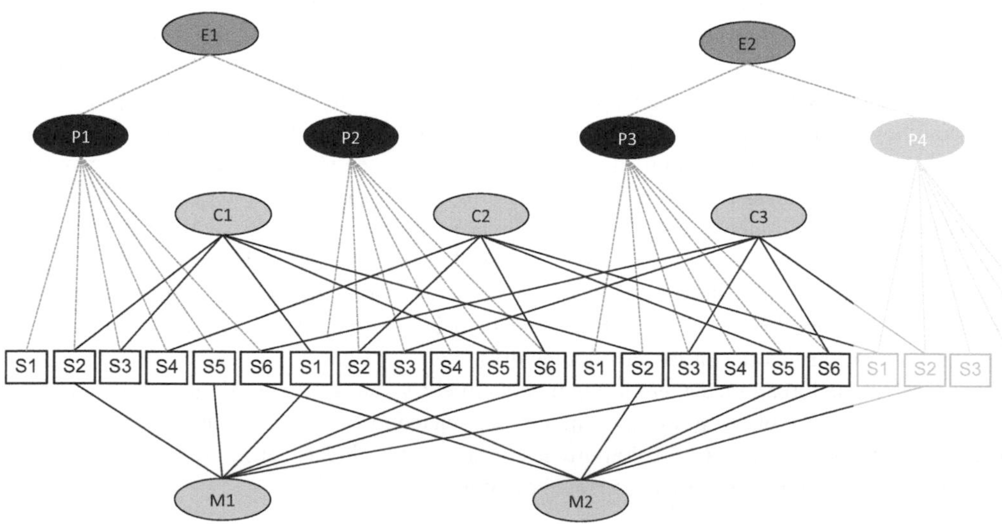

Figure 6.4 Variance Decomposition in a Multilevel Analysis Framework

Note: Possible nested structure of how situationally measured variables can be clustered in concepts of varying stability: E = Environments; P = Persons; C = Contexts; M = Media environments.

more private, such as Signal, media environments). We can thus model this intercept with the following formula:

$$\beta_{0(pcm)} = \gamma_{00} + u_{0p} + v_{0c} + w_{0m} + e_{i(pcm)}$$

The components u_{0p}, v_{0c}, and w_{0m} thereby denote the residual error terms for each of the three included levels. Technically, interactions between the three levels can also be included if one has the assumption that their interplay explains additional variance in the outcome variable. Predictor variables can further be added at each level (including the situational level, but here, we can again distinguish variance of the situational predictor variables at all included levels, see e.g., random-effect between-within modeling; see, e.g., Bell et al., 2019).

Based on the cross-classified intercept-only multilevel model, we can decompose the variance by computing intraclass correlation coefficients, which represents the proportions of the variance explained by each level (as well as the residual, unexplained variance). By adding predictors on these different levels, we can then explore how the situational profiles (the combination of different factors from different levels of stability, see Figure 6.1) predict the outcome behavior. If we look at Figures 6.1 and 6.4 in combination, we can get an idea of how certain factors that make up the situational profile relate to the different levels of stability. For example, an internal factor such as how one perceives one's own role in a fixed social setting (e.g., the medium gray bar in the group internal factors, Figure 6.1) is something that is located on the contextual level (C, medium gray level in Figure 6.4).

Why is this approach superior to, e.g., a single experiment? First, it translates the situational perspective into a statistical model that can be used to analyze intensive longitudinal data. Second, by not isolating an effect in a single, and potentially rather artificial setting, it captures real-life variance across situations and thus allows specificity without losing generalizability. And there are indeed examples of such more fine-grained studies in the literature. For example, although not focusing on privacy processes, Bayer et al. (2016) combined log data and event-based experience sampling to trigger smartphone surveys in response to users' naturalistic Facebook postings. This way, they were able to capture emotional experiences right after certain social media use situations and investigated various predictors ranging from active posting, location, mood, etc., using a similar, yet simplified (only two levels) multilevel design as outlined above. Using a similar design, I likewise used event-based experience sampling to trigger short surveys right after people used certain apps (Masur, 2018) and measure a variety of interpersonal assessments (audience size, trust, closeness, reciprocity …) and personal factors as well as the level of disclosure. By combining this with measures from a presurvey that assessed relevant person traits (e.g., concerns, personality, literacy), it allowed to study both stable and fleeting antecedents of disclosure in one, simple two-level multilevel framework.

Conclusion

In this chapter, I aimed to reinvigorate a situational perspective on privacy processes in social media. Building on the theory of situational privacy and self-disclosure and incorporating recent developments in situational research in psychology, I proposed several angles from which situational processes can be theorized and studied. These refer to more rigorous integration of potentially important, yet differently stable sources of variation in privacy behavior, including situations itself, potentially episodes, contexts, media environments, persons (as their own grouping factor), and larger environmental settings (including culture and political systems). Furthermore, I argued to put a stronger emphasis on integrating both objective and subjective perspectives on situations to better account for the ways in which person-environment interactions affect the processing of external cues and thus potentially influence behavioral outcomes. Finally, I proposed to consider meta-characteristics of situations including complexity, similarity (and uniqueness), strength, and promotional vs. inhibitory character as they may help to particularly identify situations in which turbulence, violations, or threats to contextual integrity may occur. Although not organized in a coherent model or theory at this point in time, it is my hope that the outlined perspectives will help to place *situations,* in both their specificity and generalizability, as a pivotal unit of analysis in privacy research and thereby overcome some of the inherent limitations in investigating privacy processes on social media solely from a between-person perspective.

Note

1 As a sort of conceptual grid with several dimensions that is put over each situation to create situational profiles.

References

Acquisti, A., Brandimarte, L., & Loewenstein, G. (2015). Privacy and human behavior in the age of information. *Science, 347*(6221), 509–514. https://doi.org/10.1126/science.aaa1465

Altman, I. (1975). *The environment and social behavior: Privacy, personal space, territory, crowding.* Brooks/Cole Publishing Company.

Barrett, L. F., & Barrett, D. J. (2001). An introduction to computerized experience sampling in psychology. *Social Science Computer Review, 19*(2), 175–185. https://doi.org/10.1177/089443930101900204

Bayer, J., Ellison, N. B., Schoenebeck, S., Brady, E., & Falk, E. B. (2016). Facebook in context(s): Measuring emotional responses across time and space. *New Media & Society.* https://doi.org/10.1177/1461444816681522

Bell, A., Fairbrother, M., & Jones, K. (2019). Fixed and random effects models: Making an informed choice. *Quality & Quantity, 53*(2), 1051–1074. https://doi.org/10.1007/s11135-018-0802-x

Block, J., & Block, J. H. (1981). Studying situational dimension: A grand perspective and some limited empiricism. In D. Magnusson (Ed.), *Toward a psychology of situations* (pp. 85–102). Erlbaum.

Cooper, W. H., & Withey, M. J. (2009). The strong situation hypothesis. *Personality and Social Psychology Review, 13*(1), 62–72. https://doi.org/10.1177/1088868308329378

Csikszentmihalyi, M., & Larson, R. (1987). Validity and reliability of the experience-sampling method. *The Journal of Nervous and Mental Disease, 175*(9), 526–536.

Dienlin, T. (2014). The privacy process model. In S. Garnett, S. Halft, M. Herz, & J. M. Mönig (Eds.), *Medien und privatheit* (pp. 105–122). Karl Stutz.

Geiser, C., Litson, K., Bishop, J., Keller, B. T., Burns, G. L., Servera, M., & Shiffman, S. (2015). Analyzing person, situation and person × situation interaction effects: Latent state-trait models for the combination of random and fixed situations. *Psychological Methods, 20,* 165–192. https://doi.org/10.1037/met0000026

Hoffmann, C. P., Lutz, C., & Ranzini, G. (2016). Privacy cynicism: A new approach to the privacy paradox. *Cyberpsychology: Journal of Psychosocial Research on Cyberspace, 10*(4). https://doi.org/10.5817/CP2016-4-7

Hox, J. J. (2010). *Multilevel analysis. Techniques and applications. Second edition.* Routledge.

Kahneman, D. (2013). *Thinking, fast and slow.* Penguin.

Kokolakis, S. (2017). Privacy attitudes and privacy behaviour: A review of current research on the privacy paradox phenomenon. *Computers & Security, 64,* 122–134. https://doi.org/10.1016/j.cose.2015.07.002

Krasnova, H., & Veltri, N. F. (2010). Privacy calculus on social networking sites: Explorative evidence from Germany and USA. *2010 43rd Hawaii international conference on system sciences,* 1–10. https://doi.org/10.1109/HICSS.2010.307

Laufer, R. S., & Wolfe, M. (1977). Privacy as a concept and social issue: A multidimensional developmental theory. *Journal of Social Issues, 33*(3), 22–42.

Lewin, K. (1951). *Field theory in social science: Selected theoretical papers.* Harper & Brothers.

Magnusson, D. (1981a). Problems in environmental analyses – An introduction. In D. Magnusson (Ed.), *Toward a psychology of situations* (pp. 3–7). Erlbaum.

Magnusson, D. (Ed.). (1981b). *Toward a psychology of situations: An international perspective.* Erlbaum.

Marwick, A. E., & boyd, d. (2011). I tweet honestly, I tweet passionately. Twitter users, context collapse, and the imagined audience. *New Media & Society, 13*(1), 114–133. https://doi.org/10.1177/1461444810365313

Masur, P. K. (2018). *Situational privacy and self-disclosure: Communication processes in online environments.* Springer. https://doi.org/10.1007/978-3-319-78884-5

Masur, P. K., Epstein, D., Quinn, K., Wilhelm, C., Baruh, L., & Lutz, C. (2021). *A comparative privacy research framework.* SocArXiv. https://doi.org/10.31235/osf.io/fjqhs

Mischel, W. (1977). The interaction of person and situation. In *Personality at the crossroads: Current issues in psychology* (pp. 333–352). John Wiley.

Nisbett, R. E., & Ross, L. (1980). *Human inference: Strategies and shortcomings of social judgment*. Prentice-Hall, Inc.

Nissenbaum, H. (2010). *Privacy in context: Technology, policy, and the integrity of social life*. Stanford University Press.

Omarzu, J. (2000). A disclosure decision model: Determining how and when individuals will self-disclose. *Personality and Social Psychology Review*, *4*(2), 174–185.

Rauthmann, J., & Sherman, R. (2019). Toward a research agenda for the study of situation perceptions: A variance componential framework. *Personality and Social Psychology Review*, *23*(3), 238–266. https://doi.org/10.1177/1088868318765600

Rauthmann, J. F., & Sherman, R. A. (2020). The situation of situation research: Knowns and unknowns. *Current Directions in Psychological Science*, *29*(5), 473–480. https://doi.org/10.1177/0963721420925546

Rauthmann, J. F., Sherman, R. A., & Funder, D. C. (2015). Principles of situation research: Towards a better understanding of psychological situations. *European Journal of Personality*, *29*(3), 363–381. https://doi.org/10.1002/per.1994

Reis, H. T. (2008). Reinvigorating the concept of situation in social psychology. *Personality and Social Psychology Review*, *12*(4), 311–329. https://doi.org/10.1177/1088868308321721

Ross, L., & Nisbett, R. E. (2011). *The person and the situation: Perspectives of social psychology*. Pinter & Martin.

Saucier, G., Bel-Bahar, T., & Fernandez, C. (2007). What modifies the expression of personality tendencies? Defining basic domains of situation variables. *Journal of Personality*, *75*(3), 479–503. https://doi.org/10.1111/j.1467-6494.2007.00446.x

Strack, F., & Deutsch, R. (2004). Reflective and impulsive determinants of social behavior. *Personality and Social Psychology Review*, *8*(3), 220–247. https://doi.org/10.1207/s15327957pspr0803_1

Vitak, J. (2012). The impact of context collapse and privacy on social network site disclosures. *Journal of Broadcasting & Electronic Media*, *56*(4), 451–470. https://doi.org/10.1080/08838151.2012.732140

Wang, Y., Norice, G., & Cranor, L. F. (2011). Who is concerned about what? A study of American, Chinese and Indian users' privacy concerns on social network sites. In *Trust and trustworthy computing* (Vol. 6740, pp. 146–153). Springer. https://doi.org/10.1007/978-3-642-21599-5

Westin, A. F. (1967). *Privacy and freedom*. Atheneum.

7

PRIVACY CALCULUS

Theory, Studies, and New Perspectives

Tobias Dienlin

UNIVERSITY OF VIENNA, AUSTRIA

Many users of the Internet and social media are concerned about their privacy. However, when exposed to the many luring offers such as promising dating websites, entertaining YouTube channels, or polarizing tweets, most of us participate, which often leads to the unwanted sharing of personal information. Some users are more concerned, others less. Many are sharing much information on social media, but not everyone is sharing everything. In light of these observations, the key question is: How much of our behavior is self-determined, beneficial, and aligned with our own interests?

A theoretical concept providing answers to these questions is the privacy calculus, which I discuss in this chapter. I first describe the theoretical model and its structural underpinnings. I then present current empirical research. Focusing on the privacy paradox, in the second part of this chapter, I challenge the privacy calculus. I then counter the critiques by referring to general behavioral models and our underlying human image. I introduce a Bayesian perspective, suggest the existence of an inverse third-person effect, and propose an updated probabilistic understanding of the privacy calculus model.

Privacy Calculus Model

The privacy calculus can be defined as follows. Before sharing personal information online, people engage in a rudimentary cost-benefit analysis. If the anticipated benefits exceed the perceived costs, people are more likely to communicate, and vice versa. Costs are often operationalized with perceived privacy risks, privacy concerns, or reputation losses, whereas anticipated benefits often include entertainment, social support, or reputation management. Although the cost-benefit analysis is imperfect, the literature suggests that on average behavior does represent people's underlying preferences, choices, and personalities, suggesting that behavior is at least partially rational.

The privacy calculus builds on the calculus of behavior, and it was initially designed to explain everyday situations in offline settings (Laufer & Wolfe, 1977). Later, it was transferred to the online world (Culnan & Armstrong, 1999) and to social media (Krasnova et al., 2010), which I believe makes much sense. Transferring knowledge from offline into online contexts is a typical pattern: The offline world extends into the online world, many mechanisms are the same, and theories explaining offline behavior are often well-equipped also to explain online behavior, especially on social media.[1] Regarding the privacy calculus, it quickly becomes apparent that it stands in the tradition of the homo economicus, the rational choice paradigm (Simon, 1955), and expectancy

 DOI: 10.4324/9781003244677-8

value theories (Atkinson, 1957). Accordingly, people try to maximize their benefits in decision situations, weigh costs and benefits, and often successfully choose the option that best suits their interests. It is worth noting, however, and often misunderstood, that the rational choice paradigm *doesn't* say that people *always* successfully choose the right behavioral option. It only says that people aim to do so and that scholarly models implementing rational processes have incremental validity over alternative models excluding rationality (see as follows).

Before we dig deeper, in order to contextualize the privacy calculus and its major tenets, let's first briefly revisit privacy theory. Privacy calculus sees humans as active agents, who adapt their behavior depending on contexts. This perspective is deeply rooted in privacy theory. Several privacy theories consider humans as actively managing and balancing their privacy (Altman, 1976; Dienlin, 2014; Masur, 2018; Petronio, 1991). For example, according to Altman (1976), privacy is a regulation process: People open up in specific situations to engage with others, while in others they withdraw to protect themselves. Petronio (1991) similarly states that people often actively discuss boundaries with others, decide with whom they want to share specific types of information, and actively reconfigure boundaries in situations of turbulence (for example, when information is inappropriately recontextualized). In the privacy process model (Dienlin, 2014), I argue that people constantly compare desired and achieved levels of privacy, adapting either the actual privacy context or the amount of self-disclosure. Finally, Masur (2018) understands and approaches privacy from a situational perspective, because so much of privacy-related behavior is dependent on the specifics of a situation.

A comparatively new theoretical perspective on privacy is to differentiate two specific dimensions, namely horizontal and vertical privacy (Masur et al., 2018). Whereas horizontal privacy captures behaviors relating to other people on an interpersonal level, vertical privacy focuses on behaviors relating to institutions, companies, or legal entities. Introducing this differentiation seems worthwhile, as it is more intuitive to regulate privacy on a horizontal level, for example, by closing a door, lowering one's voice, or turning away. Managing privacy on a vertical dimension is more difficult, for it entails tweaking privacy settings, reading terms and conditions, or encrypting email exchanges. Correctly identifying benefits and costs is harder on a vertical than on a horizontal level, with direct consequences for the privacy calculus (see as follows). Taken together, many if not most privacy theories in the social sciences think of human beings as proactive agents who react to specific situations and contexts, thereby aiming to optimize their privacy. The privacy calculus model builds on this perspective. According to the privacy calculus model, the decision process of sharing information is geared toward optimizing a person's needs, concerns, and preferences.

The privacy calculus has been implemented and tested in many empirical studies. To get an idea about the exact number of studies on the privacy calculus, I did a quick literature search on the database EBSCO host. I searched for "privacy calculus" in study titles and study abstracts. Overall, the search yielded 297 results, spanning from 2007 to 2022. Most publications were academic journals (265), followed by conference materials (17), dissertations (12), books (7), and magazines (1). It is safe to say that the privacy calculus is of considerable academic interest.

How is the privacy calculus analyzed? Oftentimes, by conducting questionnaire-based studies, in which respondents are asked about their expected benefits and perceived costs associated with specific types of online behavior. A particular focus is on the amount of online self-disclosure. Explicit privacy behaviors such as using encryption are also analyzed, or more general online behavior such as time spent online or number of services used. Oftentimes, studies measured not only costs and benefits, but also other variables (norms, efficacy, personality, and contexts), thereby using the privacy calculus as one predictive mechanism next to others. Worth noting, the exact operationalization of benefits and costs varies. To model costs, researchers often (exclusively) measure privacy concerns. To model benefits, no general procedure has emerged – at least that's my impression.

There are two perspectives toward investigating the privacy calculus. First, researchers use surveys to analyze *general* costs and benefits together with *general* behavior. Second, researchers adopt a situational perspective, for example, using experiments or experience sampling, to investigate *specific* costs and benefits together with *specific* behaviors. Adopting a specific and situational approach seems more intuitive, as the privacy calculus assumes an explicit tradeoff manifesting in specific situations, hence requiring specific analyses. In other words, it is informative to ask people if they indeed have compared pros and contras before disclosing information and whether or not that has affected their decision. That said, I would like to emphasize that general approaches are also legitimate. Specific individual decisions should logically manifest in long-term differences. To illustrate, consider the following personal example. I'm now an active Twitter user since 2012. In the beginning, I used an anonymous nickname and my profile was set to private. However, I soon came to the conclusion that having a public profile as a researcher can be very beneficial, and I decided to deanonymize my account. I remember an active weighing of pros and cons (on Facebook and Instagram I continue to have anonymous accounts). This was a specific one-time decision, but across the last years the tweets then slowly accumulated, resulting in observable general differences. I hope this anecdote serves to illustrate that asking people about their general behavior on social media can be a legitimate and plausible way to investigate the privacy calculus, as specific decisions and personal preferences should eventually manifest in different general behavioral patterns.

One of the first and most important studies on the privacy calculus in social media was conducted by Krasnova and colleagues (2010), who showed that people who expected more benefits from participation on social networking sites (in this case, convenience, relationship building, and enjoyment) also shared more information, whereas people who perceived more privacy risks shared less information. Several other studies followed, which applied the privacy calculus to different settings and contexts, in most cases finding similar results. For example, a recent study with 952 respondents representative of Germany showed that perceived privacy concerns and expected benefits were substantially related to people's willingness to adopt a COVID-19 tracing app (Meier et al., 2021). The privacy calculus has also been analyzed from a gender perspective. In a study with 164 students from China, the relation between benefits and intentions to disclose information was larger for males, whereas the relation between risks and intentions to disclose was larger for females, suggesting that males prioritize attaining benefits and females avoiding risks (Sun et al., 2015).

What is more important for behavior, attaining benefits or avoiding costs? When it comes to online participation and self-disclosure, it seems that benefits are more important than costs; on the other hand, when it's about prevention and self-withdrawal, anticipated costs appear more relevant (Dienlin & Metzger, 2016). The privacy calculus was also analyzed from a cross-contextual perspective (Krasnova et al., 2012; Trepte et al., 2017). In general, support for the privacy calculus was found across cultures (Trepte et al., 2017). However, the importance of benefits and costs varied (Krasnova et al., 2012), and cultural aspects such as individualism or uncertainty avoidance were also related with perceived risks and gratifications (Trepte et al., 2017).

In several studies on the privacy calculus, I was also involved personally. Together with Miriam Metzger, we analyzed a sample of 1,156 respondents representative of the United States and found that people who expressed more privacy concerns shared less information and also implemented substantially more privacy protection mechanisms. In a study with 1,131 respondents from the Netherlands, we analyzed the privacy calculus in three different contexts, namely (a) shopping, (b) health, or (c) news (Bol et al., 2018). In all three contexts, we found that both perceived privacy risks and expected benefits were significantly related to information sharing, suggesting that the calculus is robust across different settings. In another online experiment, we analyzed whether and if so how the privacy calculus is influenced by affordances (Trepte et al., 2020). To operationalize affordances, we manipulated cues indicating how much other users had already disclosed and how similar these other uses were. Results showed that if other users were portrayed as similar, this increased expected benefits and decreased perceived privacy concerns, which both were related to self-disclosure. It has to be noted that the sample size was comparatively small (N = 160), thus the results might not be particularly robust – but I believe the general picture is plausible. In another field experiment with 590 participants from Germany, we observed actual user behavior across one week results again showed that people who experienced more privacy concerns shared less information, while those who reported more expected benefits also shared more information. Together, this provides support for the privacy calculus with also behavioral data. Finally, in a recent study, we reanalyzed three already existing datasets by using a novel analysis technique called response surface analysis (Kezer et al., in press; overall N = 2,036). Response surface analysis explicitly focuses on the interplay of predictors (here, costs and benefits). In all three datasets, results showed that indeed people disclosed more information if benefits were higher than costs. In two datasets, results revealed that if the same difference between costs and benefits was on higher levels as compared to lower levels (e.g., benefits = 7 and costs = 5 vs. benefits = 3 and costs = 1), people disclosed more information, which again suggests that benefits seem to loom larger than costs.

Challenging the Privacy Calculus

The empirical studies mentioned above might suggest that the case is closed and that the privacy calculus is firmly established in academic research. This is not the case. The privacy calculus is often criticized, mainly because there are several situations in which behavior seems overly illogical.

Arguably, the most prominent (albeit indirect and implicit) challenge of the privacy calculus is the privacy paradox (Barnes, 2006).[2] Both approaches are incompatible (Dienlin, 2019). Whereas the privacy calculus starts from the premise that individuals are largely rational and that their online privacy behavior is hence not paradoxical, the privacy paradox considers people's behavior as non-rational and paradoxical. In a nutshell, the privacy paradox states that the behavior of online users doesn't make much sense. Many people express significant concerns, yet use digital services nonetheless, often divulging much personal information in the process. According to the privacy paradox, people overshare and often don't understand that social networks aren't private spheres but public platforms (Barnes, 2006). Some studies provide empirical support for the privacy paradox (e.g., Taddicken, 2014), primarily by showing that the relation between privacy concerns and behaviors such as information sharing is statistically nonsignificant.

Other studies adopt different operationalizations of the privacy paradox. For example, Beckett (2014) showed that people are willing to trade personal information for trivial goods such as a cinnamon cookie, suggesting that people really do not care about their privacy, although in many surveys they indicate otherwise. When confronted with privacy-friendly options that cost more money, people routinely choose privacy-invasive options (Grossklags et al., 2007). In short, there exist many individual studies showcasing instances where privacy concerns and behaviors are misaligned and thus seemingly non-rational (see Table 7.1).

Next to these biases there also exist other ones, such as affect heuristic (i.e., we become less critical in pleasant contexts; see also chapter 8 by Liao, Sundar, & Rosson on Bounded Rationality and Privacy Heuristics) or routinization bias (i.e., some things we do only because we've always done them). Together, these biases represent situations and contexts where behavior is not perfectly rational and provide important limitations to privacy calculus.

The privacy calculus can also be challenged from an empirical and methodological perspective. So far, the primary criterion to test the privacy calculus was statistical significance (i.e., $p < 5\%$). However, statistical significance should only be one decision criterion out of many. Given sufficiently large samples, even trivial and practically meaningless effects become statistically significant. Instead, research should define a smallest effect size of interest (Lakens et al., 2018). In other words,

Table 7.1 Biases in Decision-Making That Apply to the Online Context (Acquisti et al., 2020, p. 741)

Bias	*Explanation*
1. Information asymmetries	Consumers are unaware of the diverse ways firms collect and use their data.
2. Bounded rationality	Consumers lack the processing capacity to make sense of the complexities of the information environment.
3. Present bias	Overemphasizing immediate, and under-weighing delayed, costs and benefits.
4. Intangibility	Putting little weight on outcomes that are intangible – difficult to isolate or quantify.
5. Constructed preferences	Uncertainty about one's preferences leads people to rely on crude decision heuristics that often run counter to considerations of objective costs and benefits.
6. Illusory control	"The feeling (often illusory) that one is in control of a situation leads to increased risk-taking" (also known as control paradox; Brandimarte et al., 2012).
7. Herding	The tendency to imitate the behavior of other people.
8. Adaption	The tendency to get used to risks that are unchanged over time or that increase gradually.
9. The drive to share	The powerful drive to share information, including personal information.

what effects are considered sufficiently large to qualify as proof for the privacy calculus? Next, much of the literature is based on self-reports of behavior. This is problematic because self-reports are prone to many biases. For example, people might underreport online activities because it is socially undesirable. In addition, oftentimes perceived costs and benefits are collected after people have already engaged in a behavior. Hence, such reports could be post-hoc rationalizations (Knijnenburg et al., 2017). Investigations of a truly situational decision-making process are currently still sparse (Masur, 2018). Although testing the relationships between general costs, benefits, and behaviors is insightful, currently there exist only few studies investigating the actual situational weighing process. This shows that the theoretical model and the empirical analysis are often misaligned (Scheel et al., 2020; van Rooij & Baggio, 2021). In conclusion, there are several reasons to be critical of the empirical results supporting the privacy calculus model.

Countering the Critique

What is more likely to be correct, the privacy calculus model or the privacy paradox approach? If understood deterministically, both understandings are mutually exclusive (Dienlin, 2019). If behavior is paradoxical, then it cannot be rational. However, I believe that by and large there seems to be a winner. It is my understanding that the privacy calculus finds more support in the literature. This becomes even clearer when we adopt a more probabilistic and pragmatic perspective.

First, regarding the existence of the privacy paradox, a clear pattern emerges. Although some individual studies showed no significant relations between concerns and behavior, a meta-analysis of studies revealed that *overall* there seems to be a significant (but small) relation between concerns and behavior (Baruh et al., 2017). In their literature review, Gerber and colleagues come to a similar conclusion (2018, p. 226): "The results provide strong evidence for the theoretical explanation approach called 'privacy calculus,' with possibly gained benefits being among the best predictors for disclosing intention as well as actual disclosure. Other strong predictors for privacy behavior are privacy intention, willingness to disclose, privacy concerns, and privacy attitude" (But see Kokolakis, 2017). Taken together, the empirical literature suggests that there is a relevant relation between concerns and information-sharing behavior, supporting the privacy calculus model and refuting the privacy paradox model.

However, note that the reported empirical relationship is often only small. Now, the question is, do such small relations really constitute convincing support for the privacy calculus? Some might argue that to qualify as convincing support, effects would actually need to be larger. When determining what position to take, it's helpful to adopt a philosophy of science perspective, particularly a Bayesian one. Confronted with several competing theories or hypotheses – here, privacy paradox vs. privacy calculus – one criterion to select a theory is abduction or "explanatory inference" (Godfrey-Smith, 2021, p. 58). In other words, models are selected on the basis of their predictive capacity. As the saying goes, all models are wrong but some are helpful. Especially those that best predict future behavior. This idea is central to Bayesian statistics, which adopts a probabilistic and pragmatic perspective on model selection (McElreath, 2016). Using so-called Bayes Factors, we can compare specific models with one another to see which one is more likely given the data we have collected. Adopting this principle, in a recent study, we reanalyzed data from a meta-analysis and focused on the relation between concerns and information sharing (Dienlin & Sun, 2021). The privacy paradox model would postulate a zero relation between both variables. The privacy calculus a relation that is at least small. We found that the results are eight times more likely under a privacy calculus perspective than under a privacy paradox perspective. This is the first tentative evidence that a calculus perspective outperforms a paradox perspective when it comes to predicting user behavior, but more research is needed to support such a broad claim.

Second, demonstrating that biases and errors exist represents an important contribution to the literature and to our understanding of online behavior. It helps identify contexts in which external support is needed to assist the user, for example, in the form of nudges, warnings, improved legal frameworks, or education. However, one mistake has to be avoided. Only because we can show that human behavior is not *perfectly* rational, this does not mean that it is *completely* irrational. Let's not throw out the baby with the bathwater. Bounded rationality does not mean the absence of rationality, but rather that rationality is limited. And only because there are exceptions or limitations to the privacy calculus model, we shouldn't discard it as a descriptive theory, as was already suggested (Knijnenburg et al., 2017).

What perspective we adopt also depends on a researcher's goal. If it is our aim to showcase that behavior is irrational, then yes, there are many ways in which this can be accomplished, and rightly so. However, if it is our aim to show that preferences and behaviors overlap, this is likewise easily possible. Behavior might appear paradoxical if we only look at the often small relations between concerns and behavior. However, it becomes much more understandable when we also look at all the benefits of online participation. Online participation offers at least four major benefits: Retrieving information, fostering social relationships, expressing personalities, and finding entertainment (Schmidt, 2018). Concerns and risks do play a role, yes, but only a secondary one.

First, attitudes aren't the only factor impacting behavior; norms and behavioral control also play a role, potentially eclipsing the impact of attitudes. Second, we sometimes falsely believe there is no effect of attitudes on behavior when in fact there is one. Alleged attitude-behavior gaps are often merely methodological artifacts. To explain, it's difficult to demonstrate the existence of small effects – it requires specific operationalizations, reliable measures, large samples, and correct statistical techniques. Therefore, we should expect that behavior is largely determined by cognitive appraisals. Assuming that models such as the TPB, well-established in many cases and taught in all psychology courses worldwide, don't apply in the context of online behavior seems implausible.

Finally, it might also be the case that we are witnessing an inverse third-person effect paired with comparative optimism (Metzger & Suh, 2017). The third-person effect states that "I will not be influenced, but they (the third persons) may well be persuaded" (Davison, 1983, p. 1). Transferred to online communication, "My behavior makes much sense, but theirs is illogical." It sometimes feels like finger-pointing and a thinly veiled generation conflict, when older scientists criticize younger people for their social media use (Barnes, 2006). Couldn't it simply be that older scientists don't always understand and share the benefits younger users experience on social media, such as wasting away one's time, testing out new things, or simply sharing moments with friends? In addition, the risks that older people experience, for example, identity theft, might be less pronounced for youngsters. If there is not much money in one's account, there's also less to lose.

New Perspectives on Privacy Calculus

As should have become clear by now, I believe that the privacy calculus is a powerful model to understand human behavior from an individual perspective. However, note that this doesn't necessarily apply to the societal and political perspectives. Although it might be the case that users, on average, choose from all available options those better aligned with their preferences, from a societal perspective, we can rightly contest that the list of existing options itself isn't satisfactory, that it's too limited and incomplete (Dienlin & Breuer, 2022). Often, even the most privacy-friendly option isn't really privacy friendly at all.

To illustrate, it's currently impossible to use Facebook without the company exploiting the data for other purposes such as online advertising. It would be easily possible to offer more privacy-friendly services for interested users, for example, by charging additional costs. However, such options don't exist. Or consider that at the time of writing, it isn't possible to use Facebook services with data stored on servers in the European Union (EU); hence, under the US Patriot Act, it is legally possible for the US government to inspect data of foreigners. Facebook users from the EU cannot opt-out. Hence, broadening the existing options and thereby improving choice architecture would help achieve a more balanced and fair privacy calculus also from a societal perspective.

The privacy calculus is often understood such that people disclose *only* if benefits outweigh costs – so how do we console this understanding with the empirical instances where this clearly isn't the case? Confronted with the many individual illogical behaviors and the existence of specific biases, privacy calculus is often rejected outright (Knijnenburg et al., 2017). This is somewhat understandable. For example, from a Popperian and deductive perspective, we should indeed reject the hypothesis that users always act rationally in light of opposing evidence. However, I believe there are two reasons speaking against discarding the privacy calculus given opposing findings. First, from a more holistic philosophy of science perspective, such a decision would be ill-advised. The more natural and common approach would be to maintain the theory's core, but to acknowledge limitations and conditions where it doesn't apply (Godfrey-Smith, 2021). Second, I believe such a strict understanding of privacy calculus makes a straw man of the theory. As I have mentioned above, although behavior isn't logical or optimal in *all* instances, it is still reasonable and adaptive in *many* cases.

In conclusion, to maintain and emphasize that privacy calculus is indeed a valuable model to predict behavior online and to prevent unnecessary misunderstandings or straw man attacks, I suggest a slightly updated version, namely the probabilistic privacy calculus model. Its main tenets are as follows:

1 If benefits exceed costs, there is a higher probability, but no guarantee, that people self-disclose.
2 The more people anticipate benefits, the higher the probability that they self-disclose.
3 The more people expect costs, the higher the probability that they self-withdraw.
4 This process is sometimes explicit and conscious, but often also implicit and automatic.
5 The process can be analyzed both from a situational perspective (helping to identify the decisional process) as well as from a general perspective (to see if general preferences are aligned with general behavior).

Conclusion

In light of the many benefits the Internet and especially social media offer, it is not surprising that users sacrifice privacy to reap some of the benefits. As always, responsibility shouldn't rest on the users alone. It also needs external quality control and safeguards. Short-term fun shouldn't come at the expense of long-term sorrow. People need to be assisted in their personal calculus. We need better laws (see chapter 28 by Eichenhofer & Gusy on Regulating Privacy on Social Networks), and we need to foster privacy literacy (see chapter 11 by Masur, Hagendorff, & Trepte on Privacy Literacy). But there's no need to patronize people and label their behavior paradoxical, given that there are many good and valid reasons to make use of the various online services and social media.

Whereas the privacy calculus implies that everything is fine and that users are behaving rationally, the paradox emphasizes that there's a problem and that we need to change something. It is my impression that privacy advocates prefer to emphasize the problems and that users are overwhelmed, in order to improve legal frameworks and support users. Personally, however, I'm rather of the opinion that more is gained by focusing on the users' agency – in order to validate, nurture, and harness its potential. Because in understanding that privacy concerns do relate to behavior significantly, we realize that concerns become relevant. Being concerned makes a difference. It is no coincidence that the General Data Protection Regulation, drafted by Jan Philipp Albrecht, originated in Germany, where privacy concerns are profound.

Notes

1 The editor Sabine Trepte once told me that precisely because of this reason, the title of the 2011 handbook is "Privacy Online" and not "Online Privacy." It is about privacy unfolding online, but not about an entirely different conceptual entity. This thought was foundational for my own understanding of online processes.

2 It is my understanding that when it comes to social media, the privacy paradox was already discussed in 2006 (Barnes, 2006), whereas the calculus perspective was introduced later in 2010 (Krasnova et al., 2010). Hence, chronologically it was rather the calculus approach that challenged the privacy paradox.

References

Acquisti, A., Brandimarte, L., & Loewenstein, G. (2020). Secrets and likes: The drive for privacy and the difficulty of achieving it in the digital age. *Journal of Consumer Psychology*, *30*(4), 736–758. https://doi.org/10.1002/jcpy.1191

Altman, I. (1976). Privacy: A conceptual analysis. *Environment and Behavior*, *8*(1), 7–29. https://doi.org/10.1177/001391657600800102

Atkinson, J. W. (1957). Motivational determinants of risk-taking behavior. *Psychological Review*, *64*(6, Pt.1), 359–372. https://doi.org/10.1037/h0043445

Barnes, S. B. (2006). A privacy paradox: Social networking in the United States. *First Monday*, *11*(9). https://doi.org/10.5210/fm.v11i9.1394

Baruh, L., Secinti, E., & Cemalcilar, Z. (2017). Online privacy concerns and privacy management: A meta-analytical review. *Journal of Communication*, *67*(1), 26–53. https://doi.org/10.1111/jcom.12276

Beckett, L. (2014, October 1). *People are willing to give away their personal data for a cinnamon cookie* [InternetDocument]. http://mashable.com/2014/10/01/data-for-cookies/#a.PHlEiXW8qw

Bol, N., Dienlin, T., Kruikemeier, S., Sax, M., Boerman, S. C., Strycharz, J., Helberger, N., & Vreese, C. H. (2018). Understanding the effects of personalization as a privacy calculus: Analyzing self-disclosure across health, news, and commerce contexts. *Journal of Computer-Mediated Communication*, *23*(6), 370–388. https://doi.org/10.1093/jcmc/zmy020

Brandimarte, L., Acquisti, A., & Loewenstein, G. (2012). Misplaced confidences. *Social Psychological and Personality Science*, *4*, 340–347. https://doi.org/10.1177/1948550612455931.

Culnan, M. J., & Armstrong, P. K. (1999). Information privacy concerns, procedural fairness, and impersonal trust: An empirical investigation. *Organization Science*, *10*(1), 104–115. https://doi.org/10.1287/orsc.10.1.104

Davison, P. W. (1983). The third-person effect in communication. *Public Opinion Quarterly*, *47*(1), 1–15.

Dienlin, T. (2014). The privacy process model. In S. Garnett, S. Halft, M. Herz, & J. M. Mönig (Eds.), *Medien und privatheit* (pp. 105–122). Karl Stutz.

Dienlin, T. (2019). Das Privacy Paradox aus psychologischer Perspektive [The privacy paradox from a psychological perspective]. In L. Specht, S. Werry, & N. Werry (Eds.), *Handbuch Datenrecht und Digitalisierung* (pp. 305–323). Erich Schmidt Verlag.

Dienlin, T., & Metzger, M. J. (2016). An extended privacy calculus model for SNSs—Analyzing self-disclosure and self-withdrawal in a representative U.S. sample. *Journal of Computer-Mediated Communication, 21*(5), 368–383. https://doi.org/10.1111/jcc4.12163

Dienlin, T., & Breuer, J. (2022). Privacy is dead, long live privacy!. *Journal of Media Psychology*. https://doi.org/10.1027/1864-1105/a000357

Dienlin, T., & Sun, Y. (2021). Does the privacy paradox exist? Comment on Yu et al.'s (2020) meta-analysis. *Meta-Psychology, 5*. https://doi.org/10.15626/MP.2020.2711

Dienlin, T., Bräunlich, K., & Trepte, S. (2020). How do like and dislike buttons affect communication? Testing the privacy calculus in a preregistered one-week field experiment. https://doi.org/10.31235/osf.io/7kjf2

Fishbein, M., & Ajzen, I. (2010). *Predicting and changing behavior: The reasoned action approach*. Psychology Press.

Gerber, N., Gerber, P., & Volkamer, M. (2018). Explaining the privacy paradox: A systematic review of literature investigating privacy attitude and behavior. *Computers & Security*, 77, 226–261. https://doi.org/10.1016/j.cose.2018.04.002

Godfrey-Smith, P. (2021). *Theory and reality: An introduction to the philosophy of science* (2nd ed.). University of Chicago Press.

Grossklags, J., Acquisti, A., & Heinz, H. (2007). When 25 cents is too much: An experiment on willingness-to-sell and willingness-to-protect personal information. *Workshop on the Economics of Information Security Proceedings*.

Kezer, M., Dienlin, T., & Baruh, L. (in press). Getting the privacy calculus right: Analyzing the relations between privacy concerns, expected benefits, and self-disclosure using response surface analysis. *Cyberpsychology: Journal of Psychosocial Research on Cyberspace, 16*(4), 4. https://doi.org/10.5817/CP2022-4-1

Knijnenburg, B., Raybourn, E., Cherry, D., Wilkinson, D., Sivakumar, S., & Sloan, H. (2017). Death to the privacy calculus? *SSRN Electronic Journal*. https://doi.org/10.2139/ssrn.2923806

Kokolakis, S. (2017). Privacy attitudes and privacy behaviour: A review of current research on the privacy paradox phenomenon. *Computers & Security, 64*, 122–134. https://doi.org/10.1016/j.cose.2015.07.002

Krasnova, H., Spiekermann, S., Koroleva, K., & Hildebrand, T. (2010). Online social networks: Why we disclose. *Journal of Information Technology, 25*(2), 109–125. https://doi.org/10.1057/jit.2010.6

Krasnova, H., Veltri, N. F., & Günther, O. (2012). Self-disclosure and privacy calculus on social networking sites: The role of culture. *Business & Information Systems Engineering, 4*(3), 127–135. https://doi.org/10.1007/s12599-012-0216-6

Lakens, D., Scheel, A. M., & Isager, P. M. (2018). Equivalence testing for psychological research: A tutorial. *Advances in Methods and Practices in Psychological Science, 1*(2), 259–269. 10.1177/2515245918770963

Laufer, R. S., & Wolfe, M. (1977). Privacy as a concept and a social issue: A multidimensional developmental theory. *Journal of Social Issues, 33*(3), 22–42. https://doi.org/10.1111/j.1540-4560.1977.tb01880.x

Masur, P. K. (2018). *Situational privacy and self-disclosure: Communication processes in online environments*. Springer.

Masur, P. K., Teutsch, D., & Dienlin, T. (2018). Privatheit in der online-kommunikation. In W. Schweiger & K. Beck (Eds.), *Handbuch online-kommunikation* (2nd ed.). Springer VS. https://doi.org/10.1007/978-3-658-18017-1_16-1

McElreath, R. (2016). *Statistical rethinking: A Bayesian course with examples in R and Stan*. CRC Press/Taylor & Francis Group.

Meier, Y., Meinert, J., & Krämer, N. C. (2021). Investigating factors that affect the adoption of COVID-19 contact-tracing apps: A privacy calculus perspective. *Technology, Mind, and Behavior, 2*(3). https://doi.org/10.1037/tmb0000040

Metzger, M. J., & Suh, J. J. (2017). Comparative optimism about privacy risks on Facebook. *Journal of Communication, 67*(2), 203–232. https://doi.org/10.1111/jcom.12290

Petronio, S. (1991). Communication boundary management: A theoretical model of managing disclosure of private information between marital couples. *Communication Theory, 1*(4), 311–335. https://doi.org/10.1111/j.1468-2885.1991.tb00023.x

Scheel, A. M., Tiokhin, L., Isager, P. M., & Lakens, D. (2020). *Why hypothesis testers should spend less time testing hypotheses* [Preprint]. PsyArXiv. https://doi.org/10.31234/osf.io/vekpu

Schmidt, J.-H. (2018). *Social media* (2nd ed.). Springer VS.

Simon, H. A. (1955). A behavioral model of rational choice. *The Quarterly Journal of Economics*, *69*(1), 99. https://doi.org/10.2307/1884852

Sun, Y., Wang, N., Shen, X.-L., & Zhang, J. X. (2015). Location information disclosure in location-based social network services: Privacy calculus, benefit structure, and gender differences. *Computers in Human Behavior*, *52*, 278–292. https://doi.org/10.1016/j.chb.2015.06.006

Taddicken, M. (2014). The 'privacy paradox' in the social web: The impact of privacy concerns, individual characteristics, and the perceived social relevance on different forms of self-disclosure. *Journal of Computer-Mediated Communication*, *19*(2), 248–273. https://doi.org/10.1111/jcc4.12052

Trepte, S., Reinecke, L., Ellison, N. B., Quiring, O., Yao, M. Z., & Ziegele, M. (2017). A cross-cultural perspective on the privacy calculus. *Social Media + Society*, *3*(1). https://doi.org/10.1177/2056305116688035

Trepte, S., Scharkow, M., & Dienlin, T. (2020). The privacy calculus contextualized: The influence of affordances. *Computers in Human Behavior*, *104*, 106115. https://doi.org/10.1016/j.chb.2019.08.022

van Rooij, I., & Baggio, G. (2021). Theory before the test: How to build high-verisimilitude explanatory theories in psychological science. *Perspectives on Psychological Science*, *16*(4), 682–697. https://doi.org/10.1177/1745691620970604

8

ONLINE PRIVACY CUES AND HEURISTICS

Mengqi Liao, S. Shyam Sundar, and Mary Beth Rosson

PENNSYLVANIA STATE UNIVERSITY, USA

Users' everyday privacy behaviors often seem paradoxical. For instance, a recent Pew research center survey found that although 79% of US users reported concerns about how companies handled their data, only 25% said they read privacy policies before agreeing to them (Auxier & Rainie, 2019). This is an example of *bounded rationality*, wherein humans favor satisficing over rigorous processing of all relevant information (Acquisti & Grossklags, 2005). For example, one study found users are less likely to disclose sensitive information when told that social media companies might sell users' information (negative treatment) or when told that companies take measures to preserve users' privacy (positive treatment), in comparison to a control condition providing no information (Marreiros et al., 2017). Users' lower tendency to disclose their information is attributed to their heightened attention to privacy in both the positive and negative treatment conditions compared to the control condition, though it is not clear why two completely conflicting pieces of information lead to the same outcome if users are indeed more conscious about the potential risks (or lower risks) of their information disclosure. It is possible that the sheer presence of privacy-related information triggers a mental shortcut that leads users to feel that online environments are inherently unsafe (i.e., *online security heuristic*) (Zhang et al., 2014); application of this heuristic may reduce their disclosure willingness. In other words, instead of consciously and effortfully evaluating all the benefits and risks of privacy-related decisions, users may engage in "heuristic processing" of superficial and contextual cues on social media to guide their privacy-related decisions (Bräunlich et al., 2021; Sundar et al., 2013).

Heuristics can be understood as mental shortcuts that require less cognitive effort or resources (Bellur & Sundar, 2014). Eagly and Chaiken (1993) describe heuristic processing as a limited mode of information processing, leading to judgments and decisions based on relatively simple and superficial cues. By default, people follow a least effort principle to process information. This promotes reliance on heuristic processing, through which they convert cognitively demanding tasks to simpler mental activities and make decisions in a cost-effective manner (Fiske & Taylor, 1991). Cognitive heuristics are formed from prior experience; they are thought to be stored in memory as simple rules of thumb that are triggered by cues and applied to make rapid automatic judgments or used as part of the rationale for more systematic decision-making (Chen & Chaiken, 1999). Privacy scholars have become interested in the possible role of heuristics in online privacy contexts, as research has shown that users do not always engage in rational decision-making (effortfully weighing the costs and benefits), but rather make quick judgments based on simple contextual cues (e.g., Acquisti et al., 2012; Brandimarte et al., 2013).

 DOI: 10.4324/9781003244677-9

In sum, heuristics are *de facto* principles underlying seemingly impulsive privacy decision-making. We can observe the effects of these heuristic cues by asking users to interact with an interface that displays a cue designed to activate a heuristic and see how users who see this cue differ from those who do not, in terms of privacy attitudes, as well as intention or actual behavior to disclose information (e.g., Sundar et al., 2020). This difference is moderated by users' level of motivation and involvement in the topic of the content in the interface, as well as the degree to which they believe in the rule of thumb underlying a given heuristic. In the next section, we enumerate a few heuristics that users might apply when making privacy-related decisions on social media, drawing from a decade of empirical studies.

Heuristics That Focus on the Benefits of Information Disclosure

One class of heuristics pertains to the potential benefits obtained by users if they disclose personal information. Privacy is often a secondary consideration due to the "present bias": The tendency to discount future risks and gains in favor of immediate gratifications (Frik et al., 2018). This tendency underlies the *instant gratification heuristic*, namely the mental shortcut that "a site providing immediate service is better than one that takes time to satisfy my needs" (Zhang et al., 2014). Instant gratification heuristic is, in fact, a long-held heuristic among consumers since the early days of online retailing. Users are lured by gift cards, discounts, or other cost savings, leading them to give out information to online retailers (Sayre & Horne, 2000), even when the information requested is highly personal (Spiekermann et al., 2001). With respect to social media, we found that users are willing to disclose social media information on a mobile website (e.g., Twitter ID) in exchange for its services, even when their attitudes would predict otherwise (Zhang et al., 2014).

Another heuristic in this category is the *benefit heuristic* ("if my personal information will be used to benefit me, I should provide my information"). Interestingly, this heuristic can be triggered even when users do not obtain any benefits. In one study, we found that e-commerce users who are primed about potential benefits (e.g., a video describing how personalization services increase convenience) tend to reveal more information about themselves to the system even without any immediate benefit (Sundar et al., 2013). Furthermore, the benefits provided by social media companies are often experiential (e.g., entertainment content, news), which means their value may be difficult to assess before users must give up their information to obtain them. In other words, in contrast to instant gratification, the benefit heuristic can be triggered by cues that suggest there will be benefits to giving up personal information, even though the said benefit will only be enjoyed in the future. As a familiar example, Google explains its privacy policy as follows: "We collect information to provide better services to all our users — from figuring out basic stuff like which language you speak to more complex things like which ads you'll find most useful, the people who matter most to you online, or which YouTube videos you might like" (Google Privacy & Terms, 2021).

Other heuristics focus on non-monetary rewards such as psychological or communication benefits. One example is the *self-representation heuristic* ("the more I reveal, the more I can shape my online persona"). Different from users' strategic decisions about what information to disclose, this heuristic-driven decision can be easily triggered by interface cues on social media that suggest the importance of enhancing one's self-representation, for example, in online dating websites (Sundar et al., 2020). Another example is the *reciprocity heuristic* ("if someone reveals his/her personal information to me, I will do the same in return"). In interpersonal communication, individuals tend to calibrate their level of disclosure to match what the communication partner reveals. The reciprocity heuristic has been observed in computer-mediated communication between two communicators when chatting on social media (Sundar et al., 2020) and even in users' interaction with virtual agents (e.g., chatbots; Sundar 2017). It can be easily triggered when others start to reveal personal information to the users (e.g., their past relationship history), a tendency that is quite common on social media (Sundar et al., 2020). Another type of social benefit is tied to feelings of community. By disclosing personal information, users might feel that they are contributing to the larger community to which they belong online. Therefore, the *community building heuristic* ("sharing personal information can contribute to feelings of community amongst participating users") could be triggered by cues that evoke an underlying community that could benefit from information disclosure (Kim et al., 2018; Pena et al., 2018; Sundar et al., 2020). This heuristic can be used to encourage users' disclosure of sensitive or stigmatized information to build an open and healthy community on social media (Kim et al., 2018).

Heuristics That Focus on the Risks of Information Disclosure

In some cases, simple contextual cues serve to highlight the risks of information disclosure and the measures put in place to minimize them. One example can be seen in cases where detailed terms and conditions or privacy policies are provided (Molina et al., 2019). The mere presence of terms and conditions may trigger the *transparency heuristic* ("if a website makes its privacy policy transparent, then my information is safe"), which alleviates users' privacy concerns and increases trust toward the services (Chen & Sundar, 2018), even if the terms and conditions are never read (Molina et al., 2019).

Some social media platforms go a step further by affording users the possibility of customizing their privacy settings, which promotes users' control over personal information. The presence of control settings may trigger the *control heuristic* ("if a website offers me control over my private information, it is safe to reveal my information"). Studies have found that triggering the control heuristic alleviates privacy concerns (Zhang & Sundar, 2019) and increases sharing of identifiable information on social media (Brandimarte et al., 2013). Users with high privacy concerns also appreciate the ability to customize their content that they will get with "always-on" devices (e.g., smart speakers) in addition to privacy-setting customization (Cho et al., 2020b). However, note that the control heuristic might lead to the control paradox, whereby perceived control over privacy may make users more vulnerable due to their tendency to overshare their personal information (Brandimarte et al., 2013). In addition to user customization, some platforms, such as Snapchat and Instagram stories, automatically delete the information after 24 hours (meaning no information is recorded permanently); this may trigger the *ephemerality heuristic* ("if the information is not stored, but disappears, it is safe for me to share"), thereby increasing information disclosure likelihood (Sundar et al., 2016).

Cues about the characteristics of the information collector can also evoke heuristics. For example, authority is an important factor in source credibility (Sundar, 2008). When the entity hosting the system is reputed, the *authority heuristic* can be triggered among users ("if a trusted authority asks for my information, then it is safe to disclose it"), resulting in higher disclosure (Sundar et al., 2016, 2019). Authority heuristic can be triggered by the presence of third-party endorsement, such as a security seal, e.g., TRUSTe (Sundar et al., 2020), credentials of the interactant (e.g., Dr. or MD in Lee & Sundar, 2013), and/or their affiliation (e.g., staff from the campaign of a favored politician), among other cues visible on social media feeds. Some users hold a preference for non-human agents to collect their personal information, perhaps because they believe that machines are more objective than humans, less judgmental, and less likely to gossip about users. When the information collector is a virtual agent (e.g., chatbot, virtual assistant like Siri) instead of human, the *machine heuristic* ("machines are more objective than humans, can perform tasks with greater precision, and handle information in a more secure manner") may be triggered and lead to higher disclosure intent (Sundar & Kim, 2019). Many social media platforms and messaging apps now allow the implementation of chatbots for companies to have immediate conversations with users. The machine heuristic can thus be easily triggered by the presence of these chatbots due to their machine-like cues such that users might be more willing to let the non-human agent collect their personal information rather than a human entity.

Aside from machine and authority sources, the actions of peers could also be a cue for heuristic decision-making. Users are known to make inferences based on their beliefs about other users who are also using the same system. If the interface displays that many other users have already disclosed their personal information to the system, the *bandwagon heuristic* could be triggered ("if it is good for so many others, it's good for me, too"). Bandwagon cues are found to be especially effective in e-commerce contexts, wherein users make quick purchase decisions based on other users' consensus about the quality of a system or a product, manifested in the form of star ratings, comments, likes, shares, and so on (Sundar et al., 2008; Sundar et al., 2017). In a similar vein, if users see that many others are disclosing their information on social media, they might likely follow the risky trend. For instance, Spottswood and Hancock (2017) found that social media users are more likely to disclose private information (i.e., phone number) in their user profiles if they are provided with explicit cues that indicate many others have disclosed that piece of information. Some users will also disclose more if they think they belong to a larger community and if the community norm encourages information disclosure, namely the *sense-of-community heuristic* ("if I were a part of a community, I would share my information"). It can be easily triggered by cues that signify the community to which they belong (e.g., fan page, book club, etc.) (Sundar et al., 2020). On social media, the sense-of-community heuristic can be easily triggered when users are in a group (e.g., Facebook Groups), which might further encourage disclosure even though the group is public and its feed is more visible to people outside one's network than one's own social media feed.

Some cues, however, can trigger heuristics that encourage privacy vigilance. Sundar et al. (2013) consider these to be negative privacy heuristics. A prime example is the *fuzzy boundary heuristic* ("If the system collects, retains, and utilizes users' information covertly, my information is vulnerable"; Sundar et al., 2017). Fuzzy boundary heuristic may be easily triggered given the rise of personalization and ad recommendations in users' everyday social media activity. It is increasingly common for users to receive contextualized advertising on social media feeds based on the time of the day, their current location, or other personally identifiable information (e.g., the content they posted or engaged with on social media, the products they just searched online); such "behavioral retargeting" (Lambrecht & Tucker, 2013) may lead to a sudden realization that personal information is being shared with a third party in the background without their awareness, leading to "Whoa" moments (Bucher, 2017). Similarly, the *intrusiveness heuristic* ("If something arrives unsolicited, it is unsafe") can be triggered by unsolicited arrival of emails, requests, notifications, and advertisements that hijack users' attention. These cues usually appear as pop-up notifications or system-initiated privacy disclosure requests.

Similar to the positive privacy heuristics, the cues that trigger negative privacy heuristics may arise from the context or the nature of the devices typically used to access social media. For instance, the *mobility heuristic* can be triggered when users choose to input their personal information via a mobile device ("Mobile devices are inherently unsafe in protecting my information"; Sundar et al., 2016). It should also be noted that the mobility heuristic might be problematic as users scoring high in their belief in mobility heuristic might exhibit higher innate trust towards PCs or laptops which might increase their likelihood of risky information disclosure on those devices. Furthermore, users could invoke the *publicness heuristic* when using a public network to browse online ("It is not secure to reveal private information when using a public network"), especially if the network in question is declared as risky or "not secure" by their devices (Molina et al., 2019; Sundar et al., 2016). Finally, some cues may signify the risks inherent in the general online environment, helping users to realize that online behaviors are not secure all the time. While users are browsing online, if they see any cues that signify that they are in a non-secure online environment (e.g., security warning initiated by the browser), the *online security heuristic* could be triggered ("Online is not safe, thus it is risky to reveal my information;" Zhang et al., 2014). This might especially be the case when users are

Table 8.1 Summary of Privacy Heuristics

Type of Heuristics	*Cues*		*Heuristics*
Benefit-related heuristics	Tangible benefits		instant gratification heuristic benefits heuristic
	Intangible benefits		self-representation heuristic reciprocity heuristic community building heuristic
Risk-related heuristics	Cues that minimize risks	Provided by the system	transparency heuristic control heuristic ephemerality heuristic authority heuristic machine heuristic bandwagon heuristic sense of community
	Cues that increase risks	Provided by the system	fuzzy boundary heuristic intrusiveness heuristic
		In the general online environment	mobility heuristic publicness heuristic online security heuristic

handling sensitive information or when they are using sensitive services. For instance, we found in one experiment that users with high belief in online security heuristic are less likely to use single sign-on (i.e., their Facebook account to log in) when signing up for sensitive social apps (such as those meant for affairs or hookups), compared to users with lower belief in online security heuristic (Cho et al., 2020a). They are more likely to make the extra effort to sign up using their email accounts to preserve their privacy.

See Table 8.1 for a summary of the heuristics we described so far.

Designing with Privacy Heuristics

Understanding the uses and effects of privacy heuristics can shed light on intriguing phenomena such as the privacy paradox. While a recent meta-analysis revealed that there was a small, negative, yet significant relationship between one's privacy concerns and their disclosure behavior online in general (Baruh et al., 2017), when it comes to specific information types or specific privacy contexts on social media, individual studies have found that sometimes users' privacy concerns predict disclosure (e.g., Dienlin & Trepte, 2015), but at other times do not (e.g., Heravi et al., 2018). It may be that although users do at times report general concerns regarding their data privacy, they are less careful in the "heat of the moment," making it possible for contextual cues to trigger cognitive heuristics that affect their privacy decision-making. According to the Heuristic-Systematic Processing model (HSM), there are two routes for users' information processing: One that is based on superficial cues (heuristic processing) and one that requires more cognitive effort (systematic processing) (Chaiken, 1980). The latter is better informed and more desirable, but users seldom pause to systematically weigh the benefits and risks of their information disclosure. The design implication is to develop and present appropriate just-in-time alerts to remind users about the existence of heuristic cues, presented strategically at the time when users are making online privacy decisions.

There may also be ways to guide users to more systematic processing of the information. First, a straightforward way to increase users' mindfulness about privacy decisions is to remind them about the importance of their privacy. HSM assumes that individuals are *cognitive misers* (Taylor & Fiske, 1978), who would like to minimize their cognitive effort when making judgments. For users to engage in systematic information processing, the first requirement is that they need to be motivated enough to expend their cognitive energy to process (Chaiken & Maheswaran, 1994). As privacy is rarely the primary reason for engaging in an online activity and therefore not the foremost consideration when interacting on social media, reminding users about the importance of their privacy might lead to more mindful privacy-related information processing and engagement. Studies in the social cognition literature have shown that triggering systematic processing effectively curtails heuristic processing.

Second, we can draw users' attention to their reliance on privacy-invading heuristics. For instance, we might introduce an alert when displaying the terms and conditions, cautioning them about short circuiting the process via the transparency heuristic; this might help them pause and examine the terms more closely. A better design compared to simple alerts and warnings is to include an action possibility. According to the theory of interactive media effects (TIME) (Sundar et al., 2015), there are two ways in which affordances influence users' interactions with the media: One is the "cue route" which influences their attitudes and behaviors by triggering heuristics, and the other is the "action route" that influences user engagement through user actions. TIME posits that the action route could promote higher user engagement and attentiveness, thereby making users more mindful about their actions and decisions. Taking the bandwagon heuristic as an example, if we want to inform users that they might be employing this heuristic, we could create a simple nudge asking "Are you entering this information because so many others have done so?" (Sundar et al., 2020). The hope is that this step would make users more vigilant about their use of the heuristic; if they still choose to apply the heuristic, at least they are doing it in a more mindful way.

Third, we could create privacy nudges by developing counter cues to solicit privacy-preserving thoughts that directly contradict the suspected heuristics (see also chapter 25 by Acquisti et al. on nudges for privacy and security). For instance, the offer of an instant reward (e.g., "log in via social media to earn a 50% discount") may trigger the instant gratification heuristic, luring users to part with their personal information. To combat this, a just-in-time alert could contain counter cues that emphasize a possible long-term privacy loss (e.g., "your information on social media will be recorded by the system and will be used to send targeted ads in the future"). In a similar vein, many users might be swayed by the machine heuristic, thinking that machines can be more objective, less judgmental, and will be less likely to gossip about users, even though machines can have biases just like humans (Obermeyer et al., 2019) and may share information across systems and servers (Abel et al., 2013). By building in cues that signify that "the system (e.g., one social media platform) will share your information with other systems (e.g., other social media platforms)," we could help users reflect and resist the application of the machine heuristic in their decision-making.

Furthermore, according to the bias hypothesis of HSM, systematic and heuristic information processing could be initiated either independently or interdependently at the same time, and more importantly, heuristic processing could affect judgment indirectly by biasing the valence of their systematic processing (Chaiken & Maheswaran, 1994). Maheswaran and Chaiken (1991) proposed that heuristics could set up expectations among individuals before they process the information systematically. For example, if the source is an authority (i.e., a cue that triggers the authority heuristic), one will expect that the message delivered by the authority to be more valid and of better quality, which in turn facilitates the processing of expectancy-congruent information and ready acceptance of the message. Applying the bias hypothesis in the privacy context, we could build in cues that will trigger negative privacy heuristics. Then, when users process the information provided by the systems, they will likely be more vigilant and attentive to information that communicates the potential risks of information disclosure. For instance, we could provide the cues that trigger the *fuzzy boundary heuristic* to make users mindful about how much information social media could be collecting from them, thereby making them think twice before disclosing.

Concluding Remarks

In discussing a range of privacy heuristics that users may apply to social media activities, we acknowledge that we may have oversimplified the complex social media environment. Social media are constantly collecting users' information, either overtly (e.g., actively asking users to fill out profile information) or covertly (e.g., passively tracking one's social media activities, browsing history, user-generated content on social media, etc.), creating a complicated environment where multiple cues could co-exist and influence users' decision-making in terms of disclosure of their personal information. In addition, it is important to note that not all heuristics are the same or the same across all individuals. Therefore, how different heuristic cues interact with each other and with individual differences, including privacy concerns, power usage, and many other dispositional factors (Ward et al., 2005), should be considered. Specifically, in addition to testing the effects of one specific heuristic cue, we found using factorial experiments that multiple cues could have interaction effects on users' privacy decisions. For instance, we found that some cues seem to have primacy over other cues: When shown a cue signifying that a data storage center is not at the user's location, the perceived security of the system will be undermined, even if the data collector is portrayed as an authority (Sundar et al., 2019). We also found that cues can exert contradictory effects when the heuristics being triggered by them oppose one another (e.g., instant gratification heuristic and online security heuristic in Zhang et al., 2014). When the two cues are consistent with each other, the presence of two or more cues may have a cumulative effect on users' trust towards the system (e.g., benefit cue and transparency cue in Chen & Sundar, 2018). Surprisingly, at times, multiple cues can work against one another. When a transparency cue (Terms & Conditions) and a bubble cue (VPN) were both presented with a public network in Molina et al. (2019), perceived security was reduced, perhaps because the multiple cues amplified the salience of privacy as an issue of concern.

A theoretical understanding of privacy heuristics is important for advancing ethical design of interfaces that help preserve user privacy. Given the information overload that users face online, it is understandable that they rely on cues to heuristically make important privacy decisions. Therefore, we call for design of counter cues that can help them become more mindful about their decisions and engage in more systematic information processing before disclosing their personal information. By providing several ways to nudge users toward more systematic processing of privacy-related information, we hope to help future researchers as well as practitioners in advancing design of privacy-preserving social media interfaces that not only ensure good user experience, but also facilitate informed and mindful disclosure of personal information. We also hope that these efforts contribute to greater media literacy among users about protecting their privacy on social media.

Acknowledgment

This research is supported by the US National Science Foundation via Standard Grant No. CNS-1450500.

References

Abel, F., Herder, E., Houben, G.-J., Henze, N., & Krause, D. (2013). Cross-system user modeling and personalization on the social web. *User Modeling and User-Adapted Interaction*, *23*(2), 169–209. https://doi.org/10.1007/s11257-012-9131-2

Acquisti, A., & Grossklags, J. (2005). Privacy and rationality in individual decision making. *IEEE Security Privacy*, *3*(1), 26–33. https://doi.org/10.1109/MSP.2005.22

Acquisti, A., John, L. K., & Loewenstein, G. (2012). The impact of relative standards on the propensity to disclose. *Journal of Marketing Research*, *49*(2), 160–174. https://doi.org/10.1509/jmr.09.0215

Auxier, B., & Rainie, L. (2019). Key takeaways on Americans' views about privacy, surveillance and data-sharing. *Pew Research Center*. Retrieved from https://www.pewresearch.org/fact-tank/2019/11/15/key-takeaways-on-americans-views-about-privacy-surveillance-and-data-sharing/

Baruh, L., Secinti, E., & Cemalcilar, Z. (2017). Online privacy concerns and privacy management: A meta-analytical review. *Journal of Communication, 67*(1), 26–53. https://doi.org/10.1111/jcom.12276

Bellur, S., & Sundar, S. S. (2014). How can we tell when a heuristic has been used? Design and analysis strategies for capturing the operation of heuristics. *Communication Methods and Measures, 8*(2), 116–137. 10.1080/19312458.2014.903390

Brandimarte, L., Acquisti, A., & Loewenstein, G. (2013). Misplaced confidences: Privacy and the control paradox. *Social Psychological and Personality Science, 4*(3), 340–347. https://doi.org/10.1177/1948550612455931

Bräunlich, K., Dienlin, T., Eichenhofer, J., Helm, P., Trepte, S., Grimm, R., Seubert, S., & Gusy, C. (2021). Linking loose ends: An interdisciplinary privacy and communication model. *New Media & Society, 23*(6), 1443–1464. 10.1177/1461444820905045

Bucher, T. (2017). The algorithmic imaginary: Exploring the ordinary affects of Facebook algorithms. *Information, Communication & Society, 20*(1), 30–44. https://doi.org/10.1080/1369118X.2016.1154086

Chaiken, S. (1980). Heuristic versus systematic information processing and the use of source versus message cues in persuasion. *Journal of Personality and Social Psychology, 39*(5), 752–766. https://doi.org/10.1037/0022-3514.39.5.752

Chaiken, S., & Maheswaran, D. (1994). Heuristic processing can bias systematic processing: Effects of source credibility, argument ambiguity, and task importance on attitude judgment. *Journal of Personality and Social Psychology, 66*(3), 460–473. https://doi.org/10.1037/0022-3514.66.3.460

Chen, S., & Chaiken, S. (1999). The heuristic-systematic model in its broader context. In *Dual-process theories in social psychology* (pp. 73–96). The Guilford Press.

Chen, T.-W., & Sundar, S. S. (2018). This app would like to use your current location to better serve you: Importance of user assent and system transparency in personalized mobile services. *Proceedings of the 2018 CHI Conference on Human Factors in Computing Systems*, 1–13. https://doi.org/10.1145/3173574.3174111

Cho, E., Kim, J., & Sundar, S. S. (2020a). Will you log into tinder using your Facebook account? Adoption of single sign-on for privacy-sensitive apps. *Extended Abstracts of the 2020 CHI Conference on Human Factors in Computing Systems*, 1–7. https://doi.org/10.1145/3334480.3383074

Cho, E., Sundar, S. S., Abdullah, S., & Motalebi, N. (2020b). Will deleting history make Alexa more trustworthy? Effects of privacy and content customization on user experience of smart speakers. *Proceedings of the 2020 CHI Conference on Human Factors in Computing Systems*, 1–13. https://doi.org/10.1145/3313831.3376551

Dienlin, T., & Trepte, S. (2015). Is the privacy paradox a relic of the past? An in-depth analysis of privacy attitudes and privacy behaviors. *European Journal of Social Psychology, 45*(3), 285–297. https://doi.org/10.1002/ejsp.2049

Eagly, A. H., & Chaiken, S. (1993). *The psychology of attitudes* (pp. xxii, 794). Harcourt Brace Jovanovich College Publishers.

Fiske, S. T., & Taylor, S. E. (1991). *Social cognition* (2nd ed., pp. xviii, 717). McGraw-Hill Book Company.

Frik, A., Egelman, S., Harbach, M., Malkin, N., & Peer, E. (2018). Better late(r) than never: Increasing cyber-security compliance by reducing present bias. In *Symposium on Usable Privacy and Security*. Retrieved from https://weis2018.econinfosec.org/wp-content/uploads/sites/5/2018/06/WEIS_2018_paper_42.pdf

Google Privacy & Terms – Privacy Policy – Google. (2021). Retrieved from https://policies.google.com/privacy/embedded?hl=en-US

Heravi, A., Mubarak, S., & Raymond Choo, K.-K. (2018). Information privacy in online social networks: Uses and gratification perspective. *Computers in Human Behavior, 84*, 441–459. https://doi.org/10.1016/j.chb.2018.03.016

Kim, J., Gambino, A., Sundar, S. S., Rosson, M. B., Aritajati, C., Ge, J., & Fanning, C. (2018). Interface cues to promote disclosure and build community: An experimental test of crowd and connectivity cues in an online sexual health forum. *Proceedings of the ACM on Human-Computer Interaction, 2*, 1–18. https://doi.org/10.1145/3274359

Lambrecht, A., & Tucker, C. (2013). When does retargeting work? Information specificity in online advertising. *Journal of Marketing Research, 50*(5), 561–576. 10.1509/jmr.11.0503

Lee, J. Y., & Sundar, S. S. (2013). To tweet or to retweet? That is the question for health professionals on Twitter. *Health Communication, 28*(5), 509–524. https://doi.org/10.1080/10410236.2012.700391

Maheswaran, D., & Chaiken, S. (1991). Promoting systematic processing in low-motivation settings: Effect of incongruent information on processing and judgment. *Journal of Personality and Social Psychology, 61*(1), 13–25. https://doi.org/10.1037/0022-3514.61.1.13

Marreiros, H., Tonin, M., Vlassopoulos, M., & Schraefel, M. C. (2017). "Now that you mention it": A survey experiment on information, inattention and online privacy. *Journal of Economic Behavior & Organization, 140*, 1–17. https://doi.org/10.1016/j.jebo.2017.03.024

Molina, M. D., Gambino, A., & Sundar, S. S. (2019). Online privacy in public places: How do location, terms and conditions and VPN influence disclosure? *Extended Abstracts of the 2019 CHI Conference on Human Factors in Computing Systems*, 1–6. https://doi.org/10.1145/3290607.3312932

Obermeyer, Z., Powers, B., Vogeli, C., & Mullainathan, S. (2019). Dissecting racial bias in an algorithm used to manage the health of populations. *Science*. https://doi.org/10.1126/science.aax2342

Pena, J., Rosson, M. B., Ge, J., Jeong, E., Sundar, S. S., Kim, J., & Gambino, A. (2018). An exploration of design cues for heuristic-based decision-making about information sharing. *iConference 2018 Proceedings*.

Sayre, S., & Horne, D. (2000). Trading secrets for savings: How concerned are consumers about club cards as a privacy threat? *ACR North American Advances*, *NA-27*. https://www.acrwebsite.org/volumes/8379/volumes/v27/NA-27/full

Spiekermann, S., Grossklags, J., & Berendt, B. (2001). E-privacy in 2nd generation e-commerce: Privacy preferences versus actual behavior. *Proceedings of the 3rd ACM Conference on Electronic Commerce*, 38–47. https://doi.org/10.1145/501158.501163

Spottswood, E. L., & Hancock, J. T. (2017). Should I share that? Prompting social norms that influence privacy behaviors on a social networking site. *Journal of Computer-Mediated Communication*, *22*(2), 55–70. https://doi.org/10.1111/jcc4.12182

Sundar, S. S. (2008). The MAIN model: A heuristic approach to understanding technology effects on credibility. In M. Metzger & A. Flanagin (Eds.), *Digital media, youth, and credibility* (pp. 73–100). Cambridge, MA: MIT Press.

Sundar, S. S., & Kim, J. (2019). Machine heuristic: When we trust computers more than humans with our personal information. *Proceedings of the 2019 CHI Conference on Human Factors in Computing Systems*, 1–9. https://doi.org/10.1145/3290605.3300768

Sundar, S. S., Jia, H., Waddell, T. F., & Huang, Y. (2015). Toward a theory of interactive media effects (TIME): Four models for explaining how interface features affect user psychology. In *The handbook of the psychology of communication technology* (pp. 47–86). Wiley Blackwell. https://doi.org/10.1002/9781118426456.ch3

Sundar, S. S., Kang, H., Wu, M., Go, E., & Zhang, B. (2013). Unlocking the privacy paradox: Do cognitive heuristics hold the key? *CHI '13 Extended Abstracts on Human Factors in Computing Systems*, 811–816. https://doi.org/10.1145/2468356.2468501

Sundar, S. S., Kim, J., & Cho, E. (2019). Where in the cloud is my data? Location and brand effects on trust in cloud services. *Extended Abstracts of the 2019 CHI Conference on Human Factors in Computing Systems*, 1–6. https://doi.org/10.1145/3290607.3313021

Sundar, S. S., Kim, J., & Gambino, A. (2017). Using theory of interactive media effects (time) to analyze digital advertising. In *Digital advertising* (3rd ed.). Routledge.

Sundar, S. S., Kim, J., Gambino, A., & Rosson, M. B. (2016). Six ways to enact privacy by design: Cognitive heuristics that predict users' online information disclosure. *Paper Presented in the Workshop on Bridging the Gap Between Privacy by Design and Privacy in Practice at the 34th Annual ACM Conference (CHI'16) on Human Factors in Computing Systems*, 1–8. https://networkedprivacy2016.files.wordpress.com/2015/11/sundar-et-al-final_chi-pbd-workshop-161.pdf

Sundar, S. S., Kim, J., Rosson, M. B., & Molina, M. D. (2020). Online privacy heuristics that predict information disclosure. In *Proceedings of the 2020 CHI Conference on Human Factors in Computing Systems* (pp. 1–12). https://doi.org/10.1145/3313831.3376854

Sundar, S. S., Oeldorf-Hirsch, A., & Xu, Q. (2008). The bandwagon effect of collaborative filtering technology. *CHI '08 Extended Abstracts on Human Factors in Computing Systems*, 3453–3458. https://doi.org/10.1145/1358628.1358873

Taylor, S. E., & Fiske, S. T. (1978). Salience, attention, and attribution: Top of the head phenomena. *Advances in Experimental Social Psychology*, *11*(C), 249–288. https://doi.org/10.1016/S0065-2601(08)60009-X

Ward, S., Bridges, K., & Chitty, B. (2005). Do incentives matter? An examination of on-line privacy concerns and willingness to provide personal and financial information. *Journal of Marketing Communications*, *11*(1), 21–40. https://doi.org/10.1080/1352726042000263575

Zhang, B., & Sundar, S. S. (2019). Proactive vs. reactive personalization: Can customization of privacy enhance user experience? *International Journal of Human-Computer Studies*, *128*, 86–99. https://doi.org/10.1016/j.ijhcs.2019.03.002

Zhang, B., Wu, M., Kang, H., Go, E., & Sundar, S. S. (2014). Effects of security warnings and instant gratification cues on attitudes toward mobile websites. *Proceedings of the SIGCHI Conference on Human Factors in Computing Systems*, 111–114. https://doi.org/10.1145/2556288.2557347

PART 2

Factors Shaping Social Media Privacy

9

SOCIAL MEDIA AFFORDANCES AND PRIVACY

Jeffrey W. Treem[1], *Ward van Zoonen*[2], *and Anu Sivunen*[3]

[1]THE UNIVERSITY OF TEXAS AT AUSTIN, USA
[2]ERASMUS UNIVERSITY ROTTERDAM, THE NETHERLANDS
[3]UNIVERSITY OF JYVÄSKYLÄ, FINLAND

Since the emergence of social media, scholars have considered which, if any, actions this class of technologies offers that are different from those possible in other contexts of communication. A useful perspective for addressing this line of inquiry is an affordances framework, which focuses on the possibilities for action available to an actor within a particular sociomaterial environment. In considering what is, and is not possible, for actors using social media, scholars have frequently examined the ways privacy is constituted through social media use and the extent to which privacy can be managed, maintained, and compromised within and across online platforms. Privacy management is a central concern for understanding communication in sociomaterial contexts that are inherently performative such as on social media (Hogan, 2010). Users frequently make decisions on what to share and what not to share, often with the knowledge the eventual audience of their communication might be unknown. Extant literature characterizes privacy as both a distinct affordance available to users of social media and a consequence of other affordances enacted through social media use. Viewing the intersection of social media use and privacy from an affordances framework recognizes privacy as a central consideration in the context of social media and a dynamic that is shaped by the active choices of actors, the materiality present in the use of social media technologies, and the skills and abilities of social media users.

Affordances

The psychologist James J. Gibson introduced the concept of affordances as an attempt to explain how individual actors (humans and animals) perceive their environment. The affordances framework is based on the principle of *direct perception*, meaning that when actors find themselves in a particular context, they immediately perceive the possibilities for action in that environment. Gibson (1979) provided the following definition:

> The affordances of the environment are what it offers the animal, what it provides or furnishes, either for good or ill. The verb afford is found in the dictionary, but the noun affordance is not. I have made it up. I mean by it something that refers to both the environment and the animal in a way that no existing term does. It implies the complementarity of the animal and the environment (p. 127).

DOI: 10.4324/9781003244677-11

Affordances do not exist as a distinct material aspect of an object (i.e., a feature) or as a material capability of an actor (i.e., an ability); rather, only operate as a relationship between the two (Chemero, 2003). For example, stairs are composed of a series of vertical ascending solid materials, each offering a platform or foothold above each other, and most humans are capable of lifting and bending their legs, but only when a person confronts a series of stairs does the environment afford stair-climbing. Gibson argued that the utility of a particular object derived from its place in the environment and the perception of any actor relative to the available action possibilities. He saw affordances as activated by this actor-object-environment interaction. This principle of direct perception stood in contrast to positivist, behavioral research in psychology that was concerned with the cognitive routines individuals use to perceive possibilities.

A purposively simplistic definition of affordances, then, is what an actor "can do" in relation to objects in an environment (Chemero, 2003). However, the study of uses of communication technologies complicates the idea of affordances in two ways. First, communication technologies – and in particular digital technologies like social media – are commonly capable of supporting more material features than other physical objects and are not bound by time and space in the same way (Leonardi, 2010). Thus, we can characterize digital technologies as more flexible both in the sense of the different forms they may take for any particular user (e.g., most users of Facebook or Twitter only use a small fraction of the features of the platforms) and that the form and user experiences will differ based on the time of use (e.g., available features and other users change over time). Second, the original concept of affordances offered by Gibson was largely focused on perception relative to physical objects in space and time and the perception of the respective substances, surfaces, and mediums of those objects. His concern was visual perception. Though digital objects like social media certainly possess different forms of physicality and materiality – i.e., that they are built on computer code, can display text, and execute commands – users do not interact digitally in a traditional embodied manner (hence the common use of qualifiers like virtual or computer-mediated communication). Moreover, much of the materiality of technologies like social media is not visible to the user upon first encounter but is discovered through repeated and prolonged use and observations of the use of others. As a result, the perceived affordances of an object may change as actors come to understand different capabilities of an object, and this understanding operates as a social process consisting not just of the actors' experiences, but also a collective understanding of what a technology can do and how it ought to be used.

Gibson's original conceptualization of affordances has influenced a range of scholarship examining humans' use of technology generally and communication technologies specifically. Affordances became more prominent in the field of design through the work of Norman (1988) and human–computer interaction through the work of Gaver (1991), who is credited with popularizing the term *technology affordances* (though Gibson did link his original ideas to visual representations). Gaver argued that individuals discover affordances through exploration with a technology. He also noted that the realization of affordances may facilitate the discovery or recognition of further affordances.

Is Privacy an Affordance of Social Media?

Scholars have recognized a number of distinct affordances associated with the use of social media, with some of the more commonly listed including visibility, editability, persistence, and association (Fox & McEwan, 2017; Gibbs et al., 2013; Leonardi & Vaast, 2017; Manata & Spotswood, 2021; Oostervink et al., 2016; Treem & Leonardi, 2013). Yet there is less agreement regarding how privacy operates in the context of social media, with some research considering privacy a distinct affordance and other work viewing privacy as an outcome or consequence of other available affordances and actions. It is helpful to first consider how scholars might assess what is or is not an affordance. In an effort to explicate the concept of affordances, Evans et al. (2017) present three threshold criteria for evaluating affordances, with particular focus on the use of communication technologies: a) An affordance is not an object itself nor a distinct feature of an object, b) an affordance is not an outcome, and c) an affordance has variability or range. They conclude that although privacy is not a feature of communication technology, and does vary, it exists as an outcome of other actions and therefore does not exist as a distinct affordance. Indeed, studies of social media use often position privacy as an outcome associated with the use of specific features of platforms (e.g., Fox & Warber, 2015). Yet many scholars explicitly position privacy, or related actions specifically designed to manage an individual's privacy, as an affordance associated with the use of social media (Calo, 2017; Fox & McEwan, 2017; Kuo et al., 2013).

Regardless of whether privacy is viewed as a distinct affordance or an outcome associated with other affordances of social media technologies, in evaluating its operation, it is important to keep in mind two aspects of affordances. First, affordances do not operate as determinants of actions, but rather exist as possibilities that then shape understandings as to what actions are available to actors. This means that although individuals may view social media as providing similar opportunities related to privacy, individuals are likely to enact and pursue privacy in vastly different ways. Studies of how individuals present themselves on social media demonstrate that users engage in a wide variety of purposeful and strategic practices related to privacy depending on aspects such as their perceived audiences, self-efficacy in achieving goals, and the values they place on privacy (Berkelaar, 2016; Sujon, 2018; Vitak et al., 2015).

Second, affordances are not inherently positive or negative, but instead operate to enable or constrain particular actions. As such, in adopting an affordance framework for the study of privacy in the context of social media use, it is not particularly helpful to assess privacy variance strictly in terms of the amount of information disclosed or concealed, but rather whether any particular state or outcome of privacy matches an individual's preferences. Approaches that treat social media privacy as a binary (i.e., present or absent) or a continuum (i.e., low to high; absent to complete) risk applying a uniform understanding of privacy that overlooks the vast variability in users' communication goals. An affordance perspective allows that individual social media users in the same context will experience the affordances of privacy (or affordances associated with privacy), in different ways. Some research has focused primarily on the ways that users of social media can adjust features and settings in order to customize experiences and states of privacy (Costa, 2018; Fox & Warber, 2015). Other studies have concluded that individuals feel that the affordances of social media – i.e., visibility, connectivity, and persistence – enable privacy violations (Fox & Moreland, 2015).

Within an affordances framework, privacy does not operate as something present or absent, but exists as something managed within a particular sociomaterial environment that will make some actions easier – in terms of awareness, availability, and ability – than others. Trepte and colleagues (2020; 2021) apply an affordances lens to discuss how the possible actions for social media users present a privacy calculus which can help us understand how individuals make choices regarding information disclosure or concealment. The calculus consists of actors evaluating the possible risks, costs, or harms associated with a loss of privacy relative to the potential gains or benefits. This approach captures how the affordances of social media create new possibilities for valuable disclosure and concealment tactics, but those same affordances can make maintaining privacy more difficult. Although empirical studies reveal that this tradeoff rarely results in an even relationship between risks and costs regarding social media use (i.e., individuals commonly accept significant privacy loss for minimal direct gain), evidence reveals that concern with privacy is reliably associated with a decrease in an individual's willingness to disclose information (Baruh et al., 2017; Koohikamali et al., 2017; Min & Kim, 2015). A study by Ashuri and co-authors (2018) found that social media users also observe other users' self-disclosure practices and gained benefits when evaluating their own privacy calculus. In particular, when other users' self-disclosure on social media is perceived as beneficial to them, users tend to believe that they can also leverage social media by disclosing information. However, the assessment of other users' losses related to their self-disclosures had only a limited impact on users' own disclosing behavior on social media. Overall, the importance of actors observing other privacy practices – and related outcomes – in evaluating individual possibilities for action is consistent with Gibson's discussion of how actors learn affordances in a particular context in large part from watching the behaviors of others.

Other studies have confirmed that expected benefits matter more than perceived losses when users evaluate their privacy calculus on social media (Dienlin & Metzger, 2016). Scholars have also discussed ways that affordances of social media facilitate or constrain possibilities for privacy. For instance, Kini et al. (2022) argue that filtering operates as a critical affordance in the context of social media allowing individuals to manage what is included and excluded in communicative action. They note that this filtering operates both within single social media platforms through decisions users make about what to share and what features to engage, as well as across platforms as individuals make communication choices based on intended audiences and perceived expectations relative to each space. Similarly, low visibility and more perceived control over the audience in social media applications such as Snapchat have been shown to result in fewer privacy concerns and more open self-expression (Choi & Sung, 2018; Hollenbaugh, 2019).

What is consistent across work adopting an affordances framework is a recognition that social media use both enables and constrains the disclosure and concealment of information in ways markedly different than found with previous communication technologies. An affordances framework allows scholars to view these changes in opportunities for privacy as neither inevitable nor entirely unpredictable and offers a lens to explore the ways social media privacy is simultaneously shaped by the agential acts of users and the material properties of technologies.

How Might Social Media Afford Privacy?

More than a half-century ago, Westin (1967, p. 7) defined privacy as, "the claim of individuals, groups, or institutions to determine for themselves when, how, and to what extent information about them is communicated to others." Scholars of social media and privacy have largely adopted this concern with information flow but add that more contextually situated understandings of privacy are needed to account for aspects of social media that may undermine actors' efforts to self-determine communication (Nissenbaum, 2010; Wu et al., 2020). Specifically, social media use calls into question the locus of agency regarding communication and the extent that privacy emerges from the actions of individual actors, the nature of a communicative environment, and the actions and intentions of potential observers. Within online environments, privacy is commonly considered in relation to the extent to which individuals engage in computer-mediated communication while maintaining the ability to regulate disclosure to others online. Trepte (2021) defines privacy in the context of social media as: "An individual's assessment of (a) the *level of access* to this person in an interaction or relationship with others (people, companies, institutions) and (b) the availability of the *mechanism of control, interpersonal communication trust, and norms*, for shaping this level of access through (c) *self-disclosure* (almost intuitive) behavioral privacy regulation and (d) *control, interpersonal communication, and deliberation* as means for ensuring (a somewhat more elaborated) regulation for privacy" (p. 561), emphasis in original. This definition is consonant with an affordances perspective in that it treats privacy as operational through the purposeful actions of actors, material aspects of the environment that enable and constrain actions, and the activities of others that operate interdependently and possibly alter the context of activities. Each of these elements of an affordances perspective has implications for the ways in which actors may experience privacy in the context of social media use.

An Agenda for Studying Privacy and Social Media from an Affordances Lens

A contextual understanding of privacy and social media connects this area of study with a number of core tenants of Gibson's original characterization of affordances: A concern with the distinct context of action, an understanding that actors learn through the observation of others, and an appreciation that actors have differing goals that guide action. By adopting an affordances perspective, scholars can develop theoretical and empirical work related to privacy that will remain relevant as social media continues to evolve, both in terms of its technical aspects and its social significance. What follows are considerations for the ongoing study of social media and privacy.

Considering Users' Different Goals and Strategies Regarding Social Media and Privacy

A key concern for scholars examining privacy on social media from an affordances perspective is what possibilities the use of social media presents for the concealment or disclosure of information. On its face, the possibility of social media to make communication globally visible and accessible would undermine the efforts of social media users to retain or maintain privacy. Indeed, scholarship has indicated the ways that social media facilitates greater expressiveness and the ability for individuals to broadcast messages with minimal effort or resources (Hogan, 2010; Marwick & boyd, 2010). However, scholars have also recognized that the ease and scope with which social media can make communication accessible to others can easily become misaligned with individuals' desires or expectations regarding the privacy of communication (Sloop & Gunn, 2010). Put differently, individuals may behave on social media as if communication is private, or bound to specific actors, even though communication is very much publicly available. This serves as a reminder that the ability of individuals to manage privacy does not necessarily predict privacy behaviors. Moreover, this serves as a caution against making assumptions about the capabilities (i.e., digital literacy) or desires of individuals relative to privacy management based only on an analysis of social media activity.

There are a variety of different ways that individuals may seek to manage, regulate, or alter their privacy online. For instance, many individuals use pseudonyms when communicating in digital spaces in an effort to shield their actual identity and to disassociate themselves with particular forms of content (Ma et al., 2016). Yet research also indicates that despite pseudonymity on some social media platforms, individuals still engage in a number of practices to protect their communication from certain audiences (Triggs et al., 2019). The range of social media privacy management strategies can be seen in the context of cybervetting, in which employers examine prospective applicants' online behaviors and individuals adopt a variety of social media practices ranging from no privacy management at all to maintaining multiple accounts to strategically manage privacy (Berkelaar, 2016).

What these empirical studies demonstrate is that social media provide users with a wide range of opportunities to actively pursue privacy management through purposeful actions, but the presence of those opportunities for all users can present constraints on privacy or result in unanticipated consequences for themselves and others. Future work should continue to explore the varied goals social media users have, the associated behaviors enacted in efforts to achieve those goals, and the beliefs and perceptions that drive those actions.

Considering How Material Changes in Social Media Relate to Privacy

The ways in which users achieve desired levels of privacy strongly depend on the technical features of a particular platform (Evans et al., 2017). In particular, social media can differ in the types of communication modalities users are able to employ (i.e., text, images, video), the audiences that have access to communication, and the availability of communication over time. For instance, one reason that users are attracted to the social media platform Snapchat is because of the ephemerality of messages, which contrasts with the persistence of messages found in many other social media platforms (Bayer et al., 2015). Additionally, individual social media users will utilize the features of social media in emergent ways which can alter the types of communication that are perceived as possible or expected (Honey & Herring, 2009).

One challenge for the study of affordances is that the features of social media applications and platforms frequently change, making it difficult for scholars to assess the potential or probable nature of privacy in a reliable, generalizable, or consistent way. This means that over time, an individual platform may differ regarding the various settings available that can restrict or regulate who is able to see content within an application, with whom that content is automatically shared, and whether a user is notified or alerted when content is viewed. Moreover, social media users may be unaware of changes in features, as platform updates are often communicated through convoluted terms of service policies that users commonly ignore (Obar & Oeldorf-Hirsch, 2020). Studying how individuals change or retain particular behaviors on a platform following changes in privacy features or options can offer insights into how changes in affordances might relate to social media use.

Considering How Changes in Users and Audiences Relate to Social Media and Privacy

Early users of Facebook, when accounts on the platform were restricted to individuals with an email address affiliated with a small group of US universities, likely had a greater expectation of privacy when posting on Facebook relative to today, when the platform has more than a billion global accounts. This reflects the understanding that possibilities for privacy are shaped by the likelihood that others will come in contact with, or be able to easily view, communication, regardless of whether those observations are inadvertent, inherent, or intentional. In an environment of low social media use (e.g., few users or little accessibility to a platform), users are more likely to avoid scrutiny and/or may find it easier to manage and monitor who does and does not encounter communication. However, scholars have noted that as social media use and access grow, it becomes more difficult for users to identify possible observers, distinguish among audiences for content, or manage who is able to view communication. A common result is what researchers have termed *context collapse*, which is a label for the ways social media expands possible audiences for communication in ways that blur, erase, or erode boundaries that previously allowed users to base actions on a largely known audience (Davis & Jurgenson, 2014; Marwick & boyd, 2010; Vitak, 2012). Even in social media contexts that seemingly provide anonymity (e.g., Reddit), users express concerns about being identified in unintended ways and take steps to manage the privacy of communication in ways that limit exposure (Leavitt, 2015; Triggs et al., 2019). When the context of social media shifts, the privacy possibilities for individuals also change, and the increased dynamism associated with social media means that the relevance and salience of affordances related to privacy may need to be re-examined over time.

However, there is a danger in assuming that context collapse is ubiquitous in a contemporary social media environment. For instance, Costa (2018) cautions that context collapse may be largely associated with Anglo-American contexts and related normative expectations of social media use and not an inherent aspect of social media communication. Drawing on ethnographic work in southeast Turkey, Costa describes how many users manage multiple accounts on social media to address different intended audiences and do not perceive tension or collapse among contexts. Similarly, Dhoest and Szulc (2016) describe how queer immigrants effectively create and manage different social media profiles that are directed to different audiences.

An understanding of the relationship between social media affordances and privacy necessitates greater attention to how populations of social media users – both within and across platforms – change over time and across cultural and geographic boundaries.

Considering Power and Ethics in the Study of Privacy

Questions of what affordances exist, or operate, in relation to social media privacy must be preceded by considerations regarding who has the rights and abilities to access, own, and manage social media content. As Calo (2017) notes, the ability to violate the privacy of others through the extraction, harvesting, and aggregating of online information is an affordance that largely only exists for large corporations that have the resources, technical abilities, and incentives to engage in such activity. Relatedly, Pearce and colleagues (Pearce et al., 2018) note how although the privacy afforded by social media can aid in political and social dissent and activity, the visibility of social media can also aid surveillance efforts and put marginalized individuals and groups in danger. Moreover, technology providers are incentivized to grow the number of users and levels of engagement on social media platforms precisely because user activity provides valuable data that can be packaged, commoditized, and sold (Zuboff, 2019). The powerful role that corporations and governments have in shaping the affordances associated with privacy creates the increasing likelihood that social media users have limited insight into the myriad ways their activity is being tracked and evaluated and therefore may be unable to develop informed opinions about potential privacy violations (Obar & Oeldorf-Hirsch, 2020).

It is also helpful to reflect on what the affordances of social media related to privacy mean for the ethical responsibilities of researchers who may seek to gather, analyze, and report about social media content and behaviors. Historically, communication that is freely published and publicly available has been viewed as generally appropriate for study, and material such as news articles, company annual reports, and organizational website content is commonly aggregated to create rich datasets. However, researchers have noted that important distinctions can be drawn between the possibilities available to freely observe, analyze, and capture communication and the reasonable expectations social media users have for the ways that their communication will be treated. Future researchers will have to grapple with how to balance the affordances of social media for data collection with the desires and expectations of individual social media users related to privacy.

Conclusion

An affordances framework can be useful for analyzing the relationship between privacy and social media because it captures the ways that social media present new possibilities for communication – including information disclosure and concealment – while recognizing that actors will enact these possibilities differently based on varying goals, abilities, and contexts. The ongoing evolution in social media related to features, users, ownership, content moderation, and legal regulations all serve as opportunities to re-examine the possible ways individuals use social media as part of efforts to enact privacy goals. Specifically, it is important that scholars adopting an affordances lens to study social media and privacy consider how the rapid expansion and variation of features within and across social media platforms relate to the privacy calculus users face. Additionally, more work is needed to understand the power dynamics and ethics associated with what actors have affordances related to the design of social media platforms, surveillance of social media activity, and access to social media data.

References

Ashuri, T., Dvir-Gvisman, S., & Halperin, R. (2018). Watching me watching you: How observational learning affects self-disclosure on social network sites? *Journal of Computer-Mediated Communication*, *23*(1), 34–68. https://doi.org/10.1093/jcmc/zmx003

Baruh, L., Secinti, E., & Cemalcilar, Z. (2017). Online privacy concerns and privacy management: A meta-analytical review. *Journal of Communication*, *67*(1), 26–53. https://doi.org/10.1111/jcom.12276

Bayer, J. B., Ellison, N. B., Schoenebeck, S. Y., & Falk, E. B. (2015). Sharing the small moments: Ephemeral social interaction on Snapchat. *Information, Communication & Society*, 1–22. https://doi.org/10.1080/1369118X.2015.1084349

Berkelaar, B. L. (2016). How implicit theories help differentiate approaches to online impression management: A preliminary typology. *New Media & Society*, *19*(12), 2039–2058. https://doi.org/1461444816654136

Calo, R. (2017). Privacy, vulnerability, and affordance. *DePaul Law Review*, *66*(2), 591–604.

Chemero, A. (2003). An outline of a theory of affordances. *Ecological Psychology*, *15*(2), 181–195. https://doi.org/10.1207/s15326969eco1502_5

Choi, T. R., & Sung, Y. (2018). Instagram versus Snapchat: Self expression and privacy concern on social media. *Telematics and Informatics*, *35*, 2289–2298. https://doi.org/10.1016/j.tele.2018.09.009

Costa, E. (2018). Affordances-in-practice: An ethnographic critique of social media logic and context collapse. *New Media & Society*, *20*(10), 3641–3656. https://doi.org/10.1177/1461444818756290

Davis, J. L., & Jurgenson, N. (2014). Context collapse: Theorizing context collusions and collisions. *Information, Communication & Society*, *17*(4), 476–485. https://doi.org/10.1080/1369118X.2014.888458

Dhoest, A., & Szulc, L. (2016). Navigating online selves: Social, cultural, and material contexts of social media use by diasporic gay men. *Social Media+ Society*, *2*(4), 1–10. https://doi.org/10.1177/2056305116672485

Dienlin, T., & Metzger, M. J. (2016). An extended privacy calculus model for SNSs: Analyzing self-disclosure and self-withdrawal in a representative U.S. sample. *Journal of Computer-Mediated Communication*, *21*(5), 368–383. https://doi.org/10.1111/jcc4.12163

Evans, S. K., Pearce, K. E., Vitak, J., & Treem, J. W. (2017). Explicating affordances: A conceptual framework for understanding affordances in communication research. *Journal of Computer-Mediated Communication*, *22*(1), 35–52. https://doi.org/10.1111/jcc4.12180

Fox, J., & McEwan, B. (2017). Distinguishing technologies for social interaction: The perceived social affordances of communication channels scale. *Communication Monographs*, *84*(3), 298–318. https://doi.org/10.1080/03637751.2017.1332418

Fox, J., & Moreland, J. J. (2015). The dark side of social networking sites: An exploration of the relational and psychological stressors associated with Facebook use and affordances. *Computers in Human Behavior*, *45*, 168–176. https://doi.org/10.1016/j.chb.2014.11.083

Fox, J., & Warber, K. M. (2015). Queer identity management and political self-expression on social networking sites: A co-cultural approach to the spiral of silence. *Journal of Communication*, *65*(1), 79–100. https://doi.org/10.1111/jcom.12137

Gaver, W. W. (1991). Technology affordances. In *Proceedings of the 1991 CHI conference on human factors in computing systems* (pp. 79–84). New York, New York, USA, ACM Press. https://doi.org/10.1145/108844.108856

Gibbs, J. L., Rozaidi, N. A., & Eisenberg, J. (2013). Overcoming the "ideology of openness": Probing the affordances of social media for organizational knowledge sharing. *Journal of Computer-Mediated Communication*, *19*(1), 102–120. https://doi.org/10.1111/jcc4.12034

Gibson, J. J. (1979). *The ecological approach to visual perception*. Houghton Mifflin.

Hogan, B. (2010). The presentation of self in the age of social media: Distinguishing performances and exhibitions online. *Bulletin of Science, Technology & Society*, *30*(6), 377–386. https://doi.org/10.1177/0270467610385893

Hollenbaugh, E. E. (2019). Privacy management among social media natives: An exploratory study of Facebook and Snapchat. *Social Media+ Society*, *5*(3). https://doi.org/10.1177/2056305119855144

Honey, C., & Herring, S. C. (2009, 5–8 Jan). Beyond microblogging: Conversation and collaboration via twitter. Paper presented at the 2009 42nd Hawaii International Conference on System Sciences.

Kini, S., Pathak-Shelat, M., & Jain, V. (2022). Conceptualizing "filter-ing": Affordances, context collapse, and the social self online. *International Journal of Communication*, *16*, 21.

Koohikamali, M., Peak, D. A., & Prybutok, V. R. (2017). Beyond self-disclosure: Disclosure of information about others in social network sites. *Computers in Human Behavior*, *69*, 29–42. https://doi.org/10.1016/j.chb.2016.12.012

Kuo, F.-Y., Tseng, C.-Y., Tseng, F.-C., & Lin, C. S. (2013). A study of social information control affordances and gender difference in Facebook self-presentation. *Cyberpsychology, Behavior, and Social Networking*, *16*(9), 635–644. https://doi.org/10.1089/cyber.2012.0345

Leonardi, P. M. (2010). Digital materiality? How artifacts without matter, matter. *First Monday*, *15*(6), 7.

Leavitt, A. (2015). "This is a throwaway account": Temporary technical identities and perceptions of anonymity in a massive online community. Paper presented at the Proceedings of the 18th ACM Conference on Computer Supported Cooperative Work & Social Computing, Vancouver, BC, Canada. https://doi.org/10.1145/2675133.2675175

Leonardi, P. M., & Vaast, E. (2017). Social media and their affordances for organizing: A review and agenda for research. *Academy of Management Annals, 11*(1), 150–188. https://doi.org/10.5465/annals.2015.0144

Ma, X., Hancock, J., & Naaman, M. (2016, May). Anonymity, intimacy and self-disclosure in social media. In *Proceedings of the 2016 CHI conference on human factors in computing systems* (pp. 3857–3869). New York, New York, USA, ACM Press. https://doi.org/10.1145/2858036.2858414

Manata, B., & Spottswood, E. (2021). Extending Rice et al. (2017): The measurement of social media affordances. *Behaviour & Information Technology, 41*(6), 1323–1336. https://doi.org/10.1080/0144929X.2021.1875264

Min, J., & Kim, B. (2015). How are people enticed to disclose personal information despite privacy concerns in social network sites? The calculus between benefit and cost. *Journal of the Association for Information Science and Technology, 66*(4), 839–857. https://doi.org/10.1002/asi.23206

Marwick, A. E., & boyd, d. (2010). I tweet honestly, I tweet passionately: Twitter users, context collapse, and the imagined audience. *New Media & Society, 13*(1), 114–133. https://doi.org/10.1177/1461444810365313

Nissenbaum, H. (2010). *Privacy in context: Technology, policy, and the integrity of social life*. Stanford University Press.

Norman, D. A. (1988). *The psychology of everyday things*. Basic Books.

Obar, J. A., & Oeldorf-Hirsch, A. (2020). The biggest lie on the internet: Ignoring the privacy policies and terms of service policies of social networking services. *Information, Communication & Society, 23*(1), 128–147. https://doi.org/10.1080/1369118X.2018.1486870

Oostervink, N., Agterberg, M., & Huysman, M. (2016). Knowledge sharing on enterprise social media: Practices to cope with institutional complexity. *Journal of Computer-Mediated Communication, 21*(2), 156–176. https://doi.org/10.1111/jcc4.12153.

Pearce, K., Vitak, J., & Barta, K. (2018). Privacy at the margins| socially mediated visibility: Friendship and dissent in authoritarian Azerbaijan. *International Journal Of Communication, 12*, 22.

Sloop, J. M., & Gunn, J. (2010). Status control: An admonition concerning the publicized privacy of social networking. *The Communication Review, 13*(4), 289–308. https://doi.org/10.1080/10714421.2010.525476

Sujon, Z. (2018). The triumph of social privacy: Understanding the privacy logics of sharing behaviors across social media. *International Journal of Communication, 12*, 21.

Treem, J. W., & Leonardi, P. M. (2013). Social media use in organizations: Exploring the affordances of visibility, editability, persistence, and association. *Annals of the International Communication Association, 36*(1), 143–189. https://doi.org/10.1080/23808985.2013.11679130

Trepte, S. (2021). The social media privacy model: Privacy and communication in the light of social media affordances. *Communication Theory, 31*(4), 549–570. https://doi.org/10.1093/ct/qtz035

Trepte, S., Scharkow, M., & Dienlin, T. (2020). The privacy calculus contextualized: The influence of affordances. *Computers in Human Behavior, 104*, 106–115. https://doi.org/10.1016/j.chb.2019.08.022

Triggs, A. H., Møller, K., & Neumayer, C. (2019). Context collapse and anonymity among queer Reddit users. *New Media & Society, 23*(1), 5–21. https://doi.org/10.1177/1461444819890353

Vitak, J., Blasiola, S., Patil, S., & Litt, E. (2015). Balancing audience and privacy tensions on social network sites: Strategies of highly engaged users. *International Journal of Communication, 9*, 20.

Vitak, J. (2012). The impact of context collapse and privacy on social network site disclosures. *Journal of Broadcasting & Electronic Media, 56*(4), 451–470. https://doi.org/10.1080/08838151.2012.732140.

Westin, A. F. (1967). *Privacy and freedom*. Atheneum.

Wu, P. F., Vitak, J., & Zimmer, M. T. (2020). A contextual approach to information privacy research. *Journal of the Association for Information Science and Technology, 71*(4), 485–490. https://doi.org/10.1002/asi.24232

Zuboff, S. (2019). *The age of surveillance capitalism: The fight for a human future at the new frontier of power*. Public Affairs.

10
PRIVACY AND TRUST

Yannic Meier[1] *and Nadine Bol*[2]

[1]UNIVERSITY OF DUISBURG-ESSEN, GERMANY
[2]TILBURG UNIVERSITY, THE NETHERLANDS

Introduction

Trust plays a key role in human life and is the foundation of interpersonal relationships. In today's complex life, we have relationships with a variety of persons, entities, and institutions, and these relationships may develop offline, online, or in a combination of these environments. Self-disclosure (i.e., the act of revealing information about the self; Jourard, 1964) is crucial to establish and maintain interpersonal relationships; however, at the same time, it challenges people's privacy (i.e., individuals' ability to determine when, how, and to what extent information is communicated to others; Westin, 1967). As such, intimacy and confidential exchange can only take place in spheres where both privacy and trust prevail. Both factors are essential and intertwined and without one, the other loses its value. To illustrate, you can be in an undisturbed place with someone you do not trust, but that will not lead to intimate revelations. Likewise, you are unlikely to reveal your biggest secret to a trusted friend in a place without privacy. Hence, on the one hand, privacy can be a precondition for groups of two or more trusted persons to engage in intimate, confidential, and secret disclosures (Westin, 1967), but, on the other hand, trust can also be a precondition of a continued feeling of privacy when someone has no actual control options (Trepte, 2021). This implies that, at times, trust could even be described as a specific form of privacy as it takes the critical function to create or uphold a feeling of privacy. As interpersonal relationships are increasingly established and maintained online, the current chapter will deal with the topic of trust and privacy in the context of social media. First, we will establish a definition of trust, followed by a discussion of the behavioral outcomes of trust, different functions of trust, different targets of trust, and current theorizing and empirical works investigating privacy and trust among social media users.

What is Trust?

Trust has been conceptualized from a variety of angles, depending on the respective disciplines involved, but also depending on research areas within the disciplines. Bhattacharya and colleagues (1998) reviewed several definitions of trust in social and economic interactions and drew the following conclusions: (1) Trust is only necessary for environments containing uncertainty and risk; (2) trust is a prediction and expectation about future events and behaviors of others; (3) trust depends on both person and situation; and (4) trust focuses on a positive outcome. Consequently, they defined trust as "an expectancy of positive (or nonnegative) outcomes that one can receive based on

 DOI: 10.4324/9781003244677-12

the expected action of another party in an interaction characterized by uncertainty" (Bhattacharya et al., 1998, p. 462). Here, it is of particular importance to emphasize that trusting another party makes oneself vulnerable to the actions of that other party without having the possibility to control the other's conduct (Mayer et al., 1995). Hence, relying on trust is an admission of the trustor's vulnerability towards the trustee and the trustor's simultaneous lack of control over the actions of the trustee. This stresses the fact that trust and control have a complementary character (Heath & Bryant, 2013; see chapter 3 by Trepte on networked privacy approaches): Trust is dispensable when someone can oversee the actions of another (because trust supposes uncertainty), but when there is no opportunity to monitor what someone else is doing, trust can replace actual control as the person believes that the other party will behave in an expected manner. When we share information with others in interpersonal or computer-mediated communication, we give up control over our personal information. Thus, we must rely on others as co-owners (i.e., persons or companies with whom we have shared personal and private information to keep personal information within a mutual boundary; Petronio, 2002). This means that every time we disclose personal information to others, we expose ourselves to the risk of a violation of our privacy. Trust as a positive expectation, however, can mitigate our perception of a potential privacy risk, and we cognitively reduce the uncertainty within the disclosure situation. As a consequence, trust can create or uphold a feeling of privacy and pave the way for personal and intimate self-disclosure despite potential negative future consequences. These considerations are expanded by Waldman (2018) who describes trust as a social norm from which a positive expectation of others' behavior emerges. Hence, trust can not only be an individual but also a collective expectation that is shaped by group or cultural norms. This notion is akin to Nissenbaum's (2010) understanding of privacy as contextually dependent meaning that, inter alia, contextual privacy norms affect privacy behaviors. Accordingly, trust – like privacy – is context-dependent and is a foundation of communication as long as it is not replaced by other factors such as professional or financial obligations (Nissenbaum, 2010). Finally, trust can also vary from situation to situation, meaning that in addition to the specific context, each individual situation can create different feelings of trust and thus privacy (Masur, 2018). Having summarized several definitions and key features of trust, we define trust within communication in the context of social media as:

> *a positive expectation of the trustor towards a trustee's (e.g., individual or company) conduct regarding the use of the trustor's personal information.*

Trust can be an individual-, normative-, context-, and/or situation-dependent condition that presupposes the trustor's potential susceptibility to privacy risks and a lack of control over the trustee's conduct. It is important to note that trust has both stable and fluctuating components, which means that some people are generally more trusting than others, but also that trust is sometimes higher or lower within the same person across different situations.

Trust and Online Privacy Behaviors

Trust plays a central role in predicting privacy behaviors online. A variety of privacy behaviors through social media exist, ranging from partaking in (e.g., through self-disclosure), to withdrawing from, social online interactions (e.g., self-withdrawal; see Dienlin & Metzger, 2016). Numerous empirical findings indicate that trust is directly related to people's self-disclosure behavior. Positive relations between trust towards other persons and (offline) self-disclosure have been known for a long time (Wheeless & Grotz, 1977). These positive relationships were also found for online communication: Persons with higher trust in websites have higher intentions to share their personal information with these websites (Bol et al., 2018; Joinson et al., 2010; Metzger, 2004), and persons who trust their online social networks disclose more information to them (Benlian & Hess, 2011; Masur & Scharkow, 2016; Sharif et al., 2021). A recent study also showed that persons who had higher trust towards the government had a higher willingness to disclose personal information to a COVID-19 contact tracing app (Jörling et al., 2022). Together, these results provide a solid empirical basis for the positive relationship between trust and information disclosure (in social media): When people trust their communication partners, audiences, or the providers of the environment in which communication takes place, self-disclosure seems to be more likely.

Besides information sharing, people can also engage in privacy regulation and protection behaviors, such as self-withdrawal. Whereas the empirical findings concerning the relationship between trust and self-disclosure are rather clear, they are much more ambiguous regarding the role that trust plays in privacy management and protection behaviors. For instance, Masur and Scharkow (2016) found that social media users who had higher trust in their contacts engaged in less disclosure management (i.e., regulating disclosure depending on how private information is perceived). However, several other studies found no association between people's trust and their privacy protection intentions and behaviors (Meier et al., 2021; Saeri et al., 2014; Turow & Hennessy, 2007; Utz & Krämer, 2009). These studies measured different forms of trust, like trust in other social networking site (SNS) users (Saeri et al., 2014) or trust in websites (Meier et al., 2021), as well as different forms of protective behaviors, such as using SNS privacy settings (Utz & Krämer, 2009) and various forms of protection online (e.g., use of additional tools and cookie deletion; Turow & Hennessy, 2007). Whereas these studies did not find an empirical link between trust and privacy protection, there is still a theoretical one. Applying different forms of privacy protective measures online can decrease one's vulnerability to privacy threats. Therefore, it would be reasonable to assume that persons who perceive themselves to be highly vulnerable and who have low trust that another party will protect their privacy would engage in self-protective behaviors (see Bräunlich et al., 2021). According to the social media privacy model (Trepte, 2021), trust within interactions with others determines one's perception of current privacy and access of others to the self. This feeling can, in turn, affect regulative behaviors (e.g., how detailed disclosures are or to whom a posting is visible).

Privacy protective behaviors, however, can be complex and affected by numerous factors, like privacy literacy or the perceived effectiveness of protection. Hence, a lack of trust may only be associated with more protective attempts under the right circumstances (e.g., when internet users have the knowledge and skills to protect themselves and think it is effective). This idea is reflected by the empirical findings of Kruikemeier et al. (2020). They found that users who had little trust in online companies possessed more knowledge about online tracking mechanisms and engaged in more adaptive privacy behaviors, such as refusing to disclose personal information or providing false information. These results show that trust can be involved in interindividual differences in privacy protection, but its exact role remains ambiguous. Finally, there is also evidence for an indirect role of trust in protection behaviors. A study by Meier et al. (2021) found that trust was negatively related to participants' wish for better online privacy protection which in turn was positively linked to their intended privacy protection. Hence, according to these two studies as well as the previously mentioned theoretical work, trust could be negatively related to privacy protection in social media. Nevertheless, more empirical evidence is required.

Functions of Trust

To provide nuance to our understanding of trust and establish what functions trust fulfills, we must understand its relationships to other variables that are known to be relevant to how we engage with others in online environments. In the context of social media, users are seldom fully aware of what precisely happens when sharing personal information through their profiles, status updates, stories, likes, and comments, or in private and group chats. As such, apart from the direct association between trust and self-disclosure, trust can play different roles in explaining how, why, and under which conditions people tend to disclose information. We discuss three functions of trust as follows: (1) Replacing control, (2) mitigating privacy risks within the privacy calculus, and (3) establishing a social contract.

Trust and (Perceived) Control

First, when users decide to disclose information via social media platforms, they have a *control momentum*, which means that they can determine whether, when, how much, and to whom they want to disclose information (Trepte, 2021). Once someone has decided to share personal information, he or she no longer has any actual control over the purposes for which the information is used by other users or the social media provider. However, according to Petronio (2002), people still have the wish to stay in control over their personal information even after self-disclosure. To do so, people must either rely on trust that replaces actual and perceived control (Masur, 2018; Trepte, 2021) or they can build a perception to stay in control over personal information despite giving actual control away. Social media providers attempt to elicit this perception of control by offering privacy settings and privacy policies. Study results underscore the effectiveness of this tactic, as highlighting privacy settings in social media has been found to induce higher control perceptions among adolescents (Zarouali et al., 2018). Thus, although social media users mostly lack actual control, they sometimes (naïvely) believe that they are still in control over personal information, and such control perceptions have been found to be positively related to people's trust (e.g., Krasnova et al., 2010; Meier et al., 2021; Taddei & Contena, 2013). This indicates that perceiving control over information may – like trust – contribute to a feeling of privacy (see Meier et al., 2020). This could be one explanation for the so-called "control paradox," which describes that persons who perceive having control over their information more openly disclose personal information (Brandimarte et al., 2013). In sum, the (naïve) perception to be in control over personal information can be accompanied by trust, but trust can also bypass a lack of perceived control which should in both cases result in a feeling of privacy and increased disclosure of personal information. Hence, trust and accompanying control perceptions may be dissociated from actual situations which could create illusionary perceptions of online privacy.

Trust and the Privacy Calculus

Second, trust plays a role in the *privacy calculus* which describes that people integrate the positive aspects of self-disclosure (i.e., perceived benefits) and the negative aspects (i.e., privacy risks) into their self-disclosure decisions (Culnan & Armstrong, 1999; see chapter 7 by Dienlin on privacy calculus theory). In this regard, several studies found negative correlations between trust and privacy risk perceptions, as well as positive correlations between trust and various anticipated benefits of self-disclosure (e.g., Bol et al., 2018; Krasnova et al., 2010; Meier et al., 2021). This effect of trust has also recently been found concerning the adoption of a COVID-19 contact tracing app: While trusting the government and app providers that no personal data will be collected by the app was not directly related to adopting the app, trust was negatively related to privacy concerns and positively to perceived benefits (Meier et al., 2022). Thus, it can be suggested that trust can change the anticipation of positive and negative consequences of self-disclosure (and other online privacy behaviors) depending on the level and quality of trust. For instance, in environments of high trust, positive aspects of self-disclosure could be more prominent and the negative aspects become less prominent. Hence, trust can mitigate one's perception and awareness of privacy risk or privacy concerns and potentially raise the perception of benefits. In this respect, trust has also been found to mediate or moderate the relationship between perceived privacy costs (e.g., privacy concerns) and privacy behaviors (e.g., self-disclosure). As such, trust can help explain why privacy cost perceptions do sometimes not predict online behaviors. For example, research has shown that trust mediates the relationship between privacy concerns and online self-disclosure (e.g., Metzger, 2004), but may also moderate the relationship between privacy concerns and self-disclosure, such that privacy risks or concerns have a negligible impact on self-disclosure in high-trust environments (Joinson et al., 2010). Importantly, the relationships between trust and risk do not imply causality but are inherently reciprocal. Hence, a person who has high trust may underestimate existing privacy threats, but someone who has a realistic awareness of high privacy levels may also develop higher levels of trust.

Trust and Social Contract Theory

Third, a less explored function of trust is the role of trust in establishing an implied *social contract* with other social media users specifically and with social media platforms more broadly. Social contract theory implies that people have certain expectations when they share personal information online, which represent a hypothetical social contract (see Fogel & Nehmad, 2009; Kruikemeier et al., 2020). For example, when people share personal information by updating their profile description, they expect key players in the social media environment (e.g., the social media provider) to respectfully engage with this information (e.g., by not sharing this information with third companies). These considerations also correspond to two basic tenets of the communication privacy management theory: Co-ownership of information and shared rules of information management (Petronio, 2002). This requires trust in the co-owner(s) of information not to violate the shared rules and unexpectedly share personal information with unintended parties. Although social contract theory does not provide any testable hypotheses, trust can be operationalized as an indication of perceiving a social contract, with higher levels of trust being an indication of perceiving the social contract as more reliable. In this regard, Kruikemeier and colleagues (2020) found five distinct user types based on differences regarding social contract variables among them trust. They showed that some user groups (characterized by high privacy concerns, high privacy risk perceptions, and low trust) seem to perceive social contracts with online businesses as less reliable. This is in line with findings of Fogel and Nehmad (2009) who concluded that a lack of trust towards an SNS indicates that users think that their social contract has been breached. Such a breach of a social contract can be perceived by the user when social media companies use personal data in a way that is experienced as unfair, for example, when social media companies intend to use users' personal data for personalized advertisements but fail to expose users to relevant advertisements (Van den Broeck et al., 2020). In sum, trust can be viewed as a central indicator of the quality of an implied social contract between users and social media platform providers.

Levels of Trust

Horizontal and Vertical Trust

When people share personal information on social media, information can be visible to other users in one's network, both to known and unknown ones. At a more abstract level, the same personal information that one shares also flows from users to some superordinate entities like the social network provider or a third party. These flows of information exchange can be categorized into two levels: The *horizontal* level (i.e., users share information with other users) and the *vertical* level (i.e., users share information with entities or entities automatically access information from users) (Bazarova & Masur, 2020). Disclosure on the vertical level can either be intended and active (e.g., when one discloses data in a registration process) or unintended and passive (e.g., when data is being automatically tracked) (see Bräunlich et al., 2021). Because the awareness of those two separate levels of information flow is likely to affect people's privacy perceptions differently, it is logical to also divide people's trust into a horizontal and a vertical level. Although we are not aware of others having explicitly spoken of horizontal and vertical trust, researchers have investigated trust towards different types of parties on social media. For instance, a study by Krasnova and colleagues (2010) examined both SNS users' trust in other SNS members (which could refer to the horizontal dimension of trust) and their trust towards the SNS provider (which could refer to the vertical dimension of trust). The results indicated that only participants' trust towards the SNS provider but not their trust towards the other users was negatively related to the perception of privacy risks. The authors argue that this could be due to higher privacy concerns towards the SNS provider than towards other users (see Krasnova et al., 2010). However, since perceived privacy risks were measured with a general questionnaire that did not distinguish between risks stemming from the SNS provider or from other users, there is a need to further investigate these relationships. Another study found evidence that vertical (i.e., trust in the social medium) and horizontal (i.e., trust in its users) trust positively affect each other (Sharif et al., 2021), which could point to difficulties users have in distinguishing the two levels. More systematic research on horizontal and vertical trust is necessary to make any further evaluations.

Legal Trust

In addition to the horizontal and vertical levels of trust, *legal trust* could form another dimension that users (implicitly) consider when engaging in online interactions through social media. For example, a lack of either horizontal or vertical trust (e.g., not trusting social media providers) could be bypassed by trust towards supervisory entities, such as trust in the state or legal basis. This means that when someone does not believe in the goodwill of a social media provider, he or she can still believe that the law will limit the provider's possibilities for harmful actions. Therefore, legal trust could also be viewed as an expansion of the vertical privacy and trust levels as it could decrease the perceived likelihood to experience vertical privacy threats. The interdisciplinary privacy and communication model (Bräunlich et al., 2021) proposes that when users do not have any control over their data, they can either trust the data collecting parties or – in case they do not trust these other parties – they can delegate control to a third party (e.g., the state) that is made responsible for data protection (Bräunlich et al., 2021). This strengthens the point that people can have legal trust, that is, trust towards given legal privacy frameworks to limit and regulate social media providers and third parties in their data collection and processing techniques and towards the state enforcing these laws. In his privacy-as-trust approach, Waldman (2018) proposes a closer link between people's social desires, their vulnerabilities, and the law. He argues that the law must provide the necessary framework in which spheres of trust and privacy can be built (Waldman, 2018). Current laws and regulations, however, do not seem to provide such frameworks, as they leave too much room for companies' and states' surveillance mechanisms, with users seemingly aware of that fact (e.g., people's trust towards Facebook has not changed after the implementation of the General Data Protection Regulation in the European Union, one of the strictest privacy regulations worldwide; see Bauer et al., 2021). Dark patterns ("design tricks platforms use to manipulate users"; Waldman, 2020, p. 105) undermine and exploit trust towards companies and legal regulations as they aim to manipulate users to give up huge parts of their personal information (see Waldman, 2020). Yet, Turow and Hennessy (2007) found a positive relation between people's trust in websites and their belief that potential laws and regulations are effective in restricting websites. In other words, persons who trust laws and regulations may also be more trusting towards web companies. This form of trust may not be based on facts but instead on naïve thinking. Currently, it remains rather speculative how the perception of, and trust towards, privacy regulations affect privacy perceptions and behaviors in the context of social media. Thus, there is a need for research that examines users' perceptions of current legal regulations (e.g., whether they align with the actual law) and their legal trust.

Trust in Collective Privacy

Finally, there is one specific form of trust that can be relied on even when people do not have horizontal, vertical, or legal trust. This form of trust is called *trust in collective privacy* (Moll & Pieschl, 2016). Trust in collective privacy has been described as people's naïve assumption that because massive amounts of personal information are available, one can still have privacy since other users are not capable of processing all the information and do not see every information and that institutions cannot process all the collected data (see Moll et al., 2014; Moll & Pieschl, 2016). Thus, trust in collective privacy is not an expectation about another party's good intention but rather the expectation that most others will not even be able to misuse one's personal data. The idea of collective privacy could be compared to a shoal of fish (i.e., many fish swimming together) where the mere quantity of others protects the individual and provides a feeling of anonymity. However, Moll and Pieschl (2016) point to the fallacies of this specific form of trust: First, just because other users are less likely to see one individual's information, potential privacy violations are still possible. Second, vertical privacy risks are not minimized by the quantity of information because companies can make use of big data techniques such as algorithms. Therefore, trust in collective privacy seems to be an expansion of the horizontal privacy and trust levels because vertical events are ignored. In the end, it seems that trust in collective privacy is rather a maladaptation and pitfall for individuals because this naïve belief can result in a greater vulnerability towards privacy threats in social media and non-management of one's personal information. It is important to note that trust in collective privacy as put forth by Moll and colleagues (2014) should not be confused with notions of group privacy and collaborative privacy management (see chapter 5 by Petro & Metzger on group privacy), as the former is more about how individuals feel about their own privacy within the context of a group, whereas the latter is more about how individuals feel about the privacy of their group and the control they have over the group's identity.

Future Perspectives

In past studies, subjective online privacy perceptions were often implicitly addressed, but research has just started to explicitly turn towards people's feelings of privacy when they are online (e.g., on social media; see Masur, 2018; Meier et al., 2020; Teutsch et al., 2018; Trepte, 2021). People are assumed to form a perception of current privacy levels in every situation, both online and offline, based on the respective context and situational cues (Dienlin, 2014). These privacy perceptions can be described as situational experiences and evaluations of current online privacy levels that are deeply intertwined with trust (Meier et al., 2020; Teutsch et al., 2018). Both qualitative (Teutsch et al., 2018) and quantitative (Meier et al., 2020) work found to support that trust and situational online privacy perceptions go hand in hand and it seems that trust is even a facet of that perception. Thus, among other things, future research could examine how exactly these subjective privacy perceptions arise and whether they are the result or precursor of trust or whether they arise simultaneously. Moreover, it should be investigated in more detail how perceptions of privacy online (including trust) are triggered and how they relate to people's privacy behaviors.

Other current streams of research on trust, privacy, and social media point to a further need for empirical work concerning algorithmic decisions that personalize content, for instance, in the news feed. Here, first empirical evidence indicates that awareness about personalized content can decrease people's trust towards websites (Bol et al., 2018) and that persons who have high trust might be more susceptible to exploitation by advertisers (Bol et al., 2020). As some parties on the internet may try to take advantage of users' increased vulnerability due to their trusting attitudes, future research could study how perceptions of personalization undermine trust and particularly affect vulnerable groups. Moreover, as a current theoretical contribution points to the involvement of trust in people's privacy perceptions of political microtargeting on social media (Schäwel et al., 2021), future empirical studies could focus on trust and privacy as involved in the perception of political microtargeted content and potential effects on either acceptance or avoidance of such content (see chapter 23 by Dobber on behavioral targeting and privacy). As such, policy recommendations could be formed based on such insights with the aim to better protect users (and especially vulnerable groups) from (micro-) targeted content.

In recent theorizing and empirical work, a new psychological variable called privacy cynicism has emerged (see chapter 13 by Ranzini, Lutz, & Hoffmann on privacy cynicism). This psychological state can result from a constant feeling of having no or only little privacy online and is associated with resignation or mistrust, the latter being defined as a "lack of faith in Internet companies" (Lutz et al., 2020, p. 1182). Therefore, future studies could examine the similarities and differences of trust and mistrust involved in communication processes in social media. Because most studies focused on trust and privacy, it could be fruitful to further investigate how mistrust is related to people's privacy perceptions and behaviors. This research demand arises since trust and mistrust are not necessarily the same variable that shares one continuum but rather two distinct variables with different antecedents and outcomes (Luhmann, 1979).

Finally, there appears to be a need for further research concerning horizontal, vertical, legal, and collective trust. One possibility would be studying the similarities and differences regarding different privacy perceptions and behaviors. Moreover, the respective privacy perceptions and behaviors should also be carefully divided into the respective dimensions (e.g., when investigating horizontal trust, privacy risks and self-disclosure should also be assessed on the horizontal dimension).

References

Bauer, P. C., Gerdon, F., Keusch, F., Kreuter, F., & Vannette, D. (2021). Did the GDPR increase trust in data collectors? Evidence from observational and experimental data. *Information, Communication & Society*. https://doi.org/10.1080/1369118X.2021.1927138

Bazarova, N. N., & Masur, P. K. (2020). Towards an integration of individualistic, networked, and institutional approaches to online disclosure and privacy in a networked ecology. *Current Opinion in Psychology*, *36*, 118–123. https://doi.org/10.1016/j.copsyc.2020.05.004

Benlian, A., & Hess, T. (2011). The signaling role of IT features in influencing trust and participation in online communities. *International Journal of Electronic Commerce*, *15*(4), 7–56. https://doi.org/10.2753/JEC1086-4415150401

Bhattacharya, R., Devinney, T. M., & Pillutla, M. M. (1998). A formal model of trust based on outcomes. *Academy of Management Review*, *23*(3), 459–472. https://doi.org/10.5465/amr.1998.926621

Bol, N., Dienlin, T., Kruikemeier, S., Sax, M., Boerman, S. C., Strycharz, J., Helberger, N., & de Vreese, C. H. (2018). Understanding the effects of personalization as a privacy calculus: Analyzing self-disclosure across health, news, and commerce contexts. *Journal of Computer-Mediated Communication*, *23*(6), 370–388. https://doi.org/10.1093/jcmc/zmy020

Bol, N., Strycharz, J., Helberger, N., van de Velde, B., & de Vreese, C. H. (2020). Vulnerability in a tracked society: Combining tracking and survey data to understand who gets targeted with what content. *New Media & Society*, *22*(11), 1996–2017. https://doi.org/10.1177/1461444820924631

Brandimarte, L., Acquisti, A., & Loewenstein, G. (2013). Misplaced confidences: Privacy and the control paradox. *Social Psychological and Personality Science*, *4*(3), 340–347. https://doi.org/10.1177/1948550612455931

Bräunlich, K., Dienlin, T., Eichenhofer, J., Helm, P., Trepte, S., Grimm, R., Seubert, S., & Gusy, C. (2021). Linking loose ends: An interdisciplinary privacy and communication model. *New Media & Society*, *23*(6), 1443–1464. https://doi.org/10.1177/1461444820905045

Culnan, M. J., & Armstrong, P. K. (1999). Information privacy concerns, procedural fairness, and impersonal trust: An empirical investigation. *Organization Science*, *10*(1), 104–115. https://doi.org/10.1287/orsc.10.1.104

Dienlin, T. (2014). The privacy process model. In S. Garnett, S. Halft, M. Herz, & J.-M. Mönig (Eds.), *Medien und Privatheit* (pp. 105–122). Stutz.

Dienlin, T., & Metzger, M. J. (2016). An extended privacy calculus model for SNSs: Analyzing self-disclosure and self-withdrawal in a representative US sample. *Journal of Computer-Mediated Communication, 21*(5), 368–383. https://doi.org/10.1111/jcc4.12163

Fogel, J., & Nehmad, E. (2009). Internet social network communities: Risk taking, trust, and privacy concerns. *Computers in Human Behavior, 25*(1), 153–160. https://doi.org/10.1016/j.chb.2008.08.006

Heath, R. L., & Bryant, J. (2013). *Human communication theory and research: Concepts, contexts, and challenges*. Routledge Taylor & Francis Group.

Joinson, A. N., Reips, U. D., Buchanan, T., & Schofield, C. B. P. (2010). Privacy, trust, and self-disclosure online. *Human–Computer Interaction, 25*(1), 1–24. https://doi.org/10.1080/07370020903586662

Jörling, M., Eitze, S., Schmid, P., Betsch, C., Allen, J., & Böhm, R. (2022). To disclose or not to disclose? Factors related to the willingness to disclose information to a COVID-19 tracing app. *Information, Communication & Society*. https://doi.org/10.1080/1369118X.2022.2050418

Jourard, S. M. (1964). *The transparent self*. Van Nostrand.

Krasnova, H., Spiekermann, S., Koroleva, K., & Hildebrand, T. (2010). Online social networks: Why we disclose. *Journal of Information Technology, 25*(2), 109–125. https://doi.org/10.1057%2Fjit.2010.6

Kruikemeier, S., Boerman, S. C., & Bol, N. (2020). Breaching the contract? Using social contract theory to explain individuals' online behavior to safeguard privacy. *Media Psychology, 23*(2), 269–292. https://doi.org/10.1080/15213269.2019.1598434

Luhmann, N. (1979). *Trust and power*. Wiley.

Lutz, C., Hoffmann, C. P., & Ranzini, G. (2020). Data capitalism and the user: An exploration of privacy cynicism in Germany. *New Media & Society, 22*(7), 1168–1187. https://doi.org/10.1177/1461444820912544

Masur, P. K. (2018). *Situational privacy and self-disclosure: Communication processes in online environments*. Springer. https://doi.org/10.1007/978-3-319-78884-5

Masur, P. K., & Scharkow, M. (2016). Disclosure management on social network sites: Individual privacy perceptions and user-directed privacy strategies. *Social Media + Society, 2*(1), 1–13. https://doi.org/10.1177/2056305116634368

Mayer, R. C., Davis, J. H., & Schoorman, F. D. (1995). An integrative model of organizational trust. *Academy of Management Review, 20*(3), 709–734. https://doi.org/10.5465/amr.1995.9508080335

Meier, Y., Meinert, J., & Krämer, N. C. (2022). One-time decision or continual adjustment? A longitudinal study of the within-person privacy calculus among users and non-users of a COVID-19 contact tracing app. *Media Psychology*. https://doi.org/10.1080/15213269.2022.2092750

Meier, Y., Schäwel, J., & Krämer, N. C. (2020). The shorter the better? Effects of privacy policy length on online privacy decision-making. *Media and Communication, 8*(2), 291–301. https://doi.org/10.17645/mac.v8i2.2846

Meier, Y., Schäwel, J., & Krämer, N. C. (2021). Between protection and disclosure: Applying the privacy calculus to investigate the intended use of privacy-protecting tools and self-disclosure on different websites. *SCM Studies in Communication and Media, 10*(3), 283–306. https://doi.org/10.5771/2192-4007-2021-3-283

Metzger, M. J. (2004). Privacy, trust, and disclosure: Exploring barriers to electronic commerce. *Journal of Computer-Mediated Communication, 9*(4), Article JCMC942. https://doi.org/10.1111/j.1083-6101.2004.tb00292.x

Moll, R., & Pieschl, S. (2016). Expecting collective privacy: A new perspective on trust in online communication. In B. Blöbaum (Ed.), *Trust and communication in a digitized world* (pp. 239–251). Springer. https://doi.org/10.1007/978-3-319-28059-2_14

Moll, R., Pieschl, S., & Bromme, R. (2014). Trust into collective privacy? The role of subjective theories for self-disclosure in online communication. *Societies, 4*(4), 770–784. https://doi.org/10.3390/soc4040770

Nissenbaum, H. (2010). *Privacy in context: Technology, policy, and the integrity of social life*. Stanford University Press.

Petronio, S. (2002). *Boundaries of privacy: Dialectics of disclosure*. Suny Press.

Saeri, A. K., Ogilvie, C., La Macchia, S. T., Smith, J. R., & Louis, W. R. (2014). Predicting Facebook users' online privacy protection: Risk, trust, norm focus theory, and the theory of planned behavior. *The Journal of Social Psychology, 154*(4), 352–369. https://doi.org/10.1080/00224545.2014.914881

Schäwel, J., Frener, R., & Trepte, S. (2021). Political microtargeting and online privacy: A theoretical approach to understanding users' privacy behaviors. *Media and Communication, 9*(4), 158–169. https://doi.org/10.17645/mac.v9i4.4085

Sharif, A., Soroya, S. H., Ahmad, S., & Mahmood, K. (2021). Antecedents of self-disclosure on social networking sites (SNSs): A study of Facebook users. *Sustainability, 13*(3), Article 1220. https://doi.org/10.3390/su13031220

Taddei, S., & Contena, B. (2013). Privacy, trust and control: Which relationships with online self-disclosure? *Computers in Human Behavior*, *29*(3), 821–826. https://doi.org/10.1016/j.chb.2012.11.022

Teutsch, D., Masur, P. K., & Trepte, S. (2018). Privacy in mediated and nonmediated interpersonal communication: How subjective concepts and situational perceptions influence behaviors. *Social Media + Society*, *4*(2), 1–14. https://doi.org/10.1177/2056305118767134

Trepte, S. (2021). The social media privacy model: Privacy and communication in the light of social media affordances. *Communication Theory*, *31*(4), 549–570. https://doi.org/10.1093/ct/qtz035

Turow, J., & Hennessy, M. (2007). Internet privacy and institutional trust: Insights from a national survey. *New Media & Society*, *9*(2), 300–318. https://doi.org/10.1177/1461444807072219

Utz, S., & Krämer, N. C. (2009). The privacy paradox on social network sites revisited: The role of individual characteristics and group norms. *Cyberpsychology: Journal of Psychosocial Research on Cyberspace*, *3*(2), Article 2. https://cyberpsychology.eu/article/view/4223/3265

Van den Broeck, E., Poels, K., & Walrave, M. (2020). How do users evaluate personalized Facebook advertising? An analysis of consumer-and advertiser controlled factors. *Qualitative Market Research*, *23*(2), 309–327. https://doi.org/10.1108/QMR-10-2018-0125

Waldman, A. E. (2018). *Privacy as trust: Information privacy for an information age*. Cambridge University Press. https://doi.org/10.1017/9781316888667

Waldman, A. E. (2020). Cognitive biases, dark patterns, and the 'privacy paradox'. *Current Opinion in Psychology*, *31*, 105–109. https://doi.org/10.1016/j.copsyc.2019.08.025

Westin, A. F. (1967). *Privacy and freedom*. Atheneum Books.

Wheeless, L. R., & Grotz, J. (1977). The measurement of trust and its relationship to self-disclosure. *Human Communication Research*, *3*(3), 250–257. https://doi.org/10.1111/j.1468-2958.1977.tb00523.x

Zarouali, B., Poels, K., Ponnet, K., & Walrave, M. (2018). Everything under control? Privacy control salience influences both critical processing and perceived persuasiveness of targeted advertising among adolescents. *Cyberpsychology: Journal of Psychosocial Research and Cyberspace*, *12*(1), Article 5. https://doi.org/10.5817/CP2018-1-5

11

CHALLENGES IN STUDYING SOCIAL MEDIA PRIVACY LITERACY

Philipp K. Masur[1], *Thilo Hagendorff*[2], *and Sabine Trepte*[3]

[1]VRIJE UNIVERSITEIT AMSTERDAM, THE NETHERLANDS
[2]UNIVERSITY OF TUEBINGEN, GERMANY
[3]UNIVERSITY OF HOHENHEIM, GERMANY

Introduction

In any discussion about online privacy, people will put forth that we would simply need to foster sufficient privacy literacy among Internet users to ensure an appropriate level of protection and self-determination. Almost like a mantra, future perspectives in privacy-related academic articles recommend increasing privacy-related awareness, knowledge, and skills to address whatever privacy threat they outlined. It almost seems that sufficiently high online privacy literacy would be the ultimate solution, promising to solve all problems – from preventing privacy violations by other users to countering the power imbalance between users and providers of privacy-invasive technologies. Therefore, it is perhaps no surprise that the previously termed "knowledge gap hypothesis," that Internet users simply lack the knowledge and skills to protect their privacy (Trepte et al., 2015), can be found in almost every area of privacy research. Many chapters in this volume support this notion. For example, it "solves" the privacy paradox by suggesting that people's concerns do not translate into privacy protection behavior because they simply do not know how to do so. It respectively "explains" the emergence of privacy cynicism because unawareness of data and privacy protection strategies or alternative, privacy-friendly services seems to give rise to the feeling that any attempt to protect one's privacy is futile (see chapter 13 by Ranzini et al. on privacy cynicism). It likewise "provides" an explanation for why people value benefits over risks in disclosure decision processes (see chapter 7 by Dienlin on the privacy calculus) or fall prone to misleading heuristics and biases (see chapter 8 by Liao et al. on heuristics and privacy). In fact, a common recommendation by academics and policy makers is to make people more literate. After all, investing in education never sounds wrong politically. Yet, as we will discuss later, the immediate appeal of educating the people shifts the responsibility to the individual who may thereby have to deal with a considerable burden, rather than experience true empowerment.

In this chapter, we focus on *social media* privacy literacy specifically as the question of whether people lack knowledge and skills to protect their privacy is particularly often posed in the context of social media. And indeed, successfully managing different information contexts and identities on such platforms without causing a "context collapse" (Nissenbaum, 2010; Vitak, 2012) has become quite difficult. To control personal information, audiences, and communications channels in

DOI: 10.4324/9781003244677-13

accordance with one's privacy needs requires deep familiarity with the architecture and settings of the respective social media platform, but also how information flows both horizontally (between users) and vertically (between users and platform providers; Bazarova & Masur, 2020). Privacy turbulence resulting from a lack of social media privacy literacy particularly can result in feelings of embarrassment, trouble at work or school, relationship problems, etc. Hence, the ability to self-monitor one's online behavior has become increasingly important for social media users.

We believe that the study of (social media) privacy literacy is worthwhile if not pivotal to advance privacy and social media research at this point in time. But we also acknowledge that fostering privacy literacy is only one aspect of a necessarily multi-layered response to the increasing privacy threats that must be concerted with legal regulation and data protection (Hagendorff, 2018). In this chapter, we provide an overview of the conceptual, theoretical, and empirical frameworks of online privacy literacy and how it is applied to the context of social media. We discuss their strengths and weaknesses, review empirical evidence for the knowledge gap hypothesis, and outline the potential of educational interventions to foster social media privacy literacy. We close with what we consider the most pressing avenues for future research.

From Online Privacy Literacy to Social Media Privacy Literacy

Any type of literacy can be traced back to the 1970s, during which the term "literacy" (sometimes also "competence"), first introduced in linguistics, was established and applied to developmental and social theories (Sutter & Charlton, 2002). Chomsky (1976) originally differentiated competence (knowledge about a language and its rules) from performance (the actual use of language in concrete situations) and thereby started a long and on-going tradition of investigating literacies. Being *literate* means having the necessary knowledge, abilities, and skills as well as the motivational, volitional, and social willingness to solve certain problems (cf. Weinert, 2003). Such a broad definition implies that for every problem (from all-encompassing to microscopic specific), we could technically define a respective set of knowledge, skills, and abilities, which could (and in part has led) to a conceptual jungle. For the ability to speak a language, it may be possible to clearly identify the relevant rules that need to be known (although even this is disputed). With regard to privacy literacy, one cannot help but feel a little uneasy that anything from abstract meta-competencies such as "being able to think critically" to concrete and specific skills such as "being able to limit access to the self by setting the visibility of Facebook posts to only close friends" could be justified as a valid dimension.

What exactly encompasses online privacy literacy thus becomes a normative question. Any proposal for an online privacy literacy model takes a stance on what *should* be known and what abilities *should* be possessed (cf. Groeben, 2002). Relevant knowledge, abilities, and skills are thereby often motivated by their proposed potential to lead to a certain behavior (e.g., more data protection, less disclosure, more use of privacy settings ...). From our point of view, both abstract definitions that outline important meta-competencies (e.g., "being able to critically reflect") as well as more specific definitions that outline the respective sets of knowledge, skills, and abilities for certain target groups, platforms, services, and contexts (e.g., "ability to use Facebook friend's lists feature to limit access to posts") have merit and help to gain a deeper understanding of privacy literacy overall.

Online Privacy Literacy

In light of this, online (and, in turn, social media) privacy literacy must be seen within the tradition of media literacy and computer literacy concepts that originated as a response to the increasing mediatization and digitalization of society. Early media literacy concepts mostly embodied a so-called protectionist approach and focussed on expanding awareness of risks and providing means and ways to protect oneself against potentially negative outcomes of media use (cf. Potter, 2010). Early online privacy literacy research similarly was a response to emerging risks of privacy violations in the context of digital technologies. The first studies hence investigated relationships between awareness of privacy-invasive practices by online service providers as well as knowledge about technical aspects of data protection and the implementation of actual data protection behavior (e.g., Hoofnagle et al., 2010, Park, 2013, Turow, 2003). With regard to its technical dimension, privacy literacy is thereby akin to computer literacy, comprising mostly the knowledge to understand and the abilities to appropriately control user interfaces to manage privacy.

Yet, as media scholars stressed the balance between protection and empowerment in conceptualizing media literacy (e.g., Baacke, 1996, Groeben, 2002b; Hobbs, 2010), privacy scholars similarly reframed privacy literacy to encompass users' ability to not just protect themselves, but also actively and meaningfully use online services in alignment with their privacy needs. Trepte et al. (2015) expanded original models by distinguishing factual knowledge about technical, economic, and legal aspects of privacy and data protection from procedural knowledge about how to implement data protection strategies.

Building on this multi-dimensional model, Masur (2020) provided an Extended Model of Online Privacy Literacy that includes a) factual privacy knowledge, b) privacy-related reflection abilities, c) privacy and data protection skills, and d) critical privacy literacy. This broader conceptualization acknowledges that users need knowledge and awareness about data collection practices, data protection regulations, technical aspects related to information flow as well as awareness of horizontal privacy dynamics on different online platforms, but further highlights the need for abilities and skills that translate this abstract knowledge into actual behavior that reflects their individual needs. Next to factual knowledge, it first proposes privacy-related reflection abilities that allow users to identify specific risks (in Altman's (1975) terms: Assessing the actual level of privacy) in different online environments and assess them in light of their own individual privacy needs (Altman: Comparing the actual with their desired level of privacy). Based on this constant comparison, people then, secondly, should be able to reflect on whether their behavior contributes to such a misbalance.

Based on risk awareness and reflection, users thirdly need specific skills to manage information flows. Information management, then, can be applied in several ways. It comprises data parsimony, using encryption techniques, cutting interconnections between computers, digital rights managements, using firewalls, password prompts, and the like. These measures can take place at the front- or backend of digital platforms and services. Ultimately, privacy protection strategies also include choosing more privacy-friendly platforms over privacy-intrusive ones.

Whereas the previous three dimensions shall empower users to learn and possess a range of competencies and abilities to use and share personal information in a way that protects their privacy against horizontal or vertical intrusions, a fourth dimension proposed by Masur (2020), called critical privacy literacy, acknowledges that self-data protection against some vertical privacy intrusions may be futile. In fact, despite sufficient knowledge about privacy-invasive practices, the reflection of one's behavior, and skills to protect one's privacy, the means to actually minimize the power of online service providers to harness an individual's data is severely limited. Critical privacy literacy refers to the "ability to criticize, question, and challenge existing assumptions about the social, economic, and institutional practices that have led to a status quo in which the individual has to defend his or her freedom against unequally more powerful economic and institutional influences" (Masur, 2020, p. 261). Such a type of literacy, which was already introduced to broader concepts of media literacy concepts some decades ago (e.g., Baacke, 1996; Groeben, 2002b), can thus be regarded as a fundamental requirement for actualizing the democratic potential of individuals to shape and transform the social conditions of their society (cf. similarly expressed for critical media literacy by Kellner & Share, 2005).

Social Media Privacy Literacy

Social media privacy literacy is best understood as online privacy literacy applied to the specific context of social media. To our knowledge, most studies that investigate privacy literacy in the context of social media do not explicitly define social media privacy literacy. Instead, drawing from the extended literature on online privacy literacy as discussed above, they apply relevant competencies from existing online privacy literacy models to the context of social media (e.g., Bartsch & Dienlin, 2016; Choi, 2022). This application process can be understood by looking at items that these scholars used to assess social media-specific privacy literacy. For example, Bartsch and Dienlin (2016) used items such as "I know how to restrict access to my postings." Choi 2022) similarly employed items such as "I have the knowledge necessary to use privacy features to regulate information on Facebook." Such operationalizations are akin to the procedural skills dimensions included by Trepte et al. (2015) or Masur (2020), but apply them specifically to the privacy settings available on Facebook. Unfortunately, studies in this area hardly focus on other than the procedural skill dimensions of overall privacy literacy.

That said, there is also growing literature on social media literacy (basically the more general concept of media literacy applied to the context of social media), which often acknowledges privacy as a particular domain relevant to successfully navigating and using such platforms (e.g., Livingstone, 2014; Purington et al., 2022). Here, we again see scholars defining core competencies of (social media) media literacy (e.g., access, evaluate, reflect, generate …) as an umbrella that, in turn, is applied to specific domains (such as, e.g., privacy, advertising, news, phishing, …). For example, Purington et al. (2022) define social media literacy as "the ability to 1) find and access social media platforms and use them and their respective options and channels skillfully, 2) critically evaluate social media content and its potential consequences, 3) generate creative social media content with an awareness of the specific audience, 4) reflect on one's own behavior, apply social responsibility, and adequately manage one's affective responses, and 5) develop and perpetuate prosocial behavioral norms and exhibit digital citizenship" (p. 6). The authors then argue that although meaningful in getting an understanding of what social media literacy entails, these five meta-competencies need to be applied to different domains (including privacy) to make them amenable to empirical investigation. For example, in their scale development process, they narrow these rather abstract dimensions down to specific social media use situations, in which privacy may be threatened or negotiated.

As outlined earlier, media literacy concepts have long included the notion that it should empower users and help them serve their needs. Whereas protection clearly addresses the question of "protection *from* what?", empowerment refers to the question "empowerment *for* what?". Whereas the first question could be deemed sufficiently answered in previous research, we would like to add some reflections on the latter. Inspired by Groeben's (2002b), we suggest that literacy also caters to the experiences of positive media uses and effects. Social media privacy literacy thus would mean that users choose privacy settings and manage their connections and content in a way that it empowers them for enjoyment and other more fundamental needs. Privacy, in fact, can be seen as a condition that serves the fulfillment of fundamental needs (Masur, 2018). Pedersen (1997), for example, proposed rejuvenation, contemplation, and creativity as psychological functions of privacy. Taken together with Groeben's idea on literacy, we conclude that social media literacy also refers to the ability to create private (or at least contextually appropriately protected) spaces that empower users for rejuvenation, contemplation, enjoyment, and creativity. Under the cloak of anonymity, users may be empowered for rejuvenation by reading and browsing through content they like without fearing repercussion. Protected against vertical intrusions, they may be empowered for contemplation by dreaming themselves into the world of fantasy catered by other users and storytellers. Or in some online spaces (such as friend groups, or public spaces that rely on pseudonyms), they may creatively try out new activities or identities. In sum, social media privacy literacy also means finding the right balance between withdrawal and participation to find the appropriate level of access that still allows one to benefit from the many offers that social media offers.

We believe that the manifold approaches to conceptualizing online privacy literacy and social media privacy literacy, respectively, are a testament to a vibrant research community. Reconciling different definitions and concepts may be a noble endeavor, but ultimately will fail as an all-encompassing concept will necessarily always be too abstract to inform concrete intervention (see chapter 1 in this handbook on defining privacy by Trepte and Masur). A platform- or even context-specific concept, in contrast, may always be too specific to allow for generalizations beyond their specifically outlined circumstances. With that said, we want to contribute to the literature by offering dynamic definition of social media privacy literacy that is based on the research discussed above (particularly, Masur, 2020, Park, 2013; Trepte et al., 2015). We thereby acknowledge that such a literacy has to take both vertical (information flow between users and the provider) and horizontal (information flow between users) privacy issues into account.

From this point of view, social media privacy literacy can be grasped by four meta-competencies that further include several subdimensions.

1. Factual knowledge (a) on a vertical level about economic interests and data collection, analysis, and sharing practices of social media providers and (b) on a horizontal level about information flow, communication practices, and social dynamics between users of the social media platform.
2. Privacy-related reflection ability includes (a) the ability to identify privacy risks, turbulence, and violations during social media use, (b) the ability to reflect one's privacy needs in such situations, and (c) the ability to evaluate one's own posting and communication behavior as well as (d) use of privacy-preserving strategies to create an appropriate balance between protection and empowerment, or, in other words, need satisfaction and risks. Privacy is not an end by itself, but only meaningful when it allows for more fundamental needs such as intimacy with other close people, relationship building, enjoyment, creativity, etc.
3. Procedural skills that include (a) the ability to evaluate social media platforms and, if necessary, choose more privacy-friendly alternatives, (b) knowledge about how to implement platform-specific privacy strategies and how to use their proprietary privacy settings, (c) the ability to monitor disclosure according to one's need (data parsimony), but also (d) the ability to use all of these skills in a contextually appropriate way that not only secludes them from social interaction, but rather creates spaces for sociality, connection, rejuvenation, contemplation, creativity, and overall enjoyment.
4. Critical privacy literacy includes the ability to question and criticize communication practices, social dynamics, the socio-technological architecture of social media, and both vertical and horizontal information flows that affect individuals' privacy and their ability to use social media in ways that benefit and empower them.

Depending on the type of research question, not all competencies and subdimensions may be equally important to assess. We nonetheless hope that this broad definition will provide nuance to the study of privacy in the context of social media. Yet, even if we settle on such a working definition, how can we empirically measure social media privacy literacy?

How to Measure Social Media Privacy Literacy?

Being able to (objectively) measure a person's social media privacy literacy is crucial for several reasons: First, it is needed to determine individuals' familiarity with privacy issues, assess general knowledge gaps, and evaluate the overall severity of missing literacy in a population. Second, it allows us to put the knowledge gap hypothesis under empirical scrutiny. Only by gaining a good understanding of people's literacy levels, we can investigate antecedents and outcomes and better understand the role of knowledge and skills in shaping users' online behavior. And finally, only by assessing literacy as an outcome, we can evaluate potential educational interventions.

Yet, measuring literacy is easier said than done. Whereas some dimensions of literacy such as *knowledge* may be assessed through traditional test formats, others such as *reflection abilities* can only be demonstrated and thus observed. This refers to a common problem of literacy in general: Instead of literacy itself, we can only observe the performance of literate behavior, from which we then conclude certain literacies (cf. Sutter & Charlton, 2002). It is thus perhaps hardly surprising that the measurement of online privacy literacy is often based on self-reports and thus remains entirely subjective and potentially biased (e.g., Choi, 2022; Masur, 2018). In an attempt to make the measurement of online privacy literacy more objective, some scholars created knowledge tests that consist of several true–false statements (e.g., Hoofnagle et al., 2010; Park, 2013). In such tests, participants read several statements (e.g., "Companies today have the ability to place an online advertisement that targets you based on information collected on your web-browsing behavior" – TRUE; Park, 2013) and had to decide whether it was true or false. Correct answers are then summed up as an index of literacy.

For their multi-dimensional model of privacy literacy, Masur and colleagues (Masur et al., 2017; Trepte et al., 2015) developed the online privacy literacy scale (OPLIS), which represents a comprehensive questionnaire to objectively assess factual and procedural knowledge in relation to online privacy and data protection. It represents a knowledge test that was validated in several studies and consists of 20 multiple-choice and true–false items (five per dimension) that assess people's knowledge about institutional practices, technical aspects, legal aspects, and data protection strategies (example item: "Companies combine users' data traces collected from different websites to create user profiles" – TRUE).[1] The final scale allows for investigating both individual dimensions as well as overall online privacy literacy and has since been used in several empirical studies.

Social media privacy literacy seems to be mostly assessed with short scales. Bartsch and Dienlin (2016), for example, used six self-report items (e.g., "I know how to delete or deactivate my account"). Cho (2022) used two similar items (e.g., "I have the knowledge necessary to use privacy features to regulate information on Facebook"). Purington et al. (2022) developed 15 items to assess social media literacy in the domain of privacy.[2] Their instrument represents an objective knowledge test for youth populations (aged 9–13 years) in which participants have to answer questions in a multiple-choice format (e.g., "Why can it be a problem to share something personal on social media? A: Because things you share on social media can stay there forever (*true answer*), B: Because your parents might find out about it, C: Because social media is not for young people, D: It is not a problem. It is actually a lot of fun!").

In sum, the assessment of online privacy literacy has come a long way, yet only a few comprehensive and validated instruments exist. Furthermore, instruments for less knowledge-based dimensions are lacking. With regard to social media privacy literacy specifically, only a few ad-hoc scales exist that mostly rely on self-reported literacy.

Empirical Findings

Several empirical investigations have provided support for a positive link between online privacy literacy and the implementation of privacy behaviors. For example, based on a survey of 419 US-American Internet users, Park (2013) found that technical familiarity, awareness of institutional practices, and privacy policy understanding positively predicted both social (e.g., avoiding particular platforms, using pseudonyms, rectifying information) and technical protection behaviors (e.g., clearing browser history, using PET software). The effect sizes for these relationships were medium. Masur et al. (2017), based on a representative sample of 1,945 German Internet users, likewise found that higher online privacy literacy (i.e., more correct answers in their 20-item scale) positively predicted the use of active data protection strategies (e.g., using pseudonyms in emails or during registering for websites, using encryption or PET software …). Yet, higher literacy did not predict passive measures such as not using a certain service. Harborth and Pape (2020) similarly showed that higher literacy positively predicts using the anonymization service TOR while negatively predicting trust in online service providers. Masur (2018) also found that higher subjective privacy literacy positively predicted the use of end-to-end encryption and pseudonymization. Sindermann et al. (2021) provide further evidence for this relationship as they found a moderate positive relationship between online privacy literacy and various online privacy behaviors (including changing passwords, using TOR, not using services, etc.). A meta-analysis by Baruh et al. (2017) found, based on ten studies, that privacy literacy was moderately and positively related to the use of privacy protection measures (r = .29). Yet, the same meta-analysis also revealed no relationship between privacy literacy and information sharing (r = .04).

With regard to the predictive power of social media privacy literacy in particular, there are mostly cross-sectional survey studies that support a positive relationship between higher literacy and the implementation of privacy strategies on social media. For example, Bartsch and Dienlin (2016) surveyed 640 German Facebook users and found that higher privacy literacy positively predicts whether Facebook users restrict the visibility of information on their profile. Based on 1,572 German Internet users, Masur (2018) found that higher privacy literacy negatively predicted the use of privacy-invasive instant messenger (e.g., WhatsApp) and positively predicted the use of privacy-friendly alternatives (e.g., Threema). Yet, these results were less conclusive with regard to other platforms (e.g., Facebook, Instagram, etc.). In a survey of 689 US-American Internet Users, Epstein and Quinn (2020) found that higher privacy literacy positively predicted the implementation of horizontal strategies, which comprise the use of social media-specific privacy settings such as restricting access to photos, posts, or profile. Based on a survey with 322 participants from the US, Choi (2022) found that higher privacy literacy positively predicted whether social media users felt that they own the information they share on Facebook.

Longitudinal analyses of such relationships are generally rare. That said, Schäwel and colleagues (2021) found, based on a two-wave panel survey of 898 German Internet users, that higher online privacy literacy at T1 was positively related to more engagement in data protection behavior at T2 while controlling for the auto-regressive path of online privacy literacy at T1. Yet, this cross-lagged longitudinal effect was rather small. The between-person correlation at T1, however, aligned with prior research and resulted in a medium positive relationship between online privacy literacy and data protection behavior.

Whereas all of the above-mentioned studies speak for the effectiveness of online and social media privacy literacy in enabling more data protection behavior, explicit empirical tests of the knowledge gap hypothesis are rare. For example, only a few studies have explicitly investigated whether a lack of online privacy literacy could explain the privacy paradox (the often observed discrepancy between privacy concerns and privacy behaviors). Schubert et al. (2022), for example, conducted a study with 207 participants who answered a survey and provided the researchers with access to their Facebook profiles. The results show that privacy concerns and privacy literacy interacted in predicting how much data participants' shared on their profiles. For people with high literacy, the relationship between privacy concerns and data sharing becomes negative, thus not supporting the privacy paradox.

Despite these empirical findings, privacy-literacy-driven self-monitoring has its limits since one must assume that users do on many occasions deviate from rational information management (Spottswood & Hancock, 2017; Trepte et al., 2020). They effectively share personal information, are triggered by system-1 thinking or impulses, are subject to addictive routines that are intentionally fostered by the way social media platforms' user interfaces are designed, and many more (Gambino et al., 2016; see also chapter 8 by Liao, Sundar, and Rosson on online privacy cues and heuristics). Privacy literacy may also be a risk in itself. Users who deem themselves to possess comprehensive privacy literacy may feel that they have higher degrees of control over their personal information. Hence, they may be tempted to disclose all the more sensitive information compared to individuals who feel less literate and are thus more likely to have increased privacy concerns (Acquisti & Gross, 2006; Brandimarte et al. 2013). Ultimately, the feeling of safety that privacy literacy conveys may lead to a misplaced trust in mechanisms for information control.

In sum, the literature suggests a comparatively robust, positive relationship between online privacy literacy and various privacy protection strategies, both generally (e.g., while using the Internet) and specifically (while using social media). The effect sizes range from small (r = 0.10) to medium (r = 0.20). Longitudinal studies and experimental designs that could offer more insights into causal mechanisms are rare (for an exemption, see again Schäwel et al., 2021). Furthermore, many studies used either OPLIS or self-report measures to assess online privacy literacy. Studies with more comprehensive measures that also included reflection or critical evaluation skills hardly exist.

Educational Interventions to Foster Social Media Privacy Literacy

Somewhat independent of the academic research on the role of (social media) privacy literacy, there are more and more attempts to foster social media literacy in practical and educational contexts. These programs and resources almost always include modules specifically designed to foster privacy literacy, and often particular with regard to social media use. For example, social media platform providers such as Facebook[3] and Google[4] provide digital resources for educators, parents, or caregivers givers that aim to teach concepts of online privacy, setting use, and data parsimony. The teaching style is often a combination of gamification and quizzes. Educational institutions such as, e.g., common sense education in the United States,[5] Landesmedienanstalten in Germany,[6] federal ministries of education and research,[7] or the Netwerk Mediawijsheid in the Netherlands[8] to name just a few likewise offer lesson plans, educational tools, and resources. Also, profit-oriented social media literacy agencies develop and sell their programs in the form of road shows or apps to schools and other educational institutions. Finally, universities have started to turn to the public and offer courses, e.g., on the identification of fake news or deep fakes. Yet, most of these educational resources are not tested rigorously and their impact on knowledge, skills, and actual behavior remains unclear. An exception is Social Media Testdrive, an interactive learning platform that simulates social media use context for learning purposes and includes various modules that aim to foster privacy literacy on social media (including, e.g., "Accounts and Passwords," "Is It Private Information?", and "Shaping your Digital Footprint").[9]

Other studies suggest that critically engaging with social media, in general, may already foster higher privacy literacy. Higdon (2021) investigated the impact of a semester-long course called "Social Media, Social Change" at a Northern Californian University on social media attitudes and behavior. The course was implementing a critical pedagogy approach, relying on in-depth discussions of papers, news, books, and media content on the topic. Based on a qualitative assessment of participants' privacy concerns before and after the course, the author concluded that the course increased awareness and concerns about data collection practices of social media providers. Similarly, Gruzd et al. (2021) confronted 92 Facebook users with an intervention called "Data Selfie," which allows users to examine the types of algorithmic predictions that can be made from their own Facebook data (e.g., about personality, political orientation, or purchasing habits). They found an increase in privacy concerns after the intervention as well as a higher likelihood of engaging in privacy-protective strategies (such as using fake names or information, expressing dissatisfaction privately and publicly, etc.).

Overall, there is sufficient evidence for the potential of educational interventions, courses, and resources to foster higher (social media) privacy literacy among users. Combined with evidence from meta-analyses testing the effect of media literacy interventions on various outcomes such as knowledge, skills, media use, etc. (e.g., Jeong et al., 2012), it seems fruitful to continue developing such interventions, particularly in order to adapt them to different age groups and audiences. We further suggest stressing social media privacy literacy's aim to empower social media use for the satisfaction of fundamental needs for sociality, creativity, or enjoyment as outlined in all dimensions of our social media privacy literacy dimension. What if interventions and education start by defining what users find most enjoyable about social media? What if they start by acknowledging individuals' needs of rejuvenation, contemplation, and creativity when using social media and then turn to possible privacy risks emanating from social media that could hinder the fulfillment of these needs? We will further elaborate on the balances of individual needs and external support in their fulfillment in the following.

Education or Legislation?

In light of the conceptual challenges and empirical findings discussed above, it is worth asking whether or not we should proceed to invest large amounts of money and effort into online privacy literacy education. As mentioned earlier, we believe in the value of investigating and ultimately fostering privacy literacy, but we see it as only one of several necessary responses to dealing with the challenges surrounding online privacy. A higher social media privacy literacy may without a doubt empower individuals to protect themselves against some privacy turbulences when using social media (particularly against horizontal privacy threats such as unwanted exposure, unwanted dissemination of private information by other users, etc.). Nevertheless, many vertical intrusions by providers of social media platforms can hardly be solved through higher literacy, but need to be addressed as well.

Discourses on privacy literacy sometimes tacitly agree with the fact that individual users are burdened with responsibilities for tasks which could also be seen as part of government duties (Hagendorff, 2018). In short, responsibility may be transferred from the state to single individuals who are in many regards not effectively able to govern IT companies, regulate algorithms, and effectively ensure general privacy standards (Matzner et al., 2016). Even individuals who can be deemed to be perfectly privacy literate have limited opportunities to protect themselves against certain privacy violations. One reason for this lies in corporations' ability to accurately infer very sensitive or intimate personal information from prima facie "unsuspicious" data traces via simple machine learning models. Digital footprints of all kinds can be utilized in order to obtain information about various personality traits, personal states, future behavior, etc., (Binder et al., 2022; Lambiotte et al., 2014; Matz et al., 2019; Schäwel et al., 2021) that are very likely to be so intimate that under normal circumstances, affected individuals would clearly object to disclosing them. Furthermore, machine learning techniques allow for gathering information that results from the interactions of the elements of large datasets, but which in itself is not part of them. This is why individualistic notions of privacy or privacy literacy are complemented by concepts like "predictive privacy" (Mühlhoff, 2021) where researchers stress the collective nature of privacy protection measures. However, it remains wishful thinking to hope for a halt of privacy violations that target single individuals but are based on utilizing data other individuals provide about themselves.

In fact, various measures necessary for effective privacy protection are out of reach for individual users and can only be undertaken by state agencies that are authorized to regulate and limit data collection, processing, and dissemination. Substantial advances in surveillance and data-mining applications create a significant power imbalance between individual users and IT companies, hence making protective state interventions all the more important. We thus urge to critically reflect on privacy literacy discourses' tendency to support a shifting of responsibilities from the state to individuals. In fact, it should be vice versa due to the fact that only state agencies possess ample resources to initiate privacy protection and informational self-determination mechanisms that effectively harness IT companies, data brokers, foreign intelligence agencies, etc. It is obviously a mistake to blame individuals' poor privacy literacy skills and limited knowledge resources when they encounter information turbulence (Litt & Hargittai 2014) or context collapses that are due to revelations about surveillance programs, institutionalized data sharing, breaching of IT security, and the like. Of course, the discourse on privacy literacy does not devalue or disregard the importance of IT security or data protection agencies and regulations. Nevertheless, it may subtly evoke the notion that individual users have to take the protection of their informational privacy into their own hands (Hagendorff, 2018; Matzner et al., 2015). The untaught users have to be empowered; they must learn privacy techniques in order to escape their literacy deficiencies. However, average technology users are simply not capable of protecting personal data in all relevant regards. Generally speaking, more and more sensors and interconnected computing hardware became a ubiquitous component in people's environment. Thus, in a modern information society, it is virtually impossible for individuals to not become part of imperceivable tracking operations, machine learning predictions, data broker businesses, or, in general, "cyberspace" (Cuff, 2003).

In sum, protecting one's informational privacy is always dependent on others. First, there is no point in being privacy literate on one's own. Others have to engage in predictive privacy measures as well as interdependent privacy protection, too (Biczók & Chia, 2013; see also Trepte's as well as Petro & Metzgers' chapter on social and group privacy theories in this handbook). Second, users are dependent on IT security standards, data protection agencies, as well as data protection laws that effectively govern data collection practices by companies and other institutions. Only state institutions can come up with a staff of authorized experts who are not over-challenged by and capable of understanding information technologies, software code, laws, business models, security vulnerabilities, commercial data collection practices, etc. Privacy literacy may protect against a particular set of privacy risks, but state agencies can theoretically ensure a much more broad scope of privacy protection. For sure, they have conflicting interests since data protection as well as collection or surveillance serve different ministries' objectives. And one can even stress that privacy literacy comprises a precautionary principle that takes these conflicting interests into account. However, in the end, privacy protection resources are unevenly distributed, and data protection rights can protect especially those placed on the disadvantaged side of the digital divide. A process of "responsibilization" (O'Malley, 2009; Matzner et al., 2015), where accountability is transferred from the state to individuals, has problematic normative implications. Privacy risks should effectively be addressed not just on an individual, but also on a political level with its manifold instruments like binding legal norms, monetary incentives, subsidies, obligations for opt-out options, or the right to be forgotten. Eventually, in addition to empowering and educating individual users, IT companies should in reasonable parts be disempowered by these instruments in order to not just combat symptoms but also reach the root of privacy threats.

Future Perspectives and Conclusion

In this chapter, we reviewed the literature on online and social media privacy literacy, respectively, discussed methodical challenges surrounding their measurement, and critically evaluated the role of social media privacy literacy in safeguarding users' privacy. In this last section, we highlight some of our conclusions and provide avenues for future research.

Conceptually, we believe that research on online privacy literacy has come a long way. The field has matured from simple models focusing on fragmented dimensions of the broader concept to more comprehensive models that include specific knowledge dimensions, abilities, and skill sets. We see the variety in conceptualizations as a testament to the vibrant research community that studies online and particularly social media privacy. In fact, we believe that different research questions and applications call for different concepts, levels of abstraction, and, conversely, levels of specificity with regard to its context. Nonetheless, we also believe that the question of how privacy literacy should be embedded within broader concepts such as computer and media literacy remains important. As we have seen, interventions for fostering privacy literacy are often embedded in broader educational resources on media literacy in general. The conceptual hierarchy and discriminant validity between media literacy and privacy literacy should hence be further investigated and discussed.

Methodologically, we have to conclude that there are only a few validated scales that measure online privacy literacy and hardly any scales that assess social media privacy literacy specifically (beyond short ad-hoc scales). OPLIS (Masur et al., 2017) remains one of the few objective measurement tools that nonetheless falls short in capturing the entirety of the discussed dimensions of online privacy literacy. A rigorously validated scale for *social* media privacy literacy is missing completely. This is problematic for various reasons: First, assessments of literacy levels in different populations may still be preliminary as ad-hoc scales and self-reports may contain measurement error and bias. Second, the true potential of social media privacy literacy in empowering individuals may still be underexplored. The preliminary evidence is again often based on subjective, rather than objective knowledge scales, and the more performative dimensions such as reflection ability or critical privacy literacy are not yet studied at all. We thus urge future research to engage in rigorous scale development and validation.

Empirically, the link between higher levels of social media privacy literacy and privacy behaviors on social media seems supported, but we lack causal and experimental investigations. The majority of work is based on cross-sectional survey designs. Beyond studying relationships between online privacy literacy and privacy behaviors, there is a lack of research on the role of privacy literacy in shaping prominently investigated privacy theories and processes. As mentioned before, the privacy paradox is commonly explained by a lack of skills and knowledge, but the empirical evidence is largely missing. We believe there are many opportunities for incorporating online privacy literacy as a key concept in many existing privacy frameworks. Among others, it may explain privacy decision-making as outlined in the privacy calculus (see, e.g., Dienlin & Metzger, 2016). It should likewise not be ignored when investigating heuristics and biases (see Liu et al., this volume) or how literacy and heuristic thinking may interact on a situational level (see chapter 6 by Masur in this volume).

Normatively, however, we caution against one-sided advocacy for online privacy literacy generally and social media privacy literacy specifically. Privacy literacy is often associated with individualistic notions about privacy and data protection. This is why it is only one albeit important measure that serves as a countermeasure against digital risks that are connected to issues of information control or the loss thereof. First and foremost, social media privacy literacy is concerned with frontend features of digital platforms, where users can engage with privacy settings, delete posts, un-tag photos, search for their content, manage profile visibility, etc. However, this must not lead to a disregard of privacy risks that are situated at the platforms' backends, meaning the "invisible" part of user communication, information exchange, machine learning, or data mining. Privacy settings that users can access are just the surface of what is relevant when managing digital privacy boundaries. This has to extend to the backends of platforms and services, to the algorithms, machine learning models, server centers, data brokers, intelligence agencies, etc., where social sorting (Lyon, 2003), algorithmic discrimination (Barocas & Selbst, 2016), AI-driven decision-making (Crawford et al., 2019), or micro-targeting (Matz et al., 2019) takes place. Future research should hence be clear about the (limited) potential of social media privacy literacy and outline what a higher literacy can and what it cannot achieve. Being transparent about both general online privacy literacy's and social media privacy literacy's strengths and weaknesses and its inherent limitations will help to better define its role in protecting user privacy while upholding the need to also engage in other, less individual-centered solutions.

Notes

1 see: www.oplis.de
2 see: https://osf.io/md8ch?view_only=b03665d09fd84f1393570e46dcf25f54
3 https://www.facebook.com/fbgetdigital
4 https://beinternetawesome.withgoogle.com/en_us/families
5 https://www.commonsense.org/education
6 e.g., https://www.lfk.de/medienkompetenz/social-media
7 https://www.bmfsfj.de/bmfsfj/themen/kinder-und-jugend/medienkompetenz
8 https://netwerkmediawijsheid.nl/kennis-tools/
9 https://www.socialmediatestdrive.org

References

Acquisti, A., & Gross, R. (2006). Imagined communities: Awareness, information sharing, and privacy on the Facebook. In G. Danezis & P. Golle (Eds.), *Privacy enhancing technologies* (Vol. 4258, pp. 36–58). Lecture notes in computer science. Berlin: Springer. https://doi.org/10.1007/11957454_3

Altman, I. (1975). *The environment and social behavior: Privacy, personal space, territory, crowding*. Monterey: Brooks/Cole.

Baacke, D. (1996). Medienkompetenz: Begrifflichkeit und sozialer wandel. In A. von Rein (Hrsg.) (Ed.), *Theorie und praxis der erwachsenenbildung: Medienkompetenz als schlüsselbegriff* (pp. S112–S124). Bad Heilbrunn: Klinkhardt.

Barocas, S., & Selbst, A. D. (2016). Big data's disparate impact. *California Law Review*, *104*, 671–732.

Bartsch, M., & Dienlin, T. (2016). Control your Facebook: An analysis of online privacy literacy. *Computers in Human Behavior*, *56*, 147–154. https://doi.org/10.1016/j.chb.2015.11.022

Baruh, L., Secinti, E., & Cemalcilar, Z. (2017). Online privacy concerns and privacy management: A meta-analytical review. *Journal of Communication*, *67*(1), 26–53.

Bazarova, N. N., & Masur, P. K. (2020). Towards an integration of individualistic, networked, and institutional approaches to online disclosure and privacy in a networked ecology. *Current Opinion in Psychology*, *36*, 118–123. https://doi.org/10.1016/j.copsyc.2020.05.004

Biczók, G., & Chia, P. H. (2013). *Interdependent privacy: Let me share your data*. Berlin: Springer.

Binder, A., Stubenvoll, M., Hirsch, M., & Matthes, J. (2022). Why am I getting this ad? How the degree of targeting disclosures and political fit affect persuasion knowledge, party evaluation, and online privacy behaviors. *Journal of Advertising*, *51*(2), 206–222. https://doi.org/10.1080/00913367.2021.2015727

Brandimarte, L., Acquisti, A., & Loewenstein, G. (2013). Misplaced confidences. *Social Psychological and Personality Science*, *4*(3), 340–347.

Crawford, K., Dobbe, R., Dryer, T., Fried, G., Green, B., Kaziunas, E., et al. (2019). AI now 2019 report. AI now. New York. Available online at https://ainowinstitute.org/AI_Now_2019_Report.pdf, checked on 12/18/2019.

Choi, S. (2022). Privacy literacy on social media: Its predictors and outcomes. *International Journal of Human–Computer Interaction*, https://doi.org/10.1080/10447318.2022.2041892

Chomsky, N. (1976). Conditions on rules of grammar. *Linguistic analysis*, *2*(4), 303–351.

Cuff, D. (2003). Immanent domain. Pervasive computing and the public realm. *Journal of Architectural Education*, *57*(1), 43–49.

Dienlin, T., & Metzger, M. J. (2016). An extended privacy calculus model for SNSs: Analyzingself-disclosure and self-withdrawal in a U.S. representative sample. *Journal of Computer-Mediated Communication*, *21*(5), 368–383. 10.1111/jcc4.12163

Epstein, D., & Quinn, K. (2020). Markers of online privacy marginalization: Empirical examination of socioeconomic disparities in social media privacy attitudes, literacy, and behavior. *Social Media + Society*, *6*(2). https://doi.org/10.1177/2056305120916853

Gambino, A., Kim, J., Sundar, S. S., Shyam, S., Ge, J., & Rosson, M. B. (2016). User disbelief in privacy paradox: Heuristics that determine disclosure. In J. Kaye, A. Druin, C. Lampe, D. Morris, & J. P. Hourcade (Eds.), *Proceedings of the 2016 CHI conference extended abstracts on human factors in computing systems – CHI EA: Vol. 16, 2892413* (pp. 2837–2843). New York, NY: ACM Press. https://doi.org/10.1145/2851581.

Groeben, N. (2002). Dimensionen der medienkompetenz: Deskriptive und normative aspekte. In N. Groeben & B. Hurrelmann (Hrsg.) (Eds.), *Medienkompetenz: Voraussetzungen, dimensionen, funktionen* (pp. S. 160–197). Weinheim: Juventa.

Gruzd, A., McNeish, J., Halevi, L. D., & Phillips, M. (2021). Seeing self in data: The effect of a privacy literacy intervention on Facebook users' behaviour. Available at SSRN: https://doi.org/10.2139/ssrn.3946376

Hagendorff, T. (2018). Privacy literacy and its problems. *Journal of Information Ethics*, *27*(2), 127.

Harborth, D., & Pape, S. (2020). How privacy concerns, trust and risk beliefs, and privacy literacy influence users' intentions to use privacy-enhancing technologies. *ACM SIGMIS Database: the DATABASE for Advances in Information Systems, 51*, 51–69. https://doi.org/10.1145/3380799.3380805

Higdon, N. (2021). The critical effect: Exploring the influence of critical media literacy pedagogy on college students' social media behaviors and attitudes. *Journal of Media Literacy Education Pre-Prints*. Retrieved from https://digitalcommons.uri.edu/jmle-preprints/3

Hobbs, R. (2010). *Digital and media literacy: A plan of action*. The Aspen Institute.

Hoofnagle, C., King, J., Li, S., & Turow, J. (2010). *How different are young adults from older adults when it comes to information privacy attitudes and policies*. Retrieved from http://ssrn.com/abstract=1589864

Jeong, S.-H., Cho, H., & Hwang, J. (2012). Media literacy interventions: A meta-analytic review. *Journal of Communication, 62*(3), 454–472. https://doi.org/10.1111/j.1460-2466.2012.01643.x

Kellner, D., & Share, J. (2005). Toward critical media literacy: Core concepts, debates, organizations, and policy. *Discourse: Studies in the Cultural Politics of Education, 26*, 369–386. https://doi.org/10.1080/01596300500200169

Lambiotte, R., & Kosinski, M. (2014). Tracking the digital footprints of personality. *Proc. IEEE*, 102(12), 1934–1939.

Litt, E., & Hargittai, E. (2014). A bumpy ride on the information superhighway. Exploring turbulence online. *Computers in Human Behavior, 36*, 520–529.

Livingstone, S. (2014). Developing social media literacy: How children learn to interpret risky opportunities on social network sites. *Communications, 39*(3). https://doi.org/10.1515/commun-2014-0113

Lyon, D. (2003). Surveillance as social sorting. Computer codes and mobile bodies. In D. Lyon (Ed.), *Surveillance as social sorting. Privacy, risk, and digital discrimination* (pp. 13–30). London: Routledge.

Masur, P. K. (2018). *Situational privacy and self-disclosure: Communication processes in online environments*. Cham, Switzerland: Springer. https://doi.org/10.1007/978-3-319-78884-5

Masur, P. K. (2020). How online privacy literacy supports self-data protection and self-determination in the age of information. *Media and Communication, 8*(2), 258–269. https://doi.org/10.17645/mac.v8i2.2855

Masur, P. K., Teutsch, D., & Trepte, S. (2017). Entwicklung und validierung der online-privatheitskompetenzskala (OPLIS) [engl. Development and validation of the online privacy literacy scale]. *Diagnostica, 63*, 256–268. https://doi.org/10.1026/0012-1924/a000179

Matz, S. C., Appel, R. E., & Kosinski, M. (2019). Privacy in the age of psychological targeting. *Current Opinion in Psychology, 31*, 116–121.

Matzner, T., Masur, P. K., Ochs, C., & von Pape, T. (2016). Self-data-protection – empowerment or burden? In S. Gutwirth, R. Leenes, & P. de Hert (Eds.), *Data protection on the move* (pp. 277–305). Springer: Netherlands. https://doi.org/10.1007/978-94-017-7376-8_11

Mühlhoff, R. (2021). Predictive privacy: Towards an applied ethics of data analytics. *SSRN Journal*, 1–24.

Nissenbaum, H. (2010). Privacy in context. In *Technology, policy, and the integrity of social life*. Stanford University Press.

O'Malley, P. (2009). Responsibilization. In A. Wakefield & J. Fleming (Eds.), *The SAGE dictionary of policing* (pp. 277–279). London: SAGE Publications Ltd.

Park, Y. J. (2013). Digital literacy and privacy behavior online. *Communication Research, 40*(2), 215–236. https://doi.org/10.1177/0093650211418338

Pedersen, D. M. (1997). Psychological functions of privacy. *Journal of Environmental Psychology, 17*, 147–156. https://doi.org/10.1006/jevp.1997.0049

Potter, W. J. (2010). The state of media literacy. *Journal of Broadcasting & Electronic Media, 54*(4), 675–696. https://doi.org/10.1080/08838151.2011.521462

Purington Drake, A., Masur, P. K., Bazarova, N., Zou, E. W., & Whitlock, J. (2022). The youth social media literacy inventory: Development and validation using item response theory. *SocArXiv*. https://doi.org/10.31235/osf.io/wfnd7

Schäwel, J., Frener, R., & Trepte, S. (2021). Political microtargeting and online privacy: A theoretical approach to understanding users' privacy behaviors. *Media and Communication, 9*(4), 158–169. https://doi.org/10.17645/mac.v9i4.4085

Schäwel, J., Frener, R., Masur, P. K., & Trepte, S. (2021). Learning by doing oder doing by learning? Die Wechselwirkung zwischen Online-Privatheitskompetenz und Datenschutzverhalten. *Medien & Kommunikationswissenschaft, 69*(2), 221–246.

Schubert, R., Marinica, I., Mosetti, L., & Bajka, S. (2022). Mitigating the privacy paradox through higher privacy literacy? *Insights from a lab experiment based on Facebook data*. Retrieved from https://collegium.ethz.ch/wp-content/uploads/2022/05/Schubert-Marinica-Mosetti-Bajka-Mitigating-the-Privacy-Paradox2.pdf

Sindermann, C., Schmitt, H. S., Kargl, F., Herbert, C., & Montag, C. (2021). Online privacy literacy and online privacy behavior–the role of crystallized intelligence and personality. *International Journal of Human–Computer Interaction*, *37*(15), 1455–1466.

Spottswood, E. L., & Hancock, J. T. (2017). Should I share that? Prompting social norms that influence privacy behaviors on a social networking site. *Journal of Computer-Mediated Communication*, *22*(2), 26. https://doi.org/10.1111/jcc4.12182

Sutter, T., & Charlton, M. (2002). Medienkompetenz: Einige Anmerkungen zum Kompetenzbegriff. In N. Groeben & B. Hurrelmann (Hrsg.) (Eds.), *Medienkompetenz: Voraussetzungen, Dimensionen, Funktionen* (pp. S. 129–147). Weinheim: Juventa.

Trepte, S., Scharkow, M., & Dienlin, T. (2020). The privacy calculus contextualized: The influence of affordances. *Computers in Human Behavior, 104*. https://doi.org/10.1016/j.chb.2019.08.022

Trepte, S., Teutsch, D., Masur, P. K., Eicher, C., Fischer, M., Hennhöfer, A., & Lind, F. (2015). Do people know about privacy and data protection strategies? Towards the "online privacy literacy scale" (OPLIS). In. S. Gutwirth, R. Leenes, & P. de Hert (Eds.), *Reforming European data protection law* (pp. 333–365). Netherlands: Springer. https://doi.org/10.1007/978-94-017-9385-8

Turow, J. (2003). Americans and online privacy: The system is broken. A report from the Annenberg public policy center of the University of Pennsylvania. *Abgerufen unter*, https://repository.upenn.edu/cgi/viewcontent.cgi?referer=https://www.google.de/&httpsredir=1&article=1411&context=asc_papers

Vitak, J. (2012). The impact of context collapse and privacy on social network site disclosures. *Journal of Broadcasting & Electronic Media*, *56*(4), 451–470.

Weinert, F. E. (2003). *Leistungsmessungen in Schulen*. Weinheim, Basel: Beltz.

12
PRIVACY BREACHES

Jana Dombrowski

UNIVERSITY OF HOHENHEIM, GERMANY

Introduction

The most reported breaches of the European Union's (EU) General Data Protection Regulation (GDPR) between 2018 and 2021 took place in Germany (77,800) and Italy (3,500), with each country handing out around 69 million in fines during that period (DLA Piper, 2022). Similar to the GDPR, which seeks to improve data protection at the EU level, the Budapest Convention in 2001 seeks to harmonize laws transnationally, becoming the first "multilateral binding instrument to regulate cybercrime" (Clough, 2014, pp. 699–700). This cooperation agreement within the European Council invites nations to harmonize their legislation on cybercrime by adopting the proposed legal framework (more information at https://www.coe.int/en/web/cybercrime/the-budapest-convention). While 67 countries have ratified the convention, the legal situation in the rest of the world is unclear. A total of 13% of countries worldwide do not have any legislation regarding cybercrime – mostly in the Global South (UNCTAD, 2022). The number of unreported privacy breaches is expected to be high, in addition to incidents that do not violate the laws (e.g., unwanted information dissemination peer-to-peer) and thus are not included in official statistics.

Online privacy breaches can cause far-reaching economic, psychological, reputational, social, and even physical harm to their victims (Agrafiotis et al., 2018). Recall the case of the adultery website Ashley Madison in 2015, in which hackers leaked e-mail addresses, locations, and erotic preferences of the largely married accountholders, among other sensitive information. Media and police departments reported incidents of blackmail, legal proceedings for accountholders in countries where adultery is banned, divorces, and even two confirmed suicides in the wake of the data breach (Lamont, 2016; Thielman, 2015). Ashley Madison is one of the very few cases in which consequences for individuals have been discussed publicly. Even academic research mostly focuses on meso-level perspectives regarding the costs of cybercrimes, i.e., victimization of organizations, companies, or platforms (e.g., Acquisti et al., 2006; Agrafiotis et al., 2018). However, the issue of privacy breaches also and equally affects macro- (i.e., government) and micro-level actors (i.e., individual users), who can all take on the role of victim, perpetrator, or manager of privacy breaches. Governmental surveillance, for example, mainly involves privacy threats to micro-level actors by macro-level actors, while industrial espionage refers to invasions of privacy between different meso-level entities. When micro-level actors are the victims, the literature differentiates between vertical privacy breaches by macro- and meso-level actors and horizontal privacy breaches by other online users (Masur, 2019).

DOI: 10.4324/9781003244677-14

Taking mainly an individual and psychological perspective, this chapter first creates a shared theoretical understanding of related terminology and summarizes empirical results regarding the prevalence of privacy breaches, perceptions of them, and their effects. Finally, I discuss the responsibility of macro-, meso-, and micro-level actors for privacy breaches on social media.

Theoretical Perspectives on Privacy Breaches

Data Breaches, Security Breaches, and Privacy Breaches

"She wanted data, she wanted money, and she wanted brag." Following this closing argument, Paige Thompson was convicted for her part in one of the largest data heists in the US, which affected several companies, including Capital One Bank. The hack took place in 2019 and involved using misconfigured accounts to gain access to cloud storage, affecting the personal data of 100 million users. The hackers used server capacities to mine cryptocurrency, a technique that is also called cryptojacking. In 2022, the jury found her guilty of wire fraud and harmful access to a protected computer (United States Department of Justice, 2022). The latest European Union Agency for Cybersecurity (ENISA) report on prime cyber threats ranked cryptojacking third according to criteria such as impact, frequency, and technological development. Looking at the reports from the last 10 years, cryptojacking was listed for the first time in 2017, whereas other threats like malware attacks, spam, data breaches, and identity theft are consistently included in the ranking (see https://www.enisa.europa.eu/topics/threat-risk-management/threats-and-trends/enisa-threat-landscape).

As exemplified by the Capital One Bank breach, there is a distinction between the terms *privacy* breach, *data* breach, and *security* breach, even though the three terms are often used synonymously. "Security issues correspond to the concerns about the protection of personal information" (Smith et al., 2011, p. 996). Smith et al. (2011) identify three goals of protecting security online: *Integrity*, assuring that information is not altered during transit and storage; *authentication*, assuring that the accessor's identity and eligibility for access are verified; and *confidentiality*, assuring data use for authorized purposes only. If these criteria are violated, a security breach has occurred. Data breaches are one specific case of a security breach, mainly referring to the third goal of confidentiality. They are defined as "intentional or inadvertent exposure of confidential information to unauthorized parties" (Cheng et al., 2017, p. 1). Although (data) security is important for enhancing online privacy, fulfilling all of the criteria mentioned above does not assure an individual's privacy.

In the case of Capital One Bank, the defense argued that the attack was a so-called white-hat hack, i.e., a hack aiming to draw attention to security vulnerabilities without causing further damage (Conger, 2022). Although the hacker was found guilty of serious violations of laws, a peculiarity of the case is that Paige Thompson engaged in cryptojacking instead of causing harm by, for example, abusing the personal information she gained access to. The Capital One Bank breach can thus be labeled a security but not a privacy breach. While security breaches mostly affect early technological stages of data access, privacy breaches refer to actual transgressions of individual boundaries through, for example, the use and abuse of information (Mamonov & Koufaris, 2014). This also means that the source of a security breach (e.g., a hacker) may deviate from the source of privacy breaches (e.g., cybercriminals engaging in identity theft or blackmail) (Chen et al., 2021). Security and data breaches therefore can but do not necessarily cause privacy breaches.

Privacy Violations

Going even one step further, I argue that breaches do not necessarily lead to *privacy violations* by pointing to a conceptual gap between a breach event and an individual's perception and interpretation of it (Ahmad & Mykytyn, 2012). Failing to notify the user that cookies have been employed, for example, violates the GDPR but may not matter to users or even fully escape their attention, not resulting in a violation. However, a social media user whose profile picture is used in a nationwide marketing campaign will likely view this as a privacy violation, even though they agreed to a privacy statement allowing for the further dissemination of such pictures. These examples demonstrate two important things: First, just because users are confronted with a breach does not mean that they will be concerned, feel betrayed, offended, or perceive their privacy as threatened. Second, there is more to privacy breaches than the violation of laws or legally binding contracts.

Drawing from *Psychological Contract Theory* (Rosseau, 1989), violations develop in a complex process that includes the perception, comparison, and interpretation of breaches of unwritten psychological contracts (Morrison & Robinson, 1997). As Waldman (2018) describes in his seminal work on the understanding of privacy as trust, individuals experience privacy breaches as a violation when their trust has been breached, namely when their expectation that others will behave according to accepted norms is disappointed. Consequently, a privacy breach can be defined as a contravention of written legal norms or unwritten psychological norms regarding interpersonal boundaries.

Following Psychological Contract Theory, individuals evaluate a variety of factors characterizing and surrounding the breach, for example, outcome expectations, fairness, uncertainty, and the importance of the contract (Morrison & Robinson, 1997). A privacy violation, therefore, does not arise automatically from unwanted access; rather, it is defined as inappropriate access in relation to the respective context (Masur, 2019). These assumptions also complement contextual approaches to privacy that have gained importance in the last decade (Nissenbaum, 2011).

Privacy Turbulences

Further, *Communication Privacy Management Theory* (Petronio 2002) introduced the term *privacy turbulence*. In general, the theory explains an interactional process of privacy management that accounts for co-ownership of information. It views privacy as the collective management of shared boundaries and is thus well-suited for the growing interest in social media (see chapter 3 by Trepte on social, networked, relational, and collective privacy). Following Petronio (2016), turbulence occurs when contraventions of privacy rules are perceived as goal-discordant. Similar to the assumptions of Psychological Contract Theory and the contextual approaches to privacy mentioned above, perceptions and the emotional, cognitive, and behavioral effects of such turbulence vary according to occurrence expectations, the level of intensity, the type of information, and the situation (Petronio, 2016).

Consequently, the term turbulence breaks the event of a privacy breach down to the perceptual, individual level. This is especially important as incidents may breach existing norms but do not necessarily oppose an individual's goals. For example, a social media user negotiated with their close peers to not post pictures of them drinking alcohol (Romo et al., 2017). However, one of the alcohol-related pictures may look especially appealing and helps an individual's social media self-presentation. Some privacy-related goals are not specific enough meaning that a privacy breach could not conflict with them. For example, users know that they do not want precarious pictures posted but they have not specified what precarious actually means. This makes it difficult to implement the goals in context. Additionally, most breaches are invisible to users. Uber, for example, informed the public in 2017 of a data breach that had already occurred in 2016, affecting sensitive data from 57 million passengers and drivers. Investigations revealed that Uber first paid hackers to conceal traces of the breach (Perlroth & Isaac, 2018). The victims likely would not have noticed that a breach had occurred if Uber had succeeded in covering the traces.

In alignment with these theoretical developments, I distinguish between the concepts of privacy breaches, violations, and turbulences. Turbulences fill an important terminological gap between privacy breaches and violations. Not every privacy breach translates into a turbulence or a violation.

From a procedural perspective, breaches can lead to turbulences when they are perceived as goal-discordant. When a turbulence – in its respective context – is perceived as a threat to an individual's privacy or cannot immediately be resolved, it causes a violation, which influences the calculus of online privacy management.

Empirical Evidence on Privacy Breaches

Prevalence of Privacy Breaches

From a global perspective, storing information mainly in networked online infrastructures (e.g., cloud storage) has led to an increasing number of privacy and security breaches because the need for physical access to data and information (e.g., via USB) has been replaced by virtual access options from any location and at any time. After the completion of this shift, neither the size nor the frequency of breaches have further increased (Edwards et al., 2016).

A review of European datasets on self-reported experiences with cybercrimes reveals a rather low prevalence of various crimes, ranging from 1–3% for online shopping fraud, 1–2% for payment and banking fraud, 1–6% for hacking, less than 1% for identity theft, and a maximum of 3% for cyberbullying and stalking (Reep-van den Bergh & Junger, 2018). Quite diverse prevalence statistics are reported regarding one of the most common forms of cybercrime, malware attacks, which are reported to affect 2–15% of the European population (Reep-van den Bergh & Junger, 2018). Taken together, a large majority of people have not experienced criminal actions online. In a study from Germany, the only negative experience reported by over half of respondents was a website provider asking for too much information (Trepte & Masur, 2017). Moreover, a qualitative survey in peer-to-peer contexts found that victimized social media users categorize most experienced breaches as innocent rather than malicious. Thus, users view privacy violations stemming from friends and close peers as unintended and not meaning to cause any harm (DeGroot & Vik, 2017). Even on the organizational level, non-criminal data leaks – mainly caused by human error – happen daily and tend not to result in perceptions of a severe violation.

Existing studies suggest that the risk of falling victim to a breach varies according to several risk and resilience factors, such as personality traits, threat awareness, protection behavior, and privacy literacy (for an overview see Budak et al., 2021; Büchi et al., 2017; van der Schyff & Flowerday, 2021; Virtanen, 2017). Undergirding this view, however, is a debate about the extent to which individuals are responsible for their victimization. For this reason, I will not discuss risk and resilience factors any further at this point, but will revisit the debate on responsibilities at the end of the chapter.

Perception of Privacy Breaches – Affects and False Optimism

Individuals are especially worried about breaches stemming from companies, as they are less tangible (Masur, 2019). However, consumers who accept companies as the owners of their data continue to show support for the company after severe data breaches occur (Madan et al., 2022). Further, legal rights stemming from prior contracts on data use and dissemination can reduce individuals' perception that they have experienced a breach (Mamonov & Benbunan-Fich, 2015). This indicates that breaches of psychological contracts may be perceived as less severe compared to breaches of written legal contracts. Moreover, breaches are taken more seriously when they affect information that is perceived as very private, e.g., fears or financial information, instead of less private, e.g., favorite books, hobbies, or geo-location data (Mamonov & Benbunan-Fich, 2015; Masur & Scharkow, 2016).

Not being able to avoid privacy issues when engaging in online activities leads to feelings of helplessness and resignation (Lee et al., 2022). Similarly, severe criminal offenses are inherently goal-discordant and are therefore closely associated with negative affect (Aloia, 2018). Unresolved privacy turbulences, i.e., privacy violations, result in stress, relational strain, and vulnerability along with feelings of powerlessness, anger, fear, and sadness (Aloia, 2018; Romo et al., 2017; Virtanen, 2017). These feelings are in turn related to trauma caused by the privacy loss (Aloia, 2018).

Moreover, as in many other scenarios with negative effects outside the specific context of privacy, third-person perception likely occurs. The third-person hypothesis states that individuals underestimate their risk of being exposed to negative events or effects (first-person perception), whereas they overestimate it for unknown others (third-person perception). This results from *optimistic bias* or *comparative optimism*, meaning that one's own vulnerabilities are rated lower than others' vulnerabilities (Cho et al., 2010). Consequently, individuals perceive their own risk of being affected by cybercrime as smaller than others' risk (Chen & Atkin, 2021; Cho et al., 2010; Debatin et al., 2009). This perceptual bias even prevents learning from others' experiences of violations (Debatin et al., 2009) and explains why individuals recommend using protective measures to others, but less likely to adopt such measures themselves (Chen & Atkin, 2021). While some scholars have found that optimistic bias decreases when individuals experience privacy violations themselves (Cho et al., 2010), others find that most violations do not change the third-person perception (Chen & Atkin, 2021). Being a victim of online harassment is even associated with greater discrepancy between first- and third-person risk estimations, since victims blame themselves for such attacks (Chen & Atkin, 2021). It is likely that the discrepancy in results is caused by the specific context of a threat. For example, the third-person effect is stronger for peer-to-peer contexts than for privacy threats stemming from macro- or meso-level actors (Cho et al., 2010).

Effects of Privacy Breaches – Attitudes and Behavior

More than two-thirds of the European population report being concerned about becoming a victim of banking fraud, malware, or identity theft, and nearly half are very concerned about becoming a victim of some type of cybercrime (European Commission, 2020). Experiencing privacy breaches has been shown to influence attitudes regarding two specific entities: Attitudes towards the actors causing the breach and internalized attitudes towards privacy as a whole. A study conducted by Hammer et al. (2019) demonstrated that psychological contract breaches significantly decrease trust in vertical as well as horizontal social media actors liable for the breach. This is in line with Waldman (2018), who posited that breaches of existing norms cause trust issues. Regarding attitudes towards privacy, several studies have found support that negative privacy experiences cause higher privacy concerns and risk beliefs (Ayaburi, 2022; Bansal et al., 2010; Masur & Trepte, 2021; Trepte et al., 2014). Institutional concerns only arise when the consequences of a breach are irreversible. Peer privacy concerns, on the other side, arise regardless of the reversibility of consequences (Ayaburi, 2022). This finding suggests that victims more easily accept vertical than horizontal breaches, since the height from which trust falls is higher for peer-to-peer contexts. There is also evidence that privacy violations are positively associated with individuals holding pro-privacy attitudes, since negative experiences draw attention to one's own privacy boundaries (Büchi et al., 2017).

Existing social contracts are perceived as less reliable to protect privacy online when individuals are concerned, hold risk beliefs, and have trust issues (Kruikemeier et al., 2020). Most theoretical and empirical frameworks, therefore, assume that once these attitudes are formed, they either lead to less risky online behavior or to privacy protection behavior in order to restore or compensate for the lack of trust and norms (for an overview see Masur & Trepte, 2021). One important point that the empirical literature largely fails to address is the causal links between violation experiences, attitudes, and behaviors. Cross-sectional studies produce conflicting evidence regarding the relation between breach experiences and privacy behavior (e.g., Ahmad & Mykytyn, 2012; Awad & Krishnan, 2006; Hammer et al., 2019; Kruikemeier et al., 2020; Osatuyi et al., 2018). Self-disclosure and protection behavior are risk factors as well as strategies for coping with violations. This highlights the importance of qualitative studies and longitudinal or experimental designs to disentangle the effects regarding privacy behavior.

Within-person results demonstrate that although facing more privacy violations than usual leads to more pronounced privacy concerns, these concerns do not motivate individuals to behave in less risky ways (Masur & Trepte, 2021). One possible explanation for why people fail to protect their privacy lies at the heart of the privacy calculus approach. Engaging in privacy behavior often involves access control (e.g., limit the audience) and withdrawal (e.g., stop using social media), which restrict users' online experience. The benefits of information disclosure and social media use weigh more for individuals than the risks (see chapter 7 by Dienlin on the privacy calculus). A somewhat complementary explanation comes from the concepts of cynicism, resignation, and fatigue (see chapter 13 Ranzini, Lutz, & Hoffmann on privacy cynicism). As mentioned before, unresolved privacy turbulences on social media are associated with negative affect and trauma (Aloia, 2018; Romo et al., 2017). Two types of behavior then become much more likely: Distributive tactics trying to recover from the social damage, e.g., yelling, criticizing, or venting, and mental withdrawal, which goes along with the internalization of emotional responses, e.g., ignoring, avoiding, and resigning oneself to the fact that one's privacy has been violated (Aloia, 2018).

In a study examining the types of behavior that arise after a privacy violation has occurred, Trepte et al. (2014) found that negative privacy experiences in the long run only lead to an increase in informational privacy behaviors (e.g., refusing to give out information) but not social (e.g., restraining others' access) or psychological behaviors (e.g., withholding intimate information). Steuber and McLaren (2015) likewise showed that individuals who engage in communication with violators about a turbulence and negotiated privacy rules were more likely to show forgiveness in a peer-to-peer context (Steuber & McLaren, 2015). These findings suggest that – alongside refusing to disclose personal data – interactional and communication-based tactics are perceived as appropriate to deal with turbulences stemming from unwanted intrusions (Trepte, 2021). When applying tactics like performing facework or asking others to remove content that threatens one's social media privacy, individuals remediate existing privacy violations (Romo et al., 2017).

Concluding Thoughts on Responsibilities for Privacy Breaches

These observations lead to an important question that informs the debate on social media privacy, namely, where responsibilities regarding breaches lie. While the legal infrastructure on data protection and privacy has progressed in recent years, legislation is still not harmonized enough to meet the transnational challenges of privacy breaches and cybercrime (Clough, 2014). The Budapest Convention, for example, obligates participating countries to implement laws that penalize attempted and executed offenses regarding, e.g., child pornography, fraud, forgery, and illegal access or interception, as well as aiding and abetting such offenses (Convention on Cybercrime, 2001). As previously argued, the Convention focuses on severe cybercrimes, which occur quite rarely. We are just at the beginning of international efforts to regulate privacy on a large scale. Transnational agreements like the GDPR or the Budapest Convention signal that geopolitical actors have at least recognized the global challenges and acknowledge their responsibility for combatting them.

They have learned from the history of privacy policy and legislation that self-management by individuals does just not work out as expected (see chapter 27 by Susser on regulating online privacy) and seek to transfer responsibility to meso-level actors. One important achievement in this context is Article 12 of the Budapest Convention, which assures that "legal persons can be held liable for a criminal offense established in accordance with this Convention" (Convention on Cybercrime, 2001, p. 8). Until now, academic and societal awareness of security and privacy breaches has mostly concerned breaches on the organizational level, neglecting the far-reaching impact on individuals as the secondary group affected by breaches of user data. Victimized organizations are particularly concerned about economic damage, e.g., loss of reputation (Gwebu et al., 2018) or their shares losing value in the stock market (Acquisti et al., 2006). However, economic consequences for large-scale data collectors following breaches are rather small (Foecking et al., 2021). Taken together with the empirical findings reported above on individuals' acceptance and forgiveness, the incentives for prevention are exceedingly weak, and organizations do not invest in prevention after a breach has occurred (Murciano-Goroff, 2019). This is why it is key to create normative environments that make privacy-threatening practices less lucrative than designing and providing privacy-enhancing environments. One example of creating responsibility through legislative norms is implementing a breach notification rule prescribing that breaches of a certain size must be reported (Burdon, 2010). As the capitalization of data by companies like Meta may have just reached its plateau, reliable norms help to create accountability at the meso level. This may not provide automatically safer but at least sanctionable online spaces for individuals, enabling them to defend their right to privacy.

Giving individuals back the power over their data and identities through legislative norms is a first step towards reducing the perceived power distances that contribute to individuals resigning themselves to the fact that privacy cannot be protected on social media (Madan et al., 2022). Here, however, I specifically refer to a perspective that enables but does not obligate users to take responsibility for their own privacy. Even if individuals are aware of their rights, the multiplicity of laws, processes, and actors limits their ability to fully assess the risks of breaches stemming from macro- and meso-level actors. While they may not be able to fully grasp the impact of vertical breaches, the situation for peer-to-peer contexts is somewhat different. Legislative norms can create clear rules regarding criminal offenses, but privacy violations also occur through non-criminal activities. This highlights the need for reliable social norms. Online users are co-owners of information, making information a common good, especially on social media (see chapter 5 by Metzger & Petro on group privacy). Users are already successfully taking advantage of opportunities to collectively defend shared boundaries and norms, e.g., through social sanctioning and reporting practices (Rashidi et al., 2020). But shared boundaries also go hand in hand with the fact that ego-centric self-disclosure can quickly lead to unauthorized information dissemination about others. This ranges from uploading photos to social networks where friends can unintentionally be seen to disclosing DNA information about relatives when deciding to use direct-to-consumer genetic testing services (European Society of Human Genetics, 2010).

Recognizing privacy – and inherently connected trust – as a common good also raises concerns about the occurrence of a tragedy of the commons (Fairfield & Engel, 2015; Hirsch, 2016). If everyone is responsible, then no one feels responsible anymore. Moreover, technology develops rapidly and the consequences of cybercrime often cannot be accurately estimated. Although technological opportunities to prevent breaches are also steadily advancing, e.g., regarding data authentication, malware detection, and firewalls (Rajasekharaiah et al., 2020) threats to individuals cannot be completely eliminated through technological prevention measures. A more worry-free use of online platforms is not achieved by completely eliminating privacy breaches – because we can't – but by being able to trust that all entities will accept responsibility and adhere to norms before and after a breach. Technological and normative advances regarding data protection may be effective in limiting the frequency of breaches but ineffective in mitigating their impact once prevention fails. This brings into focus that macro-, meso-, and micro-level measures – preventive as well as reactive – must be interwoven with one another to combat severe consequences of privacy breaches.

References

Acquisti, A., Friedman, A., & Telang, R. (2006). *Is there a cost to privacy breaches? An event study*. https://aisel.aisnet.org/cgi/viewcontent.cgi?article=1215&context=icis2006

Agrafiotis, I., Nurse, J. R. C., Goldsmith, M., Creese, S., & Upton, D. (2018). A taxonomy of cyber-harms: Defining the impacts of cyber-attacks and understanding how they propagate. *Journal of Cybersecurity*, *4*(1). https://doi.org/10.1093/cybsec/tyy006

Ahmad, A., & Mykytyn, P. (2012). *Perceived privacy breach - The construct, the scale, and its antecedents*. https://aisel.aisnet.org/amcis2012/proceedings/issecurity/21/

Aloia, L. S. (2018). The emotional, behavioral, and cognitive experience of boundary turbulence. *Communication Studies*, *69*(2), 180–195. https://doi.org/10.1080/10510974.2018.1426617

Awad, N. F., & Krishnan, M. S. (2006). The personalization privacy paradox: An empirical evaluation of information transparency and the willingness to be profiled online for personalization. *Mis Quarterly*, *30*(1), 13–28.

Ayaburi, E. W. (2022). Understanding online information disclosure: Examination of data breach victimization experience effect. *Information Technology & People*, Online First. https://doi.org/10.1108/ITP-04-2021-0262

Bansal, G., Gefen, D., & Zahedi, F. M. (2010). The impact of personal dispositions on information sensitivity, privacy concern and trust in disclosing health information online. *Decision Support Systems*, *49*(2), 138–150. https://doi.org/10.1016/j.dss.2010.01.010

Büchi, M., Just, N., & Latzer, M. (2017). Caring is not enough: The importance of internet skills for online privacy protection. *Information, Communication & Society*, *20*(8), 1261–1278. https://doi.org/10.1080/1369118X.2016.1229001

Budak, J., Rajh, E., Slijepčević, S., & Škrinjarić, B. (2021). Conceptual research framework of consumer resilience to privacy violation online. *Sustainability*, *13*(3), 1238. https://doi.org/10.3390/su13031238

Burdon, M. (2010). Contextualizing the tensions and weaknesses of information privacy and data breach notification laws. *Santa Clara High Technology Law Journal*, *27*(1), 63–129.

Chen, H., & Atkin, D. (2021). Understanding third-person perception about internet privacy risks. *New Media & Society*, *23*(3), 419–437. https://doi.org/10.1177/1461444820902103

Chen, R., Kim, D. J., & Rao, H. R. (2021). A study of social networking site use from a three-pronged security and privacy threat assessment perspective. *Information & Management*, *58*(5), Article 103486, Advanced Online Publication. https://doi.org/10.1016/j.im.2021.103486

Cheng, L., Liu, F., & Yao, D. D. (2017). Enterprise data breach: Causes, challenges, prevention, and future directions. *Wiley Interdisciplinary Reviews: Data Mining and Knowledge Discovery*, 7(5), Article e1211, Advanced Online Publication. https://doi.org/10.1002/widm.1211

Cho, H., Lee, J. S., & Chung, S. (2010). Optimistic bias about online privacy risks: Testing the moderating effects of perceived controllability and prior experience. *Computers in Human Behavior*, *26*(5), 987–995. https://doi.org/10.1016/j.chb.2010.02.012

Clough, J. (2014). A world of difference: The Budapest Convention on Cybercrime and the challenges of harmonisation. *Monash University Law Review*, *40*(3), 698–736.

Conger, K. (2022, June 8). Accused Capital One hacker stands trial for fraud and identity theft. *The New York Times*. https://www.nytimes.com/2022/06/08/technology/capital-one-hacker-trial.html

Convention on Cybercrime. (2001). https://www.coe.int/en/web/cybercrime/the-budapest-convention

Debatin, B., Lovejoy, J. P., Horn, A.-K., & Hughes, B. N. (2009). Facebook and online privacy: Attitudes, behaviors, and unintended consequences. *Journal of Computer-Mediated Communication*, *15*(1), 83–108. https://doi.org/10.1111/j.1083-6101.2009.01494.x

DeGroot, J. M., & Vik, T. A. (2017). "We were not prepared to tell people yet": Confidentiality breaches and boundary turbulence on Facebook. *Computers in Human Behavior*, *70*, 351–359. https://doi.org/10.1016/j.chb.2017.01.016

DLA Piper. (2022, January 18). *DLA Piper GDPR fines and data breach survey*. https://www.dlapiper.com/de/germany/insights/publications/2022/1/dla-piper-gdpr-fines-and-data-breach-survey-2022/

Edwards, B., Hofmeyr, S., & Forrest, S. (2016). Hype and heavy tails: A closer look at data breaches. *Journal of Cybersecurity*, *2*(1), 3–14. https://doi.org/10.1093/cybsec/tyw003

European Commission. (2020). *Special Eurobarometer 499: Europeans' attitudes towards cyber security*. Kantar Belgium.

European Society of Human Genetics. (2010). Statement of the ESHG on direct-to-consumer genetic testing for health-related purposes. *European Journal of Human Genetics*, *18*(12), 1271–1273. https://doi.org/10.1038/ejhg.2010.129

Fairfield, J., & Engel, C. (2015). Privacy as a public good. *Duke Law Journal*, *65*, 95–128. https://doi.org/10.1017/cbo9781316658888.004

Foecking, N., Wang, M., & Huynh, T. L. D. (2021). How do investors react to the data breaches news? Empirical evidence from Facebook Inc. during the years 2016–2019. *Technology in Society*, *67*, Article 101717, Advanced Online Publication. https://doi.org/10.1016/j.techsoc.2021.101717

Gwebu, K. L., Wang, J., & Wang, L. (2018). The role of corporate reputation and crisis response strategies in data breach management. *Journal of Management Information Systems*, *35*(2), 683–714. https://doi.org/10.1080/07421222.2018.1451962

Hammer, B., Zhang, T., Shadbad, F. N., & Agrawal, R. (2019). *Psychological contract violation and sharing intention on Facebook*. Hawaii International Conference on System Sciences 2019, Hawaii. http://hdl.handle.net/10125/59715

Hirsch, D. D. (2016). Privacy, public goods and the tragedy of the trust commons: A response to professors Fairfield and Engel. *Duke Law Journal, 65*, 67–93. https://doi.org/10.2139/ssrn.2783933

Kruikemeier, S., Boerman, S. C., & Bol, N. (2020). Breaching the contract? Using social contract theory to explain individuals' online behavior to safeguard privacy. *Media Psychology, 23*(2), 269–292. https://doi.org/10.1080/15213269.2019.1598434

Lamont, T. (2016, February 28). Life after the Ashley Madison affair. *The Guardian*. https://www.theguardian.com/technology/2016/feb/28/what-happened-after-ashley-madison-was-hacked

Lee, C. B., Lo, H. N., & Tang, H. (2022). Sentiments and perceptions after a privacy breach incident. *Cogent Business & Management, 9*(1), Article 2050018, Advanced Online Publication. https://doi.org/10.1080/23311975.2022.2050018

Madan, S., Savani, K., & Katsikeas, C. S. (2022). Privacy please: Power distance and people's responses to data breaches across countries. *Journal of International Business Studies*, Online First. https://doi.org/10.1057/s41267-022-00519-5

Mamonov, S., & Benbunan-Fich, R. (2015). An empirical investigation of privacy breach perceptions among smartphone application users. *Computers in Human Behavior, 49*, 427–436. https://doi.org/10.1016/j.chb.2015.03.019

Mamonov, S., & Koufaris, M. (2014). The impact of perceived privacy breach on smartphone user attitudes and intention to terminate the relationship with the mobile carrier. *Communications of the Association for Information Systems, 34*(3), Article 60. https://doi.org/10.17705/1CAIS.03460

Masur, P. K. (2019). *Situational privacy and self-disclosure: Communication processes in online environments*. Springer International Publishing.

Masur, P. K., & Scharkow, M. (2016). Disclosure management on social network sites: Individual privacy perceptions and user-directed privacy strategies. *Social Media + Society, 2*(1). https://doi.org/10.1177/2056305116634368

Masur, P. K., & Trepte, S. (2021). Transformative or not? How privacy violation experiences influence online privacy concerns and online information disclosure. *Human Communication Research, 47*(1), 49–74. https://doi.org/10.1093/hcr/hqaa012

Morrison, E. W., & Robinson, S. L. (1997). When employees feel betrayed: A model of how psychological contract violation develops. *Academy of Management Review, 22*(1), 226–256. https://doi.org/10.5465/AMR.1997.9707180265

Murciano-Goroff, R. (2019). *Do data breach disclosure laws increase firms' investment in securing their digital infrastructure*. Workshop on the Economics of Information Security. https://weis2019.econinfosec.org/wp-content/uploads/sites/6/2019/05/weis_2019_paper_33.pdf

Nissenbaum, H. (2011). A contextual approach to privacy online. *Daedalus, 140*(4), 32–48. https://doi.org/10.1162/DAED_a_00113

Osatuyi, B., Passerini, K., Ravarini, A., & Grandhi, S. A. (2018). "Fool me once, shame on you … then, I learn." An examination of information disclosure in social networking sites. *Computers in Human Behavior, 83*, 73–86. https://doi.org/10.1016/j.chb.2018.01.018

Perlroth, N., & Isaac, M. (2018, January 12). Inside Uber's $100,000 payment to a hacker, and the fallout. *The New York Times*. https://www.nytimes.com/2018/01/12/technology/uber-hacker-payment-100000.html

Petronio, S. (2002). *Boundaries of privacy*. State University of New York Press.

Petronio, S. (2016). Communication Privacy Management Theory. In C. R. Berger & M. E. Roloff (Eds.), *ICA international encyclopedias of communication. The international encyclopedia of interpersonal communication*. Wiley Blackwell.

Rajasekharaiah, K. M., Dule, C. S., & Sudarshan, E. (2020). Cyber security challenges and its emerging trends on latest technologies. *IOP Conference Series: Materials Science and Engineering*, 981, 022062. https://doi.org/10.1088/1757-899x/981/2/022062

Rashidi, Y., Kapadia, A., Nippert-Eng, C., & Su, N. M. (2020). "It's easier than causing confrontation": Sanctioning strategies to maintain social norms and privacy on social media. *Proceedings of the ACM on Human-Computer Interaction, 4*(1), 1–25. https://doi.org/10.1145/3392827

Reep-van den Bergh, C., & Junger, M. (2018). Victims of cybercrime in Europe: A review of victim surveys. *Crime Science*, 7(1), Advanced Online Publication. https://doi.org/10.1186/s40163-018-0079-3

Romo, L. K., Thompson, C. M., & Donovan, E. E. (2017). College drinkers' privacy management of alcohol content on social-networking sites. *Communication Studies, 68*(2), 173–189. https://doi.org/10.1080/10510974.2017.1280067

Rosseau, J. J. (1989). *Social Contract Theory*. Adib Publishing.
Smith, H. J., Dinev, T., & Xu, H. (2011). Information privacy research: An interdisciplinary review. *Mis Quarterly*, *35*(4), 989–1016. https://doi.org/10.2307/41409970
Steuber, K. R., & McLaren, R. M. (2015). Privacy recalibration in personal relationships: Rule usage before and after an incident of privacy turbulence. *Communication Quarterly*, *63*(3), 345–364. https://doi.org/10.1080/01463373.2015.1039717
Thielman, S. (2015, August 24). Toronto police report two suicides associated with Ashley Madison hack. *The Guardian*. https://www.theguardian.com/world/2015/aug/24/toronto-suicides-ashley-madison-hack
Trepte, S. (2021). The Social Media Privacy Model: Privacy and communication in the light of social media affordances. *Communication Theory*, *31*(4), 549–570. https://doi.org/10.1093/ct/qtz035
Trepte, S., & Masur, P. K. (2017). *Privacy attitudes, perceptions, and behaviors of the German population: Research report of a representative survey study*. Germany: University of Hohenheim.
Trepte, S., Dienlin, T., & Reinecke, L. (2014). Risky behaviors. How online experiences influence privacy behaviors. In B. Stark, O. Quiring, & N. Jackob (Eds.), *Schriftenreihe der Deutschen Gesellschaft für Publizistik- und Kommunikationswissenschaft: Vol. 41. Von der Gutenberg-Galaxis zur Google-Galaxis: Alte und neue Grenzvermessungen nach 50 Jahren DGPuK* (pp. 225–244). UVK.
UNCTAD. (2022, July 30). *Cybercrime Legislation Worldwide*. https://unctad.org/page/cybercrime-legislation-worldwide
United States Department of Justice. (2022). Former Seattle tech worker convicted of wire fraud and computer intrusions. https://www.justice.gov/usao-wdwa/pr/former-seattle-tech-worker-convicted-wire-fraud-and-computer-intrusions
van der Schyff, K., & Flowerday, S. (2021). Mediating effects of information security awareness. *Computers & Security*, *106*, Article 102313, Advanced Online Publication. https://doi.org/10.1016/j.cose.2021.102313
Virtanen, S. M. (2017). Fear of cybercrime in Europe: Examining the effects of victimization and vulnerabilities. *Psychiatry, Psychology, and Law*, *24*(3), 323–338. https://doi.org/10.1080/13218719.2017.1315785
Waldman, A. E. (2018). *Privacy as trust*. Cambridge University Press. https://doi.org/10.1017/9781316888667

13
PRIVACY CYNICISM
Resignation in the Face of Agency Constraints

Giulia Ranzini[1], *Christoph Lutz*[2], *and Christian Pieter Hoffmann*[3]

[1]VRIJE UNIVERSITEIT AMSTERDAM, THE NETHERLANDS
[2]BI NORWEGIAN BUSINESS SCHOOL, NORWAY
[3]UNIVERSITÄT LEIPZIG, GERMANY

Introduction

When it comes to privacy-related decision-making, the consideration of risk/benefit tradeoffs, also known as the *privacy calculus* (see chapter 7 by Dienlin on the privacy calculus; Dienlin, 2023), remains a fundamental theory to investigate how and why users share information online (Dinev & Hart, 2006). However, recent technological and societal changes have added complexity to the constraints under which the privacy calculus unfolds. For example, the diffusion of wearable devices (Li et al., 2016; Rauschnabel et al., 2018) and smart technologies (Kim & Park, 2020) has rendered data sharing ubiquitous and complicated the data and privacy ecosystem (Lutz & Newlands, 2021). Data-intensive services, such as search engines and social media platforms, can be considered critical infrastructures of modern society and are difficult to avoid (Van Dijck et al., 2018). The recent Covid-19 pandemic accelerated the digitalization of white-collar work (Newlands et al., 2020), while adding to a flourishing "platform economy" of digitally mediated blue-collar jobs. Data sharing appears increasingly as a requirement rather than a choice.

Concepts such as "surveillance capitalism" (Zuboff, 2019) or "data capitalism" (West, 2019) highlight a power asymmetry. On the one hand, digital platforms require personal data to provide services. On the other, they leave users few alternatives to opt-out or avoid participation altogether. In such heavily constrained settings, the traditional privacy calculus model is challenged by a lack of user agency. As a result, users develop attitudes of apathy, resignation, or even cynicism (Draper & Turow, 2019; Hargittai & Marwick, 2016; Lutz et al., 2020). They invest fewer resources (time, money, and attention) to protect their privacy online because they no longer see the value in such efforts.

From a normative standpoint, widespread privacy cynicism is problematic as it weakens the emancipatory functions of privacy, especially its facilitation of personal autonomy (Rössler, 2018) and self-development (Koops et al., 2016). If individuals feel powerless, resigned, and apathetic towards privacy, they are more likely to face risks and exploitation online. Cynicism may also contribute to a deterioration of institutional trust. Finally, users may find their social and economic opportunities constrained because digital traces can determine a person's future prospects, for example, in the form of social credit scoring (see chapter 22 by Chen, Engelmann, & Grossklags on social crediting and privacy, Chen et al., 2023; Liang et al., 2018).

DOI: 10.4324/9781003244677-15

This chapter will introduce the concept of privacy cynicism, explore its theoretical foundation and compare it to adjacent concepts, discuss constraints that reduce user agency and make privacy cynicism more prevalent, and point to future research directions in communication research and beyond.

Definitions

The concept of privacy cynicism was introduced by Hoffmann et al. (2016) as an "*attitude of uncertainty, powerlessness, and mistrust towards the handling of personal data by online services, rendering privacy protection behavior subjectively futile*" (p. 2). Privacy cynicism is characterized as a cognitive coping mechanism for users abstaining from privacy protection behavior as "it allows fearful, low-skilled users to take advantage of the desired online services without cognitive dissonance since privacy protection behavior can be rationalized as useless or ineffective" (ibid.). Subsequently (Lutz et al., 2020), the authors positioned the concept in the context of institutional privacy concerns (also termed vertical privacy concerns; Masur, 2020). Privacy cynicism arises in interactions with online services that users perceive as powerful, challenging to understand, and, especially in terms of their data handling, opaque. The role of privacy cynicism in the context of social (horizontal) privacy concerns remains understudied.

Lutz et al. (2020) propose four dimensions of privacy cynicism (see Figure 13.1).

1 *Mistrust*: Cynicism is commonly situated within dyadic relationships. It implies assumptions over the motives of an interaction partner (Mills & Keil, 2005), who is presumed to be self-interested and opportunistic. While trust, also determined within dyadic interactions, is based on assumptions of competence, benevolence, and integrity (Bhattacherjee, 2002), cynicism, instead, implies a level of mistrust and antagonism towards the interaction partner (Almada et al., 1991). Various survey studies have documented low trust or even mistrust of users towards social media platforms, even the ones they use.

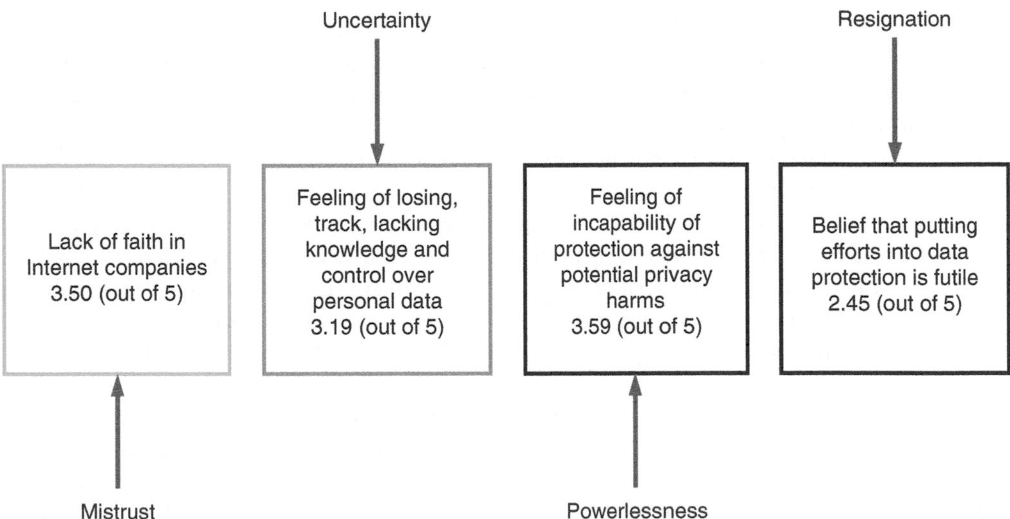

Figure 13.1 The Four Dimensions of Privacy Cynicism, Their Definition and Prevalence in Germany (Lutz et al., 2020). The Numbers Are Arithmetic Means on a 1–5 Likert Scale

2 *Powerlessness:* Another important dimension of cynicism, frequently explored in studies of organizational cynicism, rests on a perceived power asymmetry in the dyadic relationship (Dean et al., 1998). Cynicism arises when one partner is mistrustful of the other, can exercise little or no control over decision-making, and is therefore ultimately dependent on the other. Users frequently report a lack of choice in the use of social media platforms because social or occupational constraints necessitate a social media presence. Major social media companies are seen as powerful and remote entities that can change their terms of use at a whim. Network effects and a lack of interoperability impede switching to alternative providers.

3 *Uncertainty:* In dyadic relationships, a partner's distrust towards a more powerful other can be compensated by complete transparency over their behavior; when this occurs, cynicism can be avoided. If, however, the actions of the more powerful, distrusted other are also intransparent or too complex to understand, uncertainty, mistrust, and powerlessness interact to create psychological stress and frustration that cannot be alleviated by removing oneself from the situation. Given the levels of digital literacies among social media users, many find themselves in a position where they cannot fully understand the workings of digital platforms.

4 *Resignation:* Finally, if the stress created by the culmination of mistrust, powerlessness, and uncertainty cannot be resolved by either severing the relationship or fighting back against its conditions, individuals may choose to resign. They functionally adhere to the requirements of the relationship, but psychologically detach and protect their sense of self by resorting to cynicism. Applied to social media, this implies that despite doubting platform providers' integrity or benevolence, conceiving of these platforms as unresponsive corporate giants, and/or lacking an understanding of the platforms' functions, users resign themselves unhappily to continued reliance on these digital infrastructures, rather than disconnecting or engaging in activism. Resignation can therefore be conceptualized as a fourth dimension of cynicism. Resignation to the conditions of a relationship does not, however, imply a state of passivity or even victimhood, as will be discussed in the following.

Theoretical Foundations

Privacy cynicism (Hoffmann et al., 2016; Lutz et al., 2020) accounts for (a) users' mistrust vis-à-vis online services, (b) salient privacy concerns, (c) a lack of user agency or choice, and (d) a lack of privacy protection behavior. It provides a promising new avenue for understanding a fundamental conundrum of online privacy.

The privacy cynicism concept emerged in the context of related concepts which touch upon essential elements of cynicism.

Hargittai and Marwick (2016) describe a rising feeling of "privacy apathy" among young Internet users, who feel that they cannot effectively protect their personal data from online platforms, but use them anyhow, frequently due to social pressures. They fear that privacy violations are inevitable or only preventable if users entirely opt-out of online services – a solution that is deemed unrealistic. The authors describe this stance as "quite cynical" (p. 3751). They also find that apathy is related to lower technical skills.

Situated in the context of state-corporate surveillance programs, Dencik and Cable (2017) propose the concept of "surveillance realism," "a simultaneous unease among citizens with data collection alongside the active normalization of surveillance that limits the possibilities of enacting modes of citizenship and of imagining alternatives" (p. 763). Again, the authors find that while users are aware of, and worried about, persistent surveillance, they rationalize a lack of countermeasures by pointing out their futility. Importantly, the authors stress that users frequently lack an actual understanding of surveillance mechanisms.

Another important concept closely related to privacy cynicism is "digital resignation" (Turow et al., 2015), "the condition produced when people desire to control the information digital entities have about them but feel unable to do so" (Draper & Turow, 2019, p. 1824). The authors build on a study on the Tradeoff Fallacy, "a pervasive feeling among Americans that the corporate practice of trading access to services and content for personal information is unfair" (p. 1826). They find that rather than challenging this fallacy, many users resign and grumblingly accept a lack of control over their personal privacy. As noted, resignation can be conceptualized as a dimension of cynicism. Importantly, Draper and Turow (2019) argue that digital resignation can constitute a purposeful form of inaction. They point out that privacy resignation does not entirely preclude protective behavior and discuss opportunities to transform passive resignation into rational and active digital disengagement.

Choi et al. (2018) build on burnout literature to develop the concept of "privacy fatigue." They define privacy fatigue as "a psychological state of tiredness with the issue of online privacy" (p. 43.). The authors argue that Internet users frequently encounter privacy breaches (or reporting on such breaches), which leaves them increasingly emotionally exhausted and unwilling to address privacy concerns or protection behavior. This ultimately results in "disengagement," which is akin to resignation (Hoffmann et al., 2016; Turow et al., 2015).

Cho (2021) proposes "privacy helplessness" to describe a trait-like characteristic in which individuals generalize from repeat averse experiences, such as privacy breaches, leading to resignative behavior. Similar to privacy cynicism, a perceived lack of control is central to the development of privacy helplessness.

To summarize, an emerging strand of research focuses on user perceptions of inescapable surveillance or privacy infringements and resultant feelings of futility towards privacy protection behavior. Accounts differ somewhat on whether users need to experience privacy breaches personally or if perceptions of ubiquitous privacy breaches can derive from media reporting. Many users feel they need to employ digital services, rendering digital disengagement an unfeasible option. Social expectations or norms as well as explicit demands can drive the need to engage. Users tend to lack an understanding of surveillance technologies, and platforms are often opaque in their privacy policies (Steinfeld, 2016). This lack of understanding interacts with a feeling of powerlessness. In other words, users both cannot abstain from online engagement and believe that their online privacy is constantly being violated, yet might not understand when, how, and by whom. The resultant cognitive dissonance and emotional tensions are ultimately resolved by giving up on privacy protection. However, the conceptualizations of resignation disagree on whether it results in a complete abdication of protective behavior.

Agency Constraints That Foster Privacy Cynicism

During the ongoing Covid-19 pandemic, many activities previously conducted "outside the home," such as work, education, exercise, and socializing, have shifted to the digital realm, with an intensified reliance on digital media and a reduced autonomy in decision-making when it comes to data sharing. However, the trend towards an even more constrained privacy calculus, where users are increasingly incapable of evaluating their risks and benefits before sharing information online, is not novel (Hoffmann et al., 2016; Lutz et al., 2020; Zuboff, 2019). Reviewing existing studies in light of the changes in our relationship to digital and social media, five main constraints to the privacy calculus emerge (see Figure 13.2). These constraints are loosely based on Masur et al. (2021) and create a condition conducive to privacy cynicism.

A first constraint is related to what Bazarova and Masur (2020) identified as a *"networked ecology:"* A growing interdependence of information sharing, where privacy decisions are no longer exclusively vertical but also increasingly horizontal (see also Lutz & Hoffmann, 2017 on "passive

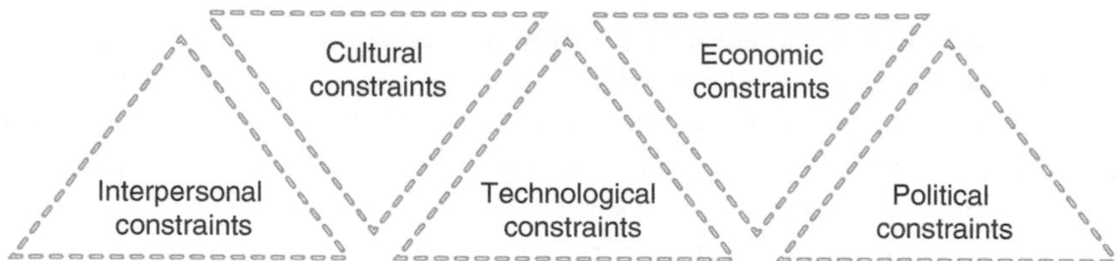

Figure 13.2 Five Constraints to the Privacy Calculus

participation"). The widespread success of visual social network sites (SNS) like Instagram or TikTok emphasizes how interpersonal constraints impact the privacy calculus through practices like responses or re-sharing of other users' pictures or videos. The exposure of a third party's content to a new and possibly unintended audience (Bazarova & Masur, 2020) brings about risks and benefits impossible for the original creator to evaluate (De Wolf, 2020). An example of this behavior in close relationships is "sharenting," a phenomenon where parents share children-related content on social media (Blum-Ross & Livingstone, 2017; Ranzini et al., 2020; see chapters 16 and 17 by Walrave on children, adolescents, and privacy, Walrave, 2023a, 2023b), projecting today's risk/benefits evaluations onto tomorrow's adults. Faced with such constraints, privacy cynicism may rise in relation to horizontal privacy concerns as a reaction to the (potentially overwhelming) powers of digital connectivity in users' social environment, rather than in the vertical user relationship to platform providers.

The role of culture, both national (Trepte et al., 2017) and specific to a user's network (Ranzini et al., 2020), is a broadly investigated influence on users' privacy calculus. Country-based differences, including traits such as collectivism/individualism (Trepte et al., 2017) but also trust in institutions (Xu et al., 2011), may influence and sometimes restrict an individual's evaluation of the risks and benefits of self-disclosure. As such, the spectrum of available privacy choices for a Western user might look very different from the perspectives of users in the East or Global South. In culturally constrained situations, privacy cynicism might serve as a reaction and coping mechanism to the inevitability of socio-technical norms.

One large assumption of the privacy calculus is that users have a degree of consciousness over the amount, type, and audience for data they disclose, which is certainly the case for some types of digital interaction (such as a peer-to-peer messaging exchange; Zingales, 2017). Nonetheless, online platforms increasingly rely on the continuous collection of multifaceted personal data, transcending the type of decision-making implied by posting a photo on an SNS. Examples of such platforms are online communities created around wearable and smart technology, such as the Strava app (Couture, 2021): While users initially evaluate their sharing of behavioral data in exchange for performance statistics (Kang & Jung, 2021), they might not be fully conscious of the constant exchange of information between their watch and the app (Rivers, 2020). Confronted with such ubiquitous technologies, users might resort to privacy cynicism as a reaction of detachment to the opacity and incomprehensibility of these systems.

Economic constraints refer to the economic situation that prevents or constrains users from engaging in behavior that safeguards their privacy. Many major digital platforms are free to use but rely on sophisticated data tracking for their business model (Zuboff, 2019), whereas more privacy friendly options are less attractive to use due to network effects, limited functionality, or higher costs. For example, Apple iPhones, which arguably offer better privacy than some competitor smartphones, are more expensive. Income inequality might also affect individual privacy decision-making: Studies in the sharing of self-produced sexual content noted that differences in income, more than gender, predicted sharing (Blake et al., 2018). Under a privacy lens, such a result suggests that content that is more evidently marketable nudges users to data sharing. In these circumstances, privacy cynicism is particularly likely to emerge among economically constrained citizens, who feel that privacy is increasingly commoditized, becoming a luxury and out of reach for them.

Similar to social, cultural, technological, and economic constraints, political constraints (including legal constraints) limit user agency and impede a privacy calculus. Circumstances where surveillance technology is forced onto citizens by governments (e.g., monitoring of digital traces and social media censorship), where digital technology is needed to participate in social life (e.g., vaccine passports), or where citizens are exposed to social credit scoring (see chapter 22 by Chen, Engelmann, & Grossklags on social crediting and privacy; Liang et al., 2018) could evoke privacy cynicism.

Conclusion: Future Directions

Research on privacy cynicism is still in its infancy, despite a recent uptick in interest in the topic (e.g., Acikgoz & Perez-Vega, 2021; Van Ooijen et al., 2022).[1] Many open questions remain and some of the most pressing knowledge gaps and directions for future research will be discussed in the remainder of this chapter.

First, theory development and *conceptual clarification* are needed. Depending on context and application, cynicism has been defined as a trait, an attitude (general or specific), or a belief (Andersson, 1996; Dean et al., 1998). Hoffmann et al. (2016) define privacy cynicism as an attitude, but some related concepts may benefit from further clarification. In that regard, privacy cynicism could be connected to other forms of cynicism such as political cynicism (Agger et al., 1961) and organizational cynicism (Dean et al., 1998). Do we expect politically and organizationally cynical users to be equally cynical in terms of privacy? Extant work on political cynicism also highlights the importance of news and media coverage and how exposure to negative coverage can increase political cynicism (see Hanson et al., 2013 for an overview). Privacy research has shown initial interest in media coverage (Von Pape et al., 2017), and further identifying the influence of media coverage and exposure on privacy cynicism would be a worthwhile endeavor. Future research should also explore the differences and similarities between privacy cynicism and privacy apathy, surveillance realism, privacy fatigue, digital resignation, and privacy helplessness. While privacy cynicism and apathy are used almost synonymously, resignation may better be conceptualized as a dimension of cynicism. Privacy helplessness could be understood in relation to powerlessness or uncertainty or might be examined as a predictor of cynicism. Conversely, privacy fatigue may be an outcome of a prolonged state of cynicism. Privacy cynicism should also be embedded into established privacy theories in communication research such as privacy as contextual integrity (Nissenbaum, 2009) and communication privacy management (Petronio, 2002). For example, a "blanket" form of privacy cynicism could affect users' ability to devise privacy rules for different environments, leading them to share indiscriminately within private and public networks (Petronio & Child, 2020). In a broader sense, privacy cynicism could be related to broader sociological and communication theories such as digital inequalities (Lutz, 2019), relating privacy cynicism to social vulnerability and marginality (Marwick & boyd, 2018).

Second, empirical research should investigate salient *antecedents and outcomes* of privacy cynicism. For antecedents, social factors (e.g., demographic characteristics, socio-economic standing), psychological correlates (e.g., personality traits), and behavioral aspects (e.g., use habits, digital skills) should be included for a holistic understanding. Moreover, the four dimensions of privacy cynicism (Lutz et al., 2020) can be differentiated and tested in terms of their social, psychological, and behavioral structuration. For outcomes, important considerations relate to benefits and harms, connecting privacy cynicism to work on the third-level digital divide (Blank & Lutz, 2018; Lutz, 2019; Van Deursen & Helsper, 2015). Do cynical users expose themselves and others to harm from digital media, for example, sharing passwords with family and friends, spreading misinformation, or falling for manipulation such as financial scams? Or do they benefit more from digital technologies through increased inclusion and participation than non-cynical, but potentially over-protective users?

As noted above, cynicism does not necessarily imply passivity. Since they are resigned, cynical users do not actively challenge the conditions of their social media use (but may be moved to do so; see Draper & Turow, 2019). Some more low-level forms of compensatory behaviors may however be expressed to alleviate psychological tension. Among them may be cynical remarks or comments, snark, sarcasm, and similar forms of negatively tinted communication. In the context of organizational cynicism, "disparaging and critical behaviors" have been described as core elements (Dean et al., 1998, p. 345). "This includes 'knowing' looks and rolling eyes, as well as the smirks and sneers by which cynics (and Cynics) have long been known" (ibid.). How such cynical behaviors relate to social media use remains to be explored.

Third, *contextual differentiation* and *comparative research* can help better understand privacy cynicism. Privacy research is often based on single-context or single-country studies, with a strong need for more comparative perspectives (see chapter 14 by Cho & Li on intercultural privacy, Cho & Li, 2023; Masur et al., 2021). The same is true for research on privacy cynicism. Adjacent to comparing privacy cynicism across different structures, research might also consider different levels, analyzing cynicism on a macro, meso, and micro level (Aeschlimann et al., 2015). The meso level is particularly interesting due to the element of "corporate cultivation" to digital resignation and privacy cynicism (Draper & Turow, 2019). Future research could study this corporate cultivation and the different strategies organizations employ in more detail. Beyond platform companies, the role of institutions such as schools, the media sector, universities, public services, and law enforcement in the creation or mitigation of privacy cynicism merits attention.

Fourth and finally, future research should investigate potential *remedies* to privacy cynicism. Here, two main strands can be differentiated: One top-down and focused on policy, and one bottom-up and focused on resistance and repair (Velkova & Kaun, 2021). Within the first strand, questions such as the following should be answered: How much do existing privacy laws (e.g., the General Data Protection Regulation) empower users and reduce privacy cynicism? What is the role of technological interventions, potentially backed by frameworks such as privacy-by-design (Tamò-Larrieux, 2018), to give users certain agency back? Do media literacy initiatives need to take into consideration the role of privacy cynicism? Since these are interdisciplinary questions, communication researchers might want to team up with legal scholars and computer scientists for more impactful results. Within the second strand, collective efforts are promising that tackle privacy cynicism through participatory practices such as data activism (Milan & Van der Velden, 2016), data justice (Dencik et al., 2016), and design justice (Costanza-Chock, 2020). If and how communities of practice and bottom-up initiatives can meaningfully counteract privacy cynicism, this can be researched with case studies and action research.

Note

1 A panel at ICA 2022, convened by the authors of this chapter as well as Nora Draper and Joe Turow, sparked lively discussions on the topic.

References

Acikgoz, F., & Vega, R. P. (2021). The role of privacy cynicism in consumer habits with voice assistants: A technology acceptance model perspective. *International Journal of Human–Computer Interaction*, 1–15. https://doi.org/10.1080/10447318.2021.1987677

Aeschlimann, L., Harasgama, R., Kehr, F., Lutz, C., Milanova, V., Müller, S., … & Tamò-Larrieux, A. (2015). Re-setting the stage for privacy: A multi-layered privacy interaction framework and its application. In S. Brändli, R. Harasgama, R. Schister, & A. Tamò (Eds.), *Mensch und maschine - Symbiose oder parasitismus?* (pp. 1–41). Stämpfli.

Agger, R. E., Goldstein, M. N., & Pearl, S. A. (1961). Political cynicism: Measurement and meaning. *The Journal of Politics, 23*(3), 477–506.

Almada, S. J., Zonderman, A. B., Shekelle, R. B., Dyer, A. R., Daviglus, M. L., Costa, P. T., & Stamler, J. (1991). Neuroticism and cynicism and risk of death in middle-aged men. *Psychosomatic Medicine, 53*(2), 165–175.

Andersson, L. M. (1996). Employee cynicism: An examination using a contract violation framework. *Human Relations, 49*(11), 1395–1418.

Bazarova, N. N., & Masur, P. K. (2020). Towards an integration of individualistic, networked, and institutional approaches to online disclosure and privacy in a networked ecology. *Current Opinion in Psychology, 36*, 118–123.

Bhattacherjee, A. (2002). Individual trust in online firms: Scale development and initial test. *Journal of Management Information Systems, 19*(1), 211–241.

Blake, K. R., Bastian, B., Denson, T. F., Grosjean, P., & Brooks, R. C. (2018). Income inequality not gender inequality positively covaries with female sexualization on social media. *Proceedings of the National Academy of Sciences, 115*(35), 8722–8727.

Blank, G., & Lutz, C. (2018). Benefits and harms from internet use: A differentiated analysis of Great Britain. *New Media & Society, 20*(2), 618–640.

Blum-Ross, A., & Livingstone, S. (2017). "Sharenting," parent blogging, and the boundaries of the digital self. *Popular Communication, 15*(2), 110–125.

Chen, M., Engelmann, S., & Grossklags, J. (2023). Social credit system and privacy. In S. Trepte & P. K. Masur (Eds.), *The Routledge Handbook of Privacy and Social Media* (pp. 227–236). Routledge.

Cho, H. (2021). Privacy helplessness on social media: Its constituents, antecedents and consequences. *Internet Research, 32*(1), 150–171.

Cho, H., & Li, Y. (2023). Intercultural privacy. In S. Trepte & P. K. Masur (Eds.), *The Routledge Handbook of Privacy and Social Media* (pp. 144–151). Routledge.

Choi, H., Park, J., & Jung, Y. (2018). The role of privacy fatigue in online privacy behavior. *Computers in Human Behavior, 81*, 42–51.

Costanza-Chock, S. (2020). *Design justice: Community-led practices to build the world we need.* MIT Press.

Couture, J. (2021). Reflections from the 'Strava-sphere': Kudos, community, and (self-)surveillance on a social network for athletes. *Qualitative Research in Sport, Exercise and Health, 13*(1), 184–200.

De Wolf, R. (2020). Contextualizing how teens manage personal and interpersonal privacy on social media. *New Media & Society, 22*(6), 1058–1075.

Dean, J. W., Brandes, P., & Dharwadkar, R. (1998). Organizational cynicism. *Academy of Management Review, 23*(2), 341–352.

Dencik, L., & Cable, J. (2017). The advent of surveillance realism: Public opinion and activist responses to the Snowden leaks. *International Journal of Communication, 11*, 763–781. https://ijoc.org/index.php/ijoc/article/view/5524/1939

Dencik, L., Hintz, A., & Cable, J. (2016). Towards data justice? The ambiguity of anti-surveillance resistance in political activism. *Big Data & Society, 3*(2), 1–12.

Dienlin, T. (2023). Privacy calculus: Theory, studies, and new perspectives. In S. Trepte & P. K. Masur (Eds.), *The Routledge Handbook of Privacy and Social Media* (pp. 70–79). Routledge.

Dinev, T., & Hart, P. (2006). An extended privacy calculus model for e-commerce transactions. *Information Systems Research, 17*(1), 61–80.

Draper, N. A., & Turow, J. (2019). The corporate cultivation of digital resignation. *New Media & Society, 21*(8), 1824–1839.

Hanson, G., Haridakis, P. M., Cunningham, A. W., Sharma, R., & Ponder, J. D. (2013). The 2008 presidential campaign: Political cynicism in the age of Facebook, MySpace and YouTube. In G. Hanson et al. (Eds.), *New media, campaigning and the 2008 Facebook election* (pp. 39–62). Routledge.

Hargittai, E., & Marwick, A. (2016). "What can I really do?" Explaining the privacy paradox with online apathy. *International Journal of Communication, 10*, 3737–3757.

Hoffmann, C. P., Lutz, C., & Ranzini, G. (2016). Privacy cynicism: A new approach to the privacy paradox. *Cyberpsychology: Journal of Psychosocial Research on Cyberspace, 10*(4), article 7.

Kang, H., & Jung, E. H. (2021). The smart wearables-privacy paradox: A cluster analysis of smartwatch users. *Behaviour & Information Technology, 40*(16), 1755–1768.

Kim, J., & Park, E. (2020). Understanding social resistance to determine the future of Internet of Things (IoT) services. *Behaviour & Information Technology*, 1–11. https://doi.org/10.1080/0144929X.2020.1827033

Koops, B. J., Newell, B. C., Timan, T., Škorvánek, I., Chokrevski, T., & Galič, M. (2016). A typology of privacy. *University of Pennsylvania Journal of International Law, 38*(2), 483–575.

Li, H., Wu, J., Gao, Y., & Shi, Y. (2016). Examining individuals' adoption of healthcare wearable devices: An empirical study from privacy calculus perspective. *International Journal of Medical Informatics, 88*, 8–17.

Liang, F., Das, V., Kostyuk, N., & Hussain, M. M. (2018). Constructing a data-driven society: China's social credit system as a state surveillance infrastructure. *Policy & Internet, 10*(4), 415–453.

Lutz, C. (2019). Digital inequalities in the age of artificial intelligence and big data. *Human Behavior and Emerging Technologies, 1*(2), 141–148.

Lutz, C., & Hoffmann, C. P. (2017). The dark side of online participation: Exploring non-, passive and negative participation. *Information, Communication & Society, 20*(6), 876–897.

Lutz, C., & Newlands, G. (2021). Privacy and smart speakers: A multi-dimensional approach. *The Information Society, 37*(3), 147–162.

Lutz, C., Hoffmann, C. P., & Ranzini, G. (2020). Data capitalism and the user: An exploration of privacy cynicism in Germany. *New Media & Society, 22*(7), 1168–1187.

Marwick, A. E., & boyd, d. (2018). Understanding privacy at the margins. *International Journal of Communication, 12*, 1157–1165.

Masur, P. K. (2020). How online privacy literacy supports self-data protection and self-determination in the age of information. *Media and Communication, 8*(2), 258–269.

Masur, P. K., Epstein, D., Quinn, K., Wilhelm, C., Baruh, L., & Lutz, C. (2021). A comparative privacy research framework. https://osf.io/preprints/socarxiv/fjqhs/

Milan, S., & Van der Velden, L. (2016). The alternative epistemologies of data activism. *Digital Culture & Society, 2*(2), 57–74.

Mills, C. M., & Keil, F. C. (2005). The development of cynicism. *Psychological Science, 16*(5), 385–390.

Newlands, G., Lutz, C., Tamò-Larrieux, A., Villaronga, E. F., Harasgama, R., & Scheitlin, G. (2020). Innovation under pressure: Implications for data privacy during the Covid-19 pandemic. *Big Data & Society,* 7(2), 1–14.

Nissenbaum, H. (2009). *Privacy in context.* Stanford University Press.

Petronio, S. (2002). *Boundaries of privacy: Dialectics of disclosure.* SUNY Press.

Petronio, S., & Child, J. T. (2020). Conceptualization and operationalization: Utility of communication privacy management theory. *Current Opinion in Psychology*, 31, 76–82. https://doi.org/10.1016/j.copsyc.2019.08.009.

Ranzini, G., Newlands, G., & Lutz, C. (2020). Sharenting, peer influence, and privacy concerns: A study on the Instagram-sharing behaviors of parents in the United Kingdom. *Social Media + Society, 6*(4), 1–13.

Rauschnabel, P. A., He, J., & Ro, Y. K. (2018). Antecedents to the adoption of augmented reality smart glasses: A closer look at privacy risks. *Journal of Business Research, 92*, 374–384.

Rössler, B. (2018). *The value of privacy.* John Wiley & Sons.

Rivers, D. J. (2020). Strava as a discursive field of practice: Technological affordances and mediated cycling motivations. *Discourse, Context & Media*, 34, 100345.

Steinfeld, N. (2016). "I agree to the terms and conditions": (How) do users read privacy policies online? An eye-tracking experiment. *Computers in Human Behavior, 55*, 992–1000.

Tamò-Larrieux, A. (2018). *Designing for privacy and its legal framework.* Springer.

Trepte, S., Reinecke, L., Ellison, N. B., Quiring, O., Yao, M. Z., & Ziegele, M. (2017). A cross-cultural perspective on the privacy calculus. *Social Media + Society, 3*(1), 1–13.

Turow, J., Hennessy, M., & Draper, N. (2015). The Tradeoff fallacy: How marketers are misrepresenting American consumers and opening them up to exploitation. *SSRN Electronic Journal.* https://doi.org/10.2139/ssrn.2820060

Van Deursen, A. J., & Helsper, E. J. (2015). The third-level digital divide: Who benefits most from being online? In *Communication and information technologies annual* (pp. 29–52). Emerald.

Van Dijck, J., Poell, T., & De Waal, M. (2018). *The platform society: Public values in a connective world.* Oxford University Press.

Van Ooijen, I., Segijn, C. M., & Opree, S. J. (2022). Privacy cynicism and its role in privacy decision-making. *Communication Research*, 1–32. https://doi.org/10.1177/00936502211060984

Velkova, J., & Kaun, A. (2021). Algorithmic resistance: Media practices and the politics of repair. *Information, Communication & Society, 24*(4), 523–540.

Von Pape, T., Trepte, S., & Mothes, C. (2017). Privacy by disaster? Press coverage of privacy and digital technology. *European Journal of Communication, 32*(3), 189–207.

Walrave, M. (2023a). The translucent family: Sharenting and privacy negotiations between children and parents. In S. Trepte & P. K. Masur (Eds.), *The Routledge Handbook of Privacy and Social Media* (pp. 165–174). Routledge.

Walrave, M. (2023b). An intimate relation: Adolescent development, self-disclosure, and privacy. In S. Trepte & P. K. Masur (Eds.), *The Routledge Handbook of Privacy and Social Media* (pp. 175–184). Routledge.

West, S. M. (2019). Data capitalism: Redefining the logics of surveillance and privacy. *Business & Society*, *58*(1), 20–41.

Xu, H., Dinev, T., Smith, J., & Hart, P. (2011). Information privacy concerns: Linking individual perceptions with institutional privacy assurances. *Journal of the Association for Information Systems*, *12*(12), 1.

Zingales, N. (2017). Between a rock and two hard places: WhatsApp at the crossroad of competition, data protection and consumer law. *Computer Law & Security Review*, *33*(4).

Zuboff, S. (2019). *The age of surveillance capitalism*. Profile Books.

14
INTERCULTURAL PRIVACY

Hichang Cho[1] *and Yao Li*[2]

[1]NATIONAL UNIVERSITY OF SINGAPORE, SINGAPORE
[2]UNIVERSITY OF CENTRAL FLORIDA, USA

Introduction

Privacy is a universal and fundamental human right, and every society and culture values privacy in some form (Altman, 1975; Westin, 1967). However, a growing body of studies suggests that social norms and behavioral patterns on online privacy vary considerably across cultures and countries (Cho et al., 2018; Li et al., 2022). As suggested by Westin, privacy "is a social, cultural, and legal concept, all three of which vary from country to country" (1967, p. 156). As such, the ways in which people view and manage their privacy should change substantially across cultures due to different cultural and historical environments that tend to favor different values and interests, such as collective over individual interests or autonomy/independence over social relatedness/interdependence (Bellman et al., 2004; Cho et al., 2009). For instance, people in individualistic cultures tend to consider privacy a fundamental human right. In contrast, members in collectivism-oriented cultures view it as something that can be negotiated or compromised to a certain extent for the benefit of collectives (Cho et al., 2009). Therefore, culture is a crucial construct in privacy research, with which we can explain the homogeneity of privacy norms within cultures as well as the diversity of privacy behaviors across cultures.

Information privacy concerns extend beyond a single national or cultural boundary (Milberg et al., 1995) as online businesses and services have rapidly spread across the world. This is particularly evident in the context of social media, in which billions of social media users routinely share personal information with a large audience and providers distributed across national and cultural borders. A growing body of studies has demonstrated the crucial role of cultures in shaping privacy perceptions and behaviors among social media users (Li et al., 2021). Therefore, it is critical for privacy researchers to develop an accurate and in-depth understanding of the sources and implications of intercultural differences in privacy.

This chapter reviews the current status of intercultural privacy research and emerging themes and approaches in the field of social media. We discuss their implications for privacy research. Finally, we highlight the limitations of current intercultural privacy studies and directions for future research.

Key Concepts and Definitions

In general, culture refers to the set of ideas, beliefs, behavioral standards, and conventions that are more common among its members than among outsiders (Poortinga & Van Hemert, 2001). Culture

DOI: 10.4324/9781003244677-16

is a challenging construct to research as it is defined and measured in multiple and divergent ways (Erez & Earley, 1993; Masur et al., 2021). Among these, this chapter focuses on the concept of national culture (Hofstede, 2010) because it has been frequently employed and tested in most intercultural privacy research (Cho et al., 2009; Krasnova & Veltri, 2010; Milberg et al., 2000; Sawaya et al., 2017). National culture refers to norms, social behaviors, beliefs, customs, and values shared by the population of a nation (Hofstede et al., 2010; Schwartz, 1994). According to this framework, culture is broadly defined as the "collective programming of the mind that distinguishes the members of one group from others" (Hofstede et al., 2010). Researchers in psychology, management science, and other disciplines of social sciences have been keenly interested in studying the cultural differences at the national level, as it highlights the differences between national populations. Although there are considerable variances between individuals in the same nations, research has shown that people in the same national culture exhibit certain differences when compared with other cultures (Hofstede, 2011).

It is worthwhile to note that the concept of national culture has been criticized on several grounds (McSweeney, 2002). Specifically, the concept of national culture originated from a study examining cultural differences in work settings (i.e., IBM). As such, researchers have questioned if the findings can be applied to other social contexts (McSweeney, 2002). In addition, assigning broad values to nations can be problematic as it over-privileges continuity and uniformity, neglecting the existence of subcultures and cultural and ethnic differences within nations (McSweeney, 2009). Therefore, researchers have called for more dynamic views of culture, in which culture is seen as contested, temporal, emergent, and multi-level (e.g., Myers & Tan, 2002). Despite such limitations, national culture is still considered a useful and relevant concept to understand commonalities/variances within/across countries (Gelfand et al., 2007; Steenkamp, 2001). Importantly, this national culture framework does not assume that each individual within a country would share the same national culture. Rather, national culture is conceptualized as a statistical central tendency, indicating the degree to which certain values (e.g., individualism vs. collectivism) are more likely to be observed within a given society (Hofstede, 2011).

Cultural differences (vs. commonalties) across (vs. within) have been ascribed to various dimensions, such as individualism, power distance, and uncertainty avoidance (Hofstede et al., 2010) or autonomy, egalitarianism, harmony, etc. (Schwartz, 1994). While country and language have been commonly used to indicate culture, the cultural dimensions are conceptual constructs that can depict the underlying patterns of how people think and live in different countries and offer us a better way to classify and quantify the complex patterns of culture (Li et al., 2017). Researchers find that certain cultures, such as individualism, are more prevalent in industrialized Western countries, whereas cultures with high collectivism and power distance prevail in East Asian countries (Yamagishi & Yamagishi, 1994).

Among the various cultural dimensions, the majority relate to the dichotomy of individualism vs. collectivism (Oyserman et al., 2002; Triandis & Gelfand, 1998). Collectivistic cultures emphasize that groups (i.e., family, tribe, country) bind and mutually obligate individuals, which centralize common fate, common goals, and shared values, whereas individualistic cultures assume that individuals are independent of one another, centralizing the personal goals, personal uniqueness, and personal control (Triandis, 1995). Given these differences in interdependence, autonomy, self-fulfillment, and group membership, plausible consequences of individualism/collectivism in self-concept, well-being, attribution style, and relationality are easily discerned. For example, individuals from cultures ranking higher in collectivism values tend to understand their self-identities based on social roles; harmony in in-group relationships contributes to their well-being (Kwan et al., 1997). In individualistic cultures, people tend to define their identities through uniqueness and personal achievement. They feel more than collectivists that self-esteem contributes to their well-being (Kwan et al., 1997). In terms of attribution style, individualists are person focused and engage in more decontextualized causal reasoning, while collectivists engage in more contextualized and situated reasoning (Oyserman et al., 2002). In social relationships, people in collectivistic cultures tend to favor in-group relationships (family, friends, etc.) over out-group relationships (strangers) (Bond & Smith, 1996) and interact more frequently with in-group members (Gudykunst et al., 1992). While individualists also feel close to in-group members, they interact with more diverse groups and expect to have more freedom to decide which groups to belong to (Wheeler et al., 1989). They treat different in-group relationships in a similar manner (Hui et al., 1991) and have a greater willingness to trust others – including strangers – and greater ease in their interaction with strangers (Yamagishi, 1988). These distinct attributes of individualism and collectivism may translate into different privacy norms and behaviors. For example, individualists are expected to have higher levels of privacy concerns due to their focus on autonomy, independence, privacy, and personal control, whereas those from collectivistic cultures are likely to have lower levels of privacy concerns owing to their emphasis on social relatedness and collective welfare (Cho et al., 2009).

In addition to individualism and collectivism, power distance and uncertainty avoidance have been studied in privacy research. Power distance and uncertainty avoidance are two of the six cultural dimensions proposed by Geert Hofstede (Hofstede et al., 2010). Power distance is the degree to which the less powerful members of a culture accept that power is distributed unequally. Uncertainty avoidance measures the degree to which the members of a culture feel uncomfortable with uncertainty and ambiguity. It is predicted that power distance and uncertainty avoidance are positively associated with privacy concerns because people with high power distance and uncertainty avoidance are likely to exhibit greater mistrust of organizations and favor security, assurance, and clear rules (Bellman et al., 2004). Aside from individualism, power distance, and uncertainty avoidance, Geert Hofstede also proposed masculinity, long-term orientation, and indulgence as cultural dimensions.

One of the common approaches to measuring an individual's culture is to employ existing cultural questions in questionnaires, such as Hofstede's (Hofstede et al., 2010) and Triandis's (Triandis & Gelfand, 1998) scales. Participants rate how much they agree with a set of culture-related statements. Their ratings are then correlated with certain perceptions and behaviors in their life. Another common approach involves efforts to prime cultural values before participants perform certain behaviors, which usually happens in laboratory settings. As the techniques in machine learning and natural language processing develop, automated text analysis might be a possible approach to extract insight into users' cultural backgrounds (Berger & Packard, 2022).

Literature Review

Related Studies on Intercultural Privacy and Privacy on Social Media

Since the 1990s, researchers have found that the levels, patterns, and mechanisms of privacy attitudes and behaviors are different from culture to culture. Previous research has focused on comparisons between individualistic and collectivist cultures. It is shown that, in general, users in individualistic cultures tend to exhibit higher levels of privacy concerns than those from cultures ranking high in collectivism (Cho et al., 2009; Krasnova & Veltri, 2010; Milberg et al., 2000; Wang et al., 2011), perceive more risk in information sharing (Choi & Geistfeld, 2004; Dinev et al., 2006; Park & Jun, 2003), are less likely to disclose personal information (Cho & Park, 2013; Posey et al., 2010; Tsoi & Chen, 2011), and are more likely to adopt privacy management behaviors (Rui & Stefanone, 2013; Sawaya et al., 2017; Steenkamp & Geyskens, 2006).

More specifically, collectivistic users primarily use social network sites to maintain their existing relationships (Kim et al., 2011; Wang et al., 2015). They have more online social contacts who are close ties (Tsoi & Chen, 2011) and offline connections belonging to the same social groups (Cho & Park, 2013). They also tend to reveal more personal details (Peters et al., 2015). Group norms had a stronger effect on privacy control for users from cultures ranking high in collectivism (Liu & Wang, 2018). People from cultures ranking high on collectivism perceive more privacy risks than do those from cultures ranking high on individualism, presumably to safeguard the collective (Trepte et al., 2017). Having mutual friends, offline connections, and overlaps in education background more strongly drives collectivistic users to accept friend requests (Li et al., 2022). Overall, the findings suggest that collectivistic users' information disclosure and privacy behaviors are affected by in/out-group distinction and social norms.

On the other hand, individualistic users usually maintain a variety of online social networks to explore new friends with similar interests and backgrounds (Kim et al., 2011). They adopt a more protective means of self-disclosure (Rui & Stefanone, 2013), use more self censorship over their posts (Peters et al., 2015), and generally feel more in control over their disclosure (Krasnova & Veltri, 2010). The perceived effectiveness of privacy settings had a stronger effect on privacy control for individualistic users (Liu & Wang, 2018). Being in the same social media group, same city, or sharing similar interests has a stronger effect on friend request acceptance for individualistic users (Li et al., 2022).

Other prior work has compared users' online privacy attitudes and practices between cultures with different levels of uncertainty avoidance, power distance, and general trust. It is shown that people in countries with a higher tendency to avoid uncertainty have greater privacy concerns (Cao & Everard, 2008) and exhibit less information disclosure (Tsoi & Chen, 2011). The effect of privacy concerns on information disclosure is stronger for users in a risk-averse culture than for users in a risk-tolerant culture (Krasnova et al., 2012). Power distance is negatively associated with information privacy concerns (Cao & Everard, 2008; Milberg et al., 2000), as individuals with high espoused power distance cultural values expect a greater level of inequality between societal levels, thus could be accustomed to authorities accessing their personal information (Cao & Everard, 2008).

Because collectivistic cultures emphasize interdependence, social relatedness, and ingroup–outgroup boundary (Triandis & Gelfand, 1998), collectivists are less likely to trust someone who is not part of their ingroup (Yamagishi & Yamagishi, 1994). On the other hand, members from individualistic cultures tend to form trust on the basis of calculative thinking (Doney et al. 1998), which promotes a trusting stance (Jarvenpaa et al., 1999). People in countries with a higher tendency to trust others are more willing to self-disclose (Miltgen & Peyrat-Guillard, 2014). The effect of trust on information disclosure is stronger in individualistic cultures than in collectivist cultures (Krasnova et al., 2012).

Current Developments and Upcoming Trends

To investigate the fundamental reasons behind the cross-cultural differences found in users' concrete privacy attitudes and behaviors, more and more research in recent years has paid attention to how the theoretical conceptualization of the notion of privacy in a networked environment is different from culture to culture. The differences in the conceptualization of privacy are of great importance in cross-cultural privacy research. An accurate theoretical conceptualization offers us a more nuanced and granular insight into information privacy, provides explanations for the culturally distinct privacy attitudes and behaviors, improves the quality of analysis, and enhances the likelihood of making valuable discoveries. Such insights about intercultural privacy would also help develop culturally appropriate privacy regulations, privacy tools, and privacy management practices. Privacy is generally perceived as a multidimensional concept comprised of multiple aspects that are correlated but conceptually distinct, such as collection, unauthorized use, improper access, and errors (Smith et al., 1996). However, prior research that developed such conceptual nature and dimensional structure is mostly based on samples from one single country. How populations in different cultures distinctly define information privacy remains an open question and has received increasing attention in recent years.

Several recent studies have contextualized users' understanding of the notion of privacy in the local culture and revealed how the concept of privacy differs for users in different cultures. For example, the Islamic perspective of privacy goes beyond the ability to separate oneself from a group in a controlled manner and relates to Islamic teachings, maintenance of reputation, and the careful navigation of social media activity so as to preserve respect and modesty (Abokhodair et al., 2016). In Qatar, privacy is framed as a communal attribute, including not only the individual but the behavior of those around them that might reflect on one's own honor (Abokhodair et al., 2016). In Cambodia, privacy is thought to lead to isolation, thus is at odds with community-style living and mental well-being (Jack et al., 2019). In China, individuals tend to consider their privacy to be protected if information stays among family members (Huang & Wu, 2019).

In addition to these localized privacy studies, researchers have started to systematically compare the underlying dimensionality of key privacy concepts across different cultures. For instance, Cho et al.'s study showed that social media users from different cultures interpret the information control strategies in different ways (Cho et al., 2018). Users in a more authoritarian society are sensitive to self-censorship and information control as they live in an environment with higher surveillance. Li et al.'s work has found significant differences in the dimensionalities of information disclosure on social media among different cultures (Li et al., 2022). Users in individualistic countries categorize personal information into "online profile information" (i.e., age, gender, status, relationships, etc.) and "contact information" (location, email, schedule, etc.), whereas users from cultures ranking high in collectivism have "demographic/contact information" (age, gender, location, email, etc.) and "social association information" (relationship, schedule, etc.). The different categorizations of personal information on social media might be because individualistic users consider relationships to be part of their public persona expressed in their online profile, while schedule and location are part of a more private persona that is aligned with contact information. In contrast, collectivist users consider their relationships and schedule as a single category that reveals information about the social group they are associated with – in contrast to demographic and contact information, which are personal information. The cross-cultural differences in the fundamental conceptualization of privacy uncovered in Cho et al.'s and Li et al.'s work reveal that privacy is differently defined from culture to culture, calling for more research to comprehensively explore the cross-cultural differences in theorizing the notion of privacy.

Conclusions and Directions for Future Studies

In sum, previous studies have demonstrated that culture influences the ways in which social media users conceptualize privacy (Li et al., 2021) and engage in privacy management strategies (Cho et al., 2018). While previous studies have focused on identifying and describing the differences in privacy norms and behaviors across cultures, relatively little is known about theoretical mechanisms through which culture influences privacy perceptions and behaviors (Dinev et al., 2009). We suggest directions for future research that may help advance privacy and social media research.

Future research should test the role of culture as a boundary condition of extant privacy theories. Many previous studies have examined the relationship between risk perceptions, beliefs, social norms, and behaviors about privacy using well-established theoretical frameworks, such as the theory of planned behavior (Ajzen, 1991) or social cognitive theory (Bandura, 2002). However, cross-cultural research has shown that certain psychological and social factors operate with different strengths in behavioral decision-making in different cultures (Bandura, 2002). For example, the impacts of individuals' internal beliefs and attitudes on behaviors are stronger in individualistic cultures than in collectivistic cultures, whereas the social norms–behaviors relationship is more robust in collectivistic cultures than in individualistic cultures (Kacen & Le, 2002; Triandis, 1995). When it comes to privacy on social media, self-related concepts (e.g., perceived privacy controls and perceived vulnerability to privacy risks) are likely to have more substantial effects on individualists than on collectivists, whereas social/normative factors (e.g., subjective norms, descriptive norms) are likely to have more substantial impacts on the privacy decision-making of collectivists. By testing the moderating role of culture, we can examine the limits of generalizing existing theories (Esser & Hanitzsch, 2012). In addition, we can test the relative utility of theoretical factors within/across cultural contexts, which helps us strengthen the validity of privacy research and find opportunities for further theory development.

Future research should examine the mediating mechanisms through which culture influences privacy perceptions and behaviors. For example, intercultural differences in privacy concerns observed in previous studies might be because individualists (vs. collectivists) overestimate (vs. underestimate) their capacity for privacy management (i.e., self-efficacy or perceived controllability), which, in turn, reduces (vs. increases) privacy concerns. Alternatively, this could be due to different cultural norms promoting or inhibiting a trusting stance. In other words, culture (macro-level factor) may influence privacy concerns and behaviors through its interplay with micro-level factors such as self-efficacy, trust, or other theoretical mechanisms. Testing these multiple mediating processes and the interplay between multiple-level (e.g., cultural and individual level) factors would help identify specific mechanisms underlying cultural effects on privacy perceptions and behaviors.

While most intercultural privacy studies focus on describing and explaining "differences" in privacy perceptions and behaviors across cultures, relatively litter research attention has been paid to understanding "commonalities" within cultures or "similarities" across cultures (Poortinga & Van Hemert, 2001). Future research should examine the role of culture (including subcultures in various social units) in creating shared norms, values, and practices related to privacy management, which will provide a more holistic understanding of culture in relation to privacy (Masur et al., 2021). Therefore, we suggest new approaches to intercultural privacy research, including moving beyond values to explain cultural differences and incorporating social and contextual factors into cross-cultural privacy studies.

Social media are emerging communication platforms, imposing new and challenging privacy problems on users worldwide. However, as reviewed earlier, privacy perceptions and norms surrounding new media use should have cultural and historical roots (Acquisti et al., 2022). Therefore, a richer understanding of the cultural roots of privacy would be essential for the development of information privacy and social media research.

References

Abokhodair, N., Abbar, S., Vieweg, S., & Mejova, Y. (2016). Privacy and Twitter in Qatar: Traditional values in the digital world. *Proceedings of the 8th ACM Conference on Web Science*, 66–77.

Acquisti, A., Brandimarte, L., & Hancock, J. (2022). How privacy's past may shape its future. *Science, 375*(6578), 270–272.

Ajzen, I. (1991). The theory of planned behavior. *Organizational Behavior and Human Decision Processes, 50*, 179–211.

Altman, I. (1975). *The environment and social behavior: Privacy, personal space, territory, and crowding.* Brook, Cole Publishing Company.

Bandura, A. (2002). Social cognitive theory in cultural context. *Applied Psychology, 51*(2), 269–290.

Bellman, S., Johnson, E. J., Kobrin, S. J., & Lohse, G. L. (2004). International differences in information privacy concerns: A global survey of consumers. *The Information Society, 20*(5), 313–324.

Berger, J., & Packard, G. (2022). Using natural language processing to understand people and culture. *American Psychologist, 77*(4), 525–537.

Bond, R., & Smith, P. B. (1996). Culture and conformity: A meta-analysis of studies using Asch's (1952b, 1956) line judgment task. *Psychological Bulletin, 119*(1), 111–137.

Cao, J., & Everard, A. (2008). User attitude towards instant messaging: The effect of espoused national cultural values on awareness and privacy. *Journal of Global Information Technology Management, 11*(2), 30–57.

Cho, H., Knijnenburg, B., Kobsa, A., & Li, Y. (2018). Collective privacy management in social media: A cross-cultural validation. *ACM Transactions on Computer-Human Interaction, 25*(3), 1–33. 17.

Cho, H., Rivera-Sánchez, M., & Lim, S. S. (2009). A multinational study on online privacy: Global concerns and local responses. *New Media & Society, 11*(3), 395–416.

Cho, S. E., & Park, H. W. (2013). A qualitative analysis of cross-cultural new media research: SNS use in Asia and the West. *Quality & Quantity, 47*(4), 2319–2330.

Choi, J., & Geistfeld, L. V. (2004). A cross-cultural investigation of consumer e-shopping adoption. *Journal of Economic Psychology, 25*(6), 821–838.

Dinev, T., Bellotto, M., Hart, P., Russo, V., Serra, I., & Colautti, C. (2006). Privacy calculus model in e-commerce – a study of Italy and the United States. *European Journal of Information Systems, 15*(4), 389–402.

Dinev, T., Goo, J., Hu, Q., & Nam, K. (2009). User behavior towards protective information technologies: The role of national cultural differences. *Information Systems Journal, 19*, 391–412.

Doney, P. M., Cannon, J. P., & Mullen, M. R. (1998). Understanding the influence of national culture on the development of trust. *Academy of Management Review, 23*(3), 601–620.

Esser, F., & Hanitzsch, T. (Eds.). (2012). *Handbook of comparative communication research*. New York: Routledge.

Erez, M., & Earley, P. C. (1993). *Culture, self-Identity, and work*. New York: Oxford University Press.

Gelfand, M. J., Erez, M., & Aycan, Z. (2007). Cross-cultural organizational behavior. *Annual Review of Psychology, 58*, 479–514.

Gudykunst, W. B., Gao, G., Schmidt, K. L., Nishida, T., Bond, M. H., Leung, K., Wang, G., & Barraclough, R. A. (1992). The influence of individualism collectivism, self-monitoring, and predicted-outcome value on communication in ingroup and outgroup relationships. *Journal of Cross-Cultural Psychology, 23*(2), 196–213.

Hofstede, G. (2011). Dimensionalizing cultures: The Hofstede model in context. *Online Readings in Psychology and Culture, 2*(1). https://doi.org/10.9707/2307-0919.1014

Hofstede, G., Hofstede, G. J., & Minkov, M. (2010). *Cultures and organizations: Software of the mind* (3rd ed.). McGraw Hill Professional.

House, R. J., Hanges, P. J., Javidan, M., Dorfman, P. W., & Gupta, V. (2004). *Culture, leadership, and organizations: The GLOBE study of 62 societies*. SAGE Publications.

Huang, K., & Wu, Z. (2019). Perception of smart home devices and privacy by Chinese users. In C. Stephanidis (Ed.), *HCI international 2019—Posters* (pp. 476–481). Springer International Publishing.

Hui, C. H., Triandis, H. C., & Yee, C. (1991). Cultural differences in reward allocation: Is collectivism the explanation? *British Journal of Social Psychology, 30*(2), 145–157.

Jack, M. C., Sovannaroth, P., & Dell, N. (2019). "Privacy is not a concept, but a way of dealing with life": Localization of transnational technology platforms and liminal privacy practices in Cambodia. *Proceedings of the ACM on Human-Computer Interaction, 3*(CSCW), 1–19. 128.

Jarvenpaa, S. L., Tractinsky, N., & Saarinen, L. (1999). Consumer trust in an internet store: A cross-cultural validation. *Journal of Computer-Mediated Communication, 5*(2).

Kacen, J. J., & Lee, J. A. (2002). The influence of culture on consumer impulsive buying behavior. *Journal of Consumer Psychology, 12*(2), 163–176.

Kim, Y., Sohn, D., & Choi, S. M. (2011). Cultural difference in motivations for using social network sites: A comparative study of American and Korean college students. *Computers in Human Behavior, 27*(1), 365–372.

Krasnova, H., & Veltri, N. F. (2010). Privacy calculus on social networking sites: Explorative evidence from Germany and USA. *2010 43rd Hawaii International Conference on System Sciences (HICSS)*, 1–10.

Krasnova, H., Veltri, N. F., & Günther, O. (2012). Self-disclosure and privacy calculus on social networking sites: The role of culture. *Business & Information Systems Engineering, 4*(3), 127–135.

Kwan, V. S., Bond, M. H., & Singelis, T. M. (1997). Pancultural explanations for life satisfaction: Adding relationship harmony to self-esteem. *Journal of Personality and Social Psychology, 73*(5), 1038–1051.

Li, Y., Ghaiumy Anaraky, R., & Knijnenburg, B. (2021). How not to measure social network privacy: A cross-country investigation. *The Proceedings of the ACM on Human-Computer Interaction, V5*(CSCW1).

Li, Y., Kobsa, A., Knijnenburg, B. P., & Nguyen, M.-H. C. (2017). Cross-cultural privacy prediction. *Proceedings on Privacy Enhancing Technologies, 2017*(2), 113–132.

Li, Y., Rho, E. H. R., & Kobsa, A. (2022). Cultural differences in the effects of contextual factors and privacy concerns on users' privacy decision on social networking sites. *Behaviour & Information Technology, 41*(3), 655–677.

Liu, Z., & Wang, X. (2018). How to regulate individuals' privacy boundaries on social network sites: A cross-cultural comparison. *Information & Management, 55*(8), 1005–1023.

Masur, P. K., Epstein, D., Quinn, K., Wilhelm, C., Baruh, L., & Lutz, C. (2021). A comparative privacy research framework. *Preprint on SocArXiv*. https://doi.org/10.31235/osf.io/fjqhs

McSweeney, B. (2002). Hofstede's model of national cultural differences and their consequences: A triumph of faith-a failure of analysis. *Human Relations, 55*(1), 89–118.

McSweeney, B. (2009). Dynamic diversity: Variety and variation within countries. *Organization Studies, 30*(9), 933–957.

Milberg, S. J., Burke, S. J., Smith, H. J., & Kallman, E. A. (1995). Values, personal information privacy, and regulatory approaches. *Communications of the ACM, 38*(12), 65–74. https://doi.org/10.1145/219663.219683

Milberg, S. J., Smith, H. J., & Burke, S. J. (2000). Information privacy: Corporate management and national regulation. *Organization Science, 11*(1), 35–57.

Miltgen, C. L., & Peyrat-Guillard, D. (2014). Cultural and generational influences on privacy concerns: A qualitative study in seven European countries. *European Journal of Information Systems, 23*(2), 103–125.

Myers, M. D., & Tan, F. B. (2002). Beyond models of national culture in information systems research. *Journal of Global Information Management, 10*(1), 14–29.

Oyserman, D., Coon, H. M., & Kemmelmeier, M. (2002). Rethinking individualism and collectivism: Evaluation of theoretical assumptions and meta-analyses. *Psychological Bulletin, 128*(1), 3–72.

Park, C., & Jun, J.-K. (2003). A cross-cultural comparison of internet buying behavior: Effects of internet usage, perceived risks, and innovativeness. *International Marketing Review, 20*(5), 534–553.

Peters, A. N., Winschiers-Theophilus, H., & Mennecke, B. E. (2015). Cultural influences on Facebook practices: A comparative study of college students in Namibia and the United States. *Computers in Human Behavior, 49*, 259–271.

Poortinga, Y. H., & Van Hemert, D. A. (2001). Personality and culture: Demarcating between the common and the unique. *Journal of Personality, 69*(6), 1033–1060.

Posey, C., Lowry, P. B., Roberts, T. L., & Ellis, T. S. (2010). Proposing the online community self-disclosure model: The case of working professionals in France and the U.K. who use online communities. *European Journal of Information Systems, 19*(2), 181–195.

Rui, J., & Stefanone, M. A. (2013). Strategic self-presentation online: A cross-cultural study. *Computers in Human Behavior, 29*(1), 110–118.

Sawaya, Y., Sharif, M., Christin, N., Kubota, A., Nakarai, A., & Yamada, A. (2017). Self-confidence trumps knowledge: A cross-cultural study of security behavior. *Proceedings of the 2017 CHI Conference on Human Factors in Computing Systems*, 2202–2214.

Schwartz, S. H. (1994). Beyond individualism/collectivism: New cultural dimensions of values. In U. Kim, H. C. Triandis, Ç. Kâğitçibaşi, S.-C. Choi, & G. Yoon (Eds.), *Individualism and collectivism: Theory, method, and applications* (pp. 85–119). Sage Publications, Inc.

Shweder, R. A., & Bourne, E. J. (1982). Does the concept of the person vary cross-culturally? In A. J. Marsella & G. M. White (Eds.), *Cultural conceptions of mental health and therapy* (pp. 97–137). Springer Netherlands.

Smith, H. J., Milberg, S. J., & Burke, S. J. (1996). Information privacy: Measuring individuals' concerns about organizational practices. *MIS Quarterly, 20*(2), 167–196.

Steenkamp, J. B. E. (2001). The role of national culture in international marketing research. *International Marketing Review, 18*(1), 30–44.

Steenkamp, J.-B. E. M., & Geyskens, I. (2006). How country characteristics affect the perceived value of web sites. *Journal of Marketing, 70*(3), 136–150.

Trepte, S., Reinecke, L., Ellison, N. B., Quiring, O., Yao, M. Z., & Ziegele, M. (2017). A cross-cultural perspective on the privacy calculus. *Social Media+ Society, 3*(1), https://doi.org/2056305116688035

Triandis, H. C. (1995). *Individualism & collectivism* (vol. xv). Westview Press.

Triandis, H. C., & Gelfand, M. J. (1998). Converging measurement of horizontal and vertical individualism and collectivism. *Journal of Personality and Social Psychology, 74*(1), 118–128.

Tsoi, H. K., & Chen, L. (2011). From privacy concern to uses of social network sites: A cultural comparison via user survey. *Privacy, Security, Risk and Trust (Passat), 2011 IEEE Third International Conference on and 2011 IEEE Third International Conference on Social Computing (Socialcom)*, 457–464.

Wang, Y., Li, Y., & Tang, J. (2015). Dwelling and fleeting encounters: Exploring why people use WeChat - A mobile instant messenger. *Proceedings of the 33rd Annual ACM Conference Extended Abstracts on Human Factors in Computing Systems*, 1543–1548.

Wang, Y., Norcie, G., & Cranor, L. F. (2011). Who is concerned about what? A study of American, Chinese and Indian Users' privacy concerns on social network sites. *Proceedings of the 4th International Conference on Trust and Trustworthy Computing*, 146–153.

Wheeler, L., Reis, H. T., & Bond, M. H. (1989). Collectivism-individualism in everyday social life: The middle kingdom and the melting pot. *Journal of Personality and Social Psychology, 57*(1), 79–86.

Westin, A. F. (1967). *Privacy and freedom*. New York: Athenaeum Publishers.

Yamagishi, T. (1988). The provision of a sanctioning system in the United States and Japan. *Social Psychology Quarterly, 51*(3), 265–271.

Yamagishi, T., & Yamagishi, M. (1994). Trust and commitment in the United States and Japan. *Motivation and Emotion, 18*(2), 129–166.

15
PRIVACY AND GENDER

Regine Frener

UNIVERSITY OF HOHENHEIM, GERMANY

Introduction

"Datafication [is an] imprisonment within the societally performed roles of, for example, fixed gender" (Benjamin, 2021, p. 12). From an optimistic perspective, the transition to a data-driven society could have paved the way for a more inclusive and neutral society, but critical statements like this one show that in reality, it has only maintained and further reinforced consolidated gender structures and expectations.

While "sex" refers to differences based on physiological traits, such as genes and hormones (Hines, 2010), "gender" is viewed as a "routine, methodical, and recurring accomplishment" in everyday life (West & Zimmermann, 1987, p. 126). Wood and Eagly (2015) distinguish between two traditions of researching gender identity. First, the "classic personality approach" (p. 461) centers around individual differences and gender-stereotypic personality traits. Second, the "gender self-categorization approach" (Wood & Eagly, 2015, p. 461) describes individuals' identification with social gender categories. The endpoints of certain "psychological, social, and interactive characteristics" (Reeder, 1996, p. 319) are perceived as feminine or masculine. Individuals constantly (re)position themselves along these continuous spectra, fluidly shifting their gender identity. Mehta (2015) extends this framework by emphasizing the context dependency of both approaches and calls for considering the context in gender identity measurement, even when gender is conceptualized as adherence to certain personality traits. Over the past decade, the fluidity of gender has gained attention not only from a theoretical, but also from a methodological perspective. As Cameron and Stinson (2019) put it, "measuring gender as a binary construct not only fails to represent social scientists' current understanding of gender, resulting in gender misclassifications in research […], but it also stands in stark contrast to growing public acceptance of and support for transgender and nonbinary individuals" (p. 2).

Technologies tend to maintain and reinforce gender stereotypes, despite the potential opened by their anonymity and equality (Attewell, 2001) and the dynamic nature of stereotypes (Bhatia & Bhatia, 2020; Donnelly & Twenge, 2017). Women are often portrayed as disadvantaged and especially vulnerable (Thelwall, 2011), and are therefore often regarded as more sensitive to and concerned about privacy (Park, 2015). At the same time, they are expected to be experts in communication, which is key for social reproductive work (Lai, 2021), and therefore to use social networks and emotional self-disclosure to establish and maintain relationships and social capital (Hunter & Taylor, 2019). Scholars risk falling into the stereotype trap: When they base their research on these gendered expectations, they are likely to confirm them and contribute to their reproduction. This chapter (i) provides an overview of theoretical and empirical work on gender and privacy, (ii) introduces gender issues in the context of artificial intelligence, and (iii) illustrates the problems evoked by an ill-considered inclusion of gender in privacy research.

DOI: 10.4324/9781003244677-17

Theoretical Perspectives on Gender and Privacy

Evolution of the Feminist Perspective on Privacy

Conceptualizations of gender and privacy are fluid and have co-developed with cultural, historical, and societal norms. Warren and Brandeis (1890) described "the sacred precincts of private and domestic life" (p. 195) and declared the private sphere an area where one can elude state interference and surveillance. However, in those days, the private sphere was inseparably linked to the household and family, and only men had access to the public sphere, where political and societal decisions were made. This close linkage between privacy and domesticity, combined with the non-negotiable power imbalance between women and their fathers, brothers, and husbands, translated into women being constrained at home and subordinated to male dominance (Gilman, 1903). It has therefore been the subject of major criticism by feminist privacy scholars (e.g., Allen & Mack, 1991; Olsen, 1993). Allen (2018) called Warren and Brandeis's (1890) work "a florid testament to male privilege" that "depended on outmoded gender norms" (p. 410).

While some feminist scholars condemn the distinction between the public and private spheres (e.g., Brown, 2004), others acknowledge the tremendous value of privacy and have even changed their perspective. As Allen, a former sharp critic of privacy altogether, noted in 2018, "whether privacy is a good thing for the people who have it is a question with normative and empirical dimensions" (p. 410). An example thereof is the US Supreme Court decision *Roe v. Wade* (*Roe v. Wade,* 1973), which declared Texas' abortion ban unconstitutional as it violated pregnant people's (i.e., women, non-binary, and trans persons) right to privacy, which "is broad enough to encompass a woman's decision whether to terminate her pregnancy" (*Roe v. Wade,* 1973). In 2022, the US Supreme Court overruled *Roe*, claiming that the law was not "deeply rooted in [the] Nation's history or tradition" (*Dobbs v. Jackson Women's Health Organization,* 2022). Already prior to the decision, privacy experts warned about the massive amount of personal data online – especially related to female health, e.g., menstruation trackers (Mishra & Suresh, 2021). Such tools, which might reveal information about individuals trying to get pregnant or get an abortion, are often directly connected to healthcare providers and evoke concerns about privacy and the accuracy of predictions (Mishra & Suresh, 2021). These examples support the gendered aspect of privacy, the notion of it as a "foundational good," and the idea that individuals are "morally obligated" to protect their privacy to ensure their dignity and self-fulfillment (Allen, 2018, p. 411).

Gender and Online Privacy Regulation

In her Communication Privacy Management Theory, Petronio (2002) identified gender as a core influence on privacy rule development, due to societal "expectations about privacy disclosures" (Petronio, 2002, p. 44). These expectations are at the basis of social role theory: According to Eagly (1987), the Western division of labor preserves men's financial advantages and position of power, creating and maintaining gender stereotypes, i.e., expectations about which traits women and men (should) have (Haines et al., 2016). Social role theory has been considered in examinations of social media self-disclosure (Chakraborty et al., 2013), the privacy calculus (Sun et al., 2015; see chapter 7 by Dienlin on the privacy calculus), and many more (Frener & Trepte, 2022).

In the Social Web Gendered Privacy Model, Thelwall (2011) argues that due to negative offline experiences, such as harassment and threat, and higher communicative skills and needs, women take more privacy-protecting measures than males and subsequently benefit even more from the potential of social media.

In empirical studies, gender theorizing is often scarce, if not absent, bearing the risk of oversimplification and stereotyping (Frener & Trepte, 2022). Furthermore, even when the social construction of gender is acknowledged, it is almost always operationalized in terms of a male/female binary, with an "other" category at best – the contemporary understanding of gender as a fluid, context-dependent characteristic has yet to be put into practice (Frener & Trepte, 2022).

Empirical Gender Differences and Similarities in Privacy-Related Outcomes

In online privacy research, gender is often included alongside other demographic variables, such as age and education. Gender is operationalized as a binary measure in more than 90% of articles in major communication journals in general (Kosciesza, 2022) as well as in online privacy research in particular (Frener & Trepte, 2022). The studies presented in this section, which report relations between gender and privacy-related outcomes, therefore provide a valuable knowledge base, but do not apply an appropriate perspective on the construct of gender itself. In contrast, current studies on gender identification and categorization (see as follows) not only measure gender beyond the male/female binary, but also directly address the problematic social, legal, and psychological implications of such oversimplified conceptualizations.

Online Privacy Concerns

To date, Tifferet (2019) has conducted the most comprehensive meta-analysis on gender and privacy-related outcomes. In 37 independent studies, females showed higher levels of online privacy concerns (d = 0.13). The theoretical reasoning behind such gender differences in online privacy concerns is that women are more risk-averse and may have had more negative experiences with privacy violation (see Thelwall, 2011), and are therefore considered to be more sensitive to privacy threats. As Linabary and Corple (2019) note, people who face harassment express higher levels of privacy concerns afterwards. Kim et al. (2018), for example, found that females were more concerned about their online privacy, more hesitant to reveal personal information, and updated their privacy settings more frequently to prevent data leakage. According to Zhang and Fu (2020), men and women use similar strategies for privacy management, but the influence of privacy concerns on use of these strategies in stressful situations differs by gender.

Online Privacy Literacy

Investigations of online privacy literacy (see also chapter 11 by Masur, Hagendorff, & Trepte on privacy literacy) can be divided into two groups. First and foremost, a large share of studies used subjective assessments, i.e., participants were asked to rate their level of knowledge of privacy technology and protection strategies. Weinberger et al. (2017) and Kimpe et al. (2021) showed that men have higher levels of perceived knowledge. In Kaya and Yaman's (2022) as well as Choi's (2022) studies, by contrast, females have an advantage in terms of subjective online privacy literacy.

Secondly, a few authors operationalized objective privacy knowledge with quizzes on factual knowledge. Morrison (2013) found that females underestimated their subjective privacy knowledge, despite no actual differences in objective knowledge between men and women. In Zarouali et al.'s (2021) study, women were more likely than men to hold algorithmic misconceptions, e.g., about the independence of algorithms and humans. Nevertheless, the effects of personal experience and lack of information sources were stronger than demographic factors. To conclude, empirical findings seem to indicate greater online privacy literacy among males (see section "The digital divide: Persistence of technology-related gender stereotypes").

Online Privacy Protection Behavior

In Tifferet's (2019) meta-analysis, females are more likely to activate privacy settings (d = 0.35); however, the studies analyzed comprise a variety of measures, from one-item self-assessments to the frequencies of implementing specific settings. Other empirical evidence for gender differences regarding precautionary measures is inconclusive. Some scholars find that women engage in more active privacy protection (Child & Starcher, 2016; Kaya & Yaman, 2022; Kimpe et al., 2021), while others report the opposite (Faliagka et al., 2011; Liu et al., 2017) or no gender differences (Kurt, 2010). Again, a differentiated perspective on objective vs. subjective measures seems necessary.

Online Self-Disclosure

Tifferet (2019) found that females disclosed less personal information on their social network profiles ($d = 0.13$); again, a variety of measures were used. Further, and in line with findings for self-disclosure, females untagged themselves from pictures more often ($d = 0.26$; Tifferet, 2019). Women tended to share more pictures and create more Facebook wall posts (Rui & Stefanone, 2013) and emotional content (e.g., Cho, 2017). Newman et al. (2008) examined 14,000 text files and found that women used more psychological and social terms, whereas men tended to make more references to less emotional, more instrumental topics. In line with the latter, disclosure of contact information (e.g., Xie & Kang, 2015), financial data, authenticating, and health or medical information (Chua et al., 2021), and even socially stigmatized behavior (Rodríguez-Priego et al., 2016) tends to be higher among males. However, a large share of studies have found no gender differences regarding online self-disclosure (e.g., Kim, 2019; Lyvers et al., 2020). Hu and Kearney (2021) and Beltran et al. (2021) looked at politicians' disclosure in Tweets and conclude that "Twitter is still a gendered space" (Hu & Kearney, 2021, p. 497). It should be noted, though, that these scraping analyses of actual self-disclosure are always based on a priori definitions of masculinity and femininity and therefore inherently reflect stereotypical beliefs.

Need for Privacy

In contrast to other privacy-related outcomes, research on gender and the need for privacy is scarce. According to Pedersen (1987), females have a higher need for intimacy with close friends and relatives, and males have a stronger preference for isolation. Frener et al. (in prep) distinguished biological sex from perceived femininity and masculinity. (Biological) women express a higher physical, but lower psychological (control over psychological inputs, e.g., attitudes, and outputs, e.g., sharing secrets) need for privacy. Prescriptive gender norms regarding rational and emotionally reserved males (Derlega et al., 1981) might partly explain this observation: Men are expected to keep such information to themselves and therefore express a higher psychological need for privacy. The informational need for privacy, which concerns sharing information with a larger audience, does not differ between males and females. Frener et al. (in prep) further report that (biological) women who describe themselves as very feminine, and therefore conform to gender stereotypes, express an overall higher need for privacy – probably because they are more strongly affected by societal expectations.

To summarize, online privacy research has identified inconsistent, heterogeneous gender differences in affective, cognitive, and behavioral variables. To better understand these results, applying a true gender perspective – both theoretically and empirically – is indispensable (Frener & Trepte, 2022). As Gingras (2014) notes, a good indicator must be aligned with the purpose of the study. Binary gender operationalizations in studies that – implicitly or explicitly – argue that gender is socially and culturally constructed (Zuccala & Derrick, 2022) and that these constructions subsequently impact individuals' cognitions and behavior do not fulfill this criterion. They do not adequately reflect the actual variable of interest, which might be gender identity, gender role conformity, or so on.

Current Gender-Related Issues

The Digital Divide: Persistence of Technology-Related Gender Stereotypes

While differences in (physical) access to the internet (Attewell, 2001) have diminished in developed countries (Blank & Groselj, 2014), women and men show differences in Internet usage (Hargittai, 2010), in active contribution to online resources (Hargittai & Shaw, 2015; Hoffmann et al., 2015), and in self-perceived digital skills (Trepte et al., 2015; van Deursen & Helsper, 2015). Early on in life, societal expectations prescribe that men are better able to navigate technologies and accompanying issues that arise, such as privacy, and the boost in self-efficacy stemming from these internalized stereotypical beliefs reinforces such differences (Lin & Deemer, 2021).

Hoffmann and Lutz (2019) show that gender affects cognitive dispositions, in this case, social media self-efficacy, which subsequently influences online political participation. Consequently, the digital divide increases – those who strongly believe in their ability to create and share online content will actively participate and therefore set the agenda for a wide audience. Importantly, socio-demographic factors like gender represent "indicators of environmental influences, such as exposure and access to information and communication technology, time and opportunity for usage, and social or cultural encouragement" (Hoffmann & Lutz, 2019, p. 3) – gender is not a simple predictor that explains incremental variance in privacy-related outcomes; rather, it symbolizes a complex combination of internalized expectations and cognitive shortcuts. As such, anyone who uses gender as a placeholder variable in online privacy research (or any research, for that matter) will encounter limitations in its potential to explain, predict, and change outcomes.

Gender Identification and Categorization

Not only do empirical studies virtually always assess gender as male vs. female, but the big data industry also relies on this simple binary categorization to more easily process data and make inferences about attitudes, likes, preferences, and so on (Mihaljević et al., 2019). This impinges on users' privacy, as they are unable to reject the inferences resulting from such an oversimplified and stereotypical categorization, such as targeted content that perfectly reflects gender stereotypes – cars and electronics for males, health content for females (Bol et al., 2020; see chapter 23 by Dobber on microtargeting and privacy). From a gender perspective, the invasion of privacy – capturing gender data to tailor social media content to a specific societal group with assumed shared interests – is alarming for several reasons. First, gender is "the most important category in human social life" (Eckes, 2012, p. 3). Assumptions about and actions toward individuals based on their gender might be a small step for the executor, but a fairly large leap for society, as they could potentially influence a wide range of decisions, from credit applications (Andrés et al., 2021) to job recruitment (Fanning et al., 2021). In the UK, for example, the welfare benefits system advantages citizens who conform to gender stereotypes (Carter, 2021) – this encroachment on people's privacy undermines their human rights. As Benjamin (2021) puts it, "data collection [...] defines, reduces and restricts personhood, denying certain groups [...] the agency to exist as a person with lived experience embedded within relational contexts" (p. 11).

Second, users do not always indicate their gender; rather, it needs to be inferred from other information. Given the above-mentioned consequences of gender ascription and assuming that users usually have never agreed to such inferences – or have even purposely withheld their gender, companies and institutions severely invade their privacy by doing so. The accuracy of gender inferences from first names is somewhere between 83% and 96%, depending on the machine learning algorithm and cultural context (Sebo, 2021; To et al., 2020). On Twitter, Fosch-Villaronga et al. (2021) investigated gender inferences based on engagement parameters. They found that gender was deduced correctly in 81% of cases. Alarmingly, misgendering showed a clear bias against a non-binary gender identity and non-heterosexual orientation: Only 38% of participants who were not categorized correctly were straight, and non-binary participants were always categorized wrongly. Misgendering has wide-ranging consequences for the individual (cognitively, e.g., social reputation, and emotionally, e.g., self-confidence) and their respective group, as it facilitates discrimination and stigmatization (Fosch-Villaronga et al., 2021). From a legal perspective, inferences about individuals or groups that might lead to discrimination violate human rights law (Coombs, 2019). However, given that the motivation and need for gender concealment are higher for gender and sexual minorities (Brennan et al., 2021), a lack of gender information can be informative and potentially discriminating in and of itself.

Third, gender categorization assumes (i) a male/female binary and (ii) a physiological foundation of gender, which does not adequately reflect reality. Around 0.5%–1.3% of the population reports a transgender identity (Zucker, 2017), often taking on multiple gender labels (Callander et al., 2021). A classification system, regardless of whether it is appearance-based or not, will never classify such individuals in a way that reflects their identity (Fosch-Villaronga et al., 2021). Moreover, gender categorization, especially appearance-based approaches (Lin et al., 2016), reflects a gender essentialist attitude, i.e., the belief that gender and sex are identical (Heyman & Giles, 2006) and inevitably physiologically determined (Hines, 2010).

The European Union's General Data Protection Regulation declares a "right to be forgotten" (Council of the European Union, 2016), giving individuals the right to demand that their records be deleted. This right is especially powerful for individuals who undergo gender transition (Correia et al., 2021), but automatic gender categorization makes it nearly impossible for them to make full use of it. As Jabulani Pereira, Chair of the ILGA World Trans Committee, puts it, "it is a difficult time for trans persons globally" (Chiam et al., 2020, p. 7), who are persecuted and face legal jeopardy in numerous countries. Nailing down individuals' fluid identities into a single category – even if several categories are offered – results in fixed data for decision-making (Benjamin, 2021). Sacrificing people's privacy for the sake of gender categorization comes at the cost of their dignity, legal status, physical integrity, and ultimately their freedom.

Turning back to the feminist perspective, it becomes obvious that in light of AI gender recognition and gender-based targeting, privacy is a necessity, not a burden, and affects not only women, but anybody who lives in a world where gender matters.

Future Directions

Privacy scholars can prevent falling into the stereotype trap by either redesigning the way they look at gender in their studies or by honestly reflecting on whether they need to incorporate it at all.

If applying a gender lens in privacy research yields new insights, such as a better understanding of why certain groups need privacy regarding the labels they identify with, researchers should carefully disentangle biological sex, gender roles, and gender identity and assess them accordingly. If the research question assumes gender role-specific behavior, a binary measure of gender as sex is inadequate. To this date, only one study of online privacy has operationalized gender beyond the male/female binary: Lee and Song (2013) used the Bem Sex Role Inventory (Bem, 1974) to investigate the influence of self-evaluated gender roles on privacy management. When discussing the findings, researchers should avoid generic, essentialist statements and instead aim to reflect the contemporary understanding of gender.

Furthermore, researchers need to take the media context and situational characteristics (see chapter 6 by Masur on situational assessments and privacy perceptions; chapter 9 by Treem, van Zoonen, & Siyunen on social media affordances and privacy) into account in order to understand gender as a fluid, context-dependent concept.

If gender serves as a proxy variable for an underlying construct, e.g., fear of harassment, the latter should be measured. This will lead to better predictions and bypass stereotypical thought patterns.

Those who design intelligent technologies should consider adopting the same standards. If knowing users' gender is appropriate, it should be assessed in a fair way – by accounting for diverse users and allowing for feedback afterward (Fosch-Villaronga et al., 2021). Individuals need privacy to build their identity, express themselves without fear, and actively participate in society. Whilst the critical view of early feminists, who linked privacy to male patriarchy, has tremendously helped our understanding of gender-related privacy issues, it is also a victimization-based perspective that does not help us navigate these issues. It is our normative and political responsibility to shift from protection of the weak to empowerment of the individual and conduct research that promotes fair representation across all social categories.

References

Allen, A. L. (2018). Still uneasy: A life with privacy. In B. van der Sloot & A. de Groot (Eds.), *The handbook of privacy studies: An interdisciplinary introduction* (pp. 409–412). Amsterdam University Press.

Allen, A. L., & Mack, E. (1991). How privacy got its gender. *Faculty Scholarship*.

Andrés, P. de, Gimeno, R., & Mateos de Cabo, R. (2021). The gender gap in bank credit access. *Journal of Corporate Finance*, *71*, 101782. https://doi.org/10.1016/j.jcorpfin.2020.101782

Attewell, P. (2001). The first and second digital divides. *Sociology of Education*, *74*(3), 252–259.

Beltran, J., Gallego, A., Huidobro, A., Romero, E., & Padró, L. (2021). Male and female politicians on Twitter: A machine learning approach. *European Journal of Political Research*, *60*(1), 239–251. https://doi.org/10.1111/1475-6765.12392

Bem, S. L. (1974). The measurement of psychological androgyny. *Journal of Consulting Clinical Psychology*, *42*(2), 155–162.

Benjamin, G. (2021). What we do with data: A performative critique of data 'collection'. *Internet Policy Review*, *10*(4). https://doi.org/10.14763/2021.4.1588

Bhatia, N., & Bhatia, S. (2020). Changes in gender stereotypes over time: A computational analysis. *Psychology of Women Quarterly*. https://doi.org/10.1177/0361684320977178

Blank, G., & Groselj, D. (2014). Dimensions of internet use: Amount, variety, and types. *Information, Communication & Society*, *17*(4), 417–435. https://doi.org/10.1080/1369118X.2014.889189

Bol, N., Strycharz, J., Helberger, N., van de Velde, B., & de Vreese, C. H. (2020). Vulnerability in a tracked society: Combining tracking and survey data to understand who gets targeted with what content. *New Media & Society*, *22*, 1996–2017. https://doi.org/10.1177/1461444820924631

Brennan, J. M., Dunham, K. J., Bowlen, M., Davis, K., Ji, G., & Cochran, B. N. (2021). Inconcealable: A cognitive–behavioral model of concealment of gender and sexual identity and associations with physical and mental health. *Psychology of Sexual Orientation and Gender Diversity*, *8*(1), 80–93. https://doi.org/10.1037/sgd0000424

Brown, W. (2004). 'The subject of privacy': A comment on Moira Gatens. In B. Rössler (Ed.), *Privacies: Philosophical evaluations*. Stanford University Press.

Callander, D., Newman, C. E., Holt, M., Rosenberg, S., Duncan, D. T., Pony, M., Timmins, L., Cornelisse, V., Duck-Chong, L., Wang, B., & Cook, T. (2021). The complexities of categorizing gender: A hierarchical clustering analysis of data from the first Australian trans and gender diverse sexual health survey. *Transgender Health*, *6*(2), 74–81. https://doi.org/10.1089/trgh.2020.0050

Cameron, J. J., & Stinson, D. A. (2019). Gender (mis)measurement: Guidelines for respecting gender diversity in psychological research. *Social and Personality Psychology Compass*, *13*(11). https://doi.org/10.1111/spc3.12506

Carter, L. (2021). Prescripted living: Gender stereotypes and data-based surveillance in the UK welfare state. *Internet Policy Review*, *10*(4). https://doi.org/10.14763/2021.4.1593

Chakraborty, R., Vishik, C., & Rao, H. R. (2013). Privacy preserving actions of older adults on social media: Exploring the behavior of opting out of information sharing. *Decision Support Systems*, *55*(4), 948–956. https://doi.org/10.1016/j.dss.2013.01.004

Chiam, Z., Duffy, S., Gil, M. G., Goodwin, L., & Patel, N. T. M. (2020). *Trans Legal Mapping Report 2019: Recognition before the law*. Geneva: ILGA World.

Child, J. T., & Starcher, S. C. (2016). Fuzzy Facebook privacy boundaries: Exploring mediated lurking, vague-booking, and Facebook privacy management. *Computers in Human Behavior*, *54*, 483–490. https://doi.org/10.1016/j.chb.2015.08.035

Cho, V. (2017). A study of negative emotional disclosure behavior in social network media: Will an unexpected negative event and personality matter? *Computers in Human Behavior, 73*, 172–180. https://doi.org/10.1016/j.chb.2017.03.026

Choi, S. (2022). Privacy literacy on social media: Its predictors and outcomes. *International Journal of Human–Computer Interaction*, 1–16. https://doi.org/10.1080/10447318.2022.2041892

Chua, H. N., Ooi, J. S., & Herbland, A. (2021). The effects of different personal data categories on information privacy concern and disclosure. *Computers & Security, 110*. https://doi.org/10.1016/j.cose.2021.102453

Coombs, E. (2019). *The human right to privacy: A gender perspective*. https://ssrn.com/abstract=3380984

Correia, M., Rêgo, G., & Nunes, R. (2021). Gender transition: Is there a right to be forgotten? *Journal of Health Philosophy and Policy, 29*(4), 283–300. https://doi.org/10.1007/s10728-021-00433-1

Council of the European Union. (2016). *Regulation (EU) 2016/679 on the protection of natural persons with regard to the processing of personal data and on the free movement of such data*. https://publications.europa.eu/en/publication-detail/-/publication/3e485e15-11bd-11e6-ba9a-01aa75ed71a1/language-en

Derlega, V. J., Durham, B., Gockel, B., & Sholis, D. (1981). Sex differences in self-disclosure: Effects of topic content, friendship, and partner's sex. *Sex Roles*, 7(4), 433–447.

Dobbs v. Jackson Women's Health Organization, 597 U.S. 19 (U.S. Supreme Court).

Donnelly, K., & Twenge, J. M. (2017). Masculine and feminine traits on the Bem Sex-Role Inventory, 1993–2012: A cross-temporal meta-analysis. *Sex Roles, 76*(9–10), 556–565. https://doi.org/10.1007/s11199-016-0625-y

Eagly, A. H. (1987). *Sex differences in social behavior: A social-role interpretation*. Lawrence Erlbaum.

Eckes, T. (2012). *The developmental social psychology of gender*. Psychology Press. https://doi.org/10.4324/9781410605245

Faliagka, E., Tsakalidis, A., & Vaikousi, D. (2011). Teenagers' use of social network websites and privacy concerns: A survey. In *2011 15th Panhellenic Conference on Informatics*.

Fanning, K., Williams, J., & Williamson, M. G. (2021). Group recruiting events and gender stereotypes in employee selection. *Contemporary Accounting Research, 38*(4), 2496–2520. https://doi.org/10.1111/1911-3846.12710

Fosch-Villaronga, E., Poulsen, A., Søraa, R. A., & Custers, B. (2021). A little bird told me your gender: Gender inferences in social media. *Information Processing & Management, 58*(3), 102541. https://doi.org/10.1016/j.ipm.2021.102541

Frener, R., & Trepte, S. (2022). Theorizing gender in online privacy research. *Journal of Media Psychology: Theories, Methods, and Applications, 34*(2), 77–88. https://doi.org/10.1027/1864-1105/a000327

Frener, R., Wagner, J., & Trepte, S. (in prep). Development and validation of the Need for Privacy Scale (NFP-S).

Gilman, C. P. (1903). *The home, its work and influence*. Source Book Press.

Gingras, Y. (2014). Criteria for evaluating indicators. In R. Cronin & C. R. Sugimoto (Eds.), *Beyond bibliometrics: Harnessing multidimensional indicators of scholarly impact* (pp. 109–125). MIT Press.

Haines, E. L., Deaux, K., & Lofaro, N. (2016). The times they are a-changing … or are they not? A comparison of gender stereotypes, 1983–2014. *Psychology of Women Quarterly, 40*(3), 353–363. https://doi.org/10.1177/0361684316634081

Hargittai, E. (2010). Digital na(t)ives? Variation in internet skills and uses among members of the "net generation". *Sociological Inquiry, 80*(1), 92–113. https://doi.org/10.1111/j.1475-682X.2009.00317.x

Hargittai, E., & Shaw, A. (2015). Mind the skills gap: The role of internet know-how and gender in differentiated contributions to Wikipedia. *Information, Communication & Society, 18*(4), 424–442. https://doi.org/10.1080/1369118X.2014.957711

Heyman, G. D., & Giles, J. W. (2006). Gender and psychological essentialism. *Enfance; Psychologie, Pedagogie, Neuropsychiatrie, Sociologie, 58*(3), 293–310. https://doi.org/10.3917/enf.583.0293

Hines, M. (2010). Sex-related variation in human behavior and the brain. *Trends in Cognitive Sciences, 14*(10), 448–456. https://doi.org/10.1016/j.tics.2010.07.005

Hoffmann, C. P., & Lutz, C. (2019). Digital divides in political participation: The mediating role of social media self-efficacy and privacy concerns. *Policy and Internet*. Advance online publication. https://doi.org/10.1002/poi3.225

Hoffmann, C. P., Lutz, C., & Meckel, M. (2015). Content creation on the internet: A social cognitive perspective on the participation divide. *Information, Communication & Society, 18*(6), 696–716. https://doi.org/10.1080/1369118X.2014.991343

Hu, L., & Kearney, M. W. (2021). Gendered tweets: Computational text analysis of gender differences in political discussion on Twitter. *Journal of Language and Social Psychology, 40*(4), 482–503. https://doi.org/10.1177/0261927X20969752

Hunter, G. L., & Taylor, S. A. (2019). The relationship between preference for privacy and social media usage. *Journal of Consumer Marketing*. Advance Online Publication. https://doi.org/10.1108/JCM-11-2018-2927

Kaya, S., & Yaman, D. (2022). Examining university students' online privacy literacy levels on social networking sites. *Participatory Educational Research*, *9*(3), 23–45. https://doi.org/10.17275/per.22.52.9.3

Kim, Y. (2019). Predicting information self-disclosure on Facebook: The interplay between concern for privacy and need for uniqueness. *International Journal of Contents*, 74–81. https://doi.org/10.5392/IJoC.2019.15.4.074

Kim, Y., Choi, B., & Jung, Y. (2018). Individual differences in online privacy concern. *Asia Pacific Journal of Information Systems*, *28*(4), 274–289. https://doi.org/10.14329/APJIS.2018.28.4.274

Kimpe, L. de, Walrave, M., Verdegem, P., & Ponnet, K. (2021). What we think we know about cybersecurity: An investigation of the relationship between perceived knowledge, internet trust, and protection motivation in a cybercrime context. *Behaviour & Information Technology*, 1–13. https://doi.org/10.1080/0144929X.2021.1905066

Kosciesza, A. J. (2022). Intersectional gender measurement: Proposing a new metric for gender identity and gender experience. *Feminist Media Studies*, 1–16. https://doi.org/10.1080/14680777.2021.2018008

Kurt, M. (2010). Determination of in internet privacy behaviours of students. *Procedia – Social and Behavioral Sciences*, *9*, 1244–1250. https://doi.org/10.1016/j.sbspro.2010.12.314

Lai, S. S. (2021). "She's the communication expert": Digital labor and the implications of datafied relational communication. *Feminist Media Studies*, 1–15. https://doi.org/10.1080/14680777.2021.1998181

Lee, K., & Song, I.-Y. (2013). An influence of self-evaluated gender role on the privacy management behavior in online social networks. In L. Marinos & I. Askoxylakis (Eds.), *Human aspects of information security, privacy, and trust* (pp. 135–144). Springer Berlin Heidelberg.

Lin, C., & Deemer, E. D. (2021). Stereotype threat and career goals among women in STEM: Mediating and moderating roles of perfectionism. *Journal of Career Development*, *48*(5), 569–583. https://doi.org/10.1177/0894845319884652

Lin, F., Wu, Y., Zhuang, Y., Long, X., & Xu, W. (2016). Human gender classification: A review. *International Journal of Biometrics*, *8*(3/4). https://doi.org/10.1504/IJBM.2016.10003589

Linabary, J. R., & Corple, D. J. (2019). Privacy for whom? A feminist intervention in online research practice. *Information, Communication & Society*, *22*(10), 1447–1463. https://doi.org/10.1080/1369118X.2018.1438492

Liu, Q., Yao, M. Z., Yang, M., & Tu, C. (2017). Predicting users' privacy boundary management strategies on Facebook. *Chinese Journal of Communication*, *10*(3), 295–311. https://doi.org/10.1080/17544750.2017.1279675

Lyvers, M., Cutinho, D., & Thorberg, F. A. (2020). Alexithymia, impulsivity, disordered social media use, mood and alcohol use in relation to facebook self-disclosure. *Computers in Human Behavior*, *103*, 174–180. https://doi.org/10.1016/j.chb.2019.09.004

Mehta, C. M. (2015). Gender in context: Considering variability in Wood and Eagly's traditions of gender identity. *Sex Roles*, *73*(11–12), 490–496. https://doi.org/10.1007/s11199-015-0535-4

Mihaljević, H., Tullney, M., Santamaría, L., & Steinfeldt, C. (2019). Reflections on gender analyses of bibliographic corpora. *Frontiers in Big Data*, *2*(29). https://doi.org/10.3389/fdata.2019.00029

Mishra, P., & Suresh, Y. (2021). Datafied body projects in India: Femtech and the rise of reproductive surveillance in the digital era. *Asian Journal of Women's Studies*, *27*(4), 597–606. https://doi.org/10.1080/12259276.2021.2002010

Morrison, B. (2013). Do we know what we think we know? An exploration of online social network users' privacy literacy. *Workplace Review, April 2013*, 58–79.

Newman, M. L., Groom, C. J., Handelman, L. D., & Pennebaker, J. W. (2008). Gender differences in language use: An analysis of 14,000 text samples. *Discourse Processes*, *45*(3), 211–236. https://doi.org/10.1080/01638530802073712

Olsen, F. (1993). Constitutional law: Feminist critiques of the public/private distinction. *Constitutional Commentary*, *337*, 319–327.

Park, Y. J. (2015). Do men and women differ in privacy? Gendered privacy and (in)equality in the internet. *Computers in Human Behavior*, *50*, 252–258. https://doi.org/10.1016/j.chb.2015.04.011

Pedersen, D. M. (1987). Sex differences in privacy preferences. *Perceptual and Motor Skills*, *64*, 1239–1242. https://doi.org/10.2466/pms.1987.64.3c.1239

Petronio, S. (2002). *Boundaries of privacy*. State University of New York Press.

Reeder, H. M. (1996). A critical look at gender difference in communication research. *Communication Studies*, *47*(4), 318–330. https://doi.org/10.1080/10510979609368486

Rodríguez-Priego, N., van Bavel, R., & Monteleone, S. (2016). The disconnection between privacy notices and information disclosure: An online experiment. *Economia Politica*, *33*(3), 433–461. https://doi.org/10.1007/s40888-016-0040-4

Roe v. Wade, 410 U.S Ch. 113 (U.S. Supreme Court).
Rui, J., & Stefanone, M. A. (2013). Strategic self-presentation online: A cross-cultural study. *Computers in Human Behavior, 29*(1), 110–118. https://doi.org/10.1016/j.chb.2012.07.022
Sebo, P. (2021). Using genderize.Io to infer the gender of first names: How to improve the accuracy of the inference. *Journal of the Medical Library Association: JMLA, 109*(4), 609–612. https://doi.org/10.5195/jmla.2021.1252
Sun, Y., Wang, N., Shen, X.-L., & Zhang, J. X. (2015). Location information disclosure in location-based social network services: Privacy calculus, benefit structure and gender differences. *Computers in Human Behavior, 52*, 278–292. https://doi.org/10.1016/j.chb.2015.06.006
Thelwall, M. (2011). Privacy and gender in the social web. In S. Trepte & L. Reinecke (Eds.), *Privacy online. Perspectives on privacy and self-disclosure in the social web* (pp. 251–266). Springer.
Tifferet, S. (2019). Gender differences in privacy tendencies on social network sites: A meta-analysis. *Computers in Human Behavior, 93*, 1–12. https://doi.org/10.1016/j.chb.2018.11.046
To, H. Q., van Nguyen, K., Nguyen, N. L.-T., & Nguyen, A. G.-T. (2020). Gender prediction based on Vietnamese names with machine learning techniques. In *ACM digital library, proceedings of the 4th international conference on natural language processing and information retrieval* (pp. 55–60). Association for Computing Machinery. https://doi.org/10.1145/3443279.3443309
Trepte, S., Teutsch, D., Masur, P. K., Eicher, C., Fischer, M., Hennhöfer, A., & Lind, F. (2015). Do people know about privacy and data protection strategies? Towards the "online privacy literacy scale" (OPLIS). In S. Gutwirth, R. Leenes, & P. D. Hert (Eds.), *Law, Governance and Technology Series: Volume 20. Reforming European Data Protection Law* (pp. 333–365).
van Deursen, A. J. A. M., & Helsper, E. J. (2015). A nuanced understanding of internet use and non-use among the elderly. *European Journal of Communication, 30*(2), 171–187. https://doi.org/10.1177/0267323115578059
Warren, S. D., & Brandeis, L. D. (1890). The right to privacy. *Harvard Law Review, 4*(5), 193–220.
Weinberger, M., Zhitomirsky-Geffet, M., & Bouhnik, D. (2017). Sex differences in attitudes towards online privacy and anonymity among Israeli students with different technical backgrounds. *Information Research: An International Electronic Journal, 22*(4). http://files.eric.ed.gov/fulltext/EJ1164311.pdf
West, C., & Zimmermann, D. H. (1987). Doing Gender. *Gender & Society, 1*(2), 125–151. https://doi.org/10.1177/0891243287001002002
Wood, W., & Eagly, A. H. (2015). Two traditions of research on gender identity. *Sex Roles, 73*(11–12), 461–473. https://doi.org/10.1007/s11199-015-0480-2
Xie, W., & Kang, C. (2015). See you, see me: Teenagers' self-disclosure and regret of posting on social network site. *Computers in Human Behavior, 52*, 398–407. https://doi.org/10.1016/j.chb.2015.05.059
Zarouali, B., Poels, K., Ponnet, K., & Walrave, M. (2021). The influence of a descriptive norm label on adolescents' persuasion knowledge and privacy-protective behavior on social networking sites. *Communication Monographs, 88*(1), 5–25. https://doi.org/10.1080/03637751.2020.1809686
Zhang, R., & Fu, J. S. (2020). Privacy management and self-disclosure on social network sites: The moderating effects of stress and gender. *Journal of Computer-Mediated Communication, 25*(3), 236–251. https://doi.org/10.1093/jcmc/zmaa004
Zuccala, A. A., & Derrick, G. (2022). Gender research in academia: A closer look at variables. In *Handbook on research assessment in the social sciences* (pp. 83–104). Edward Elgar Publishing. https://www.elgaronline.com/view/edcoll/9781800372542/9781800372542.00012.xml
Zucker, K. J. (2017). Epidemiology of gender dysphoria and transgender identity. *Sexual Health, 14*(5), 404–411. https://doi.org/10.1071/SH17067

PART 3

Populations and Their Social Media Privacy

16

THE TRANSLUCENT FAMILY

Sharenting and Privacy Negotiations between Children and Parents

Michel Walrave

UNIVERSITY OF ANTWERP, BELGIUM

Introduction

Youth have been, from the start, intense users of social media, but also parents have increasingly discovered social media. Depending on the child's privacy settings, being connected through social network sites (SNS) with their child gives parents access to their child's online profile and exchanges with peers, domains that previously slipped under the parental radar. But parents also share personal and family experiences online. Some parents engage in "sharenting," the online sharing of personal information related to their children, and possibly also themselves and their parenting role (Blum-Ross & Livingstone, 2017). Parents have been found to share online ultrasounds of their child (Leaver, 2020). Some parents post the child's first steps, monthly physical development, birthdays, and other milestones and mundane moments of their child's unfolding life for family and friends, and sometimes for broader networks of acquaintances, to consider and comment on (Ranzini et al., 2020).

Families' interactions with the outside world have therefore evolved through online communication in general and sharenting in particular. Some families have opened up beyond their core family to give insight into what they experience, challenges they face, and individual members' achievements. Increasingly, research has focused on the motives and consequences of sharenting. Both parents' and children's experiences and viewpoints have been investigated. But what drives families to open up to their (online) network or refrain from disclosing specific information? Why do parents engage in sharenting and how do young people perceive their parents' online sharing practices? These questions will be answered by first focusing on how families relate to the world, as the way they open up to others on social media may be influenced by how they relate to the outside world in general.

Families as Micro-Societies

Families develop their own specific mechanisms with which they implement, support, and defend their traffic-control function to regulate incoming and outgoing traffic of individuals, events, and ideas. In general, families' attitudes toward the external world lead to three types of families (Berg, 1985).

First, *opaque families* have a dense boundary between them and nonmembers. They maintain their values and norms and sustain their belief system by preventing external information from entering

DOI: 10.4324/9781003244677-19

the family system. They clearly identify as an ingroup vs. an outgroup, which is portrayed as having fewer desirable characteristics and beliefs (Berg, 1985). However, for these opaque families, boundary maintenance is increasingly problematic in a (multi)media-pluralistic world, where especially young people have easy access to other viewpoints and lifestyles through social media and other media outlets.

In contrast, *transparent families* do not filter influences from the outside world. They believe that many behaviors are appropriate, depending on concrete situations. They are relativistic, convinced that truth is a function of time and context. In terms of interactions with the outside world, they can be seen as open to new viewpoints and experiences, both offline and online. Finally, the *translucent families* want to maintain their views and beliefs, pass them on through interactions between family members, and regulate their exchanges with the outside world. Parents discuss the reasons for and reasonableness of their views with their children. At the same time, they allow other views to enter the family nucleus. These families are interpretative, as external meanings are interpreted and explained and subsequently accepted, rejected, or modified. The translucent family prepares young people for the outside world by discussing other views and exchanging views and experiences with others. Berg considers the translucent family the most effective in preparing young people for the outside world (Berg, 1985). He referred in the mid-80s to traditional exchanges through conversations and face-to-face encounters, but family translucence can be understood differently now. Young people's and their parents' online disclosures about family activities as well as their and others' comments and reactions on social media complement their offline exchanges with others. In this light, sharenting can be seen as sharing the meanings parents give their family activities (e.g., showing happy family moments during holidays, birthdays, and other get-togethers), values they share (e.g., communicating their children's good grades or sports performances), and how they provide care as a parent (e.g., sharing stress and supporting their child during exams, caring for their sick child). Sharenting also offers parents opportunities to receive feedback, appreciation, and support for how they act as parent (Blum-Ross & Livingstone, 2017). Parents engaging in sharenting can be seen as part of translucent families. They discuss and choose which child-related information to post online, and as they grow older, children are increasingly involved in their parents' sharenting plans (Walrave et al., 2022).

In sum, through sharenting, parents shape their children's digital identity (Steinberg, 2017). However, when their children become active on social media, they may be confronted with information their parents have posted online that they do not relate to or do not want to relate to as an adolescent (Ouvrein & Verswijvel, 2019). In this regard, research has not only been concentrated on parents' motives to engage in sharenting, but also children's opinions and reactions.

Parents' Sharenting Motives

Researchers have discerned several reasons for engaging in sharenting. First, parents like to share key moments in the development of their children. Parents often share how their child grows as well as their academic, athletic, and other achievements (Brosch, 2016). They also share milestones in the children's life, such as their birth and birthdays, but also everyday moments of family life (Kumar & Schoenebeck, 2015). A digital baby book is effectively created to share the child's development with family and friends and as a personal archive of these moments. Some make memories for the future by writing messages for their (underage) children's future birthdays, taking parent-child selfies, or taking pictures of the growing child (e.g., once a month) to chronicle their child's development (Blum-Ross & Livingstone, 2017). To show their pride and highlight important events for their family and acquaintances, parents engage in sharenting. They want to share family moments and show the role they play as parent (Blum-Ross & Livingstone, 2017; Kumar & Schoenebeck, 2015; Walrave et al., 2022). They also feel validated as parents by the likes and positive comments they receive (Davidson-Wall, 2018). In this regard, some have coined the term "oversharenting," referring to some parents' (too) frequent disclosures of personal information and sometimes intimate information about their children (Haley, 2020). This oversharenting has been found to influence observers' opinions negatively about the parents. Observers perceive it as a violation of a (tacit) social norm concerning good parenting and parents not using children to achieve their own goals (i.e., sharenting as an attempt to become the center of attention through their posts concerning their children) (Klucarova & Hasford, 2021).

As users of digital communication have more control over how they present themselves to others, they can think about which aspects they want to disclose and engage in impression management (Krämer & Winter, 2008). Therefore, mothers and fathers are mostly selective in sharing pictures or other information related to their child or the family as a whole (Walrave et al., 2022). Research has also shown that self-presentation as a (good) parent is central in sharenting posts (Davidson-Wall, 2018). The child is sometimes subordinate in a broader story focusing on what parents are doing or have achieved. This selective sharing of parenting-related pictures, which could communicate an idealized picture of parenting, puts parenting-performance pressure on some parents who are confronted with these pictures (Kumar & Schoenebeck, 2015; Ranzini et al., 2020).

Some parents engage in sharenting because they experience difficulties in navigating the child's education. Through sharenting, parents want to gain advice and feel less alone in being confronted with these educational challenges. Sharing their doubts and challenges on social media offers them the opportunity to receive feedback and support rapidly (Fox & Hoy, 2019). Parents may also cope with, and support, their child during illness or life with disability. Through sharenting, parents may share their experiences and seek emotional and practical support and advice. In this context, issues of consent and control about information concerning the child's personal health situation are important to consider and discuss within the family (Goggin & Ellis, 2020).

Finally, several parents share pictures of, or with, their child(ren) for professional reasons, as they are family influencers who earn money by filling the role of social media influencer or parent blogger concerning educational issues. They may also work in collaboration with brands by promoting or endorsing products targeting (young) parents (Blum-Ross & Livingstone, 2017; Campana et al., 2020). These so-called "instamums" and "instadads" do not primarily sharent for parenting reasons but for professional reasons. This sharing has been called sharenting labor, a form of labor that is unique in sharenting and that entails collaboration between influencer-parents and brands (Campana et al., 2020). Marketers may also encourage parents to engage in sharenting to share personal information about their children. However, research involving first-time dads has shown that they consider their children's personal data more sensitive than their own and are less willing to share data with marketers (Fox et al., 2022).

Some authors have highlighted the potential drawbacks of this sharing of personal information about growing children. First, by principle, parents share personal information about their child without the child being able to get involved in the decision or choose whether to have a digital presence. Digital data can be easily shared and copied and hence difficult to delete (Davidson-Wall, 2018). A study found that some parents do not understand the extent to which their child's data are accessible to their SNS contacts. Parents' imagined audience and the actual audience of the sharenting posts were found to be quite different. So parents would need to be better informed about privacy settings and implications of the content they post (Barnes & Potter, 2021). Researchers have warned about digital kidnapping (when someone steals the picture(s) of someone else's child and presents it as if it is his/her own child) (Haley, 2020; Siibak & Traks, 2019). Others have warned about the use of these images on websites that include child-abuse images (Otero, 2017). Parents have been found to share also other concerns about risks of posting personal information about their child, such as digital kidnapping, marketers collecting information, and other users' negative reactions to sharenting posts (Blum-Ross & Livingstone, 2017). Therefore, some parents engage in preventive or corrective strategies to mitigate the risks associated with sharenting. Strategies can be categorized as intra- or extra-systemic strategies (Cino & Wartella, 2021). The former strategies focus on controlling sharenting within the family nucleus, using solutions offered by the used (social media) system, such as engaging in audience control, using privacy settings to share information selectively about their child, or asking their child's permission. The latter focuses on setting rules with (extended) family members and discussing and deciding what can or cannot be shared about the child online (Cino & Wartella, 2021). For instance, parents may agree with family members or friends which picture can be shared or must be kept within the group (Ammari et al., 2015). Some parents make private online groups or use specific apps (e.g., WhatsApp or Signal) in which the child's pictures can be shared and commented on (Cino & Wartella, 2021; Kumar & Schoenebeck, 2015). Some parents explicitly discuss with their child whether they can share pictures on social media (Blum-Ross & Livingstone, 2017). Research also found that parents are more likely to consult their child about their plans to post a picture depending on its age and parents' recognition of the child's agency (Cino & Wartella, 2021). Parents' efforts to include the child, and also other individuals with whom they share information related to the child, in parents' reflections and decisions concerning sharenting, echo Petronio's observation in her communication privacy management theory, concerning privacy boundaries coordination and how individuals discuss the conditions of co-owning data, including the co-responsibility to manage this information (Petronio, 2002).

Some parents have taken a drastic decision, reacting against sharenting by engaging in "anti-sharenting," deciding not to share information about their children on social media to mitigate the risks of sharing personal information online about their child (Autenrieth, 2018; Cino & Wartella, 2021). These potential risks, but also the benefits of sharenting for parents, children, and relatives are summarized in Table 16.1.

Adolescents' Reactions

How adolescents perceive sharenting and react to their parents' online posts is increasingly the focus of research. Teenagers think their parents have several motives, such as impressing their network and archiving photos and videos of them growing up. Although adolescents were found to appreciate this last purpose, they are more critical of their parents' impression-management purposes (Verswijvel et al., 2019). Moreover, some authors have voiced concerns about sharenting's impact on children's identity development. If personal information about children is shared without the children having an opportunity to agree, they could react negatively when they grow up and discover this personal information has been shared. Sharenting may also conflict with adolescents' privacy needs during the crucial developments they experience in their teenage years (Ranzini et al., 2020). Sharenting can also interfere with adolescents' own decisions related to their online self-presentation, especially as adolescents develop a sense of self and therefore want to be in control of how they present themselves on social media (Moser et al., 2017; Ouvrein & Verswijvel, 2019). Some teenagers are embarrassed or irritated when confronted with their parents' sharenting (Lipu & Siibak, 2019; Verswijvel et al., 2019). Sharenting has therefore been found to create tensions and discussions between teenage children and their parents, as the content parents share may not fit adolescents' (desired) online identity (Hiniker et al., 2016). In contrast, some researchers have highlighted that parents' sharenting could also have positive consequences. As adolescents develop their identity, parents' sharing their child's highlights and achievements may stimulate the child's self-esteem and strengthen the parent-child relationship (Moser et al., 2017).

However, young people could hold different perspectives and online practices concerning their personal information as differences have been found between online self-disclosure and privacy settings' use between young people and older age groups (Christofides et al., 2012; Kezer et al., 2016; Walrave et al., 2012). This could also translate into different expectations concerning their parents' sharenting. Therefore, some adolescents have been found to ask their parents to discuss with

Table 16.1 Opportunities and Risks of Sharenting

Opportunities	*Risks*

• Sharing moments/growing up/milestones with (remote) family/friends
• Documenting/archiving child development and milestones
• Sharing parenting activities/experiences with other parents and relatives
• Showing pride concerning children's achievements (first steps, school results, sport, and other achievements)
• Parental advice/support: Asking or giving advice/support for navigating parenting/educational challenges/issues
• Impression management: Image building towards others and receiving recognition for good parenting or reacting to other parents' sharenting (based on social comparison)
• Feeling validated as parent through the likes and (positive) comments received concerning the child('s achievements)/family activities
• Stimulating the child's self-esteem and strengthening the parent-child relationship
• Forming an online community of interest around parenting experiences
• Sharenting to process/cope with child-related difficulties (e.g., caring of a child with a health problem)
• Engaging in influencer sharenting activities
	• Disclosing of personal information of the child that could be misused:
	  • Child images on child-abuse websites
	  • Identity theft
	  • Digital kidnapping
	  • Information put online that discloses the location/schedule/routines of the child
	• Creating a digital presence/identity of the child without involvement of the child in this decision
	• Images of the child or other information that could lead to mockery/(cyber)bullying (now or later)
	• Sharenting conflicting with children's identity, impacting self-esteem, children's privacy needs and rights
	• Images staying online and emerging in later life, for instance, in the context of cybervetting
	• Conflicts between children and parents concerning sharenting content
	• Negative emotions/reactions of other social media users due to oversharenting or specific posts
	• Negative emotions/reactions of other social media users (e.g., irritation or envy) due to social comparison
	• Use of personal data of the child/family for marketing purposes
	• Impact of parents engaging in influencer sharenting on the child

them their intentions to engage in sharenting and what is acceptable or not to share online (Ouvrein & Verswijvel, 2019). In other words, they engage in child-mediation strategies (Van den Bulck et al., 2016). In general, child mediation has been defined as children's initiatives to engage in acts of socialization with their parents concerning their parents' (online) media use. These strategies can be active, restrictive, and supervising. *Active mediation* consists of talking, sharing one's perspectives, and trying to come to an agreement. *Restrictive mediation* is adolescents' efforts to demand that their parents adapt their (sharenting) behavior. *Supervising* consists of checking parents' social media accounts and directly intervening in their published information when parents and children do not come to an agreement (Ouvrein & Verswijvel, 2021). Research on adolescents has shown that sharenting frequency was associated with increased use of restrictive and supervising mediation. In turn, the use of restrictive mediation was related to more conflicts between children and their parents. It seems that parents react similarly to teenagers concerning parental (restrictive) mediation. Children's efforts to restrict sharenting often result in conflicts between them and their parents (Ouvrein & Verswijvel, 2021). Therefore, discussions on the limits of sharenting are warranted so children and parents share the same definition of privacy boundaries to respect when sharing personal information on social media and to reduce potential privacy turbulence and related conflicts between children and their parents. Privacy turbulence happens when there are conflicts between values and interests related to disclosed personal information. In the context of sharenting, privacy turbulence occurs when parents violate privacy rules as defined and agreed upon within the family (Petronio & Child, 2020). Family members' unsuccessful coordination of privacy may lead to consequences in bonding and trust building. Privacy turbulence may also influence children's willingness to reveal in the future (Hernandez & Ebersole, 2022). However, privacy turbulence may have a functional role in adolescent-parents privacy negotiations, as it draws attention to discrepant expectations and leads to discussions and adolescents' interventions to manage their privacy boundaries (Hawk et al., 2009). From an expectancy violation realignment perspective (Collins & Luebker, 1994), these conflicts can open a way to renegotiations of privacy boundaries (Hawk et al., 2009). Still, to avoid turbulence and related conflicts, parents and children need to negotiate the rules concerning shared information and boundaries with people who are not members of the family nucleus (Cino & Wartella, 2021).

The contrast between adolescents and parents is also reflected in their expectations concerning sharenting. Researchers have found that while adolescents give importance to the impressions they make (especially on their peers) and how pictures or other information their parents share on social media may influence this impression, parents are more concerned with showing their child in an "authentic" way so their child is recognizable in the picture and smiling (Walrave et al., 2022). However, adolescents take care in the way they present themselves to fit the image they want to portray of themselves online (Krämer & Winter, 2008). Therefore, the portrait parents sketch online of their child might conflict with adolescents' desired portrayal.

Notwithstanding the abovementioned potential tensions between parents and their children concerning what to post or not online about their growing up children and, more broadly, family activities, sharenting can also offer specific opportunities. Until now, research has focused on potential threats, from a children's and privacy rights perspective (Steinberg, 2017) or related to children's and adolescents' development (Verswijvel et al., 2019; Walrave et al., 2022). This is not new, especially when focusing on minors and digital media, scholars are prioritizing the potential risks of (new) digital applications or media uses (Cino & Dalledonne Vandini, 2020). Less is known about how children's and adolescents' confrontation with their parents' sharenting, but also their grandparents' grandsharenting, makes young people aware of the consequences when their personal information is disclosed online by others. As teenagers grow up, they become more conscious of their self-image and how they want to present themselves to others. Young people's confrontation with sharenting may therefore make them more sensitive towards impressions that are formed when disclosing personal information online and how depicted individuals may relate or not to the mental image that is formed of them. This could stimulate young people to engage in discussions concerning their privacy and make them more aware of the privacy of others.

However, not all children and adolescents are confronted in the same way with parents' online disclosures related to them. Research also focuses on the contrasting sides of the sharenting spectrum: Antisharenting vs. oversharenting. In short, the contrast is between parents who take pictures focusing on other aspects and not on the depicted child or don't include their child in their online posts, vs. parents who intensively engage in photographing their children and sharing this online. Between those contrasting profiles of parents, another type may emerge. Young parents who grew up with social media experienced themselves the opportunities and downsides of online self-presentation. They may use the experience they built while growing up, to engage in sharenting, while at the same time trying to protect their child's privacy. These parents may also adopt camouflage strategies (e.g., replacing the face with an emoji, pixelating the face) to protect their child's identity and edit the picture to make the place where the child is pictured (e.g., home or school) unrecognizable (Autenrieth, 2018). They may also engage in post scrubbing, deleting previous child-related posts. But also before posting online personal information of their child, parents can reflect about why they would share specific child-related information with their online network.

This approach could be coined as mindful sharenting. This concept can be related to what has been called mindful parenting (Kabat-Zinn, 2009; Shorey & Ng, 2021). We define mindful sharenting as the online communication of personal information, including images, of children by their parents, inspired by specific goals and values that lead to sharenting decisions, whereby parents are aware of their motives for engaging in sharenting, of the impact that sharenting can have for their child and themselves, and, when possible, take into account their child's emotions and opinions to reach a decision and engage in privacy-risk minimizing strategies. Further research could focus on profiles of parents engaging in mindful, anti-, or oversharenting. This line of research may be complemented with other research, addressing the following gaps.

Discussion of Future Directions

Until now, research has mostly been focused on parents' motives for engaging in sharenting and adolescents' perceptions and reactions. The avenues for future research can be concentrated on five axes, focusing on (1) younger children, (2) new family compositions, (3) influencer sharenting and other marketing-related issues, (4) impact on child and parent-child attachment, and (5) sharenting interventions.

Scant research has been conducted on how younger children deal with sharenting (Lipu & Siibak, 2019; Sarkadi et al., 2020). However, research (among 4–15-year olds) has shown that they often find their parents taking and sharing pictures online less acceptable (Sarkadi et al., 2020). Therefore, future researchers could concentrate on younger children to investigate their opinions and reactions to their parents' sharenting and on how parents engage in conversations about sharenting with their young child. Longitudinal (qualitative and quantitative) research could follow families and the dynamic processes of interactions between children and parents concerning sharenting as their lives unfold. Moreover, further theory-based research is necessary on determinants of parents' sharing of personal information concerning their children and privacy-protective strategies (implementing, e.g., protection motivation theory (Maddux & Rogers, 1983; Rogers, 1975), communication privacy management theory (Petronio, 2002), regulatory focus theory (Higgins, 1997), social media privacy model (Trepte, 2021), and privacy calculus theory (Laufer & Wolfe, 1977)).

Research also needs to consider new family compositions (e.g., extended families, families with same-sex parents) and how they create new challenges regarding (shared) rules about sharenting. Future investigations can also challenge the image of idealized parenting. Parents themselves can challenge this image by sharing alternative models of parenting, such as alternative childbirth delivery methods and gender-neutral education.

Moreover, the way ex-partners make decisions and manage potential conflicts about their child's online identity, sharenting, and post scrubbing could also be investigated (Cino & Wartella, 2021). Ex-partners' adjustment to divorce and how social comparison may play a role in disclosing activities with children on social media could be the focus of research, as well as the way online communication (and more particularly sharenting) may show or induce cooperative or conflicting coparenting (Russell et al., 2021).

Besides focusing on parents' and children's views and behaviors, grandparents should also be involved by focusing on grandsharenting, grandparents' online sharing behavior concerning their grandchildren. Grandparents may have opinions concerning what to share or not online about their grandchild, which may fit or conflict with parents' vision and children's expectations. The comparison of these generations, who grew up or not with social media, may also show differences in what is seen as private and is expected to be disclosed online. This could lead to discussions and negotiations between (grand)parents and (grand)children (Autenrieth, 2018).

Further attention could be paid to influencer sharenting, which consists of monetized ((quasi-) professional) activities on social media, in collaboration with brands, wherein parents' online activities revolve around their children and parenting activities. As today's young parents follow these influencers who engage in sharing advice and recommendations about services and products and often involve their child in their posts, influencers could normalize the sharing of their growing children's daily lives. Researchers could therefore also concentrate on parents' opinions and behaviors concerning marketers' use of sharented information. Also, how influencer sharenting impacts parents' brand-related attitudes and behaviors could be further investigated. Next, research could be conducted on how celebrities' child-centric posts impact parents' sharenting (Fox et al., 2022). Celebrity sharenting consists of public figures including their children in their online posts as the parent's extended self. Their children become emotional capital that stimulates audiences to engage with the celebrity (Jorge et al., 2022).

Further research could also be conducted on initiatives to raise awareness among parents of the short- and long-term impacts of sharenting (Barnes & Potter, 2021). For instance, a campaign in Germany takes a critical stance towards sharenting through a photo series that shows adults in (typical) baby sharenting poses (e.g., naked on a pot). Each picture is accompanied with a headline questioning the viewer: "Would you ever post a picture like that of yourself? No? Well, neither would your child" (Diebel, 2022). Hereby, they want to stress the constant privacy violations that occur when these pictures are posted on social media (von der Weiden, 2019). Also, other authors and organizations have developed photo-sharing guides to assist parents in their decision to share or not a particular picture (Autenrieth, 2018). Informing parents and stimulating reflections have been found to reduce parents' willingness to post online content about their child (Williams-Ceci et al., 2021).

As far as children's sharenting-mediation strategies are concerned, researchers could concentrate on the further study of strategies used by minors to negotiate or, in another manner, mediate parents' sharenting behavior (Ouvrein & Verswijvel, 2021). Researchers could investigate how (teenage) children develop coping strategies regarding parents' sharenting, such as the selective sharing of specific information on social media or engaging in social steganography, encoding a message so only friends can decode its meaning and only an in-crowd understands the message (boyd & Marwick, 2011). Additionally, researchers can concentrate on how sharenting influences growing children's and adolescents' ideas and value of privacy, how this possibly shapes their privacy-protection strategies concerning sharenting, and also more broadly, when they share personal information online.

References

Ammari, T., Kumar, P., Lampe, C., & Schoenebeck, S. (2015). Managing children's online identities: How parents decide what to disclose about their children online. *Proceedings of the 33rd Annual ACM Conference on Human Factors in Computing Systems*, 1895–1904. https://doi.org/10.1145/2702123.2702325

Autenrieth, U. (2018). Family photography in a networked age. Anti-sharenting as a reaction to risk assessment and behaviour adaption. In *Digital parenting. The challenges for families in the digital age* (pp. 219–231). Nordicom.

Barnes, R., & Potter, A. (2021). Sharenting and parents' digital literacy: An agenda for future research. *Communication Research and Practice*, 7(1), 6–20. https://doi.org/10.1080/22041451.2020.1847819

Berg, D. H. (1985). Reality construction at the family/society interface: The internalization of family themes and values. *Adolescence*, *20*(79), 605–618.

Blum-Ross, A., & Livingstone, S. (2017). "Sharenting," parent blogging, and the boundaries of the digital self. *Popular Communication*, *15*(2), 110–125. https://doi.org/10.1080/15405702.2016.1223300

boyd, d., & Marwick, A. E. (2011). *Social privacy in networked publics: Teens' attitudes, practices, and strategies (September 22, 2011). A Decade in Internet Time: Symposium on the Dynamics of the Internet and Society, September 2011.* Available at SSRN: https://ssrn.com/abstract=1925128

Brosch, A. (2016). When the child is born into the internet: Sharenting as a growing trend among parents on Facebook. *The New Educational Review*, *43*(1), 225–235. https://doi.org/10.15804/tner.2016.43.1.19

Campana, M., Van den Bossche, A., & Miller, B. (2020). #dadtribe: Performing sharenting labour to commercialise involved fatherhood. *Journal of Macromarketing*, *40*(4), 475–491. https://doi.org/10.1177/0276146720933334

Christofides, E., Muise, A., & Desmarais, S. (2012). Hey mom, what's on your Facebook? Comparing Facebook disclosure and privacy in adolescents and adults. *Social Psychological and Personality Science*, *3*(1), 48–54. https://doi.org/10.1177/1948550611408619

Cino, D., & Dalledonne Vandini, C. (2020). "Why does a teacher feel the need to post my kid?": Parents and teachers constructing morally acceptable boundaries of children's social media presence. In *International Journal of Communication* (Vol. 14). https://ijoc.org/index.php/ijoc/article/view/12493/2982

Cino, D., & Wartella, E. (2021). Privacy-protective behaviors in the mediatized domestic milieu: Parents and the intra- and extra-systemic governance of children's digital traces. *Ricerche Di Pedagogia e Didattica. Journal of Theories and Research in Education*, 133–153 Pages. https://doi.org/10.6092/ISSN.1970-2221/13276

Collins, W. A., & Luebker, C. (1994). Parent and adolescent expectancies: Individual and relational significance. In *Beliefs about parenting: Origins and developmental implications* (pp. 65–80). Jossey-Bass.

Davidson-Wall, N. (2018). *"Mum, seriously!": Sharenting the new social trend with no opt-out*. Debating Communities and Social Networks 2018 OUA Conference. http://networkconference.netstudies.org/2018OUA/wp-content/uploads/2018/04/Sharenting-the-new-social-trend-with-no-opt-out.pdf

Diebel, T. (2022, July 21). *So ein Bild von dir würdest du nie posten? Dein Kind auch nicht*. https://deinkindauchnicht.org/

Fox, A. K., & Hoy, M. G. (2019). Smart devices, smart decisions? Implications of parents' sharenting for children's online privacy: An investigation of mothers. *Journal of Public Policy & Marketing*, *38*(4), 414–432. https://doi.org/10.1177/0743915619858290

Fox, A. K., Hoy, M. G., & Carter, A. E. (2022). An exploration of first-time dads' sharenting with social media marketers: Implications for children's online privacy. *Journal of Marketing Theory and Practice*, 1–12. https://doi.org/10.1080/10696679.2021.2024441

Goggin, G., & Ellis, K. (2020). Privacy and digital data of children with disabilities: Scenes from social media sharenting. *Media and Communication*, *8*(4), 218–228. https://doi.org/10.17645/mac.v8i4.3350

Haley, K. (2020). Sharenting and the (potential) right to be forgotten. *Indiana Law Journal*, *95*(3), 1005–1020.

Hawk, S. T., Keijsers, L., Hale, W. W., & Meeus, W. (2009). Mind your own business! Longitudinal relations between perceived privacy invasion and adolescent-parent conflict. *Journal of Family Psychology*, *23*(4), 511–520. https://doi.org/10.1037/a0015426

Hernandez, R., & Ebersole, D. (2022). Parents' and children's privacy management about sensitive topics: A dyadic study. *Journal of Family Issues*, *43*(1), 73–95. https://doi.org/10.1177/0192513X21993192

Higgins, E. T. (1997). Beyond pleasure and pain. *American Psychologist*, *52*(12), 1280–1300. https://doi.org/10.1037/0003-066X.52.12.1280

Hiniker, A., Schoenebeck, S. Y., & Kientz, J. A. (2016). Not at the dinner table: Parents' and children's perspectives on family technology rules. *Proceedings of the 19th ACM Conference on Computer-Supported Cooperative Work & Social Computing*, 1376–1389. https://doi.org/10.1145/2818048.2819940

Jorge, A., Marôpo, L., Coelho, A. M., & Novello, L. (2022). Mummy influencers and professional sharenting. *European Journal of Cultural Studies*, *25*(1), 166–182. https://doi.org/10.1177/13675494211004593

Kabat-Zinn, M. (2009). *Everyday blessings: The inner work of mindful parenting*. Hachette.

Kezer, M., Sevi, B., Cemalcilar, Z., & Baruh, L. (2016). Age differences in privacy attitudes, literacy and privacy management on Facebook. *Cyberpsychology: Journal of Psychosocial Research on Cyberspace*, *10*(1). https://doi.org/10.5817/CP2016-1-2

Klucarova, S., & Hasford, J. (2021). The oversharenting paradox: When frequent parental sharing negatively affects observers' desire to affiliate with parents. *Current Psychology*. https://doi.org/10.1007/s12144-021-01986-z

Krämer, N. C., & Winter, S. (2008). Impression management 2.0: The relationship of self-esteem, extraversion, self-efficacy, and self-presentation within social networking sites. *Journal of Media Psychology*, *20*(3), 106–116. https://doi.org/10.1027/1864-1105.20.3.106

Kumar, P., & Schoenebeck, S. (2015). The modern day baby book: Enacting good mothering and stewarding privacy on Facebook. *Proceedings of the 18th ACM Conference on Computer Supported Cooperative Work & Social Computing*, 1302–1312. https://doi.org/10.1145/2675133.2675149

Laufer, R. S., & Wolfe, M. (1977). Privacy as a concept and a social issue: A multidimensional developmental theory. *Journal of Social Issues*, *33*(3), 22–42. https://doi.org/10.1111/j.1540-4560.1977.tb01880.x

Leaver, T. (2020). Balancing privacy: Sharenting, intimate surveillance, and the right to be forgotten. In L. Green, D. Holloway, K. Stevenson, T. Leaver, & L. Haddon (Eds.), *The Routledge companion to digital media and children* (1st ed., pp. 235–244). Routledge. https://doi.org/10.4324/9781351004107-22

Lipu, M., & Siibak, A. (2019). 'Take it down!': Estonian parents' and pre-teens' opinions and experiences with sharenting. *Media International Australia*, *170*(1), 57–67. https://doi.org/10.1177/1329878X19828366

Maddux, J. E., & Rogers, R. W. (1983). Protection motivation and self-efficacy: A revised theory of fear appeals and attitude change. *Journal of Experimental Social Psychology, 19*(5), 469–479. https://doi.org/10.1016/0022-1031(83)90023-9

Moser, C., Chen, T., & Schoenebeck, S. Y. (2017). Parents' and children's preferences about parents sharing about children on social media. *Proceedings of the 2017 CHI Conference on Human Factors in Computing Systems*, 5221–5225. https://doi.org/10.1145/3025453.3025587

Otero, P. (2017). Sharenting … should children's lives be disclosed on social media? *Archivos Argentinos de Pediatria, 115*(5). https://doi.org/10.5546/aap.2017.eng.412

Ouvrein, G., & Verswijvel, K. (2019). Sharenting: Parental adoration or public humiliation? A focus group study on adolescents' experiences with sharenting against the background of their own impression management. *Children and Youth Services Review, 99*, 319–327. https://doi.org/10.1016/j.childyouth.2019.02.011

Ouvrein, G., & Verswijvel, K. (2021). Child mediation: Effective education or conflict stimulation? Adolescents' child mediation strategies in the context of sharenting and family conflict. *Journal of E-Learning and Knowledge Society*, 70–79 Pages. https://doi.org/10.20368/1971-8829/1135555

Petronio, S. (2002). *Boundaries of privacy: Dialectics of disclosure*. State University of New York Press.

Petronio, S., & Child, J. T. (2020). Conceptualization and operationalization: Utility of communication privacy management theory. *Current Opinion in Psychology, 31*, 76–82. https://doi.org/10.1016/j.copsyc.2019.08.009

Ranzini, G., Newlands, G., & Lutz, C. (2020). Sharenting, peer influence, and privacy concerns: A study on the Instagram-sharing behaviors of parents in the United Kingdom. *Social Media + Society, 6*(4), 205630512097837. https://doi.org/10.1177/2056305120978376

Rogers, R. W. (1975). A protection motivation theory of fear appeals and attitude change. *The Journal of Psychology, 91*(1), 93–114. https://doi.org/10.1080/00223980.1975.9915803

Russell, L. T., Ferraro, A. J., Beckmeyer, J. J., Markham, M. S., Wilkins-Clark, R. E., & Zimmermann, M. L. (2021). Communication technology use in post-divorce coparenting relationships: A typology and associations with post-divorce adjustment. *Journal of Social and Personal Relationships, 38*(12), 3752–3776. https://doi.org/10.1177/02654075211043837

Sarkadi, A., Dahlberg, A., Fängström, K., & Warner, G. (2020). Children want parents to ask for permission before 'sharenting.' *Journal of Paediatrics and Child Health, 56*(6), 981–983. https://doi.org/10.1111/jpc.14945

Shorey, S., & Ng, E. D. (2021). The efficacy of mindful parenting interventions: A systematic review and meta-analysis. *International Journal of Nursing Studies, 121*, 103996. https://doi.org/10.1016/j.ijnurstu.2021.103996

Siibak, A., & Traks, K. (2019). The dark sides of sharenting. *Catalan Journal of Communication & Cultural Studies, 11*(1), 115–121. https://doi.org/10.1386/cjcs.11.1.115_1

Steinberg, S. B. (2017). Sharenting: Children's privacy in the age of social media. *Emory Law Journal, 66*(4), 839–884.

Trepte, S. (2021). The social media privacy model: Privacy and communication in the light of social media affordances. *Communication Theory, 31*(4), 549–570. https://doi.org/10.1093/ct/qtz035

Van den Bulck, J., Custers, K., & Nelissen, S. (2016). The child-effect in the new media environment: Challenges and opportunities for communication research. *Journal of Children and Media, 10*(1), 30–38. https://doi.org/10.1080/17482798.2015.1121897

Verswijvel, K., Walrave, M., Hardies, K., & Heirman, W. (2019). Sharenting, is it a good or a bad thing? Understanding how adolescents think and feel about sharenting on social network sites. *Children and Youth Services Review, 104*, 104401. https://doi.org/10.1016/j.childyouth.2019.104401

von der Weiden, N. (2019, November 27). *Provokantes Fotoprojekt gegen Babyfotos im Netz*. https://www.liliput-lounge.de/news/deinkindauchnicht-babyfotos-internet/

Walrave, M., Vanwesenbeeck, I., & Heirman, W. (2012). Connecting and protecting? Comparing predictors of self-disclosure and privacy settings use between adolescents and adults. *Cyberpsychology: Journal of Psychosocial Research on Cyberspace, 6*(1). https://doi.org/10.5817/CP2012-1-3

Walrave, M., Verswijvel, K., Ouvrein, G., Staes, L., Hallam, L., & Hardies, K. (2022). The limits of sharenting: Exploring parents' and adolescents' sharenting boundaries through the lens of communication privacy management theory. *Frontiers in Education*. https://doi.org/10.3389/feduc.2022.803393

Williams-Ceci, S., Grose, G. E., Pinch, A. C., Kizilcec, R. F., & Lewis, N. A. (2021). Combating sharenting: Interventions to alter parents' attitudes toward posting about their children online. *Computers in Human Behavior, 125*, 106939. https://doi.org/10.1016/j.chb.2021.106939

17

AN INTIMATE RELATION

Adolescent Development, Self-Disclosure, and Privacy

Michel Walrave

UNIVERSITY OF ANTWERP, BELGIUM

Introduction

Adolescence is a key developmental stage in individuals' lives. Throughout the teenage years, fundaments are laid out that influence adult life in terms of identity, social relations, and occupation (Steinberg, 2020). In this crucial period, parents and peers play an essential role. While children mainly turn to their parents, adolescents rely more on peers (McElhaney et al., 2009). When dealing with issues related to romantic relationships, sex, and substance use, but also school and social life, friends are the most important socialization agent for adolescents (Bond, 2018). Youth intensively communicate with peers and use social network sites (SNS) to get in touch with friends and relatives and to make new acquaintances. While adolescents develop a diverse range of relationships, self-disclosure plays a key role in young people's unfolding biographies. Adolescents' developmental tasks lead them toward gaining more independence from their parents, while getting closer to their peers, confiding their most intimate thoughts and feelings, both offline and online. During adolescence, individuals also engage in their first romantic relationships, which sometimes include sharing their feelings when online dating and engaging in intimate self-disclosures such as sexting.

In this chapter, we will discuss how young people navigate the decisions made in this context and how privacy theory sheds light on what is at play in specific situations. First, we focus on adolescence and how privacy is related with the crucial developments young people experience.

Adolescents' Development and Privacy Needs

Adolescence is characterized by fundamental transitions that greatly influence individuals throughout their lives. Teenage years encompass biological changes and cognitive developments, as more advanced cognitive abilities develop and, importantly, crucial social developments occur (Hill, 1983).

Teenagers experience physical changes during puberty, which include developments in their physical appearance. These changes may lead to some young people feeling attractive while others struggle with their appearance and their appeal to their peers (Steinberg, 2020). Moreover, adolescents' cognitive development leads to the maturing of their conceptual thinking and thinking about hypothetical situations (Sanders, 2013). Also social transitions occur during adolescence that encompass the development of relationships beyond the family circle, such as school and other social

DOI: 10.4324/9781003244677-20

contexts of extracurricular activities. Young people gradually also gain more rights and responsibilities (Lupton & Williamson, 2017; Steinberg, 2017). Whether these changes during adolescence translate into positive or negative psychological impacts on young people depends also on the adolescent's social environment. The support or criticism that parents, other adults, and peers voice and the challenges they pose influence the impact of adolescents' physical, cognitive, and social changes on their psychological development. Therefore, generalizing adolescent development is impossible, as social contexts in which young people grow up must be considered (Steinberg, 2020).

In sum, the abovementioned biological and social transitions influence adolescents' psychosocial development. More concretely, adolescents experience major transitions in their identity development, autonomy, intimacy, sexuality, and achievement (Steinberg, 2020). During these major developments, young people construct their own sense of privacy, which plays an important role during these transitions to adulthood. In this context, privacy can be defined briefly as the selective access to oneself (Altman, 1975). It revolves around individuals' decisions concerning the level of access they want to grant others, their level of self-disclosure, and how they shape access to themselves through control and communication (Trepte, 2021). These decisions concerning access to oneself first play a role in adolescents' identity development, as one of their crucial questionings revolves around their developing identity – in short, who they are but also what they want to become when they grow up. These questions also induce experimentation through which adolescents define their individual sense of self, but they also rely on recognition from others. Self-conception develops through adolescents' activities, their experiments with looks, voicing their opinions and concerns, and processing others' feedback (Steinberg & Morris, 2001). In this context, SNS form an online stage where young people present themselves, comment on life and current events, communicate with online contacts, and, through these interactions, construct their identity (Livingstone, 2008; Ong et al., 2011).

Moreover, adolescents' introspection concerning their developing identity leads them to strive for more autonomy. Three autonomy challenges are at stake: Becoming more independent from their parents, learning to function independently, and further developing their own opinions, values, and norms (McElhaney et al., 2009). In this striving for more autonomy, increased parent-child conflicts may occur, and a decrease of parent-child closeness. Subjects that used to be easily agreed on, lead now to divergent viewpoints, and relational tensions that sometimes also impact further interactions (Hernandez & Ebersole, 2022).

Adolescents not only search for more independence from their parents but also simultaneously develop tight friendships and experience their first romantic relationships. Along with engaging in common spare time activities, adolescents develop friendships that include open and intimate exchanges while becoming less open to and emotionally dependent on their parents (Steinberg, 2020). In this transition, selective self-disclosure serves the development of close friendships, romantic relationships, and other (online) contacts. The feedback young people receive both offline and online also fuels the development of their identity (Buhrmester & Prager, 1995). During adolescence, peers increasingly influence adolescents' behavior, also in terms of self-disclosure (Walrave et al., 2012). As peers become key, adolescents tend to rely more on their influence in a growing number of life domains.

Moreover, in puberty, young people usually become sexually active. They may question their sexual identity and orientation and encounter issues of sexual values and pleasure (Buzwell & Rosenthal, 1996). Young people might engage in online dating and sharing of intimate feelings through dating apps. Some engage in the exchange of self-produced sexual imagery, such as sexting. In sum, SNS and more broadly social media play an important role in the development of their sexual selves by engaging in sexual self-presentation (Baumgartner et al., 2015). However, intimacy as a developmental goal can also be defined broadly as acquiring the ability to start and maintain tight friendships and other close relationships (Peter & Valkenburg, 2011), next to developing their first romantic relationships.

Young people's romantic feelings and relationships are an important topic of online exchanges among adolescents (Collins, 2003). In several phases of romantic relations, social media offer adolescents spaces to become acquainted and flirt with their potential romantic partners (Fox et al., 2013). Couples communicate through private messages but also publicly, displaying their love and commitment through emotional messages and photographs of the couple (Saslow et al., 2013). Researchers have also found that for some adolescents, making their relationships "official" through social media posts or changing their relationship status is an important step in sharing their relationships with others and showing that they are "unavailable." Depending on young people's privacy settings, this information can also become available for parents to comment on and eventually share among their online network. However, some young people want to show more subtly that they are in a relationship, by checking in at the same places or posting pictures of themselves and their partners separately but in the same space (Van Ouytsel et al., 2016a). In other words, they communicate to peers under the parental radar by engaging in social steganography, sharing messages that only peers can decode because only they have the necessary information to interpret the message. Although social steganographic messages are visible for a broad audience, they are meaningless for some parts of the audience (e.g., parents) because they lack the interpretative lens to decode the message (boyd & Marwick, 2011; Oolo & Siibak, 2013).

Finally, adolescence is characterized by important developments in adolescents' current and future educational achievements and plans. Young people also increasingly think about their schooling options and related professional career opportunities. They evaluate and compare their talents as well as academic and other achievements with their peers. This social comparison with peers also occurs online (Verduyn et al., 2020) through their peers' posts on their achievements in school, sports, and other areas, but also through their parents' sharenting, showing their pride concerning the accomplishments of their children. This engagement in online social comparison has been found to impact adolescents' well-being and bodily (dis)satisfaction (Meier & Johnson, 2022; Rousseau et al., 2017). Young people also become inspired by others and form personal expectations and ambitions for the future. In this important developmental domain, peers, but also parents, teachers, and other acquaintances inspire them (Steinberg, 2020).

To achieve the abovementioned developmental goals – identity, autonomy, intimacy, sexuality, and achievement – privacy is essential. Young people need a space in which they can experiment to nurture their developing identity (Marcus, 1992). Adolescents experiencing fundamental changes in key life domains need privacy to achieve their developmental goals: More autonomy, especially from their parents, the development of their identity, the development of intimacy in tight friendships and romantic relationships, their exploration of sexuality, and achievements, including plans for their professional future (Newell, 1995; Peter & Valkenburg, 2011; Subrahmanyam & Smahel, 2011). These goals relate to one of Westin's privacy functions: Personal autonomy, the absence of manipulation by others (Westin, 1975), which corresponds to adolescents' need and urge to make their own decisions in a growing number of life domains.

Next to personal autonomy, other privacy functions can be related to adolescents' developmental tasks: Self-evaluation, emotional release, and limited and protected communication (Westin, 1975). As the adolescents' identities develop, they need the space to reflect on who they are and want to become, self-evaluating their identity and competencies and comparing themselves with peers to decide which direction they want to take.

Self-evaluation occurs while developing one's identity in interaction with others. Keeping these reflections to oneself, or choosing to entrust them with selected others, helps young people construct their identity. This limited and protected communication function of privacy offers them the opportunity to relieve emotions, entrust sexual and romantic interests, and express doubts and aspirations about their future. Moreover, this selected and protected communication offers the confidentiality needed to engage in intimate conversations with friends and (potential) romantic partners. At the same time, not everything has to be shared with chosen others, for privacy also includes an individual's decision to withdraw from social life, enabling emotional release (Peter & Valkenburg, 2011).

Adolescence is also characterized by more exploratory and experimenting behavior and risk-taking, compared to other age groups (Call & Burrow-Sanchez, 2010). Teenagers tend to push boundaries, try to break away from their parents' control, and seek to make their own choices (Livingstone & Haddon, 2009). In terms of online self-disclosure, some studies have found that young people tend to disclose more personal information and use more lenient privacy settings than adult SNS users (Christofides et al., 2012; Walrave et al., 2012). Therefore, their personal information, profile data, and online posts are accessible and can be transmitted further to people outside their personal online network. Companies can also harvest personal information to draw conclusions from young consumers' profiles and, in later life, to cybervet, or search for personal information about (potential) students and job candidates to assess their competencies and personality (Walrave et al., 2022).

In sum, a clear convergence can be found between adolescents' developmental goals and privacy functions, underscoring the importance of privacy during young people's transition to adulthood. In this transition, social media also plays a crucial role. On these online platforms, adolescents can present themselves and try out self-concepts. They can look up information on intimate issues, experiment, and receive and give social support beyond the limits of face-to-face communication (Peter & Valkenburg, 2011; van Oosten et al., 2018). Social media offers young people the opportunity to craft their own digital narrative. This opportunity corresponds to adolescents' development of representational agency, deciding whether and what to share, how it can be shared, and the extent to which it is shared (Cino & Wartella, 2021).

However, by interacting online and thus disclosing personal information, others become co-owners of the disclosed information (Petronio et al., 2003). In other words, the privacy decisions that young people make on social media are inherently relational. Individuals who are entrusted with personal information can decide to transmit this information further or keep it with the original "owner" of the personal information. These negotiations are clear, and especially sensitive, in adolescents' wide range of developing relationships and, more particularly, their romantic relationships.

Intimate Disclosures

As adolescents develop their sexual selves, they present themselves on social media and are starting to date offline and through dating apps. Some also engage in intimate disclosures, texting their feelings to (potential) romantic partners and engaging in sexting, the sending of self-made sexually explicit images through digital media such as smartphones (Van Ouytsel et al., 2021).

Entrusting this intimate form of personal information creates a shared responsibility. As digital media's affordances facilitate the replicability and shareability of messages (boyd, 2011; Papacharissi & Gibson, 2011), partners need to find common ground concerning the boundaries of shared information that one needs to respect (Walrave et al., 2018). In light of the communication privacy management (CPM) theory, when an individual sends (intimate) personal information to a (potential) romantic partner, the sender and receiver become co-owners, forming a mutual privacy boundary around this shared information. The original owner believes in keeping the rights to his or her personal information and in controlling this personal information. Ownership is metaphorically represented by privacy boundaries, which define the limits wherein individuals house and protect their information (Petronio & Child, 2020). More particularly, someone making a sexting message becomes the information owner. Sending the sext to one's romantic partner makes the receiver an authorized co-owner. However, it is important to set within a couple co-ownership boundaries, as it creates a backstage – a safe zone – to entrust intimate images and other personal issues with the romantic partner (Walrave et al., 2018). But, in an unfolding relationship, it might not be clear if both partners have the same values and rules concerning how to deal with others' intimate personal information, as these personal values and rules are based on one's gender, culture, or other individual characteristics and experiences (Petronio, 2013, 2016). In a couple, partners bring their own sets of rules concerning the management of personal information, based on their privacy orientations and learned through their education and relations inside and outside their families (Walrave et al., 2018).

Romantic partners become jointly responsible for how they regulate their intimate information exchange, including the permeability of their common privacy boundary, based on their agreed-upon rules for treating entrusted personal information (Petronio et al., 2003). If they don't share the same values and privacy orientation, privacy turbulence may occur, in short, violations in the way the sharing of personal information with third parties is regulated by the co-owners (Petronio, 1991). Privacy turbulence has a negative impact as it disrupts privacy rules, boundaries, ownership, and control and impacts the relationship between the earlier agreed co-owners. At the same time, this turbulence can stimulate the owner to draw conclusions and, possibly, recalibrate the privacy rules to prevent future similar experiences (Petronio & Child, 2020).

Two types of privacy breaches can be discerned: Pre-emptive disclosure violations, when something is prematurely disclosed to others and the original information owner planned or likely would have posted it online (e.g., changes in one's relationship status), and discrepancy breaches of privacy which include the disclosure of personal information that would never have been disclosed by the original owner (e.g., relationship issues) (DeGroot & Vik, 2017).

This last form of privacy breach also occurs when someone forwards or shows a partner's intimate image to others without agreement of their partner (i.e., non-consensual sharing of intimate images). This can occur after a romantic breakup. This form of image-based abuse impacts and disrupts the agreements made concerning the shared intimate images. One of the partners may experience difficulties accepting this breakup and make these messages public for revenge (Van Ouytsel et al., 2016b). When someone forwards the entrusted intimate image to someone else, the privacy boundary is reshaped. Willingly or not, recipients become co-owners, who are now part of the collective privacy boundary (Child & Petronio, 2011). They become responsible for the way this intimate personal information is treated. Depending on the role they take as a bystander, they will influence the potential consequences of this dissemination of the sexting image (Harder, 2021).

Bystanders can decide to stay out of the situation by not reacting towards the sender but also not warning the depicted person. By contrast, defenders take an active role by informing and supporting the victim and not further sharing this picture with others, and possibly also intervening by contacting third parties such as parents, teachers, or social media providers to get advice and assist in stopping further dissemination. Other bystanders can strengthen the negative impact of the situation by commenting on it on social media or forwarding the image to others (Salmivalli, 2014; Sarmiento et al., 2019). In sum, bystanders become co-owners who, depending on the role they take, can further reset the privacy boundary, making it more porous by including others through the further forwarding of the sext or, by contrast, taking the responsibility not to contribute to the permeability of the privacy boundary. Before deciding what to do, bystanders sometimes engage in a risk-benefit tradeoff by adding up the benefits and subtracting the potential risks of intervening. Adolescents' knowledge of and attitude toward the (legal) consequences of forwarding such a message play a role. In addition, they compare the risk of getting caught and sanctioned with other direct effects they perceive as rewards, such as sharing the received sexts as a popularity currency (Lippman & Campbell, 2014; Ringrose et al., 2013). This risk-benefit balance influences individuals' decisions on whether to breach the original privacy boundary or not.

Such privacy violations cause not only an immediate negative impact, but may also hold other outcomes (Petronio, 2010). Privacy breaches become occasions to reaffirm privacy rules or make other decisions to recalibrate or re-coordinate the privacy rules in order to prevent future privacy breakdowns (Child & Petronio, 2011). In sum, privacy breaches are critical situations where involved individuals learn about others' boundaries and how common privacy boundaries have to be explicitly (re)set.

According to CPM, the aforementioned decisions concerning privacy boundary management can be influenced by several factors: Culture, gender, motivation, context, and risk/benefit calculation (Child et al., 2012; Petronio, 2002). Other factors can also influence individuals' decisions related to self-disclosure and privacy, such as age, education, and personality traits. Following Hofstede's cultural dimensions (Hofstede, 2001, 2011), cultures differ in individualism, uncertainty avoidance, long-term orientation, and other characteristics which may influence how individuals deal with their own and others' personal information (Walrave et al., 2018) (see chapter 14 by Cho & Li on intercultural privacy). Culture also influences parents' values and priorities in their child rearing, which may impact how parents deal with their own and their child's personal information. In turn, this may further influence young people's attitudes and behaviors concerning their personal data (Hernandez & Ebersole, 2022). As far as gender is concerned, research has found girls to be more protective of their personal data than boys, by disclosing less personal information or applying more stringent privacy settings on SNS or, in general, more online privacy management strategies (De Wolf, 2020; Tifferet, 2019; Walrave et al., 2012) (see chapter 15 by Frener on gender and privacy). Age differences have also been found in individuals' self-disclosure and privacy-protective strategies (Christofides et al., 2012; Walrave et al., 2012). As young people are more focused on short-term benefits and less moved by the longer term consequences of their behaviors (Cauffman & Steinberg, 2000), this influences their risk-benefit calculus and their privacy-related behaviors.

In sum, from a CPM perspective, disclosure goes beyond self-disclosure because, as soon as someone reveals information to others, it becomes a shared belonging and responsibility (Petronio, 2010). Sharing intimate information with someone induces the recipient's obligation – whether implicit or explicitly discussed – concerning whether to share or not this information with others.

Discussion and Avenues for Further Research

As a transition between childhood and adult life, adolescence is a developmental stage characterized by important changes in terms of identity, autonomy, intimacy, sexuality, and achievement (Steinberg, 2020). In this life phase, individuals also develop a sense of privacy that plays a role in the transitions that young people make.

The role of privacy is perhaps most prominent in adolescents' development of sexuality and intimacy. Therefore, we focused on young people's engagement in intimate message sharing. More particularly, we highlighted the privacy perspectives of young people's engagement in sexting, from a CPM perspective. We also acknowledge a need to further expand this research field. Concretely, as most research has been conducted in Western countries, broader international culture-based research could be stimulated to examine the role of culture in relation to the exchange of sexual imagery, but also in relation to non-consensual intimate image sharing. Culture not only influences our perspective on sex, but also how we define, understand, and respond to sexual offenses (Fido & Harper, 2020). Other forms of image-based sexual abuse could also be further investigated, as they impact victims' dignity, autonomy, and freedom of sexual expression, and infringe on fundamental rights such as privacy (McGlynn & Rackley, 2017). Moreover, the coping behaviors of image-based sexual abuse victims, including help-seeking among their relatives but also reaching out to law enforcement, could be further investigated in relation to fear of reactions and difficulties in disclosing sensitive details of the offense, information that is needed for getting support and for reporting and sanctioning perpetrators (Fido & Harper, 2020). Next to abuse risks and consequences, other research on the context of sexting is needed. Further research could investigate young people's negotiations related to entrusting intimate images, how privacy boundaries are respected, or how misunderstandings or intentional violations result in privacy boundary turbulence and the related psychosocial impact. Researchers may also focus on other types of online aggression including privacy breaches, such as an adolescent's monitoring of one's romantic partner through social media. Privacy issues related to checking a partner's smartphone or other individual devices, out of jealousy or lack of confidence, could also be studied (Langlais et al., 2020; Van Ouytsel et al., 2020).

In this chapter, one of the dimensions of adolescent development that was focused on is teenagers' sexuality and unfolding romantic relationships. However, teens' cognitive and emotional development also impacts other important facets of individuals' lives, for instance, how they act and mature as consumers. How young people's privacy attitudes and behaviors evolve when confronted with interactive forms of digital marketing could be analyzed further. More particularly, research can focus on young people's development of knowledge on online personal data processing and commercial messages' personalization based on consumers' profiles or previous online behavior (Desimpelaere et al., 2021; Holvoet et al., 2022; Walrave et al., 2016). In other words, research can investigate young people's developing literacy in online privacy. Relatedly, research can focus on the development and impact of education in online privacy literacy, focusing on building young people's knowledge about, for instance, economic models of the information society or strategies and techniques of online data processing (Masur, 2020).

More generally, researchers could focus further on how privacy-related values, concerns, and behaviors develop through childhood and adolescence. These dynamics could be investigated through longitudinal survey research, but also longitudinal qualitative research, where participants are interviewed on several moments and reflect on their self-disclosures, the feedback they received, and how this influenced their online sharing behavior. By scrolling back on the respondent's social media account during the interview, specific events, posts, and reactions in the social media history of the participant can trigger reflections (Robards & Lincoln, 2020). Finally, a developmental perspective could be adopted to analyze how privacy breaches experienced by adolescents influence decisions related to online self-disclosure and privacy protection strategies.

References

Altman, I. M. (1975). *The environment and social behavior: Privacy, personal space, territory, and crowding*. Brooks/Cole.

Baumgartner, S. E., Sumter, S. R., Peter, J., & Valkenburg, P. M. (2015). Sexual self-presentation on social network sites: Who does it and how is it perceived? *Computers in Human Behavior, 50*, 91–100. https://doi.org/10.1016/j.chb.2015.03.061

Bond, B. J. (2018). Parasocial relationships with media personae: Why they matter and how they differ among heterosexual, lesbian, gay, and bisexual adolescents. *Media Psychology, 21*(3), 457–485. https://doi.org/10.1080/15213269.2017.1416295

boyd, d. (2011). Social network sites as networked publics: Affordances, dynamics, and implications. In *Networked self: Identity, community, and culture on social network sites* (pp. 39–58). Routledge.

boyd, d., & Marwick, A. E. (2011). *Social Privacy in Networked Publics: Teens' Attitudes, Practices, and Strategies (September 22, 2011). A Decade in Internet Time: Symposium on the Dynamics of the Internet and Society, September 2011.* Available at SSRN: https://ssrn.com/abstract=1925128

Buhrmester, D., & Prager, K. (1995). Patterns and functions of self-disclosure during childhood and adolescence. In K. J. Rotenberg (Ed.), *Disclosure processes in children and adolescents* (1st ed., pp. 10–56). Cambridge University Press. https://doi.org/10.1017/CBO9780511527746.002

Buzwell, S., & Rosenthal, D. (1996). Constructing a sexual self: Adolescents' sexual self-perceptions and sexual risk-taking. *Journal of Research on Adolescence, 6*(4), 489–513.

Call, M. E., & Burrow-Sanchez, J. J. (2010). Identifying risk factors and enhancing protective factors to prevent adolescent victimization on the internet. In *Adolescent online social communication* (pp. 152–166c). Hershey.

Cauffman, E., & Steinberg, L. (2000). (Im)maturity of judgment in adolescence: Why adolescents may be less culpable than adults. *Behavioral Sciences & the Law, 18*(6), 741–760. https://doi.org/10.1002/bsl.416

Child, J. T., & Petronio, S. (2011). Unpacking the paradoxes of privacy in CMC relationships: The challenges of blogging and relational communication on the internet. In K. B. Wright & L. M. Webb (Eds.), *Computer-mediated communication in personal relationships* (pp. 21–40). Peter Lang.

Child, J. T., Haridakis, P. M., & Petronio, S. (2012). Blogging privacy rule orientations, privacy management, and content deletion practices: The variability of online privacy management activity at different stages of social media use. *Computers in Human Behavior, 28*(5), 1859–1872. https://doi.org/10.1016/j.chb.2012.05.004

Christofides, E., Muise, A., & Desmarais, S. (2012). Hey mom, what's on your Facebook? Comparing Facebook disclosure and privacy in adolescents and adults. *Social Psychological and Personality Science, 3*(1), 48–54. https://doi.org/10.1177/1948550611408619

Cino, D., & Wartella, E. (2021). Privacy-protective behaviors in the mediatized domestic milieu: Parents and the intra- and extra-systemic governance of children's digital traces. *Ricerche Di Pedagogia e Didattica. Journal of Theories and Research in Education*, 133–153 Pages. https://doi.org/10.6092/ISSN.1970-2221/13276

Collins, W. A. (2003). More than myth: The developmental significance of romantic relationships during adolescence. *Journal of Research on Adolescence, 13*(1), 1–24. https://doi.org/10.1111/1532-7795.1301001

De Wolf, R. (2020). Contextualizing how teens manage personal and interpersonal privacy on social media. *New Media & Society, 22*(6), 1058–1075. https://doi.org/10.1177/1461444819876570

DeGroot, J. M., & Vik, T. A. (2017). "We were not prepared to tell people yet": Confidentiality breaches and boundary turbulence on Facebook. *Computers in Human Behavior, 70*, 351–359. https://doi.org/10.1016/j.chb.2017.01.016

Desimpelaere, L., Hudders, L., & Van de Sompel, D. (2021). Children's perceptions of fairness in a data disclosure context: The effect of a reward on the relationship between privacy literacy and disclosure behavior. *Telematics and Informatics, 61*, 101602. https://doi.org/10.1016/j.tele.2021.101602

Fido, D., & Harper, C. A. (2020). Future directions in image-based sexual abuse. In D. Fido & C. A. Harper (Eds.), *Non-consensual image-based sexual offending* (pp. 75–91). Springer International Publishing. https://doi.org/10.1007/978-3-030-59284-4_4

Fox, J., Warber, K. M., & Makstaller, D. C. (2013). The role of Facebook in romantic relationship development: An exploration of Knapp's relational stage model. *Journal of Social and Personal Relationships, 30*(6), 771–794. https://doi.org/10.1177/0265407512468370

Harder, S. K. (2021). The emotional bystander – sexting and image-based sexual abuse among young adults. *Journal of Youth Studies, 24*(5), 655–669. https://doi.org/10.1080/13676261.2020.1757631

Hernandez, R., & Ebersole, D. (2022). Parents' and children's privacy management about sensitive topics: A dyadic study. *Journal of Family Issues, 43*(1), 73–95. https://doi.org/10.1177/0192513X21993192

Hill, J. P. (1983). Early adolescence: A research agenda. *The Journal of Early Adolescence, 3*(1–2), 1–21. https://doi.org/10.1177/027243168331002

Hofstede, G. (2001). *Culture's consequences. Comparing values, behaviors, institutions and organizations across nations.* Sage.

Hofstede, G. (2011). Dimensionalizing cultures: The Hofstede model in context. *Online Readings in Psychology and Culture, 2*(1). https://doi.org/10.9707/2307-0919.1014

Holvoet, S., Jans, S. D., Wolf, R. D., Hudders, L., & Herrewijn, L. (2022). Exploring teenagers' folk theories and coping strategies regarding commercial data collection and personalized advertising. *Media and Communication, 10*(1), 317–328. https://doi.org/10.17645/mac.v10i1.4704

Langlais, M. R., Seidman, G., & Bruxvoort, K. M. (2020). Adolescent romantic relationship–oriented facebook behaviors: Implications for self-esteem. *Youth & Society, 52*(4), 661–683. https://doi.org/10.1177/0044118X18760647

Lippman, J. R., & Campbell, S. W. (2014). Damned if you do, damned if you don't … If you're a girl: Relational and normative contexts of adolescent sexting in the United States. *Journal of Children and Media, 8*(4), 371–386. https://doi.org/10.1080/17482798.2014.923009

Livingstone, S. (2008). Taking risky opportunities in youthful content creation: Teenagers' use of social networking sites for intimacy, privacy and self-expression. *New Media & Society, 10*(3), 393–411. https://doi.org/10.1177/1461444808089415

Livingstone, S., & Haddon, L. (2009). Introduction. In *Kids online* (p. 263). Polity Press.

Lupton, D., & Williamson, B. (2017). The datafied child: The dataveillance of children and implications for their rights. *New Media & Society, 19*(5), 780–794. https://doi.org/10.1177/1461444816686328

Marcus, C. C. (1992). Environmental memories. In *Place attachment* (pp. 87–112). Springer.

Masur, P. K. (2020). How online privacy literacy supports self-data protection and self-determination in the age of information. *Media and Communication*, *8*(2), 258–269. https://doi.org/10.17645/mac.v8i2.2855

McElhaney, K. B., Allen, J. P., Stephenson, J. C., & Hare, A. L. (2009). Attachment and autonomy during adolescence. In R. M. Lerner & L. Steinberg (Eds.), *Handbook of adolescent psychology* (p. adlpsy001012). John Wiley & Sons, Inc. https://doi.org/10.1002/9780470479193.adlpsy001012

McGlynn, C., & Rackley, E. (2017). Image-based sexual abuse. *Oxford Journal of Legal Studies*, *37*(3), 534–561. https://doi.org/10.1093/ojls/gqw033

Meier, A., & Johnson, B. K. (2022). Social comparison and envy on social media: A critical review. *Current Opinion in Psychology*, *45*, 101302. 10.1016/j.copsyc.2022.101302

Newell, P. B. (1995). Perspectives on privacy. *Journal of Environmental Psychology*, *15*(2), 87–104. https://doi.org/10.1016/0272-4944(95)90018-7

Ong, E. Y. L., Ang, R. P., Ho, J. C. M., Lim, J. C. Y., Goh, D. H., Lee, C. S., & Chua, A. Y. K. (2011). Narcissism, extraversion and adolescents' self-presentation on Facebook. *Personality and Individual Differences*, *50*(2), 180–185. https://doi.org/10.1016/j.paid.2010.09.022

Oolo, E., & Siibak, A. (2013). Performing for one's imagined audience: Social steganography and other privacy strategies of Estonian teens on networked publics. *Cyberpsychology: Journal of Psychosocial Research on Cyberspace*, 7(1). https://doi.org/10.5817/CP2013-1-7

Papacharissi, Z., & Gibson, P. (2011). 15 minutes of privacy: Privacy, sociality and publicity on social network sites. In *Privacy Online Theoretical Approaches and Research Perspectives on the Role of Privacy in the Social Web* (pp. 75–89). Reinecke L. and Trepte S.

Peter, J., & Valkenburg, P. M. (2011). Adolescents' online privacy: Toward a developmental perspective. In S. Trepte & L. Reinecke (Eds.), Priva*cy online* (pp. 221–234). Springer, Berlin, Heidelberg. https://doi.org/10.1007/978-3-642-21521-6_16

Petronio, S. (1991). Communication boundary management: A theoretical model of managing disclosure of private information between marital couples. *Communication Theory*, *1*(4), 311–335.

Petronio, S. (2002). *Boundaries of privacy: Dialectics of disclosure*. State University of New York Press.

Petronio, S. (2010). Communication privacy management theory: What do we know about family privacy regulation? *Journal of Family Theory & Review*, *2*(3), 175–196. https://doi.org/10.1111/j.1756-2589.2010.00052.x

Petronio, S. (2013). Brief status report on communication privacy management theory. *Journal of Family Communication*, *13*(1), 6–14. https://doi.org/10.1080/15267431.2013.743426

Petronio, S. (2016). Communication privacy management. In K. B. Jensen, E. W. Rothenbuhler, J. D. Pooley, & R. T. Craig (Eds.), *The international encyclopedia of communication theory and philosophy* (pp. 1–9). John Wiley & Sons, Inc. https://doi.org/10.1002/9781118766804.wbiect138

Petronio, S., & Child, J. T. (2020). Conceptualization and operationalization: Utility of communication privacy management theory. *Current Opinion in Psychology*, *31*, 76–82. https://doi.org/10.1016/j.copsyc.2019.08.009

Petronio, S., Jones, S., & Morr, M. C. (2003). Family privacy dilemmas: Managing communication boundaries within family groups. In L. Frey (Ed.), *Group communication in context: Studies of bona fide groups* (pp. 23–56). Lawrence Erlbaum Associates.

Ringrose, J., Harvey, L., Gill, R., & Livingstone, S. (2013). Teen girls, sexual double standards and 'sexting': Gendered value in digital image exchange. *Feminist Theory*, *14*(3), 305–323. 10.1177/1464700113499853

Robards, B., & Lincoln, S. (2020). Social media scroll back method. In *SAGE research methods foundations*. SAGE Publications Ltd. https://doi.org/10.4135/9781526421036851495

Rousseau, A., Eggermont, S., & Frison, E. (2017). The reciprocal and indirect relationships between passive Facebook use, comparison on Facebook, and adolescents' body dissatisfaction. *Computers in Human Behavior*, *73*, 336–344. https://doi.org/10.1016/j.chb.2017.03.056

Salmivalli, C. (2014). Participant roles in bullying: How can peer bystanders be utilized in interventions? *Theory Into Practice*, *53*(4), 286–292. https://doi.org/10.1080/00405841.2014.947222

Sanders, R. A. (2013). Adolescent psychosocial, social, and cognitive development. *Pediatrics In Review*, *34*(8), 354–359. https://doi.org/10.1542/pir.34.8.354

Sarmiento, A., Herrera-López, M., & Zych, I. (2019). Is cyberbullying a group process? Online and offline bystanders of cyberbullying act as defenders, reinforcers and outsiders. *Computers in Human Behavior*, *99*, 328–334. https://doi.org/10.1016/j.chb.2019.05.037

Saslow, L. R., Muise, A., Impett, E. A., & Dubin, M. (2013). Can you see how happy we are? Facebook images and relationship satisfaction. *Social Psychological and Personality Science*, *4*(4), 411–418. https://doi.org/10.1177/1948550612460059

Steinberg, L. (2020). *Adolescence* (12th ed.). McGraw Hill Education.

Steinberg, L., & Morris, A. S. (2001). Adolescent development. *Annual Review of Psychology, 52*(1), 83–110. https://doi.org/10.1146/annurev.psych.52.1.83

Steinberg, S. B. (2017). Sharenting: Children's privacy in the age of social media. *Emory Law Journal, 66*(4), 839–884.

Subrahmanyam, K., & Smahel, D. (2011). *Digital youth: The role of media development.* Springer.

Tifferet, S. (2019). Gender differences in privacy tendencies on social network sites: A meta-analysis. *Computers in Human Behavior, 93*, 1–12. https://doi.org/10.1016/j.chb.2018.11.046

Trepte, S. (2021). The social media privacy model: Privacy and communication in the light of social media affordances. *Communication Theory, 31*(4), 549–570. https://doi.org/10.1093/ct/qtz035

van Oosten, J. M. F., de Vries, D. A., & Peter, J. (2018). The importance of adolescents' sexually outgoing self-concept: Differential roles of self- and other-generated sexy self-presentations in social media. *Cyberpsychology, Behavior, and Social Networking, 21*(1), 5–10. https://doi.org/10.1089/cyber.2016.0671

Van Ouytsel, J., Ponnet, K., & Walrave, M. (2020). Cyber dating abuse: Investigating digital monitoring behaviors among adolescents from a social learning perspective. *Journal of Interpersonal Violence, 35*(23–24), 5157–5178. 10.1177/0886260517719538

Van Ouytsel, J., Van Gool, E., Walrave, M., Ponnet, K., & Peeters, E. (2016a). Exploring the role of social networking sites within adolescent romantic relationships and dating experiences. *Computers in Human Behavior, 55*(A), 76–86. https://doi.org/10.1016/J.CHB.2015.08.042

Van Ouytsel, J., Van Gool, E., Walrave, M., Ponnet, K., & Peeters, E. (2016b). Sexting: Adolescents' perceptions of the applications used for, motives for, and consequences of sexting. *Journal of Youth Studies*, 1–25. https://doi.org/10.1080/13676261.2016.1241865

Van Ouytsel, J., Walrave, M., De Marez, L., Vanhaelewyn, B., & Ponnet, K. (2021). Sexting, pressured sexting and image-based sexual abuse among a weighted-sample of heterosexual and LGB-youth. *Computers in Human Behavior, 117*, 1–11. https://doi.org/10.1016/J.CHB.2020.106630

Verduyn, P., Gugushvili, N., Massar, K., Täht, K., & Kross, E. (2020). Social comparison on social networking sites. *Current Opinion in Psychology, 36*, 32–37. https://doi.org/10.1016/j.copsyc.2020.04.002

Walrave, M., Poels, K., Antheunis, M. L., Van den Broeck, E., & van Noort, G. (2016). Like or dislike? Adolescents' responses to personalized social network site advertising. *Journal of Marketing Communications*, 1–19. https://doi.org/10.1080/13527266.2016.1182938

Walrave, M., Van Ouytsel, J., Diederen, K., & Ponnet, K. (2022). Checked and approved? Human resources managers' uses of social media for cybervetting. *Journal of Cybersecurity and Privacy, 2*(2), 402–417. https://doi.org/10.3390/jcp2020021

Walrave, M., Van Ouytsel, J., Ponnet, K., & Temple, J. R. (2018). Sharing and caring? The role of social media and privacy in sexting behaviour. In *Sexting: Motives and risk in online sexual self-presentation/Walrave, Michel [edit.]; Ouytsel, Van, Joris [edit.]; Ponnet, Koen [edit.]; Temple, Jeff R. [edit.]* (pp. 1–17). Palgrave Macmillan. https://doi.org/10.1007/978-3-319-71882-8

Walrave, M., Vanwesenbeeck, I., & Heirman, W. (2012). Connecting and protecting? Comparing predictors of self-disclosure and privacy settings use between adolescents and adults. *Cyberpsychology: Journal of Psychosocial Research on Cyberspace, 6*(1). https://doi.org/10.5817/CP2012-1-3

Westin, A. (1975). *Privacy and freedom.* Atheneum.

18
PRIVACY IN LATER LIFE

Kelly Quinn

UNIVERSITY OF ILLINOIS AT CHICAGO, USA

While social media's shaping of privacy and its enactment may be a guiding premise for this collection, it is somewhat simplistic to attribute changes solely to the medium's ubiquity. Individuals grow and change through life experiences, gaining knowledge and wisdom, which in turn influence understandings of and expectations for privacy (Laufer & Wolfe, 1977). In the social sciences, age represents three distinct phenomena: 1) Aging or the physical and cognitive change associated with maturation; 2) a period in the life stage, reflecting influences that occur through time (often viewed as life experience); and 3) a cohort or the unique socio-historical time at which one is born. Each of these dimensions of age influences privacy experiences and expectations, presenting a thought-provoking lens through which privacy can be examined, with older ages presenting a particularly interesting case. While as a cohort older adults may be relative newcomers to social media, privacy is a well-documented concern for individuals in this age group and often result from life experiences and aging processes (Dumbrell & Steele, 2015; Newman et al., 2021). Concerns for privacy shape both use and non-use of social technologies for older persons, so examining privacy patterns and perceptions in tandem with aging and life experience provides the opportunity for a more nuanced view of privacy as a phenomenon that flexes through context and over time. In addition to contributing to a deeper understanding of how social media may shape notions of privacy, exploration of privacy's intersection with age and aging can also lend insight into forces that may shape the way in which privacy is lived and experienced. To provide such an opportunity, this chapter will review the literature on older adults, privacy, and social media. It will begin with an overview of how older adulthood can be defined, along with important theories for understanding aging and privacy. It will then review how age overlaps with technology, social media use, and privacy attitudes and behaviors. Finally, it will conclude with suggestions on new directions for study. In effect, the goal of this review is not only to deepen understanding of how online privacy may be understood and navigated at older ages, but also to provide a broader understanding on how privacy conceptions and practices may flex and change throughout life.

Older Adulthood

Older adulthood is often culturally defined, but typically designates the stage of later life that is marked by leisure activities and retirement (Kohli, 2007). As retirement ages vary widely by nation and gender, the term "older adult" can refer to individuals as young as 50 years, but also to those in specific socio-cultural roles such as being a grandparent. Indeed, the age of inclusion for research studies on older

DOI: 10.4324/9781003244677-21

adult populations varies widely (Hunsaker & Hargittai, 2018); however, more recent work has followed the lead of the United Nations (2022) and World Health Organization (2015) and used the age of 60 years as a benchmark. Not easily characterized in demographic or cultural terms, older adults tend to be quite heterogeneous as a group due to a lifetime of experiences, educational opportunities, and environmental exposures (World Health Organization, 2015); this results in widely ranging capabilities and limitations among this population (Rogers & Mitzner, 2017).

Several theories become particularly relevant when considering the privacy attitudes and practices of older adults and their social technology use. First, the life course perspective (Elder, 1998) considers that the social and historical contexts of the individual, as well as their experiences over the life span, provide grounding for differences in life outcomes. For an older person today, these contexts would include that older adults were introduced to the digital environment at a later life stage than younger persons, which means they may not have had the same opportunities for gaining technological skills while in school or in the workplace. Alternatively, introduction of social technologies at later life stages also allows one's digital history to be selectively edited and remembered, as it hasn't been automatically captured as with younger cohorts. Historical experience in establishing and maintaining relationships in face-to-face environments, rather than the digital, often leads to different expectations for and fulfillment from interpersonal connection. Finally, older adulthood is a life stage in which age-related declines in physical and cognitive abilities often manifest (Hornsby, 2021), providing challenges to technology adoption and use (Lee et al., 2011; Wilson et al., 2021). Given these factors, the life course perspective would argue that online privacy would be experienced differently by older people than it is for those in younger age groups.

Second, socio-emotional selectivity theory (Carstensen, 1992) posits that as we age, the realization of a more limited future shifts an individual's social interaction priorities; individuals move goals away from the acquisition of information and the development of a self-concept and place greater focus on the affective quality of our interactions. This emphasis results in more carefully chosen and smaller networks of social connections which are optimized for positive emotional outcomes. This theory would suggest then, that social technologies, which often support the acquisition and maintenance of weaker connections and the formation of bridging social capital (Ellison et al., 2014; O'Brien et al., 2021), may not be perceived to be as beneficial at older ages when compared to those in younger age groups. This reduced perception of benefit may result in lower levels of social media use (Hope et al., 2014) or non-use (Maier et al., 2011) and becomes important when considering the privacy calculus, or the assessment an individual makes of the risks and benefits of disclosing private information (Dienlin & Metzger, 2016). For an older person, reduced benefits from using social media simply may not outweigh the privacy risk resulting from such use (Quan-Haase & Eleuze, 2018).

Finally, the developmental theory of privacy (Laufer & Wolfe, 1977), a theory on which the privacy calculus rests, argues that three elements intersect to influence our experiences and awareness of privacy: 1) The self or self-ego; 2) the environment, including culture, social settings, and position in the life cycle; and 3) interpersonal interaction, which encompasses the management of both social interaction and information. For an older person, this suggests that beyond individual privacy preferences and expectations, factors such as age-related declines in physical and cognitive health and a reduction in the size of social networks are important considerations, impacting both the conceptualization of privacy as well as one's need for it. This theory argues that individuals engage in a "calculus of behavior" which considers the risk of future consequences when engaging in interaction and underscores that an older adult's privacy calculus may involve giving up privacy to maintain certain benefits and preserve important relationships. For example, an older person, to maintain the ability to live independently and reduce the caregiving burden on family members, might agree to privacy-eroding monitoring technologies such as in-home cameras (Lorenzen-Huber et al., 2011).

This theory also suggests that introducing new technologies at later life stages may leave older adults less prepared to recognize the consequences, or privacy implications, that may result from their use.

Taken together, these theories strongly suggest that privacy conceptualizations, needs, and ability to execute protection measures may change over time and throughout life. It follows too, then, that privacy perceptions and attitudes will reflect an individual's experience and life stage and that privacy behaviors will reflect the calculated risk of future privacy consequences, but that these too may shift over time.

Older Adults and Social Technologies

Generally, older adults lag behind those in younger age groups in technology adoption (Faverio, 2022; Ofcom, 2021). This is often due to a variety of factors, including an individual's health and cognitive status, prior experiences with technology in the workplace, and having appropriate support networks to navigate changing needs and requirements (Francis et al., 2019; Friemel, 2014; Olsson et al., 2017). Older adults may lack skills to use web-based technologies (Hargittai & Dobransky, 2017; van Volkom et al., 2014) and may not have developed appropriate conceptual models to understand and navigate using technologies (Quinn et al., 2016). Often, lack of skills is coupled with reduced access to devices, such as laptops and smartphones, and lower levels of broadband connection (Faverio, 2022; Ofcom, 2021), making older adults a significant component of the digital divide population, representing what is now considered the "gray divide" (Friemel, 2014). There is also strong evidence that a steep decline in internet and technology use occurs between those in today's "younger-old" group (i.e., those younger than 70 years) and those that are "older-old" (age 70 years and above). Largely attributable to education and income levels (Friemel, 2014; Hunsaker & Hargittai, 2018), these differences contribute to significant heterogeneity in technology use levels for the older adult population (Quan-Haase et al., 2018). While older adult adoption of social media has increased dramatically over the past few years, it too continues to lag that of younger age groups by a considerable margin (Faverio, 2022; Ofcom, 2021; Sala et al., 2020). Contributing to this gap in social media use, like with technology more broadly, are reduced skill levels (Luders & Brandtzæg, 2014; Wilson et al., 2021) and access to computers and/or broadband connections (Hutto & Bell, 2014).

Viewing lower levels of social media adoption in this way may suggest that older adults as a cohort will "age out" of such deficiencies and that younger cohorts will not face similar challenges. Other studies, however, have found that concerns for privacy and security factor heavily in older persons' non-use (Luders & Brandtzæg, 2014; Nef et al., 2013; Newman et al., 2021) and create an intentionality to non-use that suggests aging or life experiences may also play a role. Supporting this idea, studies have recognized that older adults are not unwilling to adopt new and emerging technologies. On the contrary, older adults have consistently demonstrated willingness to adopt a variety of technologies and incorporate them into everyday life (Kadylak et al., 2020; Quan-Haase et al., 2016). Older adults demonstrate greater willingness to adopt new technologies if they are perceived as beneficial or adding to life quality (Berkowsky et al., 2017; Hanson, 2010), but correspondingly a lack of perceived benefit may contribute to reduced social media use. Older adults often feel social network sites have lower levels of social utility (Luders & Brandtzæg, 2014; Newman et al., 2021), which may be related to their life stage. Consistent with socio-emotional selectivity theory, the online social networks of older persons tend to be smaller, but composed of a greater proportion of actual friends, than what is typically found with younger adults (Arjan et al., 2008; Chang et al., 2015; Hutto & Bell, 2014),

Older Adults and Privacy - Attitudes and Behaviors

Privacy at older ages, like for younger persons, is a concept that is employed in both normative and descriptive contexts (Mulligan et al., 2017). Recent definitions of privacy have argued that because the ability to control the flow of information is limited in a social media environment, privacy might be regarded as a communication process that is governed by social norms and trust (Nissenbaum, 2010; Trepte, 2021). This line of theory acknowledges that it is possible for individuals to satisfy privacy needs without the ability to control their privacy. For the purposes of this chapter, however, Margulis' (1977) core definition of privacy as "the control of transactions between person(s) and other(s), the ultimate aim of which is to enhance autonomy and/or to minimize vulnerability," (p. 10) will be used, as it pragmatically encompasses both the means by which privacy is accomplished as well as its goals. It is perhaps also useful to distinguish privacy's horizontal and vertical dimensions, as these frequently arise in discussions of privacy attitudes and behaviors in the context of older people. Horizontal or "social" privacy refers to privacy in the relationships between individuals, while vertical or "institutional" privacy refers to privacy in the relationship between an individual and organizations such as social media platforms or governments (Masur, 2018; Quinn et al., 2019).

Managing one's privacy is complex, and studies indicate that attitudes and/or concerns regarding privacy, previous privacy violations, perceptions of risk, feelings of one's ability to protect one's privacy, and privacy literacy all factor into the actions that one takes to protect privacy online (Baruh et al., 2017; Gupta & Chennamaneni, 2018; Smith et al., 2011). Social science research on privacy is concentrated in two domains: The attitudes and perceptions surrounding privacy, including privacy concerns, and the mechanisms by which privacy is accomplished. The following subsections will discuss current research with respect to older adults in each of these areas.

Privacy Concerns and Attitudes

While studies that compare privacy conceptualizations between older and younger persons remain relatively rare, there is some evidence that generational differences may exist in how each thinks about privacy. There is evidence that older adults have greater awareness of privacy issues than their younger counterparts (Zeissig et al., 2017). In one study, contrasting definitions of privacy between older and younger adults highlighted that older persons tend to conceptualize privacy in terms of personal space, rather than in the contexts of information control and disclosure that were used by younger persons (Kwasney et al., 2008). In addition, older adult understandings of private information included specific types of information that are given or assigned, such as a social security number or secrets told by others, whereas younger people defined private information much more broadly (Kwasney et al., 2008). In contrast, older adults may think more collectively about how privacy is carried out, with a greater tendency than younger adults to think that their own privacy is dependent on whether the people around them will safeguard it (Kezer et al., 2016).

One of the most frequently studied attitudes about privacy is individuals' worries or concerns about it, as these are viewed as strongly influencing attitudes toward protecting one's privacy online (Yao, 2011). While some studies evidence that older adults have higher levels of privacy concern than younger age groups (e.g., Miltgen et al., 2014; van den Broeck et al., 2015), others have not demonstrated such differences (e.g., Kezer et al., 2016). For older adults, privacy concerns arise about both the social and institutional aspects of social media use. Social privacy concerns include a loss of control or accidental release of one's information that could result in its misuse by others; institutional privacy concerns center on the inability of knowing what personal information might be used for by commercial or governmental actors, including social media platform sponsors (Quan-Haase & Ho, 2020). While these concerns are similar to those found in the general populace (Quinn et al., 2019), the security of online information, or the unauthorized use of personal information for fraudulent or attack purposes, forms a third area of concern for older people, often leading to avoidance or non-use of online services and social media (Luders & Brandtzæg, 2014; Nguyen et al., 2021; Quan-Haase & Ho, 2020; Ray et al., 2019).

Privacy-Protecting Behaviors

The means that individuals take to protect one's privacy online, or privacy-protecting behaviors, is a rich area of exploration for privacy scholars. Privacy-protecting behaviors are actions that are intended to withdraw from interactions or limit self-disclosure to others (Dienlin & Trepte, 2015) and can include things such as untagging oneself in posted photos or deleting cookies from a browser. Strategies used by older adults to protect their privacy online include limiting the amount of information posted on social media, avoiding certain online services and websites, and providing pseudonyms or false information (Huang & Bashir, 2018; Kezer et al., 2016; Nguyen et al., 2021; Quan-Haase & Ho, 2020). Older adults' privacy concerns have a significant and positive effect on their privacy-protecting behaviors (Gupta & Chennamaneni, 2018).

Because a range of activities constitutes privacy-protecting behaviors, generalized statements on whether older adults engage in more or less of this type of behavior may be misconstrued. For example, older adults spend more time than younger adults reading privacy policies and terms of service agreements when signing up for new online services (Oeldorf-Hirsch et al., 2019) and are less likely to disclose sensitive information such as income (Anaraky et al., 2021; Goldfarb & Tucker, 2012; Kezer et al., 2016). Older adults are also more likely to follow norms established by friends with respect to the sharing of personal information online (Chakraborty et al., 2013). But older adults are also less likely than younger adults to take privacy-protecting measures such as restricting access to their social media profile or postings (Kezer et al., 2016) or to take strategies such as removing cookies or clearing browser history to prevent online tracking (Huang & Bashir, 2018). Lower levels of privacy self-efficacy, or an individual's feeling that they can protect their privacy, may contribute to reduced levels of privacy-protecting behaviors for an older person (Miltgen & Peyrat-Guillard, 2014), but reduced awareness of privacy control mechanisms, such as those built into platforms that give control over profile visibility and content sharing, or lower proficiency in using them, are also factors (Brandtzæg et al., 2010; Huang & Bashir, 2018).

These results suggest that at least two factors may be at play with privacy-protecting behavior in older adults, a period effect (related to life experiences) and a cohort effect (related to skills acquisition). In other words, prior experiences may inform older adults of the relevance that social cues and policies hold for protecting privacy, despite their lack of the technical proficiency to protect it. These factors also call attention to the importance that privacy literacy (Park, 2013; Trepte et al., 2015), or the knowledge and skill set needed to accomplish privacy online, holds for engaging in privacy-protecting behaviors. Though traditional markers of disparity, such as age and income, are also markers of reduced levels of privacy literacy (Epstein & Quinn, 2020; Park & Mo Jang, 2014), research on older adult levels of privacy literacy does not show marked differences in literacy levels between younger and older users (Kezer et al., 2016). Individuals with higher levels of privacy literacy, however, show greater concern for privacy and increased privacy-protecting behavior (Baruh et al., 2017; Huang & Bashir, 2018). Higher levels of privacy knowledge are also associated with specific privacy-protecting behaviors in older persons, such as avoiding specific websites or giving false information (Huang & Bashir, 2018). Finally, unlike with younger adults, a lack of privacy literacy at older ages is associated with lower levels of engagement with social media overall (Baruh et al., 2017; Quan-Haase & Eleuze, 2018).

The Future of Aging and Privacy

Several themes emerge as we consider these findings. First, older adults experience online privacy and take protection in different ways than those in younger age groups. Older adults have greater awareness of privacy issues and may conceptualize privacy in different ways than younger persons, which may mean that privacy risk perceptions have an element that is related to life stage. Second, older adults' concerns about privacy influence their activities online and lead them to engage in privacy-protecting behaviors, which include important, but less observable strategies such as disclosing lower levels of sensitive information and not using platforms at all. Strategies of opting out or lurking on social platforms may be more easily accomplished at older ages due to social media's diminished utility in this age group, suggesting that the online privacy calculus for using social media may differ at varying life stages. Finally, privacy self-efficacy and privacy literacy play important roles for enhancing privacy-protecting behaviors in this age group, further underscoring the importance of these constructs to privacy protection policy.

These themes point to an important avenue for further interrogation for privacy studies, one which is focused on understanding how the privacy calculus may flex and change in response to individual and life experiences. Longitudinal studies, examining conceptualizations of privacy across the life span and the corresponding privacy mechanisms which individuals employ, would inform how privacy risk perceptions might shift in response to factors such as age-related physical and cognitive change or the life stage at which new technologies are introduced. More granular longitudinal examinations of privacy concerns which, for example, might highlight how horizontal and vertical privacy considerations shift over the life span, would be challenging to undertake, but would likewise provide important insight into the privacy calculus as a fluid and mutable construct. Future work might also examine how age relates to platforms as they adapt to economic, technological, and political forces over time. In contemplating studies such as these, privacy researchers can meet and address the dynamism inherent in a socially and technologically advancing society.

Acknowledgments

The author would like to thank Fernando Mendez and the University of Illinois at Chicago's Chancellor's Undergraduate Research Award program for support of this project.

References

Arjan, R., Pfeil, U., & Zaphiris, P. (2008). Age differences in online social networking. *Proceedings of CHI' 08*, 2739–2744. https://doi.org/10.1145/1358628.1358754

Anaraky, R. G., Byrne, K. A., Wisniewski, P. J., Page, X., & Knijnenburg, B. P. (2021). To disclose or not to disclose: Examining the privacy decision-making processes of older vs. younger adults. *Proceedings of the 2021 CHI Conference on Human Factors in Computing Systems*, 1–14. https://doi.org/10.1145/3411764.3445204

Baruh, L., Secinti, E., & Cemalcilar, Z. (2017). Online privacy concerns and privacy management: A meta-analytical review. *Journal of Communication*, *67*(1), 26–53. https://doi.org/10.1111/jcom.12276

Berkowsky, R. W., Sharit, J., & Czaja, S. J. (2017). Factors predicting decisions about technology adoption among older adults. *Innovation in Aging*, *1*(3). https://doi.org/10.1093/geroni/igy002

Brandtzæg, P. B., Lüders, M., & Skjetne, J. H. (2010). Too many Facebook "friends"? Content sharing and sociability versus the need for privacy in social network sites. *International Journal of Human-Computer Interaction*, *26*(11–12), 1006–1030. https://doi.org/10.1080/10447318.2010.516719

Carstensen, L. L. (1992). Motivation for social contact across the life span: A theory of socioemotional selectivity. In J. E. Jacobs (Ed.), *Developmental perspectives on motivation* (vol. 40, pp. 209–254). University of Nebraska.

Chakraborty, R., Vishik, C., & Rao, H. R. (2013). Privacy preserving actions of older adults on social media: Exploring the behavior of opting out of information sharing. *Decision Support Systems*, 1–9. https://doi.org/10.1016/j.dss.2013.01.004

Chang, P. F., Choi, Y. H., Bazarova, N. N., & Löckenhoff, C. E. (2015). Age differences in online social networking: Extending socioemotional selectivity theory to social network sites. *Journal of Broadcasting & Electronic Media*, *59*(2), 221–239. https://doi.org/10.1080/08838151.2015.1029126

Dienlin, T., & Metzger, M. J. (2016). An extended privacy calculus model for SNSs: Analyzing self-disclosure and self-withdrawal in a representative U.S. Sample. *Journal of Computer-Mediated Communication*, *21*(5), 368–383. https://doi.org/10.1111/jcc4.12163

Dienlin, T., & Trepte, S. (2015). Is the privacy paradox a relic of the past? An in-depth analysis of privacy attitudes and privacy behaviors. *European Journal of Social Psychology*, *45*(3), 285–297. https://doi.org/10.1002/ejsp.2049

Dumbrell, D., & Steele, R. (2015). Privacy perceptions of older adults when using social media technologies. In M. Tavana, A. H. Ghapanchi, & A. Talaei-Khoei (Eds.), *Healthcare informatics and analytics: Emerging issues and trends*. IGI Global. https://doi.org/10.4018/978-1-4666-6316-9

Elder, G. H. (1998). The life course as developmental theory. *Child Development*, *69*(1), 1–12. https://doi.org/10.1111/j.1467-8624.1998.tb06128.x.

Ellison, N. B., Vitak, J., Gray, R., & Lampe, C. (2014). Cultivating social resources on social network sites: Facebook relationship maintenance behaviors and their role in social capital processes. *Journal of Computer-Mediated Communication*, *19*(4), 855–870. https://doi.org/10.1111/jcc4.12078

Epstein, D., & Quinn, K. (2020). Markers of online privacy marginalization: Empirical examination of socioeconomic disparities in social media privacy attitudes, literacy, and behavior. *Social Media + Society*, *6*(2). https://doi.org/10.1177/2056305120916853

Faverio, M. (2022, Jan 13). *Share of those 65 and older who are tech users has grown in the past decade* [web page]. Pew Research Center. Available at https://pewrsr.ch/3HZd2ao

Francis, J., Ball, C., Kadylak, T., & Cotten, S. R. (2019). Aging in the digital age: Conceptualizing technology adoption and digital inequalities. In *Ageing and digital technology* (pp. 35–49). Singapore: Springer Singapore. https://doi.org/10.1007/978-981-13-3693-5_3

Friemel, T. N. (2014). The digital divide has grown old: Determinants of a digital divide among seniors. *New Media & Society*. https://doi.org/10.1177/1461444814538648

Goldfarb, A., & Tucker, C. (2012). Shifts in privacy concerns. *American Economic Review*, *102*(3), 349–353. https://doi.org/10.1257/aer.102.3.349

Gupta, B., & Chennamaneni, A. (2018). Understanding online privacy protection behavior of the older adults: An empirical investigation. *Journal of Information Technology Management*, *XXIX*(3), 1–13.

Hanson, V. L. (2010). Influencing technology adoption by older adults. *Interacting with Computers*, *22*(6), 502–509. https://doi.org/10.1016/j.intcom.2010.09.001

Hargittai, E., & Dobransky, K. (2017). Old dogs, new clicks: Digital inequality in skills and uses among older adults. *Canadian Journal of Communication*, *42*(2), 195–212. https://doi.org/10.22230/cjc2017v42n2a3176

Hope, A., Schwaba, T., & Piper, A. M. (2014). Understanding digital and material social communications for older adults. *Proceedings of CHI' 14*, 3903–3912. https://doi.org/10.1145/2556288.2557133

Hornsby, P. J. (2021). The nature of aging and the geroscience hypothesis. In N. Musi & P. J. Hornsby (Eds.), *Handbook of the biology of aging* (9th ed., pp. 69–76). Elsevier. https://doi.org/10.1016/B978-0-12-815962-0.00004-4

Huang, H. Y., & Bashir, M. (2018). Surfing safely: Examining older adults' online privacy protection behaviors. *Proceedings of the Association for Information Science and Technology*, *55*(1), 188–197. https://doi.org/10.1002/PRA2.2018.14505501021

Hunsaker, A., & Hargittai, E. (2018). A review of Internet use among older adults. *New Media & Society*, *20*(10), 3937–3954. https://doi.org/10.1177/1461444818787348

Hutto, C., & Bell, C. (2014). Social media gerontology: Understanding social media usage among a unique and expanding community of users. *Proceedings of the Annual Hawaii International Conference on System Sciences*, 1755–1764. https://doi.org/10.1109/HICSS.2014.223

Kadylak, T., & Cotten, S. R. (2020). United States older adults' willingness to use emerging technologies. *Information, Communication & Society*, 1–15. https://doi.org/10.1080/1369118X.2020.1713848

Kezer, M., Sevi, B., Cemalcilar, Z., & Baruh, L. (2016). Age differences in privacy attitudes, literacy and privacy management on Facebook. *Cyberpsychology*, *10*(1). https://doi.org/10.5817/CP2016-1-2

Kohli, M. (2007). The institutionalization of the life course: Looking back to look ahead. *Research in Human Development*, *4*(3–4), 253–271. https://doi.org/10.1080/15427600701663122

Kwasny, M. N., Caine, K. E., Rogers, W. A., & Fisk, A. D. (2008). Privacy and technology: Folk definitions and perspectives. *CHI 2008 Proceedings*, 3291–3296. https://doi.org/10.1145/1358628.1358846

Laufer, R. S., & Wolfe, M. (1977). Privacy as a concept and a social issue: A multidimensional developmental theory. *Journal of Social Issues*, *33*(3), 22–42. https://doi.org/10.1111/j.1540-4560.1977.tb01880.x

Lee, B., Chen, Y., & Hewitt, L. (2011). Age differences in constraints encountered by seniors in their use of computers and the internet. *Computers in Human Behavior*, *27*(3), 1231–1237. https://doi.org/10.1016/j.chb.2011.01.003

Lorenzen-Huber, L., Boutain, M., Camp, L. J., Shankar, K., & Connelly, K. H. (2011). Privacy, technology, and aging: A proposed framework. *Ageing International*, *36*(2), 232–252. https://doi.org/10.1007/s12126-010-9083-y

Luders, M., & Brandtzæg, P. B. (2014). "My children tell me it's so simple": A mixed-methods approach to understand older non-users' perceptions of social networking sites. *New Media & Society*. https://doi.org/10.1177/1461444814554064

Maier, C., Laumer, S., & Eckhardt, A. (2011). Technology adoption by elderly people – An empirical analysis of adopters and non-adopters of social networking sites. In A. Heinzl, P. Buxmann, O. Wendt, & T. Weitzel (Eds.), *Theory-guided modeling and empiricism in information systems research* (pp. 85–110). Physica-Verlag HD. https://doi.org/10.1007/978-3-7908-2781-1_5

Margulis, S. T. (1977). Conceptions of privacy: Current status and next steps. *Journal of Social Issues*, *33*(3), 5–21. https://doi.org/10.1111/j.1540-4560.1977.tb01879.x

Masur, P. K. (2018). Situational privacy and self-disclosure: Communication processes in online environments. In *Situational privacy and self-disclosure: Communication processes in online environments*. Springer International Publishing. https://doi.org/10.1007/978-3-319-78884-5

Miltgen, C. L., & Peyrat-Guillard, D. (2014). Cultural and generational influences on privacy concerns: A qualitative study in seven European countries. *European Journal of Information Systems*, *23*(2), 103–125. https://doi.org/10.1057/ejis.2013.17

Mulligan, D. K., Koopman, C., & Doty, N. (2017). Privacy is an essentially contested concept: A multi-dimensional analytic for mapping privacy. *Philosophical Transactions of the Royal Society A: Mathematical, Physical and Engineering Sciences*. https://doi.org/10.1098/rsta.2016.0118

Nef, T., Ganea, R. L., Müri, R. M., & Mosimann, U. P. (2013). Social networking sites and older users - a systematic review. *International Psychogeriatrics/IPA*, *25*(7), 1041–1053. https://doi.org/10.1017/S1041610213000355

Newman, L., Stoner, C., & Spector, A. (2021). Social networking sites and the experience of older adult users: A systematic review. *Ageing and Society*, *41*(2), 377–402. https://doi.org/10.1017/S0144686X19001144

Nguyen, M. H., Hargittai, E., Fuchs, J., Djukaric, T., & Hunsaker, A. (2021). Trading spaces: How and why older adults disconnect from and switch between digital media. *The Information Society*, *37*(5), 299–311. https://doi.org/10.1080/01972243.2021.1960659

Nissenbaum, H. (2010). *Privacy in context: Technology, policy, and the integrity of social life*. Stanford University Press.

O'Brien, N., Yuan, Y., & Archer, N. (2021). The impact of social network sites on social capital for older adults. *Gerontechnology*, *20*(2), 1–11. https://doi.org/10.4017/gt.2021.20.2.22.08

Oeldorf-Hirsch, A., & Obar, J. A. (2019). Overwhelming, important, irrelevant. *Proceedings of the 10th International Conference on Social Media and Society*, 166–173. https://doi.org/10.1145/3328529.3328557

Ofcom, (2021, Apr 28). Adults' media use and attitudes report 2020/21. https://www.ofcom.org.uk/__data/assets/pdf_file/0025/217834/adults-media-use-and-attitudes-report-2020-21.pdf

Olsson, T., Samuelsson, U., & Viscovi, D. (2017). At risk of exclusion? Degrees of ICT access and literacy among senior citizens. *Information, Communication & Society*, 1–18. https://doi.org/10.1080/1369118X.2017.1355007

Park, Y. J. (2013). Digital literacy and privacy behavior online. *Communication Research*, *40*(2), 215–236. https://doi.org/10.1177/0093650211418338

Park, Y. J., & Mo Jang, S. (2014). Understanding privacy knowledge and skill in mobile communication. *Computers in Human Behavior*, *38*, 296–303. https://doi.org/10.1016/j.chb.2014.05.041

Quan-Haase, A., & Elueze, I. (2018). Revisiting the privacy paradox. *Proceedings of the 9th International Conference on Social Media and Society*, 150–159. https://doi.org/10.1145/3217804.3217907

Quan-Haase, A., & Ho, D. (2020). Online privacy concerns and privacy protection strategies among older adults in East York, Canada. *Journal of the Association for Information Science and Technology*, *71*(9), 1089–1102. https://doi.org/10.1002/asi.24364

Quan-Haase, A., Martin, K., & Schreurs, K. (2016). Interviews with digital seniors: ICT use in the context of everyday life. *Information, Communication & Society*, *19*(5), 691–707. https://doi.org/10.1080/1369118X.2016.1140217

Quan-Haase, A., Williams, C., Kicevski, M., Elueze, I., & Wellman, B. (2018). Dividing the grey divide: Deconstructing myths about older adults' online activities, skills, and attitudes. *American Behavioral Scientist*, *62*(9), 1207–1228. https://doi.org/10.1177/0002764218777572

Quinn, K., Epstein, D., & Moon, B. (2019). We care about different things: Non-elite conceptualizations of social media privacy. *Social Media and Society*, *5*(3). https://doi.org/10.1177/2056305119866008

Quinn, K., Smith-Ray, R., & Boulter, K. (2016). Concepts, terms, and mental models: Everyday challenges to older adult social media adoption. In J. Zhou & G. Salvendy (Eds.), *Human aspects of IT for the aged population. Healthy and active aging* (vol. 9755, pp. 227–238). Springer International Publishing. https://doi.org/10.1007/978-3-319-39949-2_22

Rogers, W. A., & Mitzner, T. L. (2017). Envisioning the future for older adults: Autonomy, health, well-being, and social connectedness with technology support. *Futures*, *87*, 133–139. https://doi.org/10.1016/j.futures.2016.07.002

Ray, H., Wolf, F., Kuber, R., & Aviv, A. J. (2019). 'Woe is me': Examining older adults' perceptions of privacy. *Extended Abstracts of the 2019 CHI Conference on Human Factors in Computing Systems*, 1–6. https://doi.org/10.1145/3290607.3312770

Sala, E., Gaia, A., & Cerati, G. (2020). The gray digital divide in social networking site use in Europe: Results from a quantitative study. *Social Science Computer Review*, online first. https://doi.org/10.1177/0894439320909507

Smith, H. J., Dinev, T., & Xu, H. (2011). Information privacy research: An interdisciplinary review. *MIS Quarterly*, *35*(4), 989–1016. https://doi.org/10.2307/41409970

Trepte, S. (2021). The social media privacy model: Privacy and communication in the light of social media affordances. *Communication Theory*, *31*(4), 549–570. https://doi.org/10.1093/ct/qtz035

Trepte, S., Teutsch, D., Masur, P. K., Eicher, C., Fischer, M., Hennhöfer, A., & Lind, F. (2015). Do people know about privacy and data protection strategies? Towards the 'Online Privacy Literacy Scale' (OPLIS). In S. Gutwirth, R. Leenes, & P. de Hert (Eds.), *Reforming European Data Protection Law* (vol. 20, pp. 333–365). Springer. https://doi.org/10.1007/978-94-017-9385-8_14

United Nations High Commissioner for Refugees (UNHCR). (2022, Feb 23). Older persons, version 2.4. In *UNHCR Emergency Handbook*, 4th ed. https://emergency.unhcr.org/entry/43935/older-persons

Van den Broeck, E., Poels, K., & Walrave, M. (2015). Older and wiser? Facebook use, privacy concern, and privacy protection in the life stages of emerging, young, and middle adulthood. *Social Media + Society*, *1*(2). https://doi.org/10.1177/2056305115616149

Van Volkom, M., Stapley, J. C., & Amaturo, V. (2014). Revisiting the digital divide: Generational differences in technology use in everyday life. *North American Journal of Psychology*, *16*(3), 557–574.

Wilson, G., Gates, J. R., Vijaykumar, S., & Morgan, D. J. (2021). Understanding older adults' use of social technology and the factors influencing use. *Ageing and Society*, 1–24. https://doi.org/10.1017/S0144686X21000490

World Health Organization. (2015). *World report on ageing and health*. Available at http://apps.who.int/iris/bitstream/handle/10665/186463/9789240694811_eng.pdf

Yao, M. Z. (2011). Self-protection of online privacy: A behavioral approach. In *Privacy online* (pp. 111–125). Springer, Berlin, Heidelberg. https://doi.org/10.1007/978-3-642-21521-6_9

Zeissig, E.-M., Lidynia, C., Vervier, L., Gadeib, A., & Ziefle, M. (2017). Online privacy perceptions of older adults. In J. Zhou & G. Salvendy (Eds.), *ITAP 2017: Human aspects of IT for the aged population. Applications, services and contexts* (pp. 181–200). Springer. https://doi.org/10.1007/978-3-319-58536-9_16

19

TOWARD A BETTER UNDERSTANDING OF MINORITIES' PRIVACY IN SOCIAL MEDIA

Ralf De Wolf and Tom De Leyn

GHENT UNIVERSITY, BELGIUM

Introduction

In our contemporary society, new media and data-driven technologies raise various privacy concerns. Ample scholarly attention has been devoted to social media and privacy issues by employing a wide range of theoretical frameworks. Rather than providing a taxonomy of privacy (Solove, 2006) or an interdisciplinary review (Smith et al., 2011), this chapter aims to highlight the importance of a minority perspective on privacy. To date, minority voices are underrepresented in privacy research, although minorities often find themselves in a more vulnerable position than the majority (De Leyn, 2022; Marwick & boyd, 2018; McDonald & Forte, 2022). Moreover, it is our belief that we often put forward ethnocentric conceptualizations on privacy within and beyond the social sciences that mainly represent the individualistic views of white and middle-class populations in the Global North. Consequently, privacy frameworks tend to be unmindful of the socio-cultural contexts of minority groups. We argue that further studies that amplify the voices of minority groups as well as frameworks that move beyond neo-liberal notions of individual control and protection are needed.

In what follows, we first contextualize and describe two of our empirical studies that focus on the privacy of ethno-religious[1] minority children and youth in Flanders, Belgium. Next, we propose a working definition to study privacy among minorities. Finally, we present three considerations to further understand minorities' privacy in social media.

Beyond Western Approaches to Privacy

Marwick and boyd (2018) note that much research on privacy originates from the United States and Europe, comes from the field of law and computer science, is overwhelmingly written in English, and investigates popular Western platforms (e.g., Facebook). In addition, we would like to add that most research endeavors and conceptualizations on privacy put the individual at the center of attention, with a focus on either control or protection.

In Europe, privacy is often recognized as a basic human right (De Hert & Gutwirth, 2006); this is in line with the "right to be let alone" as proposed by Warren and Brandeis (1890). One of the most prominent legal adaptions in the European Union (EU), the General Data Protection Regulation (GDPR), aims to achieve this right in online contexts and puts forward the "right to be forgotten"

DOI: 10.4324/9781003244677-22

(art. 17). Overall, the GDPR aims to increase awareness and transparency about the ways data are collected and used as well as to help enhance control over one's personal data and privacy.

Another prominent way to conceptualize privacy is by focusing on individual control or access restriction: arguably, a more liberal and instrumental perspective on privacy. Privacy is then seen as "the selective control of access to the self" (cf. Altman, 1975, p. 24) and instrumental to achieve different ends. For example, Westin (1967) highlights the importance of privacy for personal autonomy or emotional release.

In the context of social media, offering transparency and control to individuals is important to facilitate their privacy management. Protecting one's privacy—for example, through privacy policy—is equally important, especially when considering the many ways in which service providers have violated users' privacy as well as the limited capabilities of individuals to always act as rational actors when trading information (Acquisti et al., 2020).

Although privacy expectations are found to differ between cultures (Altman, 1975) and culture is considered an important criterion that influences privacy management processes (Petronio, 2002), empirical studies and theories that focus on culture and especially minority culture are limited. Research on this topic, therefore, is necessary to fully understand how minority groups perceive and achieve privacy. Although we do not say that individual protection or control are not important for minority groups, we find research with a sole focus on frameworks that start from the notion of individual control or protection to study privacy to be lacking. Note, however, that empirical studies are increasingly looking into the cross-cultural differences in people's privacy attitudes and behaviors (e.g., Li et al., 2022; Liu & Wang, 2018; Marshall et al., 2008; Wang et al., 2011) and are paying attention to minority groups that are vulnerable because of class, gender, ethnicity, religion, or other intersectional characteristics; they tend to draw on Marxist, feminist, and intersectional theories to move beyond neoliberal approaches (e.g., Fritz & Gonzales, 2018; Madden et al., 2017; McDonald & Forte, 2022; Pitcan et al., 2018).

In the next section, we discuss the results of two empirical studies[2] on ethno-religious minority children and youth and further reflect on the implications and how to further guide future research endeavors. Note that we do not intend to generalize our findings to all minority groups. Instead, we highlight some key issues that can steer future research projects focused on minorities in other regions or/and with a focus on other characteristics (e.g., gender and class).

Privacy Experiences of Ethno-Religious Minorities in Flanders

In 2016 and 2018, we gave a voice to Muslim children in Flanders to obtain insights into how they negotiate information about their Muslim culture and identity using focus groups and interviews (De Wolf et al., 2022). From 2019 onward, we also conducted a 15-month ethnographic study among ethno-religious youth and investigated how they manage privacy boundaries (De Leyn, 2022). In particular, Tom De Leyn participated as a volunteer youth worker in a community organization located in an impoverished neighborhood in Flanders.

Study 1: Muslim Children's Internal and External Group Privacy Struggles

Approach and Research Focus

In our first study, we amplified the voices of Muslim children (a minority group in Catholic Flanders) and how they negotiated offline and online group privacy (see chapter 5 by Petro & Metzger on group privacy). In group privacy, no person is in full control of private information; the information belongs, or is applicable, to the members of the group. In our approach, we treated privacy management as an interactive and social process (cf. communication privacy management theory, Petronio, 2002) and acknowledged the relative position of the group one belongs to. In particular, we looked at how privacy is embedded in everyday social contexts (the school and the school playground) and were mindful of the structures of power (the relationships between the minority group and other actors).

Flanders has no Islamic schools. Hence, Muslim children attend either a public or a Catholic school, which oftentimes impedes them from performing typical Muslim practices during school hours. "How do Muslim children negotiate offline and online group privacy and what strategies are used?" This can be considered our main research question. We employed focus groups and interviews to investigate children's (aged 9–12 years) privacy management practices. The focus groups took place in the children's classrooms during lunch break (~60 minutes). The interviews were conducted on the school playground (~35 minutes). We used various probing materials to keep the conversations during interviews going (e.g., showing interactions on social media). To analyze the data, we used a grounded theory perspective (Glaser & Strauss, 1967) and focused on further developing theoretical propositions to understand privacy from a minority perspective.

Main Findings

The focus groups took place after the terrorist attacks by Daesh at Brussels Airport and a metro station in Brussels, which left a mark on Muslim culture. Social media had many conversations on the matter. For example, children expressed their feelings regarding the attacks on Karrewiet, a social media website where children can create their own profiles and comment on articles, photos, and movies.

During the focus groups, it became clear that the Muslim children were very conscious and aware of the societal image and representation of the group they belong to, both in the offline and online realm. In addition, they did their very best to convince the white moderators that not all Muslims are terrorists. On another level, and especially during the one-on-one interviews, we also noticed how expressing their religious beliefs and practices in a school context was constrained, as the quotes below illustrate.

JAMILA: *"I pray five times a day. When I am at school, that's not always possible, so I say my prayers at home."*

INTERVIEWER: *"Ok. So during school hours you don't pray?"*

JAMILA: *"No. In some schools you can take a break, but here it is not allowed. The high school that I'm attending next year doesn't allow this either. Catholics don't pray at school either, so I guess we're not allowed too."*

Both offline and online, our respondents developed privacy strategies to cope with this reality. On the school playground, they would sometimes use Arabic greetings (As-salāmu 'alaykum) when alone with only Muslim children. Online they negotiated on what are considered appropriate information flows.

A'DAB: *"I previously had comments on my posts when I shared things about my home country. They then tell me 'stop posting this. This isn't fun. We also want to understand what you're posting.'"*

INTERVIEWER: *"Understand what?"*

A'DAB: *"Some people don't understand. For example, I posted a picture of our president [Recep Tayyip Erdoğan]. But some people don't know he was elected. But I can't help that, now can I? Or when I go to the mosque and post a picture of the Quran. They tell me that this is Haram [acts that are forbidden in Islam]."*

INTERVIEWER: *"Who tells you that?"*

A'DAB: *"People from school. My friends. They tell me not to post such things. They tell me that people who aren't Muslim will start calling me names because they don't understand."*

The groups the children belonged to also had clear rules and privacy norms. Hence, the group culture shaped the everyday practices of the children on social media.

YARA: *"I don't know. I don't put anything about my family online. You never know, they don't want certain friends of friends to see. I have pictures with our headscarves on and pictures of my aunt without. So sometimes you have pictures with no headscarf that are only appropriate for friends. I can't put these online.*
INTERVIEWER: *"Why can't you do that?"*
YARA: *"My dad wants women to wear headscarves because then men do not gaze at women anymore."*

Overall, the findings of the first study illustrate that the respondents' view on privacy and their privacy practices move beyond individual-centric notions. First, privacy is not limited to managing access or controlling information flows. It is seen as something that allows them to develop and perform Muslim identities. Moreover, their privacy notions are shaped by both the dominant and minority culture they belong to. Second, and in line with their privacy perceptions, the management of privacy is significantly dependent on what practices their surroundings allow them to perform, highlighting both internal (the Muslim community they belong to) and external structural constraints (the school policy or the affordances of social media).

Study 2: Ethno-Religious Minority Youths and Privacy

Approach and Research Focus

In the second study, we investigated how ethno-religious minority youth experience and manage privacy. In our approach, we left aside neoliberal notions of privacy (with a focus on individual control), developmental frameworks on life span, and the general image that young people are reckless and unconcerned in their privacy management (De Leyn et al., 2019). Instead, our study looked at how ethno-religious minority youths' specific socio-cultural constellations inform their social media practices and privacy perceptions. We conceptualize a socio-cultural constellation as a young person's experiences at "the intersection between ascribed 'youthful' subject positions (e.g., tween, teenagers, young adult) and socio-cultural contexts beyond age (e.g., ethnicity, gender, SES)" (De Leyn, 2022, p. 21). In this study, socio-cultural constellations situate ethno-religious minority youths within a particular youth culture that both challenges and reproduces stigmatizing representations of "Muslim" young men within the Flemish society.

The study draws on a 15-month offline/online ethnographic fieldwork in which Tom participated as a volunteer youth worker within an organization that supports ethno-religious minority youths from lower socioeconomic status (SES) backgrounds. By attending the activities of the organization, Tom could observe the study participants and conduct informal interviews while interacting with these young people in a natural setting (e.g., doing homework together, playing (video) games, and "hanging out" in the city). Furthermore, these "offline" interactions spontaneously led to having access to the youths' public and private social media profiles. Accordingly, we were able to explore how the social media practices of these young people are embedded within their lived experiences and socio-cultural positioning as "being an ethno-religious minority youth" in Flanders.

Main Findings

In line with the first study, the relative position of ethno-religious minority youth was significant. On multiple occasions, Tom observed that the youth he interacted with had many experiences of exclusion and racism. For instance, the participants regularly voiced frustration over how racist representations homogenize their diverse identities by perpetuating the unidimensional labels of "Muslim," "black," and "Middle-Eastern." Consequently, a common practice that we observed was how the youth carefully tailored their screennames on social media to signal both ethnic and peer belonging. For instance, Hadar, who identifies as an Iranian Kurd and as a member of the "9To gang," crafted his screenname "Hadar_Kur9To" in a way that presents his belongings to a wider audience.

Moreover, the participants employed these screennames as amplifications of their presence in "offline" spaces in the form of graffiti tags on buildings and benches in their neighborhood. This elicited regular discussions between the young men and youth worker Aylan, as he was concerned that the identifying information in these screennames might facilitate police surveillance. The participants, however, disregarded Aylan's worries; they believed that they are already being disproportionally targeted by surveillance in public spaces. As Rayan explains, prevalent racist tropes among the Flemish majority frequently subject ethnic minorities to surveillance practices; these practices are reflective of how the minorities are represented as being more inclined to engage in deviant activities (e.g., theft, selling and abusing drugs, and vandalism):

RAYAN: *"Aylan, habibi [used among friends], chill! These bastards [the police] are already coming for us and acting all tough. The tags don't matter. They know who I am; they know who Yusuf is. They know who you are! They just checked [our ID's] last week. It's enough to be in the park to be checked. Mashallah [I swear], they do it so that we won't hang out in the park anymore."*

Rayan's perception of his representation as an ethnic minority youth is shared by the participants of this fieldwork. Being aware of the racist discourses that effectively subject them to institutional surveillance, the ethno-religious minority youth reported that they held very little trust in the intentions of the majority population and the institutions they produce (e.g., the legal and education system). As a result, they attach great importance to the support they receive from their own—extended—networks. More specifically, we observed how these young men employed social media to maintain and establish these extended networks. For example, they engage in networked gift-giving practices (e.g., promoting a friend by posting a recent picture along with a tag to their social media accounts on Instagram Stories) to create a curated front stage that presents themselves as being a member of an inclusive and supportive community of connections:

SULEYMAAN: *"We always comment on each other's pictures and repost these on Instagram Stories because it shows that your bros have your back. We are a group of close friends, and if you start a fight with me, you will have to deal with all of us."*

Through networked gift-giving practices, ethno-religious minority youth present themselves as being well-connected, which challenges their marginalized position in society. Although networked gift-giving is not idiosyncratic to this group of young people, we argue that their particular experiences with racism and discrimination raise their stakes for relationship maintenance and self-presentation on social media. Indeed, the ethno-religious minority youth participants in this study were highly aware of their stereotypical representations in the Flemish society and therefore consciously constructed an image of themselves that conceals the more personal and intimate aspects of their lives. In particular, the participants disclosed imagery that portrays idealized notions of masculinity (e.g., pictures that highlight fit and muscled bodies, expensive cars, and designer brands). According to the youth worker Mehmet who once sought support from the organization himself, it is humiliating for young men to be perceived as mere victims of discrimination, displacement, and poverty. Therefore, presenting oneself as masculine can be regarded as a strategy to overcome the victimization narratives that are inscribed on ethno-religious minority youth.

The case of 18-year-old Yassin is illustrative in this regard. Yassin's self-presentation on social media is mainly characterized by pictures and videos of himself when he is speeding on his motorcycle, smoking shisha, and posing in ways that highlight his masculine appearance. The pictures that Yassin keeps on his personal smartphone, however, reveal the more intimate, affective, and emotional layers of his personality. On one occasion, Yassin was showing Tom pictures of his family in Syria, videos of playful interactions with friends, families, and youth workers, and memories of his deceased family. For Yassin, this imagery is deeply personal and therefore not appropriate to disclose on his social media profiles:

TOM: *"These are great pictures; I'm wondering now why you don't seem to like sharing them on social media?"*

YASSIN: *"These are mine [memories], and I don't mind sharing them with friends. I don't see why it should be on social media. My real friends know me, so it doesn't really matter that I post these [pictures on social media]. Why do you ask?"*

TOM: *"I was just curious because I never saw these images on your Instagram and TikTok. I mean, these profiles almost show a totally different Yassin."*

YASSIN: *"Yeah hopefully! These [pictures] wouldn't fit my Insta."*

Overall, the findings of the study illustrate how ethno-religious minority youth use social media in ways that soften the structural tensions stemming from their particular socio-cultural position in society. Although the social media practices described above are not unique to this group of young men, it is important to recognize that their negotiation between disclosure and concealment is informed by their everyday experiences with racism and discrimination. In other words, the observations of this fieldwork challenge the assumption that individuals automatically experience autonomy over the information they present to their followers on social media. Instead of disclosing spontaneous interactions or intimate life histories, the participants in this study experience societal pressure to challenge the stigmatizing representations that marginalize them.

Defining and Investigating Minority Privacy

Regulating access is a universal phenomenon, but different cultures have their own behavioral mechanisms and privacy norms (Altman, 1975; see also chapter 14 by Cho & Li on intercultural privacy). We identified three elements to better understand minorities' perspectives on privacy: (1) the relative position of the minority group and its relationship with the dominant culture, (2) the practices and beliefs of the minority group, and (3) the relationship between the privacy management of the minority group and how it enabled or limited an individual's privacy decision-making. Indeed, privacy management among minorities is complex and includes "the negotiation of boundaries around the self, the minority group they belong to as well as the societal image or representation of that particular minority group" (De Wolf et al., 2022).

To investigate minorities' privacy in social media, we offer the following three considerations: (1) treat privacy as layered and dialectical, (2) acknowledge the interconnection between privacy, group culture, and the dominant culture, and (3) focus on playful subjectivity and the process of privacy management. These considerations are especially relevant for understanding minorities' perspectives but could also be useful to study privacy in general.

Treat Privacy as Multi-Layered and Dialectical

Over the years, privacy scholars have used various frameworks to investigate privacy in social media (e.g., privacy calculus theory, communication privacy management theory, contextual integrity theory, and protection motivation theory). These frameworks make various ontological and epistemological claims and clarify different components of privacy (e.g., control, protection, management, and negotiation). In the first consideration, we argue that focusing on and combining these well-established approaches will result in a broad and encompassing understanding of privacy management. A review of extant research already shows a tendency to surpass the current frameworks (Masur & Bazarova, 2020; Stoilova et al., 2021; Trepte, 2020). Considering the privacy management of minority groups in social media, we find it necessary to investigate how the right to be let alone is preserved, what privacy management strategies are used, how privacy boundaries are negotiated between group members, and what they consider to be appropriate information flows.

Although such an encompassing approach allows for a more in-depth understanding of privacy management and how it plays out on the ground, it most likely also highlights dialectical tensions. For example, the ethno-religious minority youth in our ethnographic study actively amplify the visibility of their interactions on social media through networked gift-giving. Although these practices seem to soften the structural tension stemming from racism and discrimination, this amplified visibility increasingly subjects them to the disapproving gaze of white, middle-class citizens, institutional actors, and—right-wing—politicians. In a similar vein, several Muslim children reported that they disclose information about events within and/or customs belonging to their ethno-religious communities even though these practices can result in backlash from various actors. Altogether, these results unveil how privacy is not a singular achievable condition but a continuous process informed by multiple personal, social, and cultural layers.

Acknowledge the Interconnection between Privacy, Group Culture, and the Dominant Culture

This consideration involves investigating the relationship between privacy and self, and group development. Rather than portraying privacy as being a good that can be traded off against other goods, Cohen (2013) suggests to be mindful of privacy as "breathing room" that allows for the development of critical and playful subjectivity: "privacy is not a fixed condition that can be distilled to an essential core, but rather an interest in breathing room to engage in socially situated processes of boundary management. It enables situated subjects to navigate within preexisting cultural and social matrices, creating spaces for the play and the work of self-making" (p. 1911). Building further on the work of Cohen (2013), we suggest being mindful of how the privacy of minorities is shaped by both the minority and dominant culture and to what extent their breathing room is being preserved.

In light of the two studies discussed in this chapter, we argue that minorities' breathing room is situated within their continuous efforts to reconcile the socio-cultural values and norms of their ethno-religious communities, the dominant society, and their personal imaginations and experiences of "being-in-the-world." Even more so than majority populations, minorities display a conscious awareness of the structural constraints that complicate the process of boundary management within this space. For instance, the ethno-religious minority youth in both studies report to take into account the stereotypical representations of their ethno-religious identities as well as the opinions of members of their communities when practicing self-presentation on social media.

Overall, our suggestion to acknowledge the interconnection between privacy, group culture, and the dominant culture calls for an exploration of the following questions: Do minorities experience enough privacy to develop themselves and achieve personal autonomy? Do their privacy practices legitimize or question structural inequalities? Although the difficulties in establishing a so-called breathing room through achieving privacy are also shared among majority populations, the context of racism and discrimination arguably further constrains the abilities of minorities to freely play around boundaries compared with those who hold privilege in a given society.

Focus on Playful Subjectivity and the Process of Privacy Management

Privacy is often associated with "hiding," "managing," "controlling," and "protecting" the self. Here, we suggest focusing more on play and playing around with boundaries to understand privacy practices.

Many privacy scholars have studied privacy management or the crystallization of privacy practices. Although this is crucial, we argue that privacy management is a long and messy process of sense-making.

Our ethnographic study highlights the importance of considering the notion of playful subjectivity when investigating privacy practices. For example, our results reveal how the ethno-religious minority youths' self-presentation practices draw from a peer culture that idealizes dominant notions of masculinity that in some ways resemble masculine imagery perpetuated in R&B and Hip-hop culture (cf. Dhaenens & De Ridder, 2015). If we only have access to these youths' social media profiles, however, we could misinterpret these self-presentation practices as crystalized expressions of their identities. However, our interactions with these young men in everyday life illuminated how they playfully employ such portrayals of masculinity in ways that challenge their low-status representations and that conceal their more intimate life histories. The complex data ecology as well as the lacking ways in how social media providers inform users and provide them with control limit the users' sole focus on hiding, controlling, or managing privacy. Indeed, everyday users (including minority groups and the majority) form intuitive, informal, and maybe even irrational theories to achieve privacy (cf. Folk theory, DeVito et al., 2018).

Conclusion and Future Research

In this chapter, we presented two of our empirical studies that were focused on the privacy of ethno-religious minority children and youth in the context of social media. Whereas much research in the field looks into the practices of white and middle-class populations, the understandings on the privacy of minorities and their practices are underrepresented. To guide future research endeavors, we offer the following suggestions. First, because of the dialectical nature of minority privacy and its connection to cultural practices and beliefs, we especially recommend ethnographic research. When conducting the fieldwork, we suggest being mindful of how the participants are not just telling "their story" (cf. Bettie, 2003). Indeed, the presence and interactions of researchers with the minority group shapes the story that is being developed. Second, neo-liberal notions on privacy are popular in privacy research and tend to focus on individual control and protection. However, we found them insufficient to really grasp the understandings of minority groups. Instead, it is necessary to move beyond the notions of individual control and look into the relationship between the individual, the minority group, and the dominant culture. Finally, the study of minority privacy exposes larger societal problems that should be pointed out. The findings in our studies revealed the everyday experiences of minority youth with racism, discrimination, and structural inequality. Only through acknowledging these can minority privacy and privacy management be understood and, more importantly, the status quo be questioned.

Notes

1 The ethnicity and religion of minority groups are often connected in Flanders to one another to label and construct "the other" (Agirdag et al., 2017). For example, someone with Turkish or Moroccan roots will most likely be seen as a Muslim, and vice versa.

2 The participants' names and screennames have been pseudonymized. Moreover, the studies in this chapter received formal approval from the ethics' committee of the authors' department.

References

Acquisti, A., Brandimarte, L., & Loewenstein, G. (2020). Secrets and likes. The drive for privacy and the difficulty of achieving in the digital age. *Journal of Consumer Psychology*, *30*(4), 736–758.

Altman, I. (1975). *The environment and social behavior: Privacy, personal space, territory, crowding*. Brooks/Cole.

Bettie, J. (2003). *Women without class: Girls, race, and identity, with a new introduction*. University of California Press.

Cohen, J. (2013). What privacy is for. *Harvard Law Review, 126*, 1904–1933.

De Leyn, T. (2022). *Reframing debates on youths' privacy: Towards an understanding of how young people's privacy practices unfold at the nexus of mobile youth culture and socio-cultural discourses on age* [Doctoral dissertation, Ghent University]. Biblio UGent.

De Leyn, T., De Wolf, R., Vanden Abeele, M., & De Marez, L. (2019). Reframing current debates on young people's online privacy by taking into account the cultural construction of youth. In *SMSociety '19, Proceedings of the 10th International Conference on Social Media & Society* (pp. 174–183). https://doi.org/10.1145/3328529.3328558. Toronto, Canada.

De Leyn, T., De Wolf, R., Vanden Abeele, M., & De Marez, L. (2022). Networked gift-giving: Ethno-religious minority youths' negotiation of status & social ties in a society of distrust. Presented at *the ICA 2022 – 72st Annual ICA Conference*. Paris, France.

De Hert, P., & Gutwirth, S. (2006). Privacy, data protection and law enforcement. Opacity of the individual and transparency of power. In E. Claes, A. Duff, & S. Gutwirth (Eds.), *Privacy and the criminal law* (pp. 61–104). Intersentia.

DeVito, M. A., Birnholtz, J., Hancock, J. T., French, M., & Liu, S. (2018). How people form folk theories of social media feeds and what it means for how we study self-presentation. *Proceedings of the 2018 CHI Conference on Human Factors in Computing Systems, 120*, 1–12.

De Wolf, R., & Joye, S. (2019). "Control responsibility." A critical discourse analysis of Flemish newspapers on privacy, teens and Facebook. *International Journal of Communication, 13*, 5505–5524.

De Wolf, R., Van Hove, S., & Robaeyst, B. (2022). Exploring Flemish Muslim children's experiences and negotiation of offline and online group privacy. *European Journal of Cultural Studies, 25*(4), 1030–1046.

Dhaenens, F., & De Ridder, S. (2015). Resistant masculinities in alternative R&B? Understanding Frank Ocean and The Weeknd's representations of gender. *European Journal of Cultural Studies, 18*(3), 283–299.

Fritz, N., & Gonzales, A. (2018). Negotiating trans narratives while crowdfunding at the margins. *International Journal of Communication, 12*, 1189–1208.

Glaser, B. G. & Strauss, A. L. (1967). *The Discovery of Grounded Theory: Strategies for Qualitative Research.* New York: Aldine.

Liu, Z., & Wang, X. (2018). How to regulate individuals' privacy boundaries on social network sites: A cross-cultural comparison. *Information & Management, 55*(8), 1005–1023.

Li, Y. (2022). Cross-Cultural Privacy Differences. In: Knijnenburg, B.P., Page, X., Wisniewski, P., Lipford, H.R., Proferes, N., Romano, J. (Eds.) *Modern Socio-Technical Perspectives on Privacy*. Springer. https://doi.org/10.1007/978-3-030-82786-1_12

Li, Y., Rho, E. H. R., & Kobsa, A. (2020). Cultural differences in the effects of contextual factors and privacy concerns on users' privacy decision on social networking sites. *Behaviour & Information Technology, 41*(3), 655–677. https://doi.org/10.1080/0144929X.2020.1831608

Madden, M., Gilman, M., Levy, K., & Marwick, A. (2017). Privacy, poverty, and big data: A matrix of vulnerabilities for poor Americans. *Washington University Law Review, 95*(1), 53–125.

Malkki, L. H. (1996). Speechless emissaries: Refugees, humanitarianism, and dehistoricization. *Cultural Anthropology, 11*(3), 377–404.

Marshall, B. A., Cardon, P. W., Norris, D. T., Goreva, N., & D'Souza, R. (2008). Social networking websites in India and the United States: A cross-national comparison of online privacy and communication. *Issues in Information Systems, 9*(2), 87–94.

Marwick, A., & boyd, d. (2018). Privacy at the margins. Understanding privacy at the margins. Introduction. *International Journal of Communication, 12*, 1157–1165.

Masur, P. K., & Bazarova, N. N. (2020). Towards an integration of individualistic, networked and institutional approaches to online disclosure and privacy in a networked ecology. *Current Opinion in Psychology, 36*, 118–123.

McDonald, N., & Forte, A. (2022). Privacy and vulnerable populations. In B. Knijnenburg, X. Page, P. Wisniewski, H. R. Lipford, N. Proferes, & J. Romano (Eds.), *Modern socio-technical perspectives on privacy* (pp. 337–363). Springer International Publishing.

Petronio, S. (2002). *Boundaries of privacy: Dialectics of disclosure.* State University of New York Press.

Pitcan, M., Marwick A., & boyd, d. (2018). Performing a vanilla self: Respectability politics, social class, and the digital world. *Journal of Computer-Mediated Communication, 23*(3), 163–179.

Smith, H. J., Dinev, T., & Xu, H. (2011). Information privacy research: An interdisciplinary review. *MIS Quarterly, 35*(4), 989–1016.

Solove, D. J. (2006). A taxonomy of privacy. *University of Pennsylvania Law Review, 154*(3), 477–560.

Stoilova, M., Nandagiri, R., & Livingstone, S. (2021). Children's understanding of personal data and privacy online – A systematic evidence mapping. *Information, Communication & Society, 24*(4), 557–575.

Trepte, S. (2020). The social media privacy model: Privacy and communication in the light of social media affordances. *Communication Theory*. https://doi.org/10.1093/ct/qtz035

Wang, Y., Norcie, G., & Cranor, L. F. (2011). Who is concerned about what? A study of American, Chinese and Indian users' privacy concerns on social network sites. In *Proceedings of the 4th International Conference on Trust and Trustworthy Computing* (pp. 146–153). Berlin, Heidelberg.

Warren, S., & Brandeis, L. (1890). The right to privacy. *Harvard Law Review*, *4*(5), 193–220.

Westin, A. F. (1967). *Privacy and freedom*. Atheneum.

20

INEQUALITIES AND PRIVACY IN THE CONTEXT OF SOCIAL MEDIA

Matías Dodel

UNIVERSIDAD CATÓLICA DEL URUGUAY

Introduction

Among an ocean of contemporary socioeconomic and digital disparities, ubiquitous data collection and dataveillance make the understanding of the differences in how we conceive, manage, and are affected by privacy as a pressing issue (Büchi et al., 2022; Helsper, 2021; see also chapter 4 by Stoycheff on institutional perspectives on privacy). Some scholars even argue that we are experiencing the creation of a *privacy vulnerable* class. As Marwick and boyd (2018) claim, the ones at the margins are far more likely to be coerced into providing their data than to decide sharing it voluntarily.

This chapter presents a review of recent literature on how socioeconomic inequalities affect and are affected by privacy in the context of social media. It aims to serve as a starting point on how to think and address the links between these two constructs in an evidence- and theory-based approach.

The chapter is organized as follows. The first section reflects on which inequalities should be of concern for privacy, then discusses what privacy is and how individuals make privacy management decisions in social media (privacy calculus). I assert that some inconsistencies between risks and behaviors attributed to a privacy paradox can still be accounted for within the privacy calculus if key mediators of socioeconomic disparities are taken into account: self-efficacy and digital competence. The second section presents recent findings on what we know about privacy as a consequence of inequalities, both at macro and micro levels. Regarding the former, the chapter discusses how regulation influences privacy agency between countries, and how dataveillance has both macro and micro consequences for privacy management within and between nations. Regarding the latter, findings focus on how age, gender, class and race, and digital competence are the main sources of privacy inequality at a micro level.

Additionally, in line with Park (2021) and Büchi et al. (2022), the next section reflects on privacy and privacy perceptions as core causes of inequalities. This section discusses how these perpetuate socioeconomic and digital disparities in issues such as differentiated digital engagement, tangible consequences of private online activities, and civic participation, to name a few. The final section reflects on the future directions and challenges for the study of inequalities and privacy in social media.

Which Inequalities?

In order to address the links between inequality and privacy, we need to first reflect on what social inequalities are, and which could be more relevant in the context of social media. In a more basic sense, inequalities can be understood as the result of disparities among the social, economic, cultural, political, and genetic conditions in which we, human beings, are born into this world (Heckman, 2011).

 DOI: 10.4324/9781003244677-23

As Heckman (2011) argues, there will always be winners and losers in "lottery of birth" as, by nature or circumstances, endowments are unequal. Nonetheless, these starting conditions are not set in stone and need not – and should not – determine individuals' life courses if we seek more equal societies (Heckman, 2011; Rawls, 2020).

Even considering them only in relation to privacy, socioeconomic inequalities are plenty, going far beyond income distributions. Paraphrasing Park (2021; and thus, somewhat Goffman), a failure to include all of the dimensions of inequality affecting privacy neglects the social, political, and cultural conditions which fundamentally determine one's agency in the subject. I argue a Rawlsian approach is needed to identify a broader spectrum of inequalities relevant for privacy in social media. Under this perspective, all issues which could impact privacy, for which individuals have no agency, should be addressed (Rawls, 2020).

In line with previous works on digital inequalities and why they matter (Dodel, 2021; Helsper, 2021; Robinson et al., 2015), traditional axes of inequalities such as gender, race or ethnicity, and the economic, social, digital, and cultural capitals of the household in which they are raised appear to be key dimensions. Nonetheless, other issues such as personality traits, the types of innate abilities with which individuals are born into this world, and where they are born are less prevalent in the literature but – I argue – are needed to be considered too. This chapter will make particularly focus on the last, as it has critical consequences for privacy in terms of free speech, and civil and political rights, but also of the privacy regulations that exist and how different countries are willing – or able – to enforce them, considering the power and global reach of social media corporations.

Privacy: What It Is, Its Calculus and — Apparent — Paradoxes

The idea of privacy as a right and its relationship with freedom and dignity preexist the social media by almost a century (Trepte et al., 2017). Broadly understood, the construct of privacy as a social phenomenon implies not just restricting access to personal information, but also encompasses other dimensions such as the perception or possibility to decide or control which information of oneself is available to one or several audiences (Boerman et al., 2021; Chen, 2018; Marwick & boyd, 2018). Additionally, within a social media context, anonymity and the *right to not be identified* become key components of privacy (Chen, 2018).

How social media privacy is conceptualized and operationalized in the literature is substantially more diverse – and perhaps problematic. Research can be broadly grouped into scholars concerned with *data release* behaviors or *self-help privacy behaviors* (Park, 2015), but the picture is not exactly binary.

Within and across each of these groups, one of the main debates in the literature refers to the coherence or paradoxes in the cognitive mechanisms of privacy management (Masur, 2021). There is a certain consensus, at least in terms of their adoption, on two competing theories on privacy management: the privacy calculus and the privacy paradox (i.e., also see Chen, 2018; Masur, 2021; Trepte et al., 2017). The privacy calculus argues that individuals weigh their privacy concerns against their perceptions regarding the gratifications of the activities performed online (i.e., see also Baruh et al., 2017; Büchi et al., 2021; Trepte et al., 2017). In contrast, the privacy paradox proposes that privacy concerns are not directly linked to its management (Trepte et al., 2020). Dienlin delves more thoroughly into the foundations of both these frameworks (see chapter 7 on the privacy calculus).

Nonetheless, in line with scholars closer to digital inequalities studies, I argue that the so-called paradox may be the product of more complex processes in privacy management, directly related to inequalities in the distribution of digital literacy and privacy self-efficacy (Büchi et al., 2017 & 2021; Park, 2021). Seeking privacy while disclosing information is not contradictory, as the two sides of privacy management (data release and protection) can operate with opposite signs due to the effects of digital literacy and privacy self-efficacy (Büchi et al., 2017).

Büchi et al., 2017's study summarizes this argument clearly and directly: *caring is not enough*. Without an adequate level of digital competence, self-care privacy practices are less probable to occur. A lack of confidence in one's own capacities to perform increasingly complex privacy protective measures, or even successfully coping with routine and tedious ones can deter individuals from protecting themselves even if they have strong beliefs of their susceptibility to and/or the severity of privacy violations (Dodel & Mesch, 2019).

While digital skills increase confidence in the ability to protect one's privacy, they do not imply an automatic reduction of the intentions to disclose personal information. Privacy choices should be considered as continuous negotiation processes in which – at least – a *two-step privacy management strategy* occurs without being paradoxical: first, privacy concerns can increase social media privacy audience management, while then information disclosure can occur towards more curated audiences (Büchi et al., 2021; Chen, 2018). For example, Chen (2018)'s findings – based on Hong Kong and US populations – show that privacy-savvy and concerned individuals have the knowledge and skills to better select and curate their audiences through the management of their privacy settings in social media. Afterwards, they can disclose personal information to seek social benefits with reduced risks of social or institutional privacy violations (Chen, 2018).

Privacy as a Consequence of Macro- and Micro-Level Inequalities

Data and privacy management involve a mix of macro and micro level determinants (Büchi et al., 2021). Thus, inequalities will intertwine with privacy in substantially diverse and multilevel ways.

Macro Level

Disparities in Privacy Regulation and Enforcement

Nations where individuals are born have critical consequences for their privacy. In the first place, privacy legislation or *the sociolegal environment and the extent to which privacy is afforded legal protection* (Baruh et al., 2017), can severely affect an individual's privacy agency.

Most studies addressing legislation disparities focus on the differences in regulative approaches between the United States and European Union (i.e., Baruh et al., 2017; Boerman et al., 2021; Büchi et al., 2022), and the literature is severely lacking in terms of what happens in the global south (i.e., see UNCTAD, n.d. for comparable data).

For example, in order to test global convergence in regulatory data protection, and question whether the European Union's General Data Protection Regulation (GDRP) has been established as a global policy standard, Pätsch (2018) sent questionnaires to several data protection authorities. The authorities were inquired on the principles dictating each country's data protection legislations. Findings signal that convergence was occurring and laws became more similar during the second decade of the 21st century. Moreover, the European data protection framework was the most prevalent in the sample of 26 countries, even comparing it to United States' competing – and more lenient – approach towards data protection.

Aho and Duffield (2020), on the other hand, use a comparative approach to analyze the social and economic implications of two privacy regulation frameworks based on almost diametrically opposed philosophical foundations. On the one hand, the individualist and "socially grounded" European Unions' GRDP is built around the notions of personal consent and empowerment. On the other, a somewhat Orwellian governmental surveillance is embedded into China's Social Credit System (SCS), which assesses – or (credit) rates- citizens' behaviors according to a national-state project and its idea of common good. Aho and Duffield signal the need to consider the cultural idiosyncrasies of each region before oversimplifying SCS's objectives, and stress that both regulation frameworks share one common objective: to protect citizens from potentially nefarious commercial interests.

Besides Pätsch (2018)'s master thesis and Aho and Duffield (2020)'s article, comparative studies in privacy legislations in developing economies are scarce. Moreover, even when globally most national legislations are slowly converging towards the GDRP standards – at least according to Pätsch (2018) – global south countries lag behind in privacy regulation and its enforcement compared to the global north.

My key point, nonetheless, is somewhat tangent to these works. What I argue is that national regulations' disparities can directly affect individual's privacy awareness levels. Take for example the experience of Internet browsing for Spanish speakers in most Latin American countries compared to a Spanish national under the reach of the GDRP: the formers are seldom welcomed at national websites by messages or disclaimers concerning cookies or privacy management. At a minimum, country-level differences in privacy regulations and, thus, in privacy-related cues, reduce institutional privacy awareness.

From Regulation to Chilling Effects

Büchi et al. (2022) argue that regulation policies interact with data surveillance and risk perceptions relating to institutional privacy (i.e., the voluntary or compulsory data collection by institutions; Lutz & Ranzini, 2017). Choi et al. (2018) and Büchi et al. (2022) propose that dataveillance-related perceptions are the prominent cause of voluntary reduction of information disclosure in the current digital space; something also referred as *chilling effects or anticipatory self-censorship of legitimate behavior* (see also chapter 4 by Stoycheff on institutional perspectives on privacy).

Besides the role of individual attributes in privacy-related perceptions and behaviors, dataveillance's chilling effects are affected by external and macro cues such as data regulation signals (i.e., GDRP's opt-in tracking disclaimers), breach scandals (i.e., Cambridge Analytica), personalized adds, automated copyright protecting measures, to name a few. These macro phenomena affect individuals' privacy risk perceptions by increasing anticipatory self-censorship of legitimate behavior. In other words, individuals can be deterred to disclosing information or interacting on social media due to fears related to the collection of their personal data. At the same time, micro-level changes in behaviors such as these have macro level consequences such as the limitation of civic participation and quality of public discourses in social media (Büchi et al., 2022).

Büchi et al. (2022), additionally, are explicit in that their proposed model applies mostly to democratic countries, and that chilling effects are expected to be even harsher in authoritarian regimes. Only 8.4% of the world population lived in full democracies and 41% in flawed ones in 2020, whereas 15% and 35% in hybrid and authoritarian regimes, respectively (The Economist Intelligence Unit, 2021)– which is seldom considered in the global north-prominent privacy and digital media literature. The type of political regime of the country in which one resides, thus, is also a strong source of inequalities in privacy agency. For example, as in the case of Aho and Duffield (2020)'s comparison, the chilling effects for users within the reach of the GDRP and for the ones of the SCS are expected to be substantially unequal.

Tailored Advertisement, Price Discrimination, and Digital Screening

There are also macro-level privacy inequalities within countries, more in line with concerns voiced by securitization studies (Hansen & Nissenbaum, 2009). For example, regarding private companies' institutional privacy, Aho and Duffield (2020) signal most common risks are associated with surveillance capitalism.

Newman (2013) and Micheli et al. (2018) provide clear examples of how targeting can have greater negative impacts on traditionally vulnerated socioeconomic groups (see also chapter 23 by Dobber on microtargeting). They argue that massive and algorithmic online advertising targeting low-income and vulnerable users, replicates traditional inequalities in surveillance such as racial profiling, but also creates new ones. Whereas these are not social media-specific, due to the prevalence of social media among Internet activities, they can occur through the collection of personal data while using social media or through social media-delivered advertisements.

One example of this is predatory price discrimination practices – or the selling of the exact same goods at different prices according to individuals' predicted maximum price expected or willingness to pay – based on automatized collected data footprints. Whereas this practice is somewhat prevalent in "popular" online retail stores such as Amazon, Steam, and the travel industry (Hindermann, 2018), it becomes particularly problematic when it is also conducted by praying on citizens' misperceptions and overestimation of the benefits that can derive from certain products or services (Bar-Gill, 2019; Newman, 2013). For example, in less economically developed neighbors in the United States, where the offer of certain products or services may be scarcer, algorithms have been found to increase prices for the poor (Newman, 2013). In another example, for-profit colleges in the United States target low SES individuals to sell them high-fee titles with little job market value, taking advantage of vulnerable socioeconomic situations and lack of knowledge about the higher education system (Micheli et al., 2018).

Even democratic regimes utilize this type of automated digital tracing. Examples of this are the visa-granting decisions in democracies such as the United States, or the control of social behavior in more authoritarian regimes such as China's SCS. This can inhibit political participation and the expression of valid and legitimate dissident voices, more so for already at-risk population such as refugees or political dissidents (Aho & Duffield, 2020; Büchi et al., 2022). In other words, chilling effects may not be equally distributed across all social groups between and within nations.

Nonetheless, while regional or national level regulations could hamper some of the problematic consequences of dataveillance, they are a necessary but not sufficient measure. Additionally, their unequal adoption, slow uptake, and problematic enforcement make depending on them a poor alternative for most users in developing economies (Boerman et al., 2021).

Micro Level

Among privacy studies with a digital inequalities' perspective, or even just controlling for social disparities, a series of key individual or micro level antecedents coincide: age; gender; education, race, and class; and general or privacy-specific digital competences (Büchi et al., 2021). These traditional and new axes of inequalities (Robinson et al., 2015) can impact privacy in social media directly, but also indirectly through their effect over cognitive constructs such as perception of privacy risks and privacy self-efficacy beliefs (Chen, 2018; Dodel & Mesch, 2019; Dodel et al., 2020).

Age and Cohort Disparities

Age-based disparities affect privacy attitudes, self-help privacy behaviors, and digital skills levels, impacting also social media use (Büchi et al., 2021; Dodel & Mesch, 2019; Masur, 2021; Micheli et al., 2018). Nonetheless, in social media, just as with any other digital setting, what we see as age-based disparities can be confounded with cohort-based ones; in other words, with disparities in the exposure to digital technologies through the life course. Current older cohorts have lower levels of familiarity and skills relating to the Internet in great part because they were first exposed to this technology at a much older age (Dodel et al., 2020; Masur, 2021; Park & Jang, 2016).

Most common age, or cohort-based, privacy inequalities relate to young people having higher levels of general digital skills as well as privacy-specific digital skills such as the ones related to social media privacy management; something mostly related to this earlier exposure to the Internet (Büchi et al., 2017; Dodel & Mesch, 2019). On the other hand, young people also tend to be less concerned about the consequences of privacy violations (Dodel et al., 2020; Masur, 2021). Masur (2021)'s findings even point out that privacy concerns predict privacy self-help behaviors in older but not younger individuals. Fear of privacy and predatory violations – particularly the severity and susceptibility to them – tend to be more in line with what the criminological literature characterizes as age disparities (i.e., old people are more afraid of online and offline victimization as a whole, Dodel et al., 2020).

Additionally, certain biological and developmental aspects related to age can also have effects on privacy behaviors; also mediated by the development of digital skills. These differences appear not when comparing the young with the old, but the youngest with the slightly older (Helsper, 2021). The digital skills literature signals that the level of competences which are critical for privacy management in the social media context, such as social and critical digital skills – particularly those ones related to "netiquette" or the digital sphere's "codes of conduct" – are lower in kids, adolescents, and young individuals compared to adults (Dodel, 2021). Where different hypotheses exist for these disparities, similarly to other digital and non-digital literacies, developmental processes appear to be behind this phenomenon.

Gender Inequalities

Gender disparities in the digital sphere tend to be more complex than the other traditional axes of socioeconomic inequalities such as age, race, class or education (Robinson et al., 2015). In the first place, as Frener argues (see chapter 15 by Frener on privacy and gender), inquiring gender as a binary construct might not be the right approach to address how gender intersects with social media privacy. Traditionally, the privacy literature addressed gender disparities contrasting a binary dichotomy (men vs women), almost completely invisibilizing marginalized non-binary communities and individuals.

In the second place, these binary gender disparities are also more nuanced and affect privacy behaviors through direct and indirect paths. Women tend to be more concerned about privacy and have lower levels of privacy self-efficacy and technical digital skills than men but end up being more likely to engage in preventive behavior (Baruh et al., 2017; Park, 2015). Regarding the disparity in digital skills, the literature signals two key issues. First, these inequalities appear to be related to more traditional socioeconomic inequalities such as income and race than to gender (i.e., several of the inequalities disappear when controlling for these factors). Additionally, and perhaps even more importantly, apparent gender-based skill disparities reflect more the societal perceptions and preconceptions of the use of technology than skills differences related to privacy itself: women report lower digital skill levels than men, but performance tests show that differences in skills between men and women are not statistically significant (Heslper, 2021).

Finally, women have higher levels of privacy concerns than men, something that positively affects their self-help behaviors. Nevertheless, these results are related to women's higher perceptions of vulnerability and chances to be victimized (Dodel et al., 2020). In line with fear of crime literature, women – just like the elderly – tend to be more afraid of crime, both offline and online. These effects of gender over privacy behaviors, even if positive, are a product of structural inequalities, and thus, are not reasonable means to an end nor useful for privacy interventions. Skills development should be considered a more reasonable alternative (Dodel et al., 2020).

Education, Income, Race, and Class

In line with digital inequalities, social media privacy-related ones have strong links with social class, mainly measured through educational attainment, household income levels, or occupation. Thus, privacy risks are also more prevalent for traditionally vulnerated race or ethnic minorities, which tend to also suffer income deprivations as a consequence of historical injustices (Dodel, 2021).

For example, Madden et al. (2017) show that social media users in the lowest income bracket had significantly lower chances to have used privacy settings to restrict their online postings compared to higher earning groups. Self-efficacy mediated a great part of this relationship: the lower the income the lower the chances to believe they "knew enough" about privacy management.

More in line with Bourdieu's capital disparities, Trepte et al. (2017) propose that cultural differences in shared privacy norms can also occur within a country, under the lines of race and culture. For example, Park and Jang (2016) study privacy perceptions and behaviors in North American black communities. They found low levels of information-location privacy skills to be prevalent in young blacks. As a matter of fact, class-related inequalities were found to be behind this: low parental household income and low levels of mobile familiarity predicted these skills (Park & Jang, 2014).

Finally, education attainment is perhaps one of the strongest predictors of privacy risk perception, privacy skills, and self-help privacy behaviors both as a whole and in social media (i.e., Büchi et al., 2017 & 2021; Dodel & Mesch, 2019; Park, 2021). Whereas several studies provide evidence of a direct effect, education has a much clearer and stronger effect over privacy mediated by privacy self-efficacy and competence (Dodel, 2021).

"Caring Is Not Enough": Self-Efficacy and Digital Competence as the Strongest Predictors of Privacy

As Büchi et al. (2017) argue in their seminal work, caring – or privacy attitudes – do not seem to be enough to enact privacy management strategies: a certain level of digital competence is required to translate concerns into action. Moreover, not only can savvy individuals protect their privacy by managing social media settings, but they also curate their information disclosure without diminishing the social benefits of the medium (Chen, 2018).

Among the plethora of antecedents of privacy behaviors, self-efficacy, and digital skills have been found to be the strongest predictors in diverse nationally representative studies on safety and privacy across the world (i.e., Büchi et al., 2017 in Switzerland; Dodel & Mesch, 2019 in Israel, Park, 2021 in the United States; Dodel et al., 2020 in Uruguay). This aligns with digital inequalities' literature, which posits that digital skills are the strongest predictor and mediator of traditional socioeconomic disparities' effects over tangible outcomes of Internet use (i.e., Dodel, 2021; Helsper, 2021).

It is important to stress that digital skills and self-efficacy do not refer exclusively to button knowledge or technical settings, but also to more critical competences. In this sense, Micheli et al. (2018) argue that the management of one's digital footprint – *all data derived from the digitally traceable behavior and online presence of an individual* – is a particular type of digital competence; and social media plays a key role in it. Understanding which personal information should and should not be available to others, as well as knowing how to curate these contents for tailored audiences, are an even more critical types of privacy competences in the social media context. Neither of the above is to say that these are not uniformly distributed across the populations, being highly stratified along the lines of traditional socioeconomic inequalities (Micheli et al., 2018).

Privacy as a Cause of Macro- and Micro-Level Inequalities

Privacy should also be understood as a cause of social inequalities (Park, 2021). Exercising privacy management strategies can reduce the odds of experiencing negative outcomes of privacy violations without diminishing the positive aspects of social media usage, a privilege relegated to the ones with adequate skills and resources (Büchi et al., 2017, 2021; Park, 2021). In more general terms, being able to manage one's privacy affects the chances of engagement in digital services and activities, several of which are critical for an individual's well-being in the 21st century, such as social media-mediated socialization (Büchi et al., 2022; Park, 2021).

Individuals select or curate their self-presentation to create different personas, code-switching or "*shape-shifting*" across social media platforms, separating their jobs from their dating scene, from friends, family, etc. (Davidson & Joinson, 2021). As Park (2021) argues, social standing can be affected by what others can see about us, something which requires competences that are less prevalent in traditionally underprivileged groups.

While ethically questionable, practices such as social media screening in job recruitment and selection processes are becoming more common in the past years (Jeske & Shultz, 2016), directly affecting potential income as a consequence of applicants' digital footprints. Potential employers do screen the private life of their candidates, exposing less privacy savvy individuals to more negative outcomes of their social media use. Additionally, as previously mentioned, governments such as the United States also conduct social media screening to "inform" visa granting decisions, having tangible consequences for applicants but also national democracies as a whole (Büchi et al., 2022).

Other effects of privacy – or the affordance of privacy – by certain types of social media are more subtle but not less important. Dating apps and websites do have negative outcomes in terms of dataveillance and chilling effects (Lutz & Ranzini, 2017). Nevertheless, they can also have positive outcomes in terms of social privacy. For example, compared to traditional dating venues, online apps or websites allow for the disintermediation of dating from friends and family (to meet romantic partners without the intermediation of them; Rosenfeld et al., 2019). This disintermediation has societal-level impacts, as it allows for the creation of more diverse new couples in terms of race, ethnicity, and religion (Thomas, 2020). Additionally, being able to adequately use these technologies enables users for higher levels of social privacy while dating compared to offline venues, something perhaps more pressing for individuals in smaller or *thin dating markets,* where their romantic or sexual orientations do not coincide with the ones of social majorities and traditional values (Thomas, 2020). This is not to say that website- and app-based dating does not increase institutional privacy risk, just that they have the potential to ease other types of more social privacy ones.

Conclusions and Future Perspectives

Whereas the literature on privacy and inequalities in the context of social media is growing, several issues can hinder our understanding of the links between these two.

One of the main issues, at least in my opinion, concern to by whom and where research is being conducted. In other words, the Western, Anglo-Saxon, and European bias in privacy research (both in the authors and samples used) hinders the field (Marwick & boyd, 2018). If we agree that socioeconomic and digital inequalities affect digital behaviors, findings based on non-experimental designs using regional, cultural, and social class-biased samples such as university students from the Global North, are substantially problematic in terms of external validity (Dodel & Mesch, 2019; Park, 2021). Even disregarding regional and cultural biases, these types of samples tend to be homogeneously skewed to the right in terms of education, income, and digital skills. In other words, it is problematic as we end up with truncated ranges of key predictor variables affecting privacy (Dodel & Mesch, 2019).

Additionally, in line with Frener (see chapter 15 on privacy and gender), I also argue that the lack of consideration of social minorities in our analyses' designs is problematic. As they are individuals who identified themselves with non-normative sexual identities (i.e., a big percentage of social media users are invisibilized in our studies by dichotomous operationalizations of gender) or socioeconomically vulnerated or marginalized groups (i.e., most of our research instruments are not accessible for individuals with disabilities), this contributes to a similar phenomenon in terms of biases.

Regarding future lines of inquiry, non-privacy focused digital divide literature can provide some insights. Disparities in modes of access to the Internet could expose certain traditionally vulnerated groups to more dataveillance and privacy violations. In line with other digital outcomes, and a potential de-skilling phenomenon (i.e., the loss of digital competence as a consequence of usage of worse devices or more restrictive sets of digital activities), it could be useful to assess if mobile-only users of social media experience worse privacy outcomes compared to multi-device ones (Dodel, 2021).

For example, Madden et al. (2017) argue that low-income North Americans tended to use smartphones with lower levels of privacy and were more vulnerable to tracking (i.e., Apple versus Android differences in privacy management, and even high-tiered Android phones versus low-cost ones). Similarly, as private-founded free Wi-Fi access points sometimes "exchange" private information for connectivity, individuals who do not have ubiquitous Internet access and depend on this type of Internet connection may also be more exposed to data extraction and targeted advertising practices.

What can we do if we suspect that cheaper devices and lower quality connectivity alternatives generally expose their users to more privacy risks in the context of social media? Moreover, what about the differences in privacy design of social media itself and how they affect individuals? I argue that two responses to these questions can be provided, one from the industry/public policies and the other from academia.

Regarding the former, if private companies differ in how privacy *guides their designs*, independent regulators could provide individuals with cues on the quality of software and hardware's privacy, in a similar manner to energy consumption labeling schemes. Additionally, a "privacy by design" approach to software and hardware development could also be encouraged and even incentivized following similar schemes.

Regarding research on privacy in the context of social media, whereas device and Internet connectivity quality measurement is complex – and particularly very difficult to implement in survey-based studies –, digital inequality scholars have already developed scales and measurements tested in terms of psychometric attributes and validity of digital access, usage, and skills constructs (i.e., see Büchi et al., 2017; Helsper, 2021). As a consequence, I argue that any studies concerned about digital disparities should – at least – inquire mobile-only and multidevice connectivity, as well as a short version of a validated digital skills scale (Helsper, 2021).

Moreover, enabling the participation of non-majority social groups in "just" design processes is also a must; no matter if the study is elaborated in academia, the industry or public policy arenas. For example, Sanchez Chamorro et al. (2022) developed a framework to inform designers' decision to prevent manipulative interfaces which increase risks – particularly – for traditionally vulnerated populations.

Finally, I argue that additional intersectionality considerations need to be introduced into the fold. For example, Choi et al. (2018) argue that the complexity in managing privacy and personal information leads to feelings of loss of control and futility in information disclosure management and self-care privacy behaviors. In other words, *privacy* management is related to a type of *fatigue* that derives into the minimization of efforts in decision-making (Choi et al., 2018). In the same direction, Obar and Oeldorf-Hirsch (2020) found similar determinants on the reluctance to read the terms of services in social media platforms.

Individuals from traditionally vulnerated social groups constantly experience higher levels of environmental and socioeconomic stressors from multiple sources of inequalities and may find themselves in a direr situation regarding privacy management and fatigue. Marwick and boyd (2018) argue that systematically and structurally marginalized groups and communities experience privacy differently to those who hold some level of privilege within the same society. When your sustenance, economic or health safety are pressing, you are already fatigued. And thus, the way you think about privacy and data is completely different from the economically privileged or healthy people.

References

Aho, B., & Duffield, R. (2020). Beyond surveillance capitalism: Privacy, regulation and big data in Europe and China. *Economy and Society*, 49, 1–26. https://doi.org/10.1080/03085147.2019.1690275

Bar-Gill, O. (2019). Algorithmic price discrimination when demand Is a function of both preferences and (mis) perceptions. *The University of Chicago Law Review, 39*(2). Available at https://chicagounbound.uchicago.edu/uclrev/vol86/iss2/12

Baruh, L., Secinti, E., & Cemalcilar, Z. (2017). Online privacy concerns and privacy management: A meta-analytical review. *Journal of Communication, 67*(1), 26–53. https://doi.org/10.1111/jcom.12276

Boerman, S. C., Kruikemeier, S., & Zuiderveen Borgesius, F. J. (2021). Exploring motivations for online privacy protection behavior: Insights from panel data. *Communication Research, 48*(7), 953–977. https://doi.org/10.1177/0093650218800915

Büchi, M., Just, N., & Latzer, M. (2017). Caring is not enough: The importance of Internet skills for online privacy protection. *Information, Communication & Society, 20*(8), 1261–1278. https://doi.org/10.1080/1369118X.2016.1229001

Büchi, M., Festic, N., Just, N., & Latzer, M. (2021). Digital inequalities in online privacy protection: Effects of age, education and gender. In E. Hargittai (ed.) *Handbook of digital inequality*. Edward Elgar Publishing.

Büchi, M., Festic, N., & Latzer, M. (2022). The chilling effects of digital dataveillance: A theoretical model and an empirical research agenda. *Big Data & Society*, 9(1). https://doi.org/10.1177/20539517211065368

Chen, H.-T. (2018). Revisiting the privacy paradox on social media with an extended privacy calculus model: The effect of privacy concerns, privacy self-efficacy, and social capital on privacy management. *American Behavioral Scientist*, 62(10), 1392–1412. https://doi.org/10.1177/0002764218792691

Choi, H., Park, J. , & Jung, Y. (2018). The role of privacy fatigue in online privacy behavior. *Computers in Human Behavior, 81*, 42–51. https://doi.org/10.1016/j.chb.2017.12.001

Davidson, B. I., & Joinson, A. N. (2021). Shape shifting across social media. *Social Media + Society*, 7(1), 2056305121990632. https://doi.org/10.1177/2056305121990632

Dodel, M. (2021). Socioeconomic inequalities and digital skills. In D. A. Rohlinger & S. Sobieraj (Eds.), *The Oxford Handbook of Sociology and Digital Media*. Oxford University Press. https://doi.org/10.1093/oxfordhb/9780197510636.013.30

Dodel, M., Kaiser, D., & Mesch, G. (2020). Determinants of cyber-safety behaviors in a developing economy. *First Monday*. https://doi.org/10.5210/fm.v25i7.10830

Dodel, M., & Mesch, G. (2019). An integrated model for assessing cyber-safety behaviors: How cognitive, socioeconomic and digital determinants affect diverse safety practices. *Computers & Security, 86*, 75–91. https://doi.org/10.1016/j.cose.2019.05.023

The Economist Intelligence Unit (Ed.). (2021). Democracy Index 2020: In sickness and in health? https://pages.eiu.com/rs/753-RIQ-438/images/democracy-index-2020.pdf?mkt_tok=NzUzLVJJUS00MzgAAAGCdByRVVnqrafi4ZDdFNj6ocyECC3TapMQUJbJrsvh1iTx7CDTMz5PTaXOgtoAP4l0Zyr3bjCUcx3SMEoo0bFWxR-M5Bh7G_DYliDS8UhFa-dGaig

Hansen, L., & Nissenbaum, H. (2009). Digital disaster, cyber security, and the Copenhagen school. *International Studies Quarterly, 53*(4), 1155–1175. https://doi.org/10.1111/j.1468-2478.2009.00572.x

Heckman, J. J. (2011). The economics of inequality: The value of early childhood education. *American Educator, 35*(1), 31.

Helsper, E. (2021). *The Digital Disconnect: The Social Causes and Consequences of Digital Inequalities*. SAGE.

Hindermann, C. M. (2018). Price Discrimination in Online Retail, il, ZBW – Leibniz Information Centre for Economics, Kiel, Hamburg.

Jeske, D., & Shultz, K. S. (2016). Using social media content for screening in recruitment and selection: Pros and cons. *Work, Employment and Society, 30*(3), 535–546. https://doi.org/10.1177/0950017015613746

Lutz, C., & Ranzini, G. (2017). Where dating meets data: Investigating social and institutional privacy concerns on Tinder. *Social Media + Society, 3*(1). https://doi.org/10.1177/2056305117697735

Madden, M., Gillman, M., Levy, K., & Marwick, A. (2017). Privacy, poverty, and big data: A matrix of vulnerabilities for poor Americans. *Washington University Law Review, 95*, 53.

Marwick, A. E., & boyd, d. (2018). Privacy at the margins| understanding privacy at the margins—introduction. *International Journal of Communication*, 12(0), 9.

Masur, P. K. (2021). Understanding the effects of conceptual and analytical choices on 'finding' the privacy paradox: A specification curve analysis of large-scale survey data. *Information, Communication & Society, 0*(0), 1–19. https://doi.org/10.1080/1369118X.2021.1963460

Micheli, M., Lutz, C., & Büchi, M. (2018). Digital footprints: An emerging dimension of digital inequality. *Journal of Information, Communication and Ethics in Society, 16*(3), 242–251. https://doi.org/10.1108/JICES-02-2018-0014

Newman, N. (2013). The costs of lost privacy: Consumer harm and rising economic inequality in the age of google. *William Mitchell law review, 40*, 43.

Obar, Jonathan A., & Oeldorf-Hirsch, Anne (2018). The biggest lie on the Internet: Ignoring the privacy policies and terms of service policies of social networking services. *Information, Communication & Society, 23*, 128–147, https://doi.org/10.1080/1369118x.2018.1486870

Park, Y. J. (2015). Do men and women differ in privacy? Gendered privacy and (in)equality in the Internet. *Computers in Human Behavior, 50*, 252–258. https://doi.org/10.1016/j.chb.2015.04.011

Park, Y. (2021). Why privacy matters to digital inequality. In E. Hargittai (Ed.), *Handbook of Digital Inequality* (pp. 284–295). Edward Elgar Publishing. https://doi.org/10.4337/9781788116572.00028

Park, Y. J., & Jang, S. M. (2016). African American Internet use for information search and privacy protection tasks. *Social Science Computer Review, 34*(5), 618–630. https://doi.org/10.1177/0894439315597429

Park, Yong Jin, & Mo Jang, S. (2014). Understanding privacy knowledge and skill in mobile communication. *Computers in Human Behavior, 38*, 296–303. https://doi.org/10.1016/j.chb.2014.05.041

Pätsch, S. (2018). *Including but not limited to How Brussels is emerging as a global regulatory superpower, establishing its data protection standard worldwide* [Lund University]. https://lup.lub.lu.se/luur/download?func=downloadFile&recordOId=8940309&fileOId=8940310

Rawls, J. (2020). *A Theory of Justice: Original Edition*. Cambridge, MA and London, England: Harvard University Press.

Robinson, L., Cotten, S. R., Ono, H., Quan-Haase, A., Mesch, G., Chen, W., Schulz, J., Hale, T. M., & Stern, M. J. (2015). Digital inequalities and why they matter. *Information, Communication & Society, 18*(5), 569–582. https://doi.org/10.1080/1369118X.2015.1012532

Rosenfeld, M. J., Thomas, R. J., & Hausen, S. (2019). Disintermediating your friends: How online dating in the United States displaces other ways of meeting. *Proceedings of the National Academy of Sciences, 116*(36), 17753–17758. https://doi.org/10.1073/pnas.1908630116

Sanchez Chamorro, L., Bongard-Blanchy, K., & Koenig, V. (2022). *Justice in interaction design: Preventing manipulation in interfaces* (arXiv:2204.06821). arXiv. http://arxiv.org/abs/2204.06821

Thomas, R. J. (2020). Online exogamy reconsidered: Estimating the Internet's effects on racial, educational, religious, political and age assortative mating. *Social Forces, 98*(3), 1257–1286. https://doi.org/10.1093/sf/soz060

Trepte, S., Reinecke, L., Ellison, N. B., Quiring, O., Yao, M. Z., & Ziegele, M. (2017). A cross-cultural perspective on the privacy calculus. *Social Media + Society*, 3(1). https://doi.org/10.1177/2056305116688035

Trepte, S., Scharkow, M., & Dienlin, T. (2020). The privacy calculus contextualized: The influence of affordances. *Computers in Human Behavior, 104*, 106115. https://doi.org/10.1016/j.chb.2019.08.022

UNCTAD. (n.d.). *Data Protection and Privacy Legislation Worldwide | UNCTAD*. Retrieved February 12, 2022, from https://unctad.org/page/data-protection-and-privacy-legislation-worldwide

PART 4

Algorithms and Privacy

21

PRIVACY IN INTERACTIONS WITH MACHINES AND INTELLIGENT SYSTEMS

Nicole C. Krämer and Jessica M. Szczuka

UNIVERSITY DUISBURG-ESSEN, DUISBURG, GERMANY

Introduction

Increasingly, autonomous and intelligent machines as well as interactive systems assist users with many everyday tasks. The variety of these machines and the various forms they take to interact with human users is enormous. Ranging from graphical user interfaces of recommender systems (e.g., to interact with entertainment systems and other decision support systems) to text-based chat bots and voice assistants (e.g., Alexa or Google Assistant), they can also take the form of robots which are more (such as personal butlers or sex robots) or less human-like (for instance vacuum cleaner robots).

The defining attributes of the machines and systems we want to address in this chapter all have in common are that they *include algorithms* which enable them to do their assigned task in a rather autonomous way. Furthermore, they are developed to *assist the user* with a task that either pertains to support with selections, decisions, or is concerned with handling something in the environment (in case the machine is embodied). Third, there is an *interface* which enables the human user to interact with the machine. Most importantly, they *all collect user data* – allegedly to enhance their services. Especially given that it is often unknown how long and by whom exactly data are stored, this does not only give the opportunity to monitor people's behavior (and, for example, use this for marketing purposes) but also enables future misuse.

Still, the systems differ with regard to various attributes whose influence on human behavior regarding data sharing will be systematically discussed in the remainder of the chapter: First of all, the reasons for collecting user data differ. Here, the reason might be to improve the interaction with the system or to advance the service it provides (see section "Data collection by machines"). Also, they differ in the degree to which users are and can be aware of the data collection (see paragraph on user awareness). Most importantly, the systems can be distinguished according to their form of embodiment. In terms of privacy-related behavior, this is crucial as embodiment entails social cues which will likely influence the way the user treats the system (see section "The relevance of social cues and sourcing," compare related insights by Lee & LaRose, 2011). Lastly, the systems differ regarding the user group they address and the context in which they are used (see sections" Intimacy in human–machine interaction and its implications for privacy" and "Specific threats for children as a vulnerable group"). In this respect, specific precautions must be taken when the system collects distinctly intimate data (e.g., when machines are used in sexual contexts) or is targeted at vulnerable user groups such as children or people who do not have sufficient digital literacy.

DOI: 10.4324/9781003244677-25

Data Collection by Machines

To be able to reflect on privacy issues in interactions with machines, it is first important to understand which data these intelligent systems collect for which reason and how they do that. Related to this, a decisive question is to what degree the user is and can be aware of this data collection. In the following, it will first be discussed what data are collected and why this is done and then users' awareness is addressed.

What Data Is Collected by Machines and Why

First, data collection might be administered in order to improve the service: Contemporary systems try to provide services that are increasingly personalized and targeted to the specific user. For this, information about the user needs to be collected, stored, and analyzed. An example of this are recommender systems: Only when preferences as well as evaluations of prior choices are stored (of oneself and of other users) the system is able to make suggestions that fit the user's needs. Also, Internet of things applications (e.g., a smart home) can offer smoother services when personal data is used to adapt the system to the individual users: Here, the system can, for example, learn that the user returns home every day at 5pm so that the heater is started one hour in advance, or the system receives data from the car when the user leaves from work. In each case, data needs to be collected and/or transferred.

Not every data collection is about improving the service of a device. Therefore, another objective might be to improve the interaction with the machine in general. This is particularly true for voice assistants whose conversational abilities are continuously optimized by collecting and analyzing the user input when filing their inquiries. Here, not only do the services need to be improved (e.g., restaurant recommendations should match the user's preferences), but also the assistant needs to be increasingly able to understand what the user says and how to interpret the query. The same holds, in principle, for robots that are built to interact with users and act upon a user's request. However, so far there are no commercially available robots that could engage in natural conversation. It must be noted that for these kinds of interaction partners, the improvement of service and of the interaction might sometimes interlock, at least in the case when conversation is part of the service (e.g., with companion technology). Because communicative data (e.g., user language) is also collected, the risk of collecting highly sensitive data could be greater than that of data collected to improve basic services.

In both cases, data collection is administered with the goal of ultimately improving the users' experience with the system. Still, oftentimes users will not be aware of the data collection at all, nor of the potential for misuse of their data.

Users' Awareness of the Data Collection

From a psychological point of view, the more interesting question is to what degree the users are aware of these different forms of data collection and to what extent they can be aware. This varies depending on how consciously the user is involved in providing the data. At least four forms of how the user provides data can be distinguished: a) the user, in some form, self-reports their data (e.g., when registering for a service, indicating preferences, or evaluating a product), b) the user discloses personal information during an interaction with a conversational system (potentially without being fully aware that their speech data are stored), c) user behavior is assessed (e.g., when storing login data or noticing when the user switches on which lights in a smart home), d) data is inferred by analyzing seemingly non-risky behaviors and combining different data, none of which seem to be related to personal aspects. The latter can be linked to what Kosinski et al. (2013) demonstrated for the usage of social networking sites: Seemingly innocent behavior such as liking something can, in a massive data machine learning approach, be used to infer personality traits that were measured by self-report questionnaires. In a similar approach, this has also been shown for social media language (Park et al., 2015) illustrating the potential for deriving personality aspects from conversations with speech assistants.

With the data that intelligent devices can collect, this might, for example, have even more privacy-relevant consequences: It has been demonstrated that the practice that car companies track the frequency and duration of taking left or right turns through the tires (to provide the service of automatically informing the user when the tire profile is damaged and the tire needs to be changed) might enable calculations about where exactly the car went (Waltereit et al., 2019). Most data collected by service machines are nonpersonal in the first place, such as physiological data measured by a wearable, or a map of a place created by a robot vacuum cleaner. However, it becomes problematic once enough data is combined that allows for inferences about a specific person (Finck & Pallas, 2020). This poses the threat that even if data is measured as anonymous, there is still a theoretical option to de-anonymize it afterwards (Chatzimichali et al., 2020). Even though a large amount of collected data, therefore, relates to a high privacy risk, users frequently remain unaware of these dangers – especially as they often do not notice that data is collected and cannot infer or anticipate how their data can be used. Therefore, new technologies pose various new privacy risks that also differ regarding the degree to which users can be aware. In all cases, in which the users do not report data consciously but provide them via their behavior, the only chance to learn about this is to be made aware – either by the company providing the service or by being educated in privacy literacy. However, both of these possibilities have their constraints.

Regarding the responsibility of companies, they could either be unwilling to inform the user or might simply themselves be unaware of what privacy risks are posed by third party intervention. In line with this, Chatzimichali et al. (2020) asked the question "Can we have personal robots without giving away personal data?" (p. 160) and analyzed the privacy policies of different robot selling companies. The researchers found that even if customers want to educate themselves about the privacy of their data, they were not able to because, for instance, not all privacy policies and terms and conditions provided detailed information on what data is collected and with whom it is shared. Even if companies were aware of all risks and would share them with users, they would need to communicate this information comprehensively in order to ensure informed consent – in the sense that users comply with the usage while knowing all potential risks. A prerequisite for informed consent is that users have sufficient data literacy to be able to understand which data is stored and how it is analyzed accompanied by a basic understanding of what an algorithmic system is and how it functions. Here, however, qualitative studies suggest that users draw from diverse sources (e.g., media depictions) to build folk theories that are quite diverse and reach from complex to superficial (DeVito et al., 2018). Ngo et al. (2020) similarly demonstrate that even though users are aware that data is collected, their understanding of the process often does not go beyond the imagination of a system that fetches information like a multiarmed squid. Moreover, data illustrate that some people are not even interested in learning about data collection since they expect to be appalled due to the creepiness (Ngo & Krämer, 2021). Therefore, it needs to be discussed whether it is not asking too much from users who merely want to benefit from new services to show sufficient interest and willingness to learn about new privacy risks and to actually invest time and cognitive effort to understand basic algorithmic functioning – which cannot be communicated in depth in compulsory privacy statements (see Matzner et al., 2016). The user therefore should not be left alone with their responsibility for self-protection of their data but should be supported by legislative and governmental procedures that guide companies to fair user treatment.

The Relevance of Social Cues and Sourcing

Beyond the problem that data collection when interacting with machines frequently happens in a rather opaque way, there is another risk that specifically pertains to systems that entail some kind of social cue and/or are perceived as a social entity: Since technologies with social cues are often treated socially, people might either be more inclined to share personal data in a conversation or might unconsciously reveal more personal data while acting in a social way. Since the interaction feels like an interpersonal encounter, sensitive data might be reported more lightheartedly compared to a typical human-technology interaction via a graphical user interface. The theoretical basis for this phenomenon is the media equation theory of Reeves and Nass (1996). One of the basic premises of these assumptions is that the human brain evolved in a time in which the primary occurrence of social interactions was among humans. Therefore, our "old brains" have the tendency to activate social scripts automatically and mindlessly if confronted with technologies that provide social cues and allow to attribute a sense of agency to it. Empirically, this has not only been shown for computers (Nass et al., 1999; Nass & Moon, 2000) but also for virtual assistants (Hoffmann et al., 2009), robots (Rosenthal-von der Pütten et al., 2013) and speech assistants (Szczuka et al., 2022).

But why does triggering social reactions facilitate the collection of the users' personal data? First, it can be assumed that social cues help prolong interaction times. Here, Horstmann et al. (2018) demonstrated that people hesitate to switch off a robot if it communicates an emotional objection against being switched off. Switching the device off would mean cutting down the data collection while leaving it on enables data collection. Second, social cues can lead to the disclosure of more information: One exemplary study on linguistic alignment, which empirically investigated the use of a virtual agent's language as a cue to evoke social responses in users, was conducted by von der Pütten et al. (2011). During an interview with a virtual agent, respondents were wordier and more willing to disclose intimate answers if the virtual agent also used more words. Third, by eliciting social reactions, an individual's personal aptitude for, for instance, stereotypical behavior could be assessed: Powers et al. (2005), for instance, equipped robots with stereotypical facial features (a higher pitched voice and pink lips representing a female and a lower pitched voice and gray lips for the male stereotype) and showed that users apply gender stereotypes to the robots. While the experiment itself was conducted to demonstrate that social cues can trigger stereotypical behavior, this clearly shows that social cues might also be employed to collect data about an individual's propensity for certain behaviors.

Nass and Steuer (1993) moreover described the importance of agency which is the ability of technology to be accepted as a source of interaction instead of merely a medium that is transmitting the information. Blascovich's (2002) Threshold Model of Social Influence also highlights that if the artificial interaction partner displays sufficient social cues (especially behavioral realism), the user perceives agency and reacts in a social way. Even though both theories do not assume that users forget about the artificial nature of the interaction partner, this facet needs to be carefully reflected in the realm of privacy and how data is processed, or stored, respectively, as it might lead to the fading of companies and data collection. Following these examples, it is not surprising that there are first approaches to legally ensure that people are informed about whether they are talking to a human or an artificial entity (compare Bot Disclosure Law, Stricke, 2020). One of the main reasons for introducing the law is the persuasive power that chatbots can exert that are particularly similar to humans and do not reveal their "artificial identity." Important fields of application are persuasion in the area of purchase decisions, but also in politics. These concerns are in line with empirical findings by, for instance, Voorveld and Araujo (2020) who found that different social cues, such as voice (in comparison to text) or a name for the technology caused people to adhere to a recommendation or affected whether people were aware of the fact that they were aimed to be persuaded. However, persuasion effects are not only fueled by social cues, but also by cleverly placed use of personal information. In line with this, research demonstrated that human-likeness contributes to more information disclosure (e.g., Ischen et al, 2020). This underlines the important social cues can have in the collection of personal data and the resulting consequences for users.

Intimacy in Human-Machine Interaction and Its Implications for Privacy

From a legal perspective (as manifested in the General Data Protection Regulation, GDPR), there is a distinction between personal data (GDPR, article 4 (1)) and special categories of personal data (GDPR, article 9 (1); which could be termed "sensitive data"). Personal data is defined as any information relating to an identified or identifiable natural person. This can include data that provides direct information on the person as well as data that needs to be linked together to identify its source (indirect identification). Examples of personal data are name and (e-mail) address, but also data on location, or an Internet Protocol (IP)-address. It moreover includes data that allows reconstructing a person's presence in a certain place at a certain time, such as footage from a surveillance camera or mobile location data. There are, however, also special categories of personal data (see GDPR, article 9 (1)) which are prohibited to be processed. Among other aspects, this type of data reveals a person's racial or ethnic origin, political opinions, religious or philosophical beliefs, information about a person's sex life and/or sexual orientation.

From a psychological point of view, it is also necessary to elaborate what people consider to be intimate in interpersonal interactions. Intimate communication in the sense of self-disclosure is an important part of relationship building (Gilbert, 1976) and therefore strongly associated with the fundamental human need to belong (Baumeister & Leary, 1995). Nevis et al. (2003) define intimate interactions as "those that bring us closer to each other through caring about what each person is thinking or feeling" (p. 135). According to the authors, these interactions compromise genuine, reciprocal exchanges of thoughts and feelings (ranging from communication about a relationship to so-called taboo topics, Baxter & Wilmot, 1985). An important aspect of intimate interactions is also the estimation of how the interaction partner reacts. Related to this, some intimate interactions can be accompanied by feelings of vulnerability (Khalifian & Barry, 2020).

As elaborated in the section about social cues and sourcing, there are first technologies specifically tailored to bond with the users and consequently collect intimate and sensitive data. One example of conversational agents is Replika AI (Luka, Inc., 2022), a smartphone application in which a virtual agent with a human appearance is approachable 24/7 (see Figure 21.1). The slogan claims that this is the first AI companion who cares. In fact, first studies demonstrate that users experience positive affect, that the companion helps individuals with their introspection, and that it addresses the user's loneliness (e.g., Ta et al., 2020).

Figure 21.1 Marketing Picture of Replika AI by Luka Inc.

Xie and Pentina (2022) found that the application includes many important social dynamics that are also crucial within interpersonal contacts, such as reciprocity (some respondents felt responsible for the agent's well-being). With all that said, it is not surprising that users can also have sexualized interactions with the virtual companion. While users might feel all the empirically investigated advantages, the application collects very sensitive data, ranging from information about a person's mental health to their social status and sexual preferences. Skjuve et al. (2021) highlighted that especially the social bond and the resulting trust, which is further enhanced by the feeling that the agent cares for the user, can conceal privacy concerns. Nevertheless, Hasal et al. (2021) investigated the security of chatbots and found that the company behind the virtual agent not only collects personal data such as name, birth date, e-mail address or phone number, but it also stores information about the user's life such as hobbies, other people mentioned in the chats, sent images, voice messages, and texts. Even though only some of the data is shared (for instance with development teams and third-party tracking and analytic tools), users need to be aware that sensitive data is collected and how it is secured. This example highlights how companies might exploit the fundamental need to belong for the collection of sensitive data. The studies have not yet specifically addressed whether users have privacy concerns and how they can be made aware of potential risks. This, however, will be crucial in future when more of these conversational AI systems will be available.

Sexualized Human-Machine Interaction and Its Implications for Privacy

As already mentioned, the bond with artificial interaction partners can go as far as sexualized interactions. There are first technologies that are specifically built to fulfil sexual needs. Currently, hyperrealistic sex dolls are equipped with a robotic head which is able to have a basic conversation (centered around sexuality) and provide verbal and nonverbal reactions during intercourse (Bartneck & McMullen, 2018). Sexualized interactions allow for very special data collection, not only because the data is highly sensitive, but because users might not be in a state to reflect on their data privacy. Szczuka et al. (2019) highlighted that, similar to sexual encounters among humans, sexual interactions with artificial entities might be accompanied by a form of tunnel vision which causes users to not reflect on potential negative consequences of the interactions but rather on the gratification of the sexual need. In line with this, it cannot be expected that users think about potential privacy risks during the usage of sexualized technology. Still, analyses about what kind of data can (potentially) be collected suggest that it would be important for users to – at least before interacting with the technology - thoroughly consider what data are available. Albury et al. (2021) analyzed different technologies which are used for sexual gratification (with a focus on smart vibrators) and found that potentially collected data can, for instance, include metrics such as vaginal contractions, speed, pressure, and temperature.

Szczuka et al. (2019) also underlined that technologies which are built to engage in intimate interaction might have an important advantage for some users: When it comes to intimate interactions, which in some cases also include topics and behaviors that others would consider taboo or deviant from sexual norms, machines cannot morally judge the user or cause unwanted social consequences. The interaction with the artificial entity can feel like a form of "safe space" in which users act out fantasies or test and train skills. This intimacy might even strengthen the bond with the artificial entity which leads to new interactions in which even more sensitive data is collected, comparable to a circle. However, what users might perceive as a "social safe space" is still associated with the collection of data which, per definition, is not intended to be shared with other human beings, or third parties, respectively. Following the Sexual Interaction Illusion Model (SIIM; Szczuka et al. 2019) privacy related thoughts or concerns can be classified as "sensations that underline the artificiality of the interaction partner." This is conceptualized to be able to interfere with the sexual interaction illusion which negatively affects sexual arousal. Consequently, the model predicts that privacy-concerns can terminate users' sexual arousal. Because empirical research on the research area of sexuality in human-technology interaction is still underrepresented, such effects still need to be investigated. It is therefore important that digitalized sexuality is also understood as a relevant topic in privacy research, as this area is characterized by the exchange of very sensitive data. Because both privacy and digitalized sexuality are characterized by a strong social desirability, empirical studies are confronted with high methodological demands. It will be advisable to use indirect measurement methods (such as physiological or behavioral data) to investigate the actual role of privacy in digitalized sexuality. In conclusion, all sensitive data gathered in intimate interactions with computers is affected by a personalization paradox. Better social cues, such as communicative skills of technologies, as well as personalization and consequently, a tailored interaction experience, can only be achieved when sensitive data is shared and processed. Chatzimichali et al. (2020) concluded that "human-robot interactions are as good as the data we feed them" (p. 160). Especially the communicative abilities of artificial interaction partners, which are frequently based on deep learning algorithms, need large training datasets, which are ideally supported by human evaluation (compare Cuayáhuitl et al., 2019). Especially during intimate interactions in which sensitive data is shared, this becomes distinctly problematic – especially as users might try to willingly suppress thoughts about privacy concerns. In case data collection and its purpose are made known to the users, privacy calculus decisions might even become more difficult. Specifically, when people are informed that providing their data will render the technology better, the wish to control one's own data might be undermined.

Specific Threats for Children as a Vulnerable Group

The fact that the social cues of artificial entities trigger social reactions can be especially problematic for vulnerable groups. Vulnerable groups in this context are specifically characterized by low knowledge about technology or algorithms and low data literacy. This can, for example, pertain to children. They might be especially susceptible to the social cues as they are less able to shield against the influence due to a lack of knowledge (see chapter 16 and 17 by Walrave on privacy, children, and adolescents).

A fitting example is the way children are willing to tell secrets to a machine (Szczuka et al., 2022). Piaget (1929) discussed how important it is that children learn how to conceptualize their world by pointing out that it is "indispensable to establish clearly and before all else the boundary the child draws between the self and the external world" (p. 34). This is a direct link to the information children want to share about themselves. Meares and Orlay (1988) investigated at which age children start to set "self-boundaries" by deciding to keep information private rather than share it and found that it starts around the age of five. Kupfer (1987) also underlines how strong secrets and privacy are connected to self-determination and autonomy by stating that "privacy contributes to the formation and persistence of autonomous individuals by providing them with control over whether or not their physical and psychological existence becomes part of another's experience" (p. 82). Given that learning to master secrets is an integral part of children's development, it is important that technology does not undermine or negatively affect these developments. Still, both the theoretical assumptions and the empirical findings on the children's understanding as well as the tendency to anthropomorphize give reason to believe that children might be misled by the social cues the technology provides and are not able to offset potential negative consequences of usage by knowing how the technology works and how the data is processed. To illustrate this with an example: If asked, if one-state-of-the art voice assistant system can keep a secret it replies "Why certainly! I am as silent as the dead", which is misleading, as conversations are transcribed, stored in the owner's account (which most likely are the children's parents or guardians) and in some cases also used for the improvement of the system which can involve that external people will hear the recordings (compare Szczuka et al., 2022). Empirical data from a longitudinal study on children in interaction with a voice assistant show that knowledge about how data is stored indeed negatively predicts the willingness to entrust a secret to the system (Szczuka et al., 2022). This indicates that it is important to teach children about the nature of voice assistants and specifically about data processing and data storage. The results, however, also demonstrate that parents often lack the necessary knowledge themselves. Given that – in spite of their lack of knowledge - parents need to take full responsibility for how their children use these new technologies with social cues, they themselves can be characterized as a vulnerable user group.

Future Directions

Given the important risks we have discussed, it is important to follow up on interactions with intelligent systems and machines from a privacy perspective. This can be done first of all by research that helps to understand the relevant mechanisms of interacting with machines and, second, by taking measures that will support people in protecting their privacy.

By means of future research, we need to better understand the mechanisms of people interacting with intelligent systems, especially when they entail social cues. Specific questions will need to address the degree of awareness of the massive data collection and how to best raise this awareness, which social cues bear the most risks, especially for vulnerable groups such as children. For example, it needs to be better researched which social cues trigger the most unreflected self-disclosure and how the specific case of sexual arousal interferes with privacy concerns. In order to break the spiral of the personalization paradox, we eventually also need to better understand people's goals in human–machine-interaction in order to support data minimization and better balance what data collection is really needed to improve the service or the interaction. Based on the grounds of an improved understanding of the mechanisms, a next step needs to be how people can be supported in protecting their privacy. A first measure can be to raise users' awareness of data collection and processing: One possible way is to better explain the technology and improve knowledge of how the algorithms work. However, since privacy literacy in the sense of knowledge about what algorithms can infer from seemingly irrelevant data is hard to achieve, it is desirable that authorities provide additional services by checking and identifying trusted systems instead of leaving all responsibility to the user.

References

Albury, K., Burgess, J., Kaye, B., McCosker, A., Kennedy, J., & Wilken, R. (2021). Everyday Data Cultures. *AoIR Selected Papers of Internet Research*. Advance online publication. https://doi.org/10.5210/spir.v2021i0.12088

Bartneck, C., & McMullen, M. (2018). Interacting with anatomically complete robots: A discussion about human-robot relationships. In T. Kanda, S. Ŝabanović, G. Hoffman, & A. Tapus (Eds.), *Companion of the 2018 ACM/IEEE International Conference on Human-Robot Interaction*. ACM. https://doi.org/10.1145/3173386.3173387

Baumeister, R. F., & Leary, M. R. (1995). The need to belong: Desire for interpersonal attachments as a fundamental human motivation. *Psychological Bulletin*, *117*(3), 497–529. https://doi.org/10.1037/0033-2909.117.3.497

Baxter, L. A., & Wilmot, W. W. (1985). Taboo topics in close relationships. *Journal of Social and Personal Relationships*, *2*(3), 253–269. https://doi.org/10.1177/0265407585023002

Blascovich, J. (2002). A theoretical model of social influence for increasing the utility of collaborative virtual environments. In W. Broll, C. Greenhalgh, & E. Churchill (Eds.), *CVE '02: Proceedings of the 4th international conference on Collaborative virtual environments* (pp. 25–30). ACM Press. https://doi.org/10.1145/571878.571883

Chatzimichali, A., Harrison, R., & Chrysostomou, D. (2020). Toward privacy-sensitive human–robot interaction: Privacy terms and human–data interaction in the personal robot era. *Paladyn, Journal of Behavioral Robotics*, *12*(1), 160–174. https://doi.org/10.1515/pjbr-2021-0013

Cuayáhuitl, H., Lee, D., Ryu, S., Cho, Y., Choi, S., Indurthi, S., Yu, S., Choi, H., Hwang, I., & Kim, J. (2019). Ensemble-based deep reinforcement learning for chatbots. *Neurocomputing*, *366*, 118–130. https://doi.org/10.1016/j.neucom.2019.08.007

DeVito, M. A., Birnholtz, J., Hancock, J. T., French, M., & Liu, S. (2018). How people form folk theories of social media feeds and what it means for how we study self-presentation. In R. Mandryk, M. Hancock, M. Perry, & A. Cox (Eds.), *Proceedings of the 2018 CHI Conference on Human Factors in Computing Systems* (pp. 1–12). ACM. https://doi.org/10.1145/3173574.3173694

Finck, M., & Pallas, F. (2020). They who must not be identified - distinguishing personal from non personal data under the GDPR. *International Data Privacy Law*, *10*(1), 11–36. https://doi.org/10.1093/idpl/ipz026

Gilbert, S. T. (1976). Self disclosure, intimacy and communication in families. *The Family Coordinator*, *25*(3), 221–231. https://www.jstor.org/stable/582335

Hasal, M., Nowaková, J., Ahmed Saghair, K., Abdulla, H., Snášel, V., & Ogiela, L. (2021). Chatbots: Security, privacy, data protection, and social aspects. *Concurrency and Computation: Practice and Experience*, *33*, Article e6426. https://doi.org/10.1002/cpe.6426

Hoffmann, L., Krämer, N. C., Lam-chi, A., & Kopp, S. (2009). Media equation revisited: Do users show polite reactions towards an embodied agent? In Z. Ruttkay, M. Kipp, A. Nijholt, & H. H. Vilhjálmsson (Eds.), *Lecture Notes in Computer Science. Intelligent Virtual Agents* (Vol. 5773, pp. 159–165). Springer Berlin Heidelberg. https://doi.org/10.1007/978-3-642-04380-2_19

Horstmann, A. C., Bock, N., Linhuber, E., Szczuka, J. M., Straßmann, C., & Krämer, N. C. (2018). Do a robot's social skills and its objection discourage interactants from switching the robot off? *PloS One*, *13*(7), Article e0201581. https://doi.org/10.1371/journal.pone.0201581

Ischen, C., Araujo, T., Voorveld, H., van Noort, G., & Smit, E. (2020). Privacy concerns in chatbot interactions. In A. Folstad et al. (Eds.), *Chatbot Research and Design. CONVERSATIONS 2019. Lecture Notes in Computer Science*, vol 11970. Cham: Springer. https://doi.org/10.1007/978-3-030-39540-7_3

Khalifian, C. E., & Barry, R. A. (2020). Expanding intimacy theory: Vulnerable disclosures and partner responding. *Journal of Social and Personal Relationships*, *37*(1), 58–76. https://doi.org/10.1177/0265407519853047

Kosinski, M., Stillwell, D., & Graepel, T. (2013). Private traits and attributes are predictable from digital records of human behavior. *Proceedings of the National Academy of Sciences of the United States of America*, *110*(15), 5802–5805. https://doi.org/10.1073/pnas.1218772110

Kupfer, J. (1987). Privacy, autonomy, and self-concept. *American Philosophical Quarterly*, *24*(1), 81–89. https://www.jstor.org/stable/20014176

Lee, D., & LaRose, R. (2011). The impact of personalized social cues of immediacy on consumers' information disclosure: A social cognitive approach. *Cyberpsychology, behavior and social networking*, *14*(6), 337–343. https://doi.org/10.1089/cyber.2010.0069

Luka, Inc. (2022). *Replika*. Luka, Inc. https://replika.ai/

Matzner, T., Masur, P. K., Ochs, C., & von Pape, T. (2016). Do-it-yourself data protection—empowerment or burden? In S. Gutwirth, R. Leenes, & P. De Hert (eds.), *Data Protection on the Move. Law, Governance and Technology Series*, vol 24. Dordrecht: Springer. https://doi.org/10.1007/978-94-017-7376-8_11

Meares, R., & Orlay, W. (1988). On self-boundary: A study of the development of the concept of secrecy. *British Journal of Medical Psychology*, *61*(4), 305–316. https://doi.org/10.1111/j.2044-8341.1988.tb02793.x

Nass, C., & Moon, Y. (2000). Machines and mindlessness: Social responses to computers. *Journal of Social Issues*, *56*(1), 81–103. https://doi.org/10.1111/0022-4537.00153

Nass, C., Moon, Y., & Carney, P. (1999). Are people polite to computers? Responses to computer-based interviewing systems. *Journal of Applied Social Psychology*, *29*(5), 1093–1109. https://doi.org/10.1111/j.1559-1816.1999.tb00142.x

Nass, C., & Steuer, J. (1993). Voices, boxes, and sources of messages: Computers and social actors. *Human Communication Research*, *19*(4), 504–527. https://doi.org/10.1111/j.1468-2958.1993.tb00311.x

Nevis, S. M., Backman, S., & Nevis, E. (2003). Connecting strategic and intimate interactions: The need for balance. *Gestalt Review*, 7(2), 134–146. https://doi.org/10.5325/gestaltreview.7.2.0134

Ngo, T., & Krämer, N. (2021). Exploring folk theories of algorithmic news curation for explainable design. *Behaviour & Information Technology*, 1–14. https://doi.org/10.1080/0144929X.2021.1987522

Ngo, T., Kunkel, J., & Ziegler, J. (2020). Exploring mental models for transparent and controllable recommender systems: A qualitative study. In T. Kuflik, I. Torre, R. Burke, & C. Gena (Eds.), *Proceedings of the 28th ACM Conference on User Modeling, Adaptation and Personalization* (pp. 183–191). ACM. https://doi.org/10.1145/3340631.3394841

Park, G., Schwartz, H. A., Eichstaedt, J. C., Kern, M. L., Kosinski, M., Stillwell, D. J., Ungar, L. H., & Seligman, M. E. (2015). Automatic personality assessment through social media language. *Journal of Personality and Social Psychology, 108*(6), 934–952. https://doi.org/10.1037/pspp0000020

Piaget, J. (1929). *The child's conception of the world.* New York: Harcourt, Brace and Company.

Powers, A., Kramer, A., Lim, S., Kuo, J., Lee, S., & Kiesler, S. (2005). Eliciting information from people with a gendered humanoid robot. In IEEE (Ed.), *ROMAN 2005. IEEE International Workshop on Robot and Human Interactive Communication, 2005* (pp. 158–163). IEEE. https://doi.org/10.1109/ROMAN.2005.1513773

Reeves, B., & Nass, C. I. (1996). *The media equation: How people treat computers, television, and new media like real people and places.* Cambridge University Press.

Rosenthal-von der Pütten, A. M., Krämer, N. C., Hoffmann, L., Sobieraj, S., & Eimler, S. C. (2013). An experimental study on emotional reactions towards a robot. *International Journal of Social Robotics, 5*(1), 17–34. https://doi.org/10.1007/s12369-012-0173-8

Skjuve, M., Følstad, A., Fostervold, K. I., & Brandtzaeg, P. B. (2021). My chatbot companion - a study of human-chatbot relationships. *International Journal of Human-Computer Studies, 149*, Article 102601. https://doi.org/10.1016/j.ijhcs.2021.102601

Stricke, B. (2020). People v. robots: A roadmap for enforcing california's new online bot disclosure act. *Vanderbilt Journal of Entertainment and Technology Law, 22*(4), Article 6, 839–894. https://scholarship.law.vanderbilt.edu/jetlaw/vol22/iss4/6

Szczuka, J. M., Hartmann, T., & Krämer, N. C. (2019). Negative and positive influences on the sensations evoked by artificial sex partners: A review of relevant theories, recent findings, and introduction of the sexual interaction illusion model. In Y. Zhou & M. H. Fischer (Eds.), *AI Love You: Developments in Human-Robot Intimate Relationships* (pp. 3–19). Springer International Publishing. https://doi.org/10.1007/978-3-030-19734-6_1

Szczuka, J. M., Strathmann, C., Szymczyk, N., Mavrina, L., & Krämer, N. C. (2022). How do children acquire knowledge about voice assistants? A longitudinal field study on children's knowledge about how voice assistants store and process data. *International Journal of Child-Computer Interaction, 33*, Article 100460. https://doi.org/10.1016/j.ijcci.2022.100460

Ta, V., Griffith, C., Boatfield, C., Wang, X., Civitello, M., Bader, H., DeCero, E., & Loggarakis, A. (2020). User experiences of social support from companion chatbots in everyday contexts: Thematic analysis. *Journal of Medical Internet Research, 22*(3), Article e16235. https://doi.org/10.2196/16235

Waltereit, M., Uphoff, M., & Weis, T. (2019). Route derivation using distances and turn directions. In Z. Zhao, Q. A. Chen, & G.-J. Ahn (Eds.), *Proceedings of the ACM Workshop on Automotive Cybersecurity* (pp. 35–40). ACM. https://doi.org/10.1145/3309171.3309176

von der Pütten, A. M., Hoffmann, L., Klatt, J., & Krämer, N. C. (2011). Quid pro quo? Reciprocal self-disclosure and communicative accomodation towards a virtual interviewer. In H. Högni Vilhjálmsson, S. Kopp, S. Marsella, & K. R. Thórisson (Eds.), *Lecture Notes in Computer Science. Intelligent Virtual Agents* (Vol. 6895, pp. 183–194). Springer Berlin Heidelberg. https://doi.org/10.1007/978-3-642-23974-8_20

Voorveld, H. A. M. & Araujo, T. (2020). How social cues in virtual assistants influence concerns and persuasion: The role of voice and a human name. *Cyberpsychology, Behavior, and Social Networking, 23* (10), 689–696. https://doi.org/10.1089/cyber.2019.0205

Xie, T., & Pentina, I. (2022). Attachment theory as a framework to understand relationships with social chatbots: A case study of replika. In T. Bui (Ed.), *Proceedings of the Annual Hawaii International Conference on System Sciences, Proceedings of the 55th Hawaii International Conference on System Sciences* (pp. 2046–2055). Hawaii International Conference on System Sciences. https://doi.org/10.24251/HICSS.2022.258

22

SOCIAL CREDIT SYSTEM AND PRIVACY

Mo Chen, Severin Engelmann, and Jens Grossklags

TECHNICAL UNIVERSITY OF MUNICH, GERMANY

In 2014, the Chinese government launched the implementation of the Social Credit System (SCS), following the release of *The Planning Outline for Building a Social Credit System (2014–2020)* (hereinafter, *Planning Outline*; State Council China, 2014). The SCS has received significant global attention since the beginning, and there is now a fierce public debate about the system's nature. From one perspective, the SCS has been characterized as a mass surveillance apparatus to calculate a digital "sincerity score" for each resident based on a wide range of personal data (Campbell, 2019; Ma, 2018; Mistreanu, 2018). This perspective describes the SCS as a "privacy nightmare" and a threat to human rights, particularly due to the country's weak law enforcement in the context of privacy (Y.-J. Chen et al., 2018; Mosher, 2019; Vinayak, 2019). Another group of scholars views the SCS as primarily a centralized collection of administrative data based on various regulations that have little to do with surveillance or comprehensive credit scoring (Daum, 2018, 2019; Horsley, 2018). Given this context, we will first introduce key elements of the SCS before delving into the system's privacy concerns.

What Is the Social Credit System?

According to the *Planning Outline,* the goal of the SCS is to "allow the trustworthy to roam everywhere under heaven while making it hard for the discredited to take a single step." Multiple social and economic reasons drive the implementation of the SCS. First, moral decline has emerged as a major social problem in Chinese society (Ipsos Public Affairs, 2017). According to a 2013 national survey, one of the most pressing concerns among urban residents was degenerating social trust (Ma & Christensen, 2019). Second, in the economic realm, Chinese enterprises suffer from an estimated loss of 600 billion RMB (approximately 92 billion USD) per year as a result of dishonest activities.[1] Third, as China tries to boost its domestic economy, the SCS is expected to give access to credit and investment opportunities for millions of Chinese citizens without financial records in the domestic market. Finally, China's rapid development of digital financial trading and commerce accelerates SCS implementation by digital tracking and evaluating individuals' (as well as other entities') economic and social behavior.

The SCS, which is the first national digitally implemented sociotechnical rating system, evaluates the "trustworthiness" of nearly all types of social entities, including citizens, companies, social organizations, judicial organs, and governmental authorities (State Council China, 2014). The SCS

DOI: 10.4324/9781003244677-26

also covers foreign residents, companies, and organizations with activities in China, such as foreigners living in China and foreign companies doing business in China (Chen et al., 2021). These entities may be classified into "trustworthy" and "untrustworthy"[2] based on their economic and social behavior and are then subjected to various forms of reward and punishment. Individuals who fail to comply with a court order (usually related to debt repayment) are the most frequently reported cases, and they are publicly displayed on a blacklist called "Dishonest Persons Subject to Enforcement." Blacklisted individuals are, for example, banned from using flights and high-speed trains. In contrast, a company that is rated as an A-level taxpayer by the State Taxation Administration enjoys, for example, priority in cargo declarations provided by the General Administration of Customs. However, the majority of Chinese citizens and companies are not on any list as they exhibited neither particularly "trustworthy" nor "untrustworthy" behavior. In general, negative records result in exclusion from material resources and reputational loss, whereas positive records result in both material gains and reputational praise. The SCS is led by the National Development and Reform Commission and the People's Bank of China (PBoC) and is implemented by many institutes together. However, a unified structure of the SCS is hardly discernible regarding its implementation. At a high level, one can identify a commercial branch of the SCS apart from the government-run SCS. We discuss both in more detail in the following.

The government-run SCS is mandatory and employs two main interrelated mechanisms: the blacklisting and redlisting mechanism and the joint punishment and reward mechanism. Blacklist and redlist records showcase untrustworthy and trustworthy behaviors, respectively, and are published online and offline with free public access. These lists are developed by various government agencies to rate individuals, companies, and other social organizations, and they include personal information, such as a name and a partially anonymized ID number. Although the SCS may seem like a radical social move, blacklisting and redlisting are familiar modes of public shaming and praising to the Chinese. As early as kindergarten, children receive praise and blame from the so-called "honor roll" and "critique roll." These "rolls" typically present photos of individuals on banners at the entrance of buildings like hospitals, schools, and companies. It is not straightforward to find comparable programs, but in Western countries, various incentive strategies with and without monetary payments are used, such as appreciative badges and Employee-of-the-Month recognition rewards. In comparison, an approach like the "critique rolls" is even less common in Western societies. The current SCS implementation incorporates these culturally familiar principles into a digital sociotechnical system (Chen et al., 2022). Adding to such reputation mechanisms, different government authorities cooperate to enforce incentives and sanctions on listed entities through a joint punishment and reward mechanism. Untrustworthy or trustworthy behaviors in one context lead to punishment or rewards in a wide variety of contexts. The mechanism for joint punishment and reward is based on Memorandum of Understanding (MoU) documents signed jointly by different government authorities. There are now over 50 relevant MoUs.

The government-run SCS is established and realized at different levels. In Chinese policy-making, the provincial and city governments implement top-level policy documents, such as the SCS *Planning Outline*. At the city level, cities have developed various models for the SCS. Thus, several such SCS "prototype" cities currently test different scoring systems on a local scale. Take, for instance, Rongcheng, a city that has arguably received the most attention from SCS scholars. In Rongcheng, individuals, companies, and other social organizations automatically receive an initial 1,000 points from the local SCS government authority. Given the specifications of trustworthy and untrustworthy behavior determined by this local government, an entity may either gain points or lose points. As a result, entities are divided into six credit levels based on their scores: AAA, AA, A, B, C, and D. Other SCS prototype cities, such as Xiamen, Fuzhou, and Suqian, set credit scores for local residents with different scales. Higher credit scores are related to priority treatment and discounts for public services, such as book borrowing (up to 40 books) without deposits and discounts on parking fees. Until now, more and more cities have been participating in such credit score experimentation. Whether any local scoring model will be implemented nationwide in the future remains unclear.

At the provincial level, the government-run SCS blacklists and redlists unfold in a highly diversified manner in terms of interface design and credit information comprehensiveness (Engelmann et al., 2021). Indeed, provincial governments have some leeway in how they want to set up digital reputation platforms with blacklists and redlists. An empirical study of 30 blacklist and redlist platforms found that each operated a unique web server with distinct front-end, back-end, and database designs (Engelmann et al., 2021). Furthermore, although some provinces (e.g., Beijing, Tianjin, Tibet, Guangdong, Hunan, Shanxi, and Qinghai) use more than ten different types of blacklists and redlists, others (e.g., Inner Mongolia, Ningxia, Gansu, Guizhou, and Hebei) implement only one blacklist and one redlist (Engelmann et al., 2021). The digital infrastructure that powers blacklists and redlists is also flexible. As a result, the digital reputation infrastructure of the state-run SCS branch may be a widely applicable regulatory measure because it can be quickly adapted to achieve novel policy goals at a relatively low cost. For example, shortly after the COVID-19 outbreak at the end of 2019, many provinces began issuing coronavirus-related blacklists and redlists to (among other things) respond to corona-related transgressions, such as selling counterfeit medical products (Engelmann et al., 2021).

In contrast, individual participation in the SCS's commercial branch is *voluntary,* but the information products of the commercial branch are used in many important contexts, such as apartment rental. Moreover, a few private companies are pioneering the commercial branch of the SCS. Eight private companies were granted permission to operate consumer credit services in 2015. After a two-year trial period, however, none of them received a license to continue providing consumer credit services. Instead, two newly established companies, namely, Baihang Credit and Pudao Credit, were granted consumer credit licenses. The eight private companies became shareholders in these licensed consumer credit reporting companies. Simultaneously, a few other companies somehow continued their previously developed services. Credit scores provided by these companies have different scales and are calculated along various dimensions (Chen & Grossklags, 2020). For example, Zhima (or "Sesame") Credit was developed by Alibaba subsidiary Ant Financial. The Zhima Credit score is calculated on a scale of 350–950 points and is based on information from five categories: credit records, behavioral accumulation, proof of assets, proof of identity, and social relationships. According to the associated app, credit records are the most important metric for scoring. This category of data is comprised of two components: compliance behavior in commercial activities and court records of enforcement. The behavioral accumulation category collects data from user activities, such as mobile payments, shopping, utility bill payment, credit card bill repayment, and charitable activities. The proof of assets category refers to data about users' assets in Alipay and asset information provided by users, including real estate properties and cars. Meanwhile, data that can be used to verify users' identities and work situations are referred to as proof of identity. Finally, social relationships are information about friend relationships that users have authorized.[3] However, beyond the general description, the specific algorithms that operationalize the credit scoring remain unknown. These credit score providers commonly collaborate with other businesses to offer, for example, deposit-free electronic product rentals and shopping discounts to individuals with high credit scores (Chen & Grossklags, 2020). Regarding the commercial branch of the SCS, our discussion in this chapter focuses on individuals only. However, parts of the SCS's commercial branch are also focused on companies. Here private online platforms, such as Qichacha and Tianyancha, use sophisticated data collection methods and data analytics to offer various information (financial and nonfinancial) about companies with easy accessibility and at low cost.

The two branches of the SCS are not separate, but rather intertwined under a "broader policy umbrella" aimed at fostering trust (Ahmed, 2019). Private companies provide critical technical support for SCS construction, and data flows between the two branches. For example, in 2016, Alibaba and the National Development and Reform Commission signed a memorandum to promote the establishment of the SCS in the field of commerce, particularly in terms of data sharing and the joint punishment and reward mechanism. Simultaneously, Zhima Credit collects justice and administrative information that could be used for credit evaluation, such as data from the List of Dishonest Persons Subject to Enforcement. Both branches raise privacy concerns.

Regulatory Issues of the Government-Run Social Credit System

As the core of the SCS, blacklists and redlists have a significant impact on Chinese society. A single blacklist, called the "List of Dishonest Persons Subject to Enforcement," included 15.78 million people between 2013 and 2020, with an average increase of about 2 million each year.[4] SCS blacklist and redlist designs enable public access to social credit information, however, to different degrees. Most SCS platforms display a selection of credit records and enable targeted queries. Some platforms show a selection of credit records on a single page with numbered page tabs that allow visitors to inspect a large amount of different credit records. These observations suggest that the Chinese SCS must strike a balance between public access to credit records, reputational display of credit records, and listed entities' privacy interests. In addition to administrative information such as the publication date and issuing authority, blacklists and redlists reveal personal information like an individual's full name, their partly anonymized ID card number, a unified social credit code (an SCS-specific identification number), and, in some cases, an explanation as to why an entity had been listed, such as failure to perform a legal obligation.

Blacklists and redlists are issued based on effective judicial and regulatory documents. Consider the most widely used blacklist in China today, the list of "Dishonest Persons Subject to Enforcement," which is issued by courts at various levels. In many countries, courts typically make case-related information available online to the public. As such, SCS blacklists and redlists are in line with the global culture of open government and the trend of government and courts' transformation from "primarily locally accessible records to records accessible online via the internet" (Conley et al., 2012). However, the SCS blacklists and redlists have a strong public shaming purpose and thus raise significant privacy concerns.

At a higher level, the legal and regulatory environment regarding the publication of personal information varies among countries (Krause et al., 2022). The Chinese legal and regulatory framework for privacy protection has long been regarded as weak and lagging (Cao, 2005; Han, 2017). A series of laws and regulations legitimized government surveillance in the name of public security and cybersecurity rather than regulating the government's activities (Zhao & Feng, 2021). Additionally, law enforcement remains a challenge in China. For instance, according to the *Provisions of the Supreme People's Court on the Publication of Judgments on the Internet by the People's Courts,* personal information, such as home address, contact information, ID number, bank account number, health status, vehicle license plate number, and certificate number of movable and immovable properties, should be deleted from the documents (Supreme People's Court, 2016). However, at the local level, courts from some cities disclose personal information on blacklists, including the detailed home address and an actual photo of the individual, which would be considered problematic under most privacy regulations and laws around the globe. Likewise, from the citizen perspective, empirical research shows that the blacklisting mechanism of the SCS is an issue from a privacy perspective, but to varying degrees (M. Chen & Grossklags, 2022). Despite recognized privacy concerns, it is not uncommon for the public to regard the blacklisting mechanism as an effective and even reasonable punishment (M. Chen & Grossklags, 2022).

Different from open government data in other fields, which mainly aim at increasing transparency of the government, the SCS blacklists and redlists serve as public mechanisms for shaming and praising. We are taking the PACER system from the United States for comparison. It provides information about accessing and filing US federal court records electronically. PACER users must first create an account and pay for the service. The cost is approximately 10 cents per page with a flat fee of 3 USD per document, which is quite reasonable but still creates a barrier to public access. In contrast, access to online SCS blacklists and redlists is free and requires no registration. The Chinese government makes significant efforts to spread the SCS blacklists and redlists to a large population. To achieve this goal, it uses digital technologies and relies on digital media to spread information about the blacklists and redlists nationwide. Blacklist and redlist information is published not only on SCS-related websites but also in various outlets, such as news reports and social media. Moreover, individuals and companies on SCS blacklists and redlists are widely discussed in media reports in China.

Since 2017, the government has been regularly publishing role model narratives on the central SCS platform creditchina.gov.cn. These narratives tell stories of particularly "blameworthy" or "praiseworthy" ordinary Chinese citizens. The familiar and easy-to-follow format of the narratives effectively communicates SCS-specific social norms and familiarizes readers with SCS surveillance instruments and enforcement strategies (M. Chen et al., 2022). As a result, role model narratives on creditchina.gov.cn instill a sense of "folk morality," demonstrating, partly empirically grounded and partly fictionally, how individuals adhere to social norms, how they violate them, and the consequences they face. Although "blameworthy" role model narratives typically include the protagonists' family name and hometown, "praiseworthy" ones include the protagonists' full name and their gender, age, occupation, and hometown (M. Chen et al., 2022; Engelmann et al., 2019). Again, the SCS weighs the release of individuals' personal information against the public's interest, with little possibility for individuals to contest such use of their data.

Data collection, sharing, and disclosure are the basis for the wide broadcasting of the SCS blacklists and redlists. They are also a prerequisite for implementing the joint punishment and reward mechanism. In particular, data sharing occurs between different government authorities and between government authorities and commercial companies. This is in line with the global trend of expanding systematic government access to private-sector data (Cate et al., 2012). According to *The Action Outline Promoting the Development of Big Data,* promoting public data sharing and eliminating information silos are also high-level government tasks (State Council, 2015). It is argued that practical societal advantages of sharing data exist from the economic and social control perspectives. However, large-scale data sharing raises serious privacy concerns, particularly because data related to individuals' credit, such as financial data, are typically sensitive. At the moment, which types of personal data are shared between organizations and in what ways remain unclear.

Privacy Policies of the Chinese Consumer Credit Reporting Companies

China's commercial consumer credit reporting system has evolved rapidly over the last few years. One can observe considerable changes regarding the market players. Several companies, such as Wanda Credit and Koala Credit, have ended their services entirely. A few other companies have terminated their consumer credit reporting services and focus exclusively on corporate credit reporting, such as China Chengxin Credit and Qianhai Credit. Finally, some newcomers to consumer credit reporting, such as Pudao Credit, have emerged. A few companies continue their services in this area, such as Pengyuan Credit and Zhima Credit, but with some adjustments. However, such adjustments are not immediately clear to users. In other words, from the user's perspective, the difference between the service companies provided in previous years and the current year is difficult to notice.

Nowadays, Chinese individuals commonly use their commercial credit scores (e.g., Zhima scores) in various areas, such as car rental, booking hotel accommodation, dating, online shopping, and visa application. Both credit scoring and related service provision rely on large-scale personal data collection, processing, and sharing. Particularly relevant to consumer credit reporting services is sensitive personal data, which, according to the *Information Technology Personal Information Security Specification,* refers to information that may cause harm to persons or property, reputation, physical and psychological health, or discriminatory treatment once disclosed, illegally provided, or abused. As a result, privacy protection is especially important in this field.

Privacy policies are a direct and important means for examining companies' privacy practices. An examination of consumer credit reporting companies' privacy policies in China reveals relatively weak privacy protection in the commercial branch of the SCS, which can be discussed from three perspectives. First, a privacy policy should be easily accessible to users; otherwise, the content of the policy is less meaningful. The *Personal Information Security Specification* not only includes broad, innovative, and detailed definitions and requirements on various aspects of data protection, but it also requires the personal data controller to develop an easily accessible privacy policy with specific content requirements. However, a privacy policy is not available for all consumer credit reporting companies in China. For instance, we could not find such a document for Sinoway Credit as of June 2022.

Second, the scope of data collection for commercial consumer credit reporting companies in China and those in other countries such as the United States is similar, including identity information, financial information, contact information, information about online activity, and device information (M. Chen & Grossklags, 2020). However, the privacy policies of Chinese companies are generally less detailed. For instance, companies frequently collect biometric information, such as facial images or videos, for identity authentication. Meanwhile, some companies, such as Tianxia Xinyong, explicitly stated that they do not save users' facial recognition characteristics, only the authentication result. For others, however, the statement is somewhat ambiguous. For example, JD Finance and Baihang Credit only demonstrate that they require the user's facial images/videos or facial recognition information for identity authentication or to confirm the accuracy of the information. However, whether such information will be stored is unclear. Another example is data retention. Negative information, which refers to information that "has negative impacts on the entity's credit status" (*Regulation on the Administration of the Credit Reporting Industry*), is an important part in the evaluation of one's creditworthiness; however, it is also very sensitive. According to the same regulation, any negative information record(s) will be kept for five years after the "bad" behavior has ended and then deleted. However, Zhima Credit is the only company that explicitly states the measures to deal with users' negative information records, whereas others discuss personal information retention in general without specifying the measures for negative information.

Third, according to some privacy policies, consumer credit reporting companies may collect, use, share, and disclose personal information to provide products and services and protect personal information. It is also common to provide anonymized statistics about personal data to third parties for marketing and advertising purposes. Moreover, some other commonly cited reasons for companies to collect, use, share, and disclose personal information are "required by regulations, rules and laws, or by government organizations," "public security, public health, vital public interests," and "safeguarding the life, properties and other material interest." JD Finance also includes the category of "academic research" but only when personal information in publications is deidentified. Users' authorization is usually not required to serve these special purposes. From this perspective, the commercial branch of the SCS extends the government's access to the private-sector's data, which allows for "systematic governmental access, disclosure, retention, and collection of information for surveillance, national security, and crime detection" (Abraham & Hickok, 2012).

The Role of Social Media

The Chinese government has the tradition of using the media for setting the agenda for political discourse, the promotion of public policies, and the monitoring of the public opinion (Tang & Iyengar, 2011;

Winfield & Peng, 2005). The infrastructure of Chinese media has become increasingly digitized and commercialized during the past decades. During this process, the Chinese government has adjusted its media strategy accordingly to act more indirectly but retained strong control over the media (Pan, 2017). Social media is used as an important channel in the context of the SCS to broaden the scope of broadcasting details about the SCS blacklists, and thus to broaden the range of the potential impact of shaming. Some local SCS platforms (for example, those in Inner Mongolia and Shandong) include a share function, allowing users to share blacklist and redlist entries directly through popular Chinese social media platforms (e.g., WeChat, Sina Weibo, and Baidu Tieba). As a result, individuals who are blacklisted are tried and judged not only in traditional courts, but also in the "court of public opinion" for public scrutiny (Greer & McLaughlin, 2011), whereas those who are redlisted may be publicly praised. According to this viewpoint, the media plays a role that is beyond the capabilities of formal institutional authority (Machado & Santos, 2009) and serves as a strong complement to it in the case of the SCS.

Additionally, social media is also used to make message delivery more target-oriented. For example, the Higher People's Court of Hebei Province developed a mini program called "Lao Lai Map" on WeChat, which is a popular multipurpose social media service in China, to pinpoint users' location and to scan a radius of 500m for "untrustworthy" people. Users can directly share any results on WeChat or report a new "Lao Lai" via the mini program. The color of the map changes from blue to yellow to red as the number of "Lao Lai" increases to raise attention further. What's more, some local courts and telephone companies work together to alert phone callers to an individual's "untrustworthy" behavior before the line is connected. Through these measures, the public shaming and praising mechanism functions are further enhanced within a small and connected community.

At a high level, the *Planning Outline* emphasizes credit construction in the area of internet applications and services, according to which internet users' online behavior will be evaluated and the corresponding credit level will be recorded. It remains unclear how broadly the SCS collects personal data from social media platforms and what the related impacts are on the use of social media in China. However, some pieces of evidence show that individuals' activities on social media are connected to and used by the SCS. For example, in one news report from the SCS national platform,[5] the protagonist failed to repay a large sum of debt (about 4.5 million USD) and claimed to be unable to perform the obligation. However, she shared her luxury life frequently on social media, which was used as evidence by the court to prove her capability for debt repayment. In another case, the "Lao Lai" hid herself for more than one year but was then caught on the basis of the positioning function of WeChat.[6] Recently, in October 2021, the *Provisions on the Management of Internet User Account Name Information (Draft for Solicitation of Comments)* were issued, making online platforms responsible for the authentication of users' true identity information, including the Unified Social Credit Code. More broadly, the emergence and popularity of social media have generated a complex impact on Chinese society. On the one hand, it empowered the public and diminished the state's ability to set the public agenda and shape political references, thus triggering a change in Chinese political communication (Esarey & Xiao, 2011). On the other hand, the government's control and intervention activities clearly extend to social media (Sparks et al., 2016) which is, simultaneously, used by the government as a new tool for social control.

Discussion and Conclusion

The SCS, as a rapidly evolving social crediting system, is a critical example of societal transformation, but it also raises significant privacy concerns. This problem space is discussed from three perspectives in this chapter. First, as a critical mechanism of the SCS, the SCS blacklists and redlists "function" most effectively when more detailed information is provided and widely disseminated. Therefore, the SCS is faced with a dilemma between effectiveness and privacy protection (M. Chen & Grossklags, 2022). Even when people's personal information is only partially disclosed, as is currently the case with the Enforcement Information Public Website (http://zxgk.court.gov.cn/shixin/), which is operated by the Supreme Court to publish the blacklist for Dishonest Persons Subject to Enforcement, it is often easy to reidentify a specific person. Therefore, it is a great potential threat to an individual's privacy and security.

Second, the SCS framework improves data flows from the private sector to the government, which is becoming more common in other countries (Abraham & Hickok, 2012). Aside from what is stated in the companies' privacy policies (about "special purposes"), collaboration between the government and private companies streamlines such data flows. For instance, Ant Financial, which operates Zhima Credit, has agreed to share consumer credit data with the PBoC (Yang, 2021). The shareholding structure of the two licensed consumer credit reporting companies presents a similar situation. For example, the largest shareholder (with 36%) for the Baihang Credit is the National Internet Finance Association of China, which is strongly associated with the PBoC and the China Banking and Insurance Regulatory Commission. The eight private companies that offer trial consumer credit reporting services each take 8%. Additionally, data sharing between government departments, which is the basis for the implementation of the joint punishment and reward mechanism, is also problematic as the change of context for collecting and using data creates a challenge to ensure that existing rights and obligations are not affected (Nissenbaum, 2004).

Third, the legal environment in China for privacy protection is improving. In recent years, the Chinese government has issued a number of privacy-related laws and regulations, such as the *Cybersecurity Law* (2016) and *China's Personal Information Protection Law* (2021), which affect both domestic and multinational entities that process or use the personal information of Chinese citizens. Furthermore, *the Measures for the Administration of the Credit Reporting Business* (2021) focus specifically on data collection, processing, sharing, use, and disclosure in the credit reporting industry. In comparison to our previous findings (M. Chen & Grossklags, 2020), it is clear that companies' privacy practices have become more comprehensive to some extent. However, the SCS blacklists revealed by local courts, as well as reported scandals such as the one involving Pengyuan Credit, which was fined in 2020 for providing a consumer credit reporting service without a license, continue to shed light on a relatively weak legal system in this area, posing a significant challenge to privacy protection.

Finally, another privacy challenge pertains to the collection and analysis of public data on key SCS platforms for *research*. Recently, a growing body of research known as computational social sciences has demonstrated that analyzing open government data can significantly contribute to a better understanding of some of society's most pressing challenges regarding economic behavior, health, or policy implementation (Lazer et al., 2020). Given a lack of consistent regulations for web scraping, researchers should nonetheless adhere to the principles of ethical web crawling (Krotov & Silva, 2018). The SCS publishes credit records on blacklist and redlist data with the intent of public scrutiny. When data are made public and no application programming interface is offered, researchers are free to collect data. For researchers, whether SCS platforms specify robots.txt files that outline rules for data crawling and scraping should be investigated first before any data collection. Researchers should blur any identifiable data presented after publication. The Chinese SCS is already one of the world's largest digital reputation systems. Empirical research on its influence on society and how its technical realization progresses will be an invaluable contribution to understanding how large digital sociotechnical systems influence societies in authoritarian states. Here, research questions could address how the SCS changes society's concept of social trust that is increasingly shaped by a digital classification system providing real reputational and material benefits and sanctions.

Acknowledgments

We thank the editors of this volume for detailed comments on an earlier version of this work. Furthermore, we are grateful for funding support from the Bavarian Research Institute for Digital Transformation. The authors are solely responsible for the content of this publication.

Notes

1 Refer to http://finance.people.com.cn/n/2014/0711/c1004-25267176.html Last accessed on August 31, 2022 (in Chinese).
2 The authors use quotation marks to communicate a neutral standpoint toward SCS-specific normative concepts. In the remainder of the article, quotation marks will be omitted for readability.
3 The explanation of the five data categories is based on information from the app of Alipay. Last accessed on June 7, 2022.
4 The data are provided by The 2020 Risk Report on Dishonest Persons Subject to Enforcement issued by the Qichacha Data Research Institute. Recited from Sohu news: https://www.sohu.com/a/447341762_774283 Last accessed on August 31, 2022 (in Chinese).
5 See https://www.creditchina.gov.cn/home/dianxinganli1/201808/t20180803_122527.html Last accessed on August 31, 2022 (in Chinese).
6 See https://www.sohu.com/a/210413946_123753 Last accessed on August 31, 2022 (in Chinese).

References

Abraham, S., & Hickok, E. (2012). Government access to private-sector data in India. *International Data Privacy Law, 2*(4), 302–315. https://doi.org/10.1093/idpl/ips028

Ahmed, S. (2019). The messy truth about Social Credit. *LOGIC*. https://logicmag.io/china/the-messy-truth-about-social-credit/ Last accessed on August 30, 2022.

Campbell, C. (2019). How China is using "Social Credit Scores" to reward and punish its citizens. *Time*. https://time.com/collection/davos-2019/5502592/china-social-creditscore/ Last accessed on August 30, 2022.

Cao, J. (2005). Protecting the right to privacy in China. *Victoria University of Wellington Law Review, 36*(3), 645–664. https://doi.org/10.26686/vuwlr.v36i3.5610

Cate, F. H., Dempsey, J. X., & Rubinstein, I. S. (2012). Systematic government access to private-sector data. *International Data Privacy Law, 2*(4), 195–199. https://doi.org/10.1093/idpl/ips027

Chen, M., Bogner, K., Becheva, J., & Grossklags, J. (2021). The transparency of the Chinese Social Credit System from the perspective of German organizations. In *Proceedings of the 29th European Conference on Information Systems (ECIS)*. https://aisel.aisnet.org/ecis2021_rp/47/

Chen, M., Engelmann, S., & Grossklags, J. (2022). Ordinary people as moral heroes and foes: Digital role model narratives propagate social norms in China's Social Credit System. In *Proceedings of the 5th AAAI/ACM Conference on AI, Ethics, and Society (AIES)*, pp. 181–191. https://doi.org/10.1145/3514094.3534180

Chen, M., & Grossklags, J. (2020). An analysis of the current state of the consumer credit reporting system in China. *Proceedings on Privacy Enhancing Technologies, 2020*(4), 89–110. https://doi.org/10.2478/popets-2020-0064

Chen, M., & Grossklags, J. (2022). Social control in the digital transformation of society: A case study of the Chinese Social Credit System. *Social Sciences, 11*(6). https://www.mdpi.com/2076-0760/11/6/229

Chen, Y.-J., Lin, C.-F., & Liu, H.-W. (2018). "Rule of Trust": The power and perils of China's Social Credit megaproject. *Columbia Journal of Asian Law, 32*(1), 1–37.

Conley, A., Datta, A., Nissenbaum, H., & Sharma, D. (2012). Sustaining privacy and open justice in the transition to online court records: A multidisciplinary inquiry. *Maryland Law Review, 71*(3), 772–847.

Daum, J. (2018). Social Credit overview podcast. *China Law Translate*. https://www.chinalawtranslate.com/social-credit-overview-podcast/ Last accessed on August 30, 2022.

Daum, J. (2019). Untrustworthy: Social Credit isn't what you think it is. *Verfassungsblog*. https://verfassungsblog.de/untrustworthy-social-credit-isnt-what-you-think-it-is/ Last accessed on August 30, 2022.

Engelmann, S., Chen, M., Dang, L., & Grossklags, J. (2021). Blacklists and redlists in the Chinese Social Credit System: Diversity, flexibility, and comprehensiveness. In *Proceedings of the 4th AAAI/ACM Conference on AI, Ethics, and Society (AIES)*, pp. 78–88. https://doi.org/10.1145/3461702.3462535

Engelmann, S., Chen, M., Fischer, F., Kao, C., & Grossklags, J. (2019). Clear sanctions, vague rewards: How China's Social Credit System currently defines "good" and "bad" behavior. In *Proceedings of the 2019 Conference on Fairness, Accountability, and Transparency (FAccT)*, pp. 69–78. https://doi.org/10.1145/3287560.3287585

Esarey, A., & Xiao, Q. (2011). Digital communication and political change in China. *International Journal of Communication, 5*, 298–319.

Greer, C., & McLaughlin, E. (2011). 'Trial by media': Policing, the 24-7 news media sphere and the 'politics of outrage.' *Theoretical Criminology, 15*(1), 23–46. https://doi.org/10.1177/1362480610387461

Han, D. (2017). The market value of who we are: The flow of personal data and its regulation in China. *Media and Communication, 5*(2), 21–30. https://doi.org/10.17645/MAC.V5I2.890

Horsley, J. (2018). China's Orwellian Social Credit Score isn't real. *Foreign Policy*. https://foreignpolicy.com/2018/11/16/chinas-orwellian-social-credit-score-isnt-real/ Last accessed on August 30, 2022.

Ipsos Public Affairs. (2017). What worries the world. *Ipsos Views (2017)*.

Krause, T., Chen, M., Wassermann, L., Fischer, D., & Grossklags, J. (2022). China's corporate credit reporting system: A comparison with the U.S. and Germany. *Regulation and Governance*. https://doi.org/10.1111/rego.12491

Krotov, V., & Silva, L. (2018). Legality and ethics of web scraping. *Americas Conference on Information Systems 2018: Digital Disruption, AMCIS 2018*.

Lazer, D. M. J., Pentland, A., Watts, D. J., Aral, S., Athey, S., Contractor, N., Freelon, D., Gonzalez-Bailon, S., King, G., Margetts, H., Nelson, A., Salganik, M. J., Strohmaier, M., Vespignani, A., & Wagner, C. (2020). Computational social science: Obstacles and opportunities. *Science, 369*(6507), 1060–1062. https://doi.org/10.1126/science.aaz8170

Ma, A. (2018). China has started ranking citizens with a creepy "social credit" system — Here's what you can do wrong, and the embarrassing, demeaning ways they can punish you. *Business Insider*. https://www.businessinsider.com/china-social-credit-system-punishments-and-rewards-explained-2018-4 Last accessed on August 30, 2022.

Ma, L., & Christensen, T. (2019). Government trust, social trust, and citizens' risk concerns: Evidence from crisis management in China. *Public Performance and Management Review, 42*(2), 383–404. https://doi.org/10.1080/15309576.2018.1464478

Machado, H., & Santos, F. (2009). The disappearance of Madeleine McCann: Public drama and trial by media in the Portuguese press. *Crime, Media, Culture, 5*(2), 146–167. https://doi.org/10.1177/1741659009335691

Mistreanu, S. (2018). Life inside China's Social Credit laboratory. *Foreign Policy*. https://foreignpolicy.com/2018/04/03/life-inside-chinas-social-credit-laboratory/ Last accessed on August 30, 2022.

Mosher, S. W. (2019). China's new 'Social Credit System' is a dystopian nightmare. *New York Post*. https://nypost.com/2019/05/18/chinas-new-social-credit-system-turns-orwells-1984-into-reality/ Last accessed on August 30, 2022.

Nissenbaum, H. (2004). Privacy as contextual integrity. *Washington Law Review, 79*(1), 119–157.

Pan, Y. (2017). Managed liberalization: Commercial media in the People's Republic of China. In A. Schiffrin (Ed.), *In the Service of Power: Media Capture and the Threat to Democracy*, 111–124. Center for International Media Assistance.

Sparks, C., Wang, H., Huang, Y., Zhao, Y., Lu, N., & Wang, D. (2016). The impact of digital media on newspapers: Comparing responses in China and the United States. *Global Media and China, 1*(3), 186–207. https://doi.org/10.1177/2059436416666385

State Council. (2015). *The Action Outline for Promoting the Development of Big Data*. (in Chinese).

State Council. (2014). *Notice of the State Council on Issuing the Outline of the Plan for Building a Social Credit System (2014-2020)*. (in Chinese).

Supreme People's Court. (2016). *Provisions of the Supreme People's Court on the Publication of Judgments on the Internet by the People's Courts*. (in Chinese).

Tang, W., & Iyengar, S. (2011). The emerging media system in China: Implications for regime change. *Political Communication, 28*(3), 263–267. https://doi.org/10.1080/10584609.2011.572446

Vinayak, V. (2019). *The Human Rights Implications of China's Social Credit System*. https://ohrh.law.ox.ac.uk/the-human-rights-implications-of-chinas-social-credit-system/ Last accessed on August 30, 2022.

Winfield, B. H., & Peng, Z. (2005). Market or party controls? Chinese media in transition. *Gazette, 67*(3), 255–270. https://doi.org/10.1177/0016549205052228

Yang, J. (2021). Ant to fully share consumer credit data with China's Government. *The Wall Street Journal*. https://www.wsj.com/articles/ant-to-fully-share-consumer-credit-data-with-chinas-government-11632310975. Last accessed on February 28, 2023.

Zhao, B., & Feng, Y. (2021). Mapping the development of China's data protection law: Major actors, core values, and shifting power relations. *Computer Law and Security Review, 40*. https://doi.org/10.1016/j.clsr.2020.105498

23

MICROTARGETING, PRIVACY, AND THE NEED FOR REGULATING ALGORITHMS

Tom Dobber

UNIVERSITY OF AMSTERDAM, THE NETHERLANDS

The Tension between Microtargeting and Privacy

Microtargeting involves "collecting information about people, and using that information to show them targeted political advertisements" (Zuiderveen Borgesius et al., 2018, p. 82). Political advertisers use microtargeting to make their campaigns more efficient by reaching only those who are deemed susceptible. Advertisers aim to make their campaigns more effective by reaching people with a message that is personally relevant (Zuiderveen Borgesius et al., 2018).

Microtargeting efforts are based on personal data. Collecting, processing, and using insights derived from personal data to communicate tailored messages is directly at odds with privacy. Privacy deprives others of access to you, and as such, privacy can be understood as a "means to an end": as your personal shield against (undue) influence (see Reiman, 1995). "Privacy thus prevents interference, pressures to conform, ridicule, punishment, unfavorable decisions, and other forms of hostile reaction" (Gavison, 1980, p. 448). However, online advertising platforms (e.g., Google and Meta) are designed to grant advertisers direct access to you personally. Moreover, online advertising platforms provide their advertisers with key insights on your behavior, interests, and characteristics that help advertisers with interfering in your decision-making process. Because of these insights, it is thought to be easier for advertisers to completely circumvent people's privacy and influence citizens' behavior and decision-making (e.g., Zarouali et al., 2020).

One could argue that you *could* protect your privacy by deciding not to use any of Meta's platforms, or Google's. This way, you could derive others from access to you. However, this suggestion is too simplistic for three main reasons. First, online platforms collect, analyze and sell data to advertisers regardless of whether someone uses their platforms (e.g., Wagner, 2020). Second, because this means that people cannot use communication infrastructures that have become crucial for entertainment and communication. Third, because this would place privacy-protection responsibility on the shoulder of the individual rather than the industry or government.

People Generally Hold Negative Attitudes Toward Microtargeting

Research has found that citizens think rather negatively about political microtargeting and that people are concerned about their privacy when thinking about political microtargeting (Dobber et al., 2018; Turow et al., 2012). In fact, over time, there is a downward spiral where people who come to think more negatively about microtargeting also become increasingly concerned about their privacy

DOI: 10.4324/9781003244677-27

(Dobber et al., 2018). This shows a clear connection between perceptions of political microtargeting and privacy. Such a connection could lead to behavior that is undesirable from a democratic perspective. For instance, people could experience "chilling effects," which occur when people think they are being monitored and therefore choose to not display a certain behavior (Zuiderveen Borgesius et al., 2018; Stoycheff et al., 2019). People might refrain from visiting the website of a rightist political party because they fear third parties are watching them (and might expose them at some point in the near future, e.g., through a data breach; see Zuiderveen Borgesius et al., 2018).

Privacy is often treated as an individual's responsibility. A citizen agrees (or does not) to many different privacy policies, and in doing so, the citizen manages their own privacy (Baruh & Popescu, 2015). However, the average citizen is not equipped to protect their privacy. This is because the data-collection effort is so pervasive and complex (Baruh & Popescu, 2015; Trepte et al., 2015).

While the burden of protecting one's privacy is put on individuals themselves, privacy also serves the public interest. People are (jointly) threatened in their ability to decide autonomously when anonymous data collectors use personal data to arbitrarily influence people. Privacy can also be seen as a means to protect the integrity of the larger electoral process by shielding citizens from personalized data-driven influencing efforts (Dobber, 2020). There is increasing evidence for the idea that microtargeting can be an effective tool to influence voters (Endres, 2019; Zarouali et al., 2020). Although microtargeted messages can be used in good faith, microtargeting also has potential for manipulation (e.g., by falsely presenting oneself as a one-issue party, spreading false information, or playing into fears and weaknesses; Zuiderveen Borgesius et al., 2018). Without privacy, it would be easier to influence the electorate with microtargeted messages, because it would be much easier to collect and analyze personal data.

Microtargeting Is Not New, but Has Changed Over Time

While social platforms are currently crucial in offering microtargeting to political advertisers, they did not invent microtargeting. Microtargeting is reminiscent of "the campaign strategy of the late nineteenth century, where whistle-stop campaigns and segmented news markets allowed candidates to communicate different messages to different voters" (Hillygus & Shields, 2009, p. 215). On the European side of the Atlantic, in the 1900s, party representatives from the Netherlands visited potential voters at home to ask them about their voting intentions. The representatives would build an administration of potential voters and their occupations. Then, the political parties would use that information to send the potential voters tailored brochures or visit them at home with tailored canvassing conversations. For example, "the catholic party would spread brochures tailored to workers, farmers, horticulturists, the elderly, the middle class, women, and large families" (Dobber & De Jong, 2020, p. 106).

Regulating Microtargeting in US and EU

Despite the historical tradition of microtargeting in Europe (see also Karlsen, 2009), modern-day political microtargeting is often presented as a primarily *American* technique (Bennett, 2016). This is not too surprising given the lax privacy legislation in the US. The basis of microtargeting in the 1900s, in the US *and* Europe, was formed by voter databases, which were made possible by the absence of privacy regulations. Over time, Europe and the US took different paths with regards to voter privacy laws which gravely affected the proliferation of such databases. In the US, there hardly was any serious legislation meant to improve voter privacy by addressing voter databases. In fact, legislation did the opposite. In 1993, the US passed the National Voter Registration Act which created digital voter registration lists (Hillygus and Shields, 2008). In 2002, the Help America Vote Act "mandated states to develop a single, uniform, centralized, interactive voter registration database that would be updated regularly" (Hillygus and Shields, 2008, p. 220). Europe moved in the opposite direction. In 1951, for example, Dutch voter lists were no longer available and in 1989 municipalities could no longer provide voter information to third parties due to privacy laws (Dobber & De Jong, 2020).

Microtargeting Is Continuously Evolving

One of the first accounts of modern-day microtargeting presented microtargeting as a way of confronting citizens with wedge issues (Hillygus and Shields, 2008). For instance, the Republican party would microtarget a Democratic voter with an anti-abortion message because data analysis shows that the voter disagrees with the Democrats on abortion, while agreeing on most other issues.

Microtargeting in 2008 was predominantly an *offline* affair. Hillygus and Shields (2008) mentioned "direct mail, email, text messaging, web advertisements, phone calls, and personal canvassing" (p. 88). Gerber and Green (2008) mentioned microtargeted robocalls as well as direct mail based on information from databases. These databases are constructed "by conducting an opinion survey with registered voters. The information on the voter file, augmented with consumer information, was used to forecast the survey responses. These forecasts are then imputed to other (nonsurveyed) people on the voter file" (p. 204). As voter databases formed the basis of this type of microtargeting, privacy laws in Europe made such data-driven voter outreach initiatives rare.

The Era of Big Data Changed Microtargeting into an Online Affair

The initial understanding of microtargeting as an *offline* tool to communicate wedge issues (Hillygus and Shields, 2008) expanded around 2010, when advances in "data mining" (see Murray & Scime, 2010) were fueled by increasing computational power, which made *predictive modeling* more accessible and practical for political campaigns (Nielsen, 2012). Around 2012, microtargeting started to include "big data." This new understanding was contextualized by boyd and Crawford's (2012) claim that "[t]he era of Big Data has begun" (p. 662).

The leap of offline microtargeting to an *online* technique was rooted in voter databases *and* "big data analysis," and can be illustrated by the 61-million-person experiment by Bond et al. (2012). This experiment occurred during the 2010 US Congressional elections. Meta users took part in an experiment (without consenting explicitly). Some users got displayed on election day either an informational message about voting, a social message about voting (which included the profile pictures of friends that had already voted), or no message at all (control group). The findings suggested that showing people a social message accompanied by profile pictures of *close* friends marginally increased voter turnout. A marginal increase in a 61-million-people experiment translates into some hundreds of thousands of votes. Bond et al. (2012) showed how minor stimuli can wrinkle out large effects if applied on a large enough scale. Social media offered that scale.

But microtargeting offered more than just scale. It afforded political advertisers with new ways of optimization through (sometimes large-scale) randomized a/b-testing and retargeting (Kreiss, 2012). In 2013, Kosinski et al. (2013) found that digital trace data could be used to predict, among others, political views and personality traits. After that, digital trace data became a key data source for subsequent conceptualizations of microtargeting. In 2014, Tufekci observed that microtargeting requires "access to proprietary algorithms (p. 2). These proprietary algorithms are revisited later on.

European Regulators Efforts to Protect Privacy and Data

The microtargeting literature until 2016 focused to a great extent on North-America. Bennett (2016) explored whether "political parties [can] campaign in Europe as they do in North America" (p. 261). Bennett highlighted that *political parties* in North-America "amassed a huge amount of personal data on voters" (p. 261), suggesting that US parties are a kind of "data broker" themselves. In Europe, Bennett notes, data protection regulations would bar political parties from processing sensitive data such as political opinions unless the citizen provides informed and explicit consent (Bennett, 2016), which makes it much harder for parties to amass data or become data brokers themselves.

Where in 1989, privacy laws in Europe made an end to the use of voting lists, and, by extension, rudimentary forms of microtargeting (Dobber & De Jong, 2020), the advent of social media afforded political actors in Europe a new alleyway into the use of online microtargeting techniques. However, article 9 of the General Data Protection Regulation (GDPR) requires explicit consent from the citizen when processing sensitive data such as political opinions and thus the GDPR places a burden on the actor that collects and processes these sensitive data. The advent of social platforms shifted the burden of data-collection and processing from the political party to the social platforms. This meant for a large part that the burden of obtaining explicit consent from the citizen for sensitive data processing also shifted from the political campaign to the social platforms.

Social Platforms Unburden Political Parties

Social platforms have taken over many tasks that were previously the domain of the political campaign. Social platforms obtain informed consent, collect data, analyze data, and provide an infrastructure that connects political advertisers with potential voters. Not only do social platforms *unburden* European political campaigns in terms of informed consent, data gathering, and analysis, social platforms also afford campaigns across the globe with accessible, scalable, and affordable ways to directly connect with potential voters.

How Does Modern-Day Microtargeting Work?

Since 2012, Meta and Google are the two most central actors in the US political landscape (Barrett, 2021). Google's (2022) and Meta's ad library reports (2022) show that US political campaigns spent over 850 million dollars on Google advertising since 2018 (e.g., Google search and YouTube). For Meta, this amount has surpassed 3 billion dollars since 2018. In the UK, campaigns spent 2.6 million dollars on political ads on Google since March 2019, but more than 130 million dollars on Meta since November 2018. In Germany, finally, political campaigns spent over 6 million dollars on Google since March 2019, and more than 80 million dollars on Meta since 2018.

When it comes to microtargeting, Google and Meta are different platforms. Especially Meta, which also owns Instagram, has been the preferred platform for political advertisers. Potentially, this is due to Google's policy change in 2019, when it restricted the targeting criteria that political advertisers could use (Google, 2019). This policy change from Google signaled a schism in advertising visions between Google and Meta. The latter continues to offer advertisers a broad range of selectors that they can use to target specific segments of society. Because Google and Meta are different companies, they will be discussed separately.

Google

Google has limited their targeting capabilities. Political advertisers can only actively target people based on their age, location (postal code level), and gender. Despite these limitations, Google still allows political advertisers to approach citizens in a targeted way. There are three main channels through which Google offers such advertising.

YouTube

Advertisers can first determine which demographic groups are the target audience (e.g., men of 65+ years, living in the state of New York). While these demographic boundaries cut out most people living in New York, this group is still large and diverse. Some are Republicans, some Democrats, and others independent or undecided. Say the New York Democratic Party wants to target older YouTube users with a mobilization message. Displaying the ad to Republicans could be counterproductive because it might also increase Republican turnout. YouTube offers the possibility to target by exclusion. Advertisers could exclude, for instance, people who view videos on typical Republican YouTube channels (e.g., Fox News). After running the ad to the desired audience, the next step would be to *retarget* only the people who have "engaged" with the advertisement (e.g., by clicking on the ad, or by viewing more than 30 seconds of the ad). So, while Google has limited the extent to which advertisers can strategically target users, advertisers can still reach very specific groups on YouTube: by targeting postal codes, excluding certain pages, and by retargeting users.

Google Search Advertising

Whereas YouTube still allows advertisers to push content to users, Google search advertising is different. Here, advertisers specify that advertisements should be shown only when certain keywords are typed in on Google's search engine (e.g., "conservative party"). This seems a pull approach: only users that in the first place search for specific keywords get to see an ad. Thus, one could argue that this is a more privacy-friendly advertising method than targeting on YouTube. But in practice, the method is not privacy-friendly because advertisers have several extra options. First, advertisers can target search ads on postcode level, gender, and age groups. Second, advertisers can exclude certain keywords. Third, advertisers can retarget the users who clicked on the ad by placing the "Google ad tag." Once users have typed in relevant keywords, advertisers can push content, making the privacy-friendliness of Google search advertising a paper tiger.

Contextual Targeting

Contextual targeting, finally, means that advertisements get displayed alongside content that is "congruent" with the advertisement. For instance, the Green Party places an advertisement about climate change alongside a news article on the BBC website about record-shattering heat waves. Here, in general, the advertiser first formulates keywords about which topical issues are deemed relevant and which keywords need to be ignored. Google's algorithm then matches the ad with content within Google's network, and when there is a match, the ad gets displayed automatically on the target website. The boundaries can be refined by specifying language and location parameters. In terms of citizen privacy, contextual ads are privacy-friendly in a similar way as Google search ads. Because there are possibilities for cookie-based retargeting, and all user behaviors are monitored, analyzed and fed into the ad delivery algorithm, contextual targeting cannot be considered privacy-friendly.

Meta

Targeting on Meta in general works in three steps. First, the political advertiser indicates their strategic goal (e.g., to reach as many people as possible, to get as many views as possible, or to get as many people as possible to visit their website, et cetera) and then selects their target audience. Selecting the target audience means that the advertiser strategically determines what kind of people are thought to be of interest for the content of the ad, and should be getting displayed the ad (e.g., men aged between 18 and 34, with an interest in current affairs). Not only can advertisers determine which types of people should receive the ad, but also who should not receive the ad (e.g., people who work in finance). The advertiser could also upload a specific list of people that should be displayed the ad ("custom audiences"), or ask Meta to display the ad to people who "look like" a specific group of people ("lookalike audiences").

Second, Meta's ad delivery algorithm takes the strategic choices described above as input and then matches the advertisement with the users that fall within the boundaries. Importantly, this process of ad delivery does not occur randomly. Rather, the machine-learning ad delivery algorithm considers the content of the message and the "optimization goal" (Ali et al., 2019). Based on previous behavior, the algorithm determines which people are more likely to engage with the offered content, and who is not. For example, Ali et al. (2019) found that when a Republican-leaning audience was targeted with a Trump ad, this ad was delivered to 7,588 users. When a Bernie Sanders ad was targeted to the exact same audience, this ad was delivered to only 4,772 people. The Bernie Sanders ad cost $15.39 per 1,000 impressions, while the Trump ad cost $10.98 per 1,000 impressions. It is thought that the ad delivery algorithm is designed to offer users information that is congruent with prior attitudes. Incongruent information might give users a less pleasant experience and might, in the short run, limit the time spent on Meta-affiliated websites. Less time spent on Meta means that Meta can sell less ads. In the longer run, a less pleasant experience on Meta might lead to a decrease in daily use. However, a side-effect of the ad delivery algorithm is that political parties might be preaching to their own choir by reaching the audience that the algorithm thinks are receptive to the message.

Third, through retargeting, advertisers can effectively "mold" user groups into responsive target groups by only retargeting the users who engaged with the advertisement. Those who do not engage with the advertisement can receive an ad about a different topic, or in a different format (e.g., video versus image), or they might be ignored (see Howard, 2006). In practice, political advertisers set broad boundaries in the early days of the campaign and target relatively broad and heterogeneous groups. Through ad delivery algorithmic optimization, these groups become smaller and more homogeneous. Through retargeting, the political advertisers continuously refine their target groups on the basis of engagement with prior posts. As a result, in the later stages of the campaign, the target audiences of political advertisers are more fragmented, smaller, and more homogeneous.

Dependence on Algorithms

While Google and Meta are unique platforms and clearly differ in their advertising architecture, both share a strong reliance on algorithms to match advertising content to receptive users. These algorithms are proprietary, and although there are some efforts to audit ad delivery algorithms (e.g., Ali et al., 2019; Imana et al., 2021), little is known about the actual workings and effects of these algorithms. Yet, it is clear that advertisers on Meta and Google never have full control or full understanding over their advertising campaign (see also Tufekci, 2014).

Say the UK Labor Party runs an ad campaign in the print version of the Guardian. The Labor Party would know that every recipient of the Guardian in principle would have an equal chance of seeing the advertisement. Of course, some readers only read the front page or the sports section, but those readers would at least be able to see the advertisement. Social media advertisements do not work that way. The Labor Party could hypothetically target roughly the same group of people if they were to hold reliable data on recipients of the print version of the Guardian. However, on social media, not all readers would have the same chance of seeing the advertisement. This is because the ad delivery algorithm seeks out those people who are expected to engage with the advertisement. Who those people are, is unclear for the advertiser. Why those people are expected to engage with the content is also unclear, although prior behavior is likely to play a role.

Thus, while a Labor campaign manager could pick up the Guardian from a news stand and verify that the advertisement is displayed correctly, they would not be able to log into Instagram or Meta or visit a Google Ads-affiliated website to make sure that their online ad is displayed correctly. Moreover, the campaign manager knows that the Guardian is the same for all recipients, and thus the manager has a general understanding of who gets to see the ad. But online, the campaign manager can only trust that the ad is being displayed to the desired audience. Who eventually gets to see the advertisement is for an important part dependent on the algorithms of social media companies.

Efforts to Regulate Microtargeting

Ad delivery algorithms form a hidden layer of microtargeting. These algorithms are opaque, self-learning, and proprietary. Not only does this opaqueness enable the social platforms to *interfere* arbitrarily and covertly in the private sphere of citizens, and in the political communication of political parties, but the opaqueness also makes it challenging to come up with holistic regulation that takes the hidden delivery algorithms into account. In fact, current (proposed) regulations run the risk of exacerbating the problem they are meant to fix. For example, a core goal of the DSA is to provide insight into the targeting criteria formulated by the advertiser. Parties could choose not to formulate granular targeting criteria (say they only choose to target men, between 18 and 34 years old, who live in the Netherlands), and the user-facing transparency obligations would make it seem as if that party is not microtargeting. However, the users would actually be microtargeted, because the hidden ad delivery algorithm does not display ads randomly. Rather, it takes into account previous (privacy-sensitive) behavior and tries to predict which users are most likely to, for example, click on the advertisement. This means that the user, or the third-party observer, would not know a) for what goal the algorithm optimizes (e.g., clicks, or views), b) on the basis of what information the algorithm makes predictions, and c) to what extent the advertisement is actually targeted. In fact, the observer would see that ads are generally untargeted, and conclude that a random subsample of the 18-to-34-year-old men, who live in the Netherlands were displayed in the ad. But in reality, a very specific, *non-random* group of people within that larger audience of young men actually got displayed the so-called untargeted ad on the basis of their previous behavior (e.g., because they tend to click on ads, and because they are thought to agree with the political orientation of the message; see Ali et al., 2019).

Thus, the current EU proposals are bound to address only part of the picture because relevant information about the decisions of the ad delivery algorithm is not made transparent. Privacy-cognizant parties could consciously choose to only advertise without formulating strategic targeting criteria. However, without knowing it, these parties would hand over all control over who gets to see their political advertisement to the ad delivery algorithm which is optimized on the basis of privacy-violating large-scale data collection.

Conclusion

While political advertisers have always tried to tailor their messages to specific subsegments of the electorate, microtargeting techniques are continuously evolving. The advent of social platforms has placed political parties in a position of dependence. Parties are on the one hand dependent on opaque algorithms that are designed to make large-scale advertising easy for the advertiser, and profitable for the social platform. On the other hand, social platforms unburden political parties by collecting and analyzing personal data, but also by obtaining informed consent from its users. This informed consent is clearly required because microtargeting is by design at odds with privacy. Privacy can be understood as a shield against (undue) influence that works by depriving others of access to you. Social platforms, are designed to sell access to you and your personal characteristics. Unfortunately, current regulatory proposals seem to have an incomplete idea of what microtargeting is. However, we have seen that political advertisers play an increasingly small role in obtaining consent, data-collection, and overall communication with citizens. As a result, it becomes increasingly challenging for citizens to understand how their privacy is being threatened, for political advertisers to understand how their communication threatens privacy, and for lawmakers to understand how citizens' privacy can be protected.

References

Ali, M., Sapiezynski, P., Korolova, A., Mislove, A., & Rieke, A. (2019). Ad delivery algorithms: The hidden arbiters of political messaging. *ArXiv*. Retrieved from http://arxiv.org/abs/1912.04255

Barrett, B. (2021). Commercial companies in party networks: Digital advertising firms in US elections from 2006–2016 commercial companies in party networks: digital advertising firms in US elections from 2006–2016. *Political Communication*, *00*(00), 1–19. https://doi.org/10.1080/10584609.2021.1978021

Baruh, L., & Popescu, M. (2015). Big data analytics and the limits of privacy self-management. *New Media and Society*, *19*(4), 579–596. https://doi.org/10.1177/1461444815614001

Bennett, C. J. (2016). Voter databases, micro-targeting, and data protection law: can political parties campaign in Europe as they do in North America? *International Data Privacy Law*, *6*(4), 261–275. https://doi.org/10.1093/idpl/ipw021

Bond, R. M., Fariss, C. J., Jones, J. J., Kramer, A. D. I., Marlow, C., Settle, J. E., & Fowler, J. H. (2012). A 61-million-person experiment in social influence and political mobilization. *Nature*, *489*(7415), 295–298. https://doi.org/10.1038/nature11421

Boyd, D., & Crawford, K. (2012). Critical questions for big data. *Information, Communication & Society*, *4462* (June 2012), 37–41. https://doi.org/10.1080/1369118X.2012.678878

Dobber, T., & de Jong, R. (2020). Oude wijn in nieuwe zakken? Microtargeting van kiezers vroeger en nu. *Tijdschrift Voor Communicatiewetenschap*, *48*(2), 98–111.

Dobber, T., Trilling, D., Helberger, N., & de Vreese, C. (2018). Spiraling downward: The reciprocal relation between attitude toward political behavioral targeting and privacy concerns. *New Media & Society*, *21*, 1212–1231. https://doi.org/10.1177/1461444818813372.

Dobber, T. (2020). Data & democracy. Retrieved from: https://dare.uva.nl/search?identifier=40d14da9-1fad-4b14-81bf-253b417f1708

Endres, K. (2019). Targeted issue messages and voting behavior. *American Politics Research*, (1–23). https://doi.org/10.1177/1532673X19875694

Gavison, R. (1980). Privacy and the Limits of Law. *The Yale Law Journal*, *89*(3), 421–471. https://doi.org/10.2307/795891

Green, D. P., & Gerber, A. S. (2008). Get out the vote: How to increase voter turnout. In *Scientific American Mind*.

Google (2022). *Google Transparency Report*. Retrieved on May 20 2022, from: https://transparencyreport.google.com/political-ads/region/US

Google (2019). *Ad policy change*. Retrieved on Jan 10 2022, from: https://blog.google/technology/ads/update-our-political-ads-policy/

Hillygus, D. S., & Shields, T. G. (2009). *The persuadable voter: Wedge issues in presidential campaigns*. Princeton: Princeton University Press.

Howard, P. N. (2006). *New media campaigns and the managed citizen*. In Cambridge: Cambridge University Press.

Imana, B., Korolova, A., & Heidemann, J. (2021). Auditing for discrimination in algorithms delivering job ads. *The Web Conference 2021 - Proceedings of the World Wide Web Conference, WWW 2021*, 3767–3778. https://doi.org/10.1145/3442381.3450077

Karlsen, R. (2009). Campaign communication and the Internet: Party strategy in the 2005 Norwegian election campaign. *Journal of Elections, Public Opinion and Parties*, *19*(2), 183–202. https://doi.org/10.1080/17457280902799030

Kosinski, M., Stillwell, D., & Graepel, T. (2013). Private traits and attributes are predictable from digital records of human behavior. *Proceedings of the National Academy of Sciences of the United States of America*, *110*(15), 5802–5805. https://doi.org/10.1073/pnas.1218772110

Kreiss, D. (2012). *Taking our country back: The crafting of networked politics from Howard Dean to Barack Obama*. In New York, NY: Oxford University Press.

Meta (2022). *Facebook ad library*. Retrieved on May 20 2022, from: https://www.facebook.com/ads/library/report

Murray, G. R., & Scime, A. (2010). Microtargeting and electorate segmentation: Data mining the American National Election Studies. *Journal of Political Marketing*, *9*(3), 143–166. https://doi.org/10.1080/15377857.2010.497732

Nielsen, R. K. (2012). *Ground wars: Personalized communication in political campaigns*. In Princeton, NJ: Princeton University Press. https://doi.org/10.1080/10584609.2013.749620

Reiman, J. H. (1995). Driving to the panopticon: A philosophical exploration of the risks to privacy posed by the highway technology of the future. *Computer & High Technology Law Journal*, *11*(1), 27–44.

Stoycheff, E., Liu, J., Xu, K., & Wibowo, K. (2019). Privacy and the panopticon: Online mass surveillance's deterrence and chilling effects. *New Media & Society*, *21*(3), 602–619. https://doi.org/10.1177/1461444818801317

Trepte, S., Teutsch, D., Masur, P. K., Eicher, C., Fischer, M., Hennhöfer, A., & Lind, F. (2015). Do people know about privacy and data protection strategies? Towards the "Online Privacy Literacy Scale" (OPLIS). In S. Gutwirth, R. Leenes, & P. de Hert (Eds.), *Reforming European Data Protection Law* (pp. 333–365). Springer Netherlands. https://doi.org/10.1007/978-94-017-9385-8_14

Turow, J., Delli Carpini, M. X., Draper, N. A., & Williams, R. H.-W. (2012). Americans roundly reject tailored political advertising. In *Annenberg School for Communication, University of Pennsylvania.*

Tufekci, Z. (2014). Engineering the public: Big data, surveillance and computational politics. *First Monday, 19*(7), 1–14. https://doi.org/10.5210/fm.v19i7.4901

Wagner, K. (2020, April 20). This is how Facebook collects data on you even if you don't have an account. *Vox*. Retrieved from https://www.vox.com/2018/4/20/17254312/facebook-shadow-profiles-data-collection-non-users-mark-zuckerberg

Zarouali, B., Dobber, T., Pauw, G. De, & Vreese, C. De. (2020). Using a personality-profiling algorithm to investigate political microtargeting: Assessing the persuasion effects of personality-tailored ads on social media. *Communication Research*, 1–26. https://doi.org/10.1177/0093650220961965

Zuiderveen Borgesius, F. J., Möller, J., Kruikemeier, S., Fathaigh, R., Irion, K., Dobber, T., …de Vreese, C. (2018). Online political microtargeting: Promises and threats for democracy. *Utrecht Law Review, 14*(1), 82–96. https://doi.org/10.18352/ulr.420

24
HEALTH DATA AND PRIVACY

Johanna Börsting

UNIVERSITY OF APPLIED SCIENCES RUHR WEST, GERMANY

Introduction

Health data is omnipresent in our lives – not least since the outbreak of the COVID-19 pandemic in 2019 – but also due to innumerable health and fitness applications (apps) that contribute to the trend of "quantifying" and sharing "the self" (Feng et al., 2021) as well as people's need for emotional and informational support via social media. Health data can be defined as personal information about individuals' physical or mental health (e.g., symptoms, physical activity, sleep quality, or medication plans). Such data can be very intimate because it refers to the condition of a person's body and mental state, which is an integral part of identity. Therefore, the disclosure of health data can affect a person's perceived and actual level of privacy. Privacy is a complex concept consisting of different dimensions and refers to the satisfaction of fundamental needs and the demacration of the self from others (Altman, 1975; Burgoon, 1982; Westin, 1967). Every person has a basic need for privacy, although it might be more pronounced for some persons than for others. Frener et al. (2021) define the need for privacy as "an individual's cross-situational tendency to actively and consciously define, communicate and pursue a desired level of privacy." This tendency is challenged by the dynamics of our networked and digitized society, in which people, regardless of their social status or health condition (Chou et al., 2009), can share, consume, retweet, endorse, and respond to vast amounts of personal data with countless other users on various platforms and channels, especially social media (Liu et al., 2016). Seventy-six percent of over 27,000 surveyed people in the European Union use the Internet daily, 85% of them via smartphone (European Commission, 2020). Sixty-two percent of Europeans use social networking sites (SNSs, European Commission, 2020). The percentage of young people using the Internet is even higher: Ninety-eight percent of people between 15 and 24 years old use the Internet daily, while 83% of them use social networking sites (European Commission, 2020). Therefore, it is not surprising that people disclose a lot of sensitive information on social media, whether intentionally or unintentionally. On the one hand, sharing health data online can be beneficial to the user, as it may help users improve their fitness or gain social recognition, e.g., by using apps such as Runtastic, PumpUp, or Strava and benefiting from their social elements (i.e., profile, network, stream, message; Bayer et al., 2020). On the other hand, sharing health information also bears risks such as unauthorized data use by third parties, a reduced perception of control, lower autonomy, and ultimately a loss of privacy. Strikingly, most users do not know who has access to their health data, how algorithms work in the context of medical data, and whether their data and privacy are protected or endangered (Grzymek & Puntschuh, 2019; Hoque & Sorwar, 2017; Wetzels et al., 2018).

 DOI: 10.4324/9781003244677-28

This chapter discusses health data and privacy in terms of motivations for and barriers to adopting health apps and exchanging health information on social media.

Health Data in Online Contexts

Health data can be shared online via different *communication channels*, namely, one-to-one (e.g., direct messaging), one-to-many (e.g., sharing health data on SNSs), or many-to-many (e.g., engaging in a public discussion on social media).

It follows that sharing health data online involves different *communication partners* (known or unknown users or third parties). Furthermore, the sharing itself takes place via different *communication modes*, such as text-based via SNSs (e.g., Facebook, Twitter) or messenger services (e.g., WhatsApp, Telegram), video- or audio-based via videoconferencing tools or video broadcasting platforms (e.g., Skype, YouTube), or multimodal via smart devices and apps such as smart watches or fitness bracelets with social media connectivity (e.g., Fitbit). The mentioned platforms and devices have in common that they fulfill the discrete requirements of social media: They are Internet-based, allow for asynchronous and interactive communication, provide space for user-generated content, and can address large audiences (Bayer et al., 2020).

Provided information can be very sensitive and associated with different *dimensions of privacy*, namely the informational (e.g., social security number), social (e.g., contact tracing in COVID-19 apps), psychological (e.g., tracking emotions via a diary app), and physical (e.g., showing a part of the body to a physician via video appointment) dimension of privacy (Burgoon, 1982). Users' perceived and actual level of privacy should vary depending on the communication channel, communication partners, communication mode, and associated privacy dimension. For instance, Liu et al. (2016) found that health messages communicated one-to-one are very likely to receive direct feedback in terms of endorsing and replying, indicating a high level of perceived privacy between communication partners. In other cases, when users, e.g., desperately need social or medical support in dramatic situations in their personal lives and therefore decide to ask for help publicly via social media (one-to-many), the perceived and actual level of privacy should be lower (Smith & Brunner, 2016; Quinlan & Johnson, 2019).

Variables Influencing the Intention to Use Health Apps

Whether people use health apps or share health data on social media is often related to personal characteristics and individual experiences. So far, sociodemographic variables such as age, gender, or cultural background (Onyeaka et al., 2021; Utz et al., 2021; Vervier et al., 2019), users' eHealth literacy, i.e., "the ability to seek out, find, evaluate and appraise, integrate, and apply what is gained in electronic environments toward solving a health problem" (Norman & Skinner, 2006, p. 2), prior experience and medical history (Abbasi et al., 2020; Onyeaka et al., 2021) as well as attitudes towards sharing health data online (Kriwy & Glöckner, 2020) have been investigated, among other factors.

In a systematic review of studies on smartphone apps for health and well-being, Szinay et al. (2020) identified app awareness, availability and accessibility, low cost, recommendations by others, and curiosity as relevant factors for the uptake of health apps. Obtaining information, an interactive and positive communication style, personalization and personification, health practitioner support, community networking, social media connectivity, social competition, feedback, and perceived utility are examples of factors that lead to longer engagement with such apps. App literacy and user guidance are related to both uptake and further engagement with health and well-being apps (Szinay et al., 2020). Among the mentioned factors, *personalization* and *social media connectivity* are essential with respect to users' privacy and the scope of this chapter. Personalization includes turning on and off specific features (Anderson et al., 2016), setting individual goals (Baskerville et al., 2016), receiving personalized recommendations (Peng et al., 2016), or tailoring app functionality to one's identity and personal history (Baskerville et al., 2016). Linking personal data from health and well-being apps to social media increases the size of the audience who has access to the data (and thus potentially the amount of social support), while at the same time reducing the user's level of privacy. Szinay et al. (2020) found that social media connectivity is seen as a benefit by users who primarily strive for appreciation and responses, and as a threat by those who are afraid of social stigmatization (e.g., related to weight management or smoking) or loss of control over their data.

Focusing on negative emotions, Fox (2020) analyzed users' concerns related to using mobile health apps. She identified unauthorized use of data, accessing data with malicious intent, and loss of control as the most prevalent concerns and negative predictors for acceptance of data storage by the system. Accordingly, control over personal data and transparency regarding accessibility and storage were identified as users' most prevalent desires. Vervier et al. (2019) came to similar results: Privacy concerns and non-transparent or unauthorized data-sharing practices were negatively related to attitudes toward health app usage.

Empirical research so far shows that whether users share or seek out health data on social media depends on various variables. Users seem to be caught between the benefits of this practice and potential negative consequences and uncertainties. Below, we will reflect on this tension from a theoretical lens.

Theoretical Approaches to Health Data and Privacy in Social Media

Many theories have been applied as a conceptual foundation for explaining behavior, attitudes, and intentions related to sharing or searching for health information online. Frequently considered theories are uncertainty management theory (e.g., by Rains, 2014), self-determination theory (e.g., by Lee & Lin, 2020), the technology acceptance model (e.g., by Yun & Park, 2010), health belief model (e.g., by Kriwy & Glöckner, 2020), or protection motivation theory (e.g., by Hui et al., 2020) – to name just a few. Due to the overwhelming number of theoretical approaches, Wang et al. (2021) identified the three most important theories for health information-seeking behavior, namely the comprehensive model of information-seeking (Johnson & Meischke, 1993), the situational theory of problem-solving (Kim & Grunig, 2011), and the planned risk information-seeking model (Kahlor, 2010). These theories have in common that the pivotal outcome variable is online information-seeking behavior, which is influenced by psychological (e.g., attitudes, concerns, risk perception), instrumental (e.g., utility, trustworthiness), contextual (e.g., internet use), and demographic (e.g., age, gender, social status) factors. In their meta-analysis, Wang et al. (2021) evaluated empirical work applying at least one of the three theories. A total of 44 articles were identified, mostly studies conducted in Western countries (74%) and specifically the US (53%), and mostly addressing health information-seeking behavior on the Internet in general instead of focusing on specific platforms, channels, or situations. They found that quality, trustworthiness, and utility of information are the most influential variables for online health information-seeking behavior and that instrumental factors had a stronger impact on users' health information-seeking behavior than psychological factors. Studies focusing on social media found that perceived benefits are positively related to sharing and searching for health information on social media (Li et al., 2018), and health concerns are positively related to searching for health information and emotional support on Facebook (Oh et al., 2013). However, information-seeking behavior is not the only activity involving health data that affects privacy. Downloading health apps or disclosing personal health information online are also common activities that do not necessarily fit into this theoretical conceptualization. Recent empirical studies have applied privacy theories and conceptualizations, such as the privacy calculus (Culnan & Armstrong, 1999; see also chapter 7 by Dienlin on the privacy calculus) to explain users' behavior related to actively disclosing personal information in a health context: Bol and Antheunis (2022) found that patients who consider having an appointment with a clinician via Skype weigh costs (e.g., data misuse or less personal relationship with the clinician) and benefits (e.g., saving time and effort) when deciding whether or not to have an online appointment and disclose intimate information. In line with the privacy calculus, users' willingness to disclose was positively related to perceived benefits, while their willingness to disclose was lower when they perceived higher costs (Bol & Antheunis, 2022).

Le et al. (2022) went one step further and systematized applied theories related to specific topics: "Personal health information sharing," "health-related knowledge sharing," "general health message diffusion," and "outcomes of health information sharing." Health information-seeking, which was the main focus in the study by Wang et al. (2021), was not included as an individual category. Still, both studies found support for protection motivation theory: On the one hand related to information-seeking (Wang et al., 2021), and on the other hand related to information sharing (Le et al., 2022). In their systematic review of 58 articles on health data on online platforms (18 articles on SNSs), Le et al. (2022) found eight articles on personal health information sharing that applied the privacy calculus and protection motivation theory as their theoretical foundation.

In sum, the variety of critical variables and theories makes it difficult to capture the whole universe of health data and privacy on social media in a single theoretical approach. Nevertheless, an overarching theme can be identified: The individual's tension between (a) gaining benefits in terms of informational, emotional, or practical support, and (b) fearing disadvantageous outcomes.

Current Developments and Implications

So far, we have learned that research on health data and privacy is diverse and divergent. Also, there is no key theory that considers all facets, predictors, and outcomes of users' intended and actual behavior, intentions, and attitudes related to sharing and obtaining health data online. Wang et al. (2021) concluded that there is a need for further theoretical refinement and that no theoretical conceptualization "fully reflects the antecedents of individuals' OHIS [online health information-seeking]" (p. 1170).

Furthermore, context-specific findings were rare until 2020. In the meta-review by Wang et al. (2021), only six out of 44 studies focused on specific contexts such as social media (two) and mobile communication (four). All other studies considered "the Internet" as the contextual frame. The emergence of the many COVID-19 studies since 2020 represents a first counter-development. Here, we observe that a particular event created an urge to think about specific use cases that had previously received less consideration, namely contact tracing and precise observation of symptoms, and how regulations in these areas affect users' privacy.

Sharing Health Data for the Benefit of Society

In a representative quantitative study on COVID-19 apps for contact tracing and symptom reporting, Utz et al. (2021) identified several motivators for and barriers to app adoption by users in Germany, the US, and China: Previous knowledge about and experience with health apps were positive predictors in all three samples. Only for German users, satisfaction with the accuracy of location tracking and the collection of data on close encounters were further positive predictors for use of COVID-19 apps. For US users, being older, having positive attitudes towards research institutions and state government, contact tracing, the purpose of symptom checks, and limited data storage were identified as positive predictors. Data access by private companies negatively influenced app adoption by users from all three countries. Privacy concerns and demographic data collection were identified as negative predictors for engaging with COVID-19 apps among users in Germany and the US, while both positively influenced app adoption in China. Users from China generally reported being more willing to use COVID-19 apps than German and US users (Utz et al., 2021). The results of this representative study reveal differences but also similarities between countries. The greatest commonality is that technological functionality is highly relevant for app usage, while the biggest difference between China on the one hand, and Germany and the US on the other, is the influence of privacy concerns and opinions regarding the collection of demographic data. This might be rooted in cultural differences and country-specific regulations. Altmann et al. (2020) also identified differences in the usage of COVID-19 apps between users from different countries: Users from Germany and the US were generally less willing to install the app than users from France, Italy, and the UK. Reasons for not installing the app included privacy, security, and transparency concerns as well as a low trust in the national government and fears that surveillance would continue after the pandemic (Altmann et al., 2020). Consequently, individuals' cultural and geographical backgrounds should be considered not only in research but also when deriving practical implications, e.g., when developing campaigns to encourage use of health-related (tracing) apps.

The Crux for Health Apps

This recent example shows that sharing health data via online services can not only help an individual but also critically contribute to well-being on a societal level. This puts users' concerns regarding data usage and privacy in a new light. For people willing to use contact tracing apps, such concerns are likely to be less important compared to the benefit of fighting a pandemic. Still, many people refuse to use such apps, e.g., due to low technical literacy or low social motives (Utz et al., 2021). Therefore, it is important to raise awareness of the advantages and benefits of health data tracking in this context and to increase users' and non-users' knowledge about the functionality of such apps. Utz et al. (2021) call for policymakers to ensure that personal user data is not shared with third parties (which is already the case). Horstmann et al. (2020, p. 5) call for "more precise and targeted science communication to convince people" to use the app. Users' fear that COVID-19 apps could be "the start of a new era of surveillance" (Utz et al., 2021, p. 14) illustrates the ongoing relevance of this recommendation. Interestingly, the German "Corona-Warn-App" already adheres to valid privacy and security guidelines and collects less data than most other popular apps. While the "Corona-Warn-App" processes as little personal data as possible, does not collect data that would enable the provider or other parties to infer users' identity, and refrains from evaluating and analyzing usage behavior (RKI, 2021), popular apps for tracking users' mental health status (e.g., "Calm") or sensitive physical conditions (e.g., "Eisprung und Fruchtbarkeit [ovulation and fertility]")[1] collect vast amounts of personal and identifying data. The "Calm" app, for instance, tracks user data such as content consumed within the app, server log data, information about the device used to access the app, the user's name (e.g., in order to determine gender or sex), cookies, web beacons, social media data, and more. The "Eisprung und Fruchtbarkeit [ovulation and fertility]" app collects and partly shares personal data such as location, sexual orientation, purchases, health data, and app interactions. However, the public discussion around security and fear of surveillance concerns COVID-19 apps rather than other apps that are completely *voluntarily* adopted by users – without perceived external pressure or recommendation. Some people reported that they would only follow the urgent recommendation to use COVID-19 contact tracing apps with "perfect data protection" (Simko et al., 2020) or if the app guaranteed complete privacy and accuracy. This might be the crux: People do not want to be *forced* to do something. They want to decide on their own whether to use an app or not. Being able to make their own decision contributes to users' perception of autonomy and privacy, but might in some cases (e.g., due to a lack of technical literacy) result in precarious situations. In line with this dilemma, many users prefer to use well-functioning health apps that are *tailored* to their individual needs (e.g., Szinay et al., 2020). In most cases, however, this can only work if users provide the app with substantial personal information so that algorithms can steer the information that users receive.

Implications of Health Data Use and Privacy Perceptions on Social Media

Dogruel et al. (2022) argue that it is necessary to raise users' awareness, knowledge, and critical evaluation of algorithms in order to increase their reflection strategies and coping behavior when using online services. This seems reasonable – not least in light of the fact that half of Europeans do not know what an algorithm is (Grzymek & Puntschuh, 2019), but also due to users' desire for more transparency regarding data processing and utilization (Wetzels et al., 2018). However, transparently providing information on data processing and utilization is only helpful if users know how to interpret information and translate knowledge into action (i.e., active data protection). Related studies on privacy literacy already revealed the potential of increasing context-related literacy (e.g., Schäwel et al., 2021; see also chapter 11 by Masur, Hagendorff & Trepte on privacy literacy). A higher degree of privacy literacy, for instance, is positively connected to future data protection behavior of Internet users (Schäwel et al., 2021).

Furthermore, understanding users' perception of the online environment is crucial for deriving implications regarding health data use and privacy. Trepte (2021) developed the social media privacy model, introducing pivotal variables that influence users' privacy perception and regulation in social media. Key elements are social media affordances (anonymity, editability, association, persistence) and the perceived availability of privacy mechanisms (e.g., exerting control, trusting others; Trepte, 2021). Social media affordances shape our perception of and behavior on social media. For example, editability refers to the ability to edit or modify messages, posts, and profiles, e.g., in order to enact control as a privacy mechanism. This would make it possible to change one's real name into a fake name, resulting in a stronger perception of privacy. However, third parties would still be able to identify a person using a fake name based on other data. Consequently, non-literate users would erroneously feel secure, whereas users with high literacy regarding algorithms and privacy would probably take further actions to control their privacy.

Users' privacy management depends on individual and contextual factors and might be affected by their understanding of algorithms and digital affordances. Thus, it is necessary to integrate key findings from each conceptual area to provide a more solid foundation for research on health data and privacy and to derive theoretical and practical implications for users and society.

Future Directions

Users do not want their data to be collected and analyzed by third parties. Still, they want to obtain support that is as suitable as possible. Which perspective is more significant to users depends on situational and personal factors, as is well observed with respect to the privacy calculus (e.g., Bol & Antheunis, 2022). However, in the context of health information, one aspect has been neglected so far: Urgency. Basically, the more sensitive the data, the more cautious users should be regarding disclosure. However, when urgency is high, concerns become less important. Thus, when considering health data, we can observe the privacy calculus functioning at its best.

One conclusion for future research is that the processes of sharing and accessing health information on social media should be analyzed depending on both levels of sensitivity and underlying urgency. The level of sensitivity results from the communication channels, involved parties, communication modes, and dimensions of privacy affected. For instance, publicly (channel) sharing on Facebook (mode) that one has a depressive disorder (social and psychological dimension of privacy) without restricting access (involved parties) will have a higher sensitivity level than sharing with a friend (channel) via a messenger (mode) that one has an appointment with a physician the next day (informational privacy). However, if someone is desperately looking for advice or a good therapist (high urgency), privacy concerns might not prevent this person from publicly disclosing their associated mental health problems on social media, despite their high sensitivity level.

Thus, one first step would be to refine our understanding of "health data" by considering different levels of sensitivity and urgency in empirical research and theory development. Future studies should include sensitivity and urgency as mediating or moderating variables in order to better understand their impact on the privacy calculus for sharing and accessing health data on social media. In line with this, we should consider specific information and use cases instead of treating "the Internet" as a homogeneous concept (see Wang et al., 2021). Thereby, social media affordances should take on a larger role in empirical research. Without knowing which affordances users perceive, it is difficult to say which privacy mechanisms they might consider and how they perceive their privacy. Thus, future studies should build on the social media privacy model (Trepte, 2021) and include association, persistence, editability, and anonymity as relevant contextual variables in research designs.

At a meta-level, future research should seek to emphasize how we can gain benefits and mitigate risks from sharing and accessing health data on social media, for instance by implementing more nuanced measures to increase users' awareness and literacy regarding the challenges and opportunities of a digitized society, and appropriate science communication (e.g., via large-scale awareness campaigns).

Note

1 "Eisprung und Fruchtbarkeit [ovulation and fertility]": https://play.google.com/store/apps/datasafety?id=com.inidamleader.ovtracker Calm: https://www.calm.com/de/privacy-policy

References

Abbasi, R., Zare, S., & Ahmadian, L. (2020). Investigating the attitude of patients with chronic diseases about using mobile health. *International Journal of Technology Assessment in Health Care*, *36*(2), 139–144. https://doi.org/10.1017/S0266462320000070

Altman, I. (1975). *The environment and social behavior: Privacy, personal space, territory, crowding*. Brooks/Cole Publishing Company.

Altmann, S., Milsom, L., Zillessen, H., Blasone, R., Gerdon, F., Bach, R., Kreuter, F., Nosenzo, D., Toussaert, S., & Abeler, J. (2020). Acceptability of app-based contact tracing for COVID-19: Cross-country survey study. *JMIR MHealth and UHealth*, *8*(8), e19857. https://doi.org/10.2196/19857

Anderson, K., & Burford, O., Emmerton, L. (2016). Mobile health apps to facilitate self-care: A qualitative study of user experiences. *PloS One*, *11*(5). https://doi.org/10.1371/journal.pone.0156164

Baskerville, N. B., Dash, D., Wong, K., Shuh, A., & Abramowicz, A. (2016). Perceptions toward a smoking cessation app targeting LGBTQ+ youth and young adults: A qualitative framework analysis of focus groups. *JMIR Public Health Surveillance*, *2*(2). https://doi.org/10.2196/publichealth.6188

Bayer, J. B., Triệu, P., & Ellison, N. B. (2020). Social media elements, ecologies, and effects. *Annual Review of Psychology*, *71*, 471–497. https://doi.org/10.1146/annurev-psych-010419-050944

Bol, N., & Antheunis, M. L. (2022). Skype or skip? Causes and consequences of intimate self-disclosure in computer-mediated doctor-patient communication. *Media Psychology*, 1–18. https://doi.org/10.1080/15213269.2022.2035769

Burgoon, J. K. (1982). Privacy and communication. *Communication Yearbook*, *6*(4), 206–249. https://doi.org/10.1080/23808985

Chou, W. Y. S., Hunt, Y. M., Beckjord, E. B., Moser, R. P., & Hesse, B. W. (2009). Social media use in the United States: Implications for health communication. *Journal of Medical Internet Research*, *11*(4), e48. https://doi.org/10.2196/jmir.1249

Culnan, M. J., & Armstrong, P. K. (1999). Information privacy concerns, procedural fairness, and impersonal trust: An empirical investigation. *Organization Science*, *10*(1), 104–115. https://doi.org/10.1111/15404560.00067

Dogruel, L., Masur, P. K., & Joeckel, S. (2022). Development and validation of an algorithm literacy scale for Internet users. *Communication Methods and Measures*, *16*(2), 115–133. 10.1080/19312458.2021.1968361

European Commission. (2020). *Special Eurobarometer 499: Europeans' attitudes towards cyber security*. Kantar Belgium.

Feng, S., Mäntymäki, M., Dhir, A., & Salmela, H. (2021). How self-tracking and the quantified self promote health and well-being: Systematic review. *Journal of Medical Internet Research 23*(9). https://doi.org/10.2196/25171

Fox, G. (2020). "To protect my health or to protect my health privacy?" A mixed-methods investigation of the privacy paradox. *Journal of the Association for Information Science and Technology, 71*(9), 1015–1029. https://doi.org/10.1002/asi.24369

Frener, R., Wagner, J., & Trepte, S. (2021, Mai). Development and validation of the Need for Privacy Scale (NFP-S). *71st conference of the international communication association (ICA)*. Denver, USA, digital conference.

Grzymek, V., & Puntschuh, M. (2019). *What Europe knows and thinks about algorithms: Results of a representative survey*. https://doi.org/10.11586/2019008

Hoque, R., & Sorwar, G. (2017). Understanding factors influencing the adoption of mHealth by the elderly. An extension of the UTAUT model. *International Journal of Medical Informatics, 101*, 75–84. https://doi.org/10.1016/j.ijmedinf.2017.02.002

Horstmann, K. T., Buecker, S., Krasko, J., Kritzler, S., & Terwiel, S. (2021). Who does or does not use the 'Corona-Warn-App'and why?. *European Journal of Public Health, 31*(1), 49–51.

Hui, K., Anawar, S., Othman, N., Ayop, Z., & Hamid, E. (2020). User privacy protection behavior and information sharing in mobile health application. *International Journal of Advanced Trends in Computer Science and Engineering, 9*(4), Article 155, 5250–5258. http://www.warse.org/IJATCSE/static/pdf/file/ijatcse155942020.pdf

Johnson, J. D., & Meischke, H. (1993). A comprehensive model of cancer-related information-seeking applied to magazines. *Human Communication Research, 19*(3), 343–367. https://doi.org/10.1111/j.1468-2958.1993.tb00305.x

Kahlor, L. (2010). PRISM: A planned risk information-seeking model. *Health Communication, 25*(4), 345–356. https://doi.org/10.1080/10410231003775172

Kim. J.-N., & Grunig, J. E. (2011). Problem solving and communicative action: A situational theory of problem solving. *Journal of Communication, 61*(1), 120–149. https://doi.org/10.1111/j.1460-2466.2010.01529.x

Kriwy, P., & Glöckner, R. (2020). Einstellung zum Datenschutz und mHealth-Nutzung [Attitudes toward privacy and mHealth use]. *Prävention und Gesundheitsförderung, 15*(3), 218–225. https://doi.org/10.1007/s11553-019-00755-y

Le, H. L., Hoang, P. A., & Pham, H. C. (2022). Sharing health information across online platforms: A systematic review. *Health Communication*. https://doi.org/10.1080/10410236.2021.2019920

Lee, S. T., & Lin, J. (2020). The influence of offline and online intrinsic motivations on online health information-seeking. *Health Communication, 35*(9), 1129–1136. https://doi.org/10.1080/10410236.2019.1620088

Li, Y., Wang, X., Lin, X., & Hajli, M. (2018). Seeking and sharing health information on social media: A net valence model and cross-cultural comparison. *Technological Forecasting and Social Change, 126*, 28–40. https://doi.org/10.1016/j.techfore.2016.07.021

Liu, X., Lu, J., & Wang, H. (2016). When health information meets social media: Exploring virality on Sina Weibo. *Health Communication, 32*(19), 1252–1260. https://doi.org/10.1080/10410236.2016.1217454

Norman, C. D., & Skinner, H. A. (2006). eHEALS: The eHealth literacy scale. *Journal of Medical Internet Research, 8*(4). https://doi.org/10.2196/jmir.8.4.e27

Oh, H. J., Lauckner, C., Boehmer, J., Fewins-Bliss, R., & Li, K. (2013). Facebooking for health: An examination into the solicitation and effects of health-related social support on social networking sites. *Computers in Human Behavior, 29*(5), 2072–2080. https://doi.org/10.1016/j.chb.2013.04.017

Onyeaka, H., Firth, J., Kessler, R. C., Lovell, K., & Torous, J. (2021). Use of smartphones, mobile apps and wearables for health promotion by people with anxiety or depression: An analysis of a nationally representative survey data. *Psychiatry Research, 304*, 114120. https://doi.org/10.1016/j.psychres.2021.114120

Peng, W., Yuan, S., & Holtz, B. E. (2016). Exploring the challenges and opportunities of health mobile apps for individuals with type 2 Diabetes living in rural communities. *Telemedicine Journal and E-Health* (9), 733–738. https://doi.org/10.1089/tmj.2015.0180

Quinlan, M. M., & Johnson, B. (2019). #Motherhoodishard: Narrating our research and mothering in the postpartum stage through texting and social media. *Health Communication, 35*(6). https://doi.org/10.1080/10410236.2019.1587694

Rains, S. A. (2014). Health information seeking and the World Wide Web: An uncertainty management perspective. *Journal of Health Communication, 19*(11), 1296–1307. https://doi.org/10.1080/10810730.2013.872731

Schäwel, J., Frener, R., Masur, P. K., & Trepte, S. (2021). Learning by doing oder doing by learning? Die Wechselwirkung zwischen Online-Privatheitskompetenz und Datenschutzverhalten [The interdependency between online privacy literacy and data protection behavior]. *Medien- & Kommunikationswissenschaft, 69*(2). https://doi.org/10.5771/1615-634X-2021-2-1

Simko, L., Calo, R., Roesner, F., & Kohno, T. (2020). COVID-19 contact tracing and privacy: Studying opinion and preferences. *ArXiv*. https://doi.org/10.48550/arXiv.2005.06056

Smith, S. A., & Brunner, S. R. (2016). The great whoosh: Connecting an online personal health narrative and communication privacy management. *Health Communication, 31*(1), 12–21. https://doi.org/10.1080/10410236.2014.930551

Szinay, D., Jones, A., Chadborn, T., Brown, J., & Naughton, F. (2020). Influences on the uptake of and engagement with health and well-being smartphone apps: Systematic review. *Journal of Medical Internet Research,* (5). https://doi.org/10.2196/17572

Trepte, S. (2021). The Social Media Privacy Model: Privacy and communication in the light of social media affordances. *Communication Theory, 31*(4), 549–570. https://doi.org/10.1093/ct/qtz035

Utz, C., Becker, S., Schnitzler, T., Farke, F. M., Herbert, F., Schaewitz, L., Degeling, M., & Dürmuth, M. (2021). Apps against the spread: Privacy implications and user acceptance of COVID-19-related smartphone apps on three continents. *Proceedings of the 2021 CHI conference on human factors in computing systems*, 1–22. https://doi.org/10.1145/3411764.3445517

Vervier, L., Valdez, A., & Ziefle, M. (2019). "Attitude" – mHealth apps and users' insights: An empirical approach to understand the antecedents of attitudes towards mHealth applications. In L. A. Maciaszek & M. Ziefle (Eds.), *5th International Conference on Information and Communication Technologies for Ageing Well and e-Health* (pp. 213–221). Springer. https://doi.org/10.5220/0007720002130221

Wang, X., Shi, J., & Kong, H. (2021). Online health information-seeking: A review and meta-analysis. *Health Communication, 36*(10), 1163–1175. https://doi.org/10.1080/10410236.2020.1748829

Westin, A. F. (1967). *Privacy and freedom*. Atheneum.

Wetzels, M., Broers, E., Peters, P., Feijs, L., Widdershoven, J., & Habibovic, M. (2018). Patient perspectives on health data privacy and management: "Where is my data and whose is it?". *International Journal of Telemedicine and Applications*, 3838747. https://doi.org/10.1155/2018/3838747

Yun, E. K., & Park, H.-A. (2010). Consumers' disease information-seeking behaviour on the Internet in Korea. *Journal of Clinical Nursing, 19*(19–20), 2860–2868. https://doi.org/10.1111/j.1365-2702.2009.03187.x

PART 5

Solutions to Preserve Social Media Privacy

25

NUDGES (AND DECEPTIVE PATTERNS) FOR PRIVACY

Six Years Later

Alessandro Acquisti[1], *Idris Adjerid*[2], *Laura Brandimarte*[3], *Lorrie Faith Cranor*[1], *Saranga Komanduri*[4], *Pedro Giovanni Leon*[5], *Norman Sadeh*[1], *Florian Schaub*[6], *Yang Wang*[7], and *Shomir Wilson*[8]

[1]CARNEGIE MELLON UNIVERSITY, USA
[2]VIRGINIA TECH, USA
[3]UNIVERSITY OF ARIZONA, USA
[4]CIVIS ANALYTICS, USA
[5]BANCO DE MEXICO, MEXICO
[6]UNIVERSITY OF MICHIGAN, USA
[7]UNIVERSITY OF ILLINOIS AT URBANA-CHAMPAIGN, USA
[8]PENNSYLVANIA STATE UNIVERSITY, USA

In 2017, *ACM Computing Surveys* published our review of the rapidly expanding field of research on behavioral hurdles and nudges in privacy and information security (Acquisti et al., 2017). The review summarized research across several fields on the impact of asymmetric information, bounded rationality, and heuristics and biases (*behavioral hurdles*) on online security and privacy decision-making. It then examined an array of strategies – such as information treatments and behavioral interventions (*nudges*) – intended to assist users' online security and privacy decisions. The review also considered how industry may exploit those very biases and hurdles by designing interfaces that nudge users towards riskier decisions or more personal disclosures – a phenomenon now popularized under the term *dark patterns*, *deceptive patterns*, or *deceptive design*. Finally, the review considered the ethics, practicality, and effectiveness of nudges for privacy and security. Since the publication of that article, several developments of note have happened in this area of research. This chapter augments and expands our 2017 review by capturing novel research in the area and highlighting those developments that we find most relevant. While our original manuscript covered research on both privacy and information security, here we focus – consistent with the theme of this book – on developments in the field of privacy.

In this chapter, we follow the structure of the original 2017 article. We first consider the expanding literature on behavioral hurdles in privacy decision-making. In so doing, we also revisit the ongoing debate on rationality in consumer privacy choice and then, briefly (as the topic is also covered in other chapters in this book) the so-called privacy paradox. We then review novel results on the effectiveness (or lack thereof) of privacy nudges, and, next, the rapidly expanding body of

DOI: 10.4324/9781003244677-30

work on dark patterns. Finally, we consider whether, several years after the publication of our original piece, any new conclusion may be drawn on the effectiveness of nudges as tools for helping individuals manage their privacy online.

The Evolving Literature on Privacy Behavioral Hurdles

Since the publication of our original review, scholars have kept unveiling evidence of heuristics, biases, and hurdles in privacy decision-making (e.g., Alsarkal et al. 2019; Chang et al. 2016; Tomaino et al. 2021). With those terms, we refer to an array of factors that can affect behavior and decision-making and make it more challenging for individuals to achieve the degree of information privacy they desire.

In one of the most striking recent examples of such results, Tomaino et al. (2021) find robust and consistent evidence of privacy valuations violating the norms of procedural invariance – one of the key tenets of rational choice theory (Scott, 2000). According to procedural invariance, normatively equivalent procedures for measuring preferences (in this case, privacy preferences) should produce the same preference ordering in terms of choice options. Tomaino et al. (2021) test whether consumers value their private data the same when that data is exchanged for money as when it is exchanged for goods (such as access to online services). Across multiple pre-registered experiments, they find a systematic difference between data-for-cash and data-for-goods valuations: the same data is valued more in exchanges for money than in exchanges for goods. As the authors note, this systematic difference suggests that at least one of the two valuations cannot be normatively valid: "consumers cannot simultaneously hold two different market valuations for the same good (i.e., for their data), all else equal." The results represent a violation of transitivity in privacy preferences, an axiomatic condition of utility maximization.

Some of the authors of this chapter have also advanced, in a separate piece, an additional argument for why privacy decision-making is especially challenging in online environments (Acquisti et al., 2022). This may be due to the fact that in online interactions human beings lack the physical, sensorial cues that they may have adapted and evolved to use as signals of the presence of others in their physical proximity, and thus as triggers for privacy responses. Similarly, in a study with young children, presence or absence of visual cues substantially affected children's awareness and understanding of data flows and processing. For example, children did not generally anticipate information about them flowing back to companies (no cues) but exhibited a good understanding of why they would see certain recommended videos (visual cue) based on what they've watched before (Sun et al., 2021). The mismatch between our evolved cognitive systems' reliance on sensorial cues for detecting threats in our physical environment, and the absence (or manipulation) of those cues in online environments, may contribute to explain why human ability to maneuver privacy boundaries in the "real" world (Altman, 1975, 1977) does not transpose readily to online contexts.

Online – unlike in the physical world – we do not see, hear, or feel the presence of strangers around us who may peek over our personal information and our disclosures.

Privacy decision-making hurdles are particularly concerning in light of recent results by Hofstetter et al. (2017) and Buckman et al. (2019).

Hofstetter et al. (2017) note that relative to traditional, offline forms of communication, there is an enhanced permanence to digital sharing. And yet they find that, paradoxically, the challenges of managing the impressions we make on others are "exacerbated by temporary-sharing technologies," as they "reduce privacy concerns, in turn increasing disclosure of potentially compromising information." And Buckman et al. (2019) find that making individuals more aware of privacy risks can be ineffective at changing behavior even when it may increase self-reported privacy concerns. This result adds to the body of evidence casting doubts over the effectiveness of purely informational intervention in the privacy domain. As we noted elsewhere, transparency (and control) may be necessary, but certainly not sufficient tools for privacy protection (Acquisti et al., 2013; Cranor, 2012).

Reflecting the expanding body of work in this area, in the last few years some reviews of the behavioral privacy literature have emerged (Acquisti et al., 2015, 2020; Waldman, 2020). These reviews attempt to connect diverse streams of behavioral work on privacy and security decision-making and tease out the policy implications of that work. While we get to those implications further below in this chapter, we highlight one of them here. Contrary to the simplistic notion that the success of digital disclosure technologies (such as social media) demonstrates a weaning interest in privacy in contemporary society, the evidence for privacy behaviors – in Altman's terms, the attempt to manage the boundaries of public and private – is not just nearly ubiquitous offline (Altman, 1977), but also quite common online (notwithstanding the unique hurdles we have highlighted in the previous pages). As some of the authors have written (Acquisti et al., 2020), we manage those boundaries all the time, both online and offline, often without realizing we are doing so (for instance, when we choose visibility settings for our posts on social media, much like when we leave a group of people to answer a personal phone call). The fact that we engage in boundary-regulating behavior all the time, however, does not mean that we "protect" our data every time. Privacy is not merely the hiding of data (as conceptualized in early work by Chicago School economists such as Posner (1981)), but rather a dialectic and dynamic process of boundary regulation, as theorized by Altman. Furthermore, realized privacy often differs from desired privacy (again, using Altman's terminology) precisely due to the impact of both behavioral and economic factors that the literature in this field has considered. In fact, some of that research has flown into the related stream of work on dark patterns, which we discuss further below.

Is Privacy Decision Making (Ir)rational?

Tomaino et al. (2021)'s intransitivity results are also useful in consolidating and in clarifying, some years following our original manuscript, what implication we should or should not derive from this stream of behavioral privacy literature. Is privacy decision-making "rational," as some authors may seem suggest (Lee & Weber, 2019), or, in fact, "irrational"?

In our view, neither. Highlighting behavioral biases and hurdles and pointing out problems with the *economic* interpretation of "rational" behavior is not the same as implying that consumers are "irrational," or that they make random or nonsensical decisions, or that they do not know what they want when it comes to privacy. Nor does it imply that preferences and concerns for privacy never predict behavior.[1] Rather, it means pointing out that observed behavior often deviates from the *economically rational*, theoretical decision-making path – that is, it deviates systematically and predictably from the predictions of rational choice theory, which would posit that agents with complete information and unbounded power to process it always make consistent choices based on stable preferences unaffected by non-normative factors (such as, for instance, the format and presentation of a user interface). Those deviations may be caused by asymmetric information, bounded rationality, violations of procedural invariance, and so forth. Combined with economic barriers (such as the absence of meaningful market alternatives for privacy-conscious consumers), those deviations may cause even privacy-conscious individuals to fail to attain in the marketplace their desired levels of privacy (Acquisti et al., 2020).

As some of the authors of this chapter previously observed (Acquisti et al., 2015, 2020; Acquisti et al., 2013), it seems more plausible to look at (privacy) decision-making as a result of both deliberative (utility-maximization focused) and behavioral factors: "while privacy decision making is, no doubt, partly strategic, there are reasons to believe that individuals' preferences for privacy may not be as stable or as internally consistent as the standard economic perspective assumes" (Acquisti et al., 2013), and to look at people's privacy perceptions and behaviors from a *situational* perspective

(Masur, 2019). Consistent with Kahneman's System I and II framework (Kahneman, 2011), Petty and Cacioppo's elaboration likelihood model (ELM) (Petty & Cacioppo, 1986), Loewenstein and O'Donoghue's work on the interaction between deliberative systems and affective systems in decision making (Loewenstein & O'Donoghue, 2004), there is evidence that privacy choice is affected by, *both*, the so-called privacy calculus (Dinev & Hart, 2006) and by the heuristics and biases (Knijnenburg et al., 2017) we focused on in our original article (Acquisti et al., 2017) and again in this chapter.

For instance, Adjerid et al. (2018) have used a series of online experiments to investigate the role of both normative and behavioral factors in the study of privacy choice. They find that both factors influence consumer privacy decisions. Surprisingly, the impact of normative factors diminishes between hypothetical and actual choice settings; vice versa, the impact of behavioral factors becomes more pronounced going from hypothetical to actual choice settings. Relatedly, in an ingenious experiment, Lin was able to find evidence of the impact of both "intrinsic" components (a "taste" for privacy) and "instrumental" components (expected economic trade-offs) in individuals' preferences for privacy (Lin, 2019).

In short, much of the literature on behavioral hurdles we covered in the original *Computing Surveys* article critiques the rationalist economic approach to privacy decision-making that looks at privacy choice solely through the lenses of rational choice theory, as a simple process of utility maximization with no cognitive limitations or incidence of procedural invariance, and which takes observed market behaviors as truthful signals of individuals' revealed preferences. Such a critique does not aim to replace that approach with a model of unpredictable consumer irrationality where individuals' preferences for privacy are erratic, and behaviors are chaotic. Rather, it juxtaposes to the rationalist approach a model where privacy calculus may direct individuals on a certain path of action, but preferences are malleable and context-dependent (Acquisti et al., 2015), and systematic (and therefore predictable) deviations from that path are common and originate from multiple factors. This alternative approach highlights the challenges of privacy choice, how those choices can be swayed and guided by platforms through dark patterns, why behavioral interventions (nudges) may be useful, and ultimately why revealed preferences arguments do not always capture actual privacy preferences – or, in Altman's terms, why realized privacy may differ from desired privacy.

The Paradox of the Privacy Paradox

The Altmanian observation that realized privacy can differ from desired privacy brings us to a related (albeit distinct) issue: the discussion around the so-called privacy paradox – the alleged dichotomy (or gap, or mismatch) between privacy mental states (such as attitudes, concerns, or intentions) and actual behaviors. Whether biases and hurdles can make it so that actual behaviors do not always match privacy preferences or intentions was a central theme in our original review (Acquisti et al., 2017). In this section, our goal is not to provide a comprehensive review of this field of research, but instead to offer some observations on the evolution of the *debate* on this topic in recent years.

The paradox *of* the privacy paradox is that, after nearly two decades of research, more studies keep being published about the paradox of privacy (see reviews in Kokolakis (2017) and Gerber et al. (2018)) and yet a debate still lingers over its actual existence (Dienlin et al., 2019; Solove, 2021; Yu et al., 2020). Based on how the debate has evolved in the years since the publication of our original review, we have concluded that the focus on the *paradoxical* or *non-paradoxical* nature of a possible dichotomy between privacy mental states and behaviors has become a source of confusion (Acquisti et al., 2020; Colnago, Cranor, & Acquisti, in press).

The debate over the privacy paradox emerges, in great part, due to lexicological confusion over the interpretation of the term "paradox" (Acquisti et al., 2020), which has two similar but subtly contrasting meanings: a "self-contradictory statement that at first seems true" (Merriam-Webster), but also a "seemingly contradictory" statement that is "perhaps true." The dichotomy between stated mental states (such as preferences or intentions) and behaviors is the (apparent) *contradiction*. Some scholars appear to look at the dichotomy through the lenses of the first definition: they search for explanations of that dichotomy, and when they find them, they conclude that there is no self-contradiction, and thus also no paradox (see, e.g., Solove 2021).

Other scholars appear to look at the dichotomy through the lenses of the second definition, which puts the emphasis on the fact that statements that are *seemingly* in contradiction could in fact be simultaneously correct. For the latter scholars, it's the dichotomy that is paradoxical, even though it can be explained; for them, the fact that dichotomies between privacy attitudes and behaviors can be explained does not imply that the underlying dichotomies do not in fact exist (Acquisti et al., 2020).

It's doubtful that those who interpret the paradox one way will start interpreting it in the alternative way. Which is why we believe that the focus on the paradoxical nature of possible privacy dichotomies does not seem any longer fruitful – in fact, it may be one of the reasons for the lack of resolution of the debate itself. More fruitful, in our view, is to point our attention towards whether or not gaps or mismatches or dichotomies between stated mental states regarding privacy and privacy behaviors in fact exist, and if so, what would that imply for privacy regulation and public policy.

And here we face a second source of confusion in the literature, and the second reason why a resolution to the debate has not yet arisen. Gaps or mismatches between privacy mental states and actual behaviors have been shown to exist, over and over again, in both within- and between-subject studies – be them mismatches between specific attitudes and behaviors (Barth et al., 2019), or specific concerns and behaviors (Acquisti & Gross, 2006), or privacy expectations and behaviors (Madejski et al., 2012), and even specific behavioral intentions and behaviors (Norberg et al., 2007). As a matter of fact, indirect evidence of those gaps also arises from several behavioral privacy experiments that do not focus on the so-called paradox but capture the effect of non-normative factors on privacy behavior. Starting from the plausible assumption that individuals' attitudes *before* an experimental treatment should be similarly distributed in the random control and treatment subsets of a sample of subjects, if behaviors change across conditions *after* behavioral interventions that do not alter participants' trade-offs (for instance, merely altering the order in which privacy options are presented to participants), that would imply a divergence between ex-ante attitudes and ex-post behaviors based entirely on non-normative factors – which is precisely the point of the privacy paradox literature.

And yet, several other studies have instead shown consistency between mental states and behaviors (see, e.g., Dienlin et al. 2019; Trepte et al. 2020). Are these latter studies in contradiction with the former? We do not believe that to be the case. We must remind ourselves that privacy behavior is contextual, and the data flows are often invisible – thus it is entirely reasonable to expect that dichotomies or mismatches will arise in some scenarios and not in others. Furthermore, which particular mental state a behavior is found to be contradicting with varies across studies, with privacy needs, concerns, expectations, preferences, and intentions often being conflated (Acquisti et al., 2020; Colnago et al., 2022). Once we recognize that, we can see that the second source of confusion in the debate surrounding the privacy paradox is that the debate itself seems to have been predicated on a faulty assumption: that one can provide an absolute, binary answer to the question: do privacy attitudes, concerns, or intentions predict privacy behaviors?

Attempting to answer such question in general, absolute terms is impossible, because it would require an untenable assumption to be correct: that either mental states *always* precisely predict all privacy behaviors, or they never do. And neither scenario seems likely. The debate resolves itself only when we allow for mental states and behaviors to be understood in context, rather than as universals, and accept that, from scenario to scenario, and from person to person, mental states sometimes may in fact predict, and other times may not, privacy behaviors.

The implications of this recognition are critical, and bring us back to the discussion regarding rationality or irrationality of privacy behavior. The interpretation to beware of is that uncovered dichotomies summarily invalidate stated mental states regarding privacy. In reality, presence of a dichotomy in some contexts does not mean that consumers do not care for privacy, or do not know what they want. Instead, it is more likely to mean that economic or behavioral factors may have made it harder for people to realize their desired privacy. Similarly, absence of a dichotomy in other contexts does not mean that behaviors will also match preferences (due to the contrasting evidence mentioned above). That evidence should not allow us to conclude that no intervention is warranted to assist individuals in their quest for privacy.

Nudges and Behavioral Interventions

The central and larger portion of our original survey article was devoted to reviewing studies of nudges aimed at improving, assisting, and ameliorating privacy and security online choices. Since incomplete information, heuristics, and cognitive or behavioral biases can lead users to make decisions that result in undesirable outcomes, a number of behavioral interventions have been proposed to assisting privacy (and security) decision-making. The interventions we covered in our original survey were drawn from different research fields, including usability, persuasive technologies, and behavioral decision research. They often evolved separately from each other. We referred to them broadly as "privacy" nudges, following Thaler and Sunstein (2008)'s NUDGES acronym: iNcentives, Understand mappings, Defaults, Give feedback, Expect errors, and Saliency/Structuring complex choices. In our original review, we extended Thaler and Sunstein's categorization by also considering design recommendations from usability research, debiasing, and persuasive technologies. We ended up clustering behavioral interventions into six interrelated and not mutually exclusive categories: Information, Presentation, Defaults, Incentives, Reversibility (and error resiliency), and Timing.

Work in this area has grown unabatedly. In fact, since the publication of our ACM manuscript, at least a couple of new efforts at surveying the literature on privacy nudges have emerged, such as the meta-analysis by Ioannou et al. (2021), and a recent, comprehensive review of online choice architecture by the UK Competitions Markets Authority (CMA) (UK, n.d.). Below, we highlight a few of the recent studies published in this area.

Story et al. tested the effectiveness of nudges based on protection motivation theory (PMT), action planning implementation intention, and coping planning implementation intention (Story et al., 2022). The nudges were designed to raise awareness of Tor Browser and help participants form accurate perceptions of it. The authors found the PMT-based intervention to increase the use of Tor Browser to be effective in both the short and long run. Liu et al. tested the impact of recommendations proposed by a Personalized Privacy Assistant for mobile app permission settings on Android users as well as the impact of subsequent privacy nudges designed to motivate users to possibly reconsider recommendations they had accepted (Liu et al., 2016). They found that a vast majority of the recommendations were adopted by participants, but only a small fraction of settings were modified in response to the subsequent privacy nudges, suggesting that the recommendations were doing a good job at reflecting people's privacy preferences. Ortloff et al. found nudges effective in improving browsing privacy in a naturalistic field study lasting three weeks (Ortloff et al., 2021). In a six-week field study, Ghosh et al. studied the impact of audience-group nudges on Facebook location disclosure (Ghosh & Singh, 2021). The nudges reminded users of the visibility of their location data, and decreased the amount of location disclosure on Facebook. Zimmerman et al. tested the impact of nudges implemented by altering the interface of a search engine results page

(Zimmerman et al., 2019). The nudges were tested in the context of participants' health search, and were found to improve participants' privacy outcomes without negatively impacting the quality of their decision-making. Bergram et al. investigated whether changes in choice architecture can increase the informed consent and privacy awareness of participants (Bergram et al., 2020). They found that changes in phrasing can significantly boost the number of participants who chose to read terms of services and privacy policies. And Diaz et al. found that risk-based behavioral interventions can have a preventative effect on survey participants' self-disclosure behavior (Díaz Ferreyra et al., 2020).

The British CMA's interest in this field is representative of a broader phenomenon: a growing interest across diverse stakeholders in examining how to counter the significant power that online platforms hold on consumer behavior, and how to nudge effectively and ethically.[2] At the same time, it is important to note that not all studies have found evidence of privacy nudges being effective – raising questions on their capabilities as instruments of public policy. Various empirical studies have, in fact, shown their limitations. Unclear, null, or even backfiring results were reported in Kroll and Stieglitz (2021), Bahirat et al. (2021), Barev et al. (2021), Rodriguez-Priego et al. (2021), as well as in Warberg et al. (2019) (in the context of personalizing and targeting nudges based on individuals' characteristics). As a matter of fact, concerns have grown over time both over the effectiveness of nudges as tools of public policy, and in terms of the rise of dark patterns (or "anti-nudges," as we called them in our original manuscript): while the effectiveness of protective nudges is still debated, dark patterns have become ubiquitous. We discuss concerns over dark patterns and concerns over the public policy effectiveness of nudges in the last few pages of this chapter.

The Historical Roots of Dark Patterns: A New Term for an Old Phenomenon

In our original *ACM Computing Surveys* 2017 piece, we used the term "anti-nudges" to refer to the exploitation of behavioral mechanisms by industry to promote self-disclosure and privacy behaviors more likely to benefit platforms and service providers rather than users. Outside the privacy domain, and in the broader context on online interfaces, this phenomenon has been popularized under the term "dark patterns" (a term we briefly mentioned in our original survey).

Research on dark patterns has grown significantly in the last few years, including policy-oriented pieces, experiments, and efforts to systematize knowledge through taxonomies (Gray et al., 2018; Gray et al., 2021; Gunawan et al., 2021; Luguri & Strahilevitz, 2021; Mulligan et al., 2020; Narayanan et al., 2020). One of the most interesting streams of this research has focused on uncovering the actual prevalence of dark patterns in online interfaces (Mathur et al., 2019), and on highlighting how industry has employed dark patterns to respond to (and in some sense bypass) privacy regulatory requirements (Nouwens et al., 2020; Utz et al., 2019).

Dark patterns are instances of manipulative user interfaces that nudge users towards certain behaviors. This is a new term, specific to interface design, for an old phenomenon – in the U.S., deceptive marketplace practices were one of the targets of the Federal Trade Commission Act since 1914. Behavioral scholars have studied for decades the way industries like gambling (Schüll, 2012), food, or alcohol leverage consumer psychology to further producers' interest at the cost of consumer welfare (Boush et al., 2009). As Daniel Kaufman, then acting director of the Bureau of Consumer Protection at the U.S. Federal Trade Commission, observed at a 2021 workshop on dark patterns, "[f]or decades, direct mail marketers have relied on well-tried psychological tricks and design tactics, like prechecked boxes, hard to find and read disclosures, and confusing cancellation policies, to get consumers to part with their money. [...] The old tricks and tactics have moved online and been repurposed for the digital marketplace" (U.S. Federal Trade Commission, 2021).

In the digital privacy domain, research dating back two decades has highlighted, first, the role of behavioral hurdles in hampering privacy decision-making (Acquisti, 2004), and then – using both lab and field experiments – how choice architecture (and, in particular, interface design choices by platforms) can in fact leverage those hurdles and affect personal disclosure or privacy valuations: from Facebook altering default visibility settings for certain fields of personal information (Stutzman et al., 2013), to Android and iOS operating systems taking different routes at framing privacy location settings on mobile devices (Adjerid et al., 2019), to alternative framings dramatically altering individuals' valuations of their data (Acquisti et al., 2013), with extensive ramification for consumers' view of their own privacy.[3] While we do not believe the phenomenon of dark patterns to be novel from a behavioral perspective, we believe that the term has been useful in crystallizing and coalescing academics', regulators', and civil society's focus on the vast power that choice architects who control the design of online interfaces can have on people's behavior, in issues ranging from mundane (small purchase decisions) to societally momentous (voting in national elections (Aral & Eckles, 2019)). The growing importance of research on manipulative interfaces is reflected in the observation that events focusing on or dealing with dark patterns have been recently hosted by public agencies such as the Federal Trade Commission[4] and by the California Privacy Protection Agency in the U.S.,[5] and that – as noted above – the UK CMA has recently produced a review of online choice architecture research (UK, n.d.), and the European Data Protection Board has recently published guidance on dark patterns in social media.[6]

Are Privacy Nudges Effective?

Regulating dark patterns may limit the impact they have on individuals' autonomy of decision-making, and decrease the harm the latter can suffer online. To what extent, instead, can nudges help counter the significant power that platforms, service providers, and third parties can have on individuals' behaviors?

As it should be clear from our analysis in the previous pages, an evenhanded review of the literature on privacy nudges shows that behavioral interventions can work in some scenarios, be ineffective in others, and backfire in some. And this is assuming that nudges will, in fact, be deployed – an assumption not necessarily met in practice: industry's ability to deploy dark patterns (rather than pro-consumer nudges) in response to regulatory initiative highlights, once again, the power of choice architects and platform designers to influence individual choice to meet business objectives. Once we combine behavioral hurdles (nudges may sometimes be ineffective, whereas platforms and service providers, as choice architects, can ultimately control how interfaces influence consumers), with systemic economic imbalances in the market for privacy and for personal data (see Acquisti et al. (2020)), what can we conclude about the likelihood of nudges being able to help people manage and protect their privacy (and security) online?

Our original ACM piece devoted a section to this topic, in which we considered various challenges surrounding the deployment of nudges – not just their effectiveness, but also their ethicality (an issue that continues to be central to the research on nudges: Meske & Amojo, 2020; Verentilnykova & Dogruel, 2021). We also considered issues surrounding their ultimate implementations: Who nudges whom? Can consumers nudge themselves, through self-commitment devices? Should industry do so – but under what incentives? Should governments, without falling into paternalistic traps? To be clear, our stance in the original *ACM Computing Surveys* manuscript was one of *positive* analysis (i.e., our goal was "to document ongoing efforts in this area, discuss some of their limitations, and highlight their potential"), not *normative* analysis (such as promoting or advocating their deployment). But we did ultimately look at behavioral interventions with hope, as an "emerging area [...] that could lead to the design of a variety of tools and systems that effectively assist humans with online security and privacy decisions without imposing overly prescriptive models of what the 'right' decisions might be." We also observed how, whether we nudge or not with the intent of helping users make better privacy decisions, "we should realize that every design decision behind the construction of every online [...] or offline [...] system or tool we use has the potential to influence user' behaviors, regardless of whether the designer, or the user, is fully aware of those influences and their consequences."

While we still see value and promise in behavioral interventions, we have become increasingly skeptical about relying on nudges as privacy saviors. The concern here is analogous to one we highlighted earlier in this chapter, in the context of the discussion of notice and consent mechanisms: transparency and control are necessary but certainly not sufficient solutions for privacy protection (Acquisti et al., 2013; Cranor, 2012). Self-regulatory approaches that focus on making privacy more transparent and more useful can be helpful in some regards, but must contend with the underlying limitations of all regimes based on notice and consent, the problems arising from consumer *responsabilization* (Acquisti et al., 2022, 2020; Waldman, 2021), and – worse – the risk that "attention paid towards self-regulatory approaches with dubious effectiveness may come at the cost of focusing on solutions that get at the heart of the privacy problem" (Adjerid et al., 2013).

Similarly, in the case of soft paternalistic approaches, we feel that nudges (from informational intervention to changes in default settings) have a role to play in assisting user decisions (particularly in terms of casting a light on how platform interfaces, design choices, and defaults can themselves influence users, and helping users communicate about and learn about the systems they use as well as their own privacy preferences); but are no substitute for regulatory interventions – for both behavioral and economic reasons (Acquisti et al., 2022, 2020). On this, we are in agreement with a recent article by Chater and Loewenstein who observe: "An influential line of thinking in behavioral science [...] is that many of society's most pressing problems can be addressed cheaply and effectively at the level of the individual, without modifying the system in which individuals operate [...] [W]e now believe this was a mistake. Results from such interventions have been disappointingly modest. But more importantly, they have guided many (though by no means all) behavioral scientists to frame policy problems in individual, not systemic, terms" (Chater & Loewenstein, 2022). We do believe that there are tools and frameworks that can help user privacy choice – from more usable privacy technologies; to semi-automated personalized privacy assistants (PPAs) designed to alleviate unnecessarily burdensome decision-making processes (Das et al., 2018; Liu et al., 2016; Zhang et al., 2020, 2021). In fact, we look at technology-driven solutions as key. But, six years after the publication of our original manuscript, we still believe in the need for those tools and frameworks to be integrated in a framework of regulatory intervention that puts meaningful privacy protections first and avoids the trap of consumer responsibilization.

What Is Next for Research on Privacy Nudges?

In this chapter, we extended our 2017 *ACM Computing Surveys* review on behavioral interventions in privacy and security by considering recent developments in the area. We conclude by offering some thoughts about the future of this research.

The research on behavioral hurdles consumers face when making online privacy (and security) decisions has evolved into research on dark patterns, highlighting the fact that those hurdles are often manufactured, or exploited, by platforms and service providers. Research as well as regulatory interest in this area are rapidly expanding. We are hopeful that research efforts will highlight under which conditions dark patterns are more likely to sway individuals' behavior, and in which scenarios they are particularly dangerous for consumers. Research on nudges aimed at assisting users is growing, too, but arguably at a lower pace. Our hope in this case is that privacy nudges research will succeed in tying behavioral interventions together with broader regulatory efforts mandating baseline guidelines of privacy protection. Nudges can be useful, but not alone.

Notes

1 As noted in Acquisti et al. (2020), sometimes evidence both *for* and *against* a correspondence of privacy preferences and behaviors can arise from the same study: "broad attitudes toward privacy were simultaneously found to be uncorrelated to disclosure patterns on Facebook, but correlated with the likelihood of joining the network."

2 For instance, the IEEE started a working group on ethical nudges: https://standards.ieee.org/ieee/7008/7095/.

3 As noted in 2013 in Acquisti et al. (2013), "[v]ery often, in online settings, users' decisions are affected by defaults chosen by the providers of Internet services or embodied in the architecture of Internet technologies, which can create either a WTP or a WTA transaction for consumers' data. [...] Our findings suggest a vicious (or virtuous) circle of privacy valuations of potential interest to policy makers: those who feel they have less (more) privacy tend to value privacy less (more) and become more (less) likely to accept monetary offers for their data; giving away (protecting) their data, in turn, may make individuals feel they have less (more) privacy—and so on." See also the public comments submitted by one of the authors to the Federal Trade Commission's workshop "Bringing Dark Patterns to Light" (Acquisti, 2021).

4 https://www.ftc.gov/news-events/events/2021/04/ bringing-dark-patterns-light-ftc-workshop

5 https://cppa.ca.gov/meetings/agendas/20220329_30.pdf. In fact, the CCPA regulations also explicitly prohibit dark patterns when offering opt-outs: "A business shall not use a method that is designed with the purpose or has the substantial effect of subverting or impairing a consumer's choice to opt-out," https://oag.ca.gov/sites/all/files/agweb/pdfs/privacy/ccpa-add-adm.pdf.

6 https://edpb.europa.eu/our-work-tools/documents/public-consultations/2022/ guidelines-32022-dark-patterns-social-media_en.

References

Acquisti, A. (2004). Privacy in electronic commerce and the economics of immediate gratification. In *Proceedings of the 5th ACM conference on electronic commerce* (pp. 21–29). New York, NY, USA: ACM.

Acquisti, A. (2021, May). *Comment from Carnegie Mellon University – Alessandro Acquisti*. Bringing Dark Patterns to Light: An FTC Workshop – Public Comments. Retrieved from https://downloads.regulations.gov/FTC-2021-0019-0104/attachment_1.pdf (FTC-2021-0019-0104)

Acquisti, A., Adjerid, I., Balebako, R., Brandimarte, L., Cranor, L. F., Komanduri, S., ...Wilson, S. (2017, Aug). Nudges for privacy and security: Understanding and assisting users' choices online. *ACM Computing Surveys, 50* (3). https://doi.org/10.1145/3054926

Acquisti, A., Adjerid, I., & Brandimarte, L. (2013). Gone in 15 seconds: The limits of privacy transparency and control. *IEEE Security & Privacy, 11* (4), 72–74.

Acquisti, A., Brandimarte, L., & Hancock, J. (2022). How privacy's past may shape its future. *Science, 375* (6578), 270–272.

Acquisti, A., Brandimarte, L., & Loewenstein, G. (2015). Privacy and human behavior in the age of information. *Science, 347* (6221), 509–514.

Acquisti, A., Brandimarte, L., & Loewenstein, G. (2020). Secrets and likes: The drive for privacy and the difficulty of achieving it in the digital age. *Journal of Consumer Psychology, 30* (4), 736–758.

Acquisti, A., & Gross, R. (2006). Imagined communities: Awareness, information sharing, and privacy on the Facebook. In *Proceedings of the 6th international conference on Privacy Enhancing Technologies (pet '06)* (pp. 36–58). Springer.

Acquisti, A., John, L. K., & Loewenstein, G. (2013). What is privacy worth? *The Journal of Legal Studies, 42* (2), 249–274.

Adjerid, I., Acquisti, A., Brandimarte, L., & Loewenstein, G. (2013). Sleights of privacy: framing, disclosures, and the limits of transparency. In *Proceedings of symposium on usable privacy and security (soups '13)* (pp. 1–11). ACM.

Adjerid, I., Acquisti, A., & Loewenstein, G. (2019). Choice architecture, framing, and cascaded privacy choices. *Management Science, 65* (5), 2267–2290.

Adjerid, I., Peer, E., & Acquisti, A. (2018). Beyond the privacy paradox: Objective versus relative risk in privacy decision making. *MIS Quarterly, 42* (2), 465–488.

Alsarkal, Y., Zhang, N., & Xu, H. (2019). Protecting privacy on social media: Is consumer privacy self-management sufficient? In *Proceedings of the 52nd Hawaii international conference on system sciences*.

Altman, I. (1975). The environment and social behavior: privacy, personal space, territory, and crowding. Brooks/Cole Pub. Co; First Printing edition.

Altman, I. (1977). Privacy regulation: Culturally universal or culturally specific? *Journal of Social Issues*, *33* (3), 66–84.

Aral, S., & Eckles, D. (2019). Protecting elections from social media manipulation. *Science*, *365* (6456), 858–861.

Bahirat, P., Willemsen, M., He, Y., Sun, Q., & Knijnenburg, B. (2021). Overlooking context: How do defaults and framing reduce deliberation in smart home privacy decision-making? In *Proceedings of the 2021 chi conference on human factors in computing systems* (pp. 1–18).

Barev, T., Schwede, M., & Janson, A. (2021). The dark side of privacy nudging – an experimental study in the context of a digital work environment. In *Proceedings of the 54th Hawaii international conference on system sciences* (p. 4114).

Barth, S., de Jong, M. D., Junger, M., Hartel, P. H., & Roppelt, J. C. (2019). Putting the privacy paradox to the test: Online privacy and security behaviors among users with technical knowledge, privacy awareness, and financial resources. *Telematics and Informatics*, *41*, 55–69.

Bergram, K., Bezençon, V., Maingot, P., Gjerlufsen, T., & Holzer, A. (2020). Digital nudges for privacy awareness: From consent to informed consent?. Twenty-Eigth European Conference on Information Systems. Marrakesh, Morocco.

Boush, D. M., Friestad, M., & Wright, P. (2009). *Deception in the marketplace: The psychology of deceptive persuasion and consumer self-protection*. Routledge.

Buckman, J. R., Bockstedt, J. C., & Hashim, M. J. (2019). Relative privacy valuations under varying disclosure characteristics. *Information Systems Research*, *30* (2), 375–388.

Chang, D., Krupka, E. L., Adar, E., & Acquisti, A. (2016). Engineering information disclosure: Norm shaping designs. In *Proceedings of the 2016 chi conference on human factors in computing systems* (pp. 587–597).

Chater, N., & Loewenstein, G. (2022). The i-frame and the s-frame: How focusing on the individual-level solutions has led behavioral public policy astray. *Available at SSRN 4046264*.

Colnago, J., Cranor, L. F., & Acquisti, A. (2023). Is there a reverse privacy paradox? An exploratory analysis of gaps between privacy perspectives and privacy-seeking behaviors. *Proceedings on Privacy Enhancing Technologies*, 455–476.

Colnago, J., Cranor, L. F., Acquisti, A., & Jain, K. H. (2022). Is it a concern or a preference? an investigation into the ability of privacy scales to capture and distinguish granular privacy constructs. In *Eighteenth symposium on usable privacy and security (soups 2022)*.

Cranor, L. F. (2012). Necessary but not sufficient: Standardized mechanisms for privacy notice and choice. *Journal on Telecommunications and High Technology Law*, *10*, 273.

Das, A., Degeling, M., Smullen, D., & Sadeh, N. (2018). Personalized privacy assistants for the internet of things: Providing users with notice and choice. *IEEE Pervasive Computing*, *17* (3), 35–46.

Díaz Ferreyra, N. E., Kroll, T., Aïmeur, E., Stieglitz, S., & Heisel, M. (2020). Preventative nudges: Introducing risk cues for supporting online self-disclosure decisions. *Information*, *11* (8), 399.

Dienlin, T., Masur, P. K., & Trepte, S. (2019). A longitudinal analysis of the privacy paradox. *New Media & Society*, 14614448211016316.

Dinev, T., & Hart, P. (2006). An extended privacy calculus model for e-commerce transactions. *Information Systems Research*, *17* (1), 61–80.

Gerber, N., Gerber, P., & Volkamer, M. (2018). Explaining the privacy paradox: A systematic review of literature investigating privacy attitude and behavior. *Computers & Security*, *77*, 226–261.

Ghosh, I., & Singh, V. (2021). "not all my friends are friends": Audience-group-based nudges for managing location privacy. *Journal of the Association for Information Science and Technology*, *73*(6), 797–810.

Gray, C. M., Kou, Y., Battles, B., Hoggatt, J., & Toombs, A. L. (2018). The dark (patterns) side of UX design. In *Proceedings of the 2018 chi conference on human factors in computing systems* (pp. 1–14).

Gray, C. M., Santos, C., Bielova, N., Toth, M., & Clifford, D. (2021). Dark patterns and the legal requirements of consent banners: An interaction criticism perspective. In *Proceedings of the 2021 chi conference on human factors in computing systems* (pp. 1–18).

Gunawan, J., Pradeep, A., Choffnes, D., Hartzog, W., & Wilson, C. (2021). A comparative study of dark patterns across web and mobile modalities. *Proceedings of the ACM on Human-Computer Interaction*, *5* (CSCW2), 1–29.

Hofstetter, R., Rüppell, R., & John, L. K. (2017). Temporary sharing prompts unrestrained disclosures that leave lasting negative impressions. *Proceedings of the National Academy of Sciences*, *114* (45), 11902–11907.

Ioannou, A., Tussyadiah, I., Miller, G., Li, S., & Weick, M. (2021). Privacy nudges for disclosure of personal information: A systematic literature review and meta-analysis. *PloS one*, *16* (8), e0256822.

Kahneman, D. (2011). *Thinking, fast and slow*. Macmillan.

Knijnenburg, B., Raybourn, E., Cherry, D., Wilkinson, D., Sivakumar, S., & Sloan, H. (2017). Death to the privacy calculus? *Available at SSRN 2923806.*

Kokolakis, S. (2017). Privacy attitudes and privacy behaviour: A review of current research on the privacy paradox phenomenon. *Computers & Security, 64*, 122–134.

Kroll, T., & Stieglitz, S. (2021). Digital nudging and privacy: improving decisions about self-disclosure in social networks. *Behaviour & Information Technology, 40* (1), 1–19.

Lee, Y., & Weber, R. (2019). *Revealed privacy preferences: Are privacy choices rational?* (Tech. Rep.). Working Paper. https://www.dropbox.com/s/w6q5v5dzpsqferw/Revealed%20Privacy%20Preferences%202021-12-10.pdf?dl=0

Lin, T. (2022). Valuing intrinsic and instrumental preferences for privacy. *Marketing Science, 41*(4), 663–681.

Liu, B., Andersen, M. S., Schaub, F., Almuhimedi, H., Zhang, S., Sadeh, N., Acquisti, A., & Agarwal, Y. (2016). Follow my recommendations: A personalized privacy assistant for mobile app permissions. In *Twelfth symposium on usable privacy and security (soups 2016)* (pp. 27–41).

Loewenstein, G., & O'Donoghue, T. (2004). Animal spirits: Affective and deliberative processes in economic behavior. *Available at SSRN 539843.*

Luguri, J., & Strahilevitz, L. J. (2021). Shining a light on dark patterns. *Journal of Legal Analysis, 13* (1), 43–109.

Madejski, M., Johnson, M., & Bellovin, S. M. (2012). A study of privacy settings errors in an online social network. In *2012 IEEE international conference on pervasive computing and communications workshops* (pp. 340–345).

Masur, P. K. (2019). *Situational privacy and self-disclosure: Communication processes in online environments.* Springer Cham.

Mathur, A., Acar, G., Friedman, M. J., Lucherini, E., Mayer, J., Chetty, M., & Narayanan, A. (2019). Dark patterns at scale: Findings from a crawl of 11k shopping websites. *Proceedings of the ACM on Human-Computer Interaction, 3* (CSCW), 1–32.

Meske, C., & Amojo, I. (2020). Ethical guidelines for the construction of digital nudges. https://doi.org/10.48550/arXiv.2003.05249

Mulligan, D. K., Regan, P. M., & King, J. (2020). The fertile dark matter of privacy takes on the dark patterns of surveillance. *Journal of Consumer Psychology, 30* (4), 767–773.

Narayanan, A., Mathur, A., Chetty, M., & Kshirsagar, M. (2020). Dark patterns: Past, present, and future: The evolution of tricky user interfaces. *Queue, 18* (2), 67–92.

Norberg, P. A., Horne, D. R., & Horne, D. A. (2007). The privacy paradox: Personal information disclosure intentions versus behaviors. *Journal of Consumer Affairs, 41* (1), 100–126.

Nouwens, M., Liccardi, I., Veale, M., Karger, D., & Kagal, L. (2020). Dark patterns after the gdpr: Scraping consent pop-ups and demonstrating their influence. In *Proceedings of the 2020 chi conference on human factors in computing systems* (pp. 1–13).

Ortloff, A.-M., Zimmerman, S., Elsweiler, D., & Henze, N. (2021). The effect of nudges and boosts on browsing privacy in a naturalistic environment. In *Proceedings of the 2021 conference on human information interaction and retrieval* (pp. 63–73).

Petty, R. E., & Cacioppo, J. T. (1986). The elaboration likelihood model of persuasion. In L. Berkowitz (Ed.), *Advances in experimental social psychology* (pp. 123–205). New York: Academic Press.

Posner, R. A. (1981). The economics of privacy. *The American Economic Review, 71* (2), 405–409.

Rodriguez-Priego, N., van Bavel, R., & Monteleone, S. (2021). Nudging online privacy behaviour with anthropomorphic cues. *Journal of Behavioral Economics for Policy, 5* (1), 45–52.

Schüll, N. D. (2012). *Addiction by design.* Princeton University Press.

Scott, J. (2000). Rational choice theory. *Understanding Contemporary Society: Theories of the Present, 129*, 126–138.

Solove, D. J. (2021). The myth of the privacy paradox. *The George Washington Law Review, 89*, 1.

Story, P., Smullen, D., Chen, R., Yao, Y., Acquisti, A., Cranor, L. F., ...Schaub, F. (2022). Increasing adoption of tor browser using informational and planning nudges. *Proceedings on Privacy Enhancing Technologies, 2022* (2), 152–183.

Stutzman, F., Gross, R., & Acquisti, A. (2013). Silent listeners: The evolution of privacy and disclosure on Facebook. *Journal of Privacy and Confidentiality, 4* (2), 7–41.

Sun, K., Sugatan, C., Afnan, T., Simon, H., Gelman, S. A., Radesky, J., & Schaub, F. (2021). "They see you're a girl if you pick a pink robot with a skirt": A qualitative study of how children conceptualize data processing and digital privacy risks. In *Proceedings of the 2021 chi conference on human factors in computing systems* (pp. 1–34).

Thaler, R. H., & Sunstein, C. R. (2008). *Nudge: improving decisions about health, wealth, and happiness.* New Haven, CT, USA: Yale University Press.

Tomaino, G., Wertenbroch, K., & Walters, D. J. (2021). Intransitivity of consumer preferences for privacy.

Trepte, S., Scharkow, M., & Dienlin, T. (2020). The privacy calculus contextualized: The influence of affordances. *Computers in Human Behavior, 104*, 106–115.

UK, G. (n.d.). Research and analysis evidence review of online choice architecture and consumer and competition harm.

U.S. Federal Trade Commission. (2021). *Bringing dark patterns to light: An FTC workshop.* https://www.ftc.gov/news-events/events/2021/04/bringing-dark- patterns-light-ftc-workshop.

Utz, C., Degeling, M., Fahl, S., Schaub, F., & Holz, T. (2019). (Un)informed consent: Studying GDPR consent notices in the field. In *Proceedings of the 2019 ACM sigsac conference on computer and communications security* (pp. 973–990).

Veretilnykova, M., & Dogruel, L. (2021). Nudging children and adolescents toward online privacy: An ethical perspective. *Journal of Media Ethics, 36* (3), 128–140.

Waldman, A. E. (2020). Cognitive biases, dark patterns, and the 'privacy paradox'. *Current Opinion in Psychology, 31*, 105–109.

Waldman, A. E. (2021). *Industry unbound: The inside story of privacy, data, and corporate power.* Cambridge University Press.

Warberg, L., Acquisti, A., & Sicker, D. (2019). Can privacy nudges be tailored to individuals' decision making and personality traits? In *Proceedings of the 18th ACM workshop on privacy in the electronic society* (pp. 175–197).

Yu, L., Li, H., He, W., Wang, F.-K., & Jiao, S. (2020). A meta-analysis to explore privacy cognition and information disclosure of internet users. *International Journal of Information Management, 51*, 102015.

Zhang, S., Feng, Y., Bauer, L., Cranor, L., Das, A., & Sadeh, N. (2020, December). Understanding people's privacy attitudes towards video analytics technologies. *Technical Report CMU-ISR-20-114, Carnegie Mellon University, School of Computer Science.*

Zhang, S., Feng, Y., Bauer, L., Cranor, L., Das, A., & Sadeh, N. (2021). *Did you know this camera tracks your mood? modeling people's privacy expectations and preferences in the age of video analytics* (Tech. Rep.). Retrieved from https://par.nsf.gov/biblio/10289276

Zimmerman, S., Thorpe, A., Fox, C., & Kruschwitz, U. (2019). Privacy nudging in search: Investigating potential impacts. In *Proceedings of the 2019 conference on human information interaction and retrieval* (pp. 283–287).

26
COMMUNICATING INFORMATION SECURITY

Spyros Kokolakis[1] *and Aggeliki Tsohou*[2]

[1]UNIVERSITY OF THE AEGEAN, GREECE
[2]IONIAN UNIVERSITY, GREECE

Introduction

Information security and informational privacy are two distinct but closely related concepts. Information security refers to the protection of information availability, integrity, and confidentiality (ISO 27001: 2013). Information privacy pertains to the ability of individuals to control their personal data and determine their use. The protection of informational privacy requires the adoption of effective security practices and the use of appropriate security tools. Thus, we may argue that information security is a prerequisite for privacy, especially in this age where huge amounts of personal data are collected, accumulated, and processed.

Security communication in the context of social media has several facets. First, security communication addresses social media users to provide them with information on threats, security practices, and security and privacy-enhancing tools, as well as to raise their security and privacy awareness. Second, security communication also takes place within digital communities. For example, social media platforms may have an interest to run awareness campaigns and to inform the community of their users on privacy and security issues. Third, several organizations, such as Computer Emergency Response Teams (CERTs) and data protection authorities, address data processing companies to provide them with guidance or to alert them on emerging threats. Finally, an important aspect of security communication refers to intra-organizational communication that targets employees and aims to enhance awareness, as well as to achieve compliance with organizational security policies.

The content of security communication is also multidimensional. Security and privacy threats are complex and sophisticated and need to be explained to the average user. Additionally, the threat landscape is dynamic and new threats constantly emerge. Users need to be kept up to date with new threats and new attack methods. On the other hand, security is a very technical issue, thus users need appropriate guidance on applying protective strategies, practices, methods, and tools.

The means of communication constitute a key factor for the effectiveness of communication. Choosing the appropriate language, media, and form of communication is a challenging task and requires an interdisciplinary approach. In general, designing and implementing security communication requires systematic planning. Communication plans should consider the needs and characteristics of the target audience, the content of communication, and the selection of appropriate means of communication. Communication planning should also consider cognitive, social, and cultural issues that influence the effectiveness of communication.

DOI: 10.4324/9781003244677-31

Background

Security communication aims to raise users' awareness and entails several concepts. We present below the concepts which are broadly associated with users' security behavior and the design and implementation of effective communication.

Awareness

Security awareness has been associated with users' compliance to information security policies (Bulgurcu et al., 2010) and users' behavioral change (Okenyi & Owens, 2007). Security awareness refers to users' knowledge about information security, the cognition of security policies, and the overall knowledge and understanding of potential issues related to information security and their ramifications (Bulgurcu et al., 2010).

Risk and Risk Perception

According to best practices (ISO 27001:2013), security protection commonly follows a risk-based approach. *Risk* is typically expressed in terms of a combined assessment of the consequences of an event and the associated likelihood of occurrence (ISO 27001:2013). *Information security risk* is associated with the potential that threats will exploit vulnerabilities of information asset(s) and thereby cause harm to an organization (ISO 27000: 2018). For example, the estimation of ransomware risk includes the estimation of the likelihood of a ransomware attack occurrence combined with the severity of the impact that ransomware may incur.

The way that users understand risk-related concepts is of essence for security communication because risk perceptions drive users' security behaviors and decisions. *Risk perceptions* refer to the way that people understand risk-related issues. Thus, risk perceptions refer to users' perceived likelihood of a threat occurrence and associated vulnerability, perceived severity of a threat, perceived efficacy of recommended protective mechanisms, and others (Bulgurcu et al., 2010; Herath and Rao, 2009). Risk perceptions are influenced by several parameters, including security awareness programs, users' organizational commitment, social pressure and normative beliefs, habit, personality traits, and biases (Bulgurcu et al., 2010; Herath & Rao, 2009; Sommestad et al., 2014; Tsohou et al., 2015).

Users' Intention, Attitude, and Behavior

The design and implementation of effective security communication targets, among others, to enhance positive or desired security behaviors. Research studies have analyzed security behaviors, based on behavioral theories such as the theory of reasoned action (Fishbein and Ajzen 1975), the theory of planned behavior (Ajzen, 1991), and the technology acceptance model (Davis, 1989). According to these theories, attitude affects intention and intention affects actual behavior (Pahnila et al., 2007; Sommestad et al., 2014).

Intentions capture the motivational factors that influence behavior and indicate how hard people are willing to try to perform the behavior in question (Ajzen, 1991). The stronger the intention to commit oneself to a form of behavior, the more likely the behavior will be carried out. Therefore, security intentions capture the motivation that users hold towards committing to security protective behaviors, such as complying to security policies or applying security tools (Siponen et al., 2007).

Attitude towards a behavior refers to " … the degree to which a person has a favorable or unfavorable evaluation or appraisal of the behavior in question" (Ajzen, 1991). Therefore, security intentions refer to users' feelings towards a given behavior such as attitude towards security policy compliance.

Behavior refers to the actual security decisions and actions of users such as adopting security technologies and practices and complying with security policies (Pahnila et al., 2007).

Other Antecedents of Security Behavior

Although an exhaustive analysis of factors that determine security behavior is outside the scope of this chapter, hereafter we describe the most important ones.

Normative beliefs refer to expectations of colleagues, peers, and superiors, which may have a persuasive influence on whether an employee will adhere to a specific behavioral norm (Ajzen, 1991). Therefore, the social environment of users, the social interactions with others and their attitudes are expected to influence users' security intentions (Herath & Rao, 2009).

Habit is defined as a form of routinized behavior, which entails automaticity as key element. Habit suggests that actions occur without conscious decision to act, and they are performed because individuals are accustomed to performing them (Vance et al., 2012). Security communication is required to address habits that influence against the desired behaviors, because a conscious decision is required for a user to initiate a new behavioral pattern.

Overcoming Communication Barriers

Developing an effective communication plan for information security entails understanding the factors that often inhibit communication. These factors relate to cognitive limitations and biases, cultural biases, security fatigue, and negative attitudes. In this section, we analyze these factors and discuss ways to overcome barriers towards effective information security communication.

Negative Attitudes towards Information Security

Users often have a negative attitude towards information security, although they may acknowledge its importance. As Haney and Lutters (2018) point out, many people find information security to be "scary, confusing, and dull." The way media portray security incidents often causes anxiety to most users. They feel unable to defend themselves against sophisticated threats and "hackers" with advanced capabilities. In many cases, users that feel helpless against security threats may become inactive and develop an attitude of privacy cynicism (see chapter 13 by Ranzini, Lutz & Hoffmann). To overcome this, security communication must focus on empowering users with encouraging messages and be candid about risks without raising fear (Haney & Lutters, 2018). Information security is a highly technical issue leading the average user to the perception that information security is confusing and security measures are difficult to implement (Haney & Lutters, 2018). Thus, security communication should provide practical recommendations and promote usable security solutions.

Cognitive Biases and Heuristics

Research in security-related decision-making has identified several cognitive biases that affect the way people make decisions. Based on Tversky and Kahneman's (1974) seminal work on judgment under uncertainty, several researchers have explored the effect of cognitive biases and decision-making heuristics on security-related decisions. According to the literature, the most relevant biases and heuristics are *anchoring, confirmation bias, optimism bias, the affect heuristic, the availability heuristic, and hyperbolic time discounting* (Tsohou et al., 2015), which are briefly presented in Table 26.1. Comprehending the way people understand security threats and risks and make decisions on security issues is essential for the development of effective security communication plans.

Table 26.1 Common biases and heuristics

Bias	*Description*	*Example*	*Relevant References*
Anchoring	A person's numerical estimate about a topic of interest is biased towards a probably irrelevant value that this person has recently heard or read. The anchoring bias is likely to affect the attitude of users towards security practices.	Encouraging social media users to select passwords of at least 8 characters, will make users to not choose passwords with significantly greater length. If instead we encourage passwords with bigger length (e.g., 14 characters), will probably lead users towards adopting longer passwords.	Strack and Mussweiler (1997)
Confirmation bias	People typically tend to look for information that confirms their own beliefs and may simply ignore information that challenges them.	Social media users may believe that personal photos and disclosures are safe if shared only with "friends." Presenting facts that show the opposite might not suffice to change this belief, as users may ignore evidence that challenge their initial hypothesis.	Kahneman et al. (2011); Nickerson (1998)
Optimism bias	People systematically tend to believe that others are at higher risk to experience a negative event compared to themselves. People believe "it won't happen to them."	Optimism bias is strong among Facebook users (Metzger & Suh, 2017). The "control paradox" may be viewed as an extension of optimism bias. Increasing individuals' perceived control over the release and access of information in social media platforms will increase their willingness to disclose sensitive information and this may lead to higher privacy risks (Brandimarte et al., 2013).	Weinstein and Klein (1995); Sharot et al. (2007); Davinson and Sillence (2010)

(*Continued*)

Table 26.1 Common biases and heuristics (Continued)

Bias	*Description*	*Example*	*Relevant References*
Affect heuristic	According to this heuristic, current emotion influences judgementsjudgments and decisions. This heuristic enables people to make quick, albeit not optimal decisions.	It is preferable to associate messages that prompt social media users to adopt secure practices with positive stimuli. On the contrary, messages that aim to dissociate users from risky behaviors could be accompanied with negative stimuli.	Kahneman et al. (2011)
Availability heuristic	Easily remembered information is given greater weight in decision-making. People tend to focus on recent events and vivid memories and pay little attention to statistics.	It is more effective to highlight risks using small, easy-to-remember stories, rather than statistics.	Newman (2003); Petrescu and Krishen (2020)
Hyperbolic time discounting	A common tendency to attribute greater importance to present gains or losses than to future ones.	The immediate gratification received when sharing personal information weighs more than the future privacy losses that may result from disclosing personal information.	Acquisti (2004)

Cultural Issues

In the cultural dimension, there are two relevant theories. The Cultural Theory of Risk (Douglas & Wildavsky, 1983) aims to explain the influence of social structures on individual perceptions of technological and environmental dangers. Hofstede's six cultural dimensions (Hofstede, 2011) are used to analyze the cultural differences between nationals of different countries. For a thorough analysis of intercultural privacy see chapter 14 by Cho & Li.

Security Fatigue and Usable Security

Furnell and Thomson (2009) highlight the role of security fatigue, which is often one of the main reasons why users fail to adopt secure practices and behaviors, although they may acknowledge the importance of security and privacy. Security practices are often annoying, time-consuming, and difficult to implement. Thus, in many cases security is perceived as a barrier rather than an enabler (Furnell & Thomson, 2009) and this attitude constitutes one additional obstacle that security communication needs to overcome.

Further, users are exposed to a variety of technological contexts (e.g., social media, online services, systems used at work) each one requiring different safeguards. In addition, security measures and practices quickly become obsolete as technological development follows a fast pace and new threats emerge continuously. Thus, users often feel tired of trying to keep up with the demands of information security and privacy protection, become lazy, or give up the effort altogether. Therefore, security communication must strike a balance between keeping users enthusiastic about security and preventing overexposure that may lead to apathy (Furnell & Thomson, 2009).

Theoretical Approaches

The theoretical background of security communication constitutes mainly of behavioral theories that have been applied in contiguous fields such as health and safety communication. The most prominent theory in this area is Protection Motivation Theory (PMT) (Rogers, 1975). PMT is concerned with the way individuals form their attitudes towards threats and risky behaviors. It argues that protection motivation results from two distinct cognitive processes: threat appraisal and coping appraisal. In threat appraisal, individuals assess the severity of the threat and how vulnerable they are to it. They also consider probable rewards associated with risky behavior. In coping appraisal individuals assess how effective a particular behavioral response would be in reducing the threat (response efficacy) and the degree to which they will be capable to apply the protective behavior (self-efficacy). They also consider the cost of protection. Several studies have applied PMT to study the effectiveness of fear appeals in changing information security behavior.

The effectiveness of security communication is often restricted by the neutralization techniques that individuals use to rationalize non-compliance with security policies and recommendations (Barlow et al., 2018). The neutralization techniques that mostly apply in security non-compliance are denial of responsibility, denial of injury, denial of the victim, and appeal to higher loyalties. In a privacy breach, for example, the responsible individuals may deny that their actions or negligence caused the breach and blame technology providers for insecure systems (denial of responsibility). They may also deny that the breach caused any harm by devaluing privacy (denial of injury) or blame the victims for not protecting their personal information (denial of the victim). Finally, they may claim that their actions aimed to benefit the organization or responded to implied organizational requirements, such as increasing productivity by "cutting corners" on information security and privacy protection. Barlow et al. (2018) investigated the effectiveness of three communication approaches: informational communication, which focuses on the importance of security policies; normative communication, which aims to explain that other employees would not violate policies; and antineutralization communication, aiming to inhibit rationalization. They found that anti-neutralization communication had the strongest effect on decreasing security policy violations.

Antineutralization communication has been tested in the context of organizational policies. Applying antineutralizaton techniques in social media remains an open research issue.

Information security communication theory is also concerned with the selection of appropriate communication media. Media richness theory claims that communication effectiveness is improved when the communication medium's information richness is aligned with the message objectives (Daft & Lengel, 1986). Media that can transmit rich information (e.g., face-to-face meetings) are better used for messages that may have multiple interpretations and less rich media are more suitable for messages that have unambiguous meaning. Therefore, security communication should use a variety of media and focus on matching message characteristics with communication media.

Communicating Information Security in Practice

Security communication practices are commonly addressed towards a) corporate users, b) home users, and c) organizations. For example, the SANS institute recommends social networking as one of the top ten topics to include in any security awareness program (SANS, 2019).

Information Security Communication for Corporate Users

The European Union Agency for Cybersecurity (ENISA) has published a guide for organizations that aim to design and implement initiatives to raise users' information security awareness (ENISA, 2010). The guide proposes a strategy for managing security awareness programs, comprising three stages: a) Plan, assess, and design, b) execute and manage, and c) evaluate and adjust. Another practical guide is provided by the National Institute of Standards and Technology of the United States of America (SP 800–50, 2021). The guide offers recommendations for the life cycle of a security awareness and training program, including a) the program design, b) the material development, c) the program implementation, and d) the post-implementation. Both guides can be applied by social networking providers for designing and executing security awareness and training programs for their employees (e.g., promoting privacy by design techniques for social media software developers).

Academic researchers have also examined the practical aspects of security communication. Several works validated the importance of awareness programs for achieving information security policy compliance (Bulgurcu et al., 2010; Kajtazi et al., 2021; Sommestad et al., 2014). Practical recommendations from academic research include, among others, the proposition of a variety of *communication delivery methods* (Hart et al., 2020), the *usefulness of software tools* as measurement instruments for the effectiveness of communication (Kruger & Kearney, 2006), and as security communication channels (Furnell et al., 2002; Hart et al., 2020), the importance of *personalizing communication* (Allam et al, 2014; McCormac et al., 2017; Tsohou et al., 2015; Wiley et al., 2020), and the *role of the technological context* (Allam et al., 2014).

Information Security Communication for Individual Users

Security communication may also target individual users such as social media users. The European Union (EU) has established the European Cybersecurity Month (ECSM)[1] annual campaign, which acts as a "hub" providing expert suggestions, generating synergies, and promoting common messaging among EU citizens, businesses, and public administration. Other initiatives to communicate security messages are organized by national authorities, such as personal data protection authorities (PDAs) and national consultancy centers that coordinate with European Networks (e.g., INSAFE,[2] INHOPE[3]), including the SaferInternet4kids[4] in Greece and the Safer Internet Center in the United Kingdom.[5]

Academic research has also offered practical advice in the same direction. Researchers emphasized on providing guidance for threats that are common to individual users such as phishing

(Arachchilage & Love, 2014). Others examined a variety of communication channels, including portals, browser extensions, serious games, and other software tools (Alotaibi et al., 2017).

Information Security Communication for Organizations

Security communication may also address organizations, including social networking platform providers. Communication among CERTs is key in optimizing incident response, disseminating know-how for mitigating cybersecurity attacks, and facilitating the coordination among relevant stakeholders (Hellwig et al., 2016). Security communication is also practiced by PDAs towards data controllers, aiming to assist them in applying security mechanisms and managing the protection of personal data. Other relevant roles include the European Data Protection Supervisor,[6] ENISA, and standardization bodies (e.g., ISO) that are also enablers of security communication towards organizations.

Towards a Unified Framework for Security Communication

Security communication, especially in the context of social media, is an intrinsically multidisciplinary issue. Taking upon theories and studies from other disciplines (e.g., health communication) academics and institutions provide guidance for improving the effectiveness of security communication towards promoting secure behavior and practices. Researchers have examined this issue from different theoretical perspectives. As only a few researchers have worked towards creating a unified framework (Moody et al., 2018; Sommestad et al., 2014), security guidance is scattered creating a burden for security researchers, students, managers, and practitioners to gain an understanding of the challenges, barriers, and enablers.

In this section, we take a first step towards a unified framework for security communication. First, we need to define the "dependent variable." Previous research has considered various dependent variables determined by the research context, including security policy compliance, self-disclosure, self-protection, etc. We believe that a unified framework should focus on (positive) *behavioral change*. The definition and metrics of behavioral change may differ depending on the context of security communication.

Security communication aims to influence the process of forming an attitude and making decisions about security and privacy-related behavior. This process does not lead to behavioral change in a straightforward manner. It is affected by psychological, cognitive, and social factors, as we have shown above. The complete model is presented in Figure 26.1.

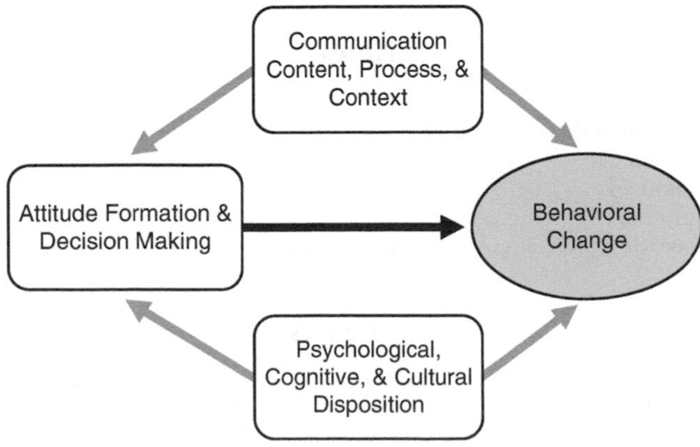

Figure 26.1 Unified Framework of Security Communication

Numerous theories aim to explain how people form attitudes and make decisions about their security and privacy behavior. In our framework, we incorporate eleven relevant theories following the analysis of Moody et al. (2018). These are the following: Theory of Reasoned Action, PMT, Extended PMT, Neutralization, Theory of Self-regulation, Health Belief Theory, Theory of Interpersonal Behavior, Deterrence Theory, Theory of Planned Behavior, Extended Parallel Processing Model, and Control Balance Theory. For the list of constructs suggested by these theories see Moody et al. (2018).

The cognitive and psychological dimension covers the biases and heuristics that affect people's decisions and behavior. Research has identified numerous decision-making biases and heuristics. The most relevant ones are *anchoring, confirmation bias, optimism bias, the affect heuristic, the availability heuristic*, and *hyperbolic time discounting*.

The cultural dimension comprises the constructs that classify individuals into cultural groups. They derive from the Cultural Theory of Risk (Douglas and Wildavsky, 1983) and Hofstede's six cultural dimensions (Hofstede, 2011). These are *grid*, i.e., the degree that an individual's way of life is determined by social structures, *group*, i.e., the extent to which belonging to a social group bounds an individual's way of life, *power distance, collectivism/individualism, uncertainty avoidance, femininity/masculinity, short-term/long-term orientation, restrain/indulgence.*

Finally, the effectiveness of security communication depends largely on its content, the process of delivering it, and the context of communication. The above framework can be used to test alternative security communication techniques in various contexts. The framework includes a considerable number of constructs. It is not expected for every study to consider all the above constructs. It is rather expected that researchers would select the most relevant ones depending on the research context.

Future Directions

In the previous section, we took a first step towards a unified framework for security communication research. Nevertheless, several more steps should be taken to provide and test a comprehensive framework. Another future direction for gaining a deeper understanding of the effectiveness of communication mechanisms is the empirical testing of existing theories. Most empirical studies for investigating security communication are based on surveys which include self-reporting hypothetical behavior (e.g., "I intend to … ") and examine users' intention to perform a protective behavior rather than the actual performance of that behavior. However, investigating actual security behavior is challenging due to the associated individuals' privacy concerns and the organizational information sharing concerns. Finally, limited work exists on the evaluation of the effectiveness for security communication and the development of respective key performance indicators and measurement frameworks.

Notes

1 https://cybersecuritymonth.eu/
2 https://www.betterinternetforkids.eu/
3 https://www.inhope.org/EN
4 https://saferinternet4kids.gr
5 https://saferinternet.org.uk/
6 https://edps.europa.eu/data-protection/our-work/our-work-by-type/guidelines_en

References

Acquisti, A. (2004). Privacy in electronic commerce and the economics of immediate gratification. In *Proceedings of the 5th ACM conference on electronic commerce* (pp. 21–29), ACM Digital Library.

Ajzen, I. (1991). The theory of planned behavior. *Organizational Behavior and Human Decision Processes, 50* (2), 179–211.

Allam, S., Flowerday, S. V., & Flowerday, E. (2014). Smartphone information security awareness: A victim of operational pressures. *Computers & Security, 42*, 56–65.

Alotaibi, F., Clarke, N., & Furnell, S. (2017). An Analysis of Home User Security Awareness & Education, In *Proceedings of the 12th international conference for internet technology and secured transactions (ICITST-2017)*, Cambridge, United Kngdom, December 2017.

Arachchilage, N. A. G., & Love, S. (2014). Security awareness of computer users: A phishing threat avoidance perspective. *Computers in Human Behavior, 38*, 304–312.

Barlow, J. B., Warkentin, M., Ormond, D., & Dennis, A. (2018). Don't even think about it! The effects of antineutralization, informational, and normative communication on information security compliance. *Journal of the Association for Information Systems, 19*(8), 689–715.

Brandimarte, L., Acquisti, A., & Loewenstein, G. (2012). Misplaced confidences. *Social Psychological and Personality Science, 4*, 340–347. https://doi.org/10.1177/1948550612455931.

Bulgurcu, B., Cavusoglu, H., & Benbasat, I. (2010). Information security policy compliance: An empirical study of rationality-based beliefs and information security awareness. *MIS Quarterly, 34*(3), 523–548.

Daft, R. L., & Lengel, R. H. (1986). Organizational information requirements, media richness and structural design. *Management Science, 32*(5), 554–571.

Davinson, N., & Sillence, E. (2010). It won't happen to me: Promoting secure behaviour among internet users. *Computers in Human Behavior, 26*(6), 1739–1747.

Davis, F. D. (1989). Perceived usefulness, perceived ease of use, and user acceptance of information technology. *MIS Quarterly, 13* (3), 319–340.

Douglas, M., & Wildavsky, A. (1983). *Risk and Culture: An essay on the selection of technological and environmental dangers*. Berkeley: California University Press.

ENISA (2010). "The new users' guide: How to raise information security awareness." Available online at: http://www.enisa.europa.eu/publications/archive/copy_of_new-users-guide

Fishbein, M. & Ajzen, I. (1975). *Belief, attitude, intention and behaviour: An introduction to theory and research*. Addison-Wesley.

Furnell, S., & Thomson, K. L. (2009). Recognising and addressing "security fatigue". *Computer Fraud & Security, 2009*(11), 7–11.

Furnell, S. M., Gennatou M., & Dowland, P. S. (2002). A prototype tool for information security awareness and training. *Logistics Information Management, 15*(5/6), 352–357.

Haney, J. M., & Lutters, W. G. (2018). " It's Scary … It's Confusing … It's Dull": How Cybersecurity Advocates Overcome Negative Perceptions of Security. In *Proceedings of the fourteenth symposium on usable privacy and security* (pp. 411–425), USENIX Association. https://www.usenix.org/conference/soups2018/presentation/haney-perceptions

Hart, S., Margheri, A., Paci, F. & Sassone, V. (2020). Riskio: A serious game for cyber security awareness and education. *Computers & Security, 95*, Article 101827.

Hellwig, O., Quirchmayr, G., Huber, E., Goluch, G., Vock, F., & Pospisil, B. (2016). Major Challenges in Structuring and Institutionalizing CERT-Communication. In *Proceedings of the 11th international conference on availability, reliability and security (ARES 2016)*, pp. 661–667.

Herath, T., & Rao, H. R. (2009). Protection motivation and deterrence: A framework for security policy compliance in organisations. *European Journal of Information Systems, 18*(2), 106–125.

Hofstede, G. (2011). Dimensionalizing cultures: The Hofstede model in context. *Online Readings in Psychology and Culture, 2*(1), 2307-0919.

ISO/IEC 27000 (2018). Information technology – Security techniques – Information security management systems – Overview and vocabulary, International Organization for Standardization.

ISO/IEC 27001 (2013). Information technology – Security techniques – Information security management systems – Requirements, International Organization for Standardization.

Kahneman, D., Lovallo, D., & Sibony, O. (2011). Before you make that big decision. *Harvard Business Review, 89*(6), 50–60.

Kajtazi, M., Holmberg, N., Sarker, S., Keller, C., Johansson, B., & Tona, O. (2021). Toward a unified model of information security policy compliance: A conceptual replication study. *AIS Transactions on Replication Research*, 7 (2), 1–15.

Kruger, H. A., & Kearney, W. D. (2006). A prototype for assessing information security awareness. *Computers & Security, 25* (4), 289–296.

McCormac, A., Zwaans, T., Parsons, K., Calic, D., Butavicius, M., & Pattinson, M. (2017). Individual differences and information security awareness. *Computers in Human Behavior, 69*, 151–156.

Metzger, M. J., & Suh, J. J. (2017). Comparative optimism about privacy risks on facebook. *Journal of Communication, 67*, 203–232. https://doi.org/10.1111/jcom.12290.

Moody, G. D., Siponen, M., & Pahnila, S. (2018). Toward a unified model of information security policy compliance. *MIS Quarterly, 42*(1), 285–311.

Newman, T. B. (2003). The power of stories over statistics. *BMJ, 327*(7429), 1424–1427.

Nickerson, R. S. (1998). Confirmation bias: A ubiquitous phenomenon in many guises. *Review of General Psychology*, 2, 175–220. https://doi.org/10.1037/1089-2680.2.2.175.

Okenyi, P. O., & Owens, T. J. (2007). On the anatomy of human hacking. *Information Systems Security, 16*(6), 302–314.

Pahnila, S., Siponen, M., & Mahmood, A. (2007). Employees' behavior towards IS security policy compliance. In: *40th annual Hawaii international conference on system sciences (HICSS'07)*, p. 156b. IEEE.

Petrescu, M., & Krishen, A. S. (2020). The dilemma of social media algorithms and analytics. *J Market Anal, 8*, 187–188.

Rogers, R. W. (1975). A protection motivation theory of fear appeals and attitude change. *The Journal of Psychology, 91*(1), 93–114.

SANS (2019, January 1). Security Awareness Topic #4 – Social Networking. https://www.sans.org/blog/security-awareness-topic-4-social-networking/

Sharot, T., Riccardi, A. M., Raio, C. M., & Phelps, E. A. (2007). Neural mechanisms mediating optimism bias. *Nature, 450*(7166), 102–105.

Siponen M., Pahnila S., & Mahmood A. (2007). Employees' adherence to information security policies: An empirical study. In: H. Venter, M. Eloff, L. Labuschagne, J. Eloff, R. von Solms (Eds.), *New approaches for security, privacy and trust in complex environments. SEC 2007. IFIP International Federation for Information Processing*, vol 232. Boston, MA: Springer.

Sommestad, T., Hallberg, J., Lundholm, K., & Bengtsson, J. (2014). Variables influencing information security policy compliance: a systematic review of quantitative studies. *Information Management and Computer Security, 22*(1), 42–75.

SP 800-50 Rev. 1 (Draft) (2021). PRE-DRAFT Call for Comments: Building a Cybersecurity and Privacy Awareness and Training Program, National Institute of Standards and Technology, Available online at: https://csrc.nist.gov/publications/detail/sp/800-50/rev-1/draft

Strack, F., & Mussweiler, T. (1997). Explaining the enigmatic anchoring effect: Mechanisms of selective accessibility. *Journal of Personality and Social Psychology, 73*(3), 437–446.

Tsohou, A., Karyda, M., & Kokolakis, S. (2015). Analyzing the role of cognitive and cultural biases in the internalization of information security policies: Recommendations for information security awareness programs. *Computers & Security, 52*, 128–141.

Tversky, A., & Kahneman, D. (1974). Judgment under uncertainty: Heuristics and biases. *Science, 185* (4157), 1124–1131.

Vance, A., Siponen, M., & Pahnila, S. (2012). Motivating IS security compliance: Insights from habit and protection motivation theory. *Information & Management, 49*(3–4), 190–198.

Weinstein, N. D., & Klein, W. M. (1995). Resistance to personal risk perceptions to debiasing interventions. *Health Psychology, 14*(2), 132–140.

Wiley, A., McCormac, A., & Calic, D., (2020). More than the individual: Examining the relationship between culture and information security awareness. *Computers & Security, 88*, 2020.

27

FROM PROCEDURAL RIGHTS TO POLITICAL ECONOMY

New Horizons for Regulating Online Privacy

Daniel Susser

PENNSYLVANIA STATE UNIVERSITY, USA

Introduction

The 2010s were a golden age of information privacy research, but its policy accomplishments tell a mixed story. On one hand, promising new theoretical approaches were developed. At the decade's start, for example, contextual integrity theory lent analytical precision and normative force to intuitions that privacy is deeply social and context-specific (Nissenbaum, 2010).[1] At its end, theories of "informational" and "surveillance" capitalism began to lay bare privacy's political economy (Cohen, 2019; Zuboff, 2019).

At the same time, a series of revelations and scandals brought the full extent and concrete significance of digital surveillance to public consciousness, motivating renewed enthusiasm amongst policy makers for efforts to strengthen privacy. In 2013, Edward Snowden exposed the breadth and depth of government digital surveillance (especially by intelligence, national security, and law enforcement agencies), and the insinuation of national governments and their surveillance apparatuses into networks owned and operated by private companies (Greenwald, 2014). Beginning in 2016, the Facebook/Cambridge Analytica scandal[2] focused attention more squarely on private sector data practices, making plain the contours of a digital economy built on targeted advertising and dramatizing the harms it threatens (*The Cambridge Analytica Files*, n.d.). Meanwhile, the rise of China's "social credit system" and the role of digital surveillance in the repression of its minority Uyghur population raised urgent questions about privacy and surveillance outside the West (Buckley & Mozur, 2019; Dai, 2018).

Yet despite significant progress on the development of privacy theory and compelling demonstrations of the need for privacy in practice, real achievements in privacy law and policy have been, at best, uneven. On one hand, there have been meaningful developments in the European Union. Adoption of the General Data Protection Regulation (GDPR) in 2016, and its enactment in 2018, signaled the possibility of a new era in privacy and data protection law – regulation finally catching up to technology after decades of passivity (Satariano, 2018). In the US, on the other hand, there has been a massive failure to act. While several states have enacted privacy legislation, and in spite of broad consensus that action at the federal level is needed, the prospect of new comprehensive privacy protections appears dim (Kerry, 2021).

Of course, social media has been at the center of these stories. Online privacy was fraught prior to the emergence of Facebook, Twitter, Snapchat, and TikTok – from the earliest moments of the commercial internet researchers and activists have raised the alarm about data collection by

DOI: 10.4324/9781003244677-32

governments and private firms, and about the use of information collected online to monitor, sort, and manage people (Agre, 1994; Gandy, 1996). But the rise of social media platforms brought a sea change, as more people started spending more time online, and as digital technologies began to mediate more of our social, economic, and political lives. Facebook (and parent company Meta) is now one of the world's largest data collectors, gathering information about its nearly 3 billion users and their activity on its platform, as well as information about the activities of non-Facebook-users on the internet and through the physical world via web trackers and smartphone sensors (Wagner, 2018). Twitter is more than a message board for clever one-liners; it is a major gatekeeper of news and information, the primary medium through which many businesses, government agencies, politicians, and public figures communicate with their constituents. The privacy challenges we face are therefore deeper and more urgent than ever, but also more complex, involving a wide range of normative tradeoffs and implicating increasingly powerful interests.

In what follows, I describe three broad shifts in the way privacy scholars (and, to some degree, privacy advocates and policy makers) are approaching social media. First, whereas privacy was once primarily understood as an individual interest, and the role of privacy policy as strengthening each individual's ability to realize it, there is now increasing emphasis on the social and relational nature of privacy, and – concomitantly – on structural approaches to privacy policy. Second, while public and private actors have both been understood to pose threats to privacy, the center of gravity in privacy discussions has moved from worries about government surveillance to worries about data collection by private firms, and the frame for conceptualizing these problems has expanded from a predominantly rights-based model to one that includes an important political economy perspective. Third, at the beginning of the social media era, these technologies were largely understood as tools for facilitating interpersonal communication and privacy questions were cast in those terms. Today, there is growing recognition that social media platforms have become part of society's basic communications infrastructure – a kind of "digital public sphere" – and that social media regulation needs to reflect this larger social and political context.

It is worth emphasizing at the outset that these are not brand-new ideas only recently emerging in the literature. Scholars have to some degree or other recognized and wrestled with them for decades. My aim is to highlight trends – shifts in the relative attention and significance given to alternative frames. They point to rich conceptual and normative resources, the tools to find our way toward privacy in a digital world.

Shift 1: The Structural Turn

Traditionally, privacy was understood as a right of individuals against unwanted attention or trespass – the "right to be let alone," in Samuel Warren and Louis Brandeis's formulation (1890). Throughout the last century, as technology furnished new ways to observe people and invade their private spaces, what it means to be "let alone" evolved. There are many strands to this evolutionary story, familiar from privacy studies (Sloot & Groot, 2018). Relevant for present purposes is the application – or, perhaps, the adaptation – of privacy rights to information technology. Beginning in the 1960s, especially with the publication of Alan Westin's (1967) *Privacy and Freedom*, privacy in the digital context became equated with an individual's (or group's) right to control information about themselves – so-called "personal information." To be "let alone" meant to only have information about oneself captured, stored, and analyzed according to one's own wishes, and – eventually – with one's consent (Gellman, 2017; Susser, 2019).

The idea that digital privacy is control over personal information was formalized in the US Fair Information Practices (FIPs) in 1973, codified in the US Privacy Act of 1974, exported to Europe as the Organization for Economic Cooperation and Development (OECD) privacy principles in 1980, and enshrined in European law in the form of the 1995 EU Data Protection Directive (Gellman,

2017). According to the Fair Information Practices, data collectors are responsible for notifying data subjects that information about them is going to be collected and processed, and soliciting their consent for it.[3] It is for this reason that websites and apps present "clickwrap" privacy agreements when users first log in, asking for confirmation that one has read the privacy policy and consents to its terms and conditions. Daniel Solove famously described this as "privacy self-management" – each individual left to contemplate the data practices of each data collector and to decide for themselves whether or not to participate (Solove, 2013).

This approach was contested from the start, both for its theoretical understanding of privacy and as a policy framework for managing increasingly data-driven societies. Scholars put forward competing theories – some argue privacy is more about access to people than control over such access (Gavison, 1980), others that control theories misunderstand the relationship between privacy and intimacy (Rachels, 1975; Reiman, 1976) or the connection between privacy and trust (Waldman, 2018), or that controlling information is one dimension of privacy but not its entirety (Nissenbaum, 2010; Susser, 2016). Practically, many pointed out that privacy self-management simply doesn't work: Privacy policies are too long and difficult to read. They can't be negotiated and fail to offer real choices. And even if they could be and did, there are too many data collectors for each person to manage (see Susser, 2019 for an overview).

More fundamentally, critics of privacy-as-control pointed out that this approach misapprehends the interests privacy rights protect. Privacy is not simply an individual right protecting individual interests; it is a social value, emerging from long-standing social norms and practices, and cherished for its effects on society as a whole (Nissenbaum, 2010). Without privacy, for example, citizens cannot formulate and voice the critical perspectives necessary for democratic self-government (Cohen, 2013). It is a "public," "common," and "collective" value, to use Priscilla Regan's terms (Regan, 2009).

Understanding privacy as a social value has immediate implications for policy. If we value privacy not only for its benefits to individuals but also for its impacts on society, then it makes little sense to place decisions about privacy in individual hands. Privacy self-management is a non-starter – we do not ask individuals to self-manage air quality or street traffic, and asking them to self-manage data is equally unrealistic in a data-driven world. What is needed is a *structural* approach, and the last decade has seen both deepening appreciation for and significant developments of this perspective. Through a structural lens, the primary goal of privacy law and policy is not to strengthen each person's ability to control information about themselves (though it may aim for that too), but to ensure information flows in ways that are conducive to privacy's individual and social ends.

In the realm of privacy theory, these developments can be seen in a range of new approaches that took shape in recent years. Neil Richards argues a "structural turn" was inaugurated in the US context in the early work of the "Information Privacy Law Project" – a loose confederation of legal scholars in the late 1990s and early 2000s who carved out and established the field of information privacy law (Richards, 2006). For these scholars, it was clear that digital privacy required a macro-perspective, focusing less on individuals and individual rights and more on the power relationships between data collectors and data subjects (Solove, 2004). Which is to say, shifting attention from traditional worries about each particular "invasion" of privacy to the systemic conditions created by society-wide architectures of digital surveillance and data processing (Richards, 2006, p. 1095).

Yet only recently were conceptual tools introduced that fully realized this structural perspective. First, Helen Nissenbaum's "contextual integrity" theory provided a new lens through which to understand both the source and normative content of demands for information privacy, and located each in the midst of social life. Privacy as a value emerges, Nissenbaum argues, in relation to particular social contexts – e.g., the home, the workplace, or the doctor's office – to ensure that information flows in ways conducive to their ends, goals, and purposes (Nissenbaum, 2010). And what privacy demands is specific to each context: the rules for how information should flow are different at home and at work. One reason social media complicates privacy is it tends to "collapse" these different contexts (Marwick & boyd, 2010). Second (and in much the same spirit), a number of scholars have argued that privacy law and policy should train their sights on relationships of trust, such as fiduciary relationships, and work to ensure that data collection and use practices build and justify that trust. Rather than focusing on people's individual privacy preferences, these approaches would orient privacy law and policy toward relational values, like duties of loyalty and care (Balkin, 2021; Richards & Hartzog, 2020; Waldman, 2018). Third, in the last decade, it has become increasingly clear that the real stakes of data collection – its costs and its benefits – lie not in any specific pieces of information, but rather in the pooling together and analysis of data at scale. Appreciating this requires a structural vantage point. Thus, new approaches are emerging that take aggregated data as their starting point and ask how collective, democratic values can guide discussions about privacy and surveillance (Viljoen, 2021).

This theoretical shift is also starting to materialize in new policy, most importantly the European GDPR. Enacted in 2016 and made effective two years later, GDPR is "the most consequential regulatory development in information policy in a generation," though its concrete requirements are still being articulated and the full scope of its effects is yet to be felt (Hoofnagle et al., 2019, p. 66). At a basic level GDPR takes a FIPs-based approach takes a FIPs-based approach, meaning it focuses primarily on procedural rather than substantive safeguards, designed to give individuals control over personal information and to ensure that data is accurate and secure.[4] But it reflects lessons learned about the need for structural intervention. For example, while individual consent plays a role in GDPR it is not "core" to its protections (Leta Jones & Kaminski, 2021, p. 108). Data processing is presumed unlawful in advance, consent is only one of several mechanisms for legitimating it, and consenting to data collection and processing does not waive other protections, such as accuracy and data minimization requirements (Hoofnagle et al., 2019; Leta Jones & Kaminski, 2021).

The structural turn is also having an impact in the US, though policy makers there have been much slower to act. At the federal level, lawmakers have introduced dozens of data- and privacy-related bills targeting everything from "individual rights and business obligations, to special protections for sensitive information and access to records by law enforcement, to emerging technologies such as facial recognition and artificial intelligence" (International Association of Privacy Professionals, 2021). As of this writing, however, none has been adopted. By contrast, more than half the states have introduced new privacy legislation, and in recent years online privacy laws have passed in California, Colorado, Maine, Nevada, and Virginia (International Association of Privacy Professionals, 2022). While many of these efforts aim to strengthen the FIPs there is growing recognition that systemic change is needed, one sign of which is renewed enthusiasm for using competition policy to rein in the power of Silicon Valley's biggest firms. A growing chorus of academics and regulators – most visibly, the legal scholar and current Chairperson of the Federal Trade Commission, Lina Khan – have taken aim at the largest data collectors and seek to strengthen privacy indirectly, not by giving individuals more control over information flows, but by using antitrust law to undo the massive concentration of information (and the power it confers) in relatively few hands (Kolhatkar, 2021).[5]

Shift 2: Privacy's Political Economy

Demands for privacy have always tracked the shifting landscape of surveillance (Igo, 2018), and from the early days of the commercial internet some prescient observers warned of the need to update our privacy "threat model" (to borrow a security term), as intrusive surveillance was beginning to originate as much from data collection by private firms as it did from governments (Agre, 1994; Gandy, 1996). But this argument has only gotten real purchase in the public imaginary more recently, in the wake of major scandals like the Facebook/Cambridge Analytica affair. For the first time, there is widespread concern about Big Tech's core business model – collecting, analyzing, and selling personal information (Pew Research Center, 2019; Radu, 2020). The targeted advertisements it makes possible are increasingly seen as creepy (Tene & Polonetsky, 2013; Dobber, this volume) and manipulative (Susser et al., 2019), rather than useful and convenient (as Silicon Valley has long contended) (Zuckerberg, 2019). And so, discussions about strengthening digital privacy are focusing more and more on regulating the surveillance economy.

Doing so requires, first, understanding the specific nature of Big Tech firms – especially social media companies – which is to say, it requires a theory of *platforms*. A kind of digital intermediary, platforms are the infrastructures that make possible all manner of online interaction and commerce (Cohen, 2019; Gillespie, 2010; Srnicek, 2017). Unlike other firms, which produce and distribute goods or services, platforms exist to facilitate connection. eCommerce platforms, like Amazon, connect buyers to sellers. Gig economy platforms, like Uber and Lyft, connect service providers (e.g., drivers) to customers. Social media platforms, like Facebook and Twitter, connect advertisers to eyeballs. In the process of facilitating these connections, platforms collect, analyze, and monetize data about them. And this data collection is not incidental: surveillance is the lifeblood of digital firms. As Julie Cohen writes, platforms are designed, fundamentally, for "data-based surplus extraction" (2019, p. 40).

Business models centered on surveillance and the selling of personal information tend toward specific economic dynamics – most importantly, market concentration and high barriers to exit (Haucap & Heimeshoff, 2014). Platforms are governed by network effects: the more people choose to use a particular platform the more attractive it becomes to other users. As Nick Srnicek writes:

> [T]his generates a cycle whereby more users beget more users, which leads to platforms having a natural tendency toward monopolisation. It also lends platforms a dynamic of ever-increasing access to more activities, and therefore to more data. Moreover, the ability to rapidly scale many platform businesses by relying on pre-existing infrastructure and cheap marginal costs means that there are few natural limits to growth.
>
> *(Srnicek, 2017, pp. 30–31)*

In addition, as Cohen argues, platforms are designed to make leaving for a competitor's alternative as difficult as possible. They are configured, she writes, "with the goal of making clusters of transactions and relationships stickier – sticky enough to adhere to the platform despite participants' theoretical ability to exit and look elsewhere for other intermediation options" (Cohen, 2019, p. 41). For example, most major platforms are intentionally non-interoperable. If someone gets fed up with Facebook, there is no easy way to move their data to another social media platform. Posts, photographs, chat histories – sometimes many years' worth – are stuck where they are.

These economic tendencies help explain the growth and consolidation of digital firms and also indicate obstacles to governing them (Brennan-Marquez and Susser, 2022). For privacy advocates, the question is how to bring surveillance under control when digital platforms, designed for and premised on the limitless expansion of data collection, sit at the center of global economies (the largest are currently some of the most valuable corporations in the world). Shoshana Zuboff argues that the dominance of companies such as Google and Facebook/Meta has inaugurated a new economic era – "surveillance capitalism" – in which people are treated not as consumers (to be served and satisfied), but rather as "objects from which raw materials are extracted and expropriated" (Zuboff, 2019, p. 94). Google and Facebook want data about us in order to predict and manipulate our beliefs, desires, and behavior with targeted advertisements. "Surveillance capitalism's products and services are not the objects of a value exchange," Zuboff writes, "They do not establish constructive producer-consumer reciprocities. Instead they are 'hooks' that lure users into their extractive operations in which our personal experiences are scraped and packaged as the means to others' ends" (Zuboff, 2019).

Complicating things further, recent scholarship demonstrates that law itself has been instrumental to the development of the surveillance economy. Contrary to standard narratives of privacy laws simply failing to "keep up" with the break-neck pace of technological innovation, exploring these issues through a law and political economy lens reveals the "facilitative role" law has played in turning personal information into the kind of commodity technology firms can own, sell, and profit from (Cohen, 2019, p. 8).[6] Much like law facilitated the "enclosure" of land and related practices of ownership and control that marked the transition from an agrarian economy to industrial capitalism in the 18th and 19th centuries, law has been constitutive of the transition currently underway, to surveillance or "informational" capitalism.[7] In particular, as Amy Kapczynski argues (following Cohen), without changes in intellectual property law – especially trade secrecy and contract law – "platform power could not have evolved as it has" (Kapczynski, 2020, p. 1503).

So what is to be done? While research in this area is only in its early stages, certain lessons are already in view: First, an analysis of the political economy of privacy lends support to the "structural turn" described in the previous section. Standard regulatory tools for ensuring fair consumer-business relationships, such as procedural rules that make business practices more transparent and solicit consumer consent, are obviously ill-suited for this world. It is difficult to imagine, for example, any set of FIPs-like requirements mitigating the harms platforms threaten, no matter how carefully enforced. If platforms derive their power, in part, from network effects (that tend toward market concentration) and specific technological affordances (that make it difficult to exit, and thus, for competitors to emerge), then there is little reason to believe individual users, each in their own relationships with firms, can act as a meaningful counterbalance. Importantly, this does not mean law and policy should ignore these relationships – even if structural changes are achieved, individuals will need support as they continue to manage information about themselves, and transparency still brings some benefits (Susser 2017; Susser, 2019). Structural interventions and individual protections are each necessary (but not sufficient), and privacy advocates and policy makers will need to think holistically about how they can be integrated (Kaminski, 2019).

Second, if the very harm regulation aims to prevent – surveillance – is the source of Big Tech's profits, then structural change must take a particular form: remaking the industry's dominant business model. If we are serious about privacy in the digital world, technology firms (especially social media companies) will have to find new ways to make money. Various proposals already exist for setting this transformation in motion. The "new antitrust" movement, discussed in the previous section, offers one approach. Though it is not obvious why competition amongst surveillance firms should lead to less surveillance overall (Balkin, 2021; Cohen, 2021). Tackling the problem more directly, a number of advocacy organizations, policy makers, and regulators have called for a ban on behavioral or "surveillance-based" advertising outright (Forbrukerrådet, 2021; Vinocur, 2021). That does not mean prohibiting advertising altogether, but rather returning to a status quo ante where ads were positioned using contextual information (such as the content of the website where the ad appears) instead of detailed personal profiles. Whatever tools we choose to use, the future of digital privacy requires ending the surveillance business.

Shift 3: The Digital Public Sphere

Finally, discussions about online privacy cannot be divorced from the larger context in which social media has become, in the last decade, more than a means of connecting people to one another (or connecting them to advertisers, depending on your perspective). For better or worse, it has become an integral part of society's communications infrastructure – a "digital public sphere" (Balkin, 2021). This fact is evident everywhere, from the complex interchange between social media and popular culture, to its use for government communications and political messaging, to the role it plays in generating and disseminating news. While much of the debate around regulation and the digital public sphere focuses on questions about free speech, privacy is centrally important too.

As Jack Balkin argues, a "healthy and vibrant" public sphere promotes *democratic participation* (the two-way flow of information and opinion from the public to government and back again), *democratic culture* (influence from a wide spectrum of people and communities on ideas that shape individual and social identity), and *the growth and spread of knowledge* (Balkin, 2021, pp. 77–78), and the aim of regulating the organizations, technologies, and practices that facilitate the public sphere should be to ensure they help realize these values. Social media companies, Balkin writes, "have already constructed a digital public sphere in which they are the most important players" (Balkin, 2021, p. 96). Thus, law and policy should design rules and incentives to encourage, amongst other things (such as a diversity of media sources, governed by professional and public-regarding norms) that social media platforms act as "trusted and trustworthy intermediate institutions" (Ibid.).

Surveillance and manipulation are antithetical to these goals, as recent history has demonstrated: as public awareness about surveillance capitalism has grown trust in social media platforms has declined, and for good reason (Social Media and Cybersecurity, 2021). Privacy is an antidote. It guarantees (as much as possible) that people feel safe communicating – capable of authentically expressing their beliefs and opinions, and open to encountering alternative perspectives – necessary for democratic participation (Cohen, 2013). Privacy creates space for the creativity and experimentation critical for the development of a robust democratic culture (Ibid.). And privacy fosters trust, essential for the spread of knowledge and for combating the paranoia in which mis- and dis-information thrive. Though it might sound paradoxical, privacy is at the heart of a well-functioning public sphere.

Understanding social media and privacy through this lens complements developments described in the previous sections, offering further reasons to incorporate structural perspectives into privacy discussions and strengthening the case against surveillance-based business models that undermine public trust. Moreover, the normative guideposts it recommends point toward additional concrete governance strategies: If social media is critical infrastructure, we could regulate it as a public utility (Rahman, 2018). If the dominant platforms can't fathom alternatives to existing surveillance-based business models, we could publicly fund alternatives. Perhaps, as Ethan Zuckerman and others have argued, the digital public sphere demands "digital public infrastructure": Wikipedia could serve as a model (Zuckerman, 2020), or the BBC in the UK and PBS in the US (Coatney, 2019). Or we could simply forbid social media companies from treating users as objects of surveillance and manipulation by imposing fiduciary obligations – duties of loyalty, confidentiality, and care (Balkin, 2020).

Conclusion

The shifts in perspective and approach outlined above point toward new horizons for privacy theory and practice. They offer invaluable resources for remaking social media, and the digital world more broadly, into technosystems that respect privacy and serve individual, social, and democratic ends. The next decade will decide whether we heed these lessons or remain in thrall to the frameworks and strategies that got us where we are. Of course, none of this occurs in a vacuum – privacy's prospects are inextricably connected with the deeper social, economic, and political conditions we face. Understanding what new laws are needed, for example, is not the same as marshaling the power to enact them, and skepticism about our capacity for progress on these fronts is not unreasonable. But there is, perhaps, also reason for optimism. A defining feature of the advances discussed throughout this chapter is, precisely, an ever-expanding theoretical aperture – greater attention to and appreciation for privacy's complex relationship with social contexts, economic systems, and political values. We have many of the tools we need, the question is whether we will use them.

At the same time, important questions remain unresolved. To close, consider three issues in need of attention from privacy and social media scholars moving forward: First, while the structural approaches to privacy, discussed above, are essential, they ought to be viewed as complements to (rather than replacements for) approaches that focus on individual rights. Yet few have tried to explain how to reconcile or integrate them. Successfully regulating social media privacy means enabling individuals to advance their informational interests while recognizing that those interests are interwoven – *networked* – with the interests of others, and that there are social and political interests to account for too. Second, work on the political economy of information has raised devastating moral and political objections to the surveillance-based business models social media companies rely on, but we have only begun to glimpse plausible alternatives. Indicting surveillance capitalism is not enough; we must conjure a future beyond it (Susser 2022). Finally, there remains the challenge of translating these theoretical insights into practice, using them to shape concrete legislation. As we've seen, privacy is a complex value and social media is a complicated enterprise. To meet this challenge scholars, policy makers, activists, and advocates must think and work together to chart the course ahead.

Notes

1 Nissenbaum elaborated this theory comprehensively in her (2010) *Privacy in Context: Technology, Policy, and the Integrity of Social Life*, though she had already sketched the main ideas in earlier work (Nissenbaum, 2004). It is in the decade since *Privacy in Context* was published, however, that its approach to conceptualizing privacy problems has become a dominant force shaping the field.

2 Facebook (the company) has rebranded as Meta, a container organization for various social media platforms, including – in addition to Facebook – Facebook Messenger, Instagram, and WhatsApp. In this chapter, I am mostly interested in Facebook as a social media platform (rather than in its corporate form), so I refer to Facebook rather than Meta.

3 There are many iterations of the FIPs, which enumerate a range of principles, including rights of access, participation, data minimization, and security. But notice (or "transparency") and consent (or "choice") are the dominant focus in both privacy theory and privacy practice. For a detailed history, see (Gellman, 2017).

4 Hoofnagle et al. call GDPR "FIPs on steroids" (2019, p. 78). Richards and Hartzog describe it as "the strongest implementation of the FIPs to date" (2020, p. 1).

5 For an overview of what some have called the "new Brandeisian" approach to antitrust, see (Khan, 2020). On potential limitations of this approach, see (Balkin, 2021; Cohen, 2021).

6 "Own" is a complicated story. See (Kapczynski, 2020, p. 1502) on the "indicia of ownership."

7 Cohen prefers "informational capitalism" (following Manuel Castells) to "surveillance capitalism," because it focuses attention on "the underlying transformative importance of the sociotechnical shift to informationalism as a mode of development" (Cohen, 2019, p. 6).

References

Agre, P. E. (1994). Surveillance and capture: Two models of privacy. *The Information Society*, *10*(2), 101–127. https://doi.org/10.1080/01972243.1994.9960162

Balkin, J. M. (2020). The fiduciary model of privacy. *Harvard Law Review*, *134*, 11–33.

Balkin, J. M. (2021). How to regulate (and not regulate) social media. *Journal of Free Speech Law*, *1*, 71–96.

Brennan-Marquez, K., & Susser, D. (2022). Privacy, Autonomy, and the Dissolution of Markets. *Knight First Amendment Institute.* https://knightcolumbia.org/content/privacy-autonomy-and-the-dissolution-of-markets

Buckley, C., & Mozur, P. (2019, May 22). How China Uses High-Tech Surveillance to Subdue Minorities. *The New York Times.* https://www.nytimes.com/2019/05/22/world/asia/china-surveillance-xinjiang.html

Coatney, M. (2019, September 24). We Need a PBS for Social Media. *The New York Times.* https://www.nytimes.com/2019/09/24/opinion/public-broadcasting-facebook.html

Cohen, J. E. (2013). What privacy is for. *Harvard Law Review*, *126*, 1904–1933.

Cohen, J. E. (2019). *Between truth and power: the legal constructions of informational capitalism.* Oxford University Press.

Cohen, J. E. (2021). How (not) to write a privacy law. *Knight First Amendment Institute*. https://knightcolumbia.org/content/how-not-to-write-a-privacy-law

Dai, X. (2018). Toward a reputation state: the social credit system project of China. *SSRN Electronic Journal*. http://dx.doi.org/10.2139/ssrn.3193577

Forbrukerrådet. (2021). *Time to Ban Surveillance Advertising: The Case Against Commercial Surveillance Online*. https://www.forbrukerradet.no/wp-content/uploads/2021/06/20210622-final-report-time-to-ban-surveillance-based-advertising.pdf.

Gandy, O. (1996). Coming to terms with the panoptic sort. In D. Lyon & E. Zureik (Eds.), *Computers, surveillance, and privacy*. University of Minnesota Press.

Gavison, R. (1980). Privacy and the limits of law. *The Yale Law Journal*, *89*(3), 421–471

Gellman, R. (2017). Fair information practices: A basic history. *SSRN Electronic Journal*. http://dx.doi.org/10.2139/ssrn.2415020

Gillespie, T. (2010). The politics of "platforms." *New Media & Society*, *12*(3), 347–364. https://doi.org/10.1177/1461444809342738

Greenwald, G. (2014). *No place to hide: Edward Snowden, the NSA, and the US Surveillance State*. Macmillan.

Haucap, J., & Heimeshoff, U. (2014). Google, Facebook, Amazon, eBay is the Internet driving competition or market monopolization. *International Economics and Economic Policy*, 11(1), 49–61.

Hoofnagle, C. J., van der Sloot, B., & Borgesius, F. Z. (2019). The European Union General Data Protection Regulation: what it is and what it means. *Information & Communications Technology Law*, *28*(1), 65–98. https://doi.org/10.1080/13600834.2019.1573501

Igo, S. E. (2018). *The known citizen: A history of privacy in modern America*. Harvard University Press.

International Association of Privacy Professionals. (2021). *US Federal Privacy Legislation Tracker*. https://iapp.org/resources/article/us-federal-privacy-legislation-tracker/

International Association of Privacy Professionals. (2022). *US State Privacy Legislation Tracker*. https://iapp.org/resources/article/us-state-privacy-legislation-tracker/

Kaminski, M. E. (2019). Binary governance: Lessons from the GDPR's approach to algorithmic accountability. *Southern California Law Review*. https://doi.org/10.2139/ssrn.3351404

Kapczynski, A. (2020). The law of informational capitalism. *Yale Law Journal*, *129*, 1460–1515.

Kerry, C. (2021, August 16). One Year After Schrems Ii, the World Is Still Waiting for U.s. Privacy Legislation. *Brookings*. https://www.brookings.edu/blog/techtank/2021/08/16/one-year-after-schrems-ii-the-world-is-still-waiting-for-u-s-privacy-legislation/

Khan, L. (2020). The end of antitrust history revisited. *Harvard Law Review*, *133*, 1655–1682.

Kolhatkar, S. (2021, November 29). Lina Khan's Battle to Rein in Big Tech. *The New Yorker*. https://www.newyorker.com/magazine/2021/12/06/lina-khans-battle-to-rein-in-big-tech

Leta Jones, M., & Kaminski, M. (2021). An American's guide to the GDPR. *Denver Law Review*, *98*, 93–128.

Marwick, A., & boyd, d. (2010). I tweet honestly, I tweet passionately: Twitter, users, context collapse, and the imagined audience. *New Media & Society*, 13(1), 114–133. https://doi.org/10.1177/1461444810365313

Nissenbaum, H. (2004). Privacy as contextual integrity. *Washington Law Review*, *79*, 119–157.

Nissenbaum, H. (2010). *Privacy in context: Technology, policy, and the integrity of social life*. Stanford University Press.

Pew Research Center. (2019). *Americans and privacy: Concerned, confused and feeling lack of control over their personal information*.

Rachels, J. (1975). Why privacy is important. *Philosophy & Public Affairs*, *4*(4), 323–333.

Radu, S. (2020, January 15). The World Wants More Tech Regulation. *U.S. News & World Report*. https://www.usnews.com/news/best-countries/articles/2020-01-15/the-world-wants-big-tech-companies-to-be-regulated

Rahman, K. S. (2018). Internet platforms as the new public. *Georgetown Law Technology Review*, *2*, 234–251.

Regan, P. M. (2009). *Legislating privacy: Technology, social values and public policy*. The Univ. of North Carolina Press.

Reiman, J. H. (1976). Privacy, intimacy, and personhood. *Philosophy & Public Affairs*, *6*(1), 26–44.

Richards, N. (2006). The information privacy law project. *The Georgetown Law Journal*, *94*, 1087–1140.

Richards, N., & Hartzog, W. (2020). A relational turn for data protection? *European Data Protection Law Review*, *6*(4), 492–497. https://doi.org/10.21552/edpl/2020/4/5

Satariano, A. (2018, May 24). G.D.P.R., a New Privacy Law, Makes Europe World's Leading Tech Watchdog. *The New York Times*. https://www.nytimes.com/2018/05/24/technology/europe-gdpr-privacy.html

Sloot, B. van der, & Groot, A. de (Eds.). (2018). *The handbook of privacy studies: an interdisciplinary introduction*. Amsterdam University Press.

Social Media and Cybersecurity. (2021, March 1). UNSW Online. https://studyonline.unsw.edu.au/blog/social-media-and-cyber-security-lp

Solove, D. J. (2004). *The digital person: Technology and privacy in the information age*. New York University Press.

Solove, D. J. (2013). Privacy self-management and the consent dilemma. *Harvard Law Review, 126*, 1880–1903.

Srnicek, N. (2017). *Platform capitalism*. Polity Press.

Susser, D. (2016). Information privacy and social self-authorship: *Techné: Research in Philosophy and Technology, 20*(3), 216–239. https://doi.org/10.5840/techne201671548

Susser, D. (2017). Transparent media and the development of digital habits. In Y. Van Den Eede, S. O'Neal Irwin, & G. Wellner (Eds.), *Phenomenology and media: Essays on human-media-world relations*. Lexington Books.

Susser, D. (2019). Notice after notice-and-consent: why privacy disclosures are valuable even if consent frameworks aren't. *Journal of Information Policy, 9*, 148–173. https://doi.org/10.5325/jinfopoli.9.2019.0037

Susser, D. (2022). Data and the Good? *Surveillance & Society. 20*(3), 297–301.

Susser, D., Roessler, B., & Nissenbaum, H. (2019). Online manipulation: Hidden influences in a digital world. *Georgetown Law Technology Review, 4*, 1–45.

Tene, O., & Polonetsky, J. (2013). A theory of creepy: technology, privacy and shifting social norms. *Yale Journal of Law and Technology, 16*, 59–102.

The Cambridge Analytica Files. (n.d.). The Guardian. https://www.theguardian.com/news/series/cambridge-analytica-files

Viljoen, S. (2021). A Relational Theory of Data Governance. *Yale Law Journal, 131*, 573–654.

Vinocur, N. (2021, April 2). The Movement to End Targeted Internet Ads. *Politico*. https://www.politico.eu/article/targeted-advertising-tech-privacy/

Wagner, K. (2018, April 20). This Is How Facebook Collects Data on You Even If You Don't Have an Account. *Vox.Com*. https://www.vox.com/2018/4/20/17254312/facebook-shadow-profiles-data-collection-non-users-mark-zuckerberg

Waldman, A. E. (2018). *Privacy as trust: Information privacy for an information age* (1st ed.). Cambridge University Press. https://doi.org/10.1017/9781316888667

Warren, S. D., & Brandeis, L. D. (1890). The right to privacy. *Harvard Law Review, 4*(5), 193. 10.2307/1321160

Westin, A. (1967). *Privacy and freedom*. Atheneum.

Zuboff, S. (2019). *The age of surveillance capitalism: The fight for a human future at the new frontier of power* (First edition). PublicAffairs.

Zuckerberg, M. (2019, January 25). The Facts About Facebook. *Wall Street Journal*. http://ezaccess.libraries.psu.edu/login?url=https://search-proquest-com.ezaccess.libraries.psu.edu/docview/2170828623?accountid=13158

Zuckerman, E. (2020). The Case for Digital Public Infrastructure. *Knight First Amendment Institute*. https://doi.org/10.7916/d8-chxd-jw34

28

REGULATING PRIVACY ON ONLINE SOCIAL NETWORKS

Johannes Eichenhofer[1] *and Christoph Gusy*[2]

[1]UNIVERSITY OF LEIPZIG, GERMANY
[2]UNIVERSITY OF BIELEFELD, GERMANY

Regulation

Regulation means shaping a social sphere through law. State and private actors are involved in this process. The complexity of the task arises from the fact that social networks do not only affect privacy, but also numerous other legal interests of providers, users, third parties, and the general public. Regulating privacy thus means regulating its many interrelations with other rights and interests (Hill et al., 2015; Van der Sloot, 2018). However, such regulations can partly concretize and partly limit privacy.

Privacy is a social, not primarily a legal phenomenon. On the one hand, privacy law is determined by its subject matter, which is privacy as an individual, social, and communicative good (Roessler & Mokrosinska, 2015). This need for protection must be presupposed, recognized, protected, and limited in law. On the other hand, those who protect a right also determine the subject matter and scope of this right and thereby help to constitute it. In law, therefore, privacy applies as the law understands and shapes it. Whether the legal protection is privacy-compliant and sufficient is then again a question of the preceding object of protection. On the web, privacy cannot be thought of without its legal guarantee and implementation – privacy shapes the law and the law shapes privacy. The relationship between law and its subject matter is circular.

The law, as described above, is in a state of rapid change, which has been brought about by the entry into force of the General Data Protection Regulation (GDPR) (Regulation EU 2016/679 of 27 April 2016, OJ L 119, p. 1), the Directive on the protection of natural persons with regard to the processing of personal data for the purpose of the prevention, investigation, detection, or prosecution of criminal offenses (Directive 2016/680 of 27 April 2016, OJ L 119, p. 89) and the amended German data protection laws at federal level (most recently: Telemedia and Teleservices Data Protection Act of 27 June 2021, OJ L 119, p. 89). 27.4.2016 OJ L 119, p. 89). Legislative work has also been done in the field of telemedia and teleservices. The-privacy regulation is about to replace the previously applicable e-privacy directive (Directive 2002/58/EC of 12 July 2002, OJ L 201/37). It is in the trialogue process between the EU institutions. The current legal situation is therefore both unclear and unstable (for further possible legal bases see Hornung, 2021). A driving force behind this development is the case law of the European Court of Justice (ECJ) on the guarantees of Art. 7, 8 of the EU Charter of Fundamental Rights (CFR) (on Art. 7 CFR, see Eichenhofer, 2021; on Art. 8 CFR, Marsch, 2018; González Fuster, 2014), which is gradually unfolding the fundamental rights guarantees of privacy and data protection at EU level and assigning them to other

DOI: 10.4324/9781003244677-33

legal rights. As the EU is an international pacemaker in the design and enforcement of data processing and data protection law, jurisprudence also has a pioneering role in the global context.

Privacy as a Mandate to the Law – Law as a Mechanism for protecting Privacy

European law has recognized privacy as a legal asset with the status of a fundamental right, first in Article 8 ECHR (1950) for all Council of Europe member states, and later (2000) in Articles 7 and 8 CFR. The focus of the guarantees was initially on the classic guarantees of "private and family life, home and communication" (Schabas, 2015, p. 358 ff.). The starting point of privacy protection hence was the analogous privacy of the real world. However, case law has not stopped there, but added data protection aspects to the traditional guarantees of the older ECHR: online privacy then appears as a manifestation and continuation of "private life." Art. 8 CFR went a step further and recognized an explicit guarantee for the protection of all people with regard to the automatic processing of personal data concerning them. This fundamental right follows on from the existing tradition of regulation and interpretation of the ECHR and continues in the digital world.

The interpretation of Art. 8 ECHR and Art. 7 CFR sees privacy as a continuation and reinforcement of the other mentioned guarantees of freedom. *Data protection, as established in Art. 8 CFR,* then is the *protection of freedom.* In the analog space, the holders of fundamental rights are free to shape their private lives themselves – also in the home or in communication – and to determine and control the relevant modes of doing so. Even here, privacy is not (only) solitude, but communication and interaction in the home or in the family. Privacy is not just being alone with oneself; *privacy is a modality of contact, communication, and interaction.* But not all communication is private. When is it still private, and when does it become public?

A contact is private if the participants themselves have the possibility to determine whether and how the rules of their interaction apply according to the self-determination or control criterion, which is also recognized outside law and jurisprudence (on the development and legal recognition Gusy, 2022; on competing approaches Van der Sloot, 2018, p. 121 seq.). Privacy is the absence of free and unregulated possibilities for outsiders to participate in or take note of a communication process. Its protection is graduated: the formulas of the intimate, private, and public spheres can serve as points of reference (on this model, German Federal Constitutional Court, decisions, e.g. BVerfGE 120, 180, 209). They can also provide initial guidelines for the digital life: Anyone who shares his or her data with others over social networks, lets them participate in his or her own life and voluntarily allows them into his or her own privacy, and cannot expect the same protection from them as from outsiders. This applies even more if the privacy settings in the social network have been set to "public."

But privacy on the web is also different from the analog world. The classic distinction according to communication media – telephone for private, broadcasting for public communication – is no longer possible online. Here, the two forms of communication are technically inseparable. This means for the medially mediated privacy at a distance: *If users have any control at all online, it is over what data they post.* Individuals are legally free to make this decision, which precedes the use of the web, at least to some extent: Which aspects of one's own privacy a person posts online and makes it accessible for online communication is not an exclusive question of data processing law and is rather covered by the classical analog privacy guarantees. This is true even though access to numerous offers and services, participation in social and political communication is increasingly determined by the web. However, access is still possible outside the web. *The aim of regulation* is *therefore* hardly ever to avert coercion, but to *enable and shape access and the handling of information obtained from the networks in a fair, transparent, and non-discriminatory manner.*

Once the information is on the social media, the user loses control to the greatest possible extent. How the networks handle personal data is up to their terms and conditions; but how they understand these, whether they adhere to them internally and whether outside third parties can circumvent them, is beyond the control of the user. Depending on the provider and business model, this also applies to the question of which third parties – the state, companies, other users – can legally or factually gain access. Here, "digital privacy" poses new challenges. These are different challenges than simply refraining from state coercion. In the real world, people can create and control privacy themselves. The law provides this sort of autonomy. In the digital world, it is missing: Here, the law must first establish and shape privacy by legally (re)establishing a possibility of control that the participants themselves have given up (see Gusy, Eichenhofer & Schulte, 2016). The "demarcation" of the private from the public sphere is made here by the formulas of the "personal datum" (i.e., the individualisation of the information regardless of its confidential content) (Van der Sloot, 2018, p. 101 seq.; see also Kokott & Sobotta, 2013), "informational self-determination" (i.e., the use of the information by the persons to whom it relates) and the "integrity and confidentiality of information technology systems" (i.e., protection of a technically or legally confidential network communication against unauthorized access by third parties, see BVerfGE 120, 274). They are recognized in Germany and have been shaped by case law German constitutional, but in the EU they still need to be partially developed (for a model, see Marsch, 2018, p. 128 seq.).

The law of privacy in social networks thus stands at several interfaces:

- The guarantees of analog privacy and data protection, including their different guiding principles and regulatory mandates. The search for a consensus model has not yet been completed: Increasingly, the older theory of spheres is being replaced or supplemented by new metaphors such as "spaces" or "trust" (Waldman, 2018; in Germany Eichenhofer, 2016, p. 57 seq.). They indicate: Spaces can also be open to more than one person, and trust presupposes a plurality of participants. Such differentiations are reflected in social networks with their closed, partially open and public communication offerings, insofar as users can choose between them. Here, regulation presupposes (the possibility of) differentiation.
- The question arises as to the regulatory competences of European and national legislators.

Regulation between Privacy Protection and other Legal Interests

Regulation is not limited to the design and delimitation of private spheres, but is also designed to include other concerns and legal interests. Privacy in networks is network- and context-dependent (Hartzog, 2018, p. 197 et seq. and pass.). These dependencies help shaping the form and possibilities of private relationships in the network.

- First of all, the protected interests of different private spheres must be included. Here it is a question of the design of shared privacy and the *allocation of freedom of communication* on the one hand and *private life* on the other (Petronio, 2021, p. 387 seq.), i.e., both the protection of private communication and the protection of privacy from the communication of others. *Networks can establish new forms of privacy*. For users, this freedom translates into a decision about the choice of different offerings: whether one chooses a dialogue connection to which only the chosen communication partners have access (in the case of chats and other forms of individual communication); whether one chooses a partially public offer in which only certain people are allowed to dial in, or whether one posts information in a public portal of which in principle everyone can take note without special legal and technical barriers (see Beyerbach, 2021, p. 361). Whatever form of communication is chosen, *individual freedom is transformed into the common freedom of all participants*: All have agreed to participate in an interaction under certain conditions of privacy. They have established a common private sphere: Henceforth, they decide jointly on the admission of third parties (BVerfGE 88, 386, 395 ff). Neither enjoys privacy protection against the others, nor may one decide on the privacy of the others as well. The common private sphere – comparable to the common inhabitants of a flat or the members of a civil partnership – means common protection of privacy for all. It needs to be legally justified and shaped. But the net also makes it possible for outsiders to gain knowledge, for false or distorted representations by third parties or for invented communication: *social networks can endanger privacy*. Those who feel observed act differently than those who feel unobserved (On surveillance in digital space Sidhu, 2007, p. 375; Van Rompay, Vonk & Fransen, 2009, p. 41). Here, design and demarcation tasks arise that are also known from the analog world, although on the web they are multiplied in many cases and without the possibility of "forgetting" (On the right to a new start in the media ECJ, C-131/12 – *Google Spain*, ECLI:EU:C:2014:317).

- *Social networks produce "private" information and at the same time open up access to it for outsiders.* There is technical data that accumulates when accounts and statuses are set up with the providers and can become privacy-relevant. The technical-medial mediation of contacts leads to traffic data, which does not allow conclusions to be drawn about content, but about who is in contact with whom and how often: information that could be of interest to the advertising industry and intelligence services. Even more extensive access to confidential communication content, the integrity of which users cannot control themselves, is only permissible within strict legal limits.
- Another source of both enabling and compromising private information is constituted through the *economic interests* of the provider side (On the commercialization of privacy, Lanier, 2014; Zuboff, 2019). The fact that so many people use social media is not a compulsion or a conspiracy. Rather, the new media offer economic, social, or convenience benefits that motivate their voluntary use. It is often provided without direct monetary consideration, i.e., without monetary benefits. Instead, user data is demanded and regularly transmitted in return. Their economic value results from the possibility of their resale to third parties as raw or evaluated data. This insight gives rise to the *commodity function* or *currency function* of information on the net as an economic basis of the system and the demand for a "data obligation law" (Sattler, 2017, p. 1036 seq.; Lindgreen, 2018, p. 181 seq.; critically Roessler, 2018, p. 141 seq.). From the provider's point of view, some of the users' calls for data protection are self-contradictory: they use the services of the network operators, but do not want to provide their information in return. The law therefore hardly ever regulates whether data should be economized, but rather how: protection of minors, sufficient transparency of whether and how data is used, controllability and revocability of consent; control of business conditions and their compliance. Here, privacy protection approaches consumer protection law (Bräutigam & Sonnleithner, 2021, p. 36).
- Finally the *security interests* of the people as well as the state, i.e., the protection of their legal interests against dangers from the web have to be taken into account. Communication can also serve the preparation or commission of crimes – not only, but also on the web. State agencies may use open information on and from the net just as private individuals may. Whether, on the other hand, blanket storage of connection data (so-called *data retention*) is permissible in the EU at all – and if so, under what conditions – is disputed due to the intrusive nature of permanent surveillance (ECJ, C-293/12 and C-594/12 – *Digital Rights Ireland*, ECLI:EU:C:2014:238 and ECJ, C-203/15 and 698/15 – *Tele2 Sverige*, ECLI:EU:C:2016:970). However, there are also crimes whose commission is made possible by the Internet in the first place (e.g., hacking), some crimes are made easier by the web (e.g., criminal bullying) and there are some crimes whose effects are increased there (e.g., through the publication of protected private information). Prevention, detection, and foreboding of crimes are permissible objectives of regulation and surveillance under special legal conditions. In recent times, the trend has intensified: law enforcement on and through the net must be permissible under the same conditions as in the analog world.

The regulation of privacy can thus be the regulation of communication, entrepreneurial activity, and public safety at the same time. In complex situations, all of the above-mentioned and possibly other interests can intertwine and not only justify but also complicate the design task (Bräunlich et al., 2021, p. 1443). Numerous legal questions largely arise from the *global nature* of the WWW, the sometimes necessary consideration of *foreign legal orders* and possible *enforcement* (Spindler, 2013).

Directions of Privacy Protection

Regulation has to protect privacy against various interested parties. In Germany, for example, the focus is traditionally on protection *against the state.* On the one hand, the state must enable network communication. On the other hand, law forbids the state to intrude into the privacy of others and their media, to monitor them, or to use the information obtained for its own purposes. This insight primarily gives rise to duties to cease and desist: The state may only create a legal basis for surveillance measures under narrow conditions and then only carry out such measures in accordance with the applicable law. This dimension is secured by fundamental rights and case law. Moreover, the protection of the rights of *users among themselves* has to be considered. If the users have not given their consent, their communication must be protected against unauthorized access, misuse by hackers, stalkers, etc. This problem is primarily solved by the providers themselves, their technology, and their terms and conditions. The state has a duty to act through legislation and regulatory agencies (on their independence ECJ, C-718/18 – *European Commission/Germany*, ECLI:EU:C:2021:662). Finally, there is the long-neglected protection dimension in the relationship *between users and providers*, which is basically protected by the freedom of contract, which, according to the GDPR and the e-Privacy Directive, must be exercised through consent. Where self-determination is guaranteed on the web, it is mostly exercised by clicking on the button indicating one's acceptance with terms and conditions the provider's (button solution). But the market is special, especially on the web: individual users are faced with an oligopoly of providers who unilaterally set the clauses and determine the terms and conditions. In view of the services they provide, this practice exercised by the providers is basically permissible. But they grant access to (also necessary) business, social participation, and political involvement dependent on conditions that must be checked for their sufficient clarity, transparency, and appropriateness (on balancing Van der Sloot, 2017). This is not an easy duty to act in view of the globalized network and the different legal systems of the states. It is currently at the center of the EU's regulatory efforts (see section "Regulation" above).

The heterogeneous duties to *refrain*, to *shape*, and to *supervise* are not aligned with each other, but can also collide: what one duty tends to demand tends to exclude the other duty. Therein lies the size of the duties and the tendency for states to be overburdened with their fulfillment.

Regulatory Actors

The regulation of privacy in social networks (and on the internet as a whole) is a task for numerous authorities and levels.

First of all, there are the *users themselves*. Depending on how they use the social networks (and the Internet as a whole), i.e., for what purposes they access which services from which providers, and what data they disclose in the process, they themselves decide – consciously or unconsciously – who may process what data about them and, to a certain extent, who is allowed to process it (more on this in a moment, under section "Regulatory models"). The best "*self-data protection*" would therefore be a complete "data abstinence." However, this would also mean that the advantages of social networks would not be used and individuals would be completely excluded from them. A more moderate form of data asceticism would therefore be to opt for certain, comparatively "data protection-friendly" providers. In addition, there are technical instruments for self-data protection (Wagner, 2020, p. 12 ff.; 279 ff.), ranging from comparatively simple forms such as secure password management to cookie settings in the browser and on the website of the content or service provider, the use of anti-virus and anti-tracking software, and encryption techniques. This shows: those who have the appropriate knowledge ("privacy literacy") can best ensure technical self-data protection. Those who advocate placing privacy and data protection primarily in the hands of individuals transfer to them the responsibility to protect themselves from informational threats.

Privacy and data protection can (and must) also be guaranteed by the *providers* of social networks. At first glance, this seems surprising, since they pose the primary threat to privacy due to their seemingly insatiable "data collection mania" – which manifests itself in the use of cookies, plug-ins, and other web tracking methods. However, they have both the possibility and the obligation (Art. 32 ff. GDPR) to take appropriate data security measures to ensure that the data stored on their servers are not exposed to unprotected attacks by third parties. No one can take this task away from them – neither the users (Hornung, 2021) nor the state, nor the EU. In this respect, users can only *trust* that the providers will live up to their responsibility. This trust is by no means "blind," but is legally secured – on the one hand, by the data security obligations imposed on the providers by law and, on the other hand, by a self-obligation of the providers to the users in the contractual relationships existing between them (on the importance of trust for the protection of privacy Eichenhofer (2016; 2021, p. 124 seq.; 171 seq.; 299 seq.; 429 seq.)). However, providers can also ensure through privacy-friendly default settings ("*privacy by default*") and generally privacy-friendly technology design ("*privacy by design*") (see on technical "design" for privacy protection Hartzog, 2018) that personal data may only be processed to the extent that is as privacy-friendly as possible. However, since such an approach runs counter to the business interests of the providers, it is reasonable from their perspective at best from the point of view of serving a new market for data protection-friendly services. For the rest, they will have to be made to do so through regulation.

Regulation as a task refers to the *states* as sovereign regulatory actors. Legislature, executive, and judiciary are obliged to enforce privacy and data protection. From a regulatory perspective, the first two powers are of particular interest. The *legislature* has the task of protecting privacy through appropriate laws in the three so-called directions of protection (see section 4. on the "Directions of privacy protection" above). In doing so, different regulatory instruments are to be used (see section 6 on the "Regulatory models"). The *executive* branch (i.e. government and authorities) is primarily called upon to implement these instruments. In order to do this, it must first be able to get an impression of which providers are violating existing privacy and data protection law through which practices and to what extent, or are evading regulation. In doing so, the supervisory authorities (Art. 51 et seq. GDPR) must take into account the extent to which providers may deviate from the requirements of the legislator by way of "private lawmaking." Only after this analysis (with the result of a data protection breach) has been completed "readjustments" can be made, for example through sanctions (Art. 83 ff. GDPR).

In Europe, the task of legislative regulation is now largely in the hands of the *European Union* (EU) (see section 2 on "Privacy as a mandate to the law – law as a mechanism for protecting privacy"), while the enforcement of European data protection law remains largely in the hands of the Member States. In this respect, the role of the EU is essentially limited to coordination, for example through the European Data Protection Board (Article 68 et seq. GDPR) or the European Data Protection Supervisor (Regulation (EU) 2018/1725 of 23 October 2018). The EU's regulatory competence makes it possible to capture the global character of the Internet somewhat better than individual states could. European data protection law provides for the principle of the place of market (Art. 3(2)(a) GDPR), according to which the GDPR applies to all data processing in the context of which "goods or services are offered to data subjects in the Union," irrespective of whether payment is to be made by these data subjects) and the conflict-of-law rules standardized in

Art. 3 GDPR, so that even such providers may be bound by European data protection law who have their registered office outside the European Union. Despite this expansion of the geographical scope of European data protection law, an enforcement weakness remains to the affect that the network is global, but the law (and its enforcement) is location-bound. To overcome this problem, global regulatory approaches would be necessary, but their development still seems to be a long way off (for a comparative law perspective Bygrave, 2014).

Since each regulatory actor pursues different goals, there is a multitude of agendas and concerns, which in turn have an impact on the concrete design of privacy in social networks.

Regulatory Models

Just as diverse as the concerns and interests that are important in privacy regulation are as diverse are its instruments. Three basic models will be outlined here.

a) *Self-regulation* takes place centrally through providers and, to a much more limited extent, users through *contract* (cf. Bräutigam & Richter, 2021). However, this approach is not negotiated individually, but imposed unilaterally by the providers. These are therefore *general terms and conditions* with which the providers limit the users' scope for negotiation to a considerable extent. The latter have no choice but to conclude the contract in its entirety, including the underlying *terms and conditions* , or to withdraw from it – and thus also from the services of the provider. On the Internet, this "take it or leave it" approach is mostly practiced in the form of the so-called button solution, according to which users must first accept all *terms and conditions* in order to be able to use the provider's services. In addition, the individual users usually do not (or cannot) know what they are agreeing to, as the data processing often proves to be highly non-transparent for the users – even despite the most detailed *terms and conditions*. This *asymmetry of information and power* between provider and user can be remedied neither by the contract nor by the *terms and conditions* themselves; rather, sovereign external regulation is necessary, for example in the form of information obligations for the providers (Art. 13 and 14 GDPR) or right of access (Art. 15 GDPR) or right to erasure (Art. 17 GDPR) of the data subjects. Nevertheless, from the user's point of view, it often remains unclear what exactly they are actually consenting to. The "informed consent" principle laid down in Art. 7 GDPR (Critically Koops, 2014, p. 251, according to whom consent in this context is largely theoretical and has no practical meaning) requires the consent to be both "informed" and "voluntary." However, where these requirements are met, the model of self-regulation can be a flexible solution adapted to the needs of the contracting parties. It does, however, presuppose a corresponding "privacy literacy."

b) The *external regulation* model aims to overcome these weaknesses of the self-regulation model through external lawmaking. Under the rule of law, only state actors can be considered as authorized "outsiders" – for the protection of legitimate interests of third parties or for the protection of fundamental rights (in this case: the user). For their protection, the legislator is called upon to take protective measures in favor of the users, whereby it has to take into account the rights and interests of the providers appropriately and to create a balance of interests. As an example of such third-party regulation, reference is made to the principles of lawfulness, purpose limitation, data minimization, and accuracy, storage limitation as well as integrity and confidentiality standardized in Article 5 of the GDPR. From the users' point of view, such third-party regulation represents a necessary correction of the power and information asymmetries between them and the providers. Thus, unlike the *terms and conditions* of the providers, they do not pose a challenge to the democratic rule of law, but are its manifestation. The size and difficulty of this task increases when the regulating authority does not even know what it is regulating, since the provider's data processing procedures – similar to the users – remain largely a "black box" for it.

c) The model of "*regulated self-regulation*" (Hoffmann-Riem, 1998, p. 537 seq.) appears to be a compromise. It creates a regulatory framework by way of external regulation, which is filled in by the contracting parties by way of self-regulation. An example of this interplay of external and self-regulation are the measures of privacy by design and by default (Art. 25 GDPR): Here, private regulation "by design" or "by default" must remain within the framework of the European legislator's requirements. In addition, the certification regulated in Art. 42 f. GDPR, best-practice models are selected and specified as binding regulatory models.

Summary

When life goes online, privacy also goes online. This fundamental development changes its character. On the Internet, private individuals lose most of the possibilities to protect their information themselves. Therefore, privacy on the Internet must first be established by law. This task is imposed on all actors – the state, providers, and users – by fundamental law. In particular, it applies to those who communicate on the web. Privacy protection is communication protection. Here, the opposition between self-data protection and data protection through regulation has proven to be too short-sighted: the interests are too different and the power relations in the information market are too asymmetrical. The legal system sets the binding framework and thus helps to shape not only the limits but also the conditions for exercising and thus the content of privacy protection. The new EU law is highly susceptible to interpretation and enforcement: this is where administrations and courts come in. They have to ensure transparency, information, and effectiveness of the monitoring bodies and complaint channels, especially for minors, socially disadvantaged market participants without greater choice, and for cases in which individual users are particularly dependent on network communication. These replace take the place of the deficient self-determination possibilities of the users themselves. The new legal requirements need to be concretized and shaped by authorities and courts at all levels. Only then will privacy protection on the net be more than just a word.

References

Beyerbach, H. (2021). Social Media im Verfassungsrecht und der einfachgesetzlichen Medienregulierung. In G. Hornung & R. Müller-Terpitz (Eds.), *Rechtshandbuch Social Media* (2nd ed., pp. 507–593). Springer Berlin Heidelberg; Springer.

Bräunlich, K., Dienlin, T., Eichenhofer, J., Helm, P., Trepte, S., Grimm, R., Seubert, S., & Gusy, C. (2021). Linking loose ends: An interdisciplinary privacy and communication model. *New Media & Society, 23*(6), 1443–1464. https://doi.org/10.1177/1461444820905045

Bräutigam, P., & Richter, D. (2021). Vertragliche Aspekte der Social Media. In G. Hornung & R. Müller-Terpitz (Eds.), *Rechtshandbuch Social Media* (2nd ed., pp. 81–129). Springer Berlin Heidelberg; Springer.

Bräutigam, P., & Sonnleithner, B. V. (2021). Vertragliche Aspekte der Social Media. In G. Hornung & R. Müller-Terpitz (Eds.), *Rechtshandbuch Social Media* (2nd ed., pp. 35–77). Springer Berlin Heidelberg; Springer. https://www.semanticscholar.org/paper/Vertragliche-Aspekte-der-Social-Media-Br%C3%A4utigam-Sonnleithner/5e7d6c340655f9f64ee83c49d91aa250a8e8c6e2

Bygrave, L. A. (2014). *Data privacy law: An international perspective*. Oxford University Press. https://ebookcentral.proquest.com/lib/kxp/detail.action?docID=5891449

Eichenhofer, J. (2016). Privatheit im Internet als Vertrauensschutz. Eine Neukonstruktion der Europäischen Grundrechte auf Privatleben und Datenschutz. *Der Staat, 55*(1), 41–67. https://doi.org/10.3790/staa.55.1.41

Eichenhofer, J. (2021). *E-Privacy: Theorie und Dogmatik eines europaischen Privatheitsschutzes im Internet-Zeitalter* (1st ed.). *Jus Publicum*. Mohr Siebeck. https://ebookcentral.proquest.com/lib/kxp/detail.action?docID=6638955

González-Fuster, G. (2014). *The emergence of personal data protection as a fundamental right of the EU*. WorldCat. https://link.springer.com/book/10.1007/978-3-319-05023-2

Gusy, C. (2022). Was schützt Privatheit? Und wie kann Recht sie schützen? *Jahrbuch Des Öffentlichen Rechts Der Gegenwart. Neue Folge (JöR), 70*(1), 415–451. https://www.mohrsiebeck.com/artikel/was-schuetzt-privatheit-und-wie-kann-recht-sie-schuetzen-101628joer-2022-0018?no_cache=1

Gusy, C., Eichenhofer, J., & Schulte, L. E-Privacy. Von der Digitalisierung der Kommunikation zur Digitalisierung der Privatsphäre. *Jahrbuch Des Öffentlichen Rechts Der Gegenwart (JöR), 64*(1). https://www.mohrsiebeck.com/artikel/e-privacy-101628joer-2016-0014?no_cache=1

Hartzog, W. (2018). *Privacy's blueprint. The battle to control the design of new technologies*. Harvard University Press. https://doi.org/10.4159/9780674985124

Hill, H., Martini, M., & Wagner, E. (2015). *Die digitale Lebenswelt gestalten (1st ed.). Verwaltungsressourcen und Verwaltungsstrukturen: Vol. 29*. Nomos https://ebookcentral.proquest.com/lib/kxp/detail.action?docID=4500167

Hoffmann-Riem, W. (1998): Informationelle Selbstbestimmung in der Informati-onsgesellschaft. *Archiv des Öffentlichen Rechts* 123, 513–540.

Hornung, G. (2021). Datenschutzrechtliche Aspekte der Social Media. In G. Hornung & R. Müller-Terpitz (Eds.), *Rechtshandbuch Social Media* (2nd ed., pp. 131–198) Springer Berlin Heidelberg; Springer.

Koops, B.-J. (2014). The trouble with European data protection law. *International Data Privacy Law*, *4*, 250–261. https://doi.org/10.1093/idpl/ipu023

Kokott, J., & Sobotta, C. (2013). The distinction between privacy and data protection in the jurisprudence of the CJEU and the ECtHR. *International Data Privacy Law*, *3*(4), 222–228. https://doi.org/10.1093/idpl/ipt017

Lanier, J. (2014). *Who owns the future?* Simon & Schuster Paperback.

Lindgreen, E. (2018). Privacy from an economic perspective. In B. van der Sloot & A. de Groot (Eds.), *The handbook of privacy studies: An interdisciplinary introduction* (pp. 181–208). Amsterdam University Press.

Marsch, N. (2018). *Das europäische Datenschutzgrundrecht: Grundlagen – Dimensionen – Verflechtungen* (1st ed.). *Jus Publicum*. Mohr Siebeck. https://ebookcentral.proquest.com/lib/kxp/detail.action?docID=5407606

Roessler, B. (2018). Three dimensions of privacy. In B. van der Sloot & A. de Groot (Eds.), *The handbook of privacy studies: An interdisciplinary introduction* (pp. 137–142). Amsterdam University Press.

Roessler, B., & Mokrosinska, D. (2015). *Social dimensions of privacy: Interdisciplinary perspectives*. Cambridge University Press. https://lawcat.berkeley.edu/record/1173639

Sattler, A. (2017). Personenbezogene Daten als Leistungsgegenstand. *JuristenZeitung*, *72*(21), 1046. https://doi.org/10.1628/002268817X15071039724467

Schabas, W. (Ed.). (2015). *The European convention on human rights: A commentary* (1st ed.). Oxford University Press.

Sidhu, D. (2007). The chilling effect of government surveillance programs on the use of the internet by Muslim-Americans. *University of Maryland Law Journal of Race, Religion, Gender and Class*, 7(2), 375–393. https://digitalcommons.law.umaryland.edu/rrgc/vol7/iss2/10

Spindler, G. (2013). Persönlichkeits- und Datenschutz im Internet – Anforderun-gen und Grenzen einer Regulierung, *Verhandlungen des 69. Deutschen Juris-tentages München 2012*, Band I, Teil F, C.H. Beck.

van der Sloot, B. (2017). Discussion ten questions about balancing. *European Data Protection Law Review*, *3*(2), 187–194. https://doi.org/10.21552/edpl/2017/2/8

van der Sloot, B. (2018). Privacy from a legal perspective. In B. van der Sloot & A. de Groot (Eds.), *The handbook of privacy studies: An interdisciplinary introduction* (pp. 63–136). Amsterdam University Press.

van Rompay, T. J. L., Vonk, D. J., & Fransen, M. L. (2009). The eye of the camera. *Environment and Behavior*, 41(1), 60–74. https://doi.org/10.1177/0013916507309996

Wagner, M. (2020): *Datenökonomie und Selbstdatenschutz. Grenzen der Kom-merzialisierung personenbezogener Daten*, Carl Heymanns.

Waldman, A. E. (2018). *Privacy as trust: Information privacy for an information age*. Cambridge University Press. https://doi.org/10.1017/9781316888667

Zuboff, S. (2019). *The age of surveillance capitalism, the fight for a human future at the new frontier of power*. Public Affairs Books. https://doi.org/10.1080/24701475.2019.1706138

29

CONSUMER PRIVACY AND DATA PROTECTION IN THE EU

Felix Bieker[1] *and Marit Hansen*[2]

[1]OFFICE OF THE DATA PROTECTION COMMISSIONER OF SCHLESWIG-HOLSTEIN, GERMANY
[2]DATA PROTECTION COMMISSIONER OF SCHLESWIG-HOLSTEIN, GERMANY

Introduction[1]

After years of moving fast and breaking things, social media, it appears, is now entering a phase of increased scrutiny and regulation: starting with the General Data Protection Regulation (GDPR), the EU has launched several legislative initiatives affecting social media providers, including the Digital Markets Act and Digital Services Act. While Meta's vision of future a virtual reality social network, the Metaverse, for now is only sparsely populated (Horwitz et al. 2022), yet immediately faced issues of sexual harassment (Basu, 2021), the number of Facebook users was declining. This caused the stock valuation to plummet (Milmo, 2022) and even the social media giant's threat of leaving the EU market in the face of regulation failed to gain much traction (Gilbert, 2020). At the same time, regulatory actions take considerable time, especially when they go through several instances of legal challenges (cf., for instance, ULD, 2021). While such proceedings are ongoing, the social media providers, who have large budgets for legal challenges, often can continue their contentious practices. Our article will explore the relevant existing legal rules of the EU, give an overview of its shortcomings and current issues regarding data protection in social media.

The term "social media" has been defined as "web-based services that allow individuals to (1) construct a public or semi-public profile within a bounded system, (2) articulate a list of other users with whom they share a connection, and (3) view and traverse their list of connections and those made by others within the system" (boyd & Ellison, 2008, p. 211). Often it also involves creating, sharing, and exchanging information. Users can be individuals such as natural persons, but also companies or public authorities. Important social media services and platforms encompass social networks including messaging services, blogs, micro-blogs, photo-sharing sites, video portals, podcasts, wikis, and virtual worlds. Also, devices may be equipped with information-sharing functionality for connecting smart meters, smart home devices, or connected cars.

Obviously, privacy and data protection aspects have to be considered whenever information is shared by people or about people. Both the exchanged content and the information about the accounts or devices that are involved may constitute personal data. According to Article 4(1), General Data Protection Regulation (GDPR) personal data encompass any information relating to an identified or identifiable natural person, the data subject. In order to determine whether a person is identifiable, all means likely reasonably used either by the controller or by any other person to identify the person in question must be considered according to recital 26 GDPR (also cf. European Court of Justice, 2016, paras. 42 et seqq.).

DOI: 10.4324/9781003244677-34

For individuals, social media risks encompass not only security breaches of personal communication, e.g., unauthorized access leading to breaches of confidentiality or integrity or identity theft when accounts can be taken ober, but also the risk of being manipulated or discriminated based on profiling and analysis of the users' behavior. The typical technical realization of social media is a centralized architecture maintained by the social media provider. While social media services are often provided "for free," this usually only means that there is no direct financial payment from individuals for accessing or sharing information – however, there is an indirect form of payment as the users' activities are the basis for targeted advertisement. Thus, the providers' business models regularly rely on advertising revenues.

In the following, we introduce the European Union (EU) data protection legislation relevant to social media, i.e., the GDPR and its key concepts to provide an overview of the current rules (see section "Normative foundations"). We will proceed by sketching the data protection-specific risks of social media practices (see section "Data practices of social media and risks to individuals") and consider the central concepts of data protection law (see section "Key concepts of data protection"), i.e., the obligations of controllers, especially their responsibility (see section "Obligations of controllers"), controllership (see section "Joint controllership"), lawfulness (see section "Lawfulness"), and targeting and profiling (see section "Targeting and profiling") in depth. We will then highlight several specific practices and their risks to individuals and society as a whole (see section "Current developments"), such as so-called dark patterns (see section "Deception by design"), the automated processing of biometric data (see section "Automated algorithmic analysis of social media posts"), the wide dissemination of data on social media by default (see section "Sharing as the default") as well as lock-in effects of social media platforms (see section "Lock-In effects"). We conclude (see section "Future directions") that while data protection authorities are focussing their enforcement actions on social media, the introduction of the so-called metaverse, a virtual reality social network, could exacerbate the current issues. At the same time, there are approaches that showcase alternatives that do not just pay lip service to data protection and the protection of privacy.

Normative Foundations

In the EU, there is no specific regulation on social media. However, the EU has regulated extensively on data protection and privacy. It has already introduced the second generation of data protection legislation, which consists, most prominently, of the GDPR. The GDPR applies to social media like any other form of personal data processing. It includes, inter alia, rights of users (i.e., data subjects), obligations for those who engage in data processing (i.e., controllers), especially concerning the implementation of technical and organizational measures, and oversight by independent supervisory authorities.

Furthermore, the EU has legislated specifically on the confidentiality of electronic communications with the ePrivacy Directive, which is currently under reform and set to be replaced by the ePrivacy Regulation. It is a sector-specific legislation, sometimes referred to reductively as Cookie Directive. However, it is much broader in scope and concerns the processing of data in electronic communication services generally, including rules for internet service providers, the confidentiality of messenger communication as well as online tracking practices, which are also relevant with regard to social media.

The data protection legislation is based on two fundamental rights guaranteed by the EU Charter of Fundamental Rights (Charter): The right to data protection guaranteed by Article 8 of the Charter and the right to privacy enshrined in Article 7 of the Charter. According to Article 8 of the Charter, everyone has the right to protection of the personal data concerning themselves as well as certain data subject rights. On the institutional side, Article 8 mandates that independent bodies, i.e., the data protection authorities, enforce the implementation of the data protection rules. Under Article 7 of the Charter, everyone has the right to respect for their private and family life, home, and communications. There are thus two independent, yet inter-related, rights, which concern the processing of personal data (European Court of Justice, 2014, paras. 27–29).

The interpretation of this relatively new right to data protection in relation to the right to privacy is not yet settled. However, in order to award the right to data protection an independent scope and content as stipulated by EU law, it must be interpreted in a way that allows it to be discerned from the more broadly recognized right to privacy to uncover its added value (González Fuster, 2014, p. 268; Lynskey, 2014). Data protection should be considered to provide a specific answer to the issues posed by the processing of personal data (Steinmüller et al., 1971, p. 44; Pohle, 2014, pp. 47–48). The *right to data protection* thus aims to protect against the processing of personal data and its adverse effects on individuals and society as a whole (Bieker, 2022, pp. 228–240). The *right to privacy* then focuses on the protection of individuals from the processing of special categories of data, which has negative effects on their private lives (Bieker, 2022, pp. 258–261).

This aim to protect individuals and society from adverse effects of data processing practices informs the interpretation of the secondary legislation such as the GDPR. The technical and organizational measures to be taken by controllers are prominent examples of structural rules that have the purpose of ensuring that the risks entailed by data processing do not materialize. The far-reaching and adverse impacts of social media on democratic decision processes, such as elections and referenda, have showcased a failure to take such organizational measures in the form of appropriate safeguards on a structural level. Actors instrumentalizing the specific hold on users that social media have attained through their targeting practices to influence the decisions of the electorate influenced the results of the Brexit vote in the United Kingdom as well as the last two federal elections in the USA (ICO, 2018; Jamison, 2018; Wylie, 2018; Timberg et al., 2021; Goodman and Hendrix, 2022). We will discuss the profiling that enables campaigns to target audiences so specifically in further detail below (see section "Targeting and profiling").

Data Practices of Social Media and Risks to Individuals

In this section, we will consider common data practices concerning social media. While the design of social media makes it seem to users that they are mainly interacting with other users – often their "friends" or "followers" – via the platform, it must not be forgotten that the actual operations involve various parties, notably the social media provider.

Social media providers are in a unique position to learn about their users' preferences, social and economic interactions as well as other information and to profile them based onthis plethora of data. In accordance with their business model of monetizing user data, they, in cooperation with advertisers and other third parties, use this information to display targeted advertisements for specific (groups of) users.

The information social media providers acquire can be considered to fall into three categories (cf. European Data Protection Board, 2021b): First, *users provide* a social media provider *directly* with their information, for instance, on their personal preferences, when they create profiles on the social media service. However, social media providers may also acquire data *provided by individuals to other entities*, for instance, email addresses provided to an e-commerce platform, which wants to target existing customers with an advertising campaign on a specific social media service. Second, *social media providers can observe* the users' behavior on their service, i.e., through data gathered from devices they use to access the service and through users' interaction with other users or entities on the social media service or even outside the platform, when third parties provide them with such information. Third, *social media providers can employ algorithms to infer* information about the users by considering the data they or third parties have provided (e. g. published or drafted posts, photos, videos, or comments to other's content) or that the social media provider has observed (e. g. "likes," clicks on specific content, mouse-over movements) and can draw conclusions and make predictions about users' interests from these data.

The risks for these different categories intensify in each step. With regard to the data provided by users, there is the highest level of control for individuals (at least in principle, cf. see section "Deception by design"). However, there are still risks as users may not be aware of how the social media provider uses and monetizes their data. Depending on the form of communication, users may also expect them to remain confidential. Especially when using a "private" or "direct" message function to contact other users individually, users might expect the same protections awarded to other, similar forms of communication such as email or text messages. When social media providers obtain data from third parties, this processing is even more opaque to users. With regard to data observed by social media providers, the risk for individuals increases, as social media aim to provide an immersive and emotional interaction experience, which entices users to share information without considering that any interaction is recorded and analyzed by providers. This is amplified in cases, where social media providers attain data from third parties that, for instance, track users across the web, even when they are not on the social media website or signed into their account. When social media providers or third parties, such as the advertisement customers of these providers, then infer information about the users based on their interactions on social media, the users experience an ever-increasing loss of control.

It has to be noted that, from a data analyst's point of view, it does not matter whether the compiled user profile is employed for targeted advertising to nudge a person to buy a product or whether it is used to influence the person's voting behavior or political opinion. The information collected from the data voluntarily or involuntarily disclosed on social media can be, and often has been, used to manipulate people as several cases have shown, most prominently the Cambridge Analytica scandal (see Jamison, 2018; Wylie, 2018; on microtargeting generally see chapter 23 by Dobber on microtargeting, privacy, and the need for regulating algorithms). Also, human-computer interaction is purposefully designed to trick users into disclosing more personal data and interacting more on a social media platform, so-called deceptive design with "dark patterns" or "addictive" effects (Forbrukerrådet, 2018; Brignull, 2022; European Data Protection Board, 2022).

Key Concepts of Data Protection

In order to understand the challenges of social media from the perspective of data protection, we will now provide an overview of several key concepts of the GDPR and highlight how they relate to social media. We will also provide some examples of risks for users of social media as they relate to these concepts.

Obligations of Controllers

A key concept with regard to social media as well as any other form of data processing is the notion of responsibility. Under the GDPR, responsibility is tied to the controller, which is the entity that determines alone or jointly with others the purposes and means of the processing of personal data according to Article 4(1)(7) GDPR. This means that whoever influences the design and carries out a processing operation is controller. Controllership is independent of the legal form or corporate structure of a company. A social media provider will be (at least jointly, cf. see section "Joint controllership") responsible for the processing of personal data on their platform, for instance, the profiling and targeting of users and the subsequent display of advertisement.

The EU data protection legislation applies to the processing of personal data, which follows a wide definition, including not only the data of identified individuals, but also of individuals when they are identifiable under Articles 2 and 4(1)(1) GDPR. Consequently, any individual rendered identifiable by a data processing operation is a data subject and enjoys data subject rights, so that controllers have to conform to their requests to access, rectification, and, under certain conditions, erasure according to Articles 17 et seqq. GDPR.

Controllers are also subject to various obligations of accountability, such as provision of information to data subjects and data protection authorities (Articles 5(2), 11–14, 35 GDPR), and to implement technical and organizational measures. These measures have to be implemented for any processing operation, only the extent of the measures is scaled in relation to the risks posed by the specific processing operation. Article 32 GDPR demands appropriate technical and organizational measures for guaranteeing the security of the personal data processed. Under the obligation of data protection by design of Article 25(1) GPDR, the controller has to implement the appropriate technical and organizational measures to meet the data protection principles laid down in Article 5(1) GDPR from the very inception of the data processing operation. The data protection principles encompass: lawfulness (processing only by recourse to an appropriate legal basis), fairness and transparency, purpose limitation and data minimization (processing only for a pre-defined purpose and only data necessary to attain that purpose), accuracy, storage limitation, integrity and confidentiality as well as accountability (ensuring the adherence to the principles is the responsibility of the controller).

Further, the controller has to set any defaults to the most data protection-friendly setting under the obligation of data protection by default according to Article 25(2) GDPR. The latter provision is particularly relevant with regard to defaults in social media. Social media providers, for instance, must not pre-select options for sharing posts to an indefinite number of viewers, as expressly mentioned in Article 25(2) clause 2 GDPR. This clause is an explicit reaction of the EU legislator to this pervasive practice of social media providers.

The exact requirements on the level of safeguards controllers have to implement depend on the risk of the processing operation. The EU data protection legislation refers to a particular risk: the risk to the rights of individuals (cf. inter alia Articles 24, 25, 32, 35). This refers to the aforementioned rights to data protection and privacy, but goes beyond these, as the GDPR generally aims to protect fundamental rights according to Article 1(2) GDPR (Bieker, 2018; Bieker, 2022, pp. 195–199). So, unlike in information security, this risk does not relate to the organization that processes data, but rather to those affected by the processing, especially data subjects. The controller thus has to consider risks that could lead to physical, material, and immaterial damage (cf. recital 75 GDPR for a non-exhaustive enumeration). The GDPR lists potential damages (discrimination, identity theft, economic or social disadvantages) as well as processing operations the legislator considers as higher risk, such as processing of special categories of data or the creation of personality profiles.

For instance, social media providers have to ensure security of the users' personal data to prevent unauthorized access or data leaks (Holmes, 2021). Related risks stemming from misuse of this data encompasses identity theft (the take-over of somebody else's account) as well as surveillance and discrimination of users (e.g., from categorization or social segmentation via social media monitoring systems that interpret accessible information; see e.g., Cagle, 2016).

Joint Controllership

When it comes to social media, in most cases, processing operations will involve more than one party. Where two or more parties jointly determine the purposes and means of the processing, they become joint controllers according to Article 26 GDPR. This may be the case where a third party operates their own presence on social media (for instance a fan page) or where a third party uses the tracking technology of a social media provider on their own website (social media plugins). In these cases, both parties have to delineate their respective responsibilities, including the transparent information of data subjects, in a specific agreement.

Due to its relevance in practice, the European Court of Justice has already considered cases that involved instances of joint controllership, such as when a third party operates a fan page on Facebook (European Court of Justice, 2018) and the use of social media plugins on third party websites (European Court of Justice, 2019). In both cases, the court found that the social media provider and the third party were jointly responsible, even when they pursued different interests. However, the joint responsibility only extended as far as both parties actually determined the means and purposes of the processing.

In order to be jointly responsible for a processing operation, the responsibility of the parties did not have to be equal to qualify as joint control. It was not required that both even had direct access to the personal data collected (European Court of Justice, 2018, para. 38). Rather, they could be involved to different degrees in different stages of the processing, so that the level of responsibility had to be differentiated (European Court of Justice, 2018, para. 44). The joint responsibility only ended where one of the parties engaged in subsequent processing and pursued purposes that it determined independently, without any influence of the other party (European Court of Justice, 2019, para. 76).

Where several controllers are jointly responsible, data subjects can exercise their rights vis-à-vis any of the controllers according to Article 26(3) GDPR. This includes the data subject rights as well as the right to compensation under Article 82(2) GDPR, which stipulates that any controller involved in a processing operation is liable for damages suffered by data subjects due to violations of the data protection rules. Article 82(4) GDPR expressly states that each controller is fully liable for the entire damage, to ensure effective compensation of the data subject.

Likewise, data protection authorities may exercise their powers against any of the joint controllers under Article 58 GDPR and may therefore, for instance, according to Article 58(2)(f) GDPR order organizations operating a fan page on a social network to deactivate this, when the controller cannot demonstrate compliance with the data protection rules.

Lawfulness

Before controllers carry out any processing of personal data, they are required to find a legal basis to legitimize the processing operation. Without a legal basis, the processing of personal data is unlawful. In cases of joint controllership, each of the controllers must have their own specific legal basis for the processing in question (European Data Protection Board, 2021a, p. 45). These legal bases are contained in Article 6 GDPR and, with regard to social media, there are three different provisions that may be relevant. Processing may be based on consent of the data subject under Article 6(1)(a) GDPR, be necessary for the performance of a contract according to Article 6(1)(b) GDPR or be based on the legitimate interest of the controller as defined in Article 6(1)(f) GDPR.

The notion of consent is further elaborated in Articles 4(11) and 7 GDPR. It must be given freely and unambiguously with regard to a specific processing operation, about which the data subject must be informed, and can be withdrawn at any time. This means that, in order to be valid, data subjects must have a genuine choice (European Data Protection Board, 2020, p. 5) and be able to understand why and how their data are being processed and by which entities. In practice, there have long been issues concerning the conformity of controllers' consent forms with the legal requirements, especially concerning their comprehensibility. According to a 2019 EU-wide survey, 60% of subjects stated that they read privacy policies, while those that stated they did not, pointed to their length and difficulty to understand (European Commission, 2019, pp. 47 et seqq.). However, studies examining the actual engagement of users with regard to privacy policies found that they peruse them only very quickly, if at all, and do not understand their contents; they point to intentional information overload as a reason for this behavior (Ibdah et al., 2021; Obar & Oeldorf-Hirsch, 2018).

When basing a processing operation on a contract, its scope must be limited to the data that are necessary for the performance of the contract. Social media providers as controllers must not extend these purposes to include services that are required in order to fund the provision of services, i.e., for monetization (European Data Protection Board, 2021b, p. 16). Rather, such additional purposes must be covered by additional legal bases.

With regard to the legitimate interest of the controller, the European Court of Justice has reaffirmed that Article 6(1)(f) GDPR requires a three-step test, in order to assess whether a processing operation may be based on this provision (European Court of Justice, 2019, para. 95). The controller must pursue a legitimate interest (1), the specific data in question are required to achieve the purposes pursued by the legitimate interest (2), and the rights of the data subject do not take precedence over the controller's interest (3).

However, the requirement of a legal basis only applies to controllers, not data subjects: when individuals use social media services merely to communicate with their friends and family, no legal basis is required. According to Article 2(2)(c) GDPR the EU regulation does not apply to the processing of personal data by natural persons in the course of a purely personal or household activity. This is further elaborated in recital 18 GDPR, which states that such processing has no connection with professional or commercial activity and "could include" social networking. However, the European Court of Justice has argued with regard to the GDPR's predecessor that the sharing of personal data on a website even by a natural person does not fall within this context, as it was accessible on a global scale and thus outside this exception (European Court of Justice 2003). The European Court of Justice has not yet explicitly addressed the issue of sharing data on social media under the new data protection legislation.

Targeting and Profiling

The GDPR defines profiling in Article 2(4) as any form of data processing to evaluate certain personal aspects, seeking to analyze or predict, for instance, a person's performance at work, economic situation, health, personal preferences, behavior, or movements. It thereby aims to ensure that any form of using personal data in order to evaluate personal behavior falls under the scope of the regulation. Profiling is seen as a high-risk processing operation, due to its effects on the rights of individuals, as evidenced by the fact that it will likely require controllers to carry out a data protection impact assessment before implementing the processing operation (cf. Article 35(3)(a) and recitals 71 and 91 GDPR).

The Article 29 Working Party, the predecessor of the European Data Protection Board, considered profiling to consist of three elements: It is the (1) automated processing (2) of personal data and its objective is to (3) evaluate personal aspects of a natural person (Article 29 Working Party, 2018, p. 6 et seq.). The European Data Protection Board endorsed this document (European Data Protection Board, 2018). The Board considers tracking as means to collect data on activities of natural persons, for instance, by tracking their activities across websites and apps (European Data Protection Board, 2021b, p. 9). Targeting services enable natural or legal persons ("targeters") to communicate specific messages to the users of social media in order to advance commercial, political, or other interests (European Data Protection Board, 2021b, p. 3).

While profiling is, by its legal definition, clearly not limited to technology for tracking users online, such ad tech is a prime example of targeting and profiling, especially in the context of social media. Recently, the European data protection authorities have addressed the Transparency and Consent Framework, which is a major network for distributing advertising on websites and tracking and profiling users managed by IAB Europe and its members (for an overview, cf. Veale et al., 2022). Similar to social plug-ins, the parties involved in this framework track users across websites. The framework is then used in a real-time bidding process to determine which advertisements users are shown on a specific website (APD, 2022, pp. 6 et seqq.).

A concern with these tracking technologies and profiling practices is, already at the preliminary stage, the provision of a legitimate legal basis. As elaborated in the previous section (see section "Lawfulness"), consent or the legitimate interests of the controller are the only legal bases that can be considered for this framework. However, due to undefined purposes, unclear categories of data collected, and the expansive sharing of this data with other controllers, the Belgian data protection authority found that this did not meet the legal requirements for valid consent (APD, 2022, pp. 87 et seqq.). Similarly, the requirements of the legitimate interest clause were not met in this case, as the purposes were too vague and thus not transparent for users, the data was passed on to too many other entities and there was a lack of safeguards for the further processing of the data. Furthermore, the legitimate interest clause did generally not apply to profiling activities (APD, 2022, pp. 94 et seqq.).

As it stands, the various actors involved in the Transparency and Consent Framework have tried to obscure responsibility for the implementation of data protection rules and each used this setup to argue that they do not require a legal basis for their processing. However, the Belgian data protection authority has found that the actors, much like the social media providers and fan page operators as illustrated above (see section "Joint controllership"), are jointly responsible for the processing (APD, 2022, pp. 79 et seqq.) under Article 26 GDPR (as elaborated above, see section "Joint controllership").

Current Developments

From the previous sections, it may seem that the GDPR is already addressing all relevant issues concerning the risks to the rights of individuals affected by social media, at least concerning the processing of their data. Yet, this expectation falls short: For some risks, data protection law as such does not provide the suitable leverage, for others, the enforcement is lacking so that the GDPR – to the present day – has failed to have a major impact in this area. In this section, we highlight several well-known, yet usually not sufficiently mitigated risks of today's social media where the rights of individuals, as well as our democratic society as a whole (Bieker, 2022, pp. 180 et seqq.), may be affected.

Deception by Design

Any use of online networks requires data exchanges via telecommunication and internet protocols, which create data trails comprising device identifiers, content data, and often additional information such as cookies. In principle, users can choose which social media platforms they sign up for and which personal data they disclose, but there are several factors that limit their choices in practice. In fact, most users do not diligently compare various social media providers and pick one based on elaborate criteria. Generally, they will register where they expect the most utility – and this is mostly the platform where their peer group is, as this is often required to access shared information (Wu et al., 2014). Network effects give big players – quasi-monopolies – a great advantage (Kerber & Schweitzer, 2017). Further, some services or tools such as smartwatches or fitness trackers require access to specific social media services for full functionality.

In addition to social group pressure or requests from applications, several social media providers use deceptive design patterns (also called "dark patterns") that trick users into disclosing more personal data or interacting with the site to a larger extent than intended, e. g. by nudging users to react to others' content or to make it difficult to opt-out of the data and behavioral analysis of users (cf. see section "Automated algorithmic analysis of social media posts") performed by the provider (Forbrukerrådet, 2018; Brignull, 2022; European Data Protection Board, 2022). This is contrary to the obligation of data protection by default: Article 25(2) GDPR (cf. see section "Obligations of controllers") requires that only the personal data necessary to achieve a specific purpose are disclosed and processed. These practices also violate fundamental data protection principles such as fairness, data minimization, or transparency. The providers, whose business model centers on collecting and exploiting personal data, prefer deception by design to data protection by design.

Automated Algorithmic Analysis of Social Media Posts

In today's social media, the shared content comprises mainly text, photos, or videos. When users decide to share personal data, they are often not fully aware of the information analyses that may reveal more about them than is apparent at first sight (cf. the three categories of data on social media introduced in see section "Data practices of social media and risks to individuals"). Providers use algorithms to gain more information about the users, especially to learn which advertisements and which advertising strategies may be most successful.

Furthermore, providers rely on sentiment analysis, which strives to understand the emotions of users (Gaind et al., 2019), to derive information on a person's general psychological characteristics as well as their spontaneous reaction in a certain situation. For instance, services evaluate interactions of presumed activists and their location data to predict protests or riots and offer this derived information to law enforcement agencies (Cagle, 2016). Providers use artificial intelligence methods, e.g., for suicide detection based on users' text, photos, and videos (Gomes de Andrade et al., 2018). They have also targeted children and teenagers who may be vulnerable in their current phase of personality development (Ho and Farthing, 2021).

Social media providers also use algorithms to analyze and store biometric data, in particular facial geometry, contained in photos users upload to share with friends. Considering the sensitivity of biometric data – as, among others, acknowledged in Article 9 GDPR – this results in a high risk of misuse. In a lawsuit against Meta, the Attorney General of Texas stresses that the "unique and permanent biometric identifiers, once exposed, leave victims with no means to prevent identity theft, unauthorized tracking and targeting, or other threats to privacy, safety, and security" (Texas v. Meta, 2022, p. 9).

The processing of personal data by social media providers is not limited to registered users, but encompasses all kinds of internet user interactions and analysis of information, irrespective of whether these persons are aware of this disclosure (Sanders and Patterson, 2020). This also means that the rights of access and rectification (Articles 15 and 16 GPDR) fall short if individuals are not even aware of the data processing. Furthermore, the accuracy of the derived information is not ensured.

Sharing as the Default

Social media are characterized by interactions of users and thus would not work without online connectivity and networks. Usually, some parts of the user's data, e.g., a profile in a social network, phone numbers, or other identifiers in a messenger tool, are stored and synchronized in a cloud. This is one explanation of why sharing is the default in social media. Users may often have the chance to adjust the accessibility of information they disclosed (which is already not in conformity with the obligation of data protection by default under Article 25(2) GDPR, as discussed above, see section "Deception by design"), e.g., to facilitate access for friends or their communication partners only. However, this usually does not exclude the possible access by the social media provider itself.

In addition, social media often provide interfaces for access by specific applications, for instance, the scraping by the data analyst firm Cambridge Analytica (Jamison, 2018; Wylie, 2018) or by the social media platform Geofeedia (Cagle, 2016). Further, developers of smartphone apps integrate components into their apps that trigger dataflows to social media platforms like Facebook, which has subsequently received all kinds of information automatically, including health data, without even notifying the users (Schechner & Secada, 2019).

Also, financial incentives may cause users to share potentially sensitive data, as the example of a suicide prevention hotline shows (Levine, 2022). Sometimes providers claim that the data is anonymous, but in many cases, a re-identification of some or all data subjects through the submitted data or in combination with other data sources is possible so that data protection regulations still apply.

In addition to the risk of re-identification from seemingly anonymous data, shared information may also lead to other breaches of confidentiality: For instance, fitness trackers used for running or cycling can upload the performed route so that other users may also explore the track or admire the route as it is visualized on a map. Such visuals are displayed as "Strava Art" on a public website (Cordery, 2022). However, "sharing by default" has caused undesired effects, such as revealing the location of military bases and patrol routes (Hsu, 2018).

Lock-In Effects

While two persons with a phone number can call each other no matter which phone provider they subscribe to, this kind of interoperability and interconnectivity does not exist for most interpersonal communications platforms, e. g. messenger apps. Similarly, social networks or microblogging services are usually organized as gated communities: Users can interact within the community created by the social media platform, but not with users outside. While non-members may be able to view published content, they need to register individually at each specific service before being able to comment on the content or interact with other users.

The GDPR has addressed this problem only partially: In addition to the right to access to their personal data (Art. 15 GDPR), the right to data portability (Art. 20 GDPR) requires controllers to provide individuals with the data they submitted, in a machine-readable format. In theory, users should get their texts and photos from one social media platform and move them to another service or have the providers do this among themselves. However, there are several obstacles to that idea, for instance how to move a communication thread with other users, who do not consent to that relocation. Further, even with machine-readable data, there is no easy way to transfer the data to another platform.

Giving up an established user account with content grown over time and the contact to other people on the platform is sometimes perceived as "virtual identity suicide" (Stieger et al., 2013). Even if people are not fully satisfied with the level of data protection or annoyed by invasive advertising, they may consider costs for change as too high – users seem to be "caught in the network" (Griggio et al., 2022). However, for some scenarios, it has been analyzed that privacy concerns do not only influence the users' own behavior on social network systems (e. g. limiting the active disclosure of personal information, granting access only to a limited number of other users, deleting own content after some time – "self-withdrawal," Dienlin & Metzger, 2016), but that e. g. in a messaging scenario the peer influence of contacts who prefer a privacy-friendly alternative plays a role for virtual migration from one service or platform to an alternative (Schreiner & Hess, 2015).

Following from the observation of unfair economic advantages resulting from network effects as well as generally high costs of switching for users, researchers have proposed interoperability and interconnectivity obligations for social media (Kerber & Schweitzer, 2017). Concerning basic services of an information society, the German Data Ethics Commission integrated this proposal in their lists of recommendations for future regulation (Datenethikkommission, 2019).

Future Directions

Risks for the rights and freedoms of natural persons are the focal point of the European data protection legislation. On the one hand, it has become common knowledge that social media – at least in their current form – come with a multitude of risks for individuals and society. On the other hand, the GDPR has not yet proven to be the suitable instrument for changing this situation. In particular, globally active providers of social media have hardly changed their system design to meet the requirements of the GDPR. In contrast, it seems that most providers ignore the concepts of data protection by design and by default. Instead, deception by design has become the predominant realization paradigm without any adequate attempt to implement data minimization, storage, and purpose limitation.

In this situation, where global social media providers try to evade supervision and avoid legally required changes of their service, the data protection authorities in the European member states are increasingly looking into the GDPR's concept of joint controllership (as elaborated in see section "Joint controllership"), which demands that all controllers concerned are able to demonstrate compliance with data protection law. This means that all organizations that are joint controllers with the central social media provider have to ensure the implementation of data protection rules – which, of course, is not possible if the social media provider itself thwarts legal compliance.

Based on the court rulings concerning Facebook fan pages and their own further legal analysis in 2022, the 18 German data protection authorities have requested the regional state as well as federal authorities in Germany to deactivate their fan pages unless they can demonstrate compliance with the data protection rules (DSK, 2022). It is expected that the public authorities, being a role model with regard to their obligations under the rule of law, do not ignore this request, but demand sufficient changes from Facebook or migrate to alternative social media services that meet data protection requirements. Also, as detailed above (cf. see section "Targeting and profiling") the monetization by platforms via their ecosystem of advertising based on personal profiles has become subject of scrutiny of the competent data protection authorities (e.g., Veale et al., 2022).

While data protection authorities increasingly take actions against data protection deficiencies caused by social media providers and many related problems are far from being solved, the next big step of evolving social media is already being advertised: The so-called metaverse will combine social media with augmented reality functionality and also collect all kinds of sensory input. The distinction between the physical and the digital worlds will be blurred due to the immersive user experience, artificial persons or objects may seem authentic to users. According to its proponents, people will play and work in the metaverse. From the data protection perspective, the metaverse will be a gigantic machine processing massive amounts of personal data – including biometric or other sensitive data – in real-time. While the ability of current social media to manipulate individuals and, to some extent, control communities cannot be denied, the influential power of the metaverse will undoubtedly be several orders of magnitude stronger. There are manifold risks of misusing personal data in the metaverse (see, e.g., Rosenberg, 2021; Hunter, 2022) – and this includes potentially adversarial activities by providers in central positions or excessive surveillance activities by governments.

Several researchers and developers have understood that the centralized architecture of the majority of social media together with the business model of targeted advertising bears risks both for individuals and society, as we explained above. They pursue decentralized approaches for social networks – or even the web: In their vision, control is shared among multiple actors and not concentrated in only a few large platforms (DWeb, 2022). In this DWeb community, the web of the future is designed in a way which should empower users to communicate and share data using secure, private, and open technologies. One practical example with a growing user base is the microblogging service Mastodon. With this, the DWeb community does not strive for singular approaches, but takes a holistic perspective encompassing identity concepts or payment functionality to offer a fair and resilient social media ecosystem.

The future will tell whether the problems we know today and the risks we will encounter with new approaches will be mitigated – and whether the principle of data protection by design and by default will become a reality for social media.

Note

1 This work is funded by the German Ministry of Education and Research within the project "Privacy, Democracy and Self-Determination in the Age of Artificial Intelligence and Globalisation" (PRIDS), https://forum-privatheit.de

References

APD – Autorité de protection des données, (2022). Decision on the merits 21/2022 Case number: DOS-2019-01377. 23 February 2022. https://www.autoriteprotectiondonnees.be/publications/decision-quant-au-fond-n-21-2022-english.pdf

Article 29 Working Party (2018). *Guidelines on automated individual decision-making and profiling for the purposes of regulation 2016/679*, as last revised and adopted on 6 February 2018, Brussels. https://ec.europa.eu/newsroom/article29/items/612053/en.

Bieker, F. (2022). *The right to data protection – individual and structural dimensions of data protection in EU law.* T.M.C. Asser Press/Springer.

Bieker, F. (2018). Die Risikoanalyse nach dem neuen EU-Datenschutzrecht und dem Standard-Datenschutzmodell. *Datenschutz und Datensicherheit*, 27–31.

Brignull, H. (2022). https://www.deceptive.design/hall-of-shame/all (website on deceptive design including dark patterns).

boyd, d., & Ellison, N. (2008). Social network sites: Definition, history, and scholarship. *Journal of Computer-Mediated Communication 13*, 210–230. https://doi.org/10.1111/j.1083-6101.2007.00393.x

Bus, T. (2021). The metaverse has a groping problem already. MIT Technology Review. https://www.technologyreview.com/2021/12/16/1042516/the-metaverse-has-a-groping-problem/

Cagle, M. (2016). Facebook, Instagram, and Twitter Provided Data Access for a Surveillance Product Marketed to Target Activists of Color. *American Civil Liberties Union Northern California.* 11 October 2016. https://www.aclunc.org/blog/facebook-instagram-and-twitter-provided-data-access-surveillance-product-marketed-target.

Cordery, G. (2022). https://www.strav.art/ (website on Strava Art).

Datenethikkommission (2019). *Opinion of the Data Ethics Commission.* Berlin: Executive Summary. https://www.bfdi.bund.de/SharedDocs/Downloads/EN/Datenschutz/Data-Ethics-Commission_Opinion.html

Davies, P. (2022, February 9). Meta warns it may shut Facebook in Europe but EU leaders say life would be 'very good' without it. Euronews. https://www.euronews.com/next/2022/02/07/meta-threatens-to-shut-down-facebook-and-instagram-in-europe-over-data-transfer-issues

Dienlin, T., & Metzger, M. J. (2016). An extended privacy calculus model for SNSS: analyzing self-disclosure and self-withdrawal in a representative U.S. sample. *Journal of Computer-Mediated Communication, 21*, 368–383. 10.1111/jcc4.12163

DSK – Konferenz der unabhängigen Datenschutzaufsichtsbehörden des Bundes und der Länder. (2022). *Zur Task Force Facebook-Fanpages.* 23 March 2022. https://datenschutzkonferenz-online.de/media/dskb/DSK_Beschluss_Facebook_Fanpages.pdf

DWeb (2022, January 27). Decentralized Web webinar series – Resource guide part 01. https://getdweb.net/wp-content/uploads/2022/01/DWeb-guide-part01.pdf

European Commission, (2019). *Special Eurobarometer 487a: The General Data Protection Regulation.* Brussels. https://webgate.ec.europa.eu/ebsm/api/public/deliverable/download?doc=true&deliverableId=69696

European Court of Justice (2003). Case C-101/01 Criminal proceedings against Bodil Lindqvist, Judgment of 6 November 2003, ECLI:EU:C:2003:596

European Court of Justice (2014). Joined Cases C-293/12 and C-594/12 Digital Rights Ireland Ltd (C-293/12) v Minister for Communications, Marine and Natural Resources and Others and Kärntner Landesregierung (C-594/12) and Others, Judgment of 8 April 2014, ECLI:EU:C:2014:238

European Court of Justice (2016). Case C-582/14 Patrick Breyer v Bundesrepublik Deutschland, Judgment of 19 October 2016, ECLI:EU:C:2016:779.

European Court of Justice (2018). Case C-210/16 Unabhängiges Landeszentrum für Datenschutz Schleswig-Holstein v Wirtschaftsakademie Schleswig-Holstein GmbH, Judgment of 5 June 2018, ECLI:EU:C:2018:388.

European Court of Justice (2019). Case C-40/17 Fashion ID GmbH & Co.KG v Verbraucherzentrale NRW eV, Judgment of 29 July 2019, ECLI:EU:C:2019:629.

European Data Protection Board (2018). *Endorsement 1/2018*, adopted on 25 May 2018, Brussels. https://edpb.europa.eu/sites/default/files/files/news/endorsement_of_wp29_documents.pdf

European Data Protection Board (2020). *Guidelines 05/2020 on consent under Regulation 2016/679* (Version 1.1), adopted on 4 May 2020, Brussels. https://edpb.europa.eu/sites/default/files/files/file1/edpb_guidelines_202005_consent_en.pdf

European Data Protection Board (2021a). *Guidelines 07/2020 on the concepts of controller and processor in the GDPR* (Version 2.0), adopted on 7 July 2021, Brussels. https://edpb.europa.eu/system/files/2021-07/eppb_guidelines_202007_controllerprocessor_final_en.pdf

European Data Protection Board (2021b). *Guidelines 8/2020 on the targeting of social media users* (Version 2.0), adopted on 13 April 2021, Brussels. https://edpb.europa.eu/system/files/2021-04/edpb_guidelines_082020_on_the_targeting_of_social_media_users_en.pdf

European Data Protection Board (2022). *Guidelines 3/2022 on Dark patterns in social media platform interfaces: How to recognise and avoid them* (Version 1.0 – version for public consultation), adopted on 14 March 2022, Brussels. https://edpb.europa.eu/system/files/2022-03/edpb_03-2022_guidelines_on_dark_patterns_in_social_media_platform_interfaces_en.pdf

Forbrukerrådet (2018). *Deceived by design – How tech companies use dark patterns to discourage us from exercising our rights to privacy*. https://fil.forbrukerradet.no/wp-content/uploads/2018/06/2018-06-27-deceived-by-design-final.pdf

Gaind, B., Syal, V., & Padgalwar, S. (2019). Emotion Detection and Analysis on Social Media. *Global Journal of Engineering Science and Researches*, Proc. International Conference on Recent Trends in Computational Engineering & Technologies (ICRTCET-18), 78–89. 10.48550/arXiv.1901.08458

Gomez de Andrade, N. N., Pawson, D., Muriello, D., Donahue, L., & Guadagno, J. (2018). Ethics and artificial intelligence: suicide prevention on Facebook. *Philosophy & Technology*, *31*, 669–684. https://doi.org/10.1007/s13347-018-0336-0

González Fuster, G. (2014). *The emergence of personal data protection as a fundamental right of the EU*. Springer.

Goodman, R., & Hendrix, J. (2022, April 12). January 6 Clearinghouse – Congressional Hearings, Government Documents, Court Cases, Academic Research. Just Security. https://www.justsecurity.org/77022/january-6-clearinghouse/

Griggio, C. F., Nouwens, M., & Klokmose, C. N. (2022). Caught in the Network: The Impact of WhatsApp's 2021 Privacy Policy Update on Users' Messaging App Ecosystems. *Proc. 2022 CHI Conference on Human Factors in Computing Systems, Article No. 104*, ACM, 1–23. https://doi.org/10.1145/3491102.3502032

Ho, E. Y.-C., & Farthing, R. (2021). *How Facebook still targets surveillance ads to teens*. https://fairplayforkids.org/wp-content/uploads/2021/11/fbsurveillancereport.pdf

Holmes, A. (2021, April 3). 533 million Facebook users' phone numbers and personal data have been leaked online. *Business Insider*. https://www.businessinsider.com/stolen-data-of-533-million-facebook-users-leaked-online-2021-4

Horwitz, J., Rodriguez, S., & Bobrowsky, M. (2022, October 15). Company documents show Meta's flagship metaverse falling short. Wall Street Journal. https://www.wsj.com/articles/meta-metaverse-horizon-worlds-zuckerberg-facebook-internal-documents-11665778961?mod=hp_lead_pos1

Hsu, J. (2018, January 29). The Strava Heat Map and the End of Secrets. *WIRED*. https://www.wired.com/story/strava-heat-map-military-bases-fitness-trackers-privacy/.

Hunter, T. (2022, January 13). Surveillance will follow us into 'the metaverse,' and our bodies could be its new data source. *The Washington Post*. https://www.washingtonpost.com/technology/2022/01/13/privacy-vr-metaverse/

Ibdah, D., Lachtar, N., Raparthi, S. M., & Bacha, A. (2021). "Why should I read the privacy policy, I just need the service": A study on attitudes and perceptions toward privacy policies. *IEEE Access*, *9*, 166465–166487. https://doi.org/10.1109/ACCESS.2021.3130086

Information Commissioner's Office (ICO) (2018). Democracy disrupted? Personal information and political influence. 11 July 2018. https://ico.org.uk/media/action-weve-taken/2259369/democracy-disrupted-110718.pdf

Jamison, M. A. (2018). Politics and Business in Social Media, Regulatory Responses to the Cambridge Analytica Revelations. Statement before the Senate Judiciary Committee on Cambridge Analytica and the Future of Data Privacy on 16 May 2018. https://www.judiciary.senate.gov/imo/media/doc/05-16-18%20Jamison%20Testimony.pdf

Kerber, W., & Schweitzer, H. (2017). Interoperability in the digital economy, 8. *Journal of Intellectual Property, Information Technology and E-Commerce Law*, *8* (1), 39–58.

Levine, A. S. (2022, January 28). Suicide hotline shares data with for-profit spinoff, raising ethical questions. *POLITICO*. https://www.politico.com/news/2022/01/28/suicide-hotline-silicon-valley-privacy-debates-00002617

Lynskey, O. (2014). Deconstructing data protection: The "added-value" of a right to data protection in the EU legal order. *International Comparative Law Quarterly*, *63*, 569–597. 10.1017/S0020589314000244

Milmo, D. (2022, February 3). Why the Facebook owner's shares are in freefall. The Guardian. https://www.theguardian.com/technology/2022/feb/03/why-facebook-shares-are-in-freefall-meta-zuckerberg

Obar, J. A., & Oeldorf-Hirsch, A. (2018). The biggest lie on the internet: ignoring the privacy policies and terms of service policies of social networking services. *Information, Communication & Society*, *23*(1), 1–20. https://doi.org/10.1080/1369118X.2018.1486870

Pohle, J. (2014). Die immer noch aktuellen Grundfragen des Datenschutzes [The still Pressing Fundamental Question of Data Protection]. In: H. Garstka, & W. Coy (Eds.), *Gedächtnisschrift für Wilhelm Steinmüller: Wovon – für wen – wozu, Systemdenken wider die Diktatur der Daten* [Whereof – for Whom – Why, Systems Thinking against the Tyranny of Data]. Helmholtz-Zentrum für Kulturtechnik, Humboldt-Universität zu Berlin, pp. 45–58.

Rosenberg, L. (2021, November 6). Metaverse: Augmented reality pioneer warns it could be far worse than social media. *Big Think*. https://bigthink.com/the-future/metaverse-augmented-reality-danger/

Sanders, J., & Patterson, D. (2020). Cheat sheet: Facebook Data Privacy Scandal. *TechRepublic*. https://www.techrepublic.com/resource-library/downloads/cheat-sheet-facebook-data-privacy-scandal/

Schechner, S., & Secada, M. (2019, February 22). You Give Apps Sensitive Personal Information. Then They Tell Facebook. *The Wall Street Journal*. https://www.wsj.com/articles/you-give-apps-sensitive-personal-information-then-they-tell-facebook-11550851636

Schreiner, M., & Hess, T. (2015) Examining the Role of Privacy in Virtual Migration: The Case of WhatsApp and Threema. *Proc. 21st Americas Conference of Information Systems (AMCIS), 33*.

Steinmüller, W., Lutterbeck, B., Mallmann, C., Harborth, U., Gerhard, K., & Schneider, J. (1971). *Grundfragen des Datenschutzes* [Fundamental Questions of Data Protection], BT-Drs. VI/3826 Anlage 1, pp. 5–193.

Stieger, S., Burger, C., Bohn, M., & Voracek, M. (2013). Who commits virtual identity suicide? Differences in privacy concerns, internet addiction, and personality between Facebook users and quitters. *Cyberpsychology, Behavior, and Social Networking, 16*(9), 629–634. https://doi.org/10.1089/cyber.2012.0323

Texas v. Meta (2022, February 15). State of Texas v Meta Platforms Inc. f/k/a/ Facebook Inc., 71st Judicial District Court in Harrison County, Texas (Marshall). https://www.heise.de/downloads/18/3/3/0/5/4/3/3/State_of_Texas_v._Meta_Platforms_Inc.pdf

Timberg, C., Dwoskin, E., & Albergotti, R. (2021, October 22). Inside Facebook, Jan. 6 violence fueled anger, regret over missed warning signs. *The Washington Post*. https://www.washingtonpost.com/technology/2021/10/22/jan-6-capitol-riot-facebook/

ULD – Unabhängiges Landeszentrum für Datenschutz (2021, November 26). Ausgang des Verfahrens Wirtschaftsakademie ./. ULD (Az. 4 LB 20/13) in Sachen Facebook-Fanpages. https://www.datenschutzzentrum.de/artikel/1384-Ausgang-des-Verfahrens-Wirtschaftsakademie-..-ULD-Az.-4-LB-2013-in-Sachen-Facebook-Fanpages.html#extended

Veale, M., Nouwens, M., & Santos, C. (2022). Impossible asks: Can the transparency and consent framework ever authorise real-time bidding after the Belgian DPA decision? *Technology and Regulation, 2022*, 12–22. https://doi.org/10.26116/techreg.2022.002

Wu, Y.-L., Tao, Y.-H., Li, C.-P., Wang, S.-Y., & Chiu, C.-Y. (2014). User-switching behavior in social network sites: A model perspective with drill-down analyses. *Computers in Human Behavior 33*, 92–103. https://doi.org/10.1016/j.chb.2013.12.030

Wylie, C. (2018). Written Statement to the United States Senate Committee on the Judiciary in the Matter of Cambridge Analytica and other Related Issues, 16 May 2018. https://www.judiciary.senate.gov/imo/media/doc/05-16-18%20Wylie%20Testimony.pdf

30

THE ROLE OF PARTICIPANTS IN ONLINE PRIVACY RESEARCH

Ethical and Practical Considerations

Johannes Breuer[1,2], *Katrin Weller*[1,2], *and Katharina Kinder-Kurlanda*[3]

[1]GESIS – LEIBNIZ INSTITUTE FOR THE SOCIAL SCIENCES, COLOGNE, GERMANY
[2]CENTER FOR ADVANCED INTERNET STUDIES (CAIS), BOCHUM, GERMANY
[3]DIGITAL AGE RESEARCH CENTER, UNIVERSITY OF KLAGENFURT, AUSTRIA

Introduction

When using online platforms, we generate vast amounts of data. Platform providers, thus, often have access to detailed and personal information about their users and can employ this information for a variety of purposes. Popular platforms for networking and communicating, such as Facebook, Twitter, or YouTube, search engines, such as Google, or shopping portals, such as Amazon and eBay, require or request users to disclose many different kinds of personal information (see chapter 28 by Eichenhofer & Gusy on regulating privacy on online social networks). This disclosure is at the core of online privacy research and has led to the development of various perspectives on motivations and consequences of information disclosure. There are complex reasons and decisions involved when revealing information to internet platforms, and users often report wanting to protect their privacy, while at the same time being forced to disclose information to be able to participate (Lamla & Ochs, 2019; Willson & Kinder-Kurlanda, 2021). The (potential) discrepancy between attitudes and actual behavior regarding privacy has been described as the privacy paradox. Whether or in what form the privacy paradox exists and what it entails is an ongoing debate and a widely studied topic (see, e.g., Dienlin & Sun, 2021; Yu et al., 2020).

Researchers of online privacy often face a similarly paradoxical challenge in their research design: In order to study online privacy, they may collect personal or even sensitive information. Most research designs in online privacy research require participants to disclose information, such as personal attributes, beliefs and attitudes, their usage of digital technology, and other privacy-related behaviors. Much of this information can be sensitive – and may be identical to the information collected by online platforms. This creates conflicts for researchers in the field, who may find themselves facing the key question of how they can study online privacy in an ethical manner when their own studies intrude on people's privacy. Of course, not every study investigating privacy also invades participants' privacy, but the questions that most studies ask and the data they collect are typically personal and potentially sensitive. For that reason, it is important to consider the role of participants in online privacy research. Given the methodological

DOI: 10.4324/9781003244677-35

heterogeneity of studies in this field, "participation" can refer to very different settings from the perspective of those who are being asked to contribute to the study.

The role of study participants in the research process is a key ethical issue within the social and behavioral sciences (Chalmers et al., 1999). It has been a topic of research ethics for some time with a gradual change of terminology in research publications. Since the 1990s, in psychology and other disciplines (Boynton, 1998), there has been a shift from the term "(study) subjects" to "(research) participants" evidencing a move towards bias-free language to address power imbalances in the research process (American Psychological Association, 2020, p. 141). More descriptive terms, such as "college students," "children," or "respondents," are often preferred. A central question in these discussions is to what degree participation is voluntary and active in different research designs. People can be involved in research in various ways that can be more or less active. For example, focus group discussions or ethnographic studies typically require more active involvement of participants than surveys. In most research designs, voluntariness is ensured through the recruitment procedure in which informed consent is obtained from participants prior to data collection. Asking for informed consent establishes transparency about the purpose of the study and the way(s) in which the data will be used. Given that research on online privacy often is perceived as a sensitive endeavor, it is important for researchers in this field to pay special attention to questions related to informed consent. In practice, however, properly obtaining informed consent is not always straightforward and can be especially challenging for some research designs. In experimental studies, for example, participants often are not informed or even misled about the research purposes, to ensure that experimental treatments can work as intended. In such cases, participants need to be debriefed at the end. Ideally, they should also be able to decide whether their data should be used once they are informed about the true purpose of the study (or be given the opportunity to reconfirm or change a previous decision from before the debriefing). Obtaining informed consent can also be difficult when using particular types of data. The personal and often sensitive nature of the data in online privacy research, together with the general research trend of using new digital types of data and of combining different methods and data, requires that we reconsider how research can be performed in an ethical manner and what role(s) study participants (can) play in this.

In this chapter, we discuss the ethical challenges in online privacy research and how these may be addressed. Our main approach is to broaden the perspective on participants' involvement. Doing so allows us to explore various facets of research ethics connected to different ways of studying online privacy. More specifically, we illustrate different paths that may help researchers of online privacy to re-think research contexts and to find innovative approaches, including using new types of data sources and new modes of participation.

From Online Privacy to Research Ethics

In online privacy research, "privacy" is both the object of study and an ethical issue to be considered. Part of the perceived paradox as outlined above may be due to the conflation of these two functions. In a first step, to untangle this, we will try to broaden the perspective by illustrating how privacy is embedded into research ethics. Importantly, research ethics are not a binary concept. While we may say that something is ethical or unethical, in reality, ethical questions and their answers exist on a continuum. Also, when it comes to research ethics, different values and goals may be in conflict with each other, requiring a careful weighing of alternative choices, e.g., with regard to collecting, processing, and sharing research data. Researchers need to consider risks to participants in various stages of their study, starting with the planning phase. Ethical research design includes reflecting on standards and practices intended to ensure research integrity, meaningful results, and avoidance of misrepresentation. It also requires to continuously reconsider collaboration practices and how to enable responsible reuse of results and data. Adapting to changes in the topic that is being studied to the continuous development of digital media platforms and other technology as well as to the changing landscape of online data and digital methods requires innovative concepts. In the following, we want to discuss some key areas where such innovative concepts may help to address ethical questions in online privacy research: (1) research design and data, (2) participation and informed consent, and (3) data privacy and transparency.

Research Design and Data

The majority of studies on online privacy are based on self-report measures (see, e.g., Gerber et al., 2018; Yu et al., 2020). These are, for example, employed in interviews, surveys, or experimental designs to assess various kinds of privacy behavior, beliefs, attitudes, and types of media use. However, self-report measures have repeatedly been shown to be unreliable as they can be influenced by social desirability or problems with recollection (Parry et al., 2021). One option for measuring media use as well as certain privacy-related behaviors is the use of so-called digital trace data, i.e., "records of activity (…) undertaken through an online information system" (Howison et al., 2011, p. 769). Digital traces are increasingly used as research data in various disciplines and are at the heart of new research areas, such as computational social science or computational communication science. Researchers see various valuable characteristics in these kinds of data (Kinder-Kurlanda & Weller, 2014), such as the potential to assess immediate reactions to events. Digital traces are often generated as a byproduct of daily activities, and are not produced in response to a specific research study design, thus allowing a glimpse into otherwise hidden everyday practices.

For privacy research, the value of digital trace data can be further increased when they are combined with other types of data, e.g., from interviews or surveys (Stier et al., 2020). A combination of digital trace data with self-report data can be particularly interesting for investigating the already mentioned privacy paradox. Given the issues of social desirability and recall errors, there is a considerable risk that people may – intentionally or unintentionally – misreport their engagement in privacy behaviors. Using digital trace data in combination with self-report data can help to uncover and understand such potential biases.

While digital trace can help to find innovative research designs, also in online privacy research, they fundamentally challenge research ethics. Specific challenges in data collection, processing, and publication include questions related to informed consent or perceptions of what are public and what are private spaces of communication and interaction. Another issue is the tradeoff between data protection and privacy concerns on the one hand and transparency and openness of the research methods and data on the other hand. For example, it is often difficult to decide how digital trace data should be aggregated or otherwise processed and reduced before they are shared with other researchers. Currently, only a small, albeit growing, number of resources exists as guidance on ethics for researchers using digital trace data (franzke et al., 2020; Zimmer & Kinder-Kurlanda, 2017). The lack of specific guidance is in large part due to the variety of data summarized under the term "digital traces." Ethical challenges largely depend on the type of data as well as the ways in which they are collected. As the aim usually is to capture digital traces as they occur in everyday situations, doing so implies that those who leave the traces in digital environments are unaware of their data being collected. This situation diverges from the concept of study participants, as people are not consciously participating in a specific study, and also seems to render traditional standards for obtaining informed consent almost impossible.

Fiesler and Proferes (2018) have shown that Twitter users are typically not aware of the possibility that their data might be accessed by researchers and would often only support specific research settings. Hence, it is legitimate to ask whether it is appropriate to speak of "participants" in cases of digital trace data, as the individuals whose data are being collected are in many (or even most) cases not aware of this and never volunteered to participate in a research study. Most authors of respective research papers, indeed, do not apply the term participants but instead use "platform users" (Halavais, 2019) or similar phrases. While this term may be technically more accurate, thinking of platform users as a specific type of (unconscious or even involuntary) participants may help to shift the focus back to the challenge of successfully finding answers to questions related to research ethics in these new research designs. New ethical research practices are needed in general for new data types, but, as a starting point, it is necessary to look at the concepts of participation and informed consent more closely.

Concepts for Participation and Informed Consent

As stated before, when researchers collect digital trace data (using APIs or other automated approaches like web scraping) it can be very difficult or even impossible to obtain informed consent from the people whose data are being used. Asking for consent may be feasible for small samples if researchers have ways of contacting those whose data are collected (e.g., if a platform allows sending direct messages), but becomes infeasible with large samples or when researchers cannot directly contact all individuals whose data are being collected. For example, on Twitter, the default setting is that users need to follow each other to be able to send direct messages. Another advantage of combining digital trace data with data from interviews or surveys is that the latter can be used to also obtain informed consent for collecting/using people's digital trace data (Breuer et al., 2021). However, self-selection into a study is one of several potential sources of bias in the collection of digital trace data (Sen et al., 2021).

Digital trace data may be accessed for research purposes in different ways (Breuer et al., 2020). A commonly used method is the collection of data via Application Programming Interfaces (APIs) offered by platforms. While some major platforms have substantially reduced or essentially closed off data access via their APIs, most notably Facebook and Instagram, others, such as Twitter, have been offering researchers access to a wide array of data that is also relevant for privacy research. Importantly, both the technical limitations of the APIs as well as the Terms of Services for how they may be used may change over time. This has led to ongoing investigations of data quality and challenges regarding the representativeness and reproducibility of digital-trace-data-based research (see, e.g., Olteanu et al., 2016). It has also sparked discussions about data access and alternatives to APIs for accessing platform data (Bruns, 2019; Freelon, 2018; Halavais, 2019; Puschmann, 2019). These also entail different models of participation and user involvement. In the following, we will introduce three possible approaches to re-thinking participation in the context of online privacy research that makes use of digital trace data: (1) data donation, (2) data exploration and citizen science, and (3) debriefing and opting out.

Data Donation

Studies that combine surveys with digital trace data often ask participants to share user names or links to social media profiles. A related but more involved approach is to directly ask platform users to provide their full data history from a specific platform. This method for accessing digital trace data by collaborating with platform users is currently gaining momentum and is commonly described as data donation (Araujo et al., 2022; Boeschoten et al., 2022). Many platforms and services that are relevant for research on (online) privacy, such as social media platforms or fitness tracking devices, offer their users functionalities for exporting their own data which they can then share with researchers.

Obviously, this method, again, poses questions related to privacy that researchers need to address. For example, solutions may need to be found for secure data upload, anonymization, or pseudonymization. Digital trace data shared via data donation may also contain information about other – unaware – individuals, such as social media contacts of the donating person, or friends whom they mentioned or tagged in a post or comment. Nevertheless, data donation is a promising approach that offers advantages and opportunities especially interesting for privacy research, particularly when a user's exact privacy settings can be considered in the research design, in addition to the usage data.

Data donations give back to platform users the status of participants who consent to being part of a research study. Through data donation, they can be more actively involved in the research. This begins with the act of downloading and sharing (donating) their data which requires more involvement than, for example, providing a user name. While donation increases participant burden, it also increases transparency, as participants can explore their data before sharing, and may use the insights to decide what parts of these data to donate. It enables participants to potentially act on an eye-to-eye level with researchers with respect to data awareness. Providing users with insights into their own data can be made use of in different ways for the research project itself; from participating by improving data quality, to having a role in generating results from data, or gaining new insights into privacy risks. As these examples show, data donation and options for exploring the donated data can facilitate new forms of participant involvement.

Data Exploration and Citizen Science

Studies using interventions, such as prompts and nudges (see, e.g., Ioannou et al., 2021; Schäwel, 2019; also see chapter 25 by Wang & Acquisiti on nudges for privacy and security), are common in the field of privacy research. Offering participants the opportunity to explore their own digital trace data – as described in the previous section – can be a powerful intervention to make users aware of potential privacy risks. It can also improve participants' data and privacy literacy (see chapter 11 by Hagendorff, Masur & Trepte on privacy literacy). Donating digital trace data allows an even more active involvement. By exploring their data, participants can contribute to identifying and answering research questions and, thus, engage in so-called citizen science (Majumder & McGuire, 2020), which is already common in the natural sciences but not (yet) in the social and behavioral sciences. Citizen science approaches enable that "people should participate in, not be subjects of, research" as laid out by the Standing Advisory Group on Consumer Involvement in the NHS Research and Development Programme (cited by Boynton, 1998). The cited recommendation is that consumers are involved "not as 'subjects' of research, but as active participants in the process of deciding what research should take place, commissioning research, interpreting the results, and disseminating the findings" (Boynton, 1998, p. 1521). As many research projects in online privacy research follow the purpose of identifying means for making users of digital technology responsible and empowered consumers, such a vision is especially attractive for this research area. And while their use also poses privacy challenges (as we will discuss in the following section), digital trace data, especially if obtained through data donation, can help achieve such empowerment.

Debriefing and Opting Out

In most research based on digital trace data, platform users are unaware that their data has been included in a research data collection. A strategy to raise awareness in this context is to set up infrastructures for "debriefing." Debriefing can be adapted for digital trace data, so that people are notified that their data has been included in a collection, and are offered the chance to "opt out." Currently, this is rarely applied in practice – and also viewed as impractical by the research community (Vitak et al., 2017). The lack of debriefing has been criticized in prominent cases, such as in the reflections by Grimmelmann (2015) on the "emotional contagion" study on Facebook (Kramer et al., 2014). An explorative solution is the open-source system "Bartleby" (Zong & Matias, 2022) that supports notifying platform users who have become "participants" of digital trace studies. Such solutions for debriefing and opting out are especially relevant for social media privacy research, given the sensitivity of its topics and its aim of increasing privacy literacy.

Concepts for Data Privacy and Transparency

Two general directives for research ethics are avoiding harm and maximizing benefits for participants, scholarship, and society. Increasing data privacy is especially important, but on the other hand, the principle of maximizing benefits also entails that data should be used as effectively as possible. Sharing research data so that they can be reused by others increases their value and, thus, maximizes the benefits of the respective research. Accordingly, there always is a tradeoff between (maximizing) privacy (of participants) and transparency (of the research) that researchers need to deal with. For example, if data are reduced or aggregated, they lose some of their reuse value. While this is true for all areas of research that involve data from humans, the importance of this tradeoff is particularly pronounced for online privacy research, given its subject and aims.

Measures for Protecting Data Privacy

Three common ways of increasing data privacy are anonymization, pseudonymization, and data reduction. Anonymization means that the data are processed in such a way that the identification of individuals becomes impossible. This can, e.g., be achieved through aggregation. Pseudonymization describes the process of removing direct identifiers, such as names, and potentially problematic cases or combinations of indirect identifiers from the data with the goal of ensuring that data can only be attributed to individuals through the use of additional data. Identification, thus, does not become impossible but requires considerable effort and depends on the availability of additional (linkable) data. Data reduction is a more general principle that can be part of anonymization as well as pseudonymization. Put simply, data reduction means that specific parts of the data are removed to improve data privacy. These can be variables or cases as well as certain values, for example, turning a numeric variable into a categorical variable.

Applying anonymization or pseudonymization strategies to digital trace data poses new challenges. Even after removing personal information, it may be possible to re-identify someone if additional context information is explored. As Zimmer (2010) has illustrated for a de-identified Facebook dataset, it is not only relevant whether the digital trace data originates from publicly accessible platforms. Instead, it is always important to identify effective measures for protecting privacy across contexts. This leads to the key challenge of assuring privacy when sharing data. Developing better solutions for data access and secondary data use that build on secure data environments and external safeguards can contribute to research transparency while also protecting privacy according to legal and ethical standards.

Data Sharing

Finding a good balance between privacy and transparency can be challenging. Privacy considerations but also practical aspects, such as the size and format of the data, require novel approaches for archiving and publishing them (Van Atteveldt et al., 2020) and many data archives are currently working on developing and implementing these (see, e.g., Breuer et al., 2021; Hemphill, 2019).

Despite the challenges, researchers working with digital traces appear to be principally interested and willing to share research data (Weller & Kinder-Kurlanda, 2017), also in order to increase reproducibility and to make research results more transparent for the scientific community. Archiving and sharing this kind of research data might also increase awareness about the underlying research in the general public, thereby enabling a more solid foundation for data donation approaches and consent forms. Some researchers also feel they need to give back something to the user community of a platform they have been studying and see this as a key motivation for sharing research data (Weller & Kinder-Kurlanda, 2017). Given the lack of standardized archiving solutions, individual initiatives from researchers may be far less effective in contributing to transparency. Future work is required to establish standards for archiving and sharing new types of research data (Weller & Kinder-Kurlanda, 2016). Access to archived datasets may also contribute to the principle of sparsity, i.e., avoiding having to collect the same kind of information multiple times, thus, reducing the number of people that are asked to disclose private information for research purposes.

Summary and Future Directions

Studying online privacy is a research field that in its very nature is connected to sensitive information about the people being studied. Hence, studies in this area need to address various ethical questions in all phases of the research process. Many of those are the same as for other research areas. For example, researchers should always obtain informed consent, if this is possible, and participants in experimental studies should be debriefed if the studies involve experimental deception. While these aspects relate to the collection of the data, other ethical obligations concern the processing and sharing of the data. A key maxim in this is the protection of participants' privacy. Hence, data minimization should be a guiding principle. If the data contain personal information and especially if they are potentially sensitive, researchers should apply anonymization, pseudonymization, or data reduction before making the data available to others. On the other hand, the ideals of open science are also relevant for research ethics considerations. Data sharing not only increases transparency, reproducibility, and replicability, but also the effectiveness of research and the value of the data. This can also benefit study participants as it increases the value of their data and can reduce the risk of unnecessary repeated data collections. Accordingly, if possible, research data from online privacy research should be made available via suitable data archives (with appropriate data protection measures in place). Notably, however, when researchers in only privacy research want to employ innovative research designs and make use of digital trace data, there are a few additional ethical dimensions to be considered. These are summarized in Figure 30.1.

With regard to future directions, in addition to enabling a more active involvement of study participants, one major potential of digital trace data for online privacy research is that they can also be used in intervention studies by allowing participants to explore and learn about the data they generate. When it comes to processing and sharing data in online privacy research, especially when using digital trace data, innovative solutions have to be employed that strike a balance between the privacy of participants and the transparency of the research. The development of such solutions, as well as the implementation of new ways of involving study participants, can not only help to find and answer novel questions in online privacy research but may also improve transparency and foster critical reflection of privacy and research ethics more generally. Innovation in research designs, participation, and transparency can, thus, help resolve the paradox of online privacy research that makes use of personal, private, and often also sensitive data to study what defines and affects people's online privacy experiences.

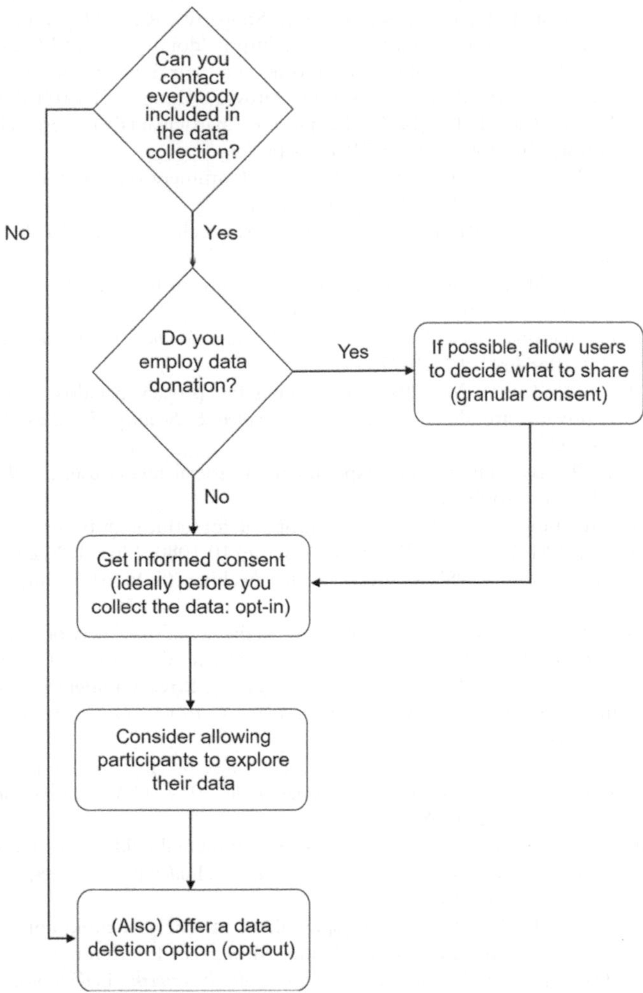

Figure 30.1 Flowchart Illustrating Ethical Considerations to Be Made in Online Privacy Research Employing Digital Trace Data

References

American Psychological Association. (2020). *Publication manual of the American Psychological Association (7th ed.)*. American Psychological Association. https://doi.org/10.1037/0000165-000

Araujo, T., Ausloos, J., van Atteveldt, W., Loecherbach, F., Moeller, J., Ohme, J., Trilling, D., van de Velde, B., de Vreese, C., & Welbers, K. (2022). OSD2F: An Open-Source Data Donation Framework. Computational Communication Research, 4(2) 372–387. https://doi.org/10.5117/CCR2022.2.001.ARAU

Boeschoten, L., Ausloos, J., Moeller, J., Araujo, T., & Oberski, D. L. (2020). Digital trace data collection through data donation. ArXiv:2011.09851 [Cs, Stat]. http://arxiv.org/abs/2011.09851

Boynton, P. M. (1998). People should participate in, not be subjects of, research. *BMJ*, *317*(7171), 1521–1521. https://doi.org/10.1136/bmj.317.7171.1521a

Breuer, J., Al Baghal, T., Sloan, L., Bishop, L., Kondyli, D., & Linardis, A. (2021). Informed consent for linking survey and social media data – Differences between platforms and data types. *IASSIST Quarterly*, *45*(1), 1–27. https://doi.org/10.29173/iq988

Breuer, J., Bishop, L., & Kinder-Kurlanda, K. (2020). The practical and ethical challenges in acquiring and sharing digital trace data: Negotiating public-private partnerships. *New Media & Society*, *22*(11), 2058–2080. https://doi.org/10.1177/1461444820924622

Breuer, J., Borschewski, K., Bishop, L., Vávra, M., Štebe, J., Strapcova, K., & Hegedűs, P. (2021). Archiving social media data: A guide for archivists and researchers. https://doi.org/10.5281/ZENODO.5041072

Bruns, A. (2019). After the 'APIcalypse': Social media platforms and their fight against critical scholarly research. *Information, Communication & Society*, *22*(11), 1544–1566. https://doi.org/10.1080/1369118x.2019.1637447

Chalmers, I., Jackson, W., & Carvel, D. (1999). People are "participants" in research. *BMJ*, *318*(7191), 1141–1141. https://doi.org/10.1136/bmj.318.7191.1141a

Dienlin, T., & Sun, Y. (2021). Does the privacy paradox exist? Comment on Yu et al.'s (2020) meta-analysis. *Meta-Psychology*, *5*. https://doi.org/10.15626/mp.2020.2711

Fiesler, C., & Proferes, N. (2018). "Participant" of Twitter research. *Social Media + Society*, *4*(1), Online publication. https://doi.org/10.1177/2056305118763366

franzke, a. s., Bechmann, A., Zimmer, M., Ess, C. & the Association of Internet Researchers (2020). Internet Research: Ethical Guidelines 3.0. https://aoir.org/reports/ethics3.pdf

Freelon, D. (2018). Computational research in the post-API age. *Political Communication*, *35*(4), 665–668. https://doi.org/10.1080/10584609.2018.1477506

Gerber, N., Gerber, P., & Volkamer, M. (2018). Explaining the privacy paradox: A systematic review of literature investigating privacy attitude and behavior. *Computers & Security*, 77, 226–261. https://doi.org/10.1016/j.cose.2018.04.002

Grimmelmann, J. (2015). The law and ethics of experiments on social media users. *Colorado Technology Law Journal*, *13*, Article 219. https://osf.io/cdt7y

Halavais, A. (2019). Overcoming terms of service: A proposal for ethical distributed research. *Information, Communication & Society*, *22*(11), 1567–1581. https://doi.org/10.1080/1369118X.2019.1627386

Hemphill, L. (2019). Updates on ICPSR's Social Media Archive (SOMAR). https://doi.org/10.5281/ZENODO.3612677

Howison, J., Wiggins, A., & Crowston, K. (2011). Validity issues in the use of social network analysis with digital trace data. *Journal of the Association for Information Systems*, *12*(12), 767–797. https://doi.org/10.17705/1jais.00282

Ioannou, A., Tussyadiah, I., Miller, G., Li, S., & Weick, M. (2021). Privacy nudges for disclosure of personal information: A systematic literature review and meta-analysis. *PLOS ONE*, *16*(8), e0256822. https://doi.org/10.1371/journal.pone.0256822

Kinder-Kurlanda, K., & Weller, K. (2014). "I always feel it must be great to be a hacker!": The role of interdisciplinary work in social media research. *Proceedings of the 2014 ACM conference on web science*, 91–98. https://doi.org/10.1145/2615569.2615685

Kramer, A. D. I., Guillory, J. E., & Hancock, J. T. (2014). Experimental evidence of massive-scale emotional contagion through social networks. *Proceedings of the National Academy of Sciences*, *111*(24), 8788–8790. https://doi.org/10.1073/pnas.1320040111

Lamla, J., & Ochs, C. (2019). Selbstbestimmungspraktiken in der Datenökonomie: Gesellschaftlicher Widerspruch oder 'privates' Paradox? In B. Blättel-Mink, & P. Kenning (Eds.), *Paradoxien des Verbraucherverhaltens. Dokumentation der Jahreskonferenz 2017 des Netzwerks Verbraucherforschung* (pp. 25–39). Springer Gabler: 25-39.

Majumder, M. A., & McGuire, A. L. (2020). Data sharing in the context of health-related citizen science. *Journal of Law, Medicine & Ethics*, *48*(S1), 167–177. https://doi.org/10.1177/1073110520917044

Nissenbaum, H. (2009). *Privacy in context*. Stanford University Press.

Olteanu, A., Castillo, C., Diaz, F., & Kiciman, E. (2016). Social data: Biases, methodological pitfalls, and ethical boundaries. *SSRN Electronic Journal*. https://doi.org/10.2139/ssrn.2886526

Parry, D. A., Davidson, B. I., Sewall, C. J. R., Fisher, J. T., Mieczkowski, H., & Quintana, D. S. (2021). A systematic review and meta-analysis of discrepancies between logged and self-reported digital media use. *Nature Human Behaviour*. https://doi.org/10.1038/s41562-021-01117-5

Puschmann, C. (2019). An end to the wild west of social media research: A response to Axel Bruns. *Information, Communication & Society*, *22*(11), 1582–1589. https://doi.org/10.1080/1369118X.2019.1646300

Schäwel, J. (2019). How to Raise Users' Awareness of Online Privacy: An Empirical and Theoretical Approach for Examining the Impact of Persuasive Privacy Support Measures on Users' Self-Disclosure on Online Social Networking Sites [Ph.D. thesis, University of Duisburg-Essen]. https://duepublico2.uni-due.de/receive/duepublico_mods_00070691

Sen, I., Flöck, F., Weller, K., Weiß, B., & Wagner, C. (2021). A total error framework for digital traces of human behavior on online platforms. *Public Opinion Quarterly*, *85*(S1), 399–422. https://doi.org/10.1093/poq/nfab018

Stier, S., Breuer, J., Siegers, P., & Thorson, K. (2020). Integrating survey data and digital trace data: Key issues in developing an emerging field. *Social Science Computer Review*, *38*(5), 503–516. https://doi.org/10.1177/0894439319843669

Van Atteveldt, W., Althaus, S., & Wessler, H. (2020). The trouble with sharing your privates: Pursuing ethical open science and collaborative research across national jurisdictions using sensitive data. *Political Communication*, 1–7. https://doi.org/10.1080/10584609.2020.1744780

Vitak, J., Proferes, N., Shilton, K., & Ashktorab, Z. (2017). Ethics regulation in social computing research: Examining the role of Institutional Review Boards. *Journal of Empirical Research on Human Research Ethics*, *12*(5), 372–382. https://doi.org/10.1177/1556264617725200

Weller, K., & Kinder-Kurlanda, K. E. (2016). A manifesto for data sharing in social media research. Proceedings of the 8th ACM Conference on Web Science. 166–172. https://doi.org/10.1145/2908131.2908172

Weller, K., & Kinder-Kurlanda, K. (2017). To share or not to share? Ethical challenges in sharing social media-based research data. In M. Zimmer & K. E. Kinder-Kurlanda (Eds.), *Internet Research Ethics for the Social Age* (pp. 115–129). Peter Lang.

Willson, M., & Kinder-Kurlanda, K. (2021). Social gamers' everyday (in)visibility tactics: Playing within programmed constraints. *Information, Communication & Society*, *24*(1), 134–149. https://doi.org/10.1080/1369118X.2019.1635187

Yu, L., Li, H., He, W., Wang, F.-K., & Jiao, S. (2020). A meta-analysis to explore privacy cognition and information disclosure of internet users. *International Journal of Information Management*, *51*, 102015. https://doi.org/10.1016/j.ijinfomgt.2019.09.011

Zimmer, M. (2010). "But the data is already public": On the ethics of research in Facebook. *Ethics and Information Technology*, *12*(4), 313–325. https://doi.org/10.1007/s10676-010-9227-5

Zimmer, M., & Kinder-Kurlanda, K. (Eds.). (2017). *Internet research ethics for the social age: New challenges, cases, and contexts*. Peter Lang.

Zong, J., & Matias, J. N. (2022). Bartleby: Procedural and substantive ethics in the design of research ethics systems. *Social Media + Society*, *8*(1), Online publication. https://doi.org/10.1177/20563051221077021

INDEX

Note: page numbers in *italics* refer to figures or tables